GREEN LANTERN

WAR OF THE GREEN LANTERNS

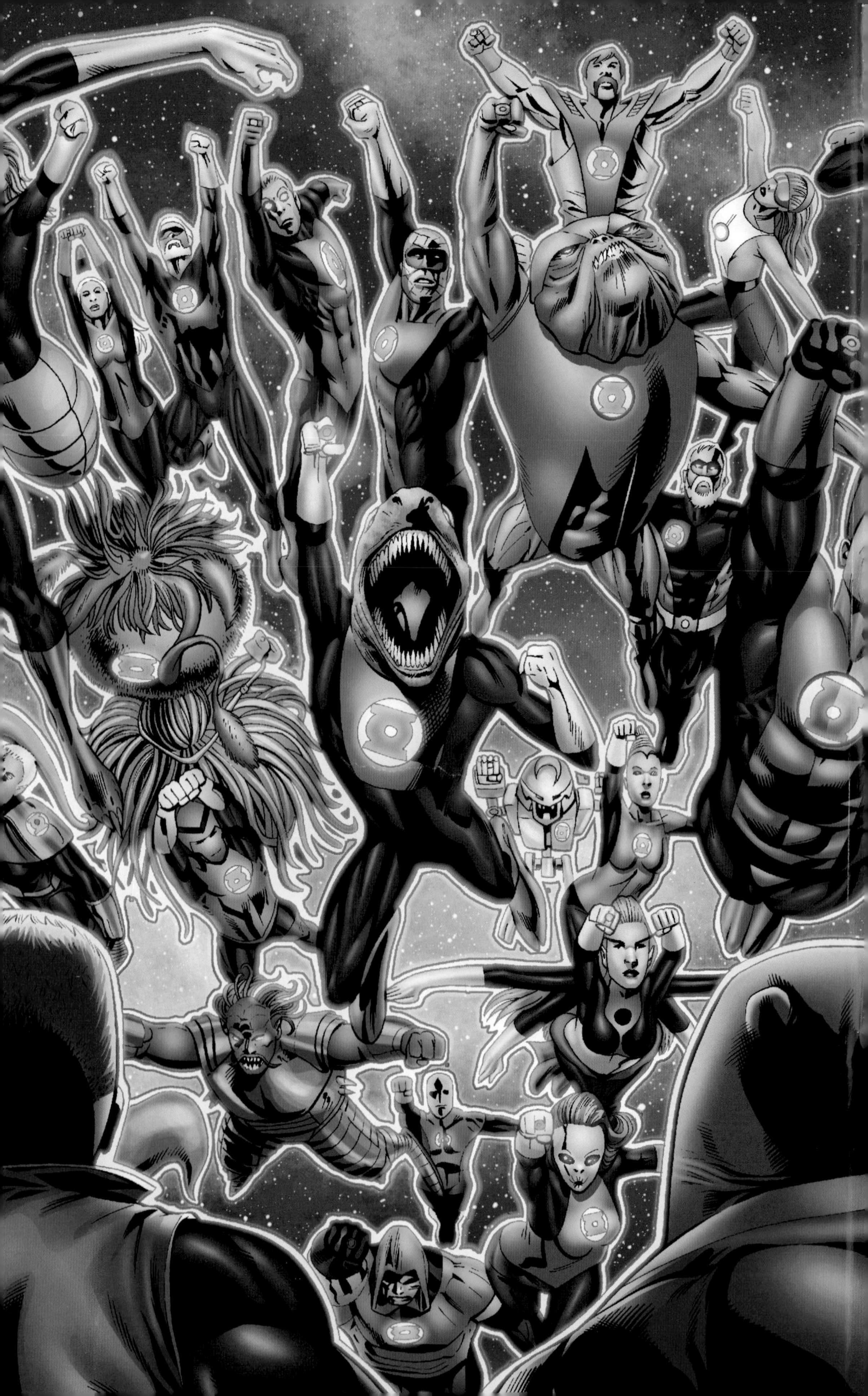

WAR OF THE GREEN LANTERNS

Geoff Johns   Tony Bedard   Peter J. Tomasi
Writers

**Doug Mahnke   Tyler Kirkham   Fernando Pasarin
Ed Benes   Ardian Syaf**
Pencillers

**Christian Alamy   BATT   Ed Benes   Vicente Cifuentes
Keith Champagne   Mick Gray   Rob Hunter   Mark Irwin
Jay Leisten   Tom Nguyen   Andy Owens   Sean Parsons
Jack Purcell   Cam Smith**
Inkers

Gabe Eltaeb   Randy Mayor   Rod Reis   Nei Ruffino
Colorists

Pat Brosseau   Rob Leigh   Nick J. Napolitano   Steve Wands
Letterers

Ivan Reis & **Oclair Albert** with **Rod Reis**
Collection cover

Brian Cunningham   Adam Schlagman   Eddie Berganza   Editors-Original Series
Darren Shan   Assistant Editor-Original Series
Ian Sattler   Director-Editorial, Special Projects and Archival Editions
Robbin Brosterman   Design Director-Books

Eddie Berganza   Executive Editor
Bob Harras   VP-Editor in Chief

Diane Nelson   President
Dan DiDio and Jim Lee   Co-Publishers
Geoff Johns   Chief Creative Officer
John Rood   Executive VP-Sales, Marketing and Business Development
Amy Genkins   Senior VP, Business and Legal Affairs
Nairi Gardiner   Senior VP-Finance
Jeff Boison   VP-Publishing Operations
Mark Chiarello   VP-Art Direction and Design
John Cunningham   VP-Marketing
Terri Cunningham   VP-Talent Relations and Services
Alison Gill   Senior VP-Manufacturing and Operations
David Hyde   VP-Publicity
Hank Kanalz   Senior VP-Digital
Jay Kogan   VP-Business and Legal Affairs, Publishing
Jack Mahan   VP-Business Affairs, Talent
Nick Napolitano   VP-Manufacturing Administration
Sue Pohja   VP-Book Sales
Courtney Simmons   Senior VP-Publicity
Bob Wayne   Senior VP-Sales

GREEN LANTERN: WAR OF THE GREEN LANTERNS

Published by DC Comics. Cover and compilation Copyright © 2011 DC Comics.
All Rights Reserved. Originally published in single magazine form in GREEN LANTERN 63-67,
GREEN LANTERN CORPS 58-60, GREEN LANTERN: EMERALD WARRIORS 8-10 © 2011 DC Comics.
All Rights Reserved. All characters, their distinctive likenesses and related elements featured in
this publication are trademarks of DC Comics. The stories, characters and incidents featured
in this publication are entirely fictional. DC Comics does not read or accept unsolicited
submissions of ideas, stories or artwork.

DC Comics, 1700 Broadway, New York, NY 10019
A Warner Bros. Entertainment Company
Printed by RR Donnelley, Salem, VA, USA. 10/14/11. First Printing.

HC ISBN: 978-1-4012-3234-4
SC ISBN: 978-1-4012-3452-2

SUSTAINABLE
FORESTRY
INITIATIVE
Certified Chain of Custody
Promoting Sustainable
Forest Management
www.sfiprogram.org
Fiber used in this product line meets the
sourcing requirements of the SFI program.
www.sfiprogram.org SGS-SFI/COC-US10/81072

GREEN LANTERN 63 Cover by Gary Frank

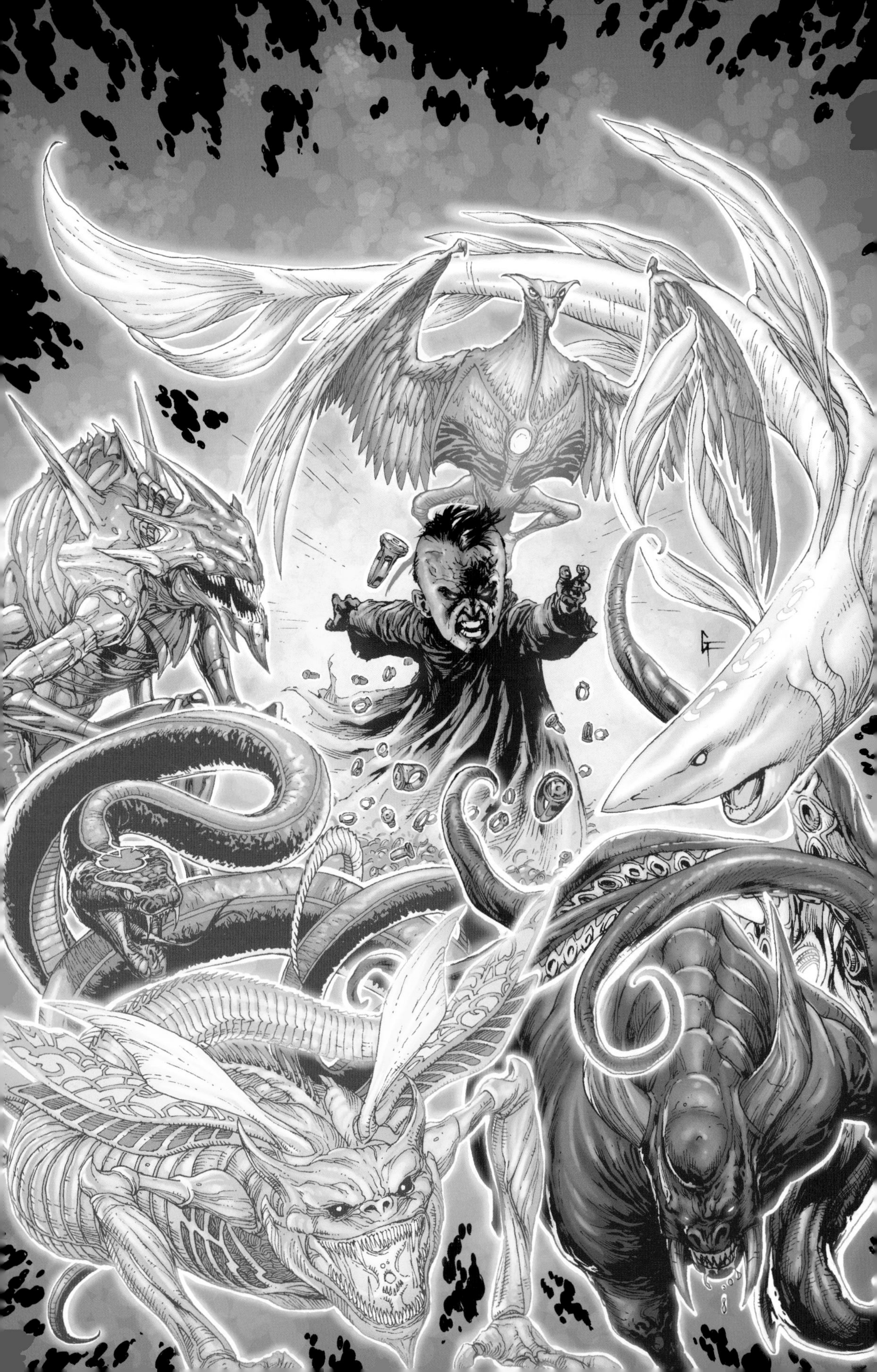

WAR OF THE GREEN LANTERNS
PROLOGUE

Geoff Johns Writer
Ed Benes & Ardian Syaf Pencillers
Ed Benes, Rob Hunter & Vicente Cifuentes Inkers

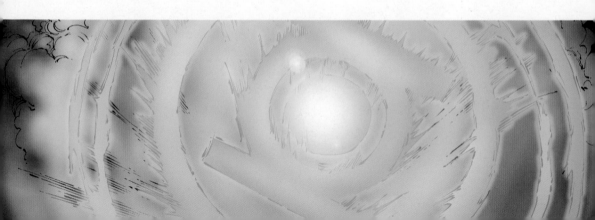

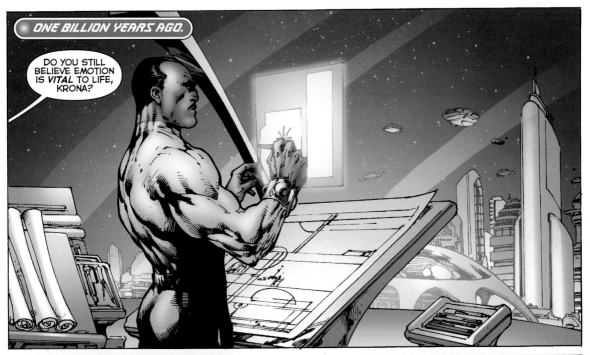

ONE BILLION YEARS AGO.
DO YOU STILL BELIEVE EMOTION IS VITAL TO LIFE, KRONA?
I STILL BELIEVE EMOTION IS LIFE, GANTHET. I ALWAYS WILL.
THEN YOU CONTINUE TO RISK YOUR IMPENDING INDUCTION INTO THE GUARDIANS OF THE UNIVERSE.
BUT IS LIFE NOT THE VERY THING THE SELF-APPOINTED "GUARDIANS" ARE DEVOTING THEMSELVES TO PROTECTING? THEY SPEAK IN CONTRADICTIONS.
MY FRIEND...YOU HAVE ALWAYS GIVEN ME YOUR SUPPORT AND I ASK FOR THAT SUPPORT NOW MORE THAN EVER.
I AM ON THE VERGE OF PEERING INTO THE PAST AND WITNESSING THE BIRTH OF THE UNIVERSE AND THEREFORE UNLOCKING THE SECRETS OF THE EMOTIONAL SPECTRUM.
WE DON'T HAVE TO BE AFRAID--
WE FEEL NO FEAR. FEAR IS FORBIDDEN.
FEAR IS HERESY.
PLEASE, GANTHET.
DO NOT DENY YOUR HEART LIKE THE OTHERS.
OUR HEARTS ARE FULL OF CHAOS, KRONA. WE MUST USE OUR MINDS AND ONLY OUR MINDS TO BRING ORDER TO THIS UNIVERSE.
I AM SORRY.

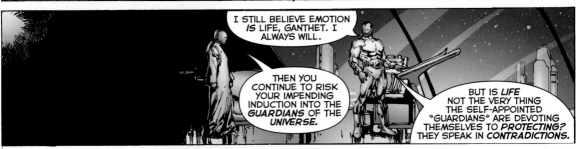

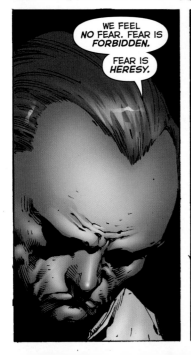

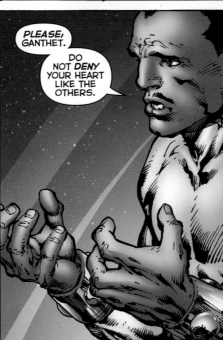

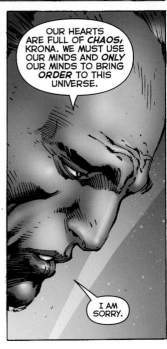

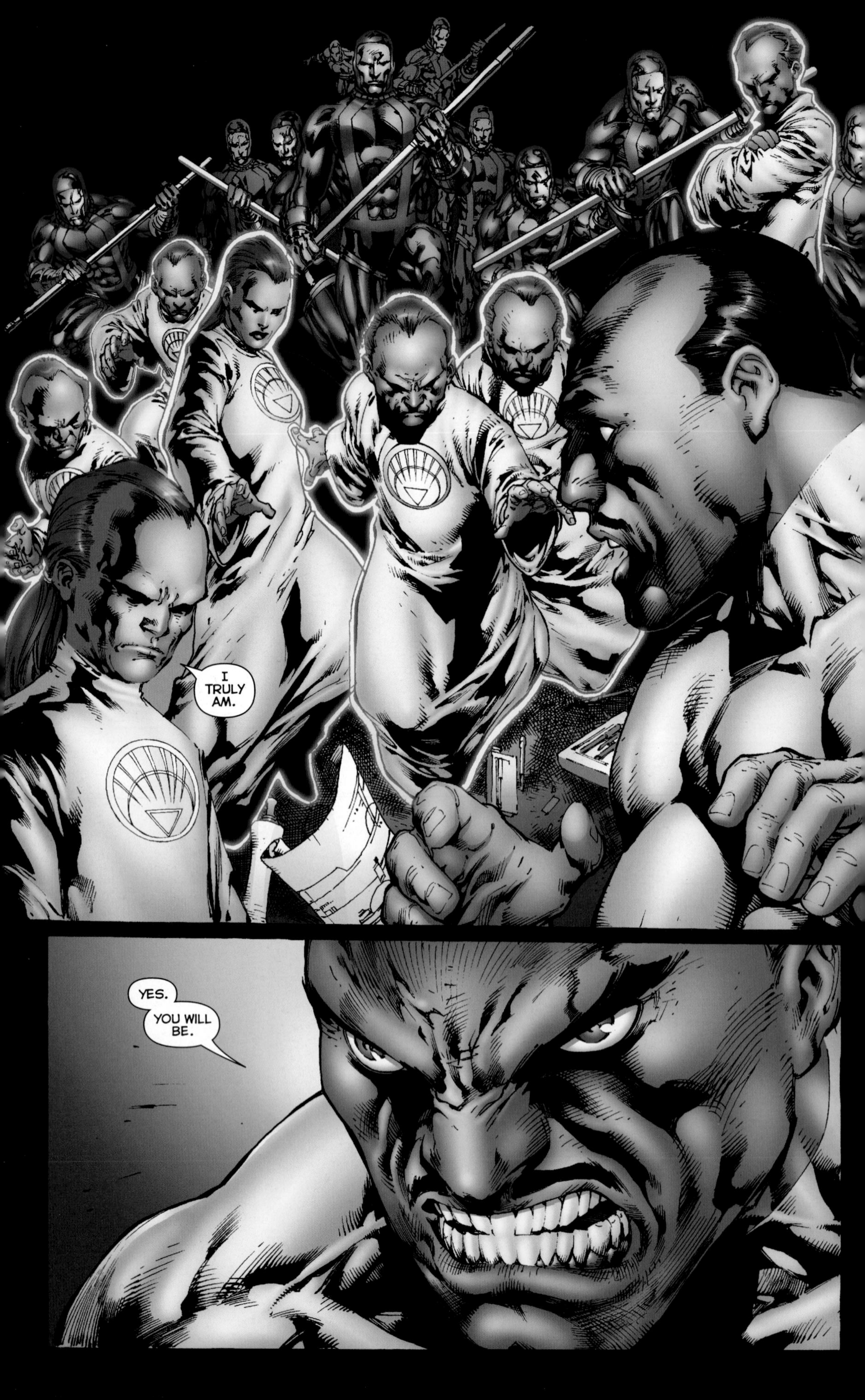
I TRULY AM.
YES.
YOU WILL BE.

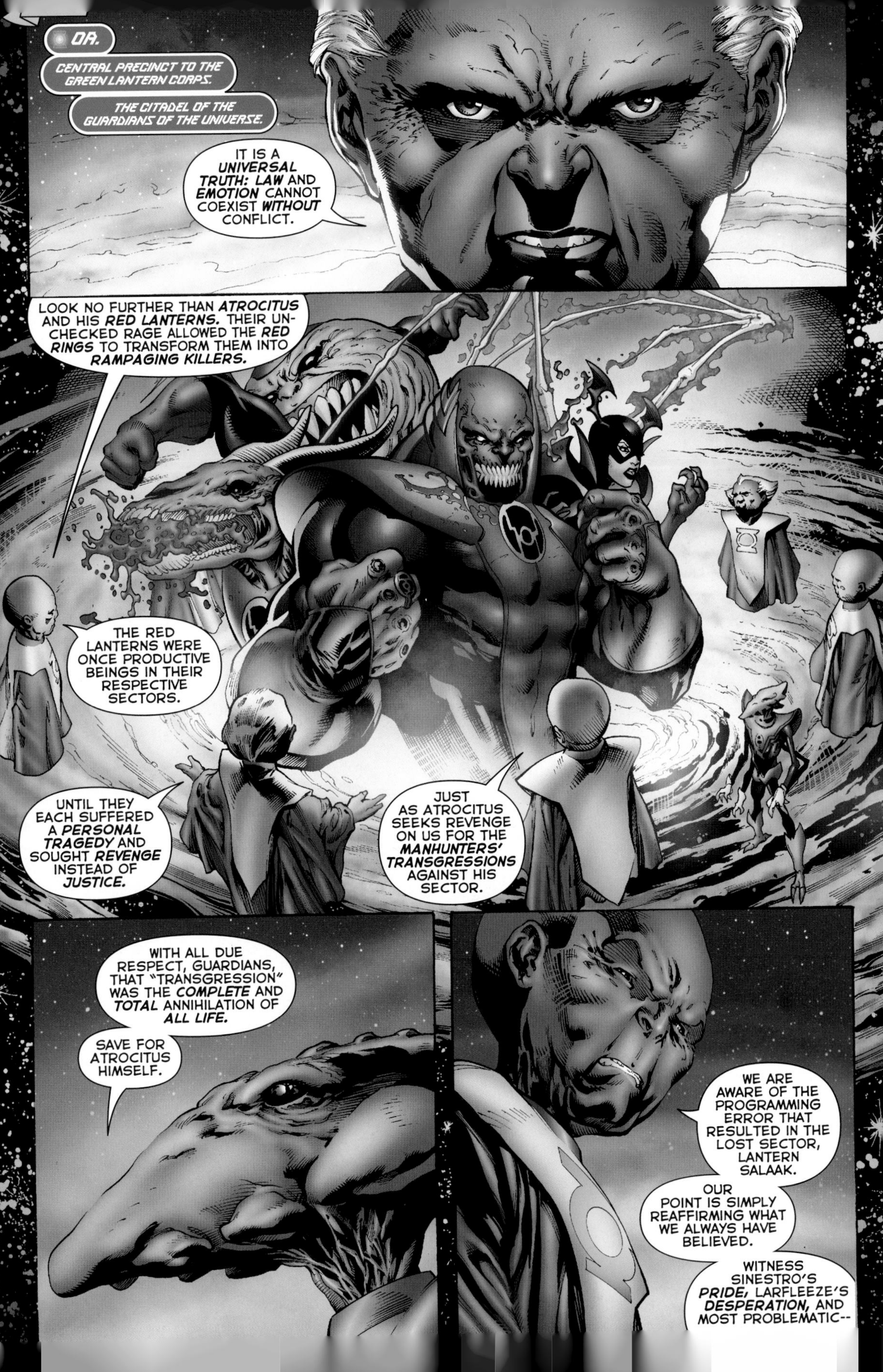
OA.
CENTRAL PRECINCT TO THE GREEN LANTERN CORPS.
THE CITADEL OF THE GUARDIANS OF THE UNIVERSE.
IT IS A UNIVERSAL TRUTH: LAW AND EMOTION CANNOT COEXIST WITHOUT CONFLICT.
LOOK NO FURTHER THAN ATROCITUS AND HIS RED LANTERNS. THEIR UNCHECKED RAGE ALLOWED THE RED RINGS TO TRANSFORM THEM INTO RAMPAGING KILLERS.
THE RED LANTERNS WERE ONCE PRODUCTIVE BEINGS IN THEIR RESPECTIVE SECTORS.
UNTIL THEY EACH SUFFERED A PERSONAL TRAGEDY AND SOUGHT REVENGE INSTEAD OF JUSTICE.
JUST AS ATROCITUS SEEKS REVENGE ON US FOR THE MANHUNTERS' TRANSGRESSIONS AGAINST HIS SECTOR.
WITH ALL DUE RESPECT, GUARDIANS, THAT "TRANSGRESSION" WAS THE COMPLETE AND TOTAL ANNIHILATION OF ALL LIFE.
SAVE FOR ATROCITUS HIMSELF.
WE ARE AWARE OF THE PROGRAMMING ERROR THAT RESULTED IN THE LOST SECTOR, LANTERN SALAAK.
OUR POINT IS SIMPLY REAFFIRMING WHAT WE ALWAYS HAVE BELIEVED.
WITNESS SINESTRO'S PRIDE, LARFLEEZE'S DESPERATION, AND MOST PROBLEMATIC--

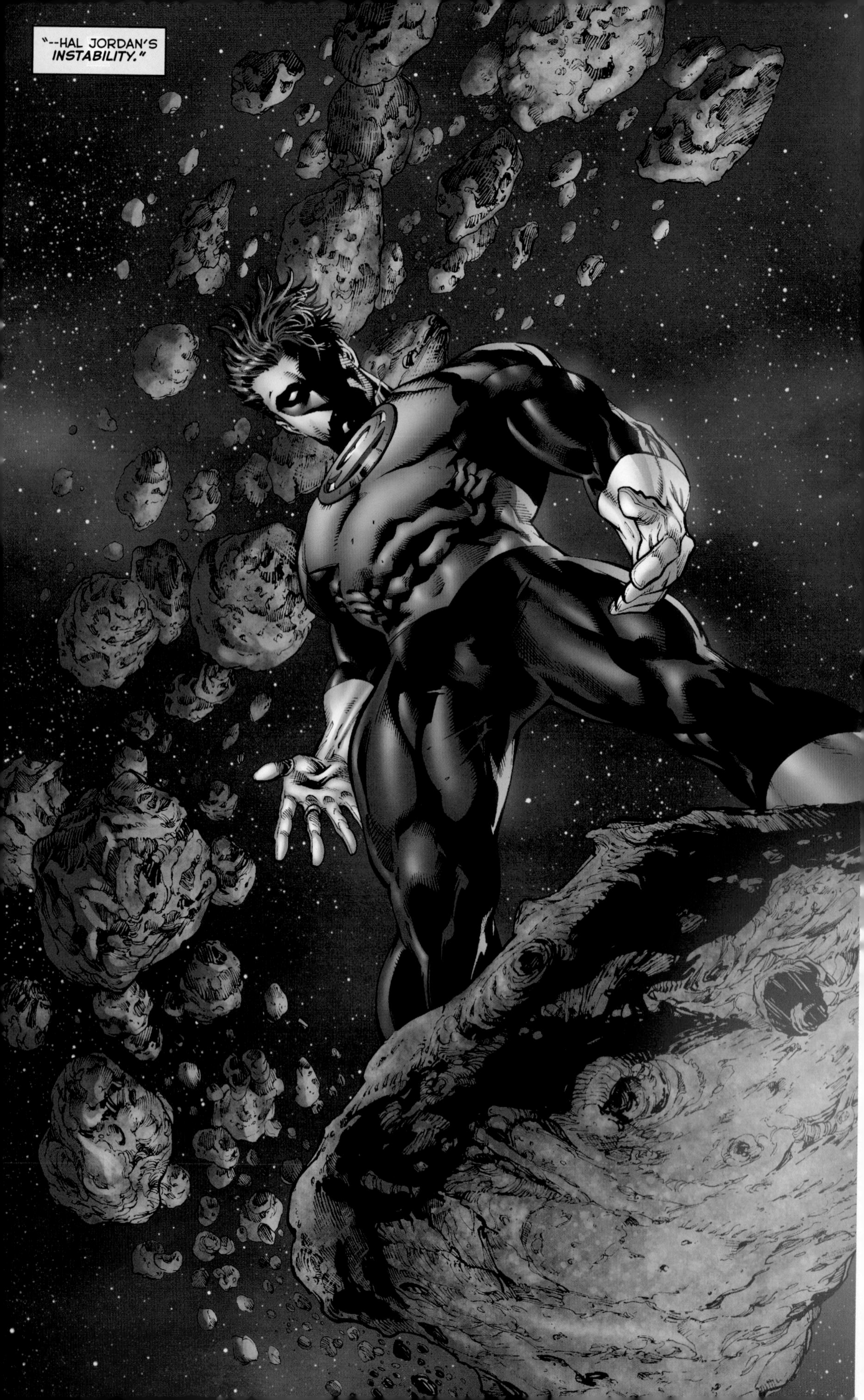
"--HAL JORDAN'S INSTABILITY."

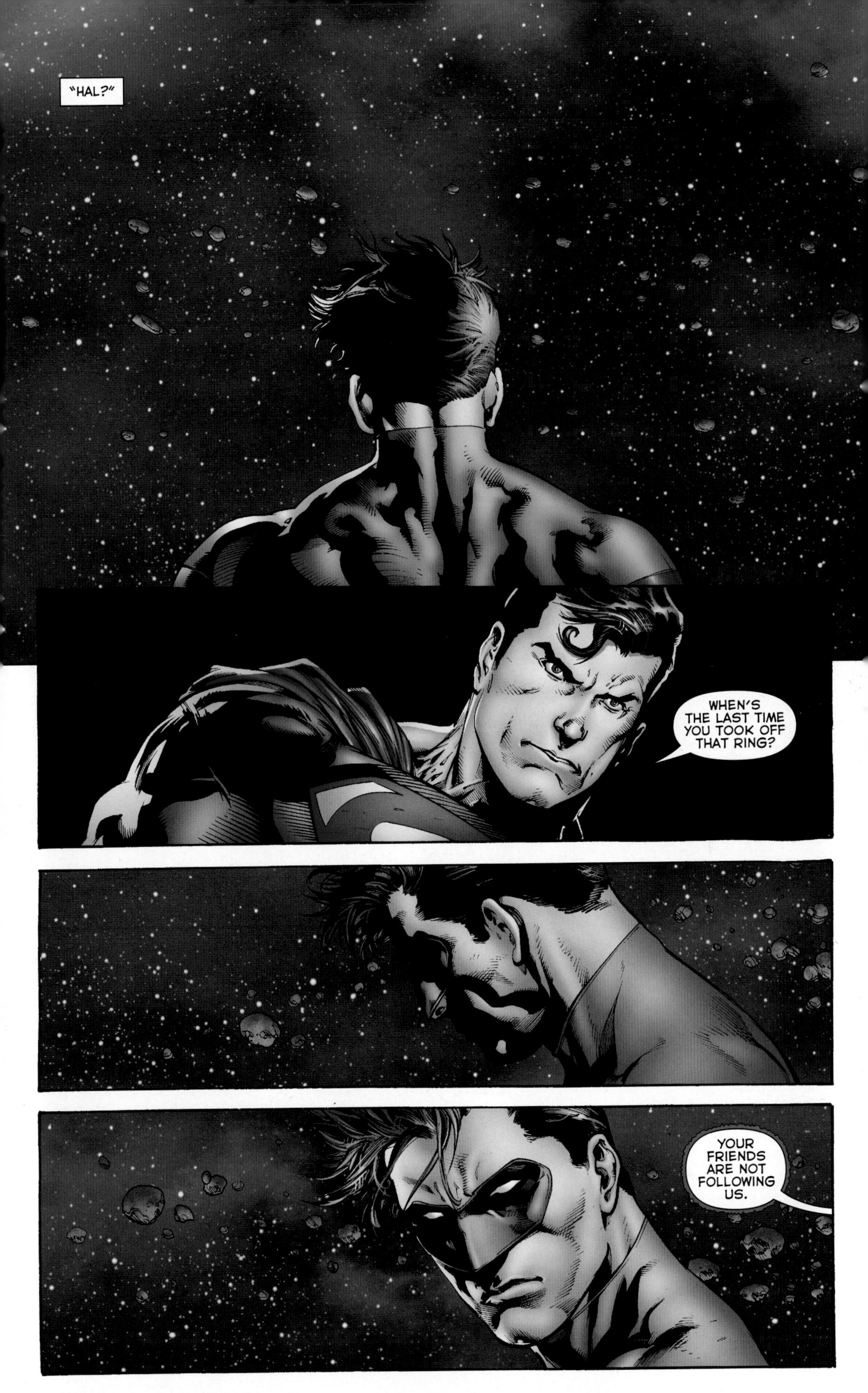
"HAL?"
WHEN'S THE LAST TIME YOU TOOK OFF THAT RING?
YOUR FRIENDS ARE NOT FOLLOWING US.

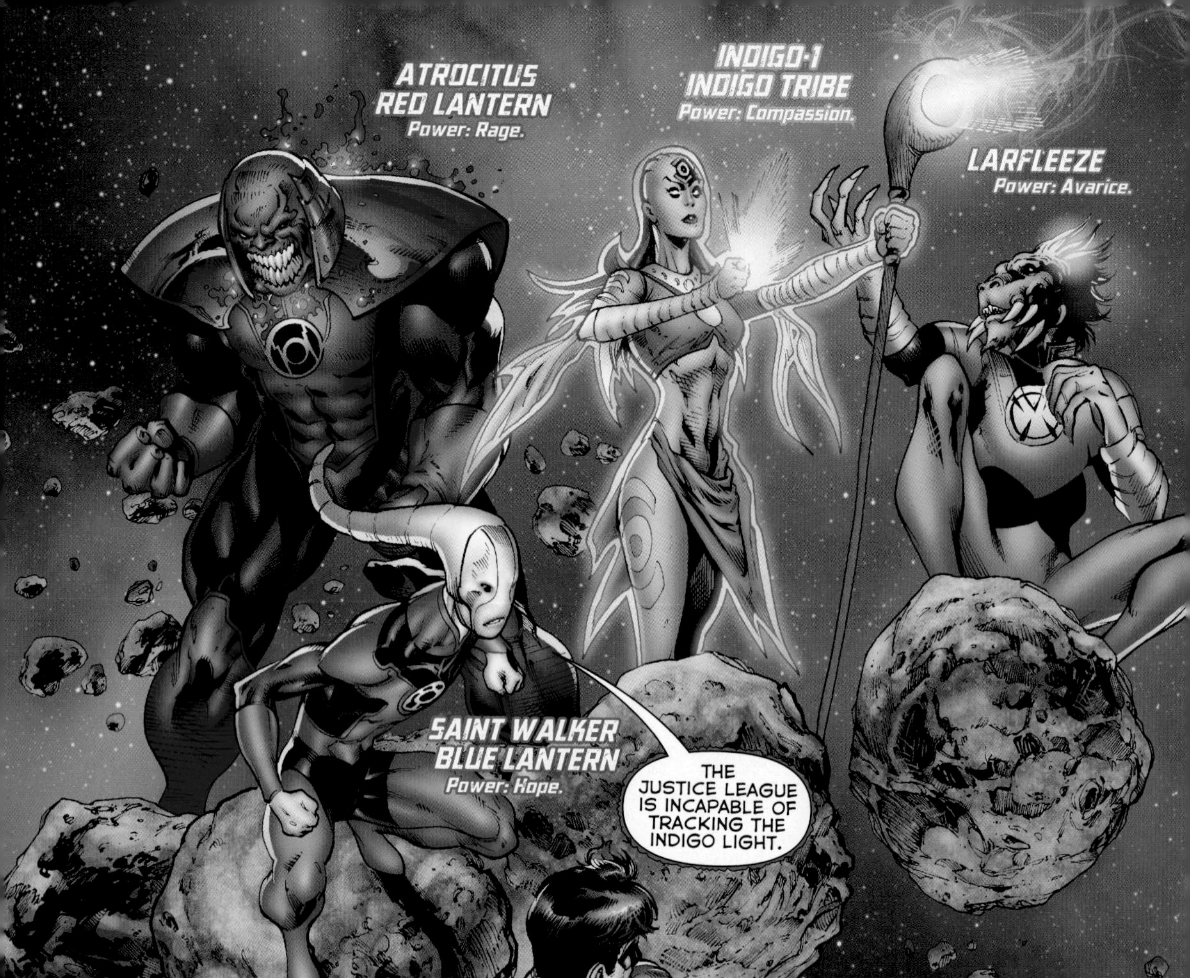
ATROCITUS
RED LANTERN
Power: Rage.
INDIGO-1
INDIGO TRIBE
Power: Compassion.
LARFLEEZE
Power: Avarice.
SAINT WALKER
BLUE LANTERN
Power: Hope.
THE JUSTICE LEAGUE IS INCAPABLE OF TRACKING THE INDIGO LIGHT.

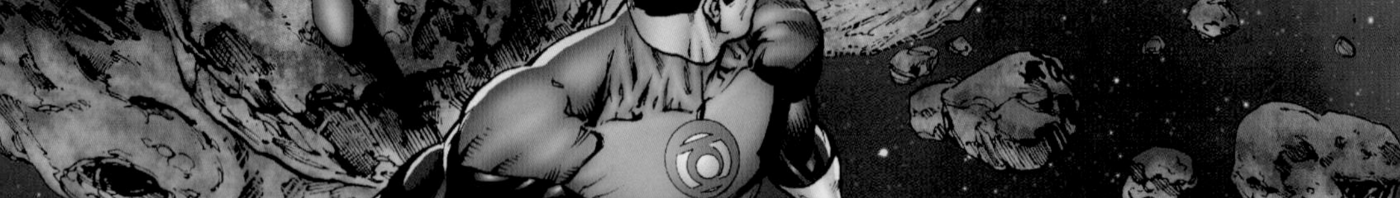
GOOD. HUNTING DOWN A *RENEGADE GUARDIAN* ISN'T THEIR JOB.
I BELIEVE YOU ARE MAKING THAT DECISION *FOR* THEM. THEY SEEMED QUITE INTERESTED IN PURSUING KRONA.
AND THE ENTITIES UNDER HIS CONTROL.
I CAN'T BELIEVE I'M SAYING THIS, BUT AFTER EVERYTHING I'VE BEEN THROUGH WITH PARALLAX AND THE OTHERS... I THINK THE GUARDIANS MIGHT ACTUALLY BE RIGHT.
ABOUT WHAT?

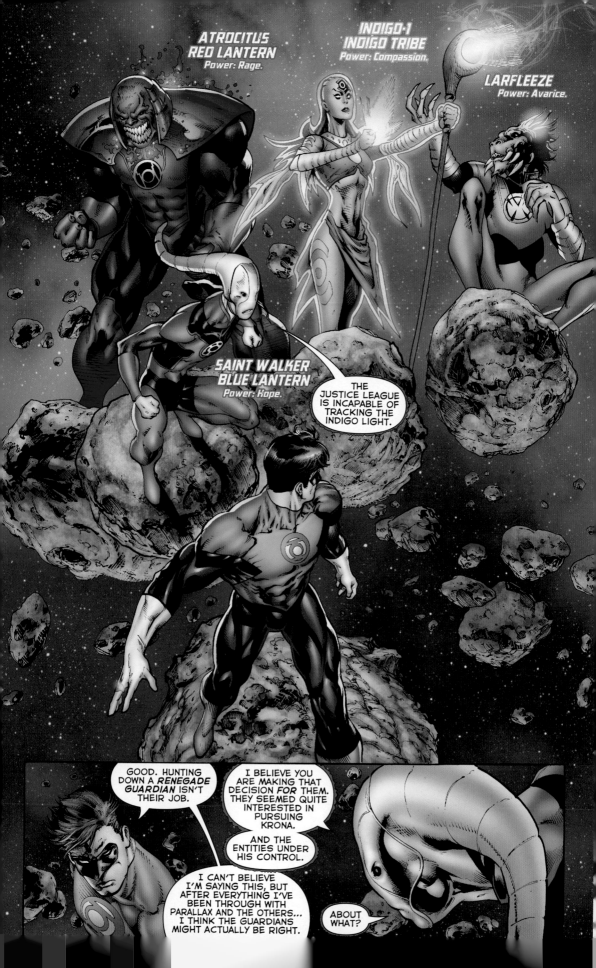

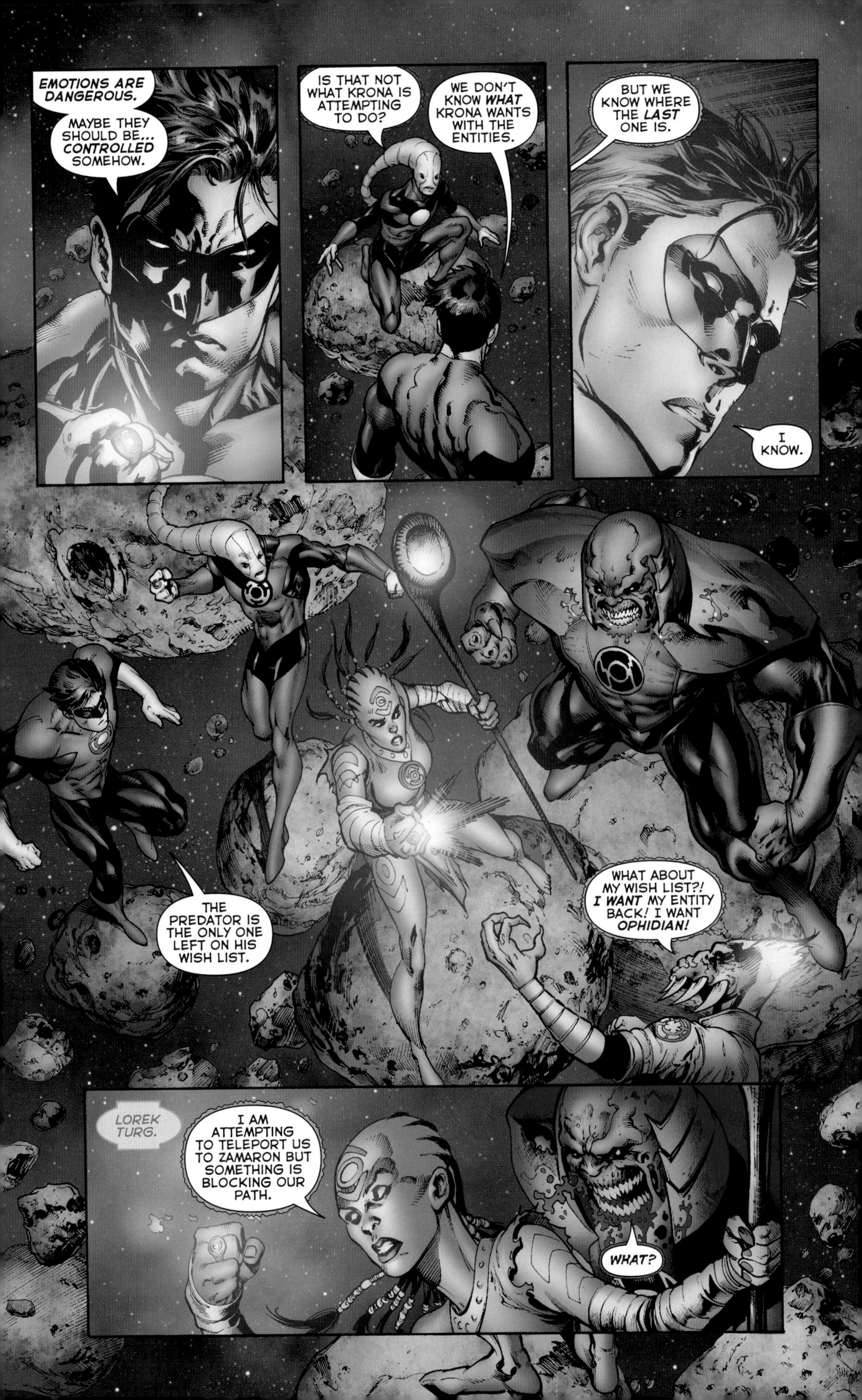
EMOTIONS ARE DANGEROUS.
MAYBE THEY SHOULD BE... CONTROLLED SOMEHOW.
IS THAT NOT WHAT KRONA IS ATTEMPTING TO DO?
WE DON'T KNOW WHAT KRONA WANTS WITH THE ENTITIES.
BUT WE KNOW WHERE THE LAST ONE IS.
I KNOW.
THE PREDATOR IS THE ONLY ONE LEFT ON HIS WISH LIST.
WHAT ABOUT MY WISH LIST?! I WANT MY ENTITY BACK! I WANT OPHIDIAN!
LOREK TURG.
I AM ATTEMPTING TO TELEPORT US TO ZAMARON BUT SOMETHING IS BLOCKING OUR PATH.
WHAT?

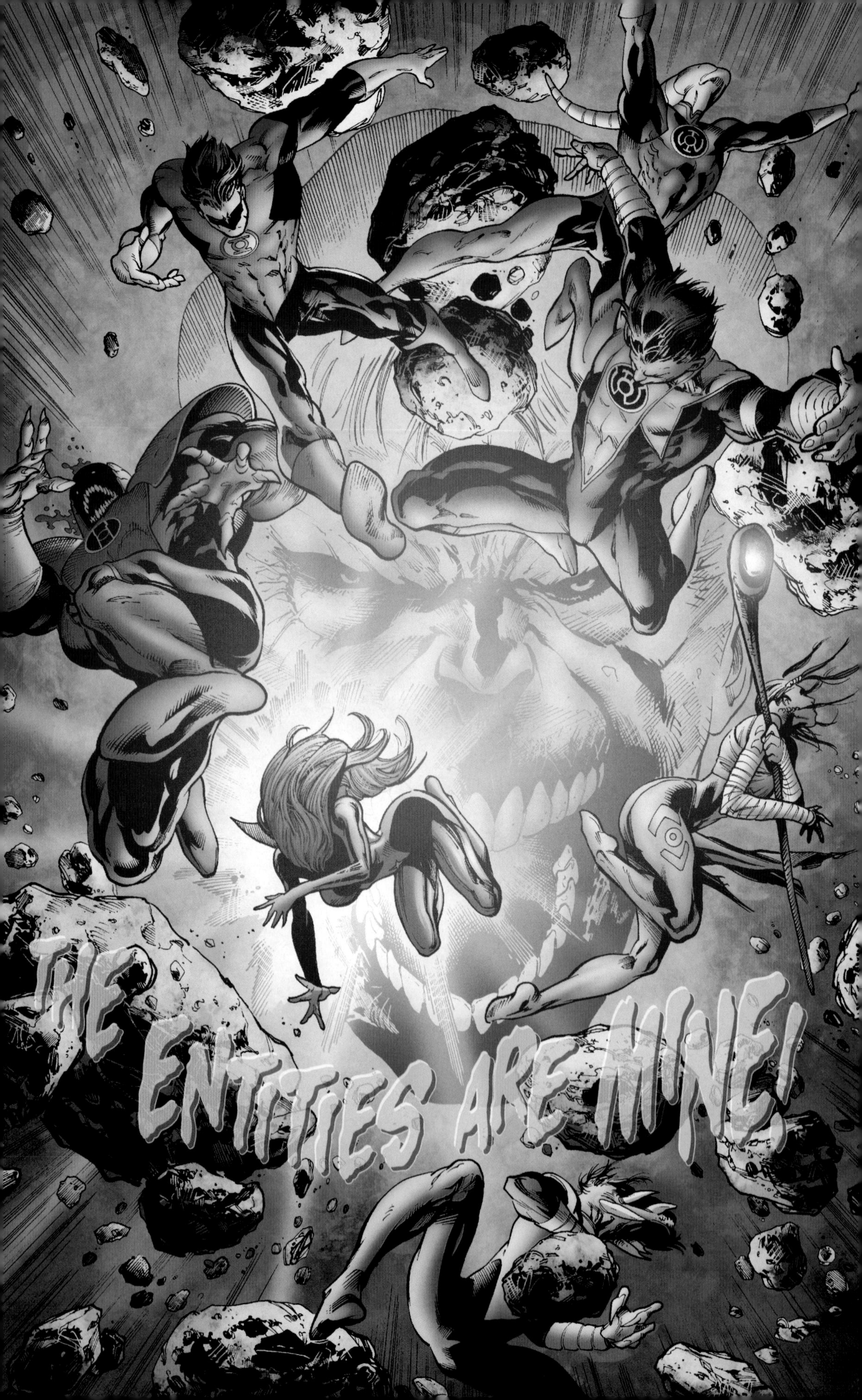
THE ENTITIES ARE MINE!

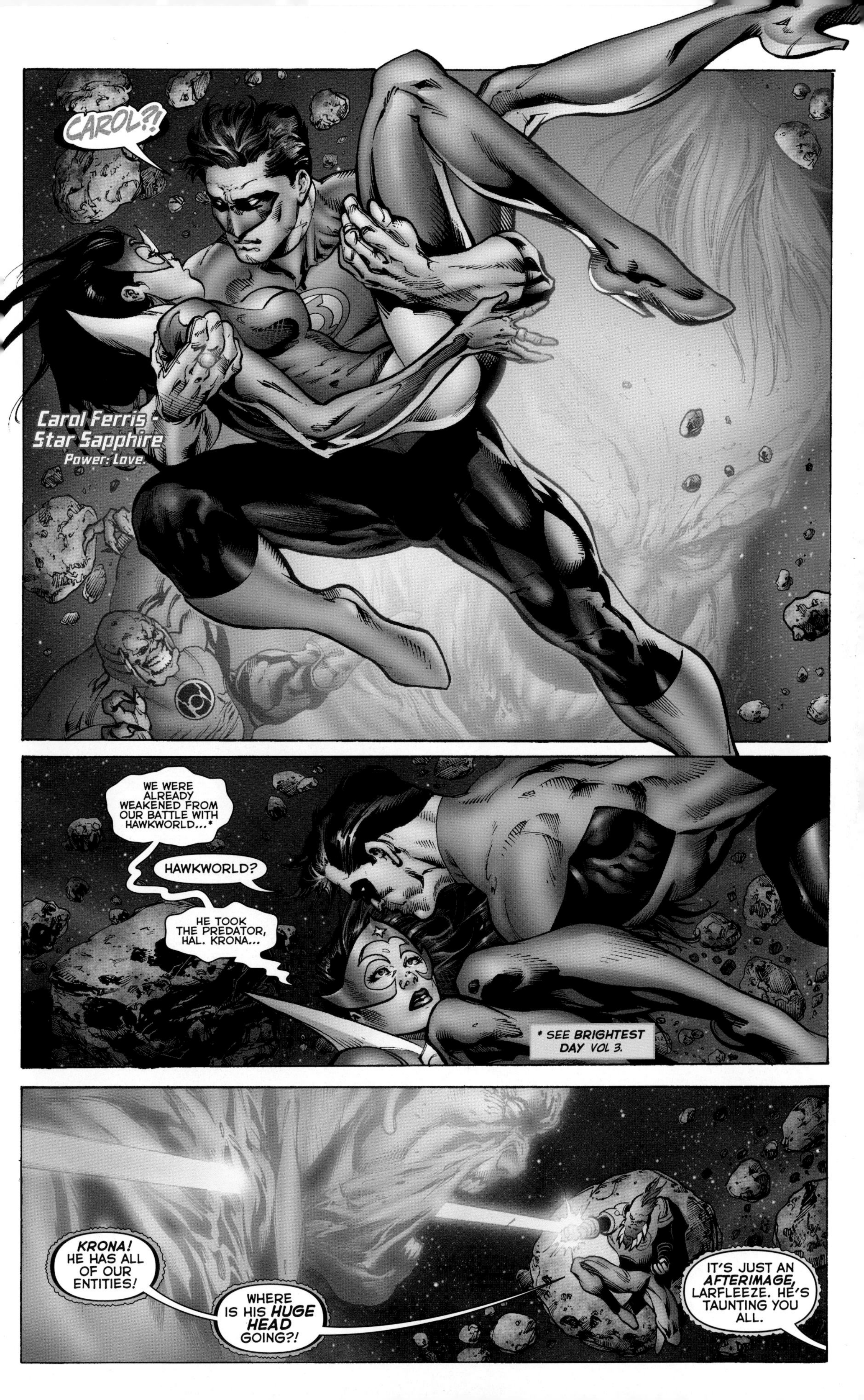
CAROL?!
Carol Ferris - Star Sapphire
Power: Love.
WE WERE ALREADY WEAKENED FROM OUR BATTLE WITH HAWKWORLD...*
HAWKWORLD?
HE TOOK THE PREDATOR, HAL. KRONA...
* SEE BRIGHTEST DAY VOL 3.
KRONA! HE HAS ALL OF OUR ENTITIES!
WHERE IS HIS HUGE HEAD GOING?!
IT'S JUST AN AFTERIMAGE, LARFLEEZE. HE'S TAUNTING YOU ALL.

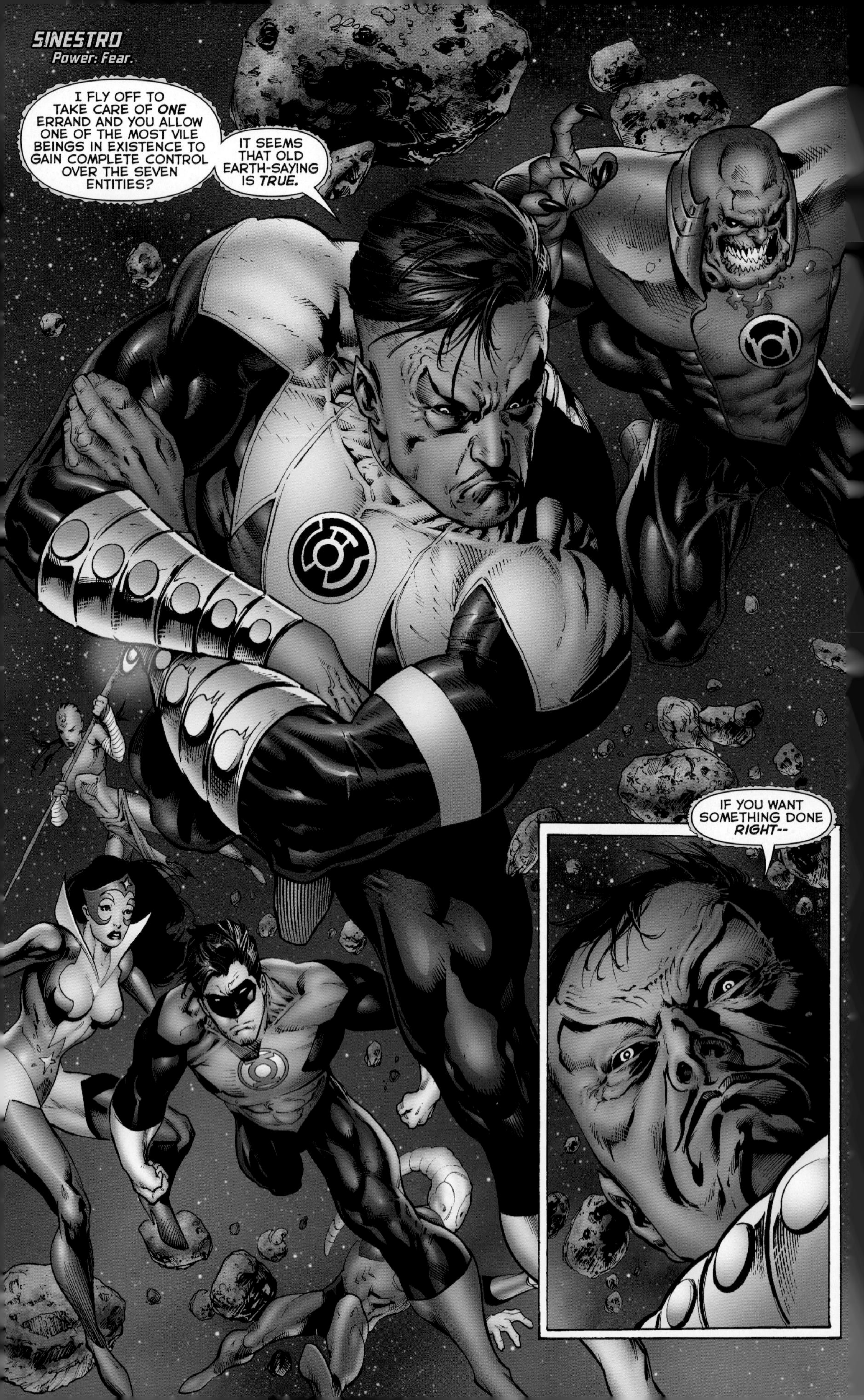
SINESTRO
Power: Fear.
I FLY OFF TO TAKE CARE OF ONE ERRAND AND YOU ALLOW ONE OF THE MOST VILE BEINGS IN EXISTENCE TO GAIN COMPLETE CONTROL OVER THE SEVEN ENTITIES?
IT SEEMS THAT OLD EARTH-SAYING IS TRUE.
IF YOU WANT SOMETHING DONE RIGHT--

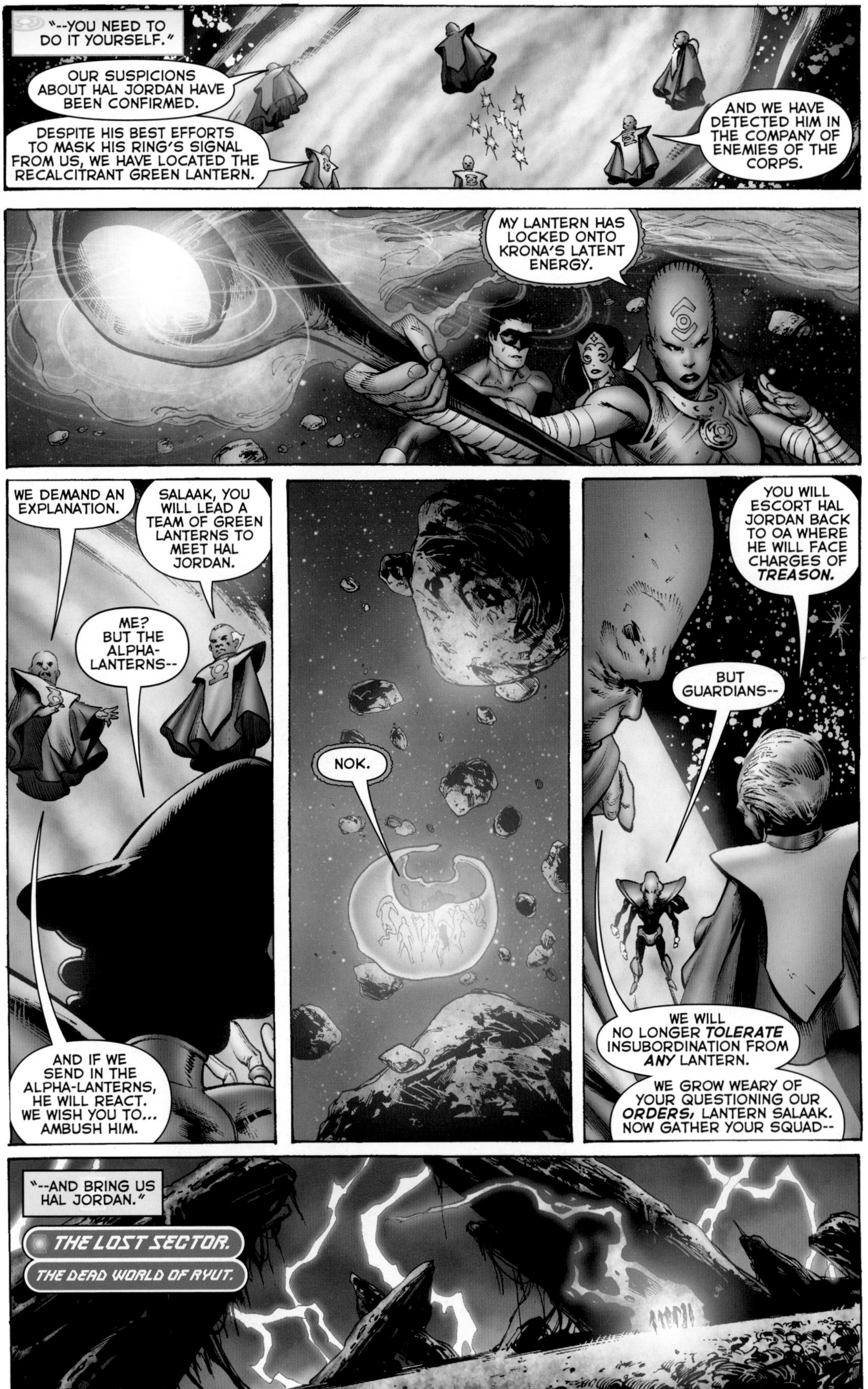
"--YOU NEED TO DO IT YOURSELF."
OUR SUSPICIONS ABOUT HAL JORDAN HAVE BEEN CONFIRMED.
DESPITE HIS BEST EFFORTS TO MASK HIS RING'S SIGNAL FROM US, WE HAVE LOCATED THE RECALCITRANT GREEN LANTERN.
AND WE HAVE DETECTED HIM IN THE COMPANY OF ENEMIES OF THE CORPS.
MY LANTERN HAS LOCKED ONTO KRONA'S LATENT ENERGY.
WE DEMAND AN EXPLANATION.
SALAAK, YOU WILL LEAD A TEAM OF GREEN LANTERNS TO MEET HAL JORDAN.
ME? BUT THE ALPHA-LANTERNS--
AND IF WE SEND IN THE ALPHA-LANTERNS, HE WILL REACT. WE WISH YOU TO... AMBUSH HIM.
NOK.
YOU WILL ESCORT HAL JORDAN BACK TO OA WHERE HE WILL FACE CHARGES OF TREASON.
BUT GUARDIANS--
WE WILL NO LONGER TOLERATE INSUBORDINATION FROM ANY LANTERN.
WE GROW WEARY OF YOUR QUESTIONING OUR ORDERS, LANTERN SALAAK. NOW GATHER YOUR SQUAD--
"--AND BRING US HAL JORDAN."
THE LOST SECTOR.
THE DEAD WORLD OF RYUT.

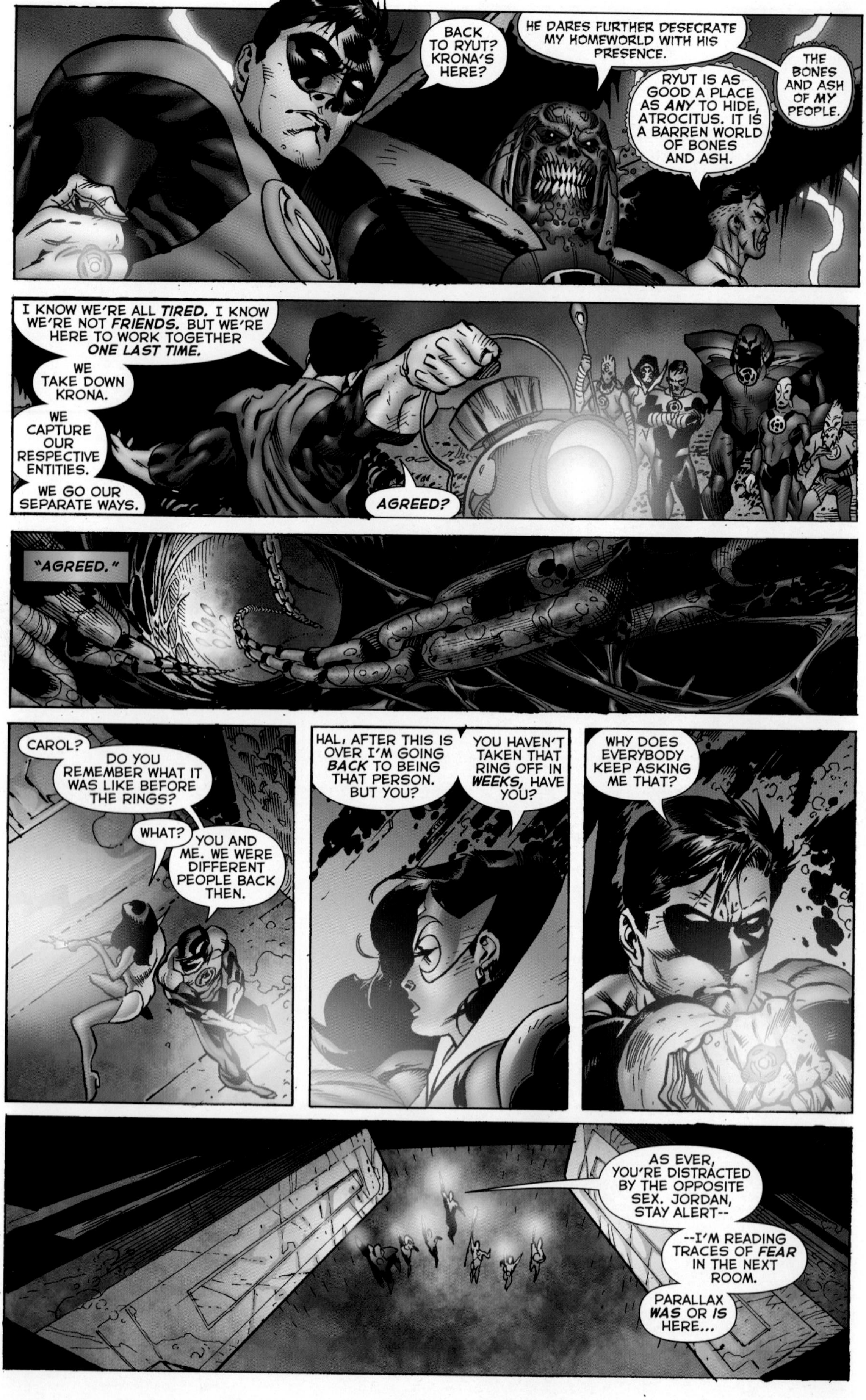
BACK TO RYUT? KRONA'S HERE?
HE DARES FURTHER DESECRATE MY HOMEWORLD WITH HIS PRESENCE.
RYUT IS AS GOOD A PLACE AS ANY TO HIDE, ATROCITUS. IT IS A BARREN WORLD OF BONES AND ASH.
THE BONES AND ASH OF MY PEOPLE.
I KNOW WE'RE ALL TIRED. I KNOW WE'RE NOT FRIENDS. BUT WE'RE HERE TO WORK TOGETHER ONE LAST TIME.
WE TAKE DOWN KRONA.
WE CAPTURE OUR RESPECTIVE ENTITIES.
WE GO OUR SEPARATE WAYS.
AGREED?
"AGREED."
CAROL?
DO YOU REMEMBER WHAT IT WAS LIKE BEFORE THE RINGS?
WHAT?
YOU AND ME. WE WERE DIFFERENT PEOPLE BACK THEN.
HAL, AFTER THIS IS OVER I'M GOING BACK TO BEING THAT PERSON. BUT YOU?
YOU HAVEN'T TAKEN THAT RING OFF IN WEEKS, HAVE YOU?
WHY DOES EVERYBODY KEEP ASKING ME THAT?
AS EVER, YOU'RE DISTRACTED BY THE OPPOSITE SEX. JORDAN, STAY ALERT--
--I'M READING TRACES OF FEAR IN THE NEXT ROOM.
PARALLAX WAS OR IS HERE...

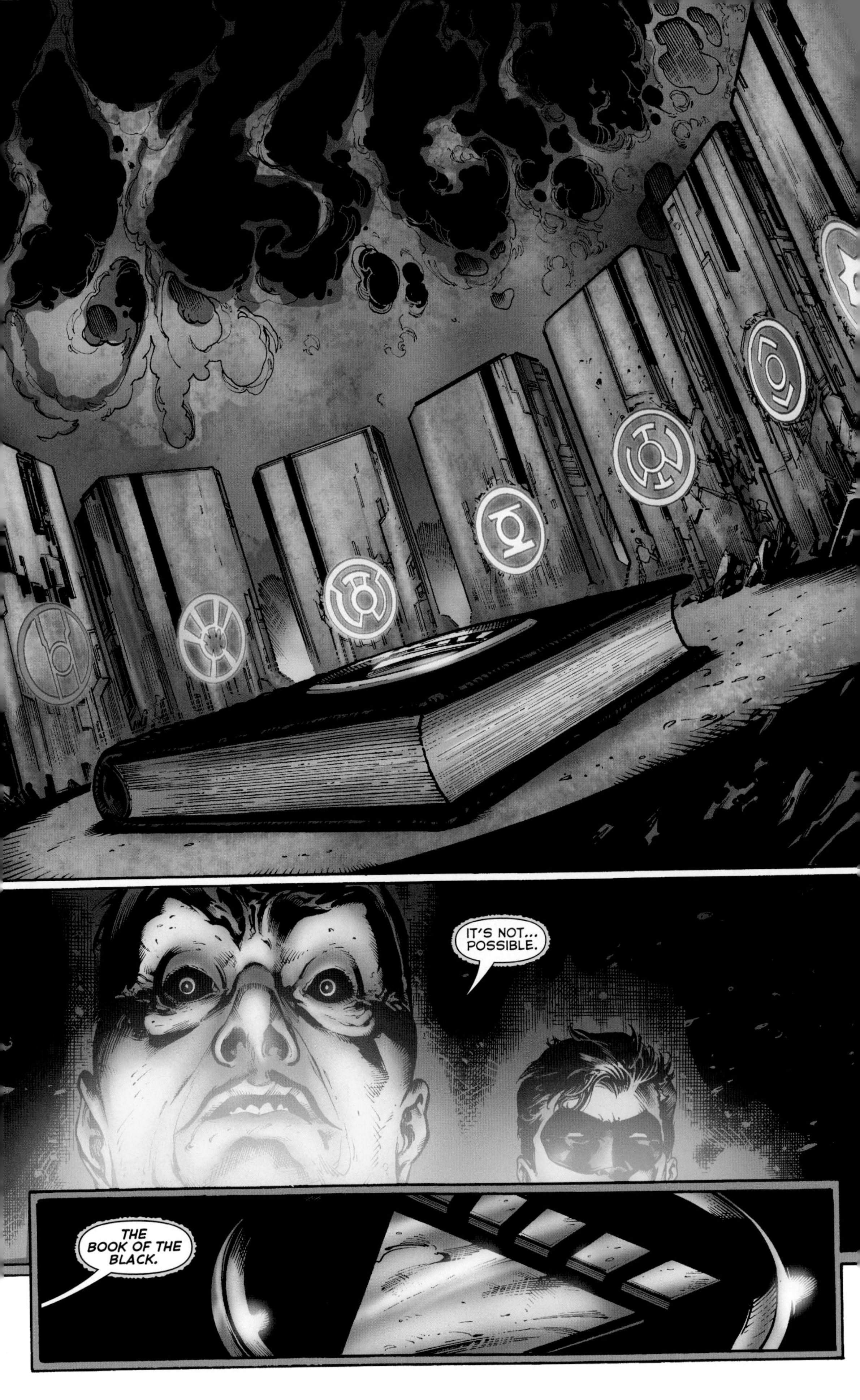
IT'S NOT... POSSIBLE.
THE BOOK OF THE BLACK.

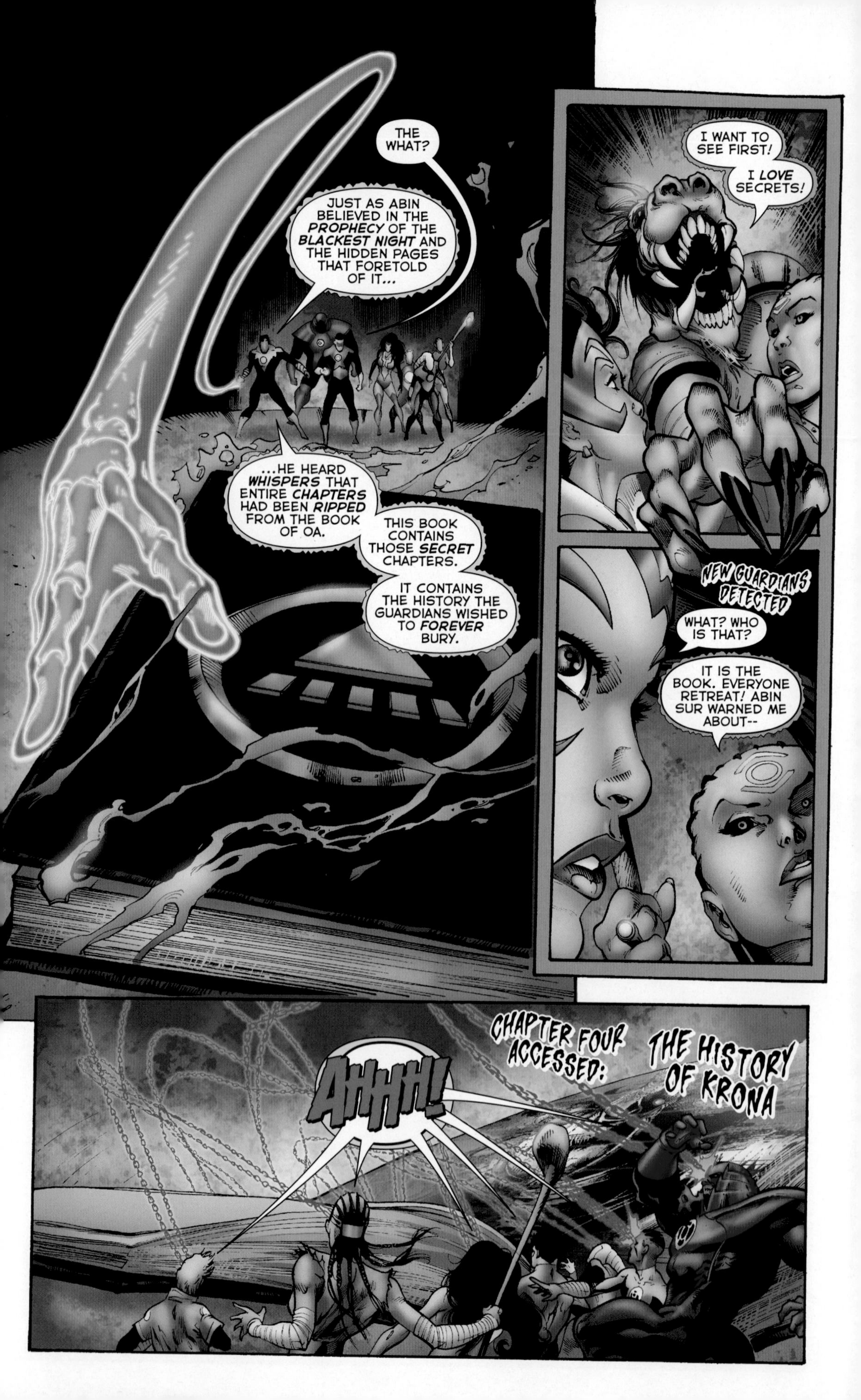
THE WHAT?
JUST AS ABIN BELIEVED IN THE PROPHECY OF THE BLACKEST NIGHT AND THE HIDDEN PAGES THAT FORETOLD OF IT...
...HE HEARD WHISPERS THAT ENTIRE CHAPTERS HAD BEEN RIPPED FROM THE BOOK OF OA.
THIS BOOK CONTAINS THOSE SECRET CHAPTERS.
IT CONTAINS THE HISTORY THE GUARDIANS WISHED TO FOREVER BURY.
I WANT TO SEE FIRST!
I LOVE SECRETS!
NEW GUARDIANS DETECTED
WHAT? WHO IS THAT?
IT IS THE BOOK. EVERYONE RETREAT! ABIN SUR WARNED ME ABOUT--
CHAPTER FOUR ACCESSED:
THE HISTORY OF KRONA
AHHH!

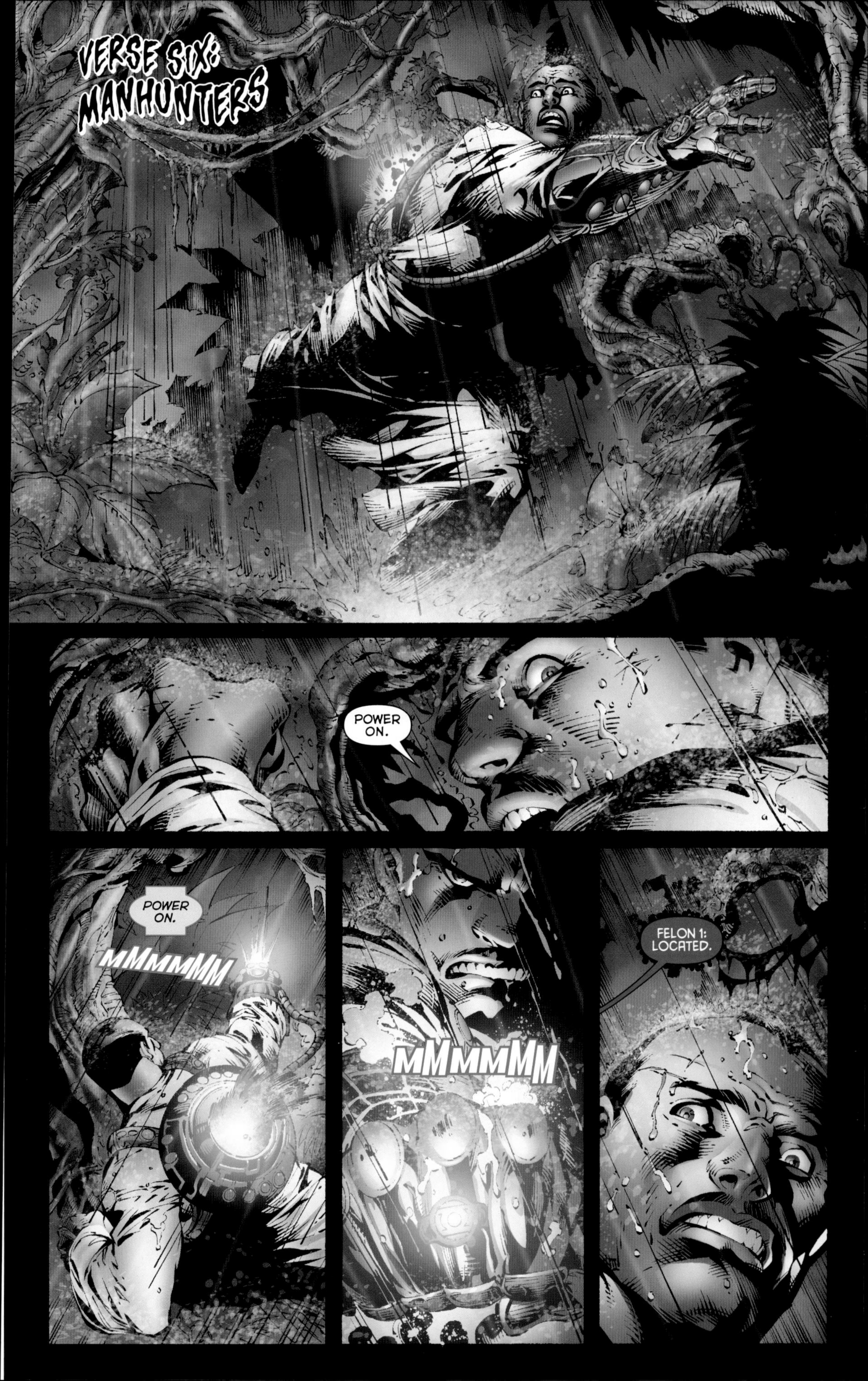
VERSE SIX: MANHUNTERS
POWER ON.
POWER ON.
MMMMMM
MMMMMM
FELON 1: LOCATED.

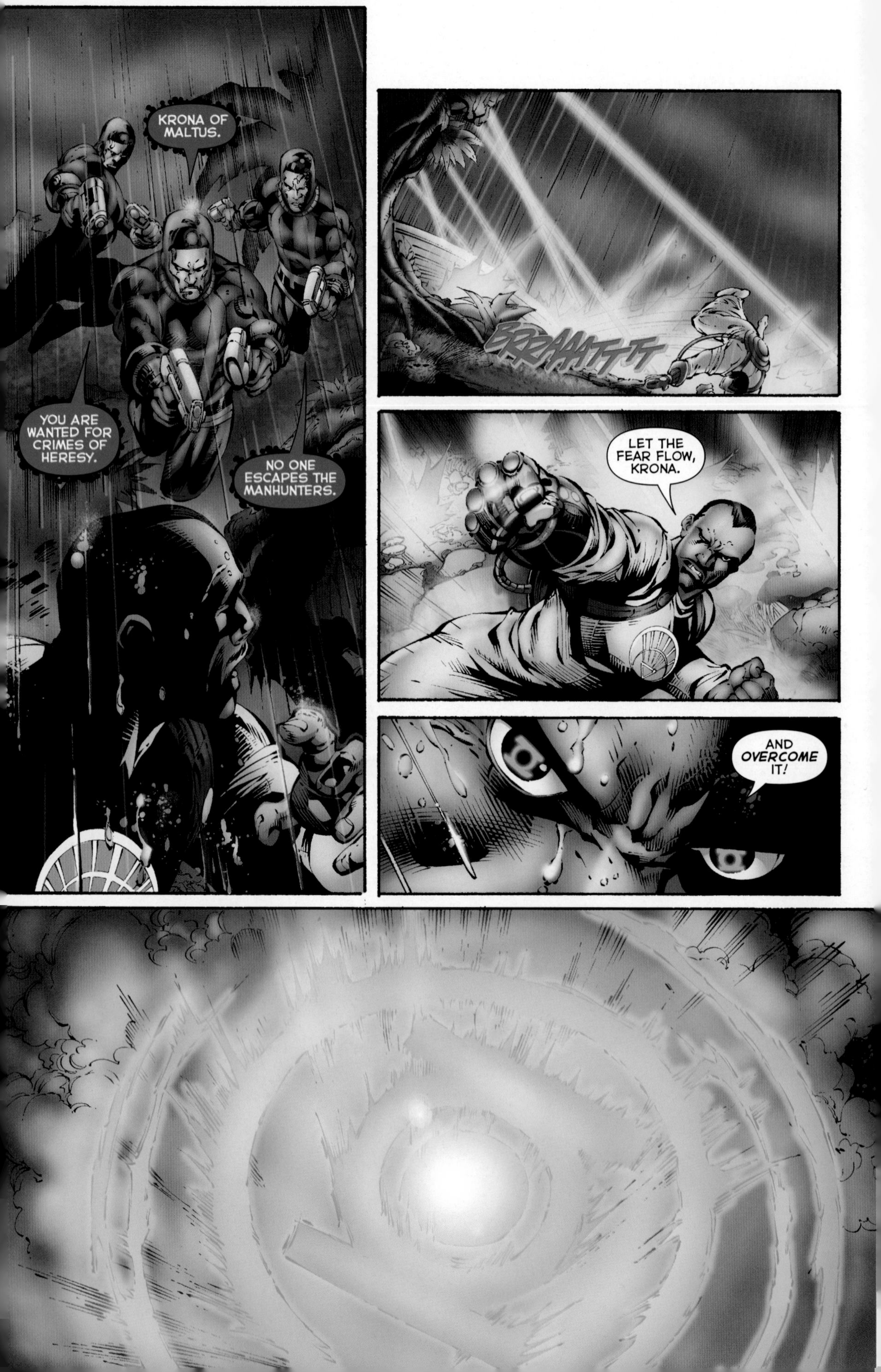
KRONA OF MALTUS.
YOU ARE WANTED FOR CRIMES OF HERESY.
NO ONE ESCAPES THE MANHUNTERS.
BRRAAATTTT
LET THE FEAR FLOW, KRONA.
AND OVERCOME IT!

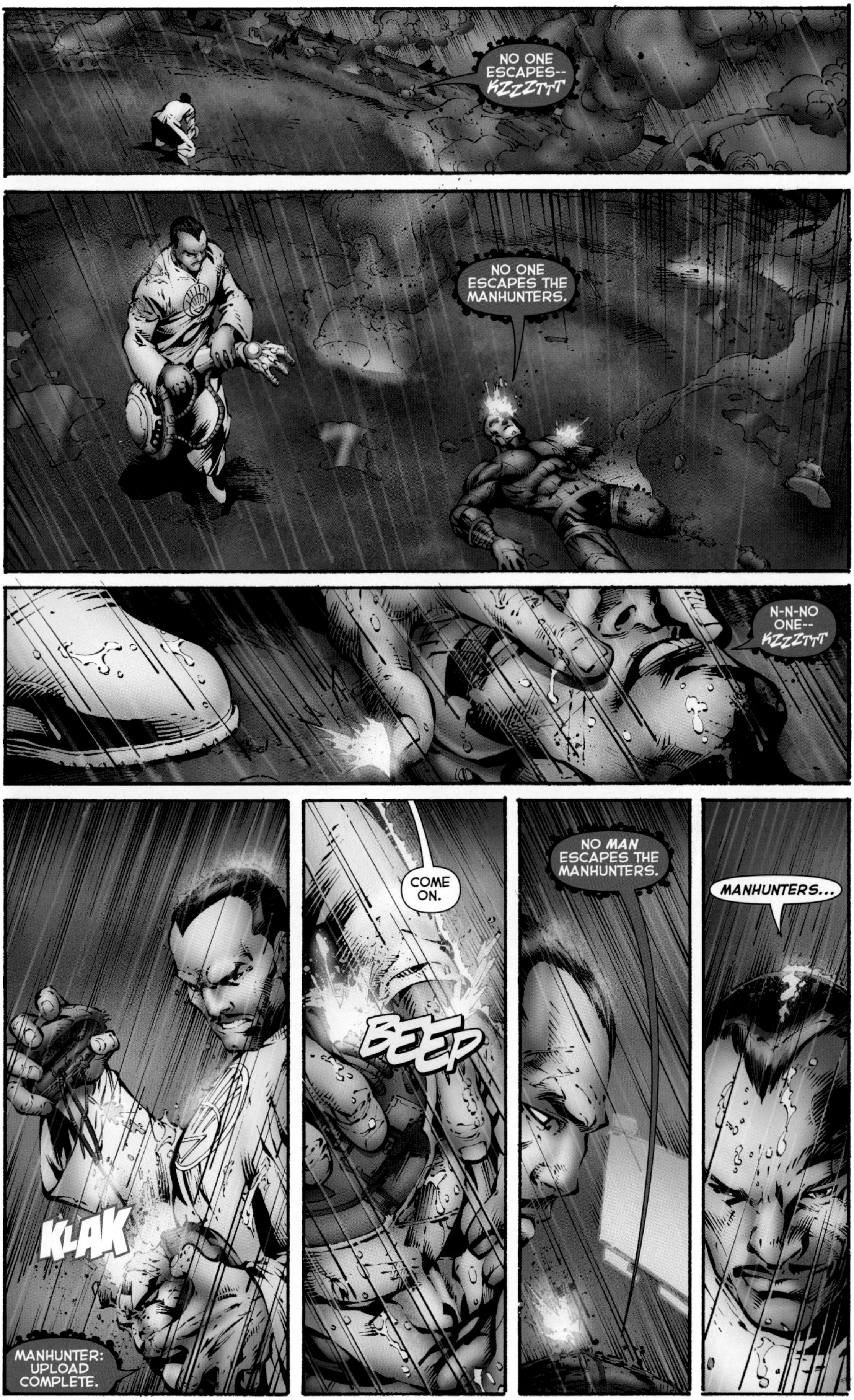
NO ONE ESCAPES-- KZZZTTT
NO ONE ESCAPES THE MANHUNTERS.
N-N-NO ONE-- KZZZTTT
KLAK
MANHUNTER: UPLOAD COMPLETE.
COME ON.
BEEEP
NO MAN ESCAPES THE MANHUNTERS.
MANHUNTERS...

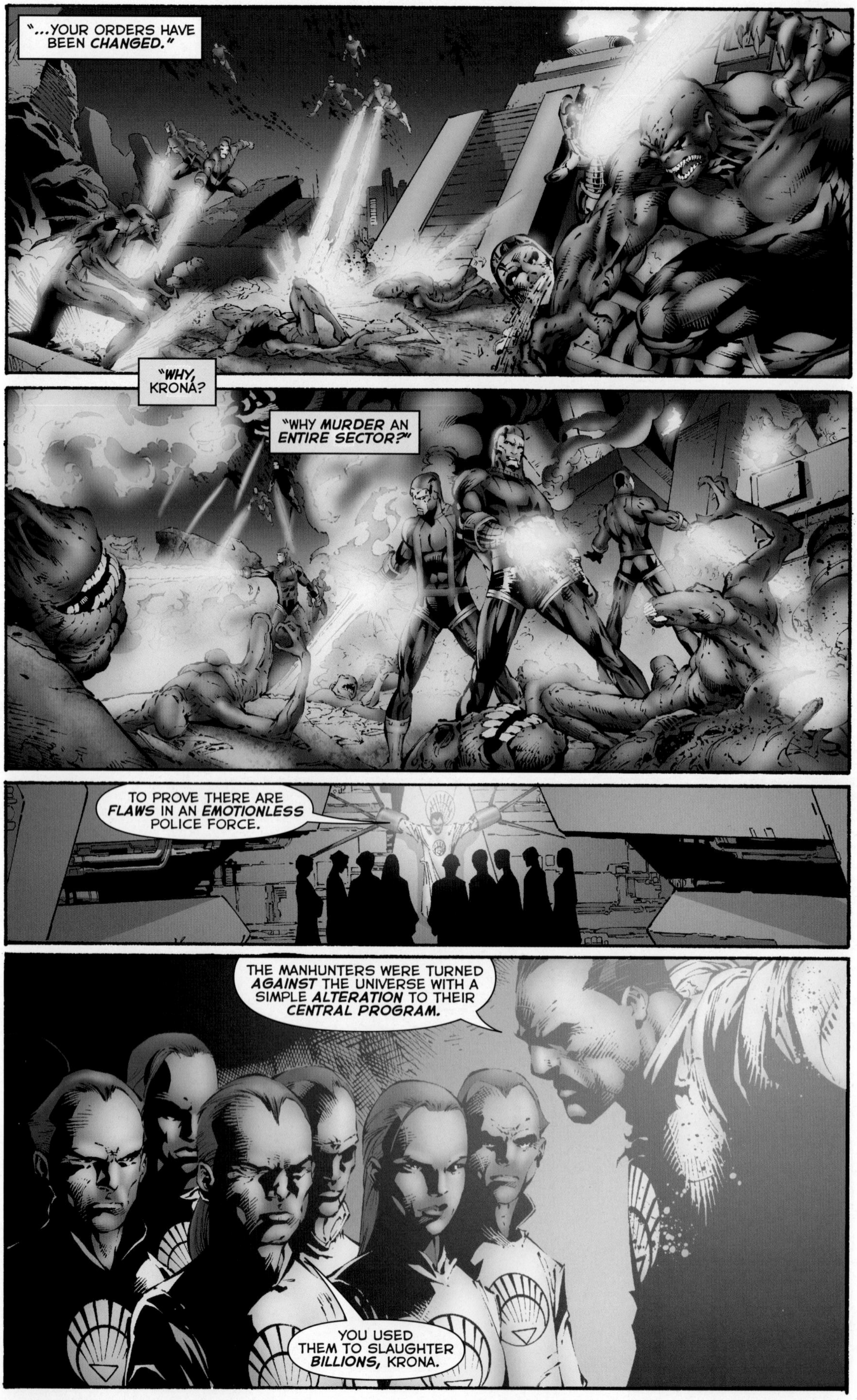
"...YOUR ORDERS HAVE BEEN CHANGED."
"WHY, KRONA?
"WHY MURDER AN ENTIRE SECTOR?"
TO PROVE THERE ARE FLAWS IN AN EMOTIONLESS POLICE FORCE.
THE MANHUNTERS WERE TURNED AGAINST THE UNIVERSE WITH A SIMPLE ALTERATION TO THEIR CENTRAL PROGRAM.
YOU USED THEM TO SLAUGHTER BILLIONS, KRONA.

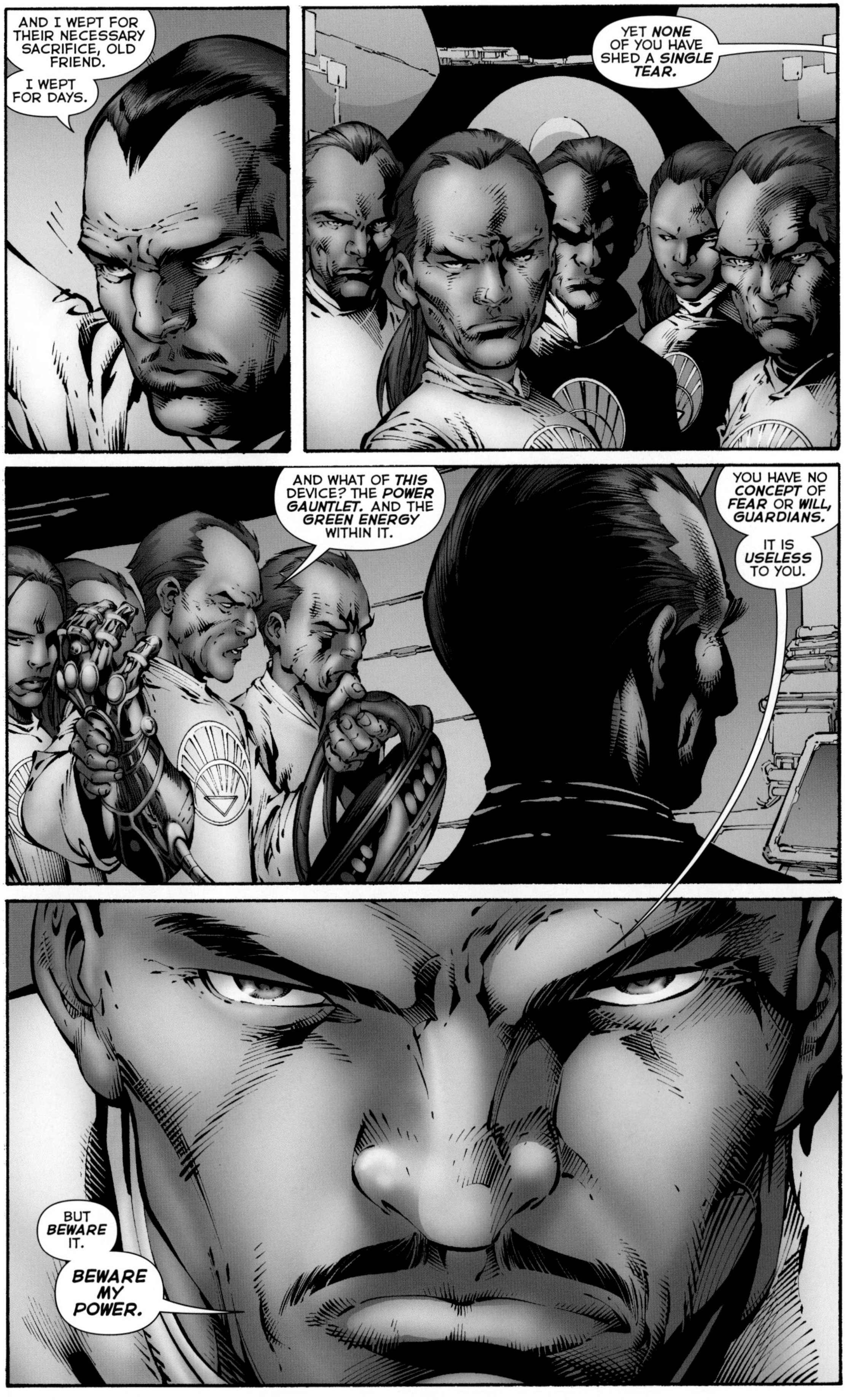
AND I WEPT FOR THEIR NECESSARY SACRIFICE, OLD FRIEND.
I WEPT FOR DAYS.
YET NONE OF YOU HAVE SHED A SINGLE TEAR.
AND WHAT OF THIS DEVICE? THE POWER GAUNTLET. AND THE GREEN ENERGY WITHIN IT.
YOU HAVE NO CONCEPT OF FEAR OR WILL, GUARDIANS.
IT IS USELESS TO YOU.
BUT BEWARE IT.
BEWARE MY POWER.

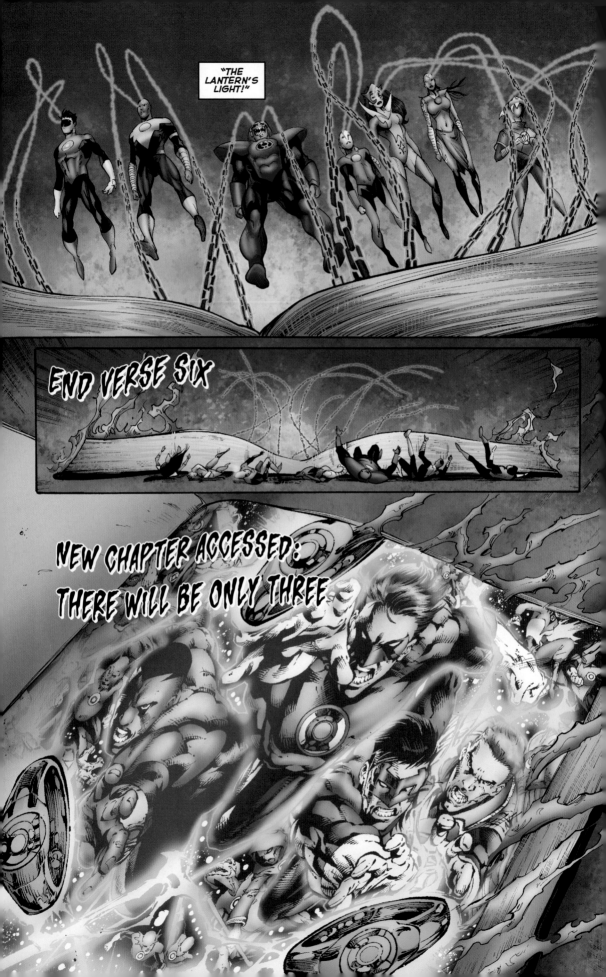

"THE LANTERN'S LIGHT!"

END VERSE SIX

NEW CHAPTER ACCESSED: THERE WILL BE ONLY THREE

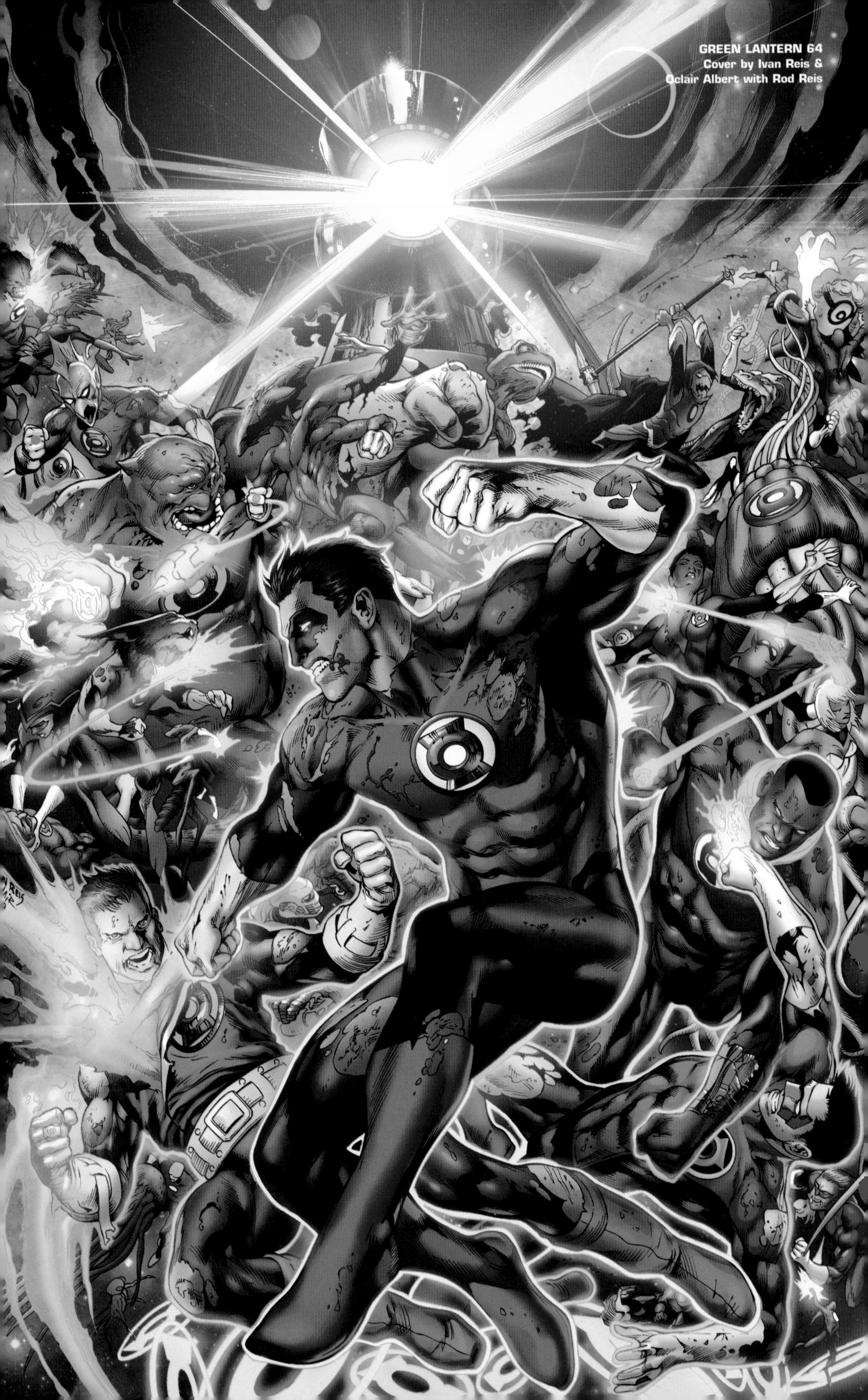

GREEN LANTERN 64
Cover by Ivan Reis &
Oclair Albert with Rod Reis

WAR OF THE GREEN LANTERNS
PART ONE

Geoff Johns Writer
Doug Mahnke Penciller
Christian Alamy, Keith Champagne, Mark Irwin & Tom Nguyen Inkers

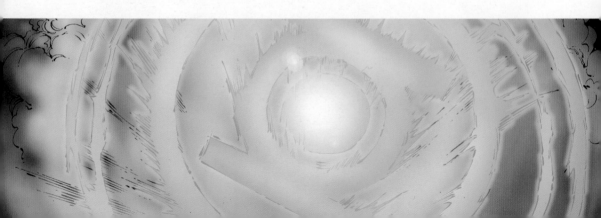

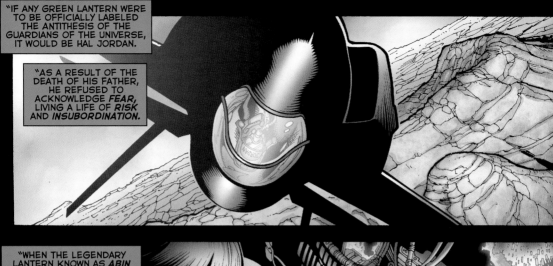

"IF ANY GREEN LANTERN WERE TO BE OFFICIALLY LABELED THE ANTITHESIS OF THE GUARDIANS OF THE UNIVERSE, IT WOULD BE HAL JORDAN.

"AS A RESULT OF THE DEATH OF HIS FATHER, HE REFUSED TO ACKNOWLEDGE *FEAR*, LIVING A LIFE OF *RISK* AND *INSUBORDINATION.*

"WHEN THE LEGENDARY LANTERN KNOWN AS *ABIN SUR* TRAGICALLY DIED, THE RING *SELECTED* HAL JORDAN AS HIS REPLACEMENT.

"DESPITE GREAT DEBATE AMONG THE GUARDIANS ON THE VERY *IDEA* OF A *HUMAN* DRAFTED INTO THE CORPS, THE RING HAD NEVER CHOSEN UNWISELY.

"AND FOR A TIME, MANY EVEN BEGAN TO BELIEVE THE RING HAD CHOSEN...*WELL.*"

"DESPITE HIS LACK OF PROFESSIONALISM AND RESTRAINT, HAL JORDAN LED THE CORPS TO VICTORY ON MORE THAN ONE OCCASION.

"HE EVEN LEARNED TO *RECOGNIZE* AND *OVERCOME FEAR*, ENABLING HIM TO DEFEAT THE LIVING EMBODIMENT OF TERROR ITSELF-- *PARALLAX.*

"HE ESCAPED THE ENTITY'S POSSESSION THROUGH SHEER *WILLPOWER.*

"BUT STILL, HAL JORDAN HAS *NEVER* BEEN ABLE TO KEEP HIS EMOTIONS IN *CHECK.* HE REMAINS *RECKLESS* AND *DISOBEDIENT* AND THEREFORE A *THREAT* TO THE CORPS.

"EVEN NOW, HE HAS GONE AGAINST LANTERN LAW AND ALLIED HIMSELF FOR AN UNKNOWN REASON WITH THE OTHER UNSANCTIONED RINGBEARERS.

"FOR THAT, THE GUARDIANS OF THE UNIVERSE HAVE ASSIGNED US A TASK I CONSIDER *LONG* OVERDUE."

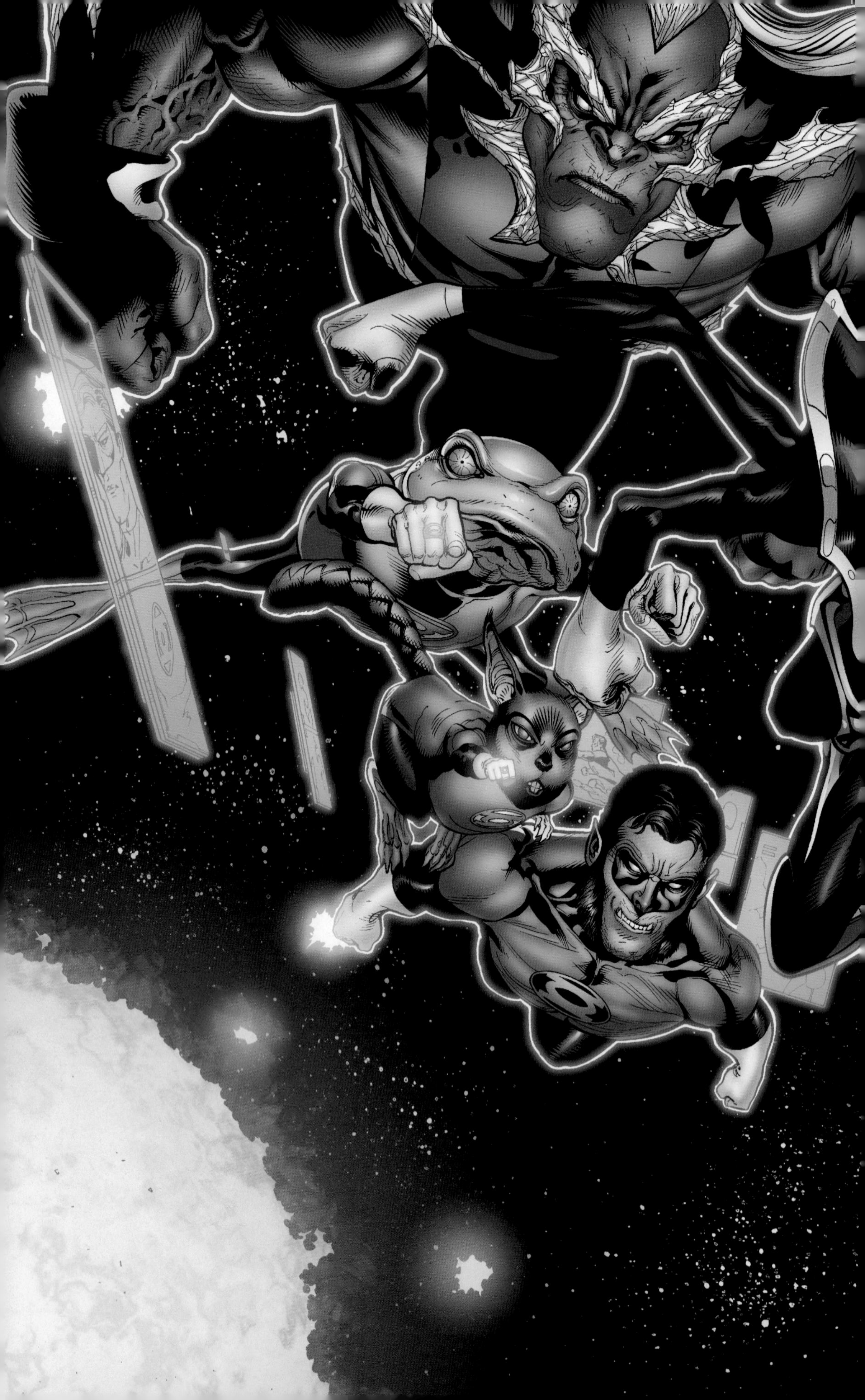

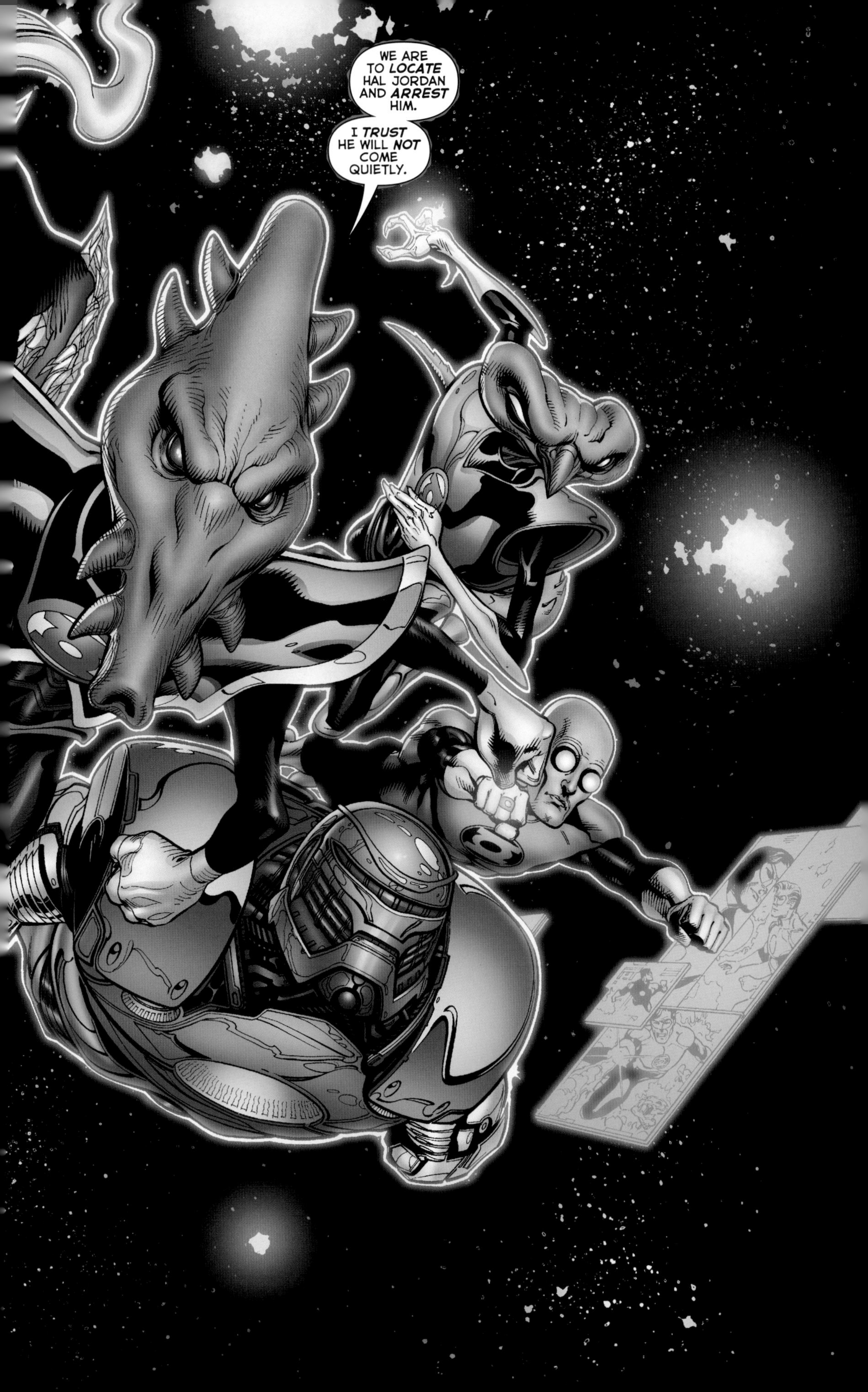
WE ARE TO LOCATE HAL JORDAN AND ARREST HIM.
I TRUST HE WILL NOT COME QUIETLY.

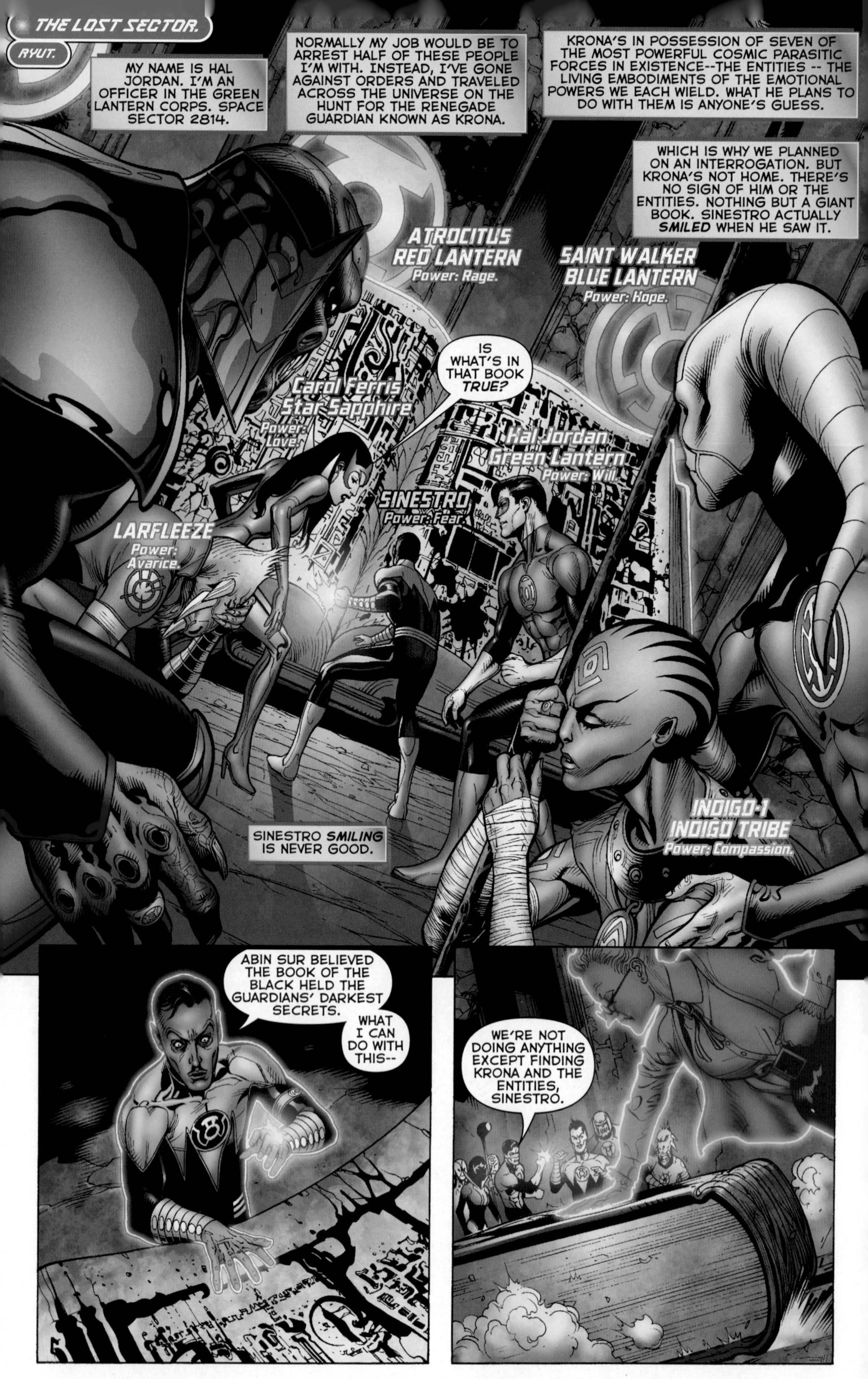
THE LOST SECTOR.
RYUT.
MY NAME IS HAL JORDAN. I'M AN OFFICER IN THE GREEN LANTERN CORPS. SPACE SECTOR 2814.
NORMALLY MY JOB WOULD BE TO ARREST HALF OF THESE PEOPLE I'M WITH. INSTEAD, I'VE GONE AGAINST ORDERS AND TRAVELED ACROSS THE UNIVERSE ON THE HUNT FOR THE RENEGADE GUARDIAN KNOWN AS KRONA.
KRONA'S IN POSSESSION OF SEVEN OF THE MOST POWERFUL COSMIC PARASITIC FORCES IN EXISTENCE--THE ENTITIES -- THE LIVING EMBODIMENTS OF THE EMOTIONAL POWERS WE EACH WIELD. WHAT HE PLANS TO DO WITH THEM IS ANYONE'S GUESS.
WHICH IS WHY WE PLANNED ON AN INTERROGATION. BUT KRONA'S NOT HOME. THERE'S NO SIGN OF HIM OR THE ENTITIES. NOTHING BUT A GIANT BOOK. SINESTRO ACTUALLY SMILED WHEN HE SAW IT.
ATROCITUS RED LANTERN Power: Rage.
SAINT WALKER BLUE LANTERN Power: Hope.
IS WHAT'S IN THAT BOOK TRUE?
Carol Ferris Star Sapphire Power: Love.
Hal Jordan Green Lantern Power: Will.
SINESTRO Power: Fear.
LARFLEEZE Power: Avarice.
INDIGO-1 INDIGO TRIBE Power: Compassion.
SINESTRO SMILING IS NEVER GOOD.
ABIN SUR BELIEVED THE BOOK OF THE BLACK HELD THE GUARDIANS' DARKEST SECRETS.
WHAT I CAN DO WITH THIS--
WE'RE NOT DOING ANYTHING EXCEPT FINDING KRONA AND THE ENTITIES, SINESTRO.

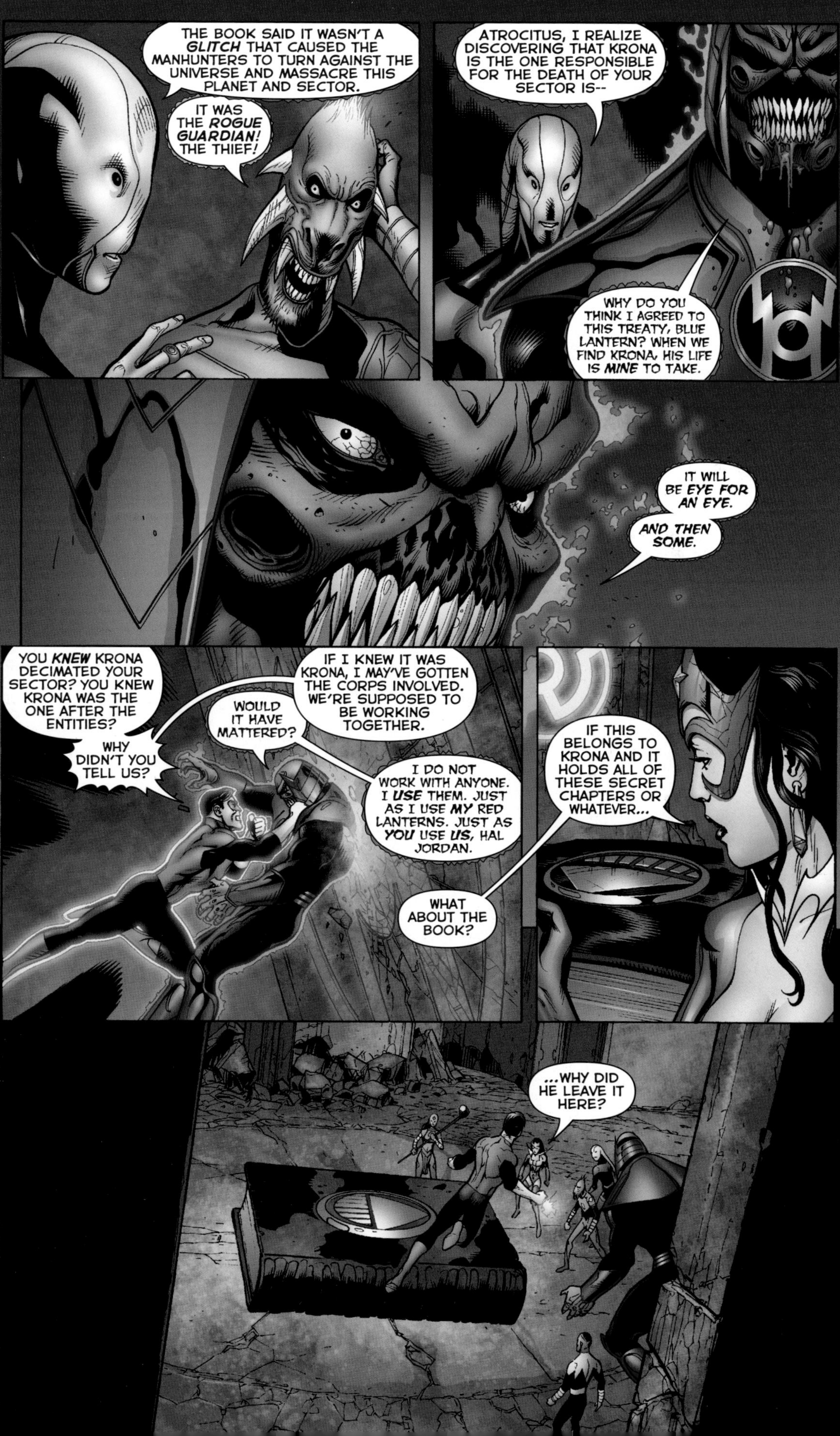
THE BOOK SAID IT WASN'T A GLITCH THAT CAUSED THE MANHUNTERS TO TURN AGAINST THE UNIVERSE AND MASSACRE THIS PLANET AND SECTOR.
IT WAS THE ROGUE GUARDIAN! THE THIEF!
ATROCITUS, I REALIZE DISCOVERING THAT KRONA IS THE ONE RESPONSIBLE FOR THE DEATH OF YOUR SECTOR IS--
WHY DO YOU THINK I AGREED TO THIS TREATY, BLUE LANTERN? WHEN WE FIND KRONA, HIS LIFE IS MINE TO TAKE.
IT WILL BE EYE FOR AN EYE.
AND THEN SOME.
YOU KNEW KRONA DECIMATED YOUR SECTOR? YOU KNEW KRONA WAS THE ONE AFTER THE ENTITIES?
WHY DIDN'T YOU TELL US?
IF I KNEW IT WAS KRONA, I MAY'VE GOTTEN THE CORPS INVOLVED. WE'RE SUPPOSED TO BE WORKING TOGETHER.
WOULD IT HAVE MATTERED?
I DO NOT WORK WITH ANYONE. I USE THEM. JUST AS I USE MY RED LANTERNS. JUST AS YOU USE US, HAL JORDAN.
WHAT ABOUT THE BOOK?
IF THIS BELONGS TO KRONA AND IT HOLDS ALL OF THESE SECRET CHAPTERS OR WHATEVER...
...WHY DID HE LEAVE IT HERE?

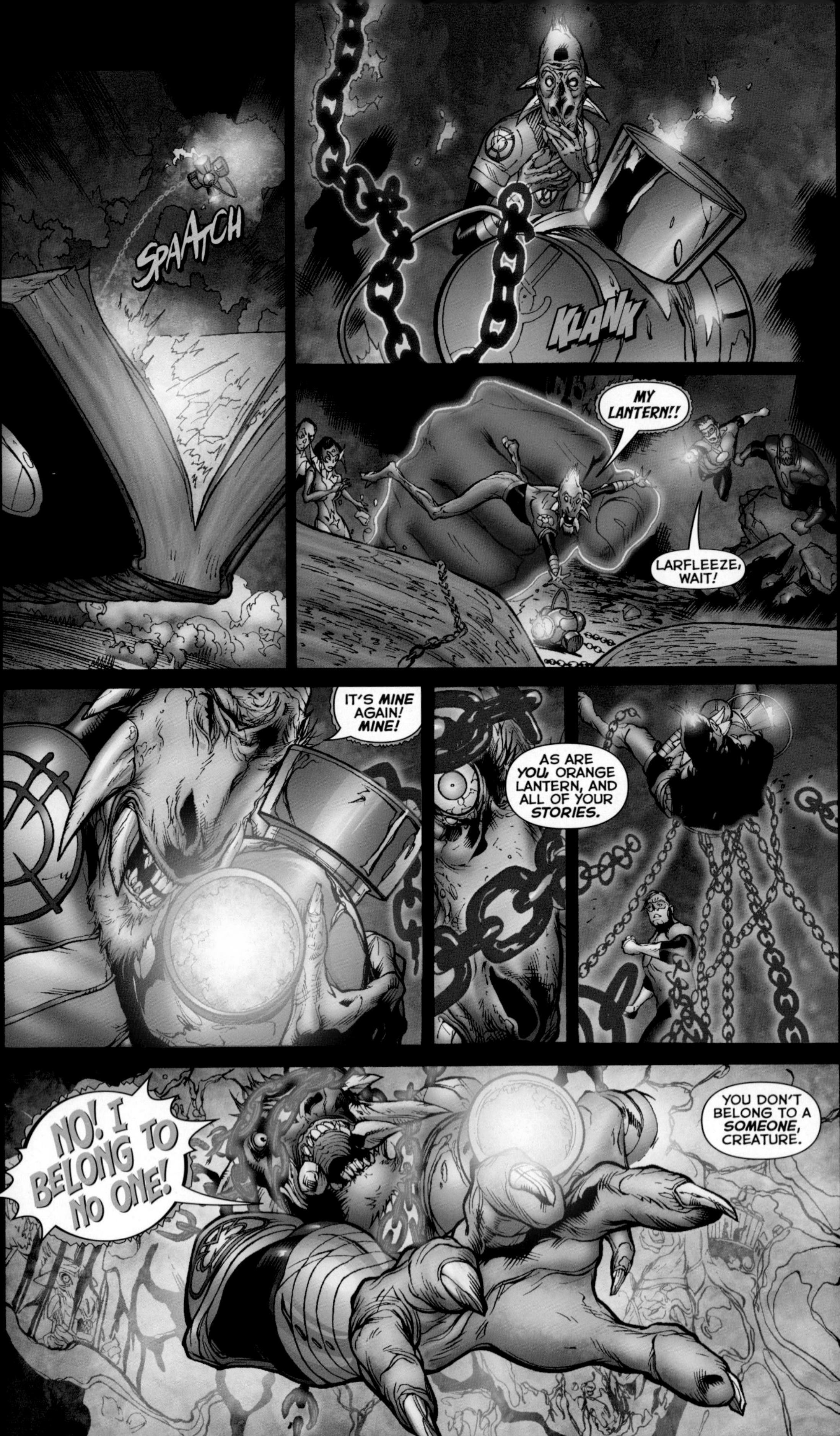
SPAATCH
KLANK
MY LANTERN!!
LARFLEEZE, WAIT!
IT'S MINE AGAIN! MINE!
AS ARE YOU, ORANGE LANTERN, AND ALL OF YOUR STORIES.
NO! I BELONG TO NO ONE!
YOU DON'T BELONG TO A SOMEONE, CREATURE.

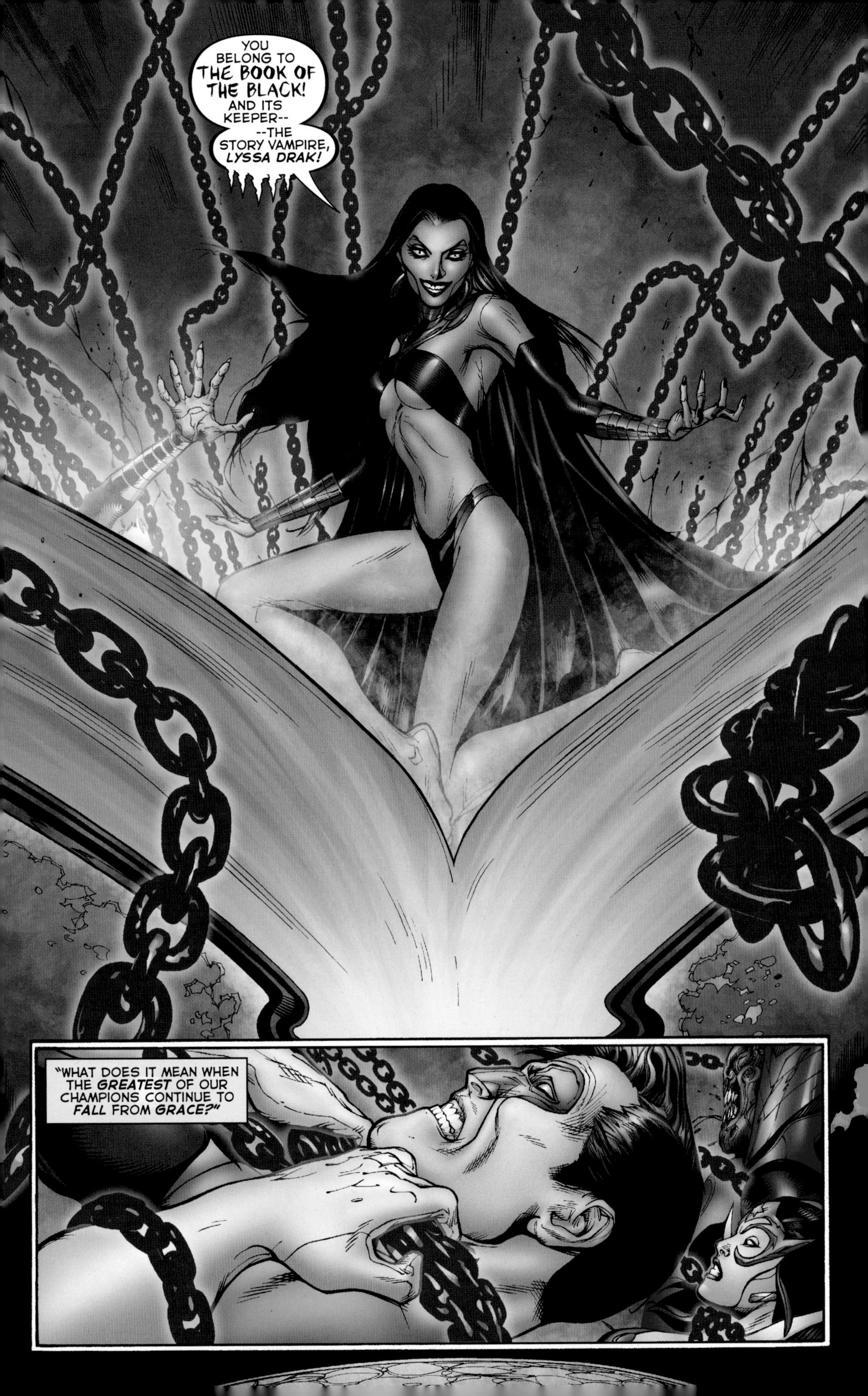
YOU BELONG TO THE BOOK OF THE BLACK! AND ITS KEEPER--
--THE STORY VAMPIRE, LYSSA DRAK!
"WHAT DOES IT MEAN WHEN THE GREATEST OF OUR CHAMPIONS CONTINUE TO FALL FROM GRACE?"

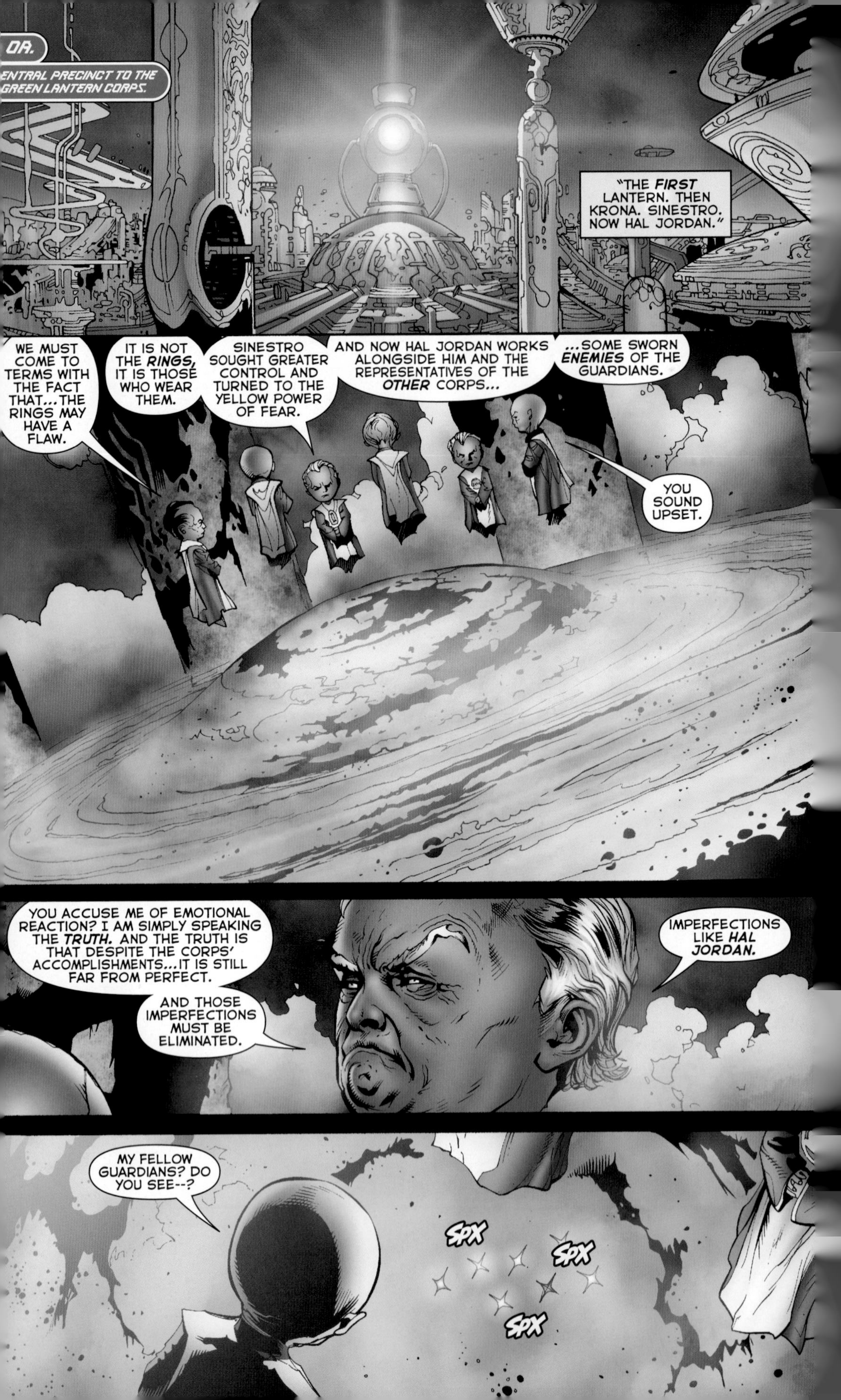
OA.
ENTRAL PRECINCT TO THE GREEN LANTERN CORPS.
"THE FIRST LANTERN. THEN KRONA. SINESTRO. NOW HAL JORDAN."
WE MUST COME TO TERMS WITH THE FACT THAT...THE RINGS MAY HAVE A FLAW.
IT IS NOT THE RINGS, IT IS THOSE WHO WEAR THEM.
SINESTRO SOUGHT GREATER CONTROL AND TURNED TO THE YELLOW POWER OF FEAR.
AND NOW HAL JORDAN WORKS ALONGSIDE HIM AND THE REPRESENTATIVES OF THE OTHER CORPS...
...SOME SWORN ENEMIES OF THE GUARDIANS.
YOU SOUND UPSET.
YOU ACCUSE ME OF EMOTIONAL REACTION? I AM SIMPLY SPEAKING THE TRUTH. AND THE TRUTH IS THAT DESPITE THE CORPS' ACCOMPLISHMENTS...IT IS STILL FAR FROM PERFECT.
AND THOSE IMPERFECTIONS MUST BE ELIMINATED.
IMPERFECTIONS LIKE HAL JORDAN.
MY FELLOW GUARDIANS? DO YOU SEE--?
SPX
SPX
SPX

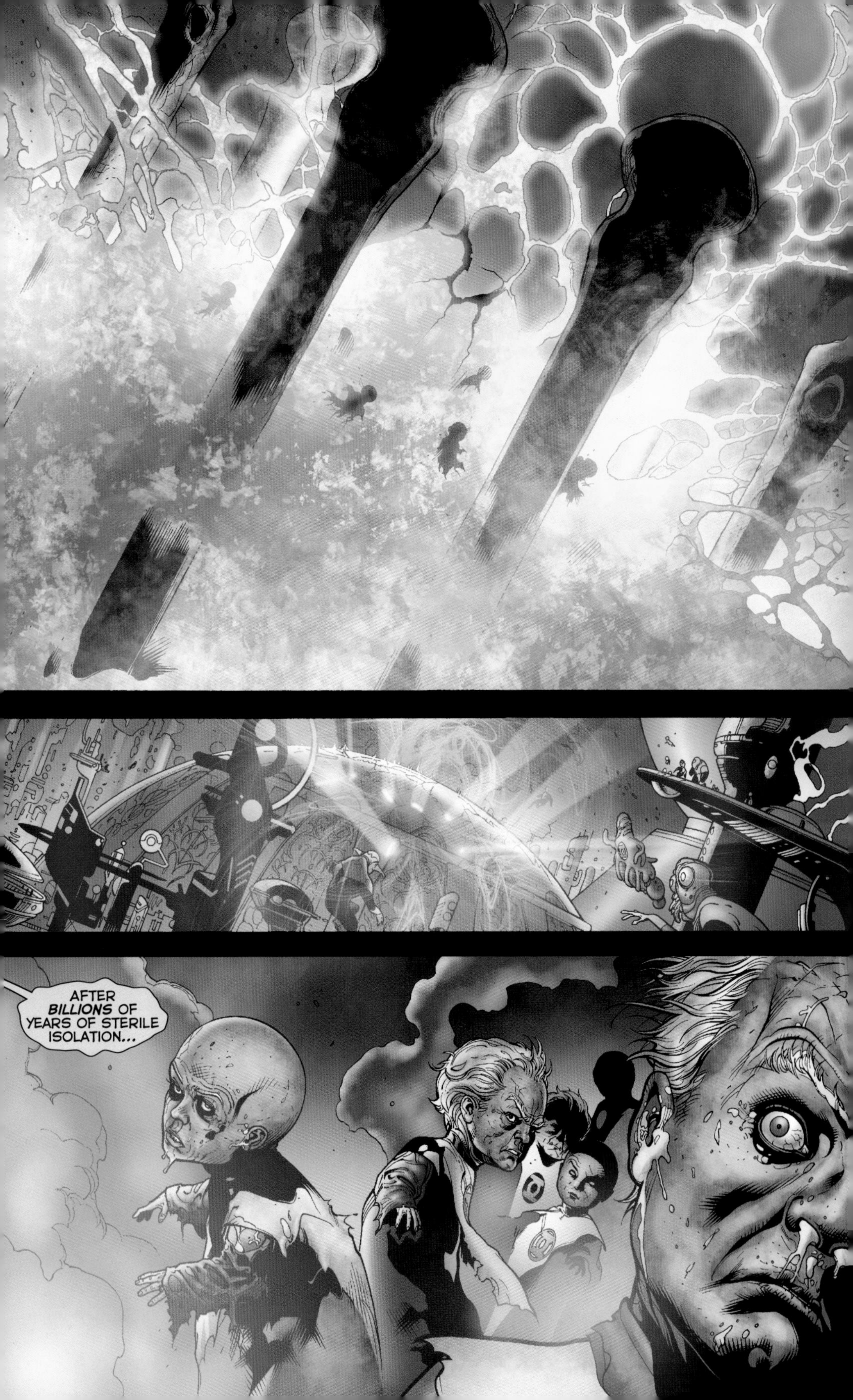
AFTER BILLIONS OF YEARS OF STERILE ISOLATION...

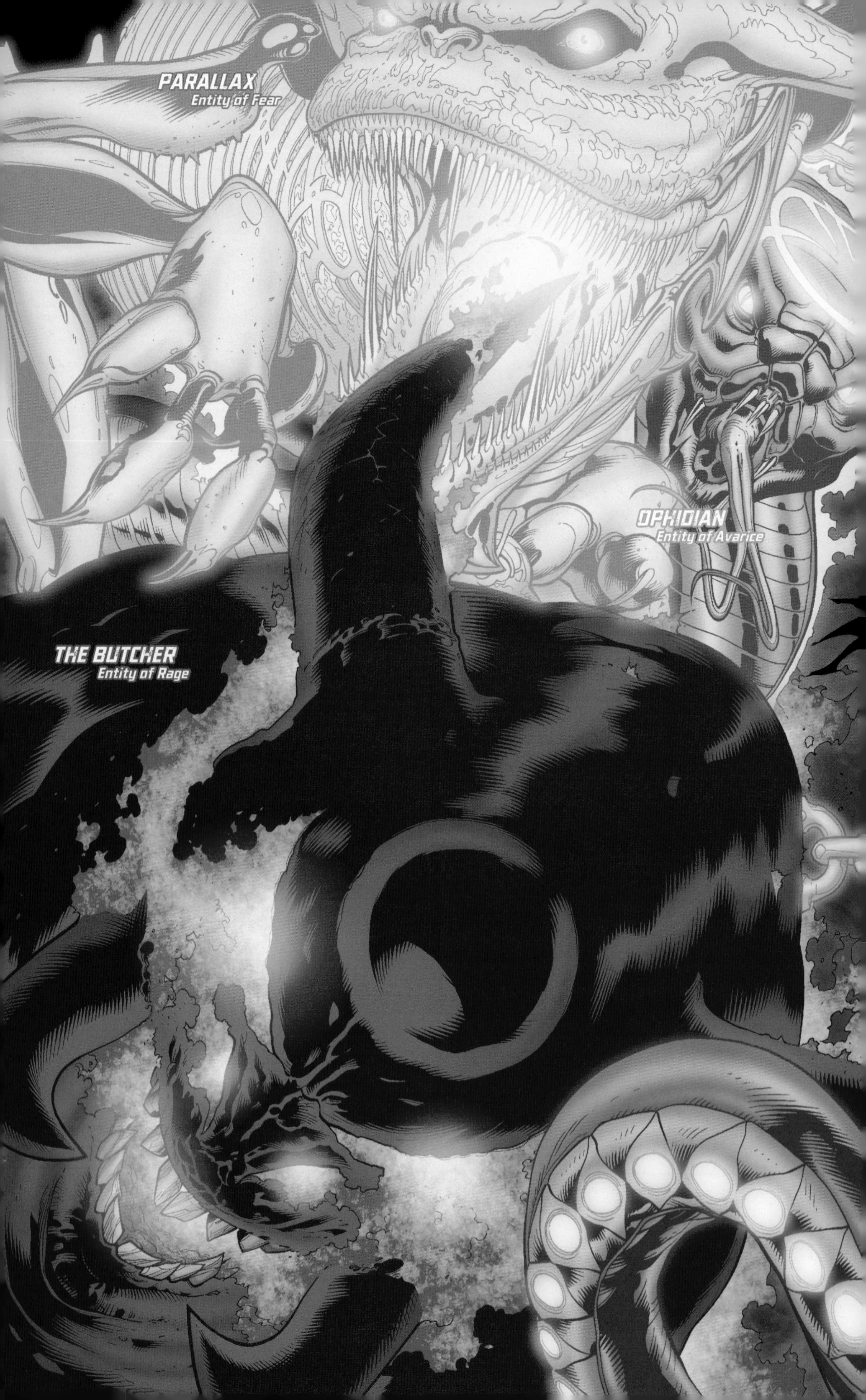
PARALLAX
Entity of Fear
OPHIDIAN
Entity of Avarice
THE BUTCHER
Entity of Rage

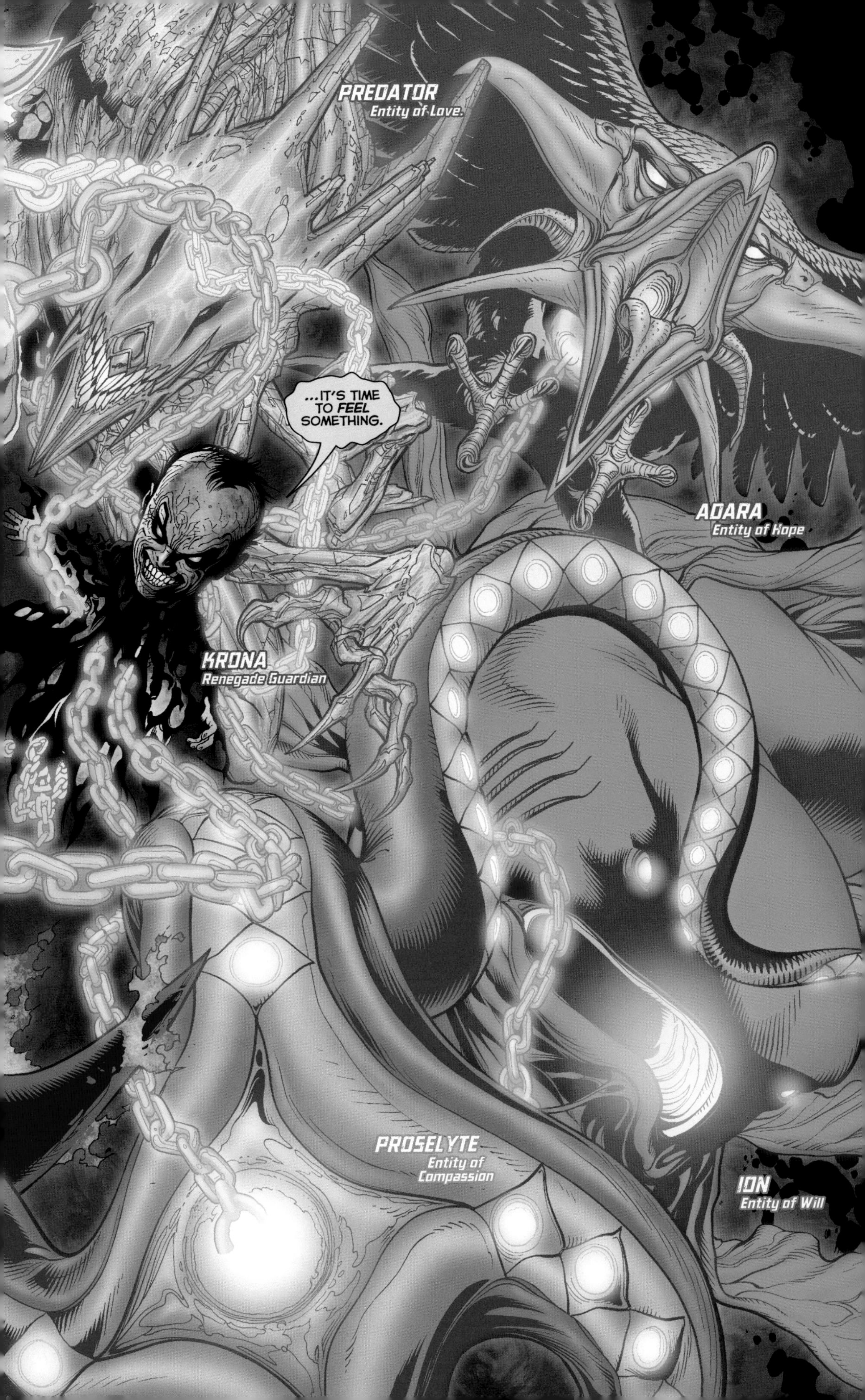
PREDATOR
Entity of Love.
...IT'S TIME TO FEEL SOMETHING.
ADARA
Entity of Hope
KRONA
Renegade Guardian
PROSELYTE
Entity of Compassion
ION
Entity of Will

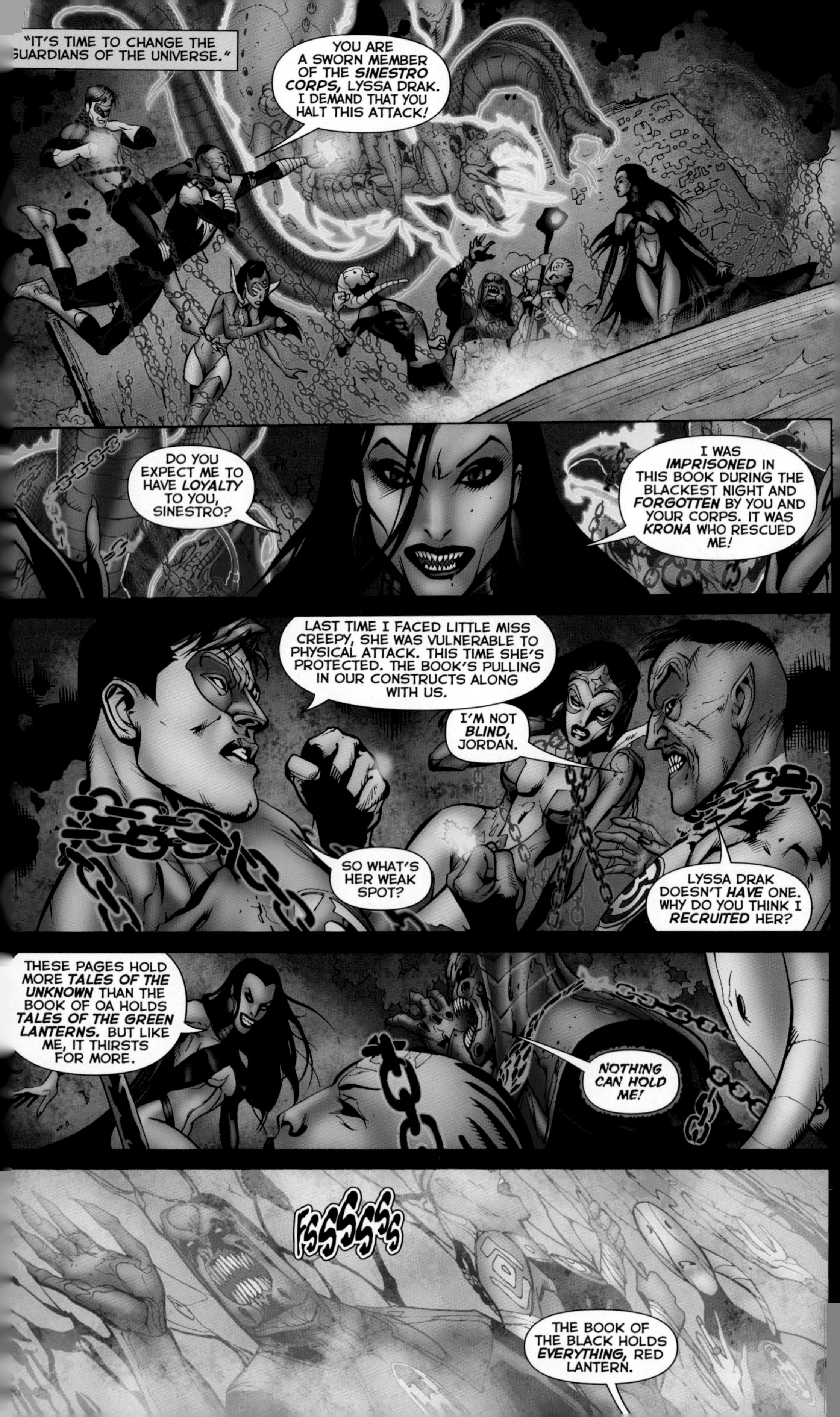
"IT'S TIME TO CHANGE THE GUARDIANS OF THE UNIVERSE."
YOU ARE A SWORN MEMBER OF THE SINESTRO CORPS, LYSSA DRAK. I DEMAND THAT YOU HALT THIS ATTACK!
DO YOU EXPECT ME TO HAVE LOYALTY TO YOU, SINESTRO?
I WAS IMPRISONED IN THIS BOOK DURING THE BLACKEST NIGHT AND FORGOTTEN BY YOU AND YOUR CORPS. IT WAS KRONA WHO RESCUED ME!
LAST TIME I FACED LITTLE MISS CREEPY, SHE WAS VULNERABLE TO PHYSICAL ATTACK. THIS TIME SHE'S PROTECTED. THE BOOK'S PULLING IN OUR CONSTRUCTS ALONG WITH US.
I'M NOT BLIND, JORDAN.
SO WHAT'S HER WEAK SPOT?
LYSSA DRAK DOESN'T HAVE ONE. WHY DO YOU THINK I RECRUITED HER?
THESE PAGES HOLD MORE TALES OF THE UNKNOWN THAN THE BOOK OF OA HOLDS TALES OF THE GREEN LANTERNS. BUT LIKE ME, IT THIRSTS FOR MORE.
NOTHING CAN HOLD ME!
FSSSSSS
THE BOOK OF THE BLACK HOLDS EVERYTHING, RED LANTERN.

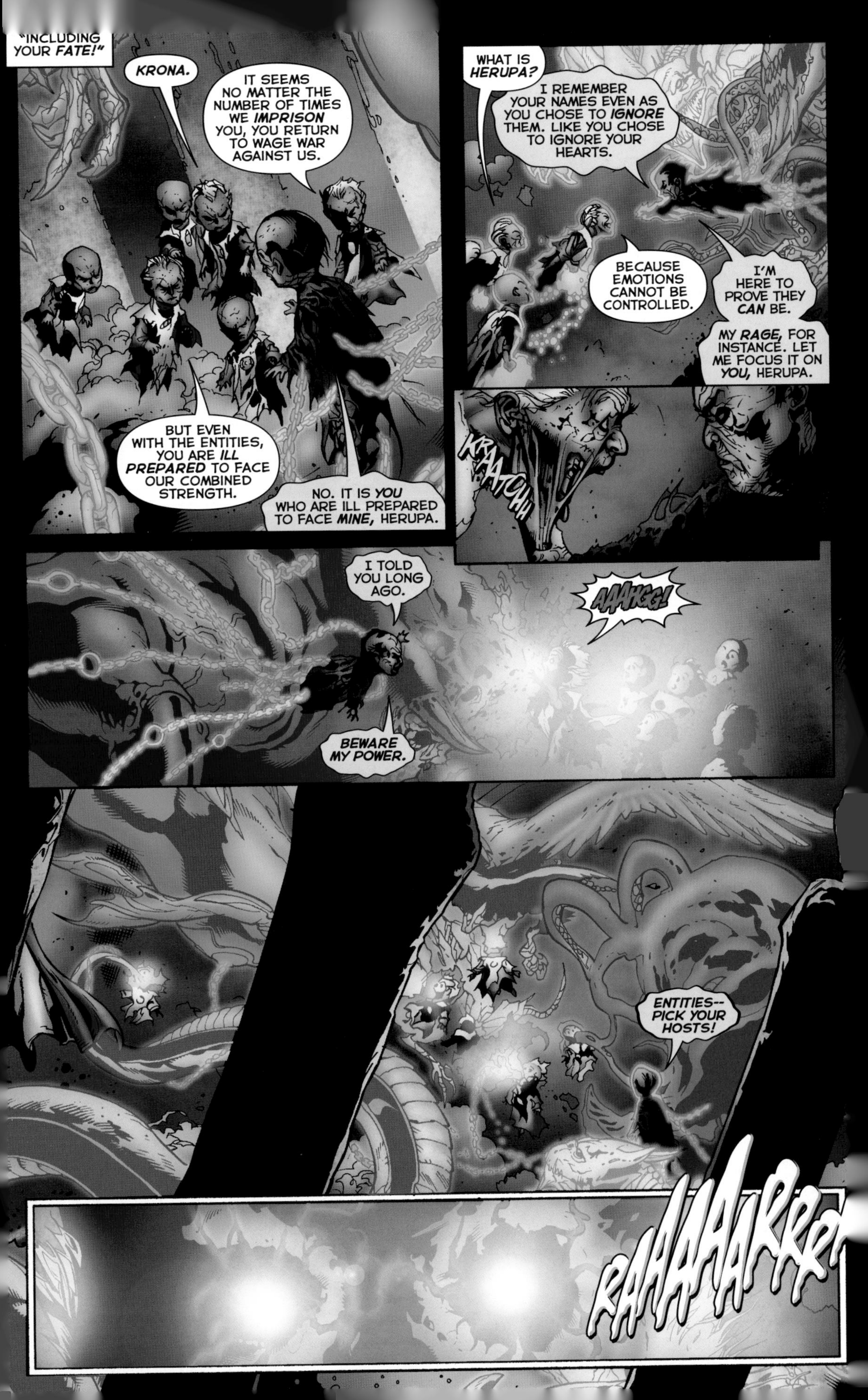
"INCLUDING YOUR FATE!"
KRONA.
IT SEEMS NO MATTER THE NUMBER OF TIMES WE IMPRISON YOU, YOU RETURN TO WAGE WAR AGAINST US.
BUT EVEN WITH THE ENTITIES, YOU ARE ILL PREPARED TO FACE OUR COMBINED STRENGTH.
NO. IT IS YOU WHO ARE ILL PREPARED TO FACE MINE, HERUPA.
WHAT IS HERUPA?
I REMEMBER YOUR NAMES EVEN AS YOU CHOSE TO IGNORE THEM. LIKE YOU CHOSE TO IGNORE YOUR HEARTS.
BECAUSE EMOTIONS CANNOT BE CONTROLLED.
I'M HERE TO PROVE THEY CAN BE.
MY RAGE, FOR INSTANCE. LET ME FOCUS IT ON YOU, HERUPA.
KRAATCHH
I TOLD YOU LONG AGO.
AAAHGG!
BEWARE MY POWER.
ENTITIES-- PICK YOUR HOSTS!
RAAAAARRR!

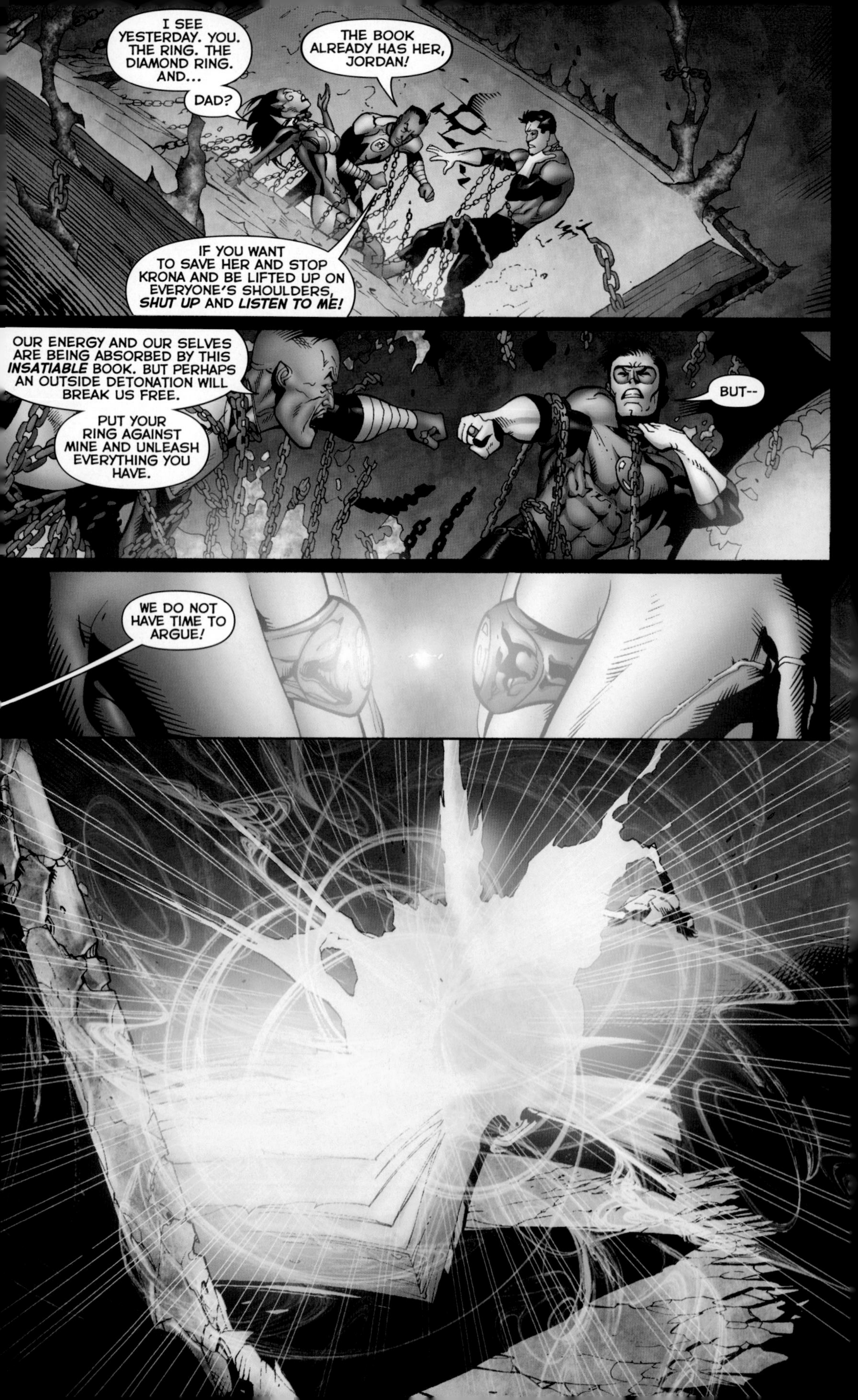
I SEE YESTERDAY. YOU. THE RING. THE DIAMOND RING. AND...
DAD?
THE BOOK ALREADY HAS HER, JORDAN!
IF YOU WANT TO SAVE HER AND STOP KRONA AND BE LIFTED UP ON EVERYONE'S SHOULDERS, SHUT UP AND LISTEN TO ME!
OUR ENERGY AND OUR SELVES ARE BEING ABSORBED BY THIS INSATIABLE BOOK. BUT PERHAPS AN OUTSIDE DETONATION WILL BREAK US FREE.
PUT YOUR RING AGAINST MINE AND UNLEASH EVERYTHING YOU HAVE.
BUT--
WE DO NOT HAVE TIME TO ARGUE!

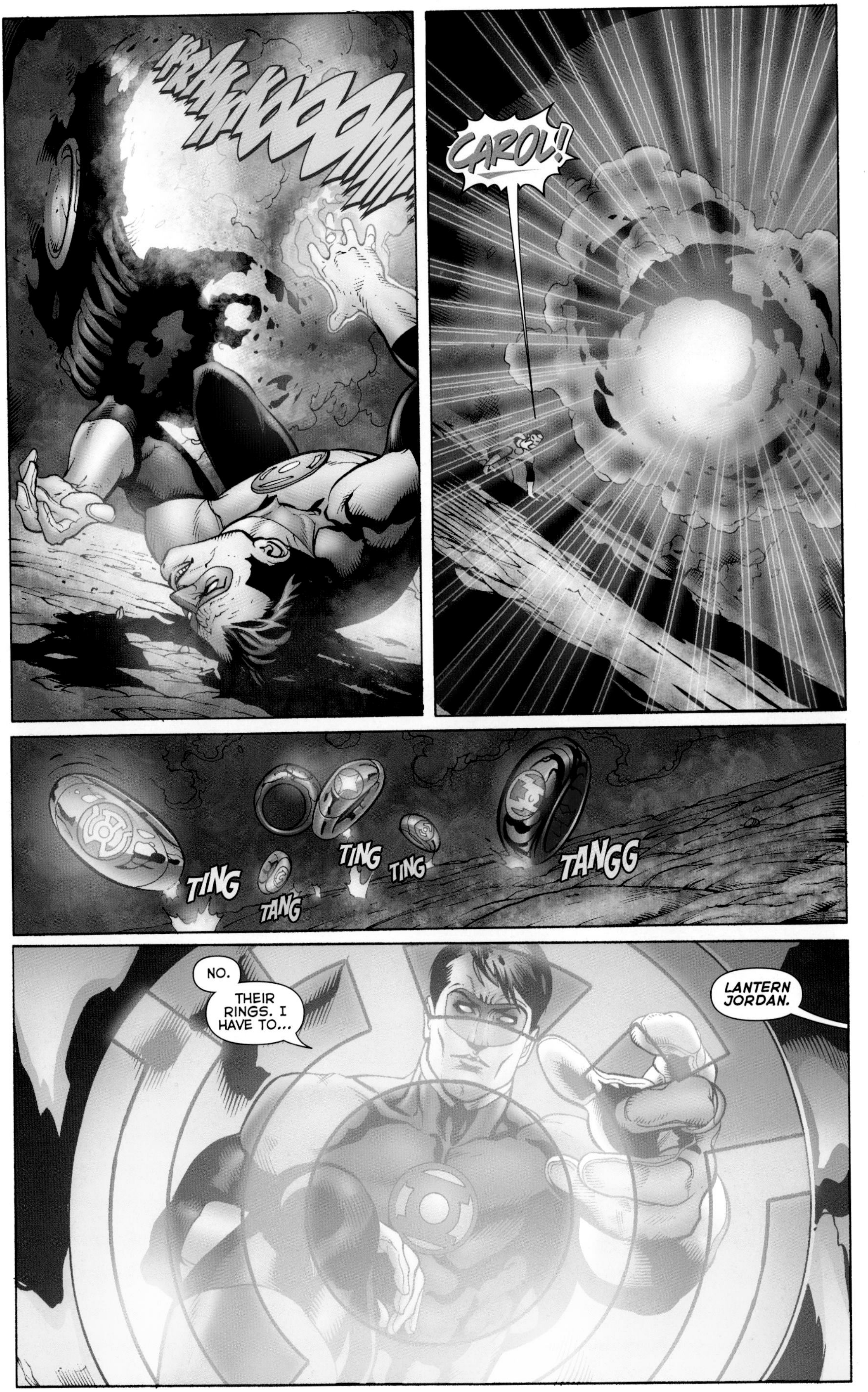
KRAKKOOOM
CAROL!
TING
TANG
TING
TING
TANGG
NO.
THEIR RINGS. I HAVE TO...
LANTERN JORDAN.

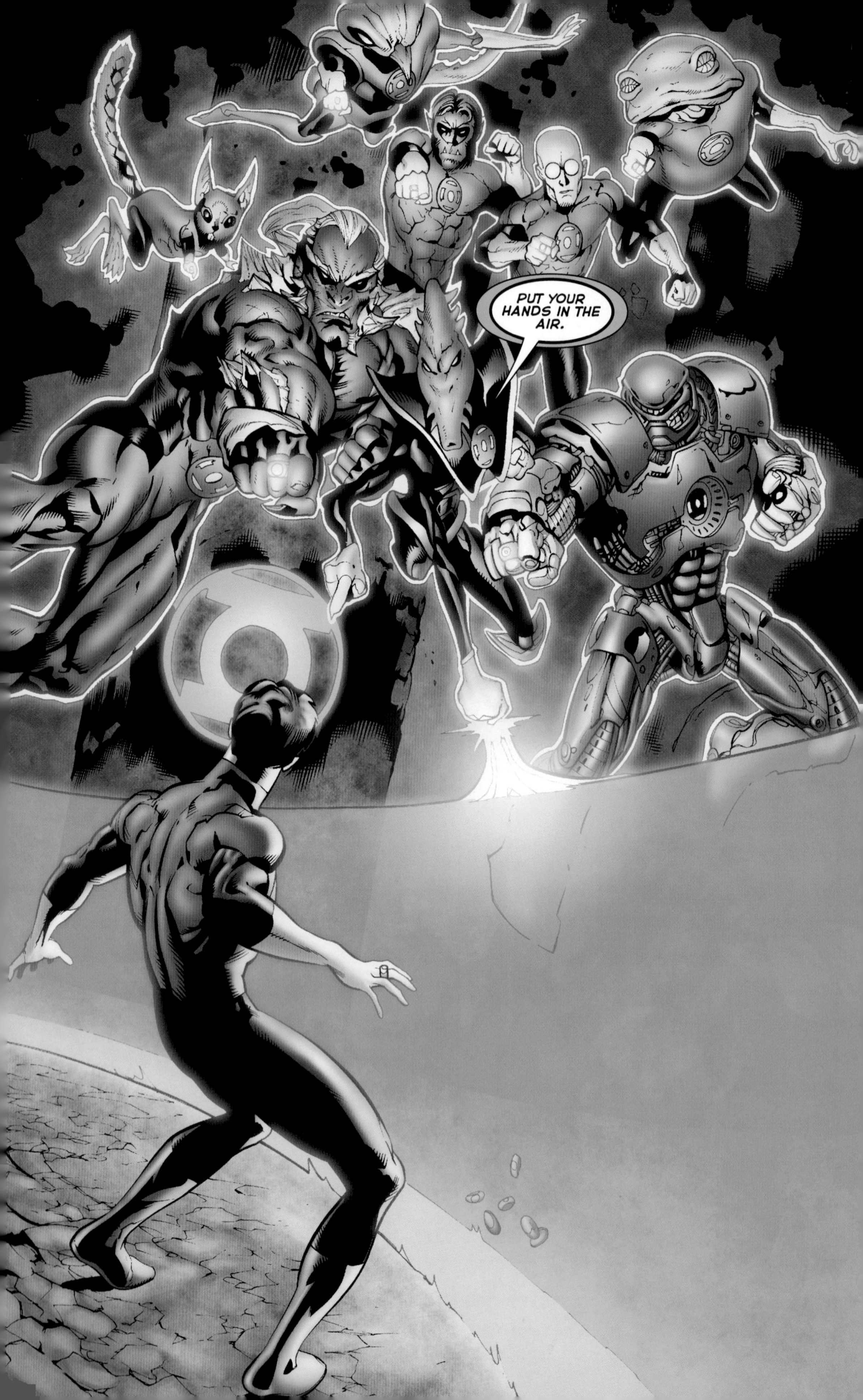
PUT YOUR HANDS IN THE AIR.

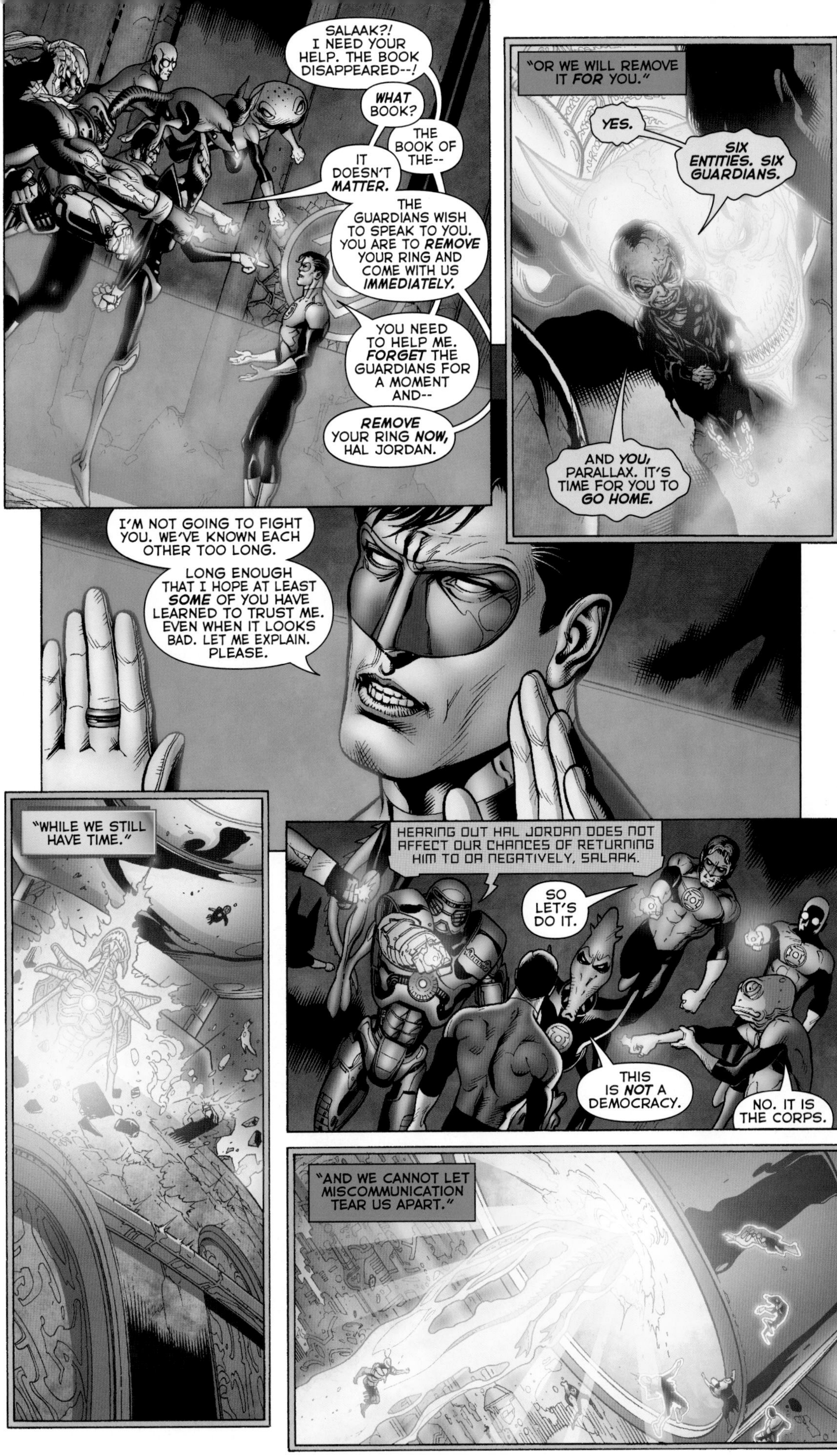
SALAAK?! I NEED YOUR HELP. THE BOOK DISAPPEARED--!
WHAT BOOK?
THE BOOK OF THE--
IT DOESN'T MATTER.
THE GUARDIANS WISH TO SPEAK TO YOU. YOU ARE TO REMOVE YOUR RING AND COME WITH US IMMEDIATELY.
YOU NEED TO HELP ME. FORGET THE GUARDIANS FOR A MOMENT AND--
REMOVE YOUR RING NOW, HAL JORDAN.
"OR WE WILL REMOVE IT FOR YOU."
YES.
SIX ENTITIES. SIX GUARDIANS.
AND YOU, PARALLAX. IT'S TIME FOR YOU TO GO HOME.
I'M NOT GOING TO FIGHT YOU. WE'VE KNOWN EACH OTHER TOO LONG.
LONG ENOUGH THAT I HOPE AT LEAST SOME OF YOU HAVE LEARNED TO TRUST ME. EVEN WHEN IT LOOKS BAD. LET ME EXPLAIN. PLEASE.
"WHILE WE STILL HAVE TIME."
HEARING OUT HAL JORDAN DOES NOT AFFECT OUR CHANCES OF RETURNING HIM TO OA NEGATIVELY, SALAAK.
SO LET'S DO IT.
THIS IS NOT A DEMOCRACY.
NO. IT IS THE CORPS.
"AND WE CANNOT LET MISCOMMUNICATION TEAR US APART."

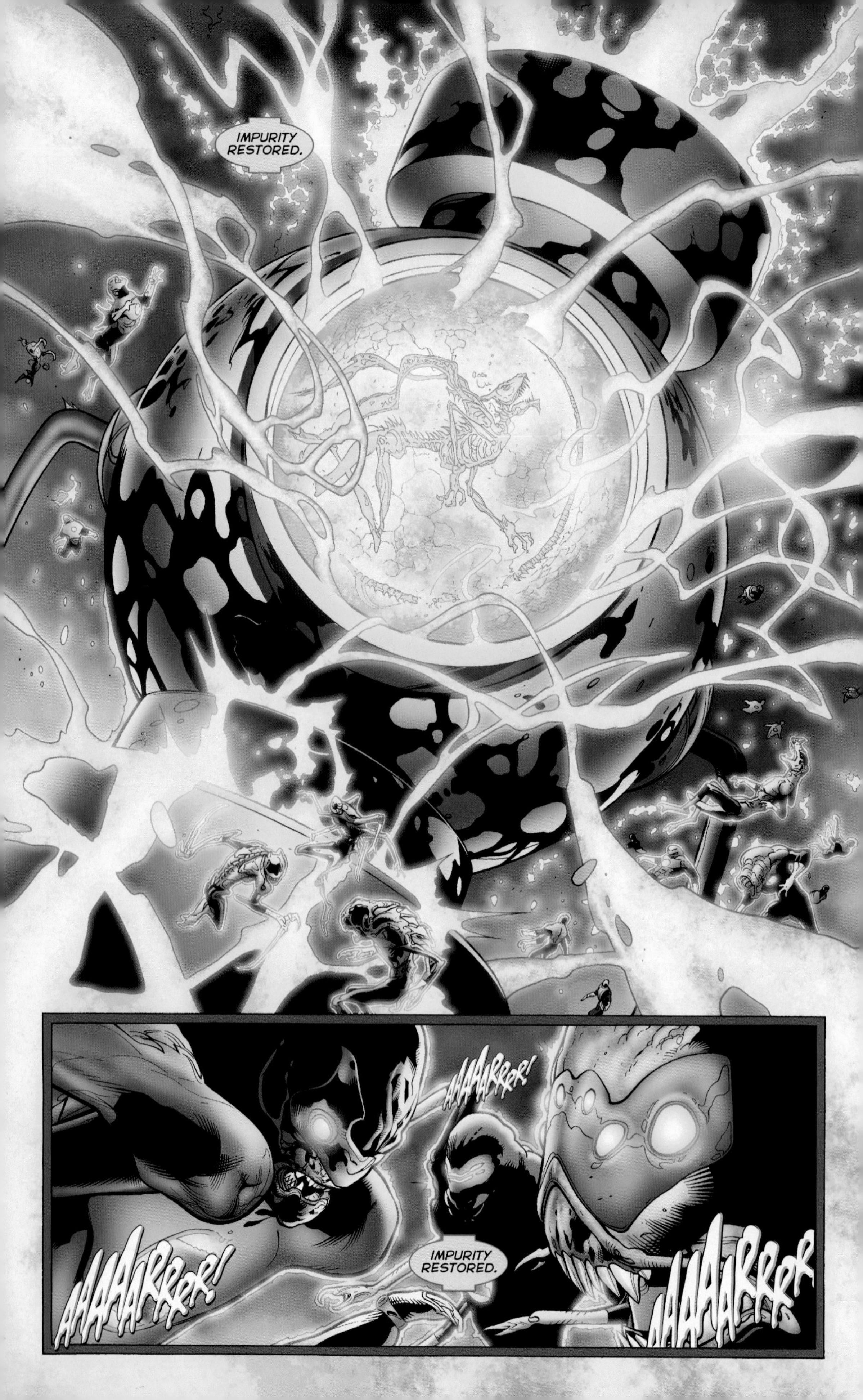
IMPURITY RESTORED.
AAAAARRRR!
AAAAAARRRR!
IMPURITY RESTORED.
AAAAARRRR

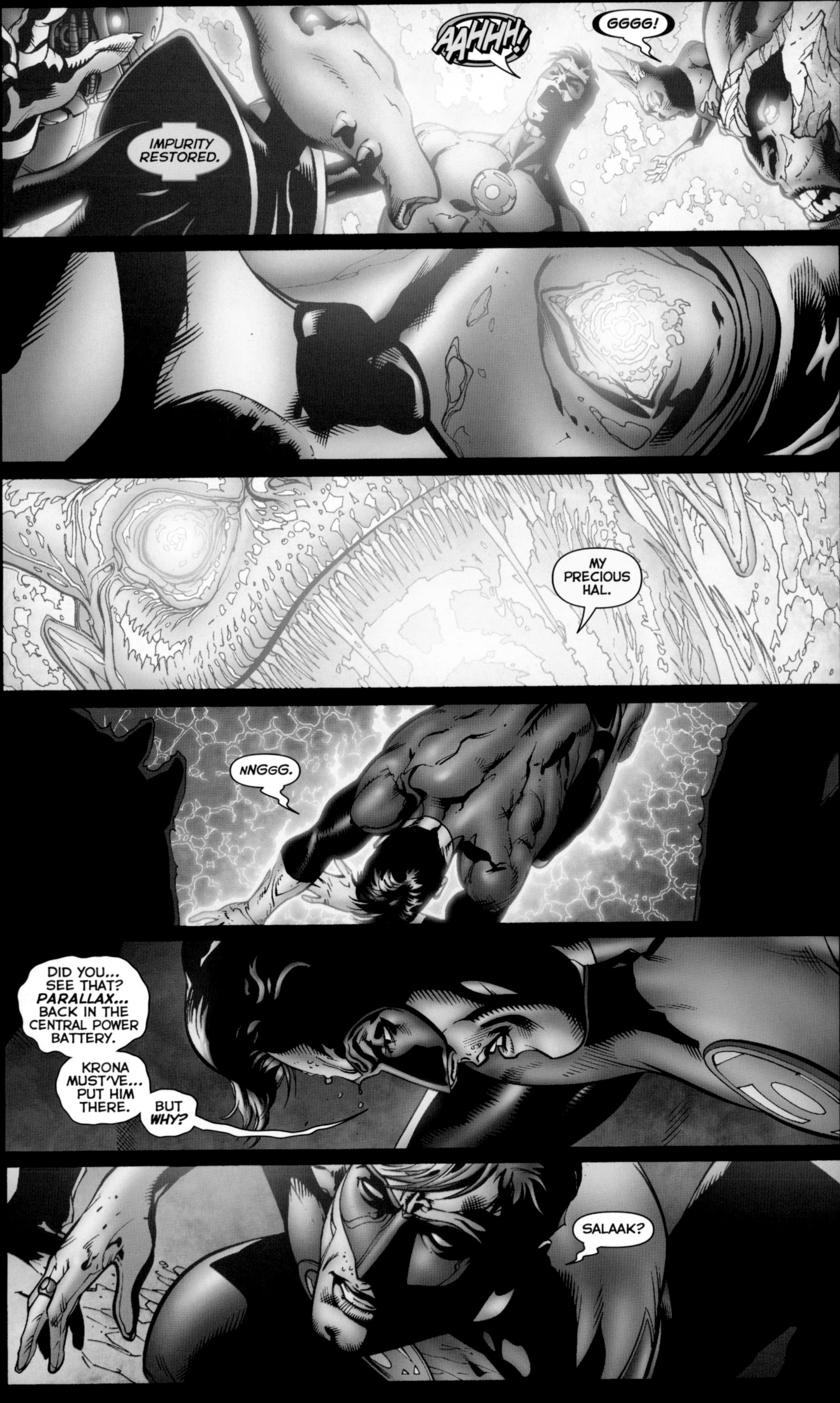
AAHHH!
GGGG!
IMPURITY RESTORED.
MY PRECIOUS HAL.
NNGGG.
DID YOU... SEE THAT? PARALLAX... BACK IN THE CENTRAL POWER BATTERY.
KRONA MUST'VE... PUT HIM THERE.
BUT WHY?
SALAAK?

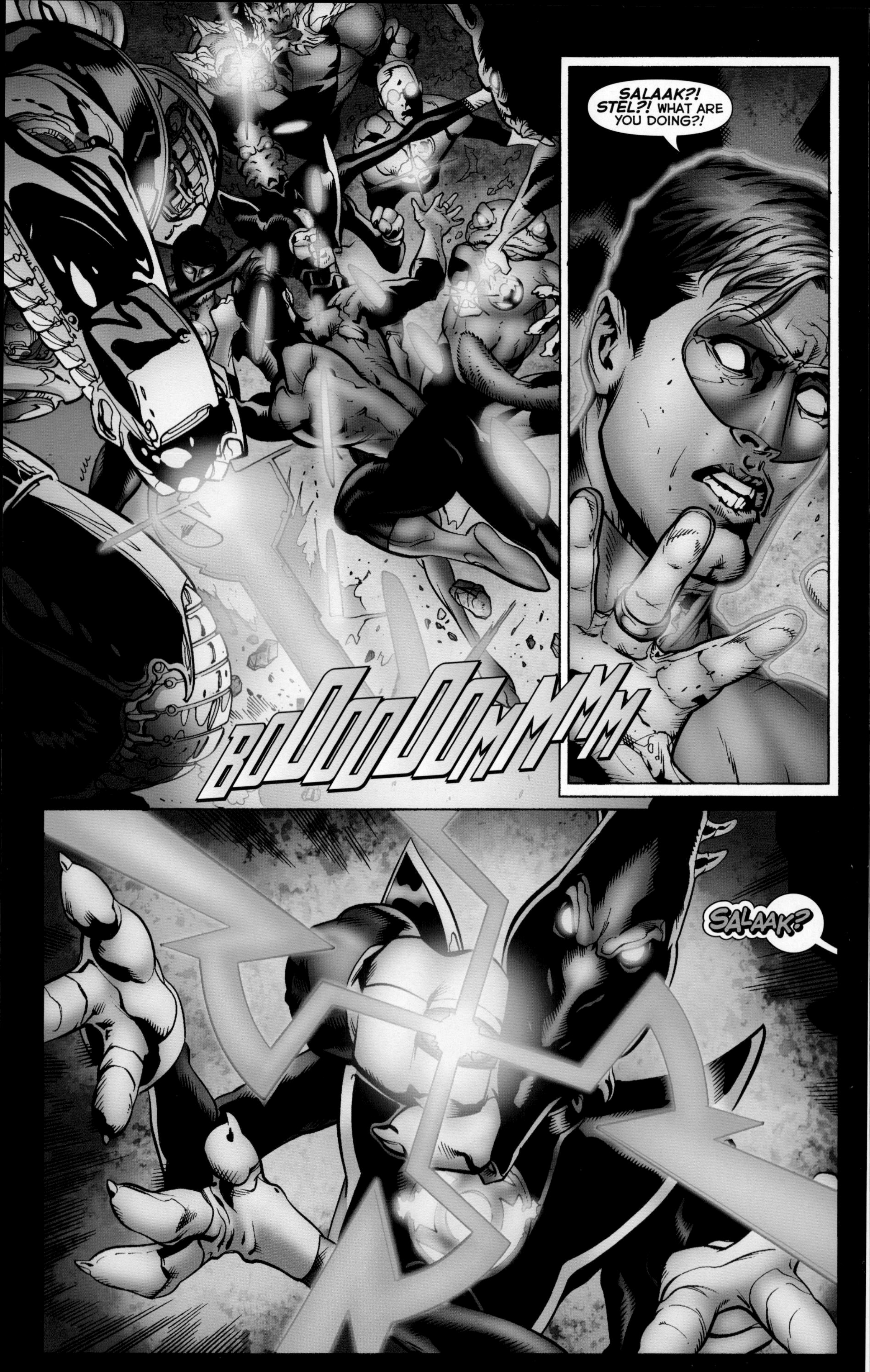
SALAAK?! STEL?! WHAT ARE YOU DOING?!
BOOOOOOMMMMM
SALAAK?

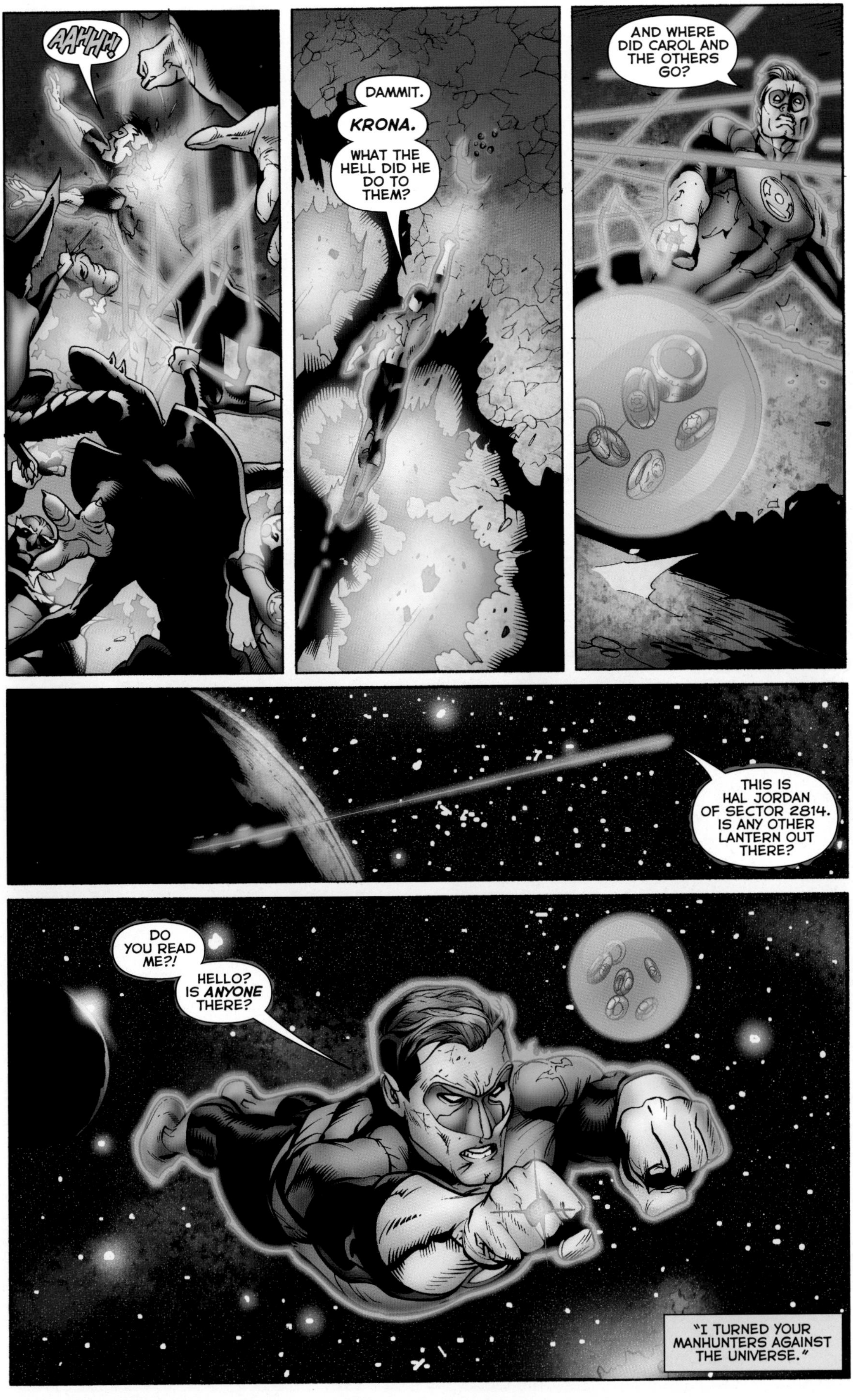
AAHHH!
DAMMIT.
KRONA.
WHAT THE HELL DID HE DO TO THEM?
AND WHERE DID CAROL AND THE OTHERS GO?
THIS IS HAL JORDAN OF SECTOR 2814. IS ANY OTHER LANTERN OUT THERE?
DO YOU READ ME?!
HELLO? IS ANYONE THERE?
"I TURNED YOUR MANHUNTERS AGAINST THE UNIVERSE."

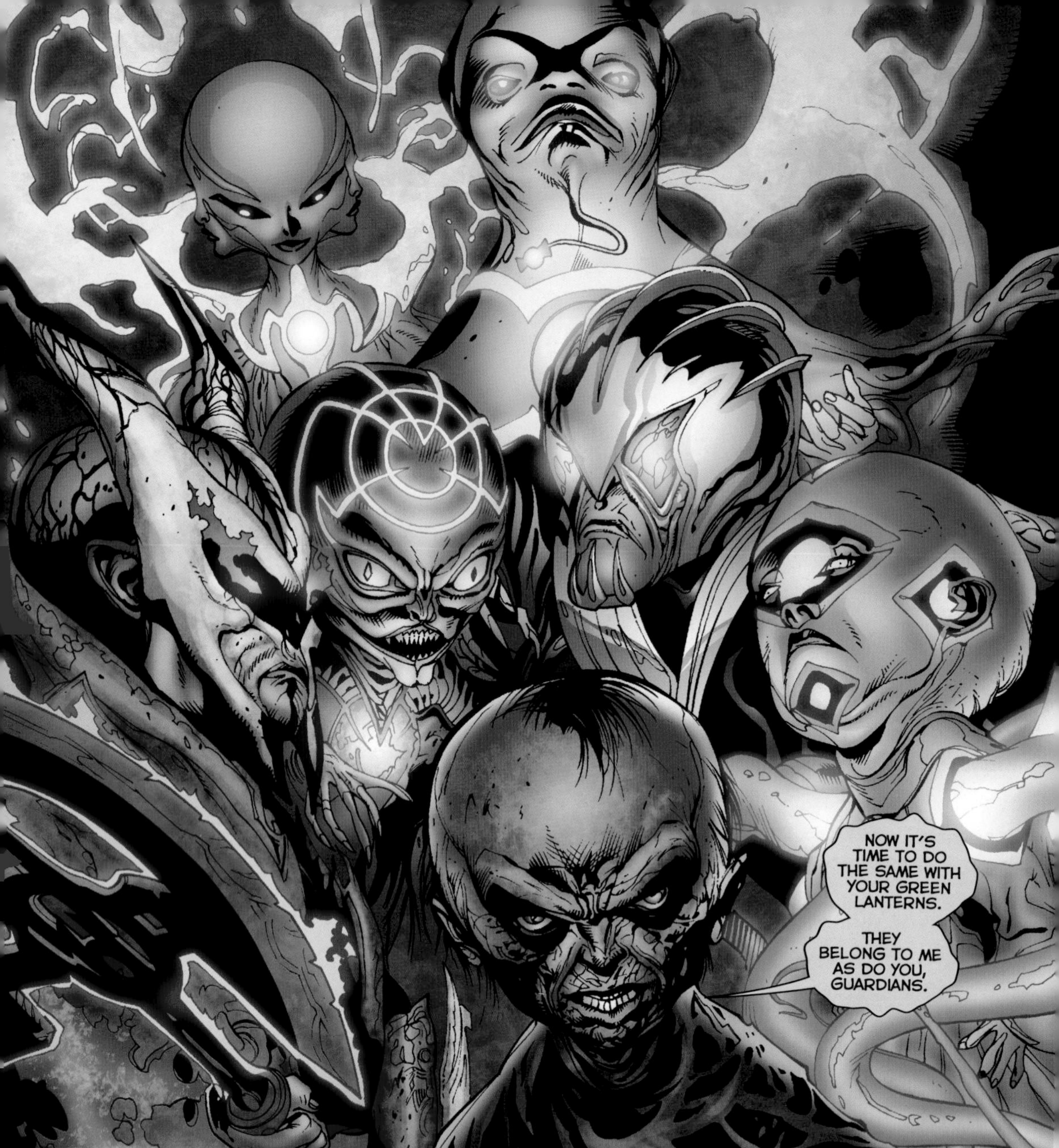
NOW IT'S TIME TO DO THE SAME WITH YOUR GREEN LANTERNS.
THEY BELONG TO ME AS DO YOU, GUARDIANS.

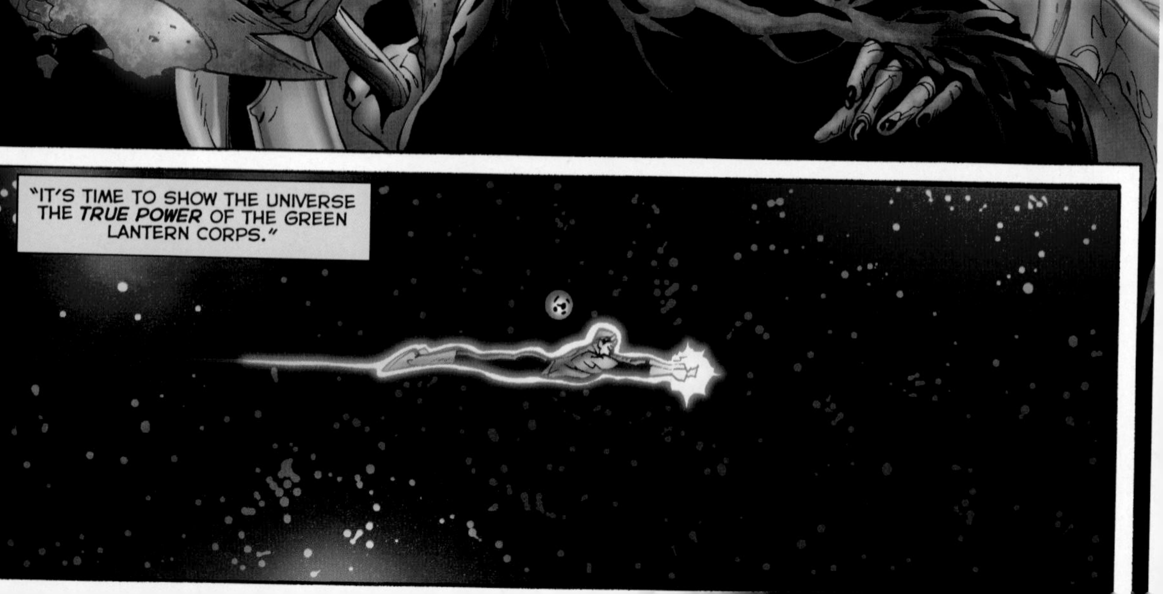
"IT'S TIME TO SHOW THE UNIVERSE THE *TRUE POWER* OF THE GREEN LANTERN CORPS."

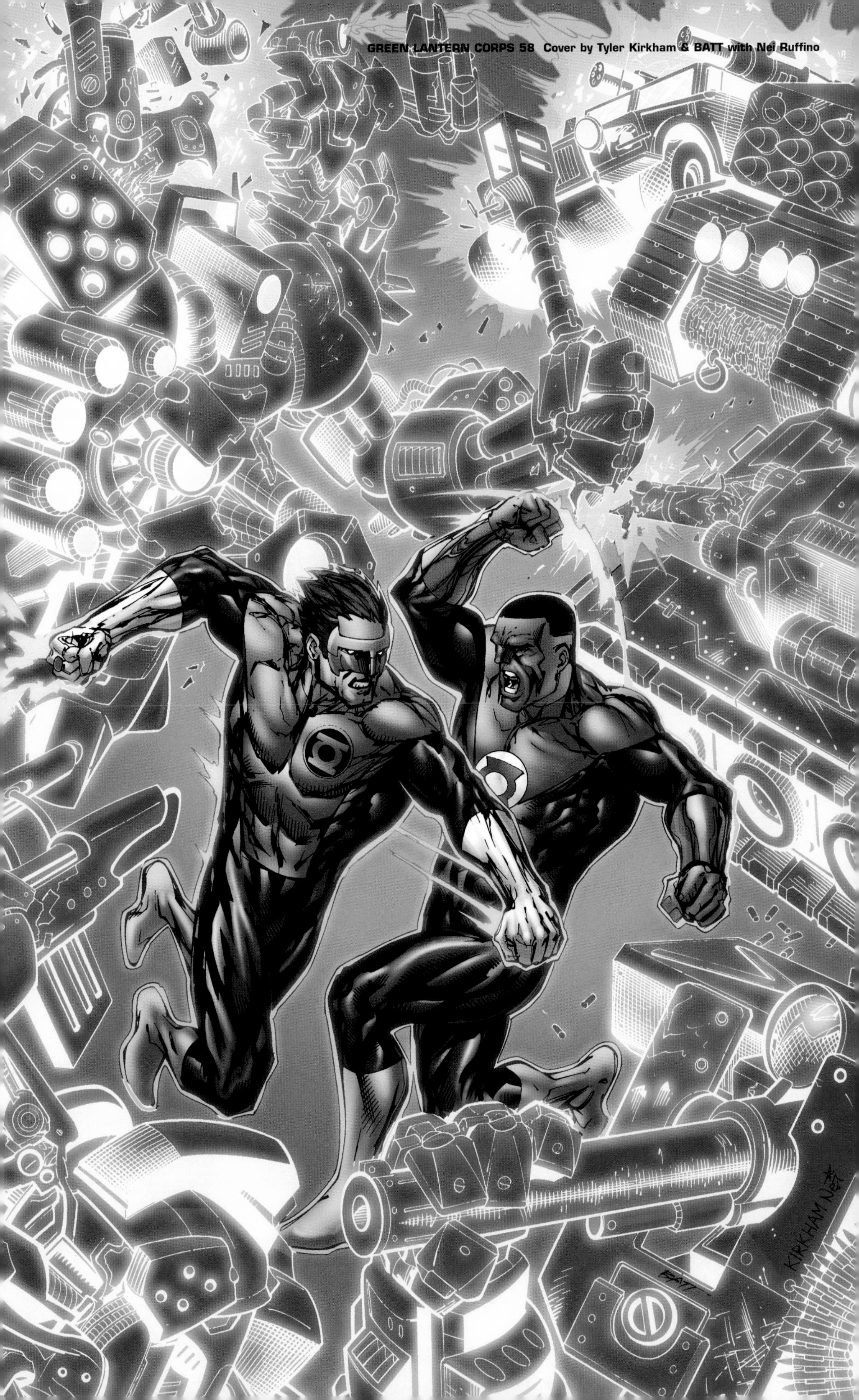
BATT
KIRKHAM Nei

GREEN LANTERN CORPS 58 Cover by Tyler Kirkham & BATT with Nei Ruffino

WAR OF THE GREEN LANTERNS
PART TWO

Tony Bedard Writer
Tyler Kirkham Penciller
BATT with Rob Hunter Inkers

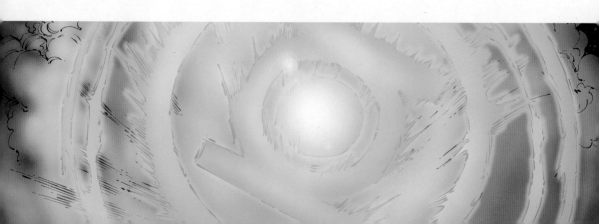

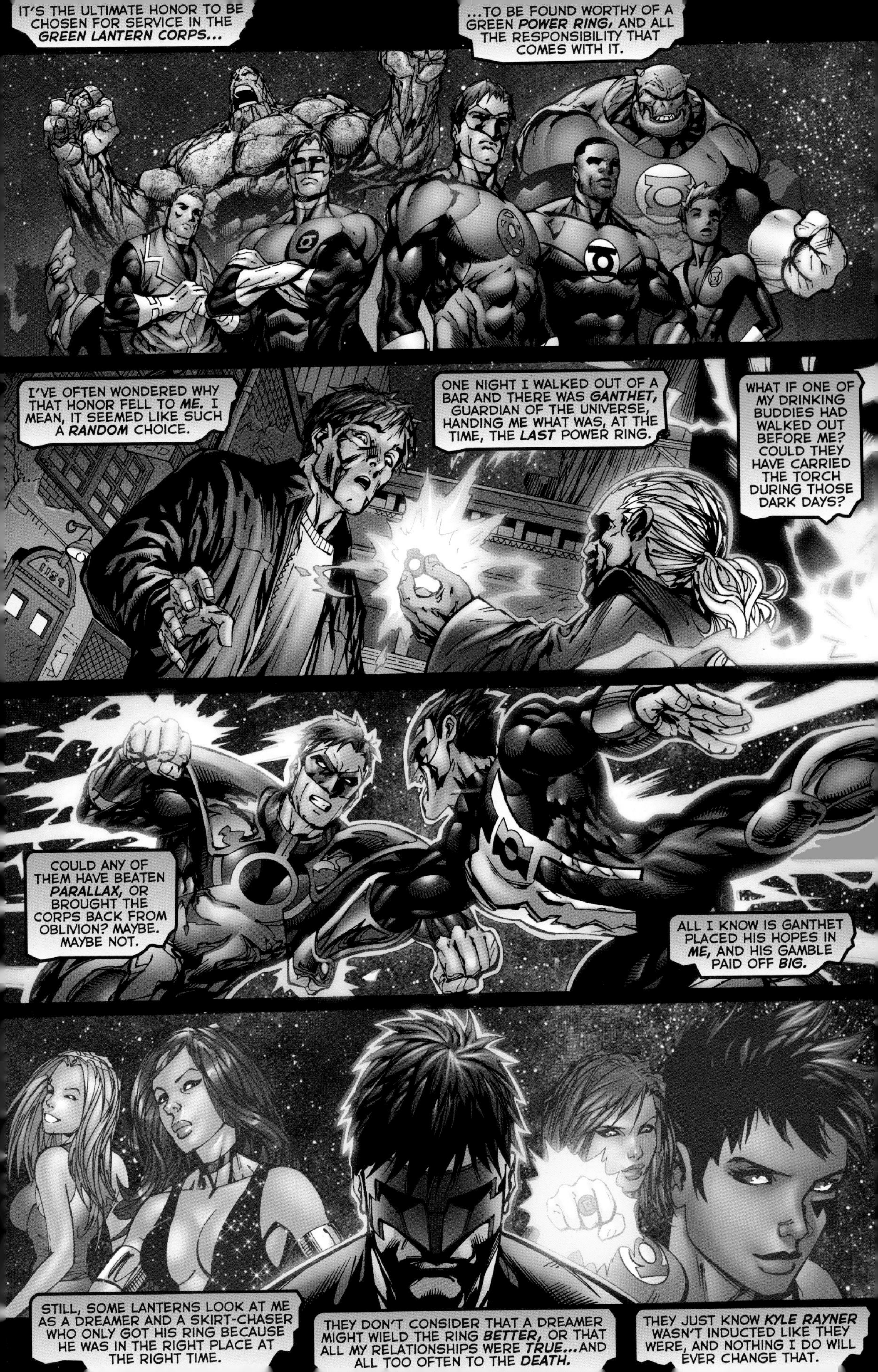

IT'S THE ULTIMATE HONOR TO BE CHOSEN FOR SERVICE IN THE GREEN LANTERN CORPS...
...TO BE FOUND WORTHY OF A GREEN POWER RING, AND ALL THE RESPONSIBILITY THAT COMES WITH IT.
I'VE OFTEN WONDERED WHY THAT HONOR FELL TO ME. I MEAN, IT SEEMED LIKE SUCH A RANDOM CHOICE.
ONE NIGHT I WALKED OUT OF A BAR AND THERE WAS GANTHET, GUARDIAN OF THE UNIVERSE, HANDING ME WHAT WAS, AT THE TIME, THE LAST POWER RING.
WHAT IF ONE OF MY DRINKING BUDDIES HAD WALKED OUT BEFORE ME? COULD THEY HAVE CARRIED THE TORCH DURING THOSE DARK DAYS?
COULD ANY OF THEM HAVE BEATEN PARALLAX, OR BROUGHT THE CORPS BACK FROM OBLIVION? MAYBE. MAYBE NOT.
ALL I KNOW IS GANTHET PLACED HIS HOPES IN ME, AND HIS GAMBLE PAID OFF BIG.
STILL, SOME LANTERNS LOOK AT ME AS A DREAMER AND A SKIRT-CHASER WHO ONLY GOT HIS RING BECAUSE HE WAS IN THE RIGHT PLACE AT THE RIGHT TIME.
THEY DON'T CONSIDER THAT A DREAMER MIGHT WIELD THE RING BETTER, OR THAT ALL MY RELATIONSHIPS WERE TRUE...AND ALL TOO OFTEN TO THE DEATH.
THEY JUST KNOW KYLE RAYNER WASN'T INDUCTED LIKE THEY WERE, AND NOTHING I DO WILL EVER CHANGE THAT.

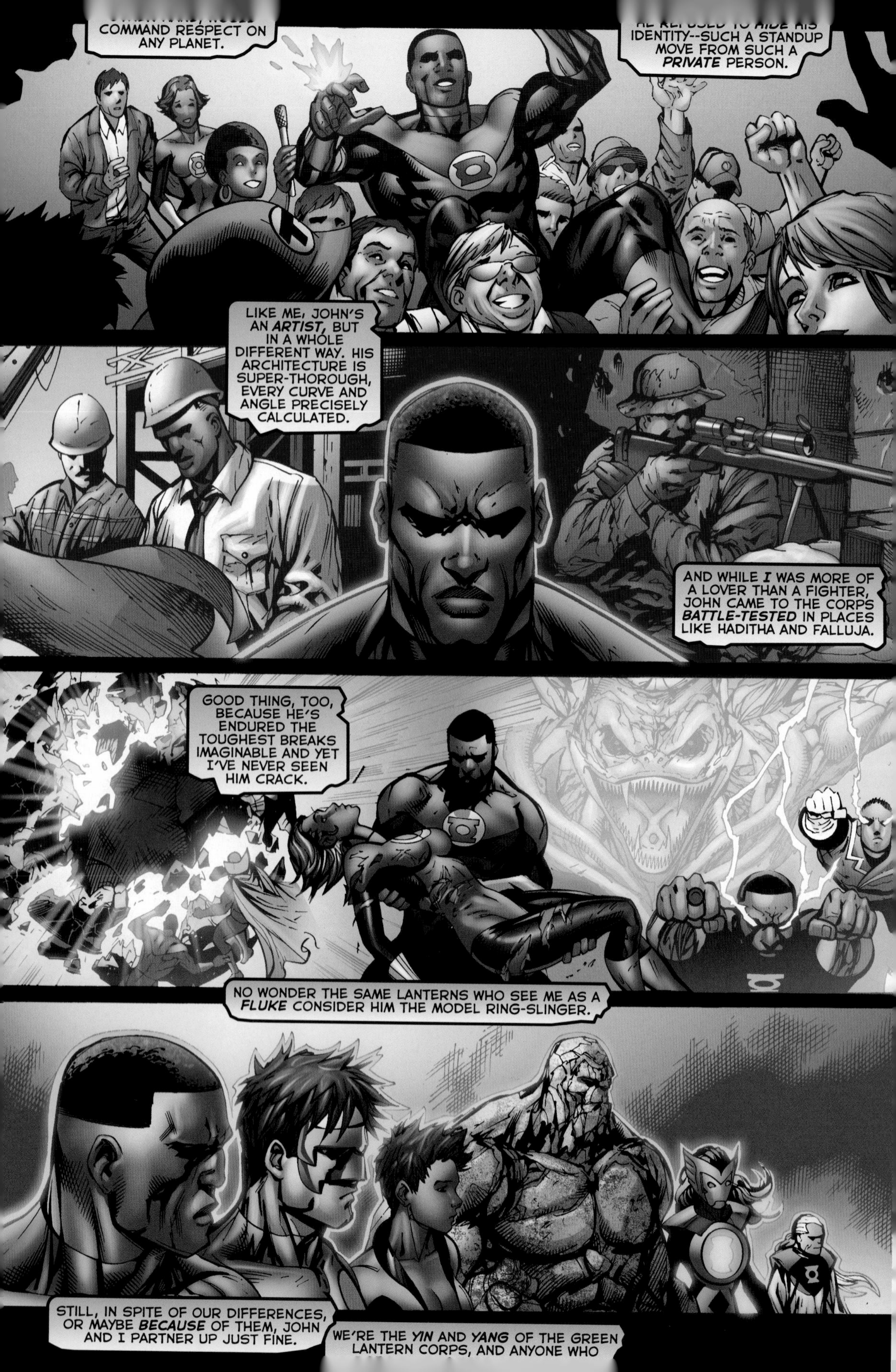
COMMAND RESPECT ON ANY PLANET.
IDENTITY--SUCH A STANDUP MOVE FROM SUCH A *PRIVATE* PERSON.
LIKE ME, JOHN'S AN *ARTIST,* BUT IN A WHOLE DIFFERENT WAY. HIS ARCHITECTURE IS SUPER-THOROUGH, EVERY CURVE AND ANGLE PRECISELY CALCULATED.
AND WHILE *I* WAS MORE OF A LOVER THAN A FIGHTER, JOHN CAME TO THE CORPS *BATTLE-TESTED* IN PLACES LIKE HADITHA AND FALLUJA.
GOOD THING, TOO, BECAUSE HE'S ENDURED THE TOUGHEST BREAKS IMAGINABLE AND YET I'VE NEVER SEEN HIM CRACK.
NO WONDER THE SAME LANTERNS WHO SEE ME AS A *FLUKE* CONSIDER HIM THE MODEL RING-SLINGER.
STILL, IN SPITE OF OUR DIFFERENCES, OR MAYBE *BECAUSE* OF THEM, JOHN AND I PARTNER UP JUST FINE.
WE'RE THE *YIN* AND *YANG* OF THE GREEN LANTERN CORPS, AND ANYONE WHO

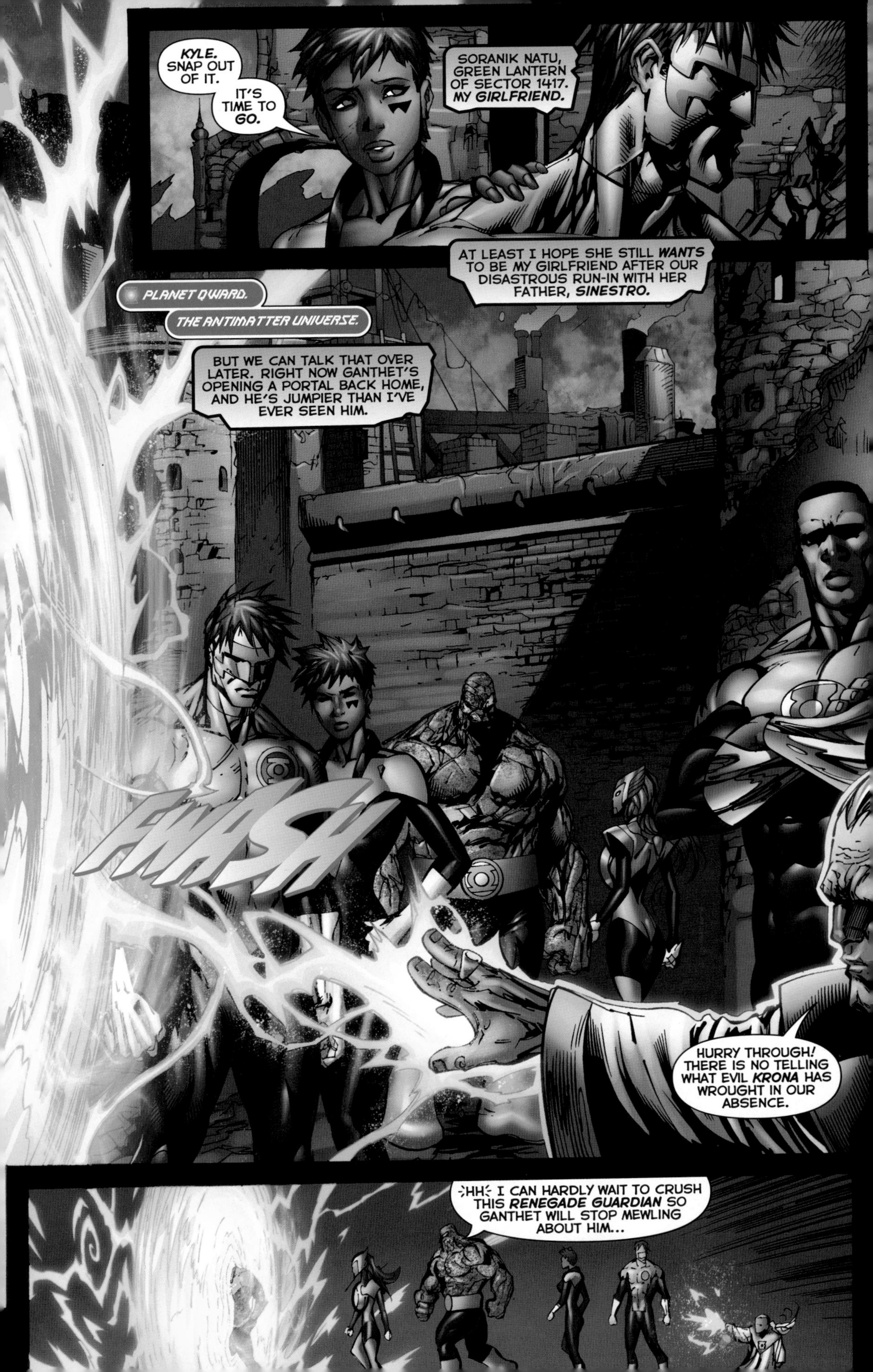
KYLE. SNAP OUT OF IT.
IT'S TIME TO GO.
SORANIK NATU, GREEN LANTERN OF SECTOR 1417. MY GIRLFRIEND.
AT LEAST I HOPE SHE STILL WANTS TO BE MY GIRLFRIEND AFTER OUR DISASTROUS RUN-IN WITH HER FATHER, SINESTRO.
PLANET QWARD.
THE ANTIMATTER UNIVERSE.
BUT WE CAN TALK THAT OVER LATER. RIGHT NOW GANTHET'S OPENING A PORTAL BACK HOME, AND HE'S JUMPIER THAN I'VE EVER SEEN HIM.
FWASH
HURRY THROUGH! THERE IS NO TELLING WHAT EVIL KRONA HAS WROUGHT IN OUR ABSENCE.
HH! I CAN HARDLY WAIT TO CRUSH THIS RENEGADE GUARDIAN SO GANTHET WILL STOP MEWLING ABOUT HIM...

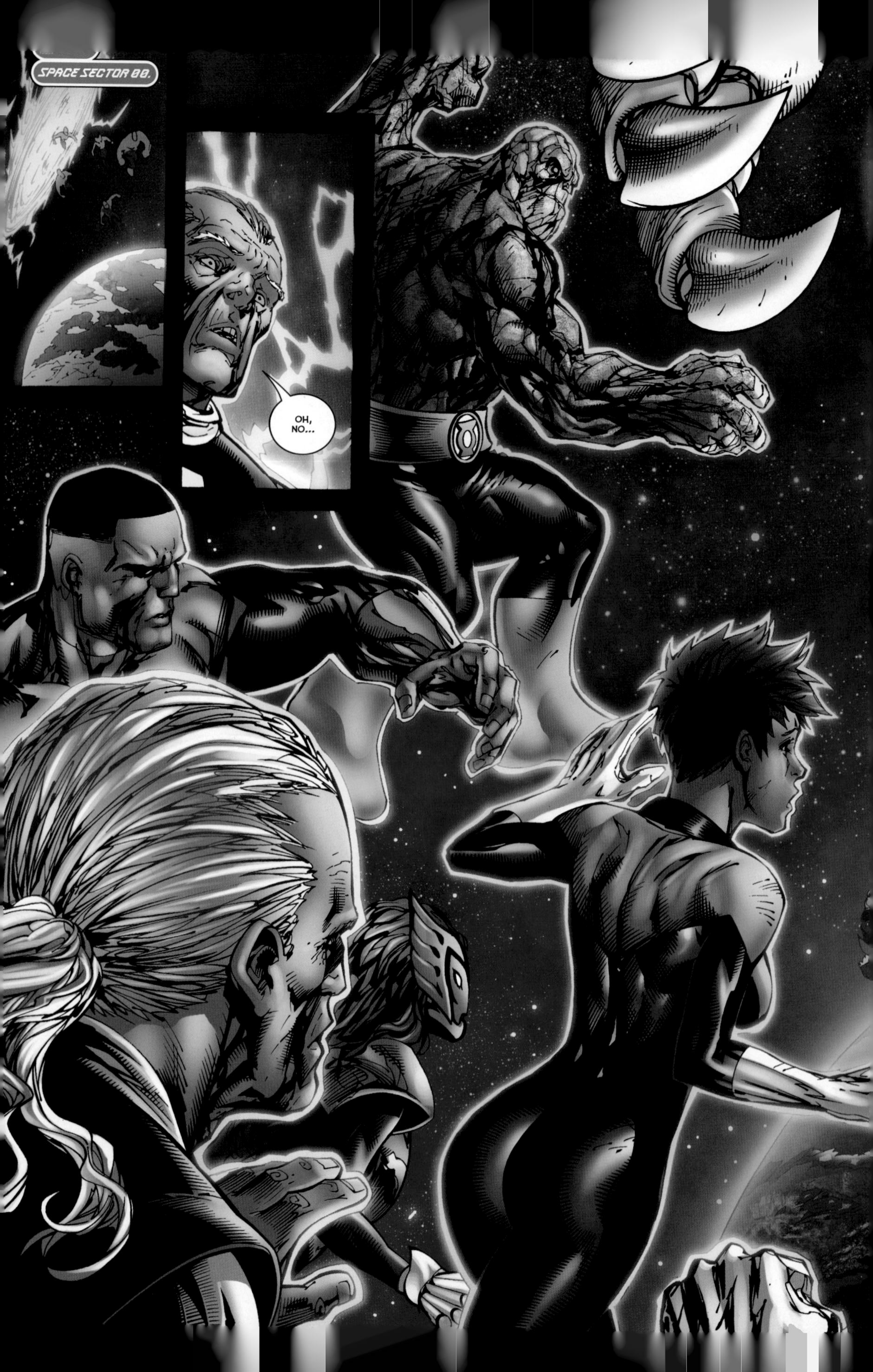
SPACE SECTOR 88.
OH, NO...

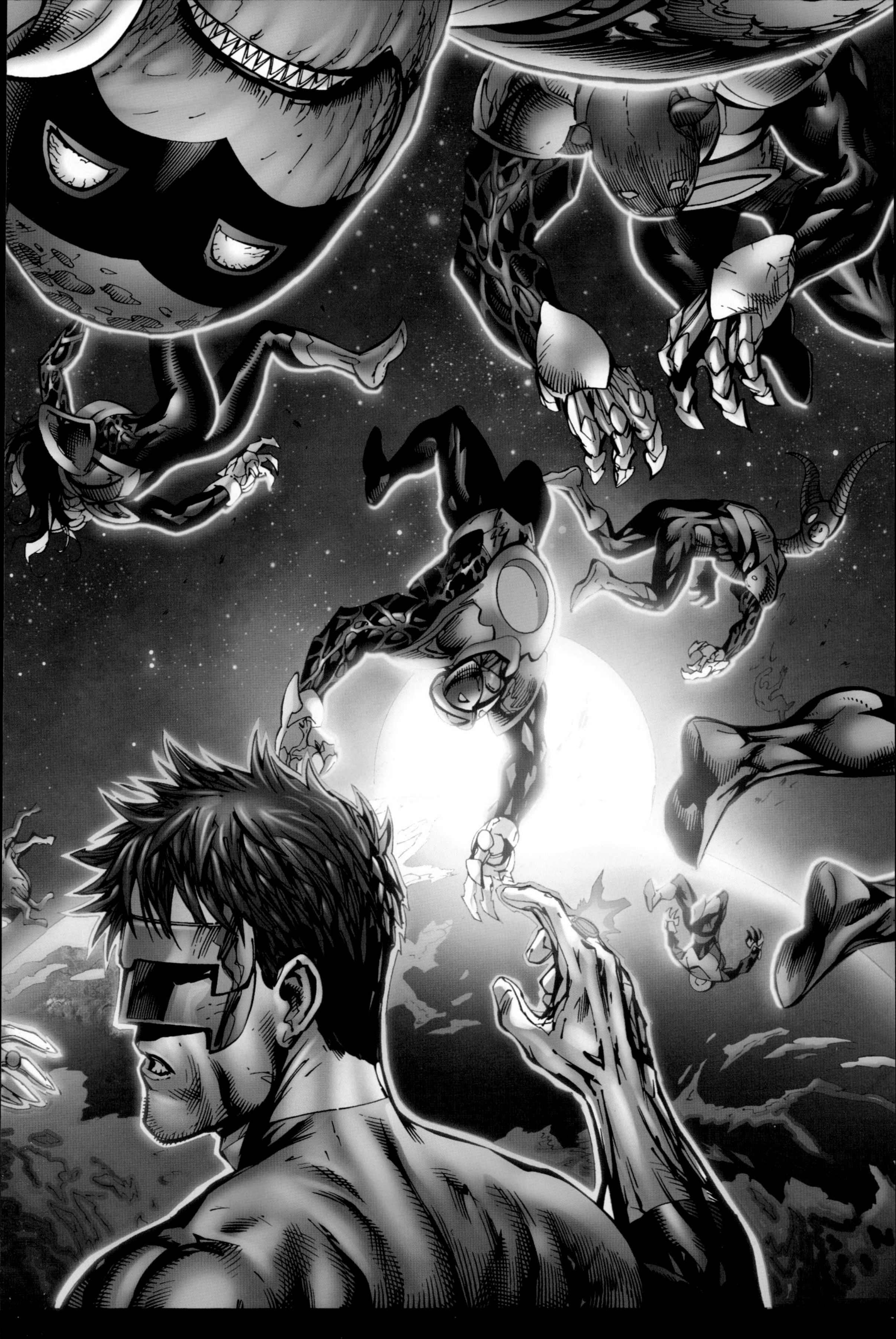

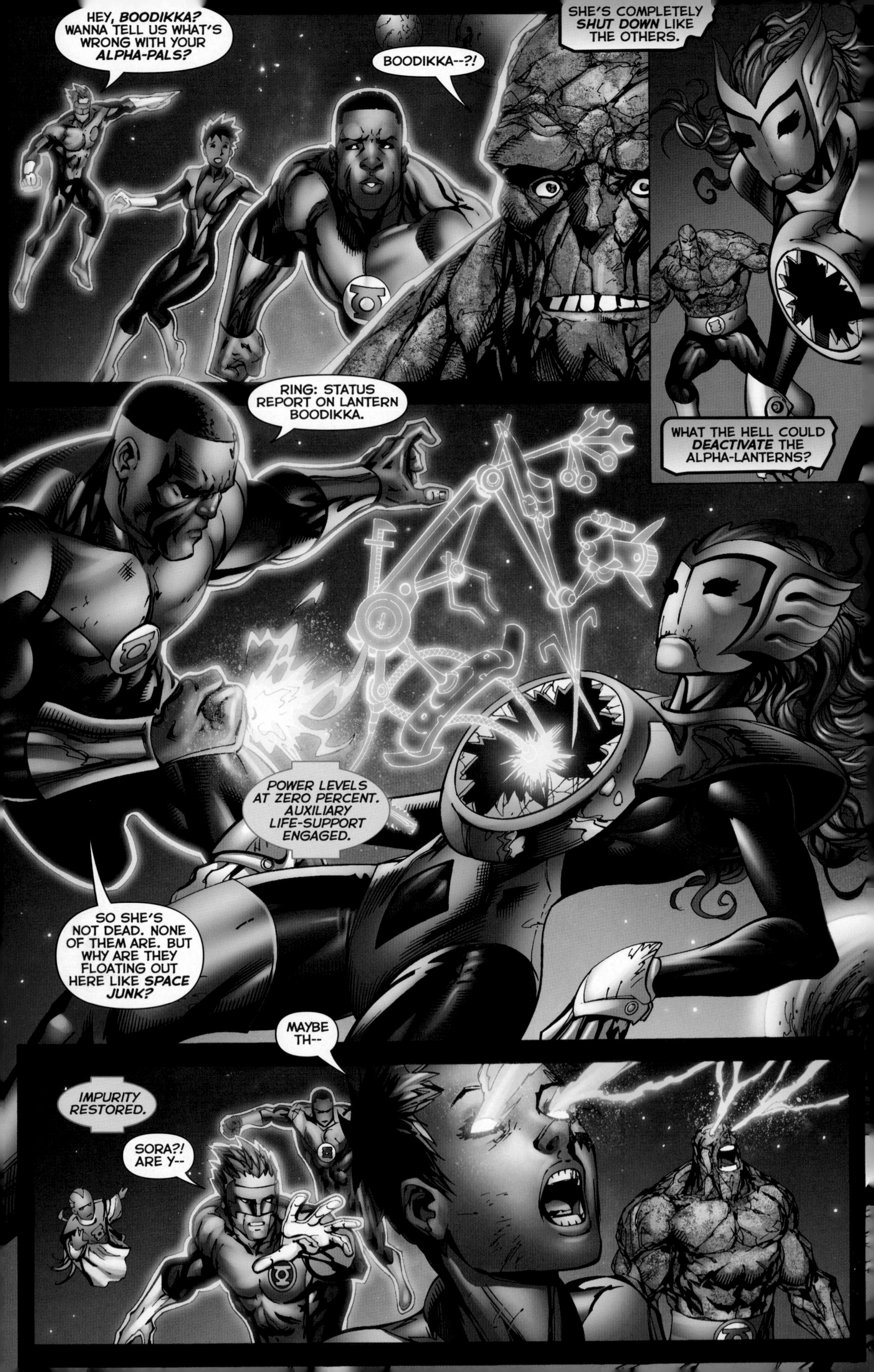
HEY, BOODIKKA? WANNA TELL US WHAT'S WRONG WITH YOUR ALPHA-PALS?
BOODIKKA--?!
SHE'S COMPLETELY SHUT DOWN LIKE THE OTHERS.
WHAT THE HELL COULD DEACTIVATE THE ALPHA-LANTERNS?
RING: STATUS REPORT ON LANTERN BOODIKKA.
POWER LEVELS AT ZERO PERCENT. AUXILIARY LIFE-SUPPORT ENGAGED.
SO SHE'S NOT DEAD. NONE OF THEM ARE. BUT WHY ARE THEY FLOATING OUT HERE LIKE SPACE JUNK?
MAYBE TH--
IMPURITY RESTORED.
SORA?! ARE Y--

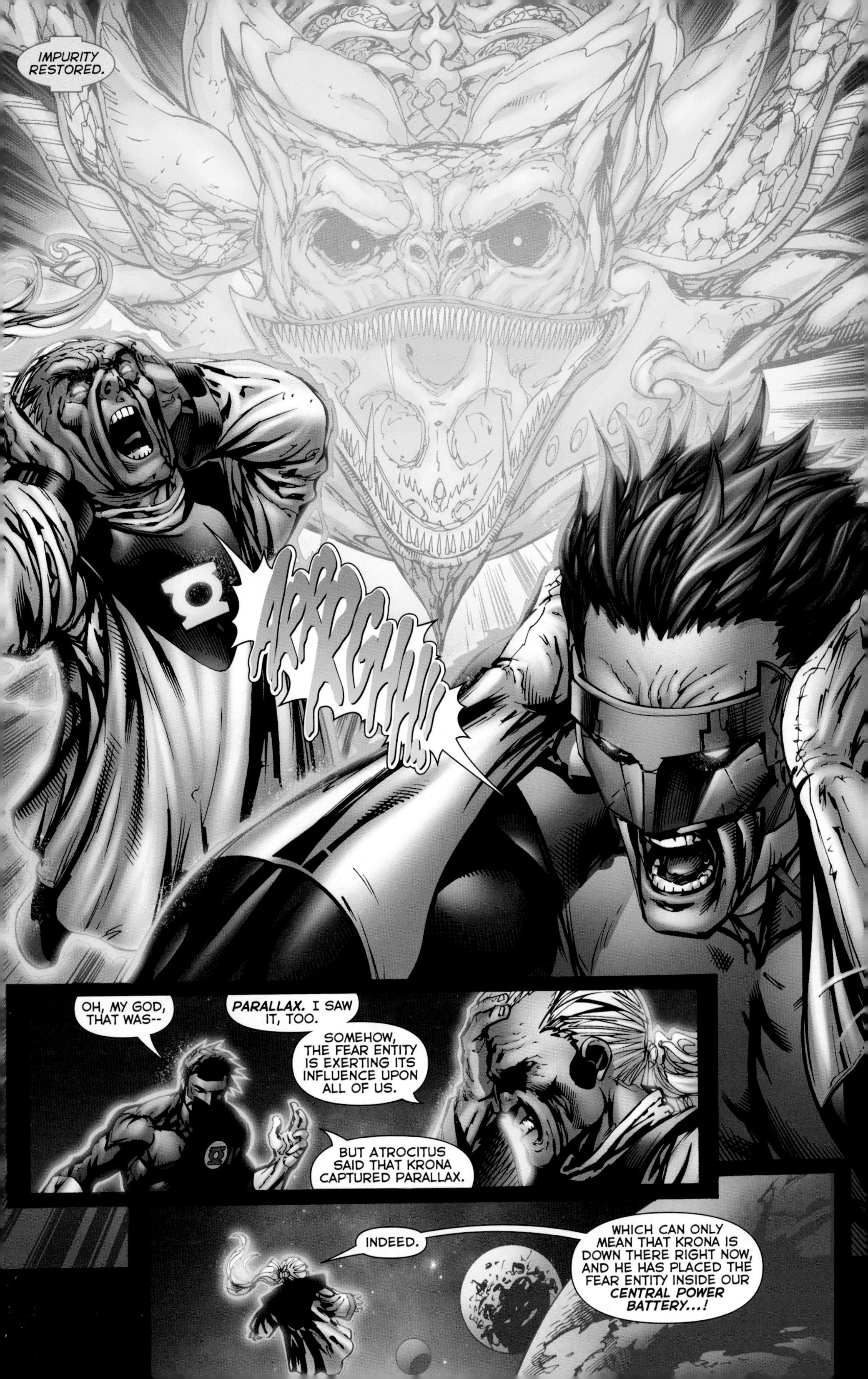
IMPURITY RESTORED.
ARRRGHH!!
OH, MY GOD, THAT WAS--
PARALLAX. I SAW IT, TOO.
SOMEHOW, THE FEAR ENTITY IS EXERTING ITS INFLUENCE UPON ALL OF US.
BUT ATROCITUS SAID THAT KRONA CAPTURED PARALLAX.
INDEED.
WHICH CAN ONLY MEAN THAT KRONA IS DOWN THERE RIGHT NOW, AND HE HAS PLACED THE FEAR ENTITY INSIDE OUR CENTRAL POWER BATTERY...!

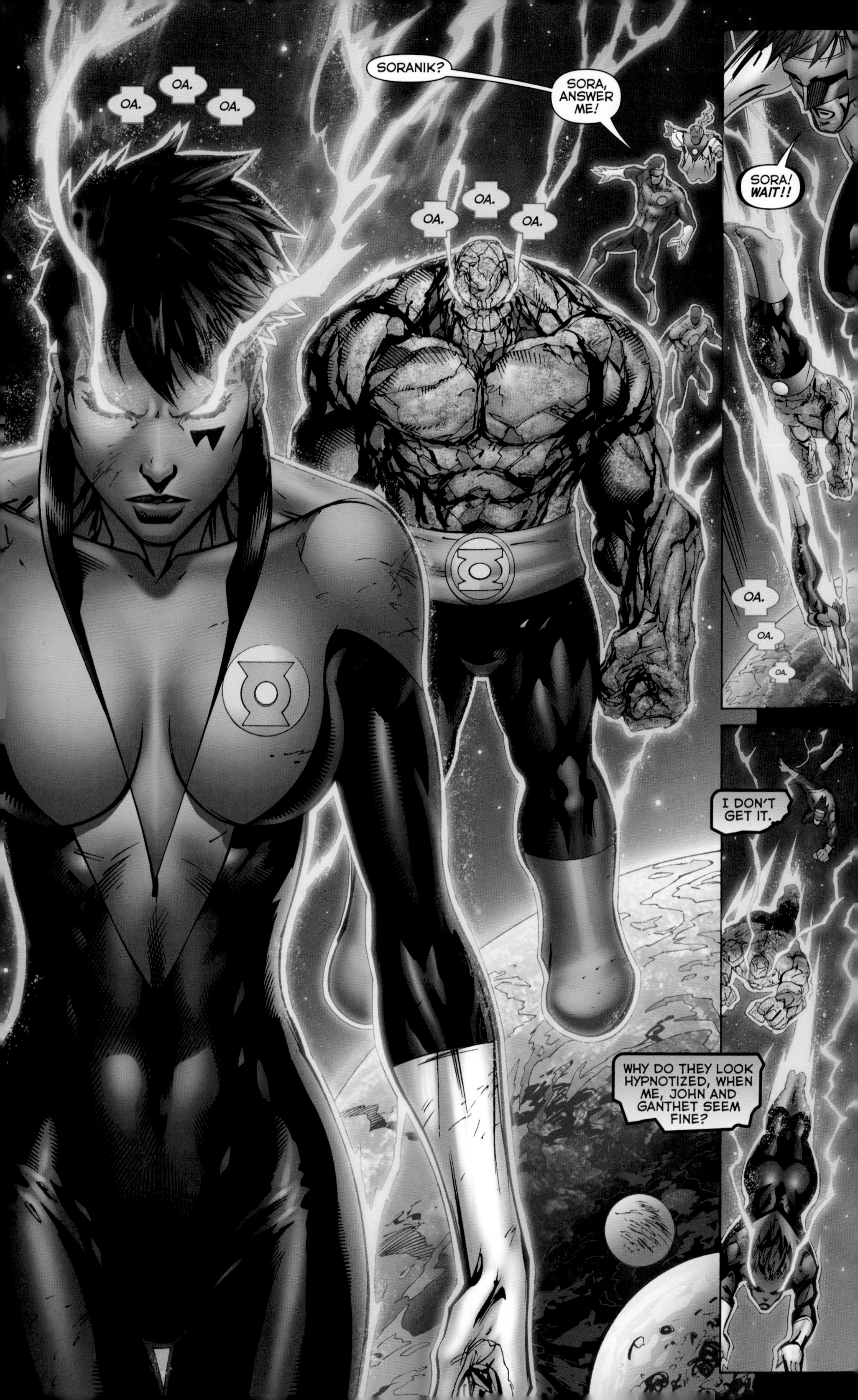
OA.
OA.
OA.
SORANIK?
SORA, ANSWER ME!
OA.
OA.
OA.
SORA! WAIT!!
OA.
OA.
OA.
I DON'T GET IT.
WHY DO THEY LOOK HYPNOTIZED, WHEN ME, JOHN AND GANTHET SEEM FINE?

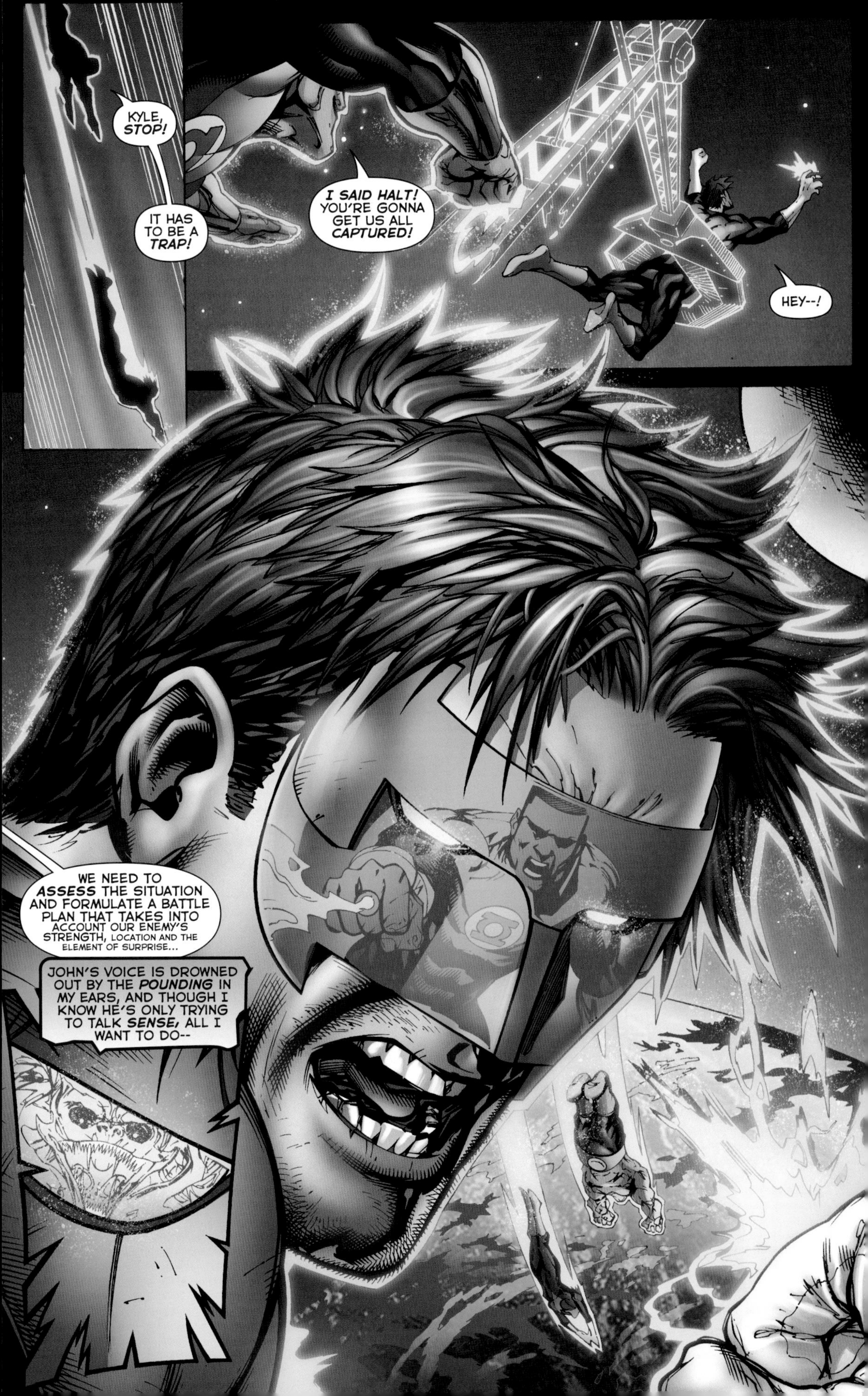
KYLE, STOP!
IT HAS TO BE A TRAP!
I SAID HALT! YOU'RE GONNA GET US ALL CAPTURED!
HEY--!
WE NEED TO ASSESS THE SITUATION AND FORMULATE A BATTLE PLAN THAT TAKES INTO ACCOUNT OUR ENEMY'S STRENGTH, LOCATION AND THE ELEMENT OF SURPRISE...
JOHN'S VOICE IS DROWNED OUT BY THE POUNDING IN MY EARS, AND THOUGH I KNOW HE'S ONLY TRYING TO TALK SENSE, ALL I WANT TO DO--

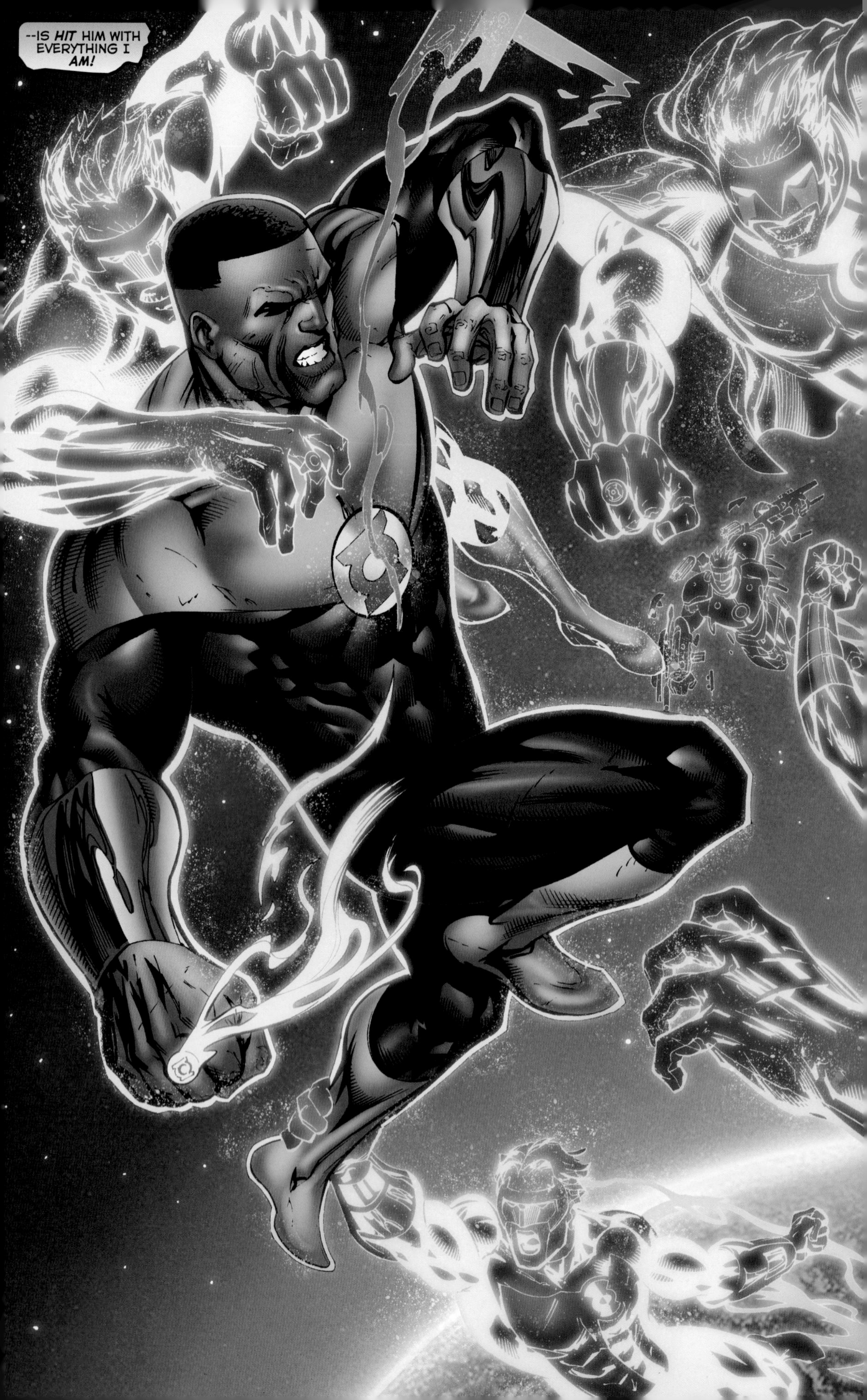
--IS HIT HIM WITH EVERYTHING I AM!

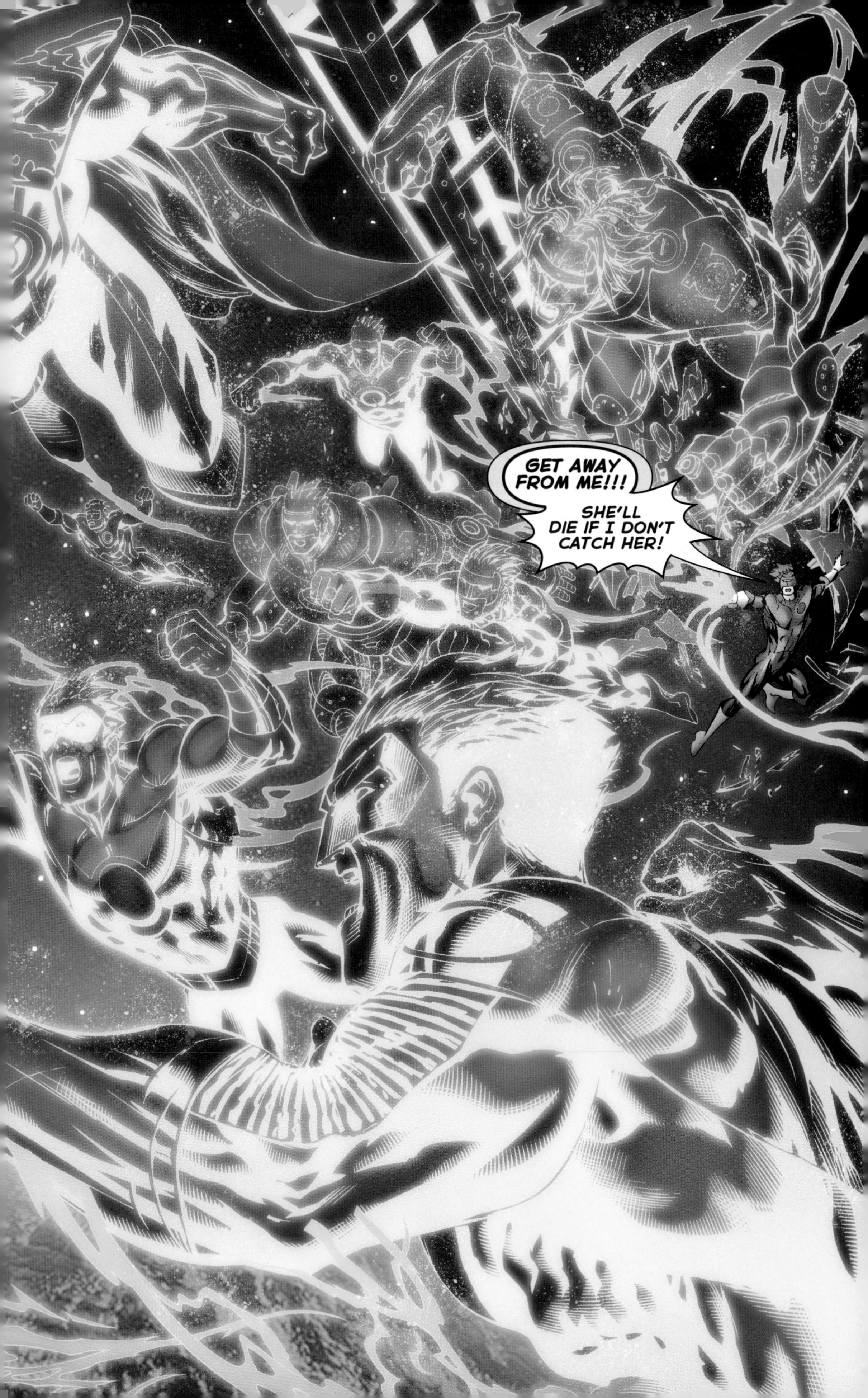
GET AWAY FROM ME!!!
SHE'LL DIE IF I DON'T CATCH HER!

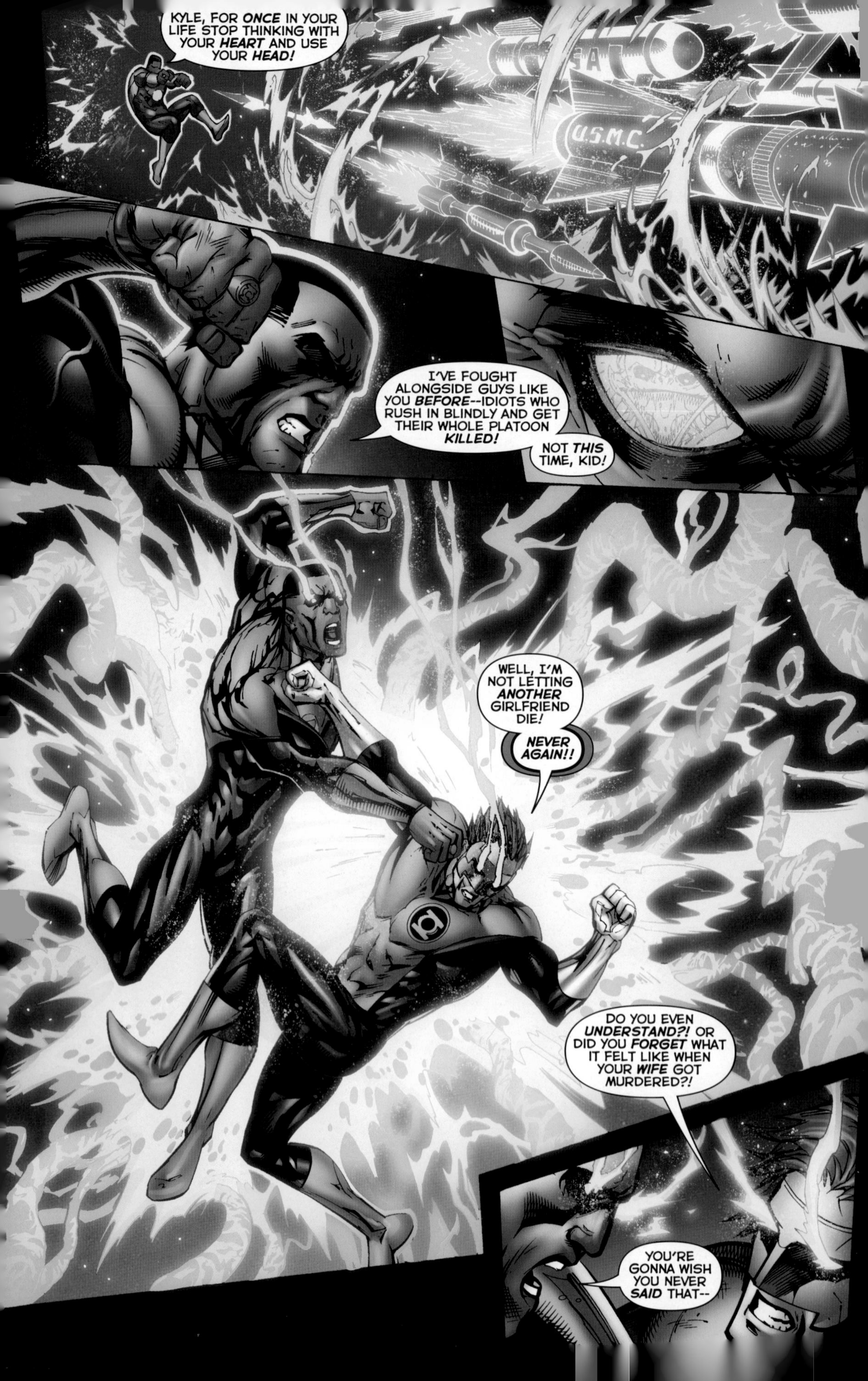
KYLE, FOR ONCE IN YOUR LIFE STOP THINKING WITH YOUR HEART AND USE YOUR HEAD!
U.S.M.C.
I'VE FOUGHT ALONGSIDE GUYS LIKE YOU BEFORE--IDIOTS WHO RUSH IN BLINDLY AND GET THEIR WHOLE PLATOON KILLED!
NOT THIS TIME, KID!
WELL, I'M NOT LETTING ANOTHER GIRLFRIEND DIE!
NEVER AGAIN!!
DO YOU EVEN UNDERSTAND?! OR DID YOU FORGET WHAT IT FELT LIKE WHEN YOUR WIFE GOT MURDERED?!
YOU'RE GONNA WISH YOU NEVER SAID THAT--

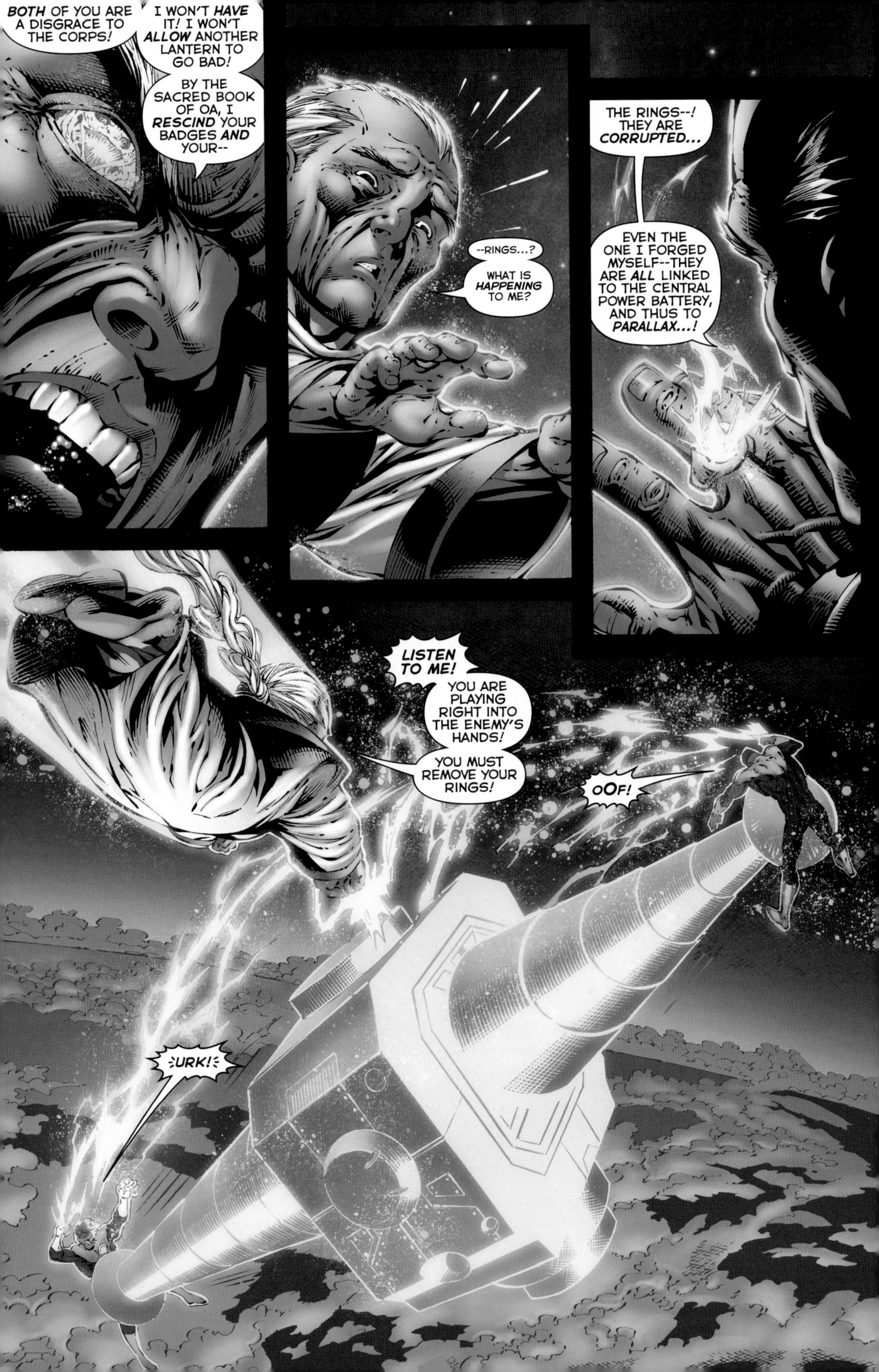
BOTH OF YOU ARE A DISGRACE TO THE CORPS!
I WON'T HAVE IT! I WON'T ALLOW ANOTHER LANTERN TO GO BAD!
BY THE SACRED BOOK OF OA, I RESCIND YOUR BADGES AND YOUR--
--RINGS...?
WHAT IS HAPPENING TO ME?
THE RINGS--! THEY ARE CORRUPTED...
EVEN THE ONE I FORGED MYSELF--THEY ARE ALL LINKED TO THE CENTRAL POWER BATTERY, AND THUS TO PARALLAX...!
LISTEN TO ME!
YOU ARE PLAYING RIGHT INTO THE ENEMY'S HANDS!
YOU MUST REMOVE YOUR RINGS!
OOF!
URK!

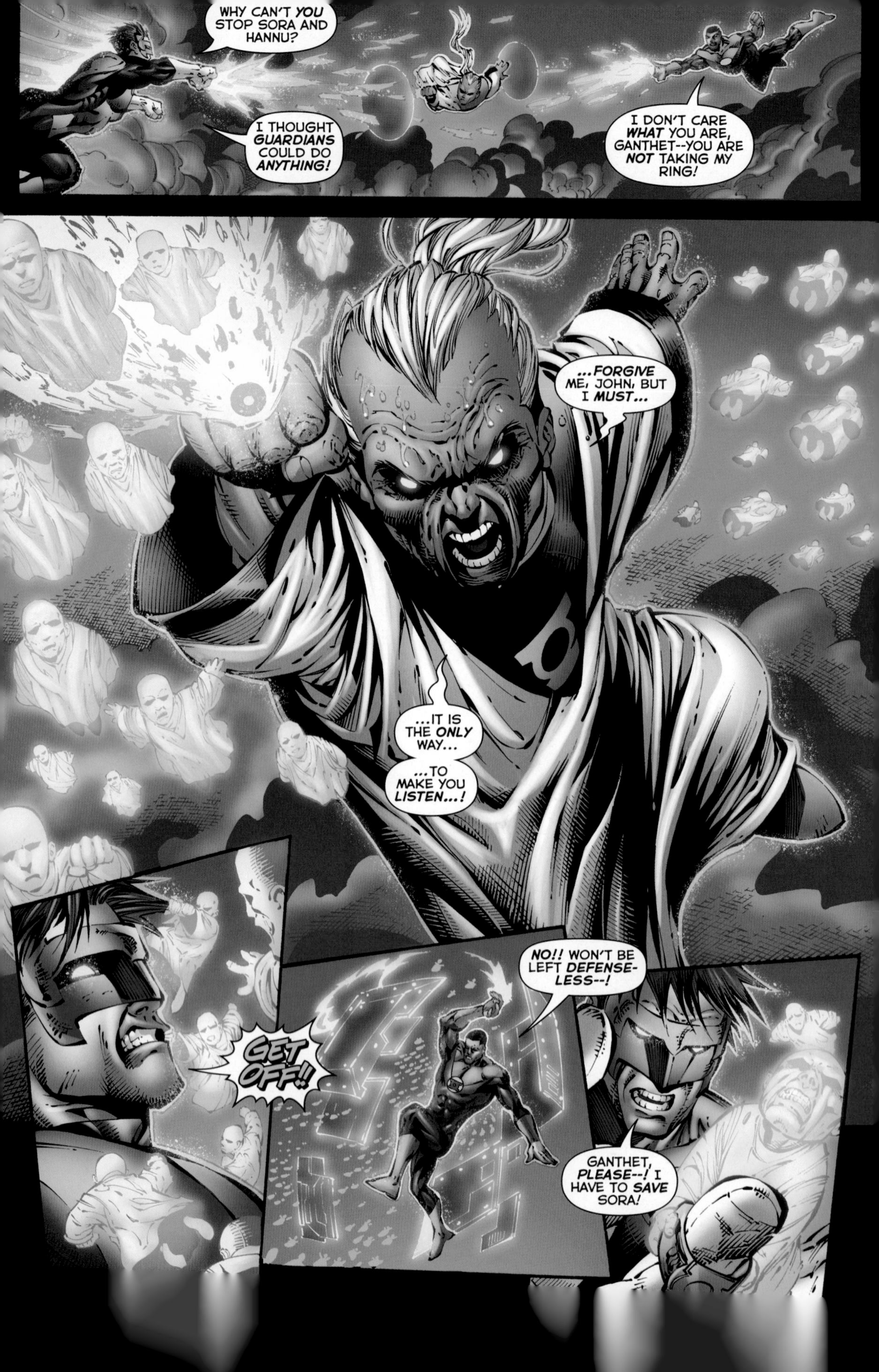
WHY CAN'T YOU STOP SORA AND HANNU?
I THOUGHT GUARDIANS COULD DO ANYTHING!
I DON'T CARE WHAT YOU ARE, GANTHET--YOU ARE NOT TAKING MY RING!
...FORGIVE ME, JOHN, BUT I MUST...
...IT IS THE ONLY WAY...
...TO MAKE YOU LISTEN...!
GET OFF!!
NO!! WON'T BE LEFT DEFENSE-LESS--!
GANTHET, PLEASE--! I HAVE TO SAVE SORA!

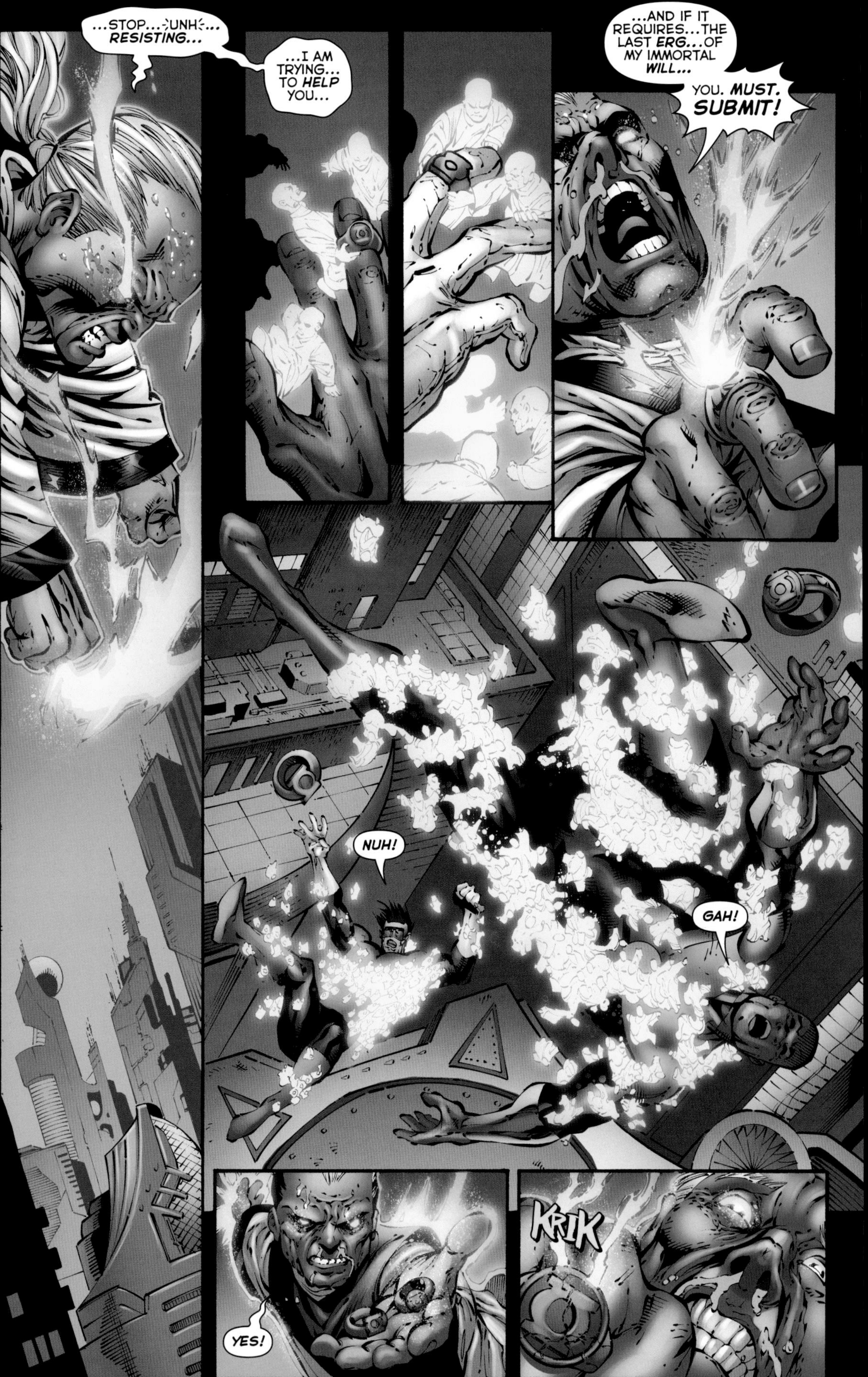
...STOP...UNH... RESISTING...
...I AM TRYING... TO HELP YOU...
...AND IF IT REQUIRES... THE LAST ERG... OF MY IMMORTAL WILL...
YOU. MUST. SUBMIT!
NUH!
GAH!
YES!
KRIK

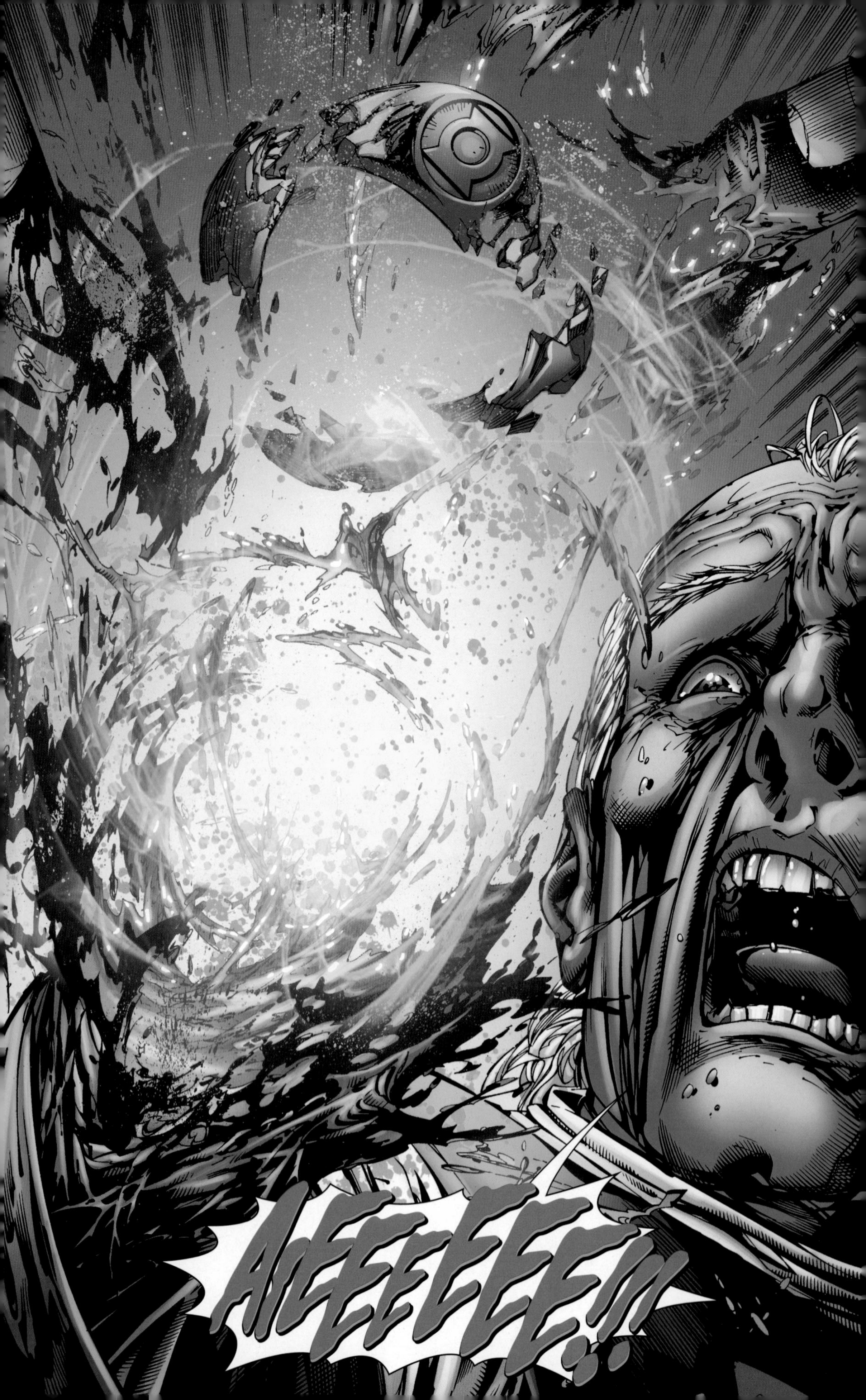
AIEEEEE!!!

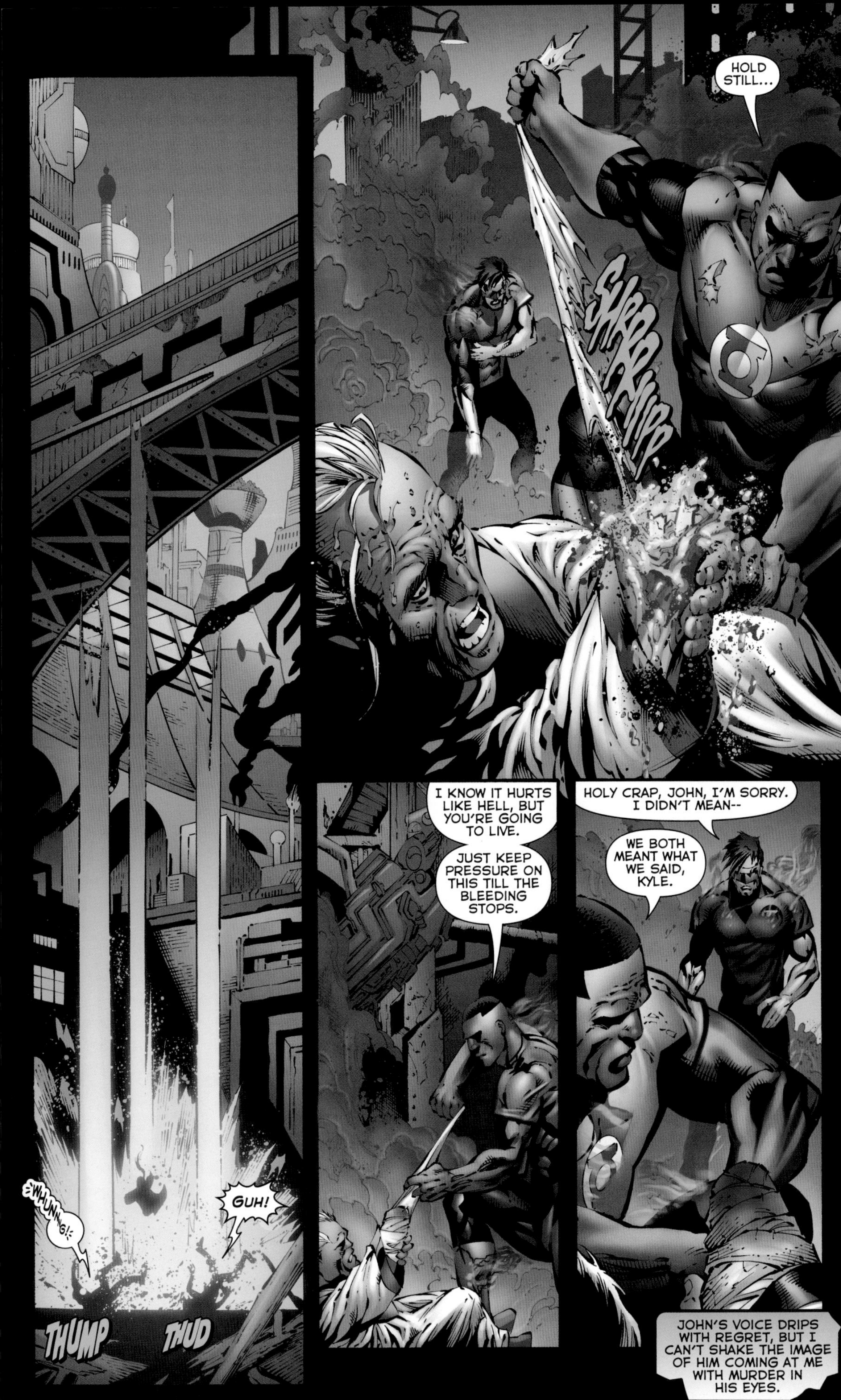
WHUNNNG!
GUH!
THUMP
THUD
HOLD STILL...
I KNOW IT HURTS LIKE HELL, BUT YOU'RE GOING TO LIVE.
JUST KEEP PRESSURE ON THIS TILL THE BLEEDING STOPS.
HOLY CRAP, JOHN, I'M SORRY. I DIDN'T MEAN--
WE BOTH MEANT WHAT WE SAID, KYLE.
JOHN'S VOICE DRIPS WITH REGRET, BUT I CAN'T SHAKE THE IMAGE OF HIM COMING AT ME WITH MURDER IN HIS EYES.

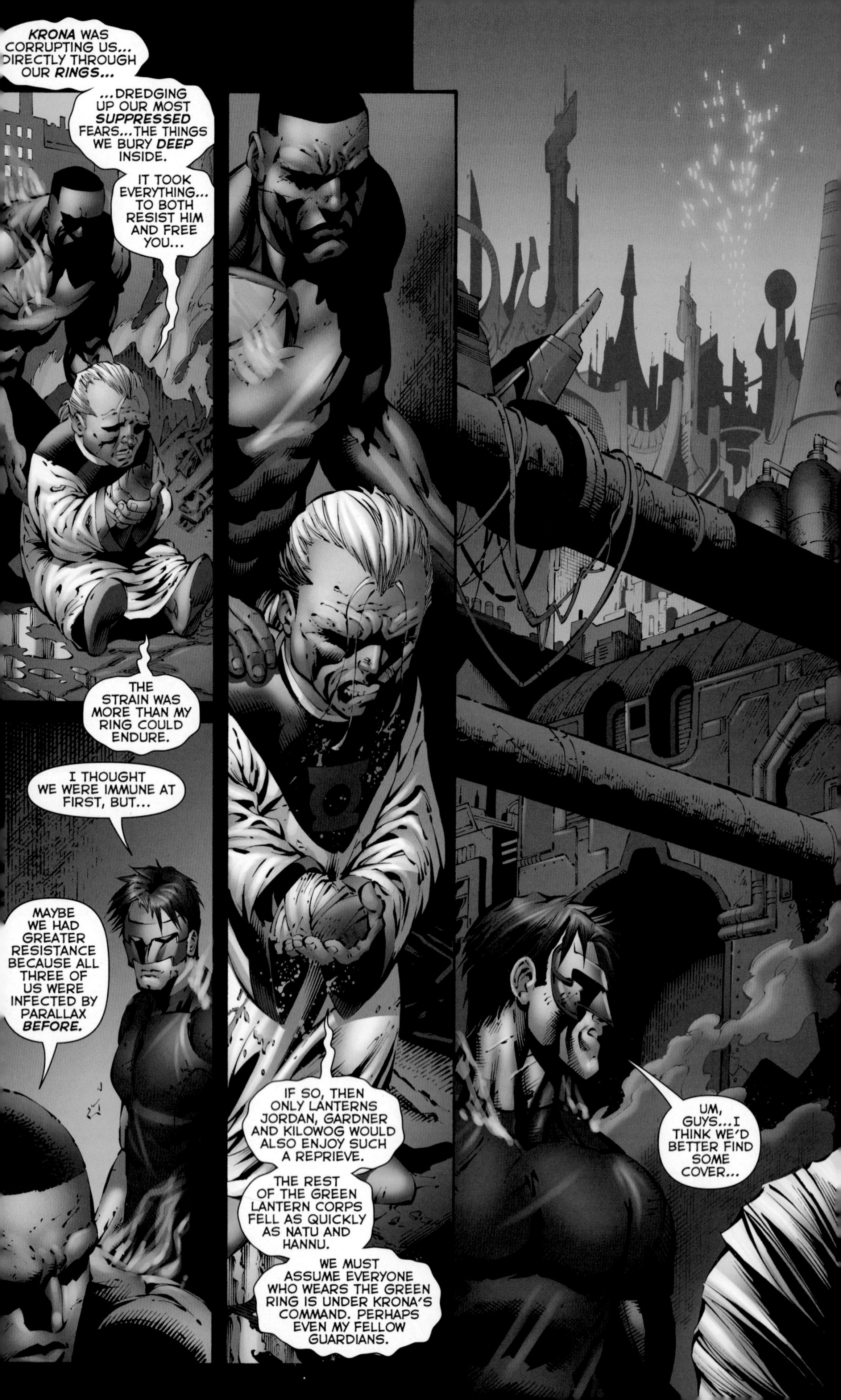
KRONA WAS CORRUPTING US... DIRECTLY THROUGH OUR RINGS...
...DREDGING UP OUR MOST SUPPRESSED FEARS...THE THINGS WE BURY DEEP INSIDE.
IT TOOK EVERYTHING... TO BOTH RESIST HIM AND FREE YOU...
THE STRAIN WAS MORE THAN MY RING COULD ENDURE.
I THOUGHT WE WERE IMMUNE AT FIRST, BUT...
MAYBE WE HAD GREATER RESISTANCE BECAUSE ALL THREE OF US WERE INFECTED BY PARALLAX BEFORE.
IF SO, THEN ONLY LANTERNS JORDAN, GARDNER AND KILOWOG WOULD ALSO ENJOY SUCH A REPRIEVE.
THE REST OF THE GREEN LANTERN CORPS FELL AS QUICKLY AS NATU AND HANNU.
WE MUST ASSUME EVERYONE WHO WEARS THE GREEN RING IS UNDER KRONA'S COMMAND. PERHAPS EVEN MY FELLOW GUARDIANS.
UM, GUYS...I THINK WE'D BETTER FIND SOME COVER...

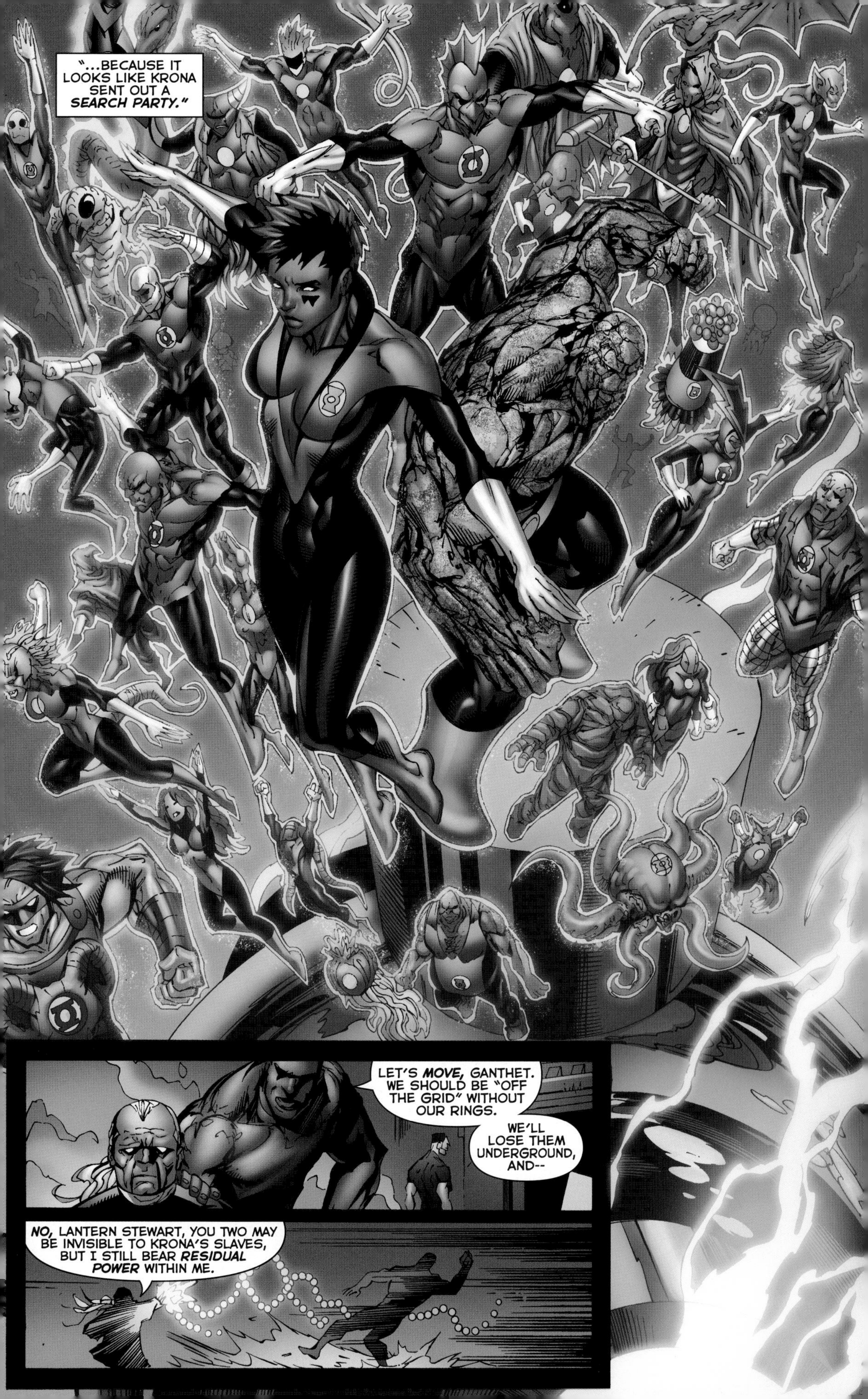
"...BECAUSE IT LOOKS LIKE KRONA SENT OUT A SEARCH PARTY."
LET'S MOVE, GANTHET. WE SHOULD BE "OFF THE GRID" WITHOUT OUR RINGS.
WE'LL LOSE THEM UNDERGROUND, AND--
NO, LANTERN STEWART, YOU TWO MAY BE INVISIBLE TO KRONA'S SLAVES, BUT I STILL BEAR RESIDUAL POWER WITHIN ME.

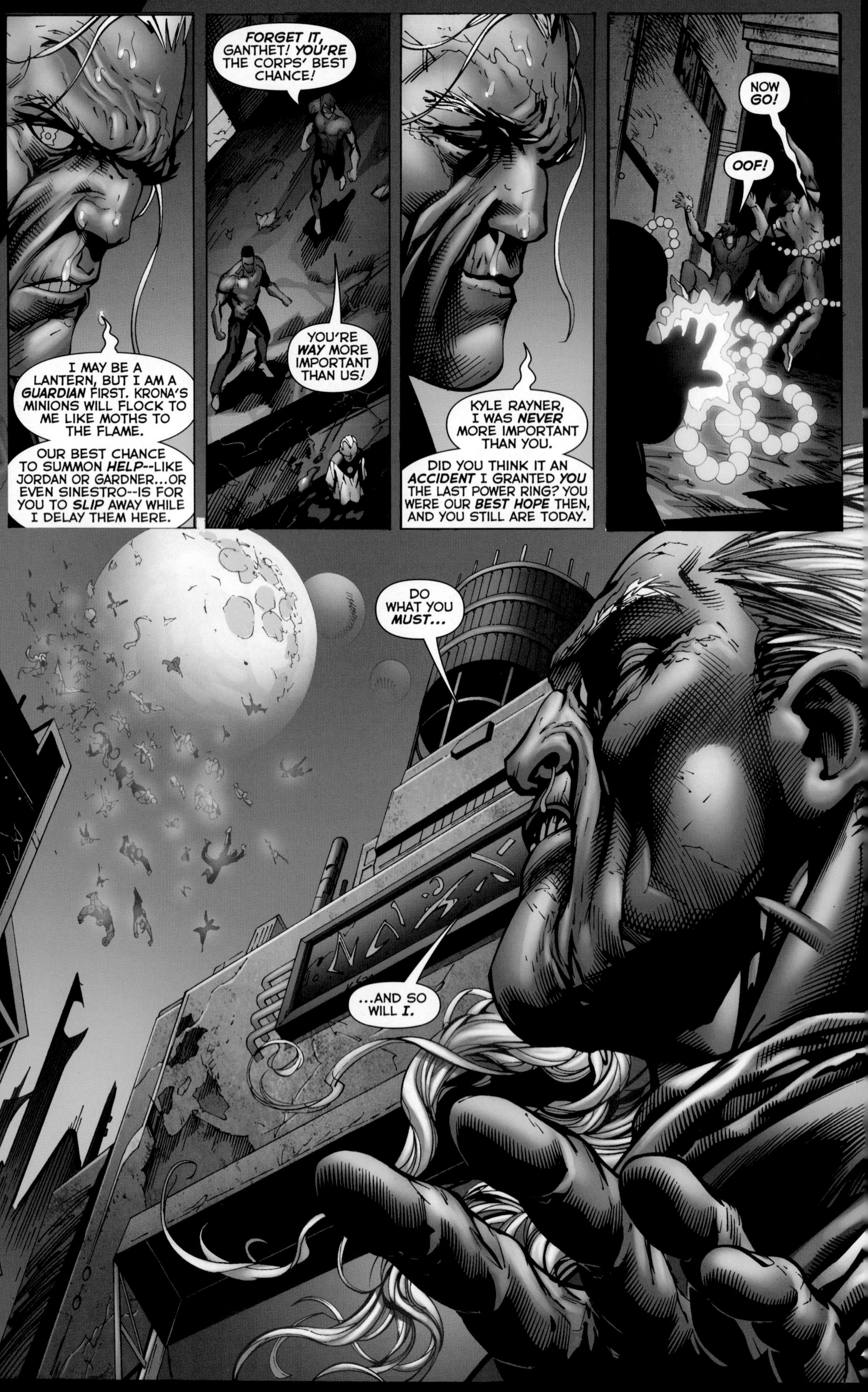
I MAY BE A LANTERN, BUT I AM A GUARDIAN FIRST. KRONA'S MINIONS WILL FLOCK TO ME LIKE MOTHS TO THE FLAME.
OUR BEST CHANCE TO SUMMON HELP--LIKE JORDAN OR GARDNER...OR EVEN SINESTRO--IS FOR YOU TO SLIP AWAY WHILE I DELAY THEM HERE.
FORGET IT, GANTHET! YOU'RE THE CORPS' BEST CHANCE!
YOU'RE WAY MORE IMPORTANT THAN US!
KYLE RAYNER, I WAS NEVER MORE IMPORTANT THAN YOU.
DID YOU THINK IT AN ACCIDENT I GRANTED YOU THE LAST POWER RING? YOU WERE OUR BEST HOPE THEN, AND YOU STILL ARE TODAY.
NOW GO!
OOF!
DO WHAT YOU MUST...
...AND SO WILL I.

GREEN LANTERN: EMERALD WARRIORS 8 Cover by Felipe Massafera

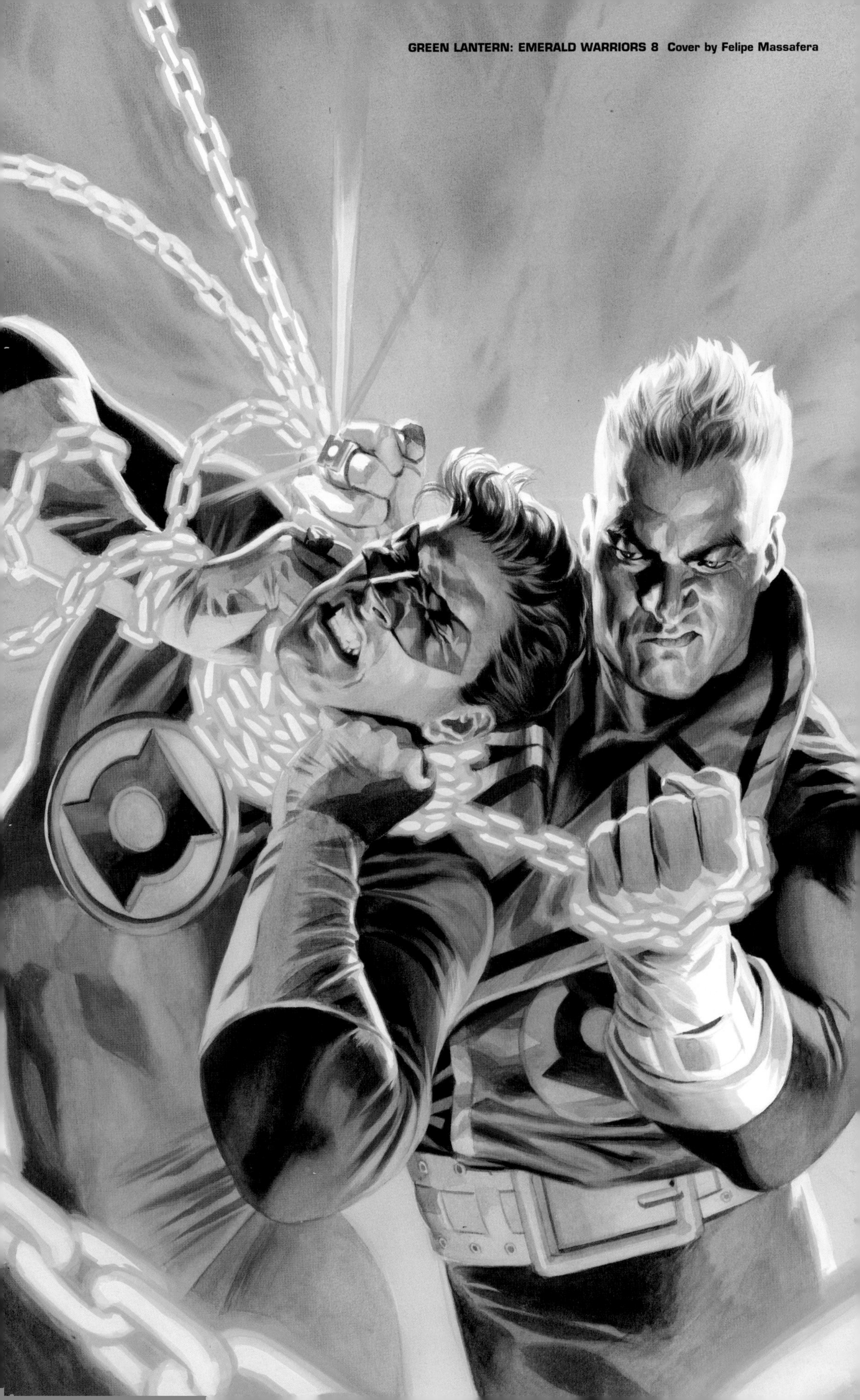

WAR OF THE GREEN LANTERNS
PART THREE

Peter J. Tomasi Writer
Fernando Pasarin Penciller
Cam Smith Inker

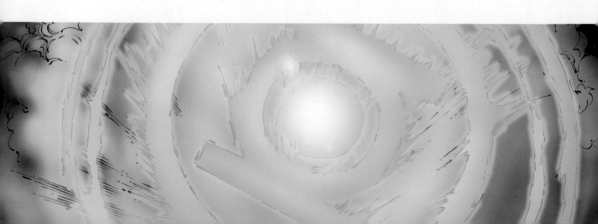

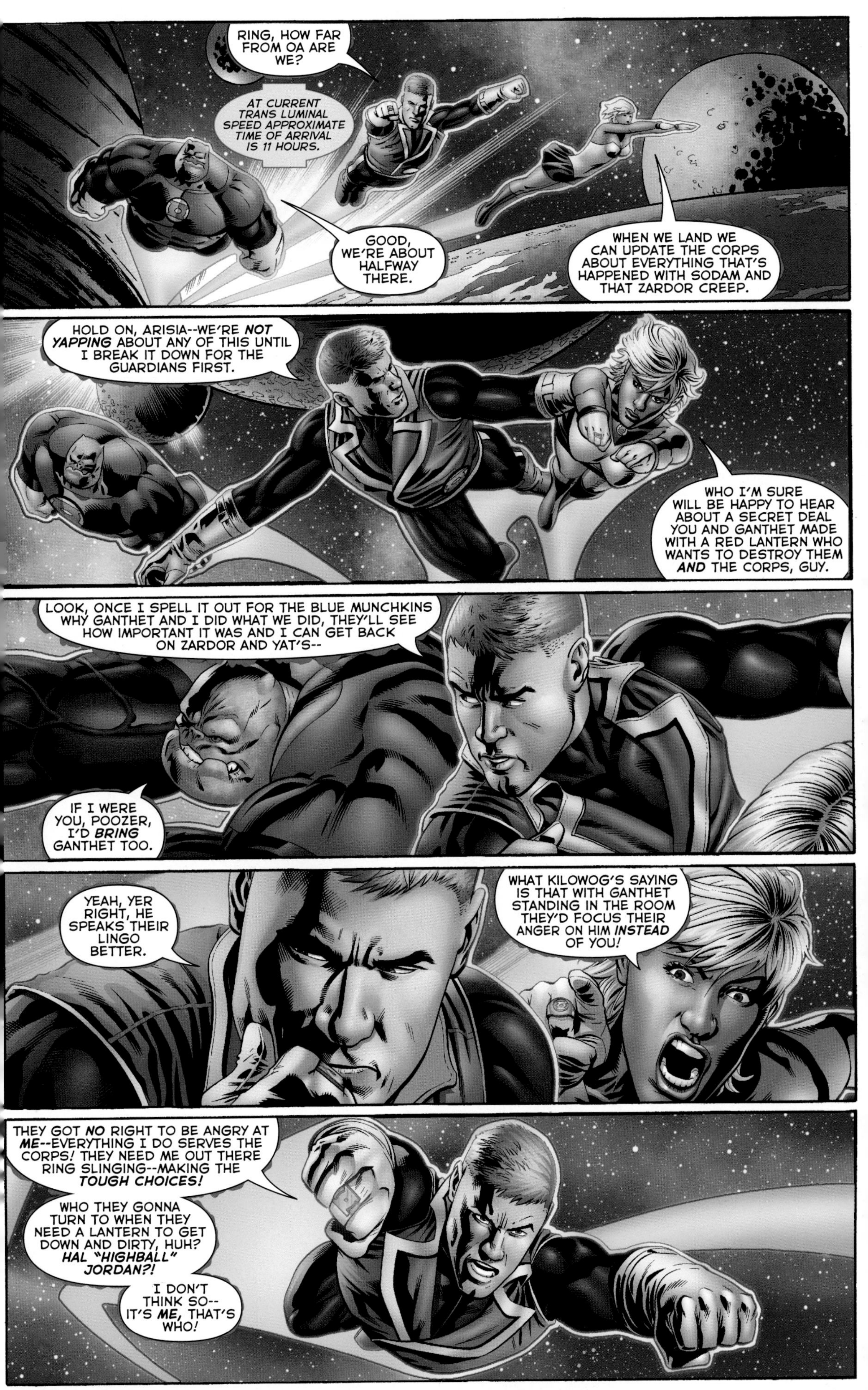

RING, HOW FAR FROM OA ARE WE?
AT CURRENT TRANS LUMINAL SPEED APPROXIMATE TIME OF ARRIVAL IS 11 HOURS.
GOOD, WE'RE ABOUT HALFWAY THERE.
WHEN WE LAND WE CAN UPDATE THE CORPS ABOUT EVERYTHING THAT'S HAPPENED WITH SODAM AND THAT ZARDOR CREEP.
HOLD ON, ARISIA--WE'RE ***NOT YAPPING*** ABOUT ANY OF THIS UNTIL I BREAK IT DOWN FOR THE GUARDIANS FIRST.
WHO I'M SURE WILL BE HAPPY TO HEAR ABOUT A SECRET DEAL YOU AND GANTHET MADE WITH A RED LANTERN WHO WANTS TO DESTROY THEM ***AND*** THE CORPS, GUY.
LOOK, ONCE I SPELL IT OUT FOR THE BLUE MUNCHKINS WHY GANTHET AND I DID WHAT WE DID, THEY'LL SEE HOW IMPORTANT IT WAS AND I CAN GET BACK ON ZARDOR AND YAT'S--
IF I WERE YOU, POOZER, I'D ***BRING*** GANTHET TOO.
YEAH, YER RIGHT, HE SPEAKS THEIR LINGO BETTER.
WHAT KILOWOG'S SAYING IS THAT WITH GANTHET STANDING IN THE ROOM THEY'D FOCUS THEIR ANGER ON HIM ***INSTEAD*** OF YOU*!*
THEY GOT ***NO*** RIGHT TO BE ANGRY AT ***ME***--EVERYTHING I DO SERVES THE CORPS*!* THEY NEED ME OUT THERE RING SLINGING--MAKING THE ***TOUGH CHOICES!***
WHO THEY GONNA TURN TO WHEN THEY NEED A LANTERN TO GET DOWN AND DIRTY, HUH? ***HAL "HIGHBALL" JORDAN?!***
I DON'T THINK SO--IT'S ***ME,*** THAT'S WHO*!*

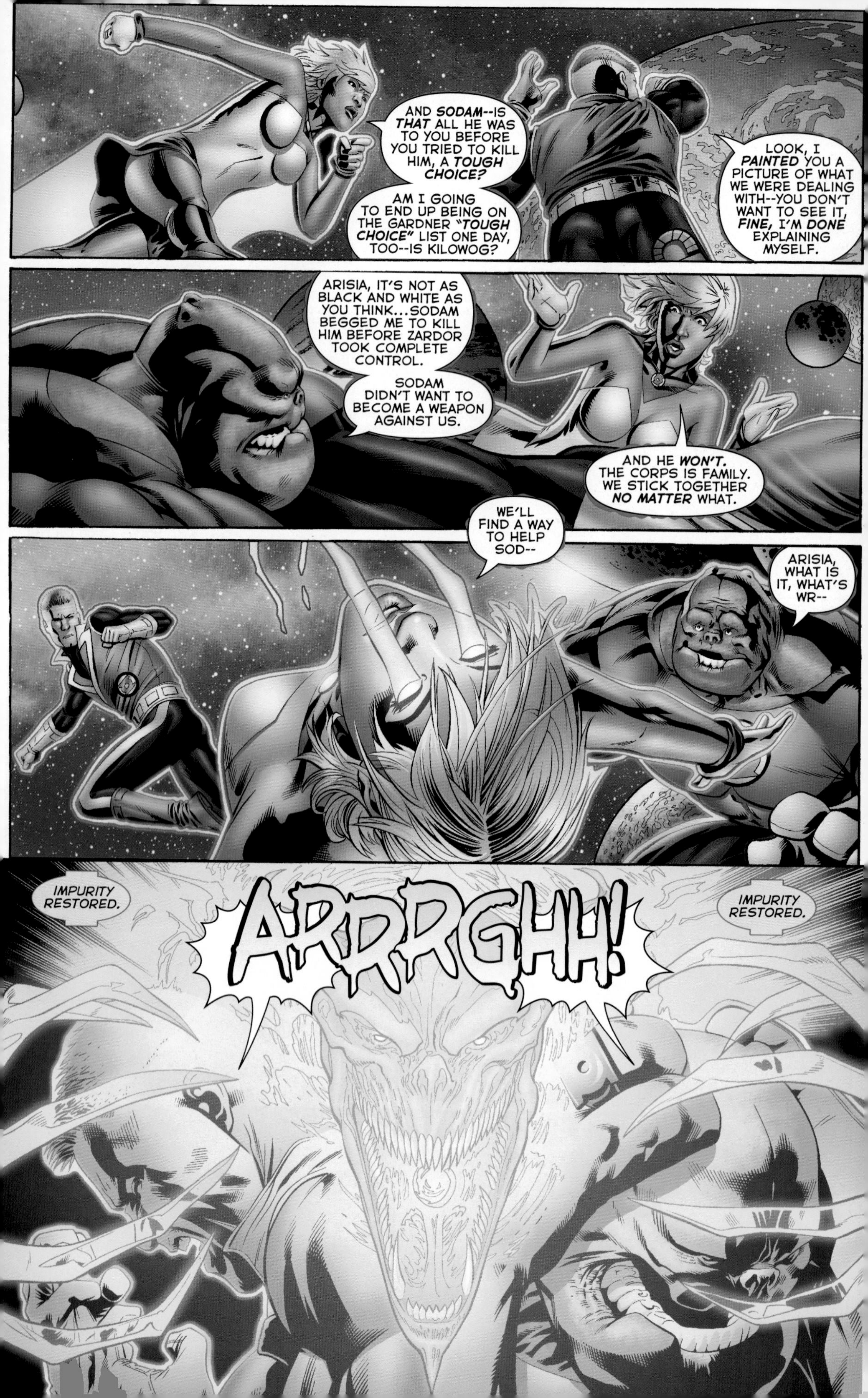
AND SODAM--IS THAT ALL HE WAS TO YOU BEFORE YOU TRIED TO KILL HIM, A TOUGH CHOICE?
AM I GOING TO END UP BEING ON THE GARDNER "TOUGH CHOICE" LIST ONE DAY, TOO--IS KILOWOG?
LOOK, I PAINTED YOU A PICTURE OF WHAT WE WERE DEALING WITH--YOU DON'T WANT TO SEE IT, FINE, I'M DONE EXPLAINING MYSELF.
ARISIA, IT'S NOT AS BLACK AND WHITE AS YOU THINK...SODAM BEGGED ME TO KILL HIM BEFORE ZARDOR TOOK COMPLETE CONTROL.
SODAM DIDN'T WANT TO BECOME A WEAPON AGAINST US.
AND HE WON'T. THE CORPS IS FAMILY. WE STICK TOGETHER NO MATTER WHAT.
WE'LL FIND A WAY TO HELP SOD--
ARISIA, WHAT IS IT, WHAT'S WR--
IMPURITY RESTORED.
ARRRGHH!
IMPURITY RESTORED.

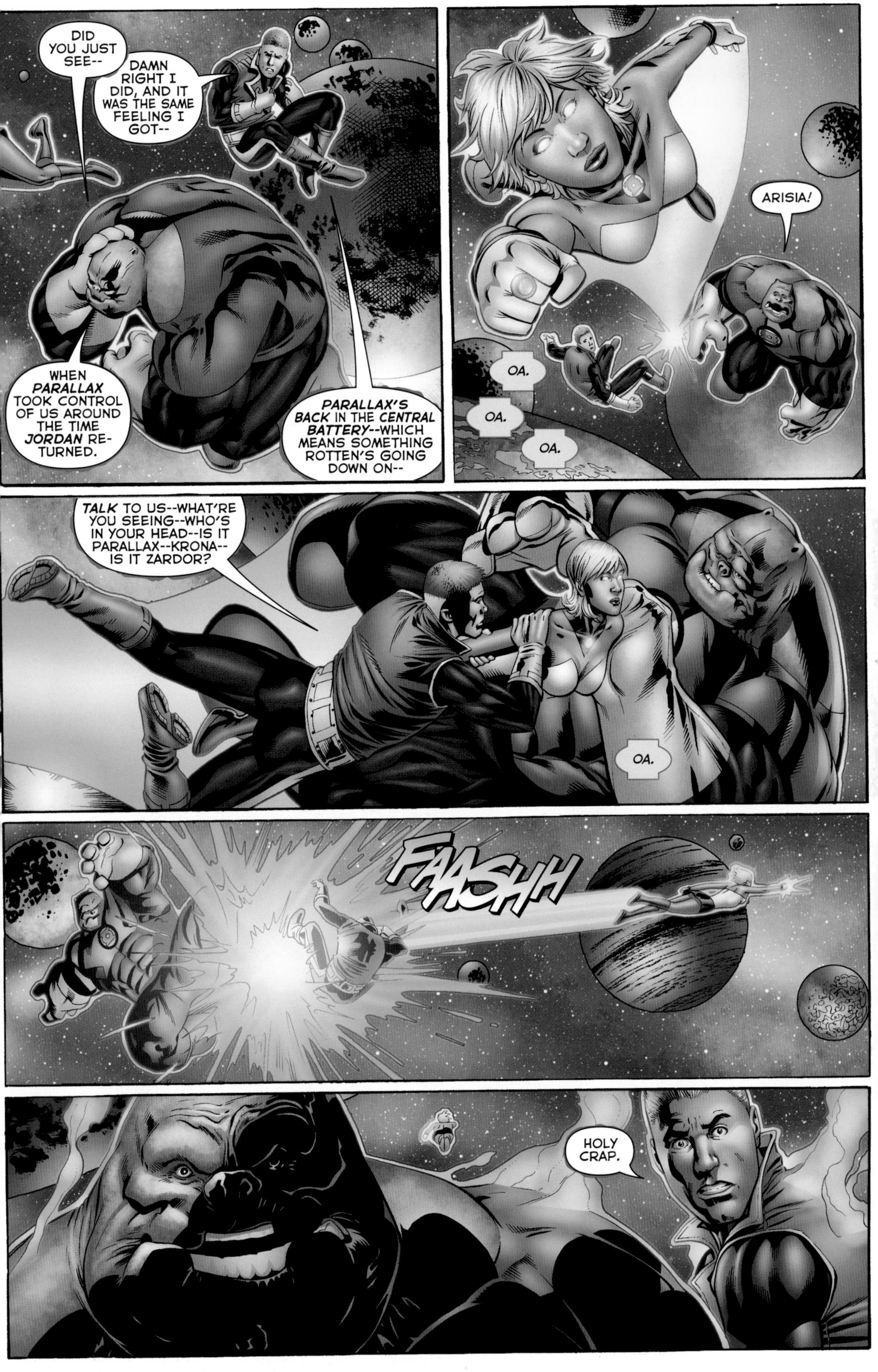
DID YOU JUST SEE--
DAMN RIGHT I DID, AND IT WAS THE SAME FEELING I GOT--
WHEN PARALLAX TOOK CONTROL OF US AROUND THE TIME JORDAN RE-TURNED.
PARALLAX'S BACK IN THE CENTRAL BATTERY--WHICH MEANS SOMETHING ROTTEN'S GOING DOWN ON--
ARISIA!
OA.
OA.
OA.
TALK TO US--WHAT'RE YOU SEEING--WHO'S IN YOUR HEAD--IS IT PARALLAX--KRONA--IS IT ZARDOR?
OA.
FAASHH
HOLY CRAP.

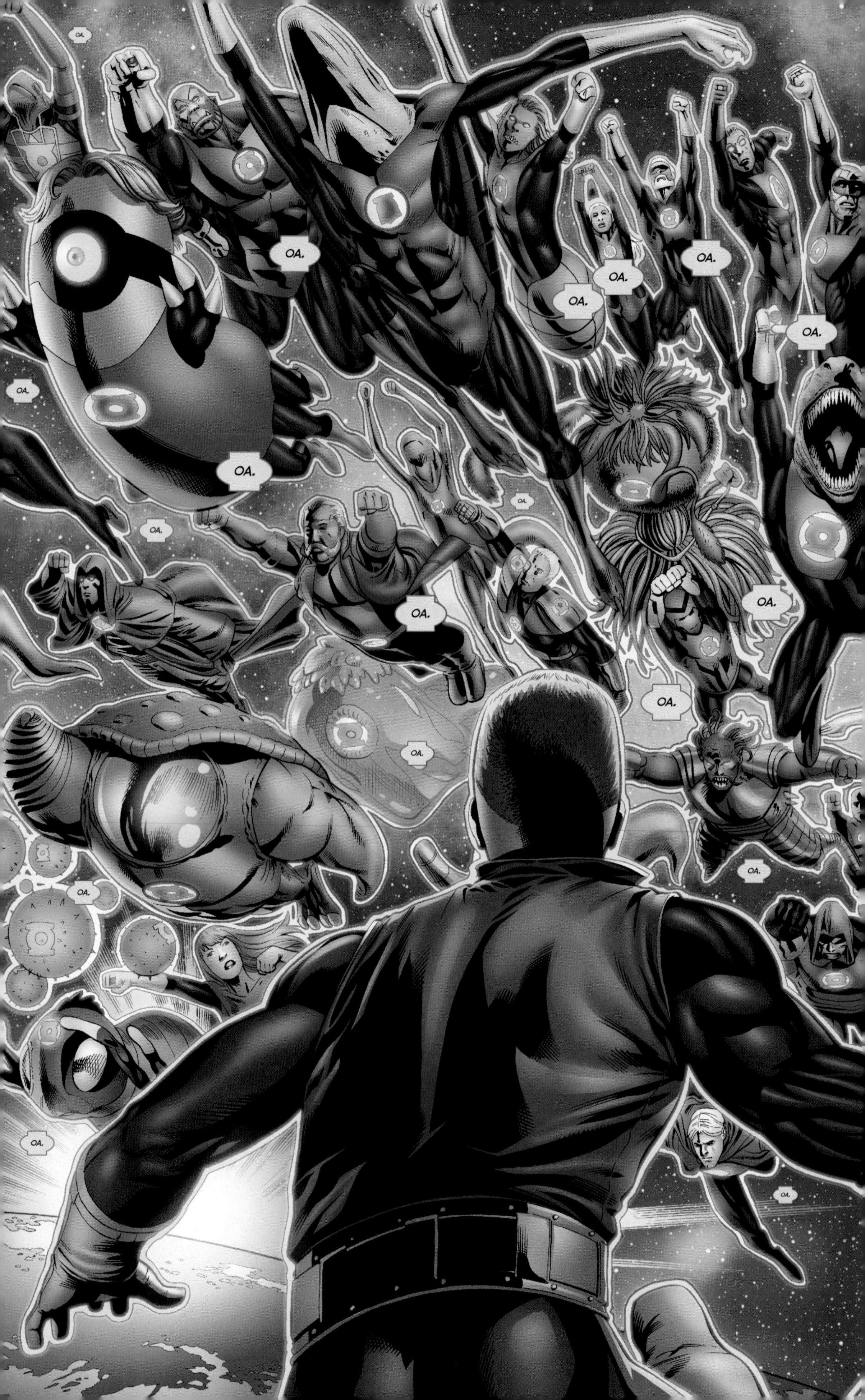

OA.
OA.
OA.
OA.
OA.
OA.
OA.
OA.
OA.
OA.
OA.
OA.
OA.
OA.
OA.
OA.
OA.
OA.

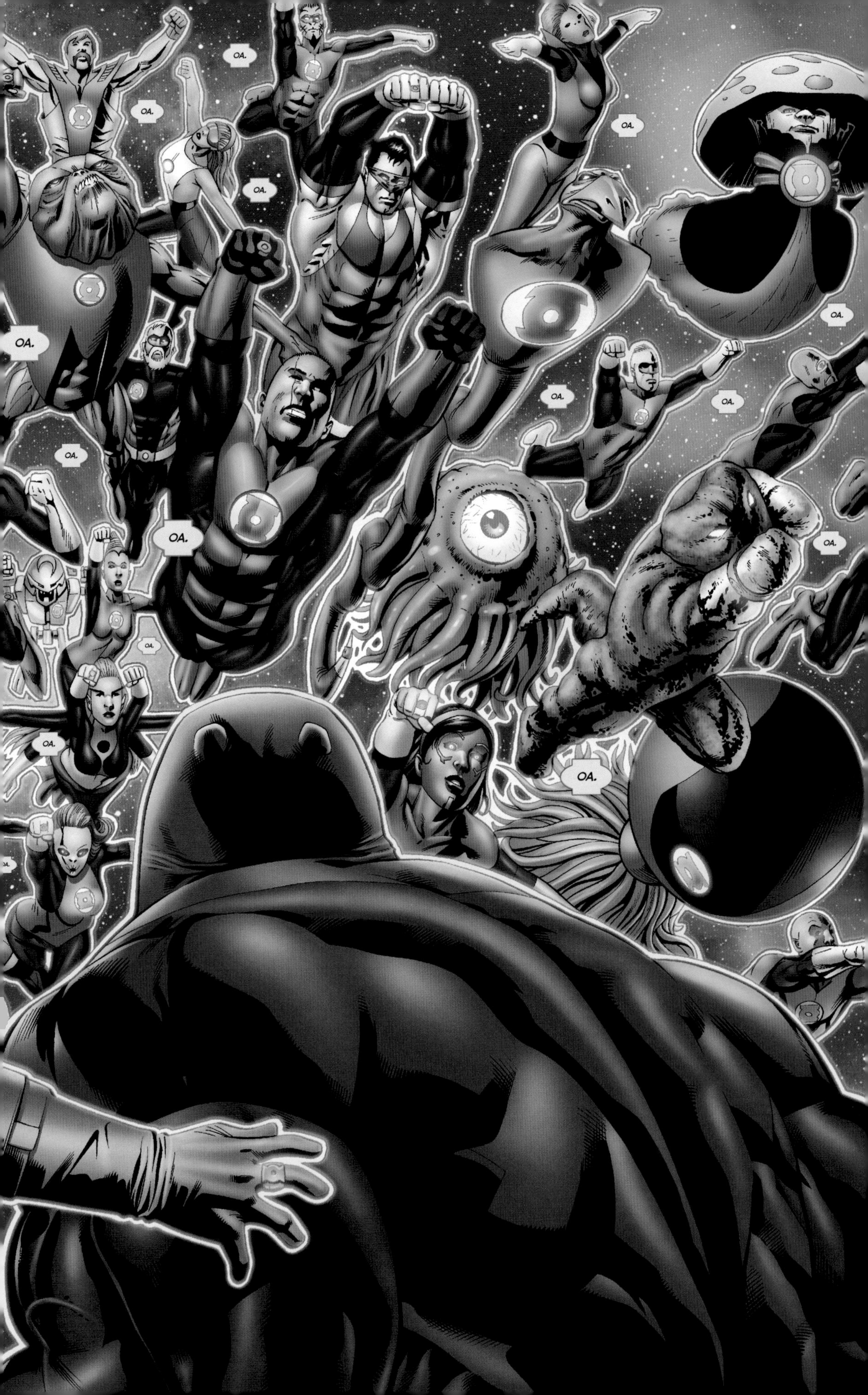
OA.
OA.
OA.
OA.
OA.
OA.
OA.
OA.
OA.
OA.
OA.
OA.
OA.
OA.
OA.

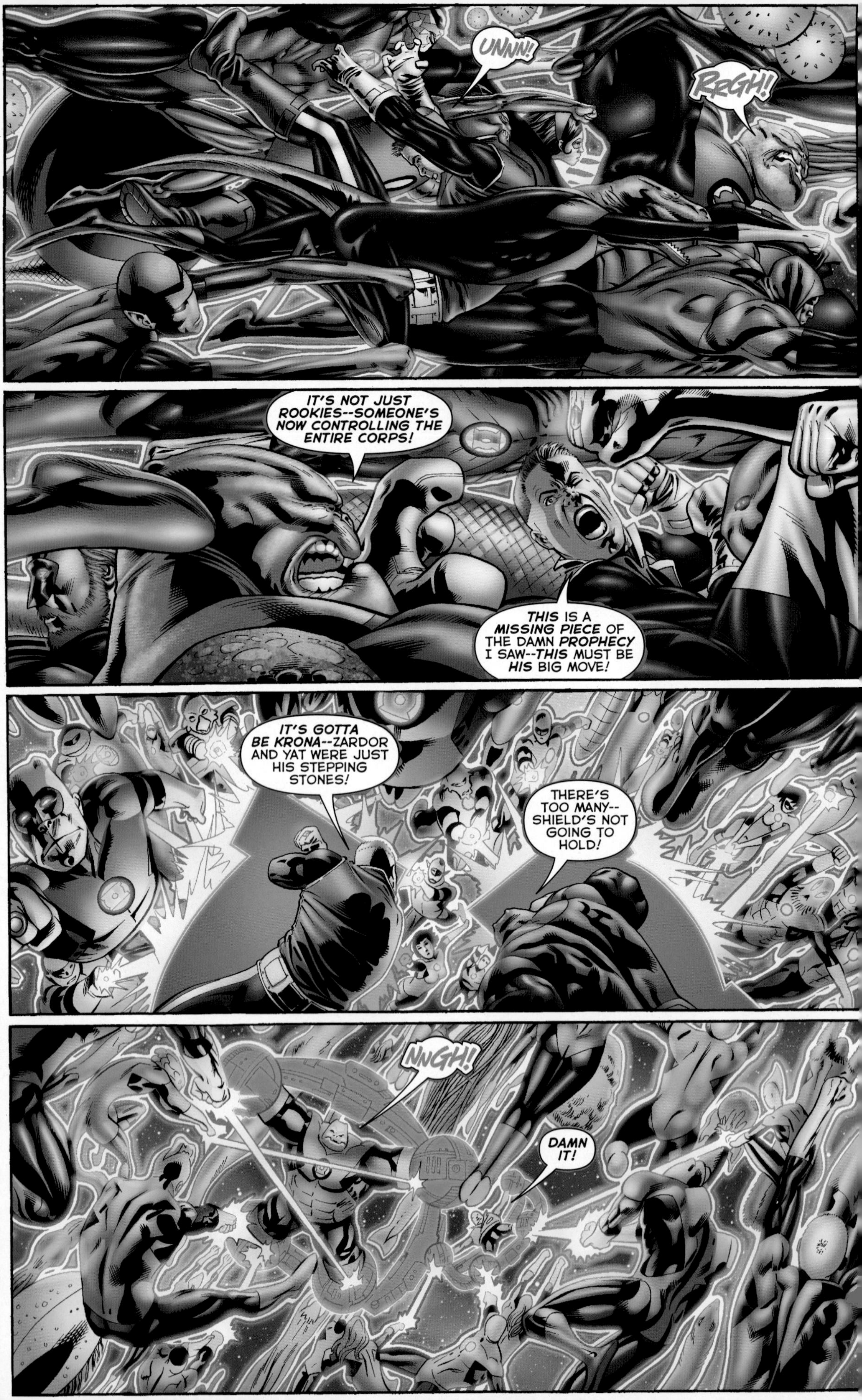
UNNN!
RRGH!
IT'S NOT JUST ROOKIES--SOMEONE'S NOW CONTROLLING THE ENTIRE CORPS!
THIS IS A MISSING PIECE OF THE DAMN PROPHECY I SAW--THIS MUST BE HIS BIG MOVE!
IT'S GOTTA BE KRONA--ZARDOR AND YAT WERE JUST HIS STEPPING STONES!
THERE'S TOO MANY--SHIELD'S NOT GOING TO HOLD!
NNGH!
DAMN IT!

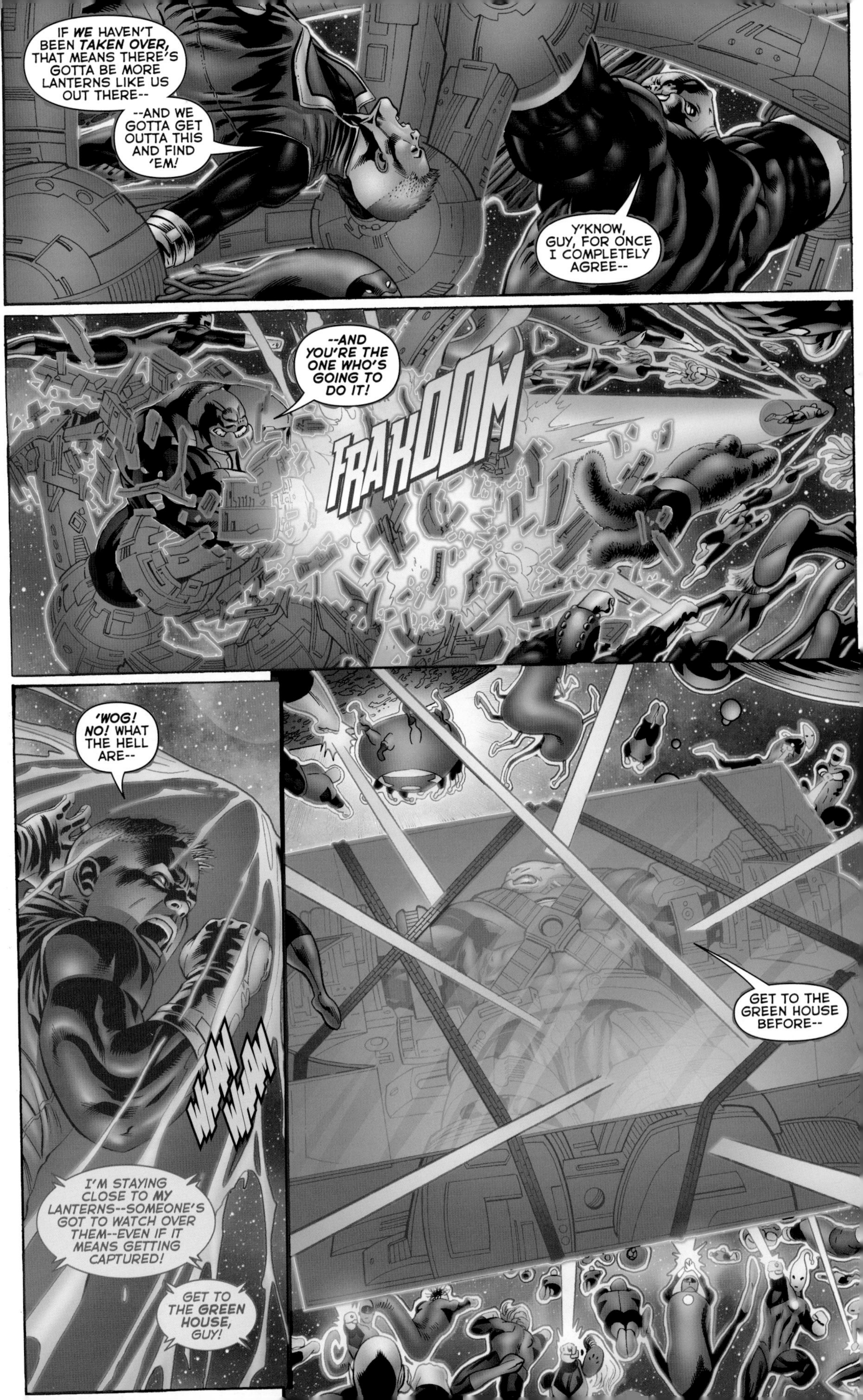
IF WE HAVEN'T BEEN TAKEN OVER, THAT MEANS THERE'S GOTTA BE MORE LANTERNS LIKE US OUT THERE--
--AND WE GOTTA GET OUTTA THIS AND FIND 'EM!
Y'KNOW, GUY, FOR ONCE I COMPLETELY AGREE--
--AND YOU'RE THE ONE WHO'S GOING TO DO IT!
FRAKOOM
'WOG! NO! WHAT THE HELL ARE--
GET TO THE GREEN HOUSE BEFORE--
I'M STAYING CLOSE TO MY LANTERNS--SOMEONE'S GOT TO WATCH OVER THEM--EVEN IF IT MEANS GETTING CAPTURED!
GET TO THE GREEN HOUSE, GUY!

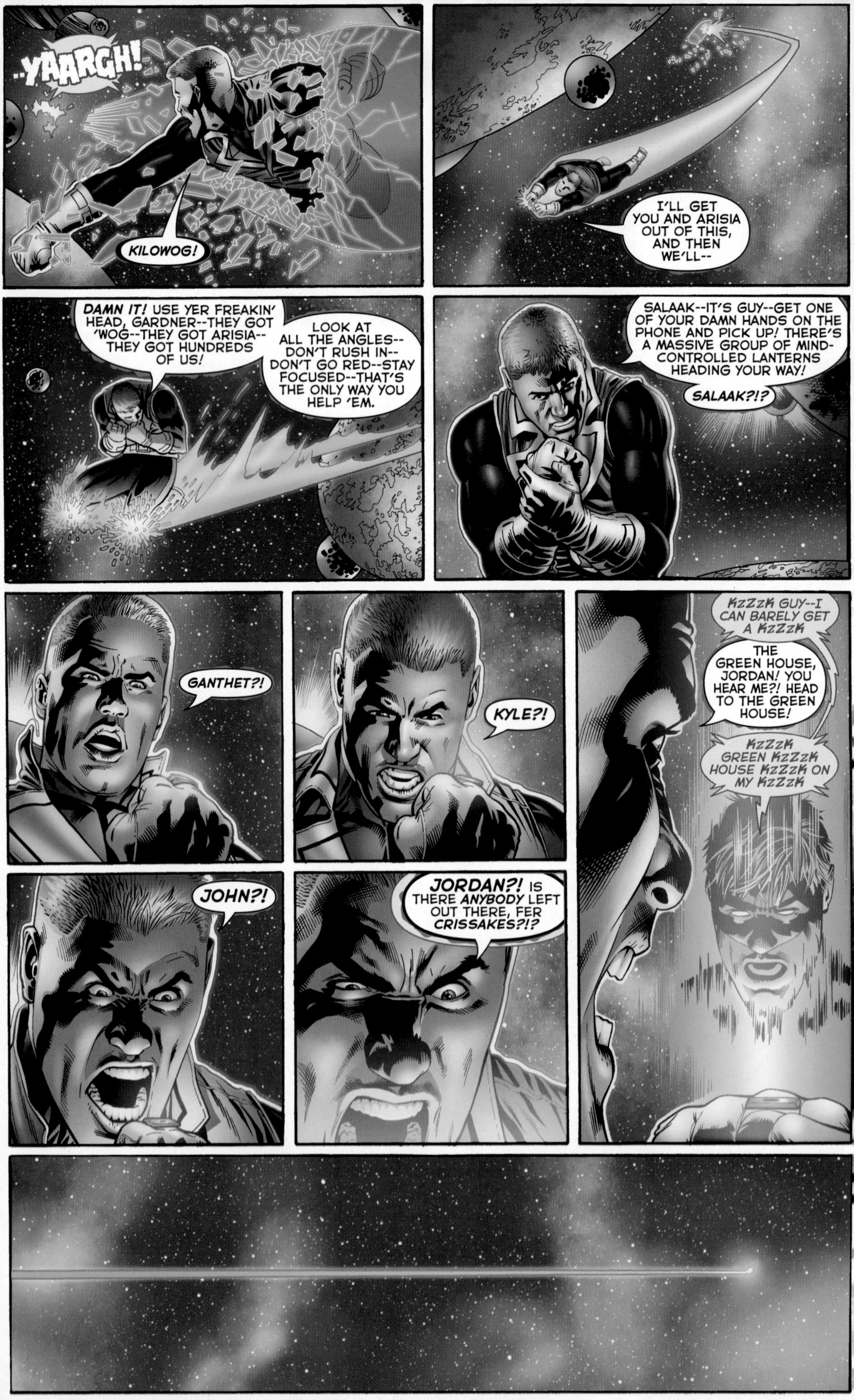
..YAARGH!
KILOWOG!
I'LL GET YOU AND ARISIA OUT OF THIS, AND THEN WE'LL--
DAMN IT! USE YER FREAKIN' HEAD, GARDNER--THEY GOT 'WOG--THEY GOT ARISIA--THEY GOT HUNDREDS OF US!
LOOK AT ALL THE ANGLES--DON'T RUSH IN--DON'T GO RED--STAY FOCUSED--THAT'S THE ONLY WAY YOU HELP 'EM.
SALAAK--IT'S GUY--GET ONE OF YOUR DAMN HANDS ON THE PHONE AND PICK UP! THERE'S A MASSIVE GROUP OF MIND-CONTROLLED LANTERNS HEADING YOUR WAY!
SALAAK?!?
GANTHET?!
KYLE?!
JOHN?!
JORDAN?! IS THERE ANYBODY LEFT OUT THERE, FER CRISSAKES?!?
KzZzK GUY--I CAN BARELY GET A KzZzK
THE GREEN HOUSE, JORDAN! YOU HEAR ME?! HEAD TO THE GREEN HOUSE!
KzZzK GREEN KzZzK HOUSE KzZzK ON MY KzZzK

FINALLY, THERE'S THE SNOWBALL.

LET'S GO, JORDAN, WE'RE BURNING DAYLIGHT HERE...

...ZERO IN ON MY LITTLE HOME FIRE...

...SO WE CAN GET THIS PARTY STARTED.

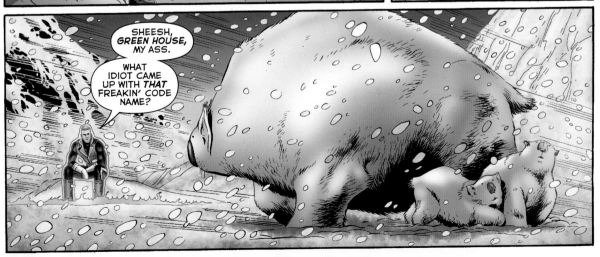

SHEESH, *GREEN HOUSE*, MY ASS.

WHAT IDIOT CAME UP WITH *THAT* FREAKIN' CODE NAME?

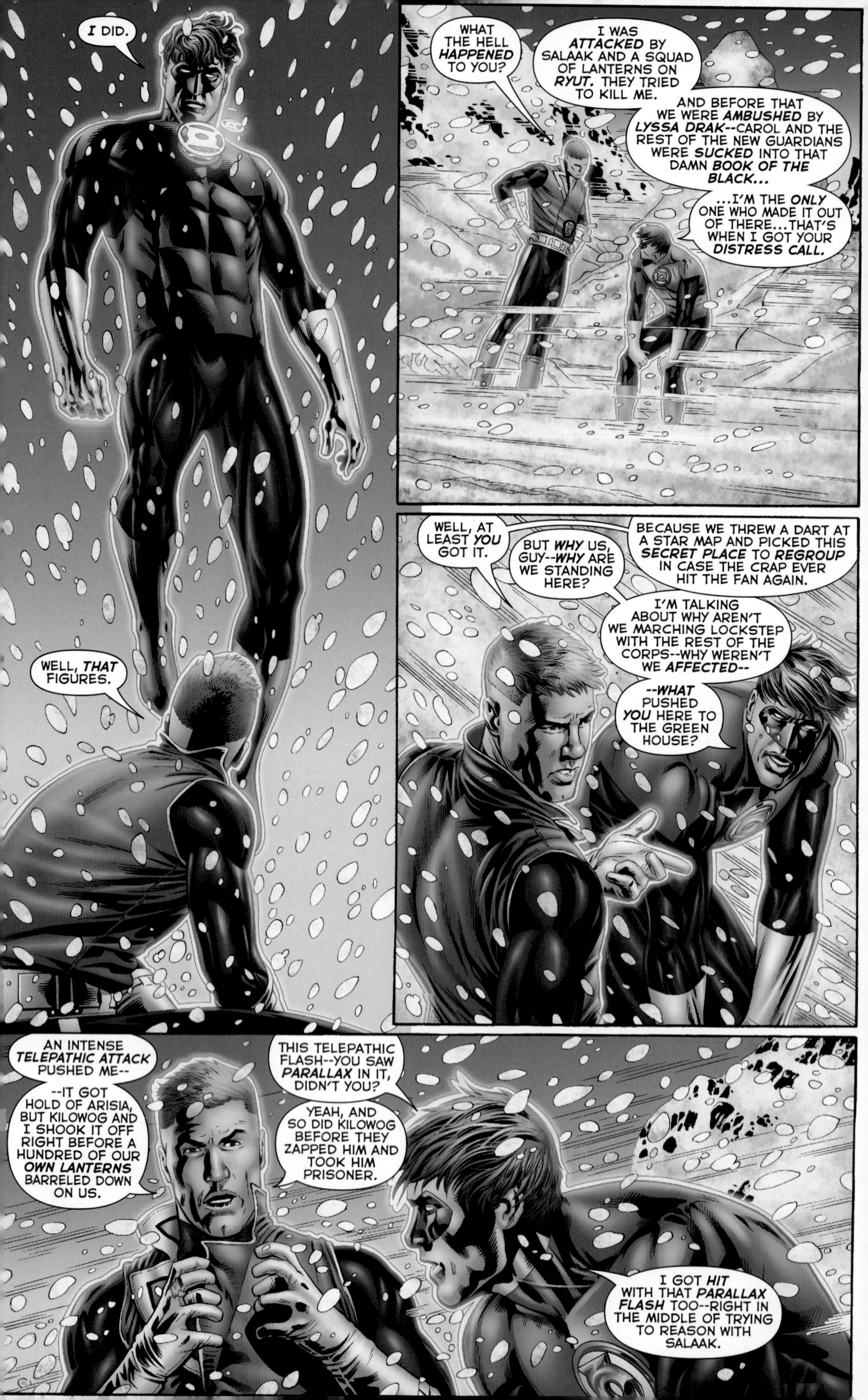
I DID.
WHAT THE HELL HAPPENED TO YOU?
I WAS ATTACKED BY SALAAK AND A SQUAD OF LANTERNS ON RYUT. THEY TRIED TO KILL ME.
AND BEFORE THAT WE WERE AMBUSHED BY LYSSA DRAK--CAROL AND THE REST OF THE NEW GUARDIANS WERE SUCKED INTO THAT DAMN BOOK OF THE BLACK...
...I'M THE ONLY ONE WHO MADE IT OUT OF THERE...THAT'S WHEN I GOT YOUR DISTRESS CALL.
WELL, THAT FIGURES.
WELL, AT LEAST YOU GOT IT.
BECAUSE WE THREW A DART AT A STAR MAP AND PICKED THIS SECRET PLACE TO REGROUP IN CASE THE CRAP EVER HIT THE FAN AGAIN.
BUT WHY US, GUY--WHY ARE WE STANDING HERE?
I'M TALKING ABOUT WHY AREN'T WE MARCHING LOCKSTEP WITH THE REST OF THE CORPS--WHY WEREN'T WE AFFECTED--
--WHAT PUSHED YOU HERE TO THE GREEN HOUSE?
AN INTENSE TELEPATHIC ATTACK PUSHED ME--
--IT GOT HOLD OF ARISIA, BUT KILOWOG AND I SHOOK IT OFF RIGHT BEFORE A HUNDRED OF OUR OWN LANTERNS BARRELED DOWN ON US.
THIS TELEPATHIC FLASH--YOU SAW PARALLAX IN IT, DIDN'T YOU?
YEAH, AND SO DID KILOWOG BEFORE THEY ZAPPED HIM AND TOOK HIM PRISONER.
I GOT HIT WITH THAT PARALLAX FLASH TOO--RIGHT IN THE MIDDLE OF TRYING TO REASON WITH SALAAK.

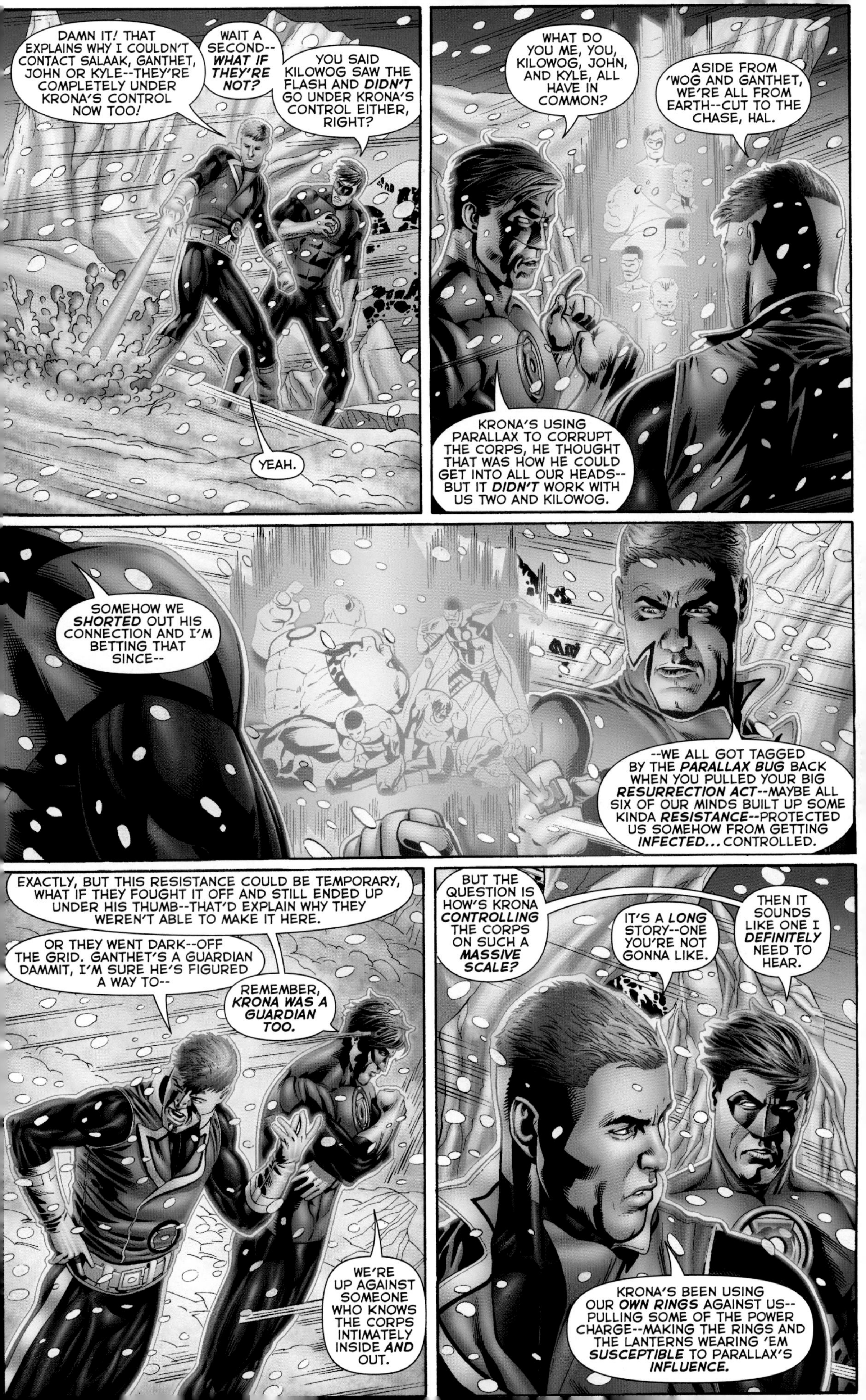
DAMN IT! THAT EXPLAINS WHY I COULDN'T CONTACT SALAAK, GANTHET, JOHN OR KYLE--THEY'RE COMPLETELY UNDER KRONA'S CONTROL NOW TOO!
WAIT A SECOND-- WHAT IF THEY'RE NOT?
YOU SAID KILOWOG SAW THE FLASH AND DIDN'T GO UNDER KRONA'S CONTROL EITHER, RIGHT?
YEAH.
WHAT DO YOU ME, YOU, KILOWOG, JOHN, AND KYLE, ALL HAVE IN COMMON?
ASIDE FROM 'WOG AND GANTHET, WE'RE ALL FROM EARTH--CUT TO THE CHASE, HAL.
KRONA'S USING PARALLAX TO CORRUPT THE CORPS, HE THOUGHT THAT WAS HOW HE COULD GET INTO ALL OUR HEADS-- BUT IT DIDN'T WORK WITH US TWO AND KILOWOG.
SOMEHOW WE SHORTED OUT HIS CONNECTION AND I'M BETTING THAT SINCE--
--WE ALL GOT TAGGED BY THE PARALLAX BUG BACK WHEN YOU PULLED YOUR BIG RESURRECTION ACT--MAYBE ALL SIX OF OUR MINDS BUILT UP SOME KINDA RESISTANCE--PROTECTED US SOMEHOW FROM GETTING INFECTED... CONTROLLED.
EXACTLY, BUT THIS RESISTANCE COULD BE TEMPORARY, WHAT IF THEY FOUGHT IT OFF AND STILL ENDED UP UNDER HIS THUMB--THAT'D EXPLAIN WHY THEY WEREN'T ABLE TO MAKE IT HERE.
OR THEY WENT DARK--OFF THE GRID. GANTHET'S A GUARDIAN DAMMIT, I'M SURE HE'S FIGURED A WAY TO--
REMEMBER, KRONA WAS A GUARDIAN TOO.
WE'RE UP AGAINST SOMEONE WHO KNOWS THE CORPS INTIMATELY INSIDE AND OUT.
BUT THE QUESTION IS HOW'S KRONA CONTROLLING THE CORPS ON SUCH A MASSIVE SCALE?
IT'S A LONG STORY--ONE YOU'RE NOT GONNA LIKE.
THEN IT SOUNDS LIKE ONE I DEFINITELY NEED TO HEAR.
KRONA'S BEEN USING OUR OWN RINGS AGAINST US-- PULLING SOME OF THE POWER CHARGE--MAKING THE RINGS AND THE LANTERNS WEARING 'EM SUSCEPTIBLE TO PARALLAX'S INFLUENCE.

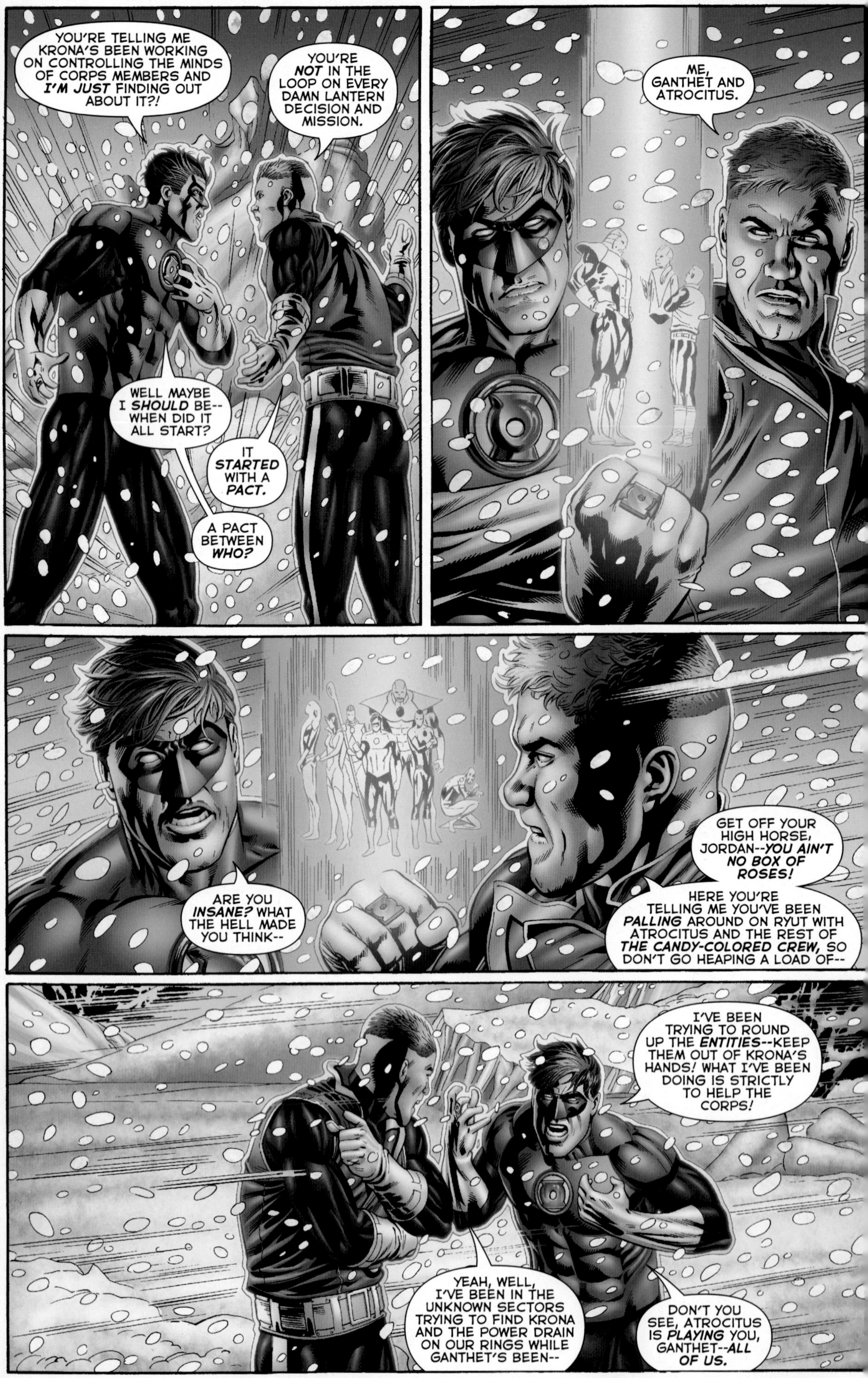
YOU'RE TELLING ME KRONA'S BEEN WORKING ON CONTROLLING THE MINDS OF CORPS MEMBERS AND I'M JUST FINDING OUT ABOUT IT?!
YOU'RE NOT IN THE LOOP ON EVERY DAMN LANTERN DECISION AND MISSION.
WELL MAYBE I SHOULD BE-- WHEN DID IT ALL START?
IT STARTED WITH A PACT.
A PACT BETWEEN WHO?
ME, GANTHET AND ATROCITUS.
ARE YOU INSANE? WHAT THE HELL MADE YOU THINK--
GET OFF YOUR HIGH HORSE, JORDAN--YOU AIN'T NO BOX OF ROSES!
HERE YOU'RE TELLING ME YOU'VE BEEN PALLING AROUND ON RYUT WITH ATROCITUS AND THE REST OF THE CANDY-COLORED CREW, SO DON'T GO HEAPING A LOAD OF--
I'VE BEEN TRYING TO ROUND UP THE ENTITIES--KEEP THEM OUT OF KRONA'S HANDS! WHAT I'VE BEEN DOING IS STRICTLY TO HELP THE CORPS!
YEAH, WELL, I'VE BEEN IN THE UNKNOWN SECTORS TRYING TO FIND KRONA AND THE POWER DRAIN ON OUR RINGS WHILE GANTHET'S BEEN--
DON'T YOU SEE, ATROCITUS IS PLAYING YOU, GANTHET--ALL OF US.

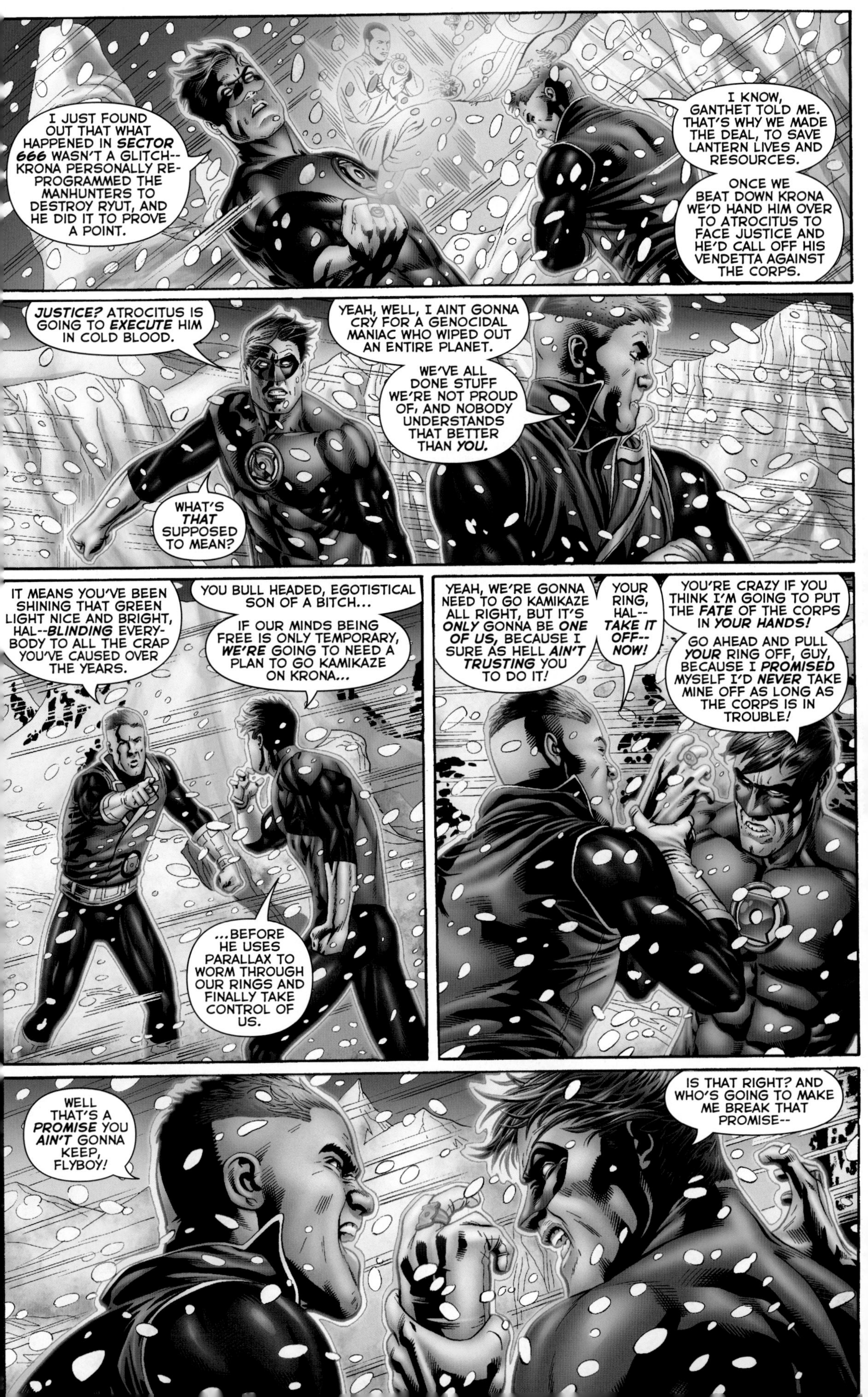
I JUST FOUND OUT THAT WHAT HAPPENED IN SECTOR 666 WASN'T A GLITCH-- KRONA PERSONALLY RE-PROGRAMMED THE MANHUNTERS TO DESTROY RYUT, AND HE DID IT TO PROVE A POINT.
I KNOW, GANTHET TOLD ME. THAT'S WHY WE MADE THE DEAL, TO SAVE LANTERN LIVES AND RESOURCES.
ONCE WE BEAT DOWN KRONA WE'D HAND HIM OVER TO ATROCITUS TO FACE JUSTICE AND HE'D CALL OFF HIS VENDETTA AGAINST THE CORPS.
JUSTICE? ATROCITUS IS GOING TO EXECUTE HIM IN COLD BLOOD.
YEAH, WELL, I AINT GONNA CRY FOR A GENOCIDAL MANIAC WHO WIPED OUT AN ENTIRE PLANET.
WE'VE ALL DONE STUFF WE'RE NOT PROUD OF, AND NOBODY UNDERSTANDS THAT BETTER THAN YOU.
WHAT'S THAT SUPPOSED TO MEAN?
IT MEANS YOU'VE BEEN SHINING THAT GREEN LIGHT NICE AND BRIGHT, HAL--BLINDING EVERY-BODY TO ALL THE CRAP YOU'VE CAUSED OVER THE YEARS.
YOU BULL HEADED, EGOTISTICAL SON OF A BITCH...
IF OUR MINDS BEING FREE IS ONLY TEMPORARY, WE'RE GOING TO NEED A PLAN TO GO KAMIKAZE ON KRONA...
...BEFORE HE USES PARALLAX TO WORM THROUGH OUR RINGS AND FINALLY TAKE CONTROL OF US.
YEAH, WE'RE GONNA NEED TO GO KAMIKAZE ALL RIGHT, BUT IT'S ONLY GONNA BE ONE OF US, BECAUSE I SURE AS HELL AIN'T TRUSTING YOU TO DO IT!
YOUR RING, HAL-- TAKE IT OFF-- NOW!
YOU'RE CRAZY IF YOU THINK I'M GOING TO PUT THE FATE OF THE CORPS IN YOUR HANDS!
GO AHEAD AND PULL YOUR RING OFF, GUY, BECAUSE I PROMISED MYSELF I'D NEVER TAKE MINE OFF AS LONG AS THE CORPS IS IN TROUBLE!
WELL THAT'S A PROMISE YOU AIN'T GONNA KEEP, FLYBOY!
IS THAT RIGHT? AND WHO'S GOING TO MAKE ME BREAK THAT PROMISE--

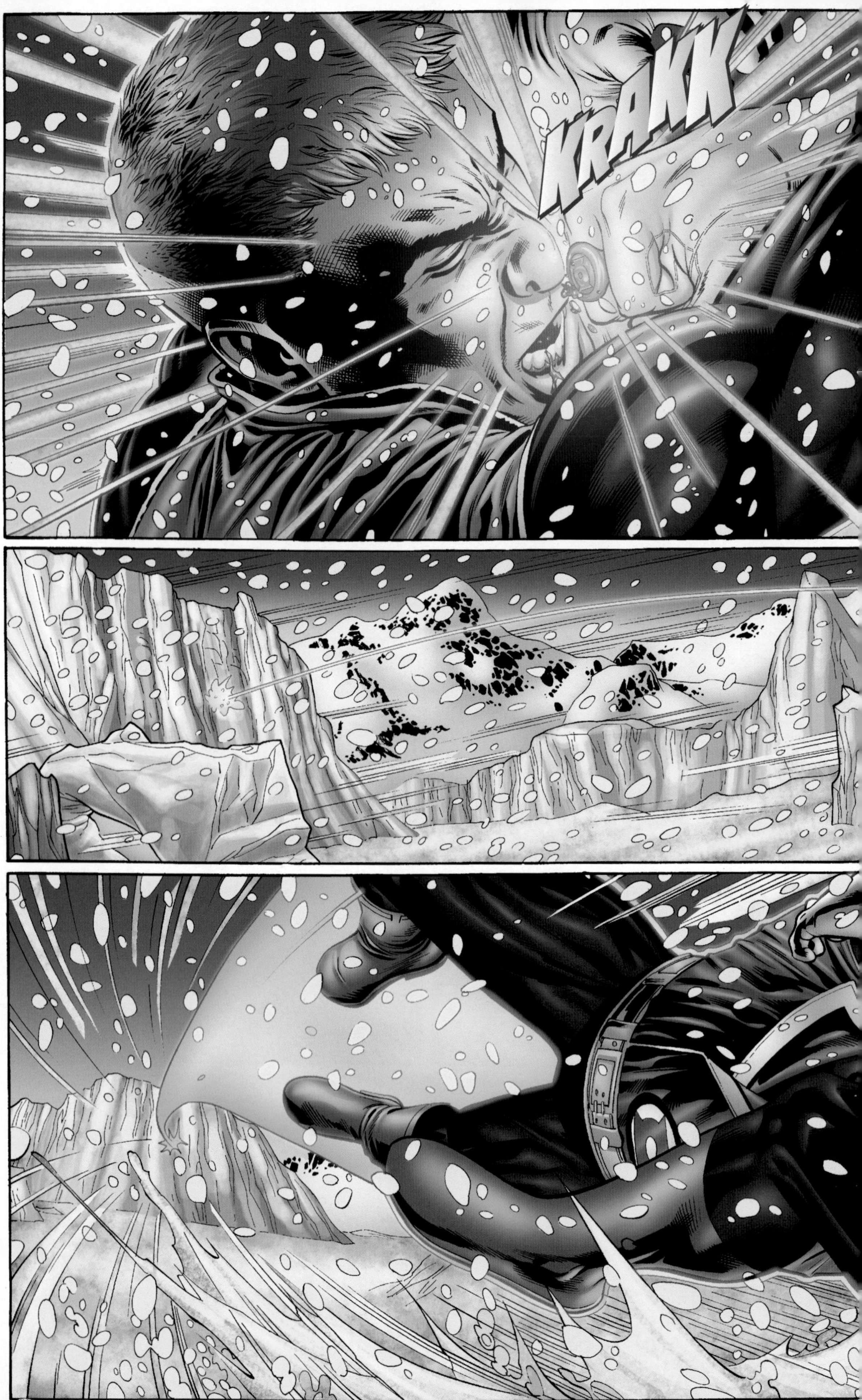
KRAKK

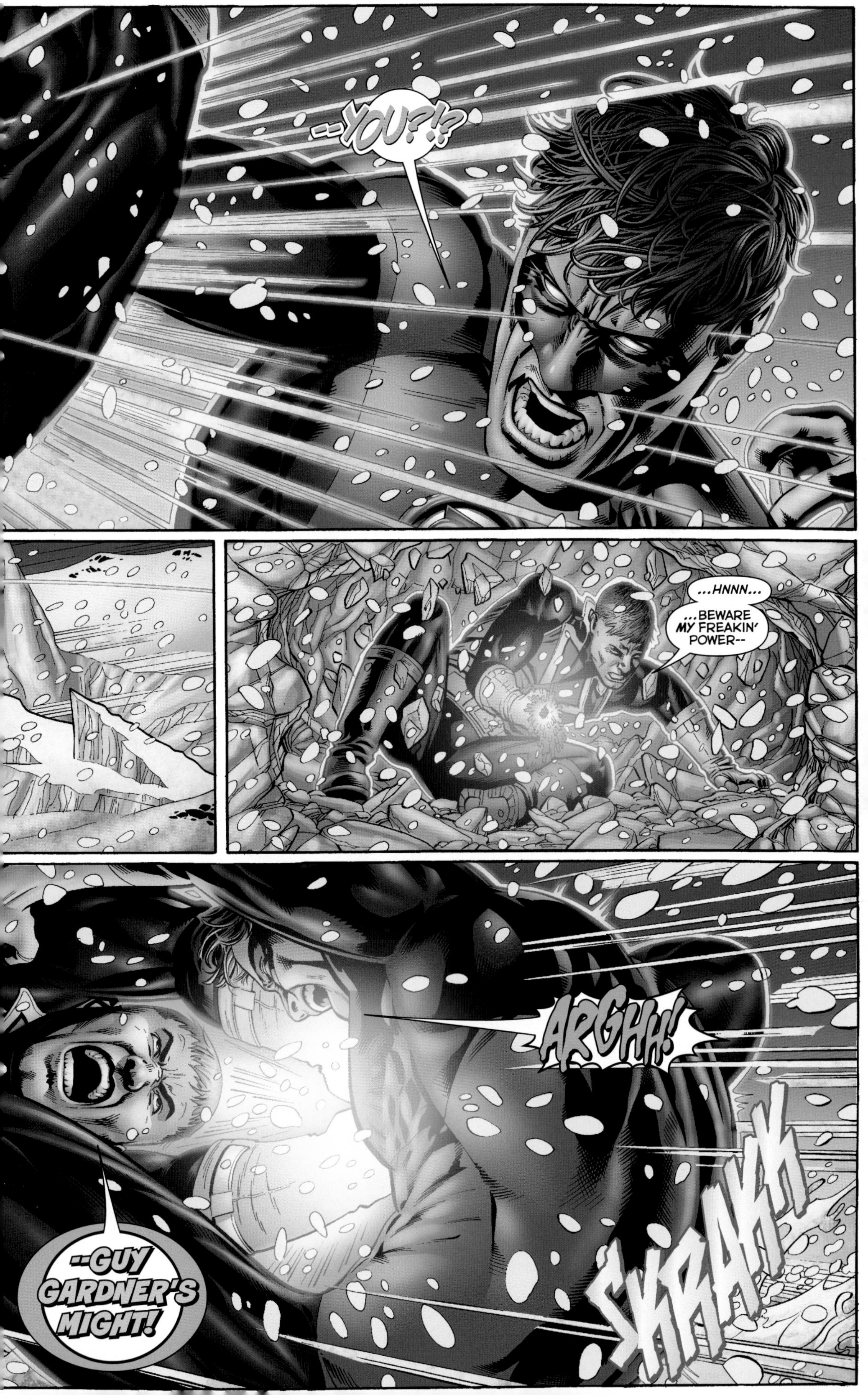
--YOU?!?
...HNNN...
...BEWARE MY FREAKIN' POWER--
ARGHH!
--GUY GARDNER'S MIGHT!
SKRAKK

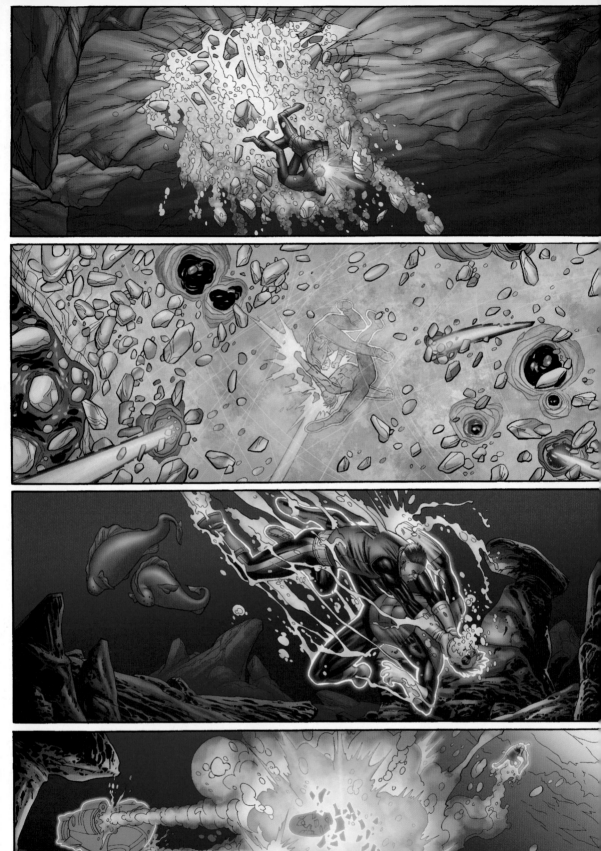

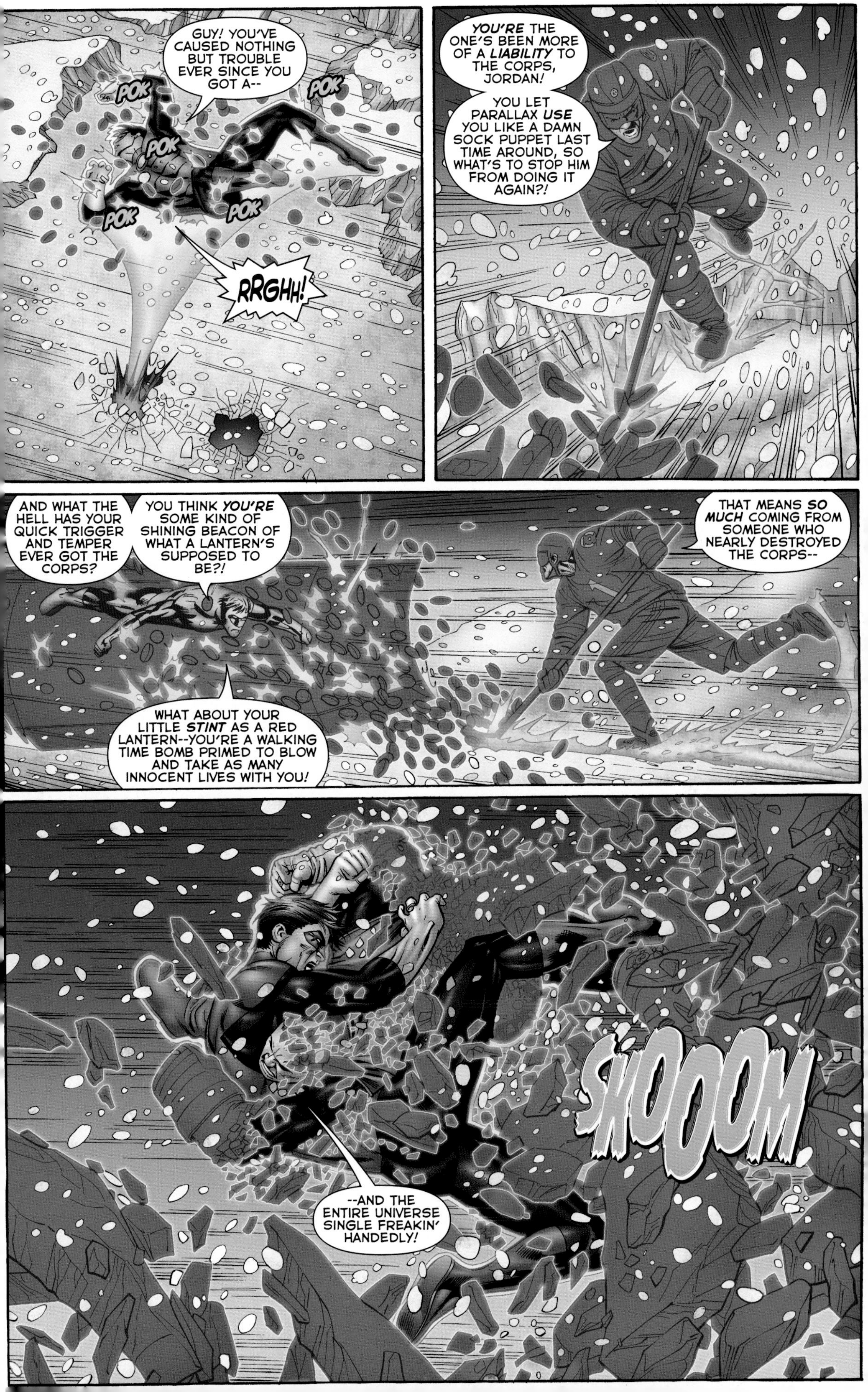
GUY! YOU'VE CAUSED NOTHING BUT TROUBLE EVER SINCE YOU GOT A--
POK
POK
POK
POK
POK
RRGHH!
YOU'RE THE ONE'S BEEN MORE OF A LIABILITY TO THE CORPS, JORDAN!
YOU LET PARALLAX USE YOU LIKE A DAMN SOCK PUPPET LAST TIME AROUND, SO WHAT'S TO STOP HIM FROM DOING IT AGAIN?!
AND WHAT THE HELL HAS YOUR QUICK TRIGGER AND TEMPER EVER GOT THE CORPS?
YOU THINK YOU'RE SOME KIND OF SHINING BEACON OF WHAT A LANTERN'S SUPPOSED TO BE?!
WHAT ABOUT YOUR LITTLE STINT AS A RED LANTERN--YOU'RE A WALKING TIME BOMB PRIMED TO BLOW AND TAKE AS MANY INNOCENT LIVES WITH YOU!
THAT MEANS SO MUCH COMING FROM SOMEONE WHO NEARLY DESTROYED THE CORPS--
SKOOOM
--AND THE ENTIRE UNIVERSE SINGLE FREAKIN' HANDEDLY!

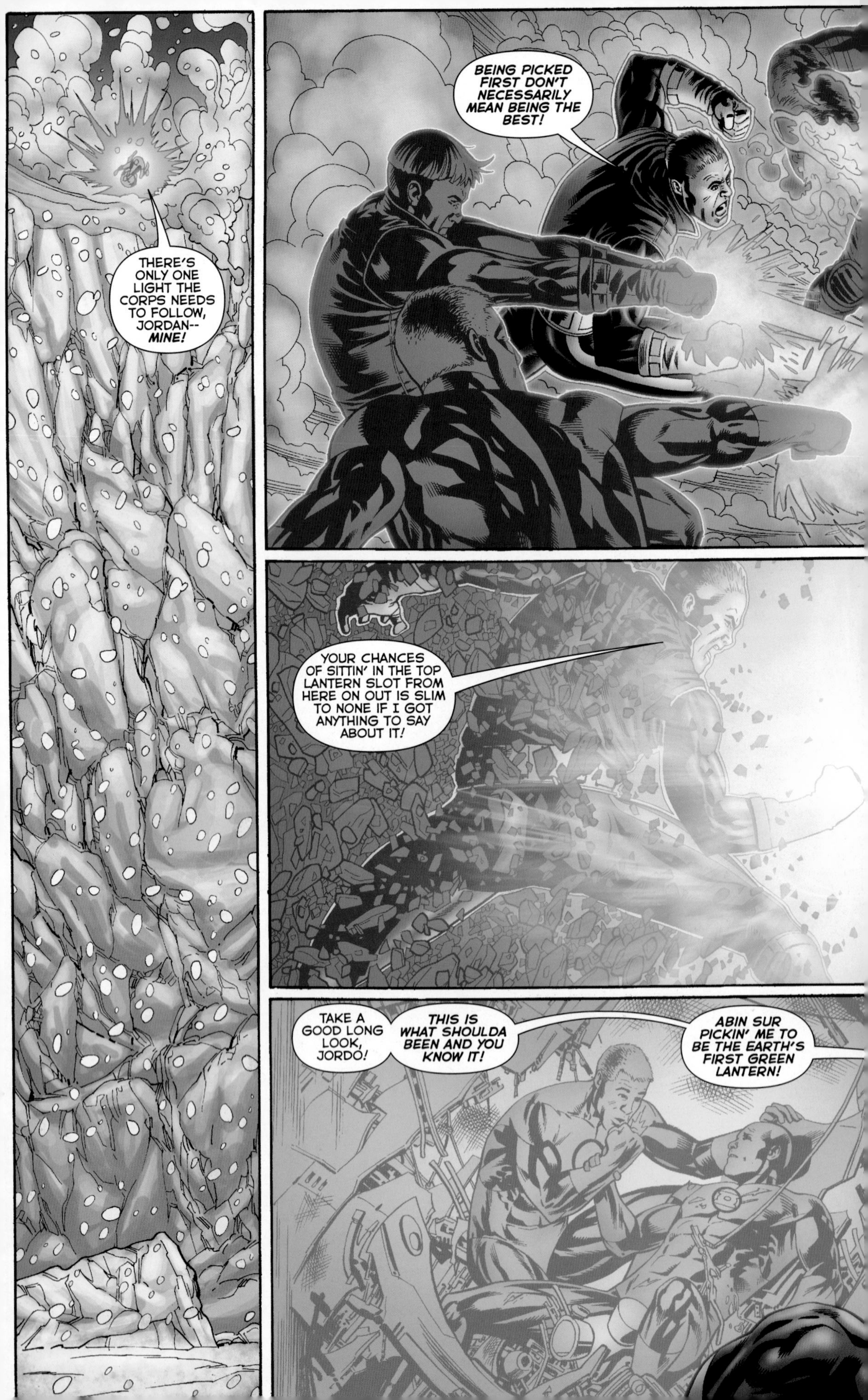
THERE'S ONLY ONE LIGHT THE CORPS NEEDS TO FOLLOW, JORDAN-- MINE!
BEING PICKED FIRST DON'T NECESSARILY MEAN BEING THE BEST!
YOUR CHANCES OF SITTIN' IN THE TOP LANTERN SLOT FROM HERE ON OUT IS SLIM TO NONE IF I GOT ANYTHING TO SAY ABOUT IT!
TAKE A GOOD LONG LOOK, JORDO!
THIS IS WHAT SHOULDA BEEN AND YOU KNOW IT!
ABIN SUR PICKIN' ME TO BE THE EARTH'S FIRST GREEN LANTERN!

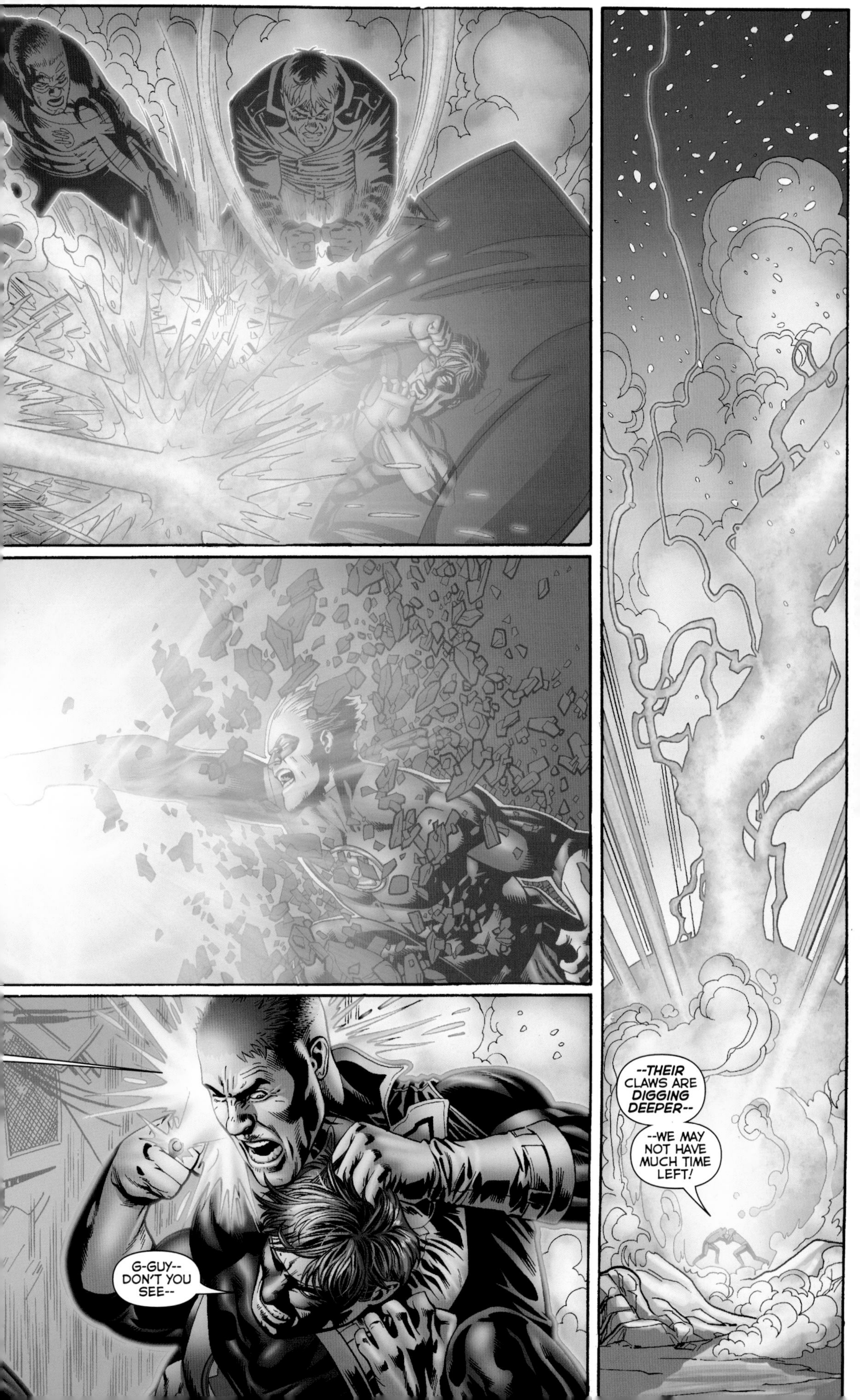
G-GUY-- DON'T YOU SEE--
--THEIR CLAWS ARE DIGGING DEEPER--
--WE MAY NOT HAVE MUCH TIME LEFT!

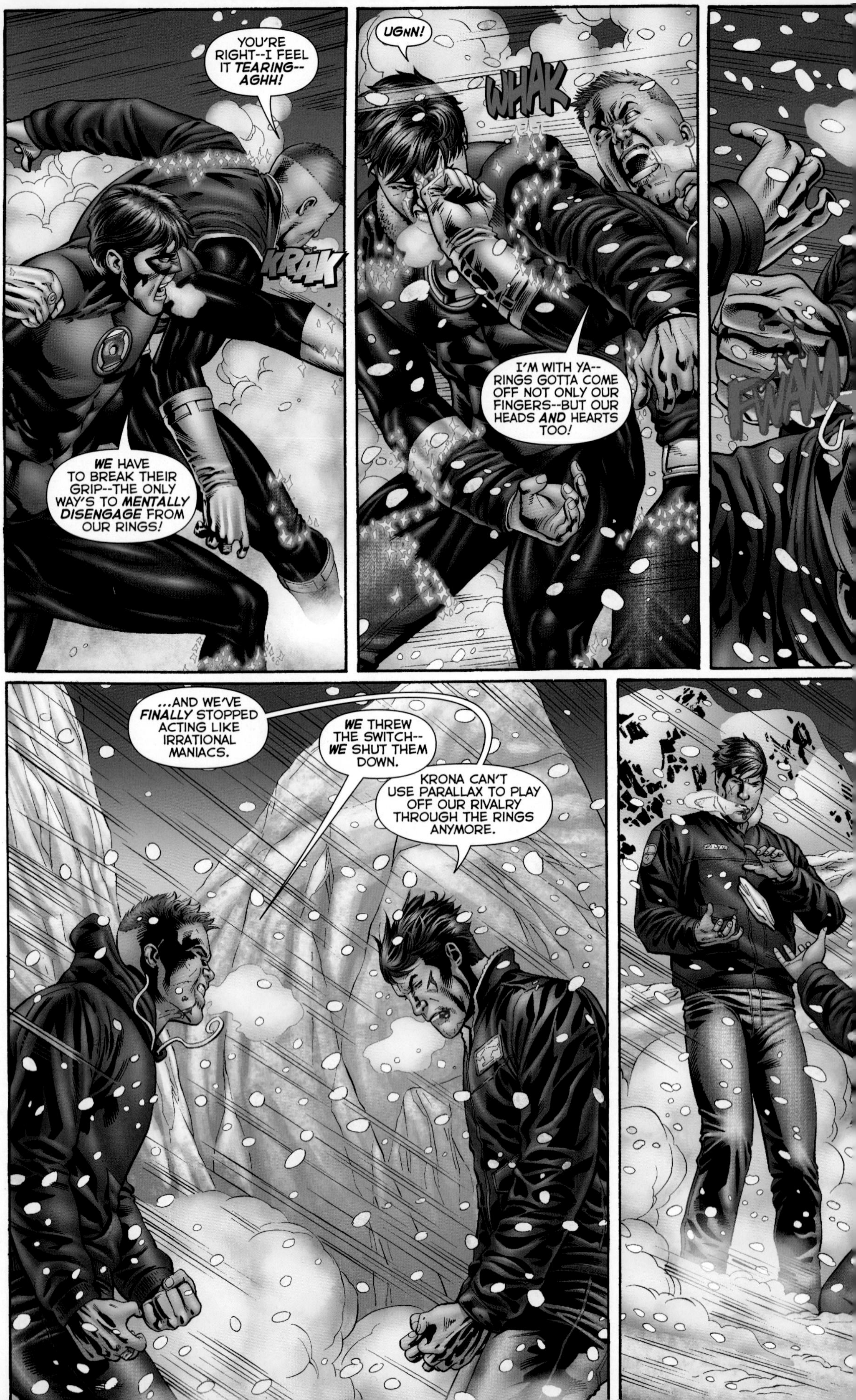
YOU'RE RIGHT--I FEEL IT TEARING-- AGHH!
KRAK
WE HAVE TO BREAK THEIR GRIP--THE ONLY WAY'S TO MENTALLY DISENGAGE FROM OUR RINGS!
UGNN!
WHAK
I'M WITH YA-- RINGS GOTTA COME OFF NOT ONLY OUR FINGERS--BUT OUR HEADS AND HEARTS TOO!
...AND WE'VE FINALLY STOPPED ACTING LIKE IRRATIONAL MANIACS.
WE THREW THE SWITCH-- WE SHUT THEM DOWN.
KRONA CAN'T USE PARALLAX TO PLAY OFF OUR RIVALRY THROUGH THE RINGS ANYMORE.

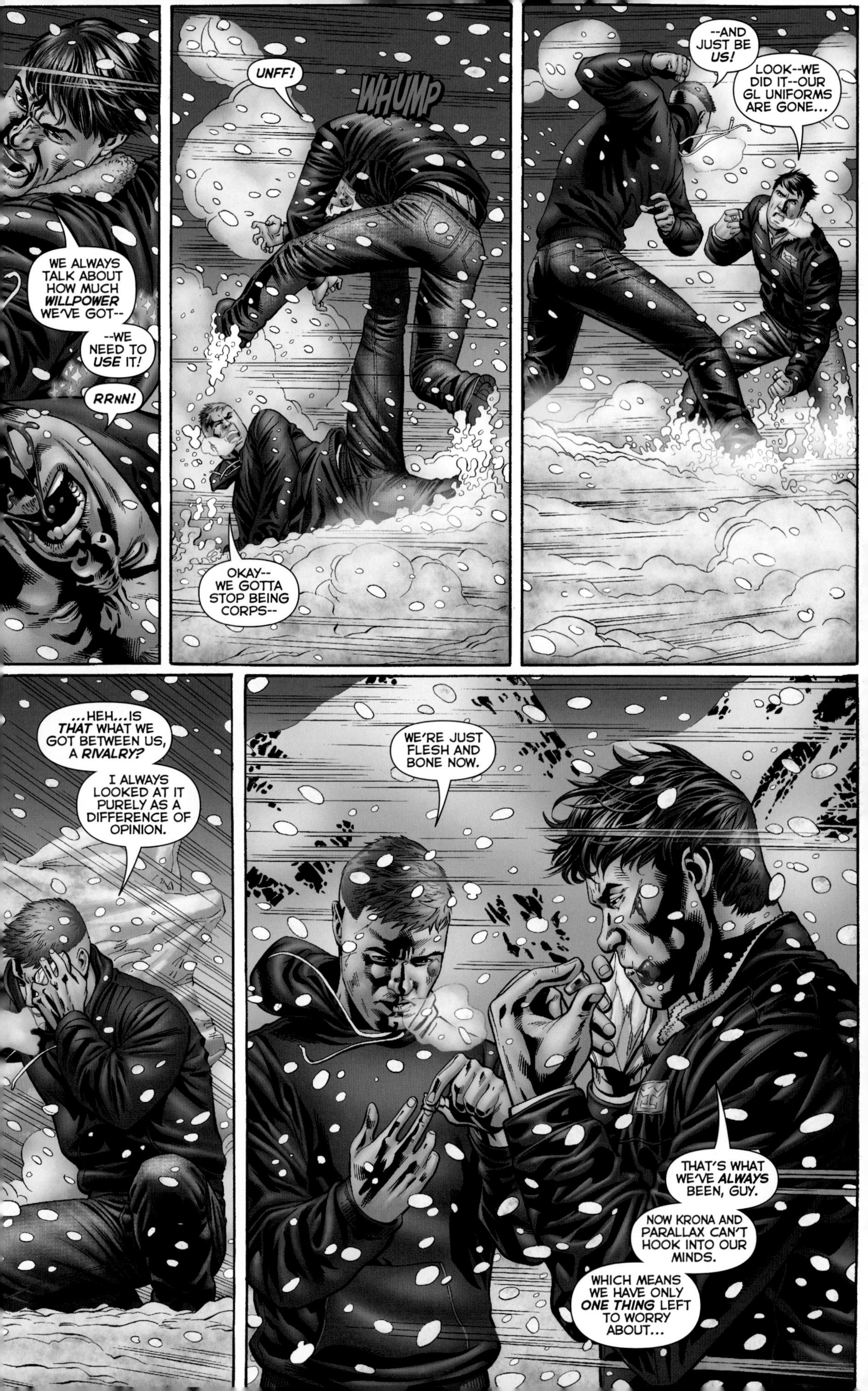
WE ALWAYS TALK ABOUT HOW MUCH WILLPOWER WE'VE GOT--
--WE NEED TO USE IT!
RRNN!
UNFF!
WHUMP
OKAY-- WE GOTTA STOP BEING CORPS--
--AND JUST BE US!
LOOK--WE DID IT--OUR GL UNIFORMS ARE GONE...
...HEH...IS THAT WHAT WE GOT BETWEEN US, A RIVALRY?
I ALWAYS LOOKED AT IT PURELY AS A DIFFERENCE OF OPINION.
WE'RE JUST FLESH AND BONE NOW.
THAT'S WHAT WE'VE ALWAYS BEEN, GUY.
NOW KRONA AND PARALLAX CAN'T HOOK INTO OUR MINDS.
WHICH MEANS WE HAVE ONLY ONE THING LEFT TO WORRY ABOUT...

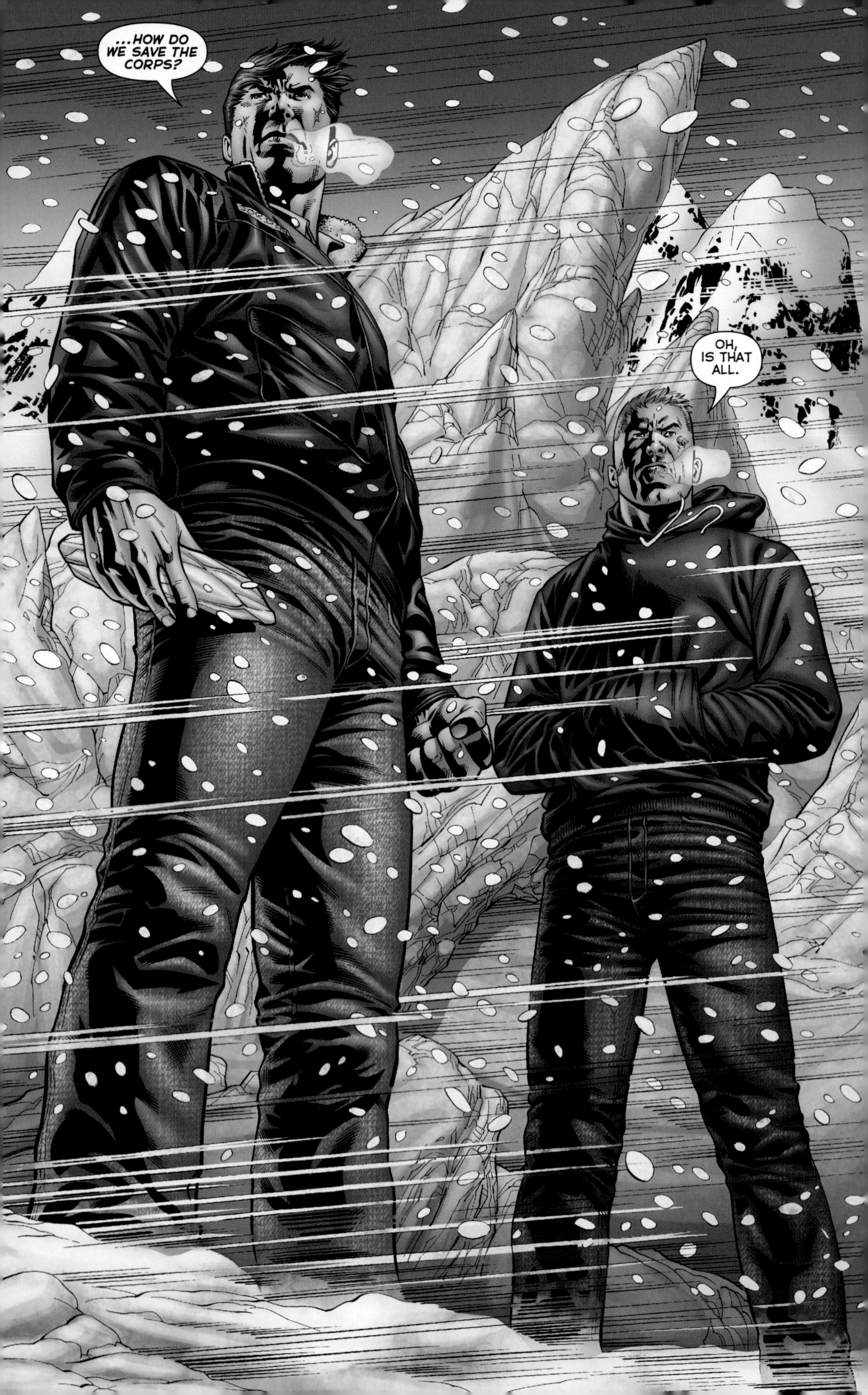
...HOW DO WE SAVE THE CORPS?
OH, IS THAT ALL.

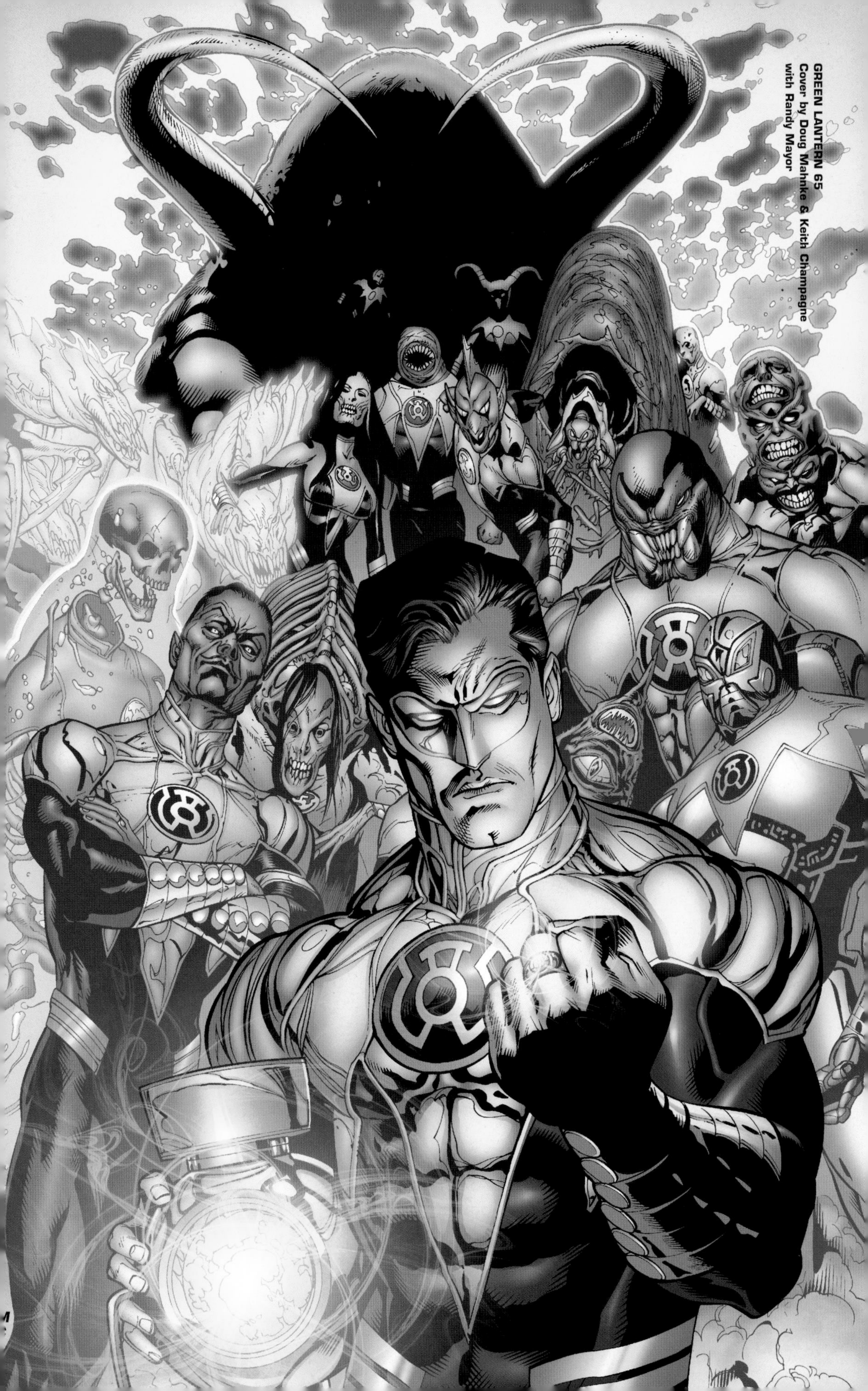

GREEN LANTERN 65
Cover by Doug Mahnke & Keith Champagne
with Randy Mayor

WAR OF THE GREEN LANTERNS
PART FOUR

Geoff Johns Writer
Doug Mahnke Penciller
Keith Champagne, Christian Alamy, Mark Irwin,
Mick Gray & Tom Nguyen Inkers

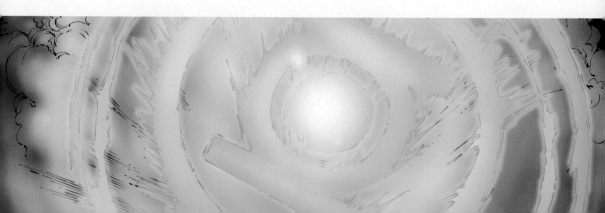

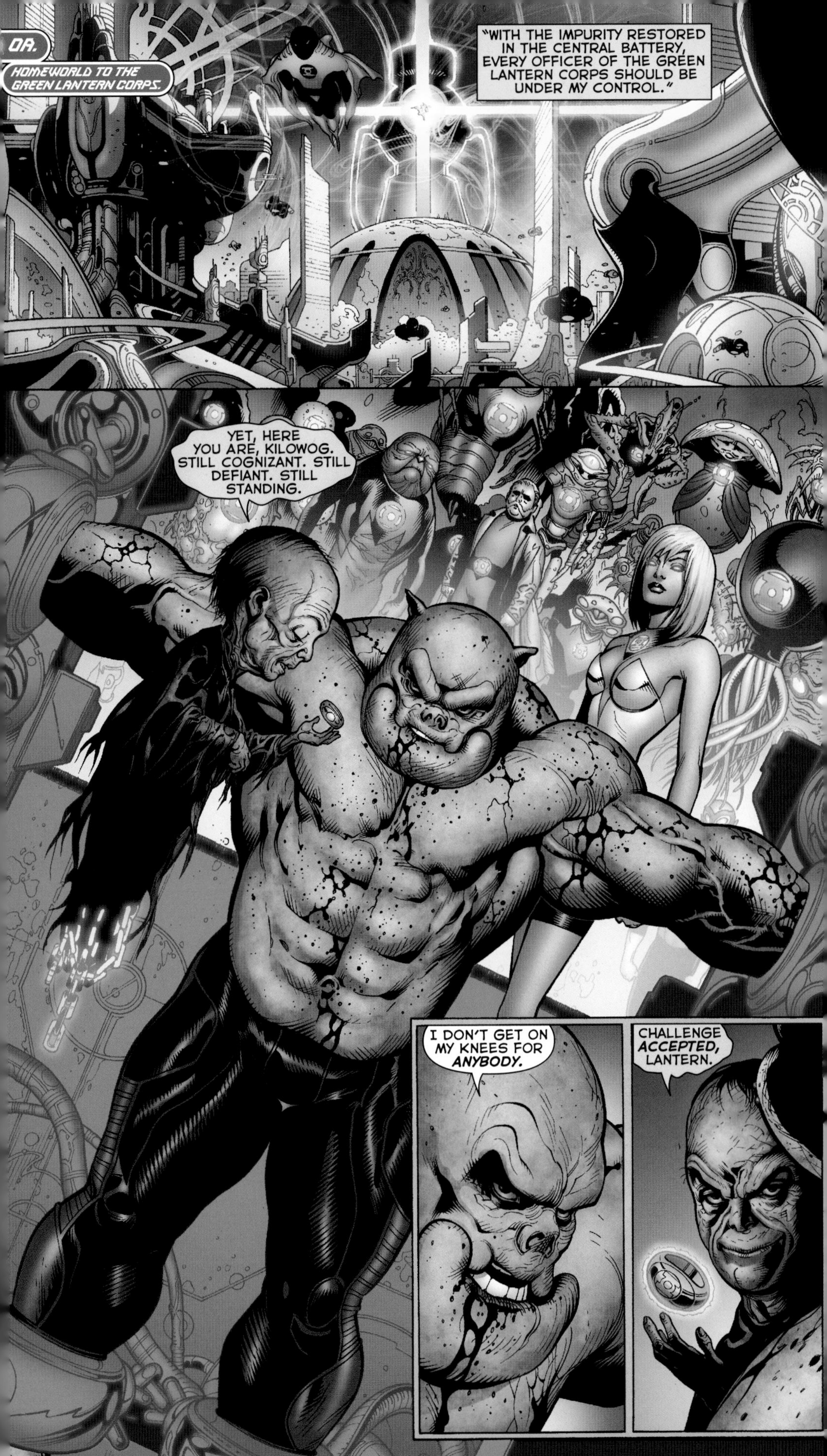
OA.
HOMEWORLD TO THE GREEN LANTERN CORPS.
"WITH THE IMPURITY RESTORED IN THE CENTRAL BATTERY, EVERY OFFICER OF THE GREEN LANTERN CORPS SHOULD BE UNDER MY CONTROL."
YET, HERE YOU ARE, KILOWOG. STILL COGNIZANT. STILL DEFIANT. STILL STANDING.
I DON'T GET ON MY KNEES FOR ANYBODY.
CHALLENGE ACCEPTED, LANTERN.

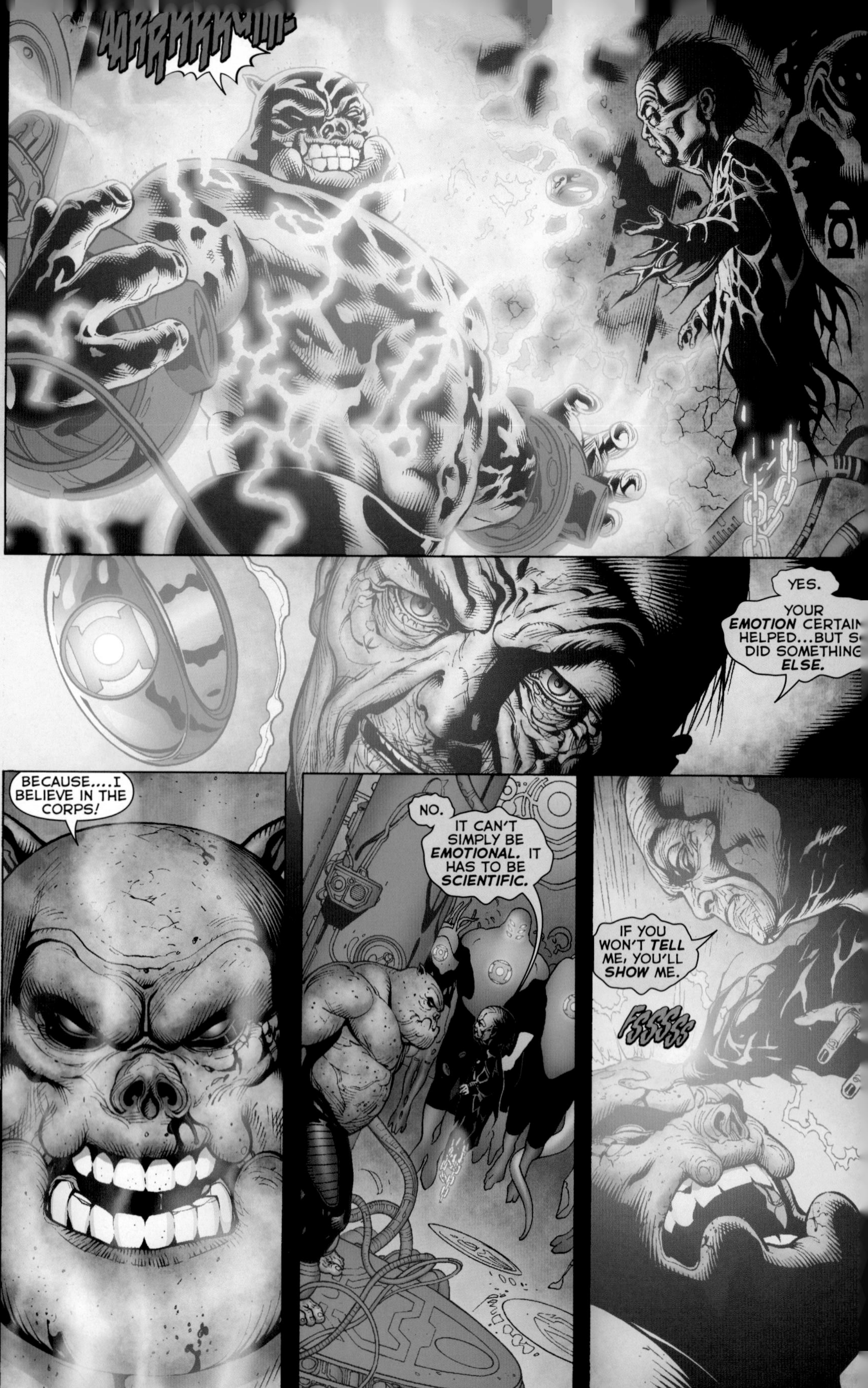
AARKKKKKK!!!!
YES.
YOUR EMOTION CERTAIN HELPED...BUT S DID SOMETHING ELSE.
BECAUSE....I BELIEVE IN THE CORPS!
NO.
IT CAN'T SIMPLY BE EMOTIONAL. IT HAS TO BE SCIENTIFIC.
IF YOU WON'T TELL ME, YOU'LL SHOW ME.
FSSSSS

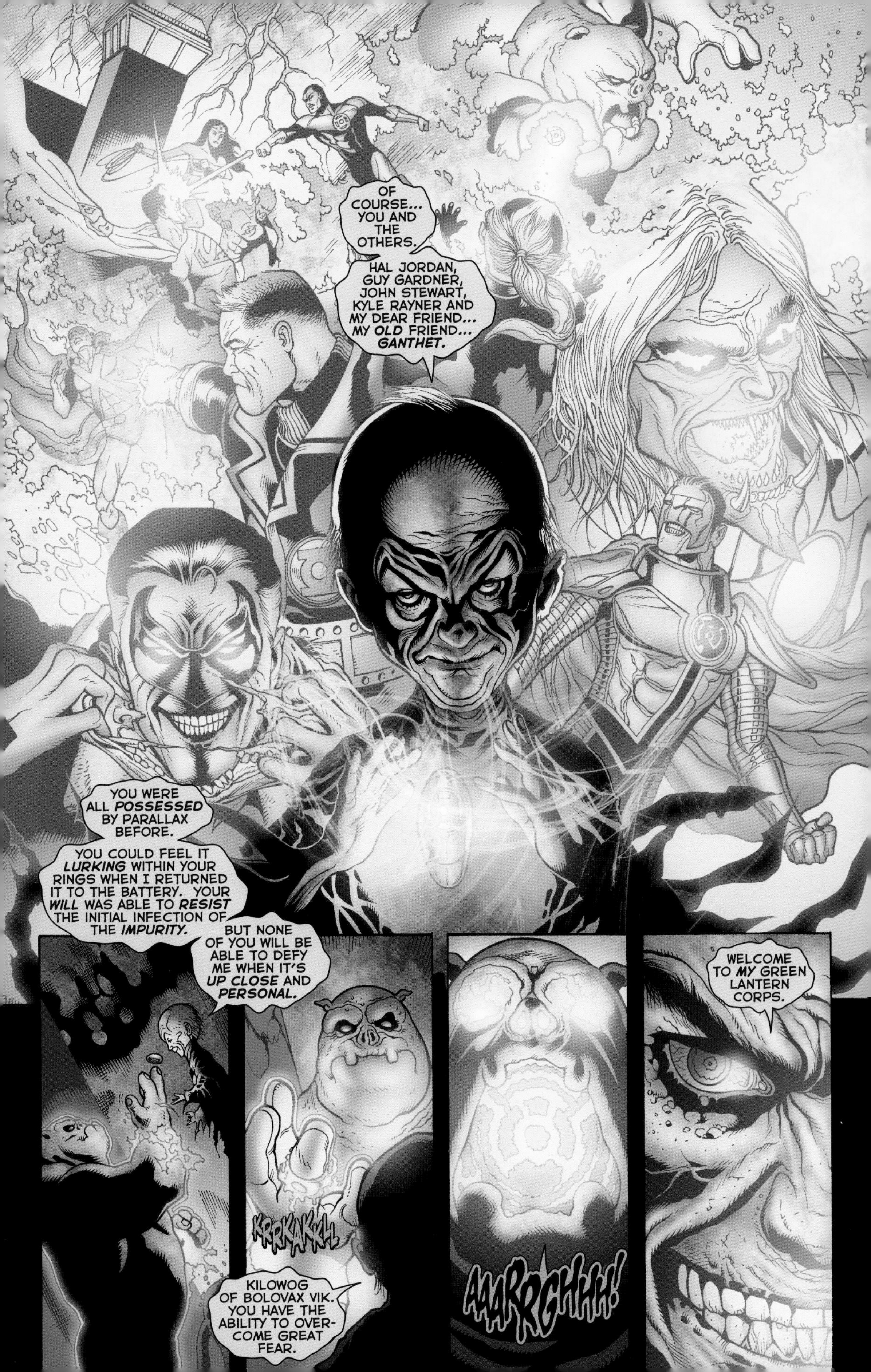
OF COURSE... YOU AND THE OTHERS.
HAL JORDAN, GUY GARDNER, JOHN STEWART, KYLE RAYNER AND MY DEAR FRIEND... MY OLD FRIEND... GANTHET.
YOU WERE ALL POSSESSED BY PARALLAX BEFORE.
YOU COULD FEEL IT LURKING WITHIN YOUR RINGS WHEN I RETURNED IT TO THE BATTERY. YOUR WILL WAS ABLE TO RESIST THE INITIAL INFECTION OF THE IMPURITY.
BUT NONE OF YOU WILL BE ABLE TO DEFY ME WHEN IT'S UP CLOSE AND PERSONAL.
KRRKAKKL
KILOWOG OF BOLOVAX VIK. YOU HAVE THE ABILITY TO OVERCOME GREAT FEAR.
AAARRGHHH!
WELCOME TO MY GREEN LANTERN CORPS.

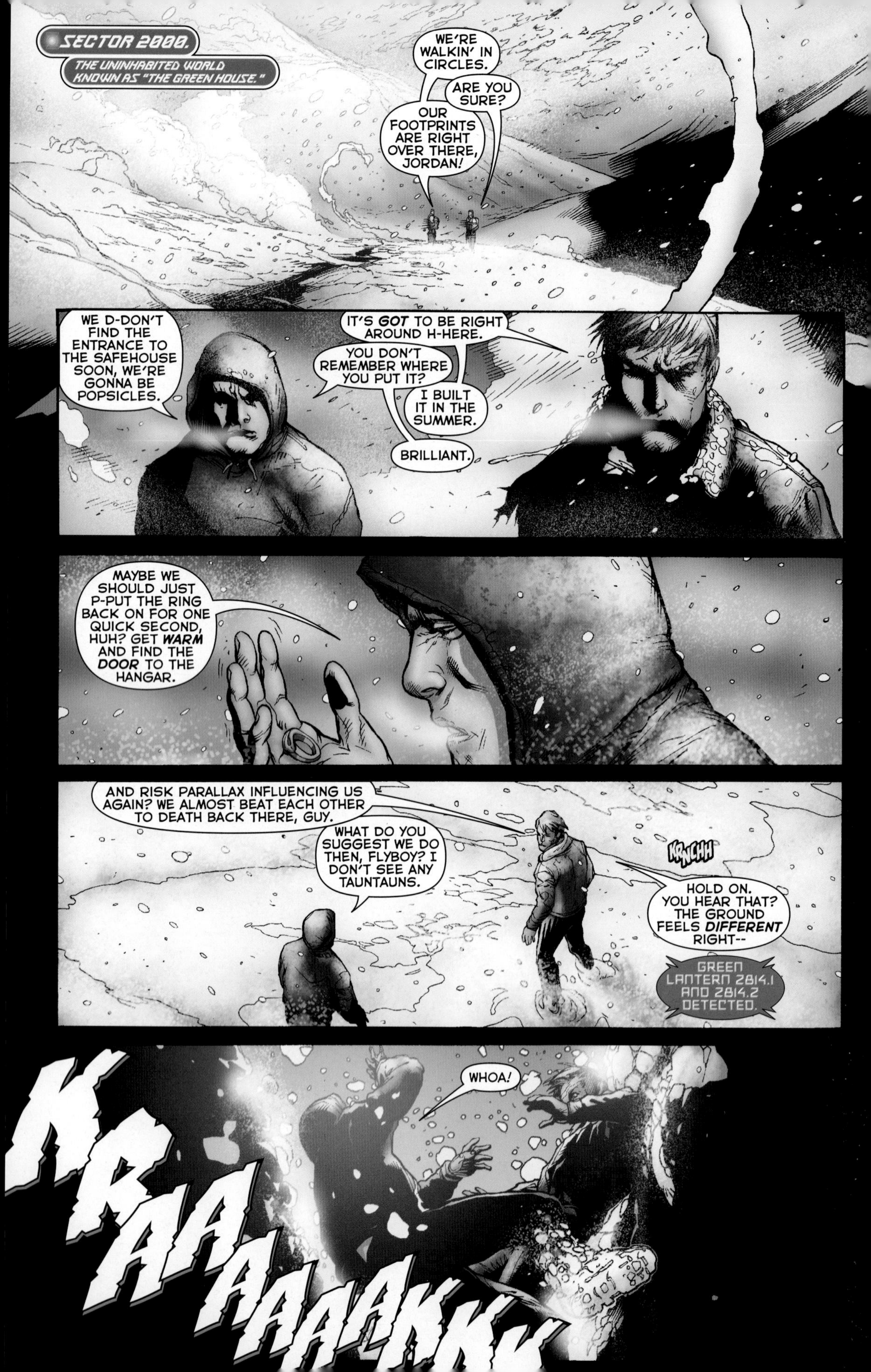
SECTOR 2000.
THE UNINHABITED WORLD KNOWN AS "THE GREEN HOUSE."
WE'RE WALKIN' IN CIRCLES.
ARE YOU SURE?
OUR FOOTPRINTS ARE RIGHT OVER THERE, JORDAN!
WE D-DON'T FIND THE ENTRANCE TO THE SAFEHOUSE SOON, WE'RE GONNA BE POPSICLES.
IT'S GOT TO BE RIGHT AROUND H-HERE.
YOU DON'T REMEMBER WHERE YOU PUT IT?
I BUILT IT IN THE SUMMER.
BRILLIANT.
MAYBE WE SHOULD JUST P-PUT THE RING BACK ON FOR ONE QUICK SECOND, HUH? GET WARM AND FIND THE DOOR TO THE HANGAR.
AND RISK PARALLAX INFLUENCING US AGAIN? WE ALMOST BEAT EACH OTHER TO DEATH BACK THERE, GUY.
WHAT DO YOU SUGGEST WE DO THEN, FLYBOY? I DON'T SEE ANY TAUNTAUNS.
KRNCHH
HOLD ON. YOU HEAR THAT? THE GROUND FEELS DIFFERENT RIGHT--
GREEN LANTERN 2814.1 AND 2814.2 DETECTED.
KRAAAAAKK
WHOA!

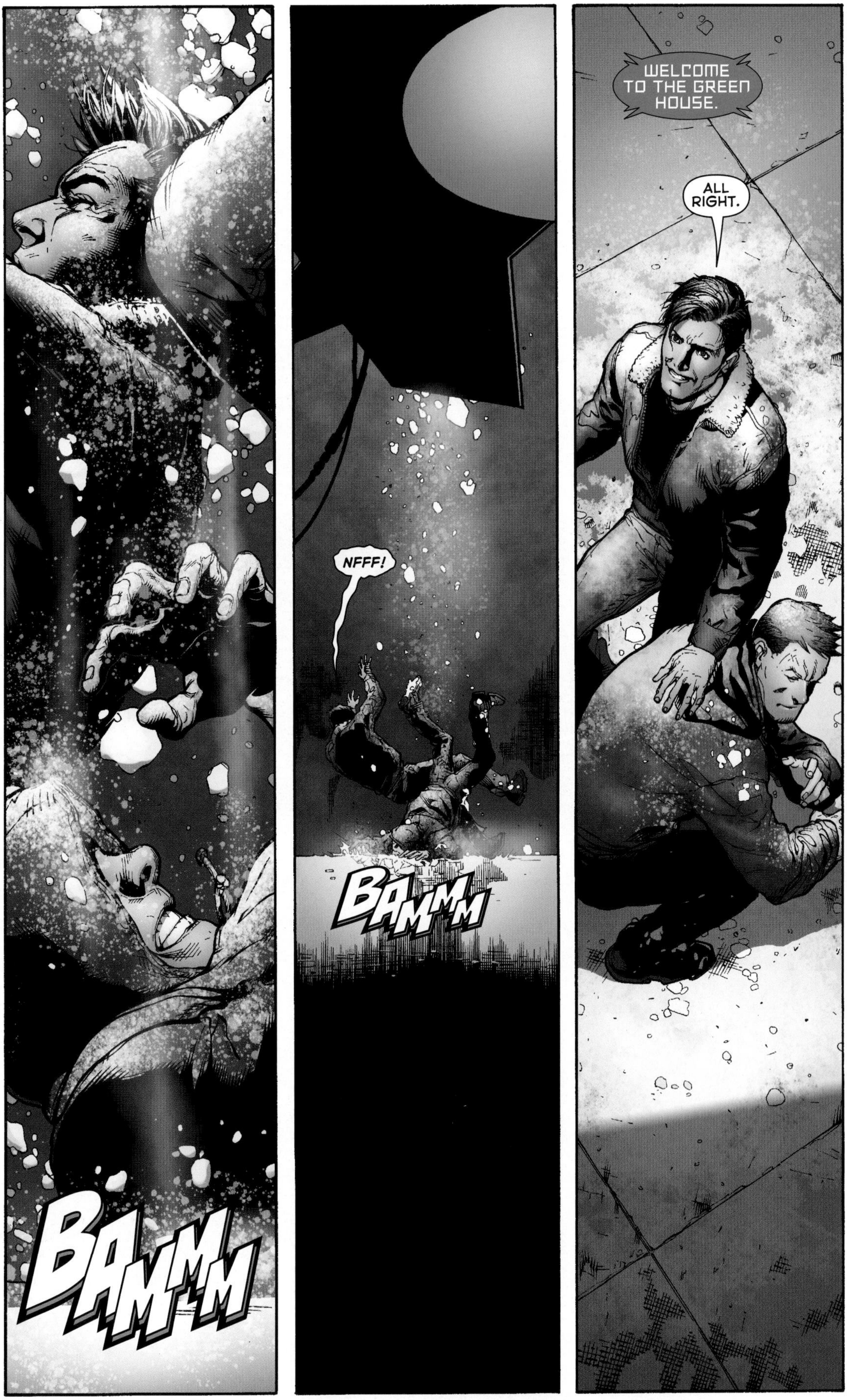
BAMMMM
NFFF!
BAMMM
WELCOME TO THE GREEN HOUSE.
ALL RIGHT.

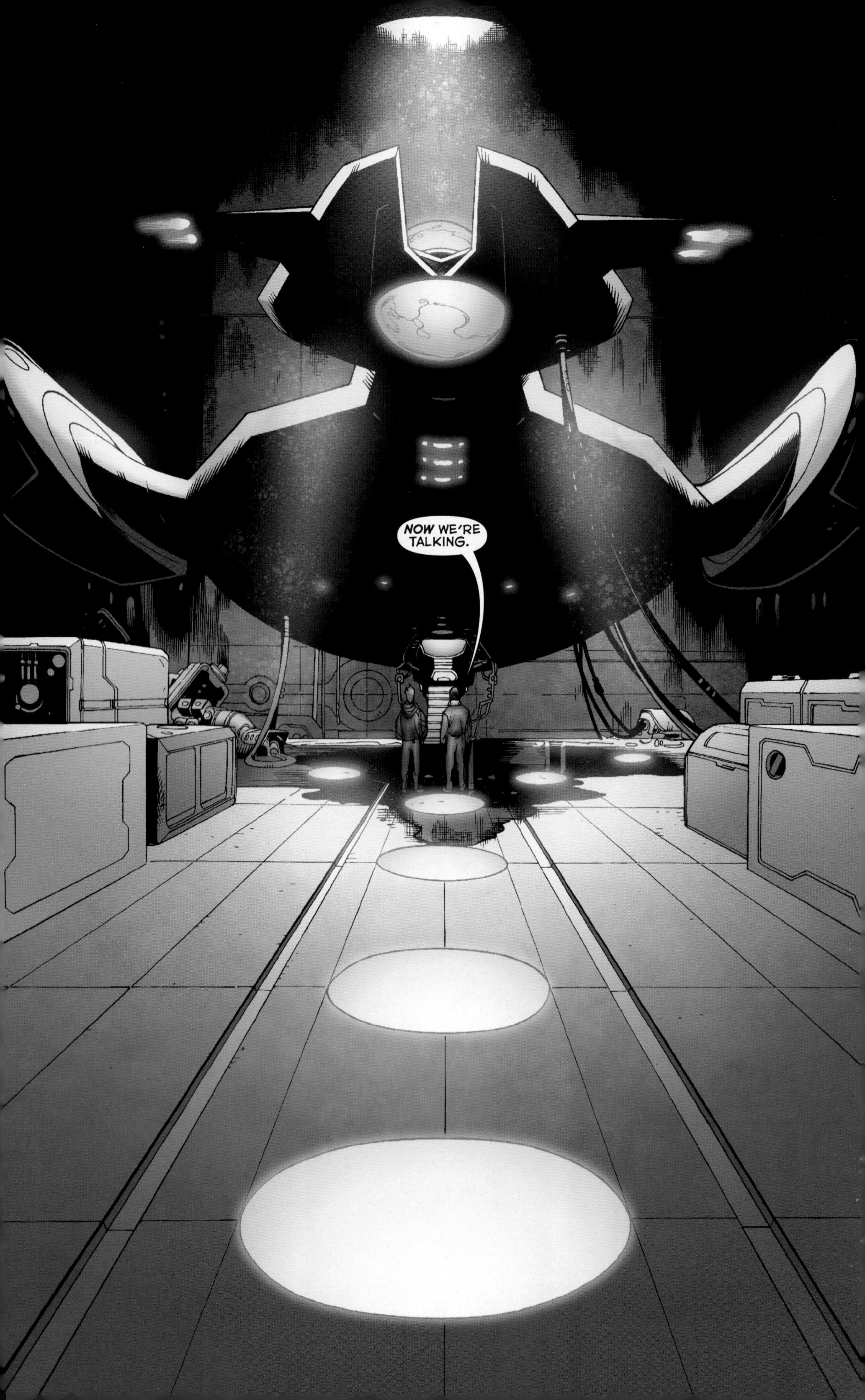
NOW WE'RE TALKING.

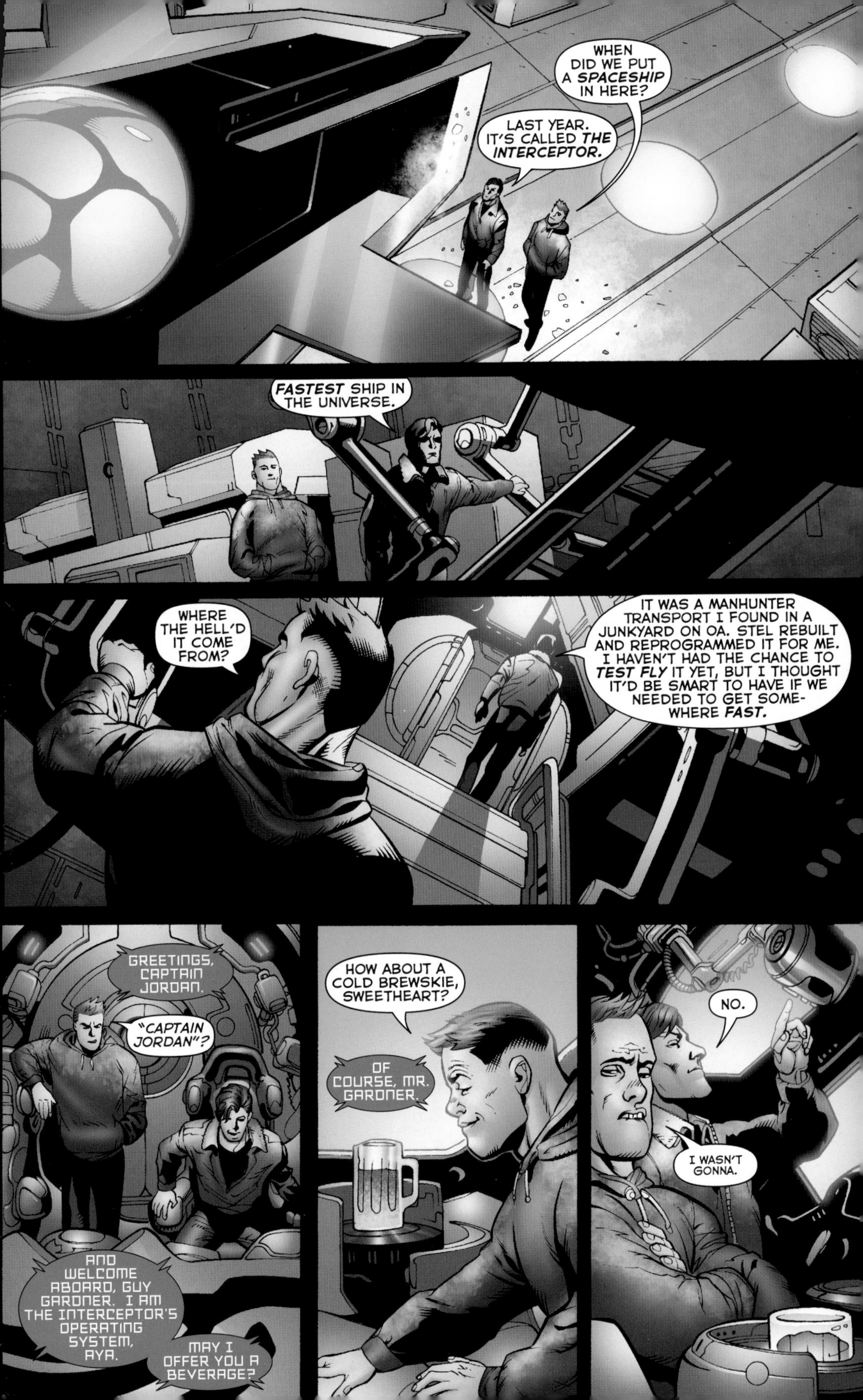
WHEN DID WE PUT A SPACESHIP IN HERE?
LAST YEAR. IT'S CALLED THE INTERCEPTOR.
FASTEST SHIP IN THE UNIVERSE.
WHERE THE HELL'D IT COME FROM?
IT WAS A MANHUNTER TRANSPORT I FOUND IN A JUNKYARD ON OA. STEL REBUILT AND REPROGRAMMED IT FOR ME. I HAVEN'T HAD THE CHANCE TO TEST FLY IT YET, BUT I THOUGHT IT'D BE SMART TO HAVE IF WE NEEDED TO GET SOME-WHERE FAST.
GREETINGS, CAPTAIN JORDAN.
"CAPTAIN JORDAN"?
AND WELCOME ABOARD, GUY GARDNER. I AM THE INTERCEPTOR'S OPERATING SYSTEM, AYA.
MAY I OFFER YOU A BEVERAGE?
HOW ABOUT A COLD BREWSKIE, SWEETHEART?
OF COURSE, MR. GARDNER.
NO.
I WASN'T GONNA.

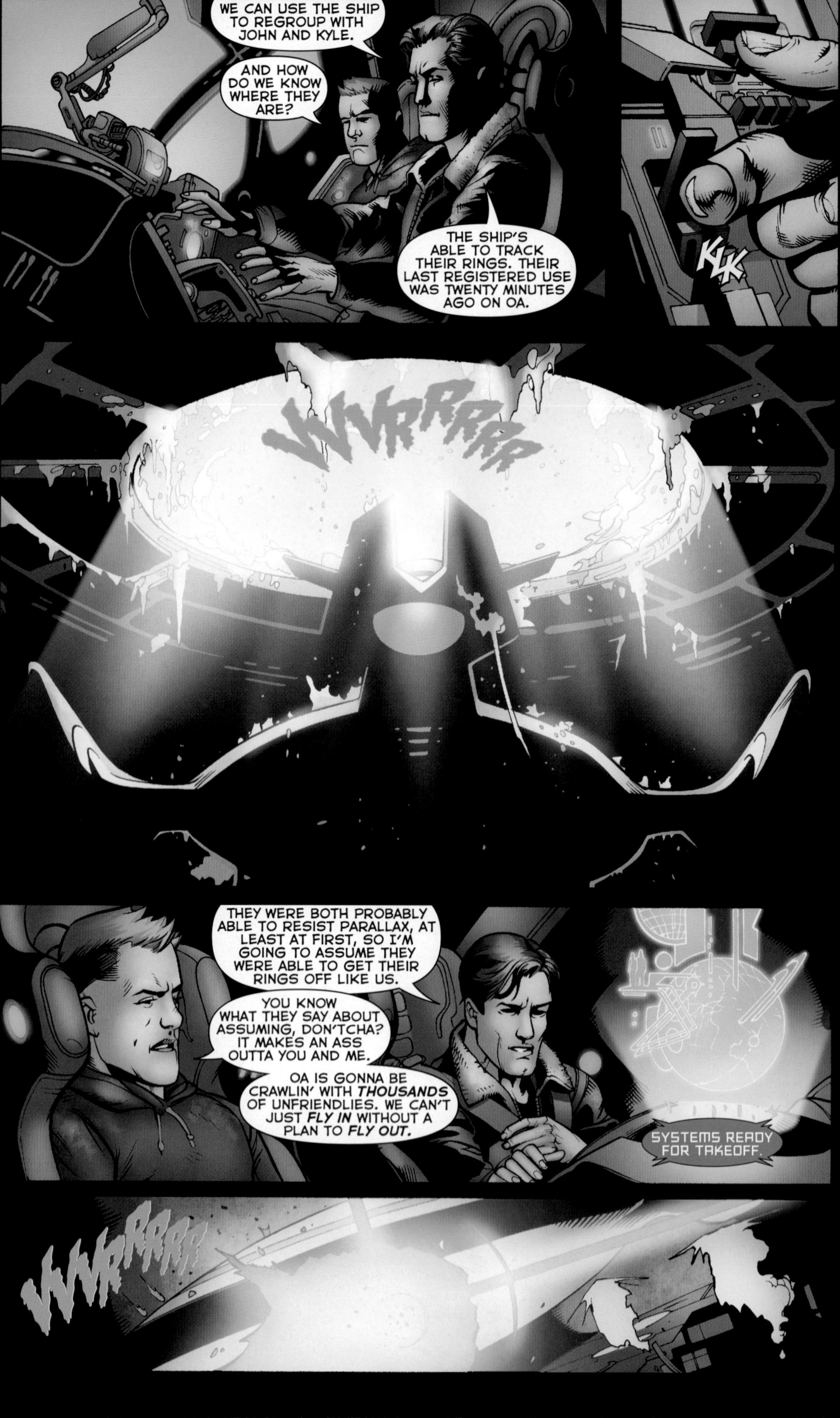
WE CAN USE THE SHIP TO REGROUP WITH JOHN AND KYLE.
AND HOW DO WE KNOW WHERE THEY ARE?
THE SHIP'S ABLE TO TRACK THEIR RINGS. THEIR LAST REGISTERED USE WAS TWENTY MINUTES AGO ON OA.
KLIK
VVVRRRRR
THEY WERE BOTH PROBABLY ABLE TO RESIST PARALLAX, AT LEAST AT FIRST, SO I'M GOING TO ASSUME THEY WERE ABLE TO GET THEIR RINGS OFF LIKE US.
YOU KNOW WHAT THEY SAY ABOUT ASSUMING, DON'TCHA? IT MAKES AN ASS OUTTA YOU AND ME.
OA IS GONNA BE CRAWLIN' WITH *THOUSANDS* OF UNFRIENDLIES. WE CAN'T JUST *FLY IN* WITHOUT A PLAN TO *FLY OUT.*
SYSTEMS READY FOR TAKEOFF.
VVVRRRRR

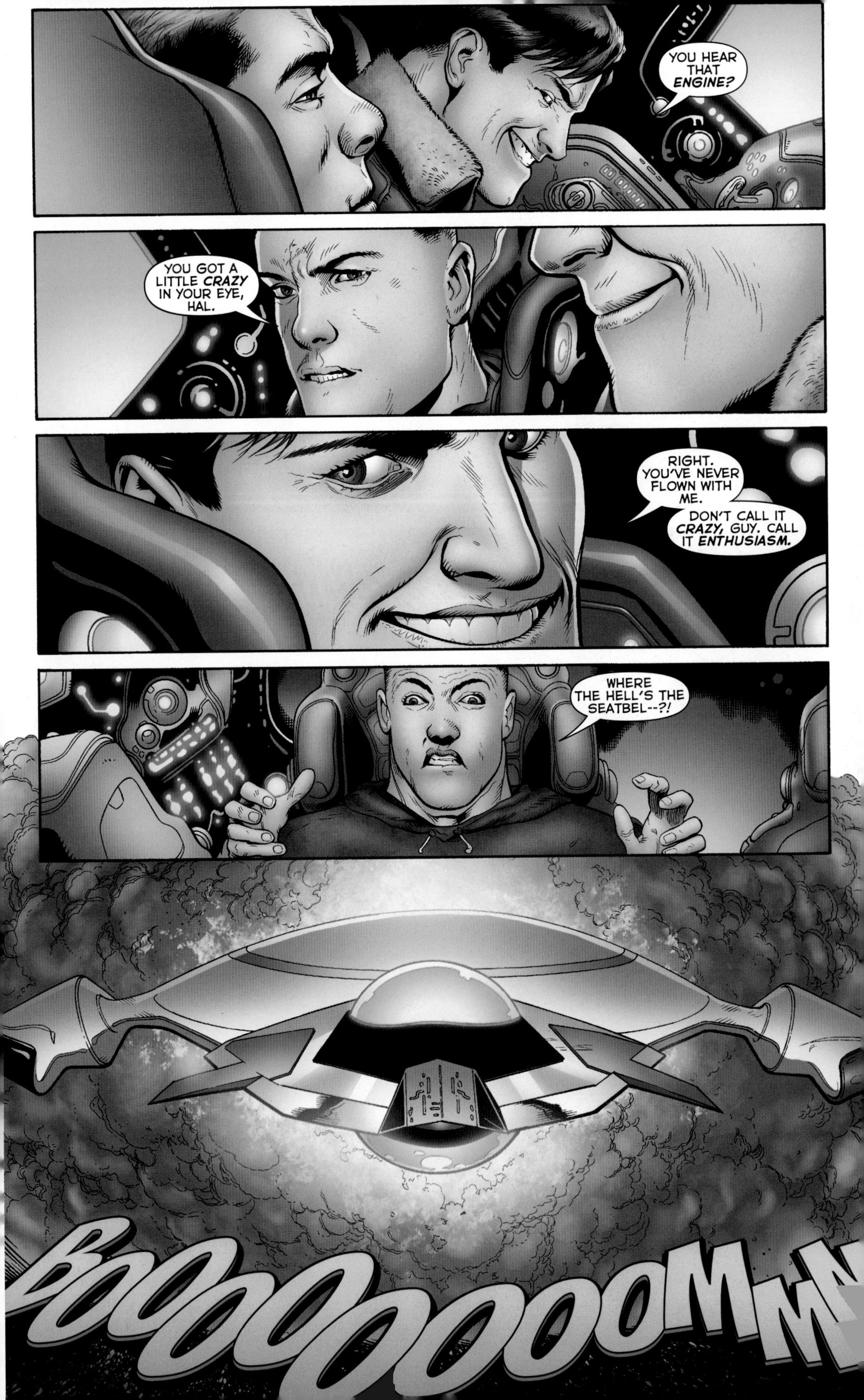
YOU HEAR THAT ENGINE?
YOU GOT A LITTLE CRAZY IN YOUR EYE, HAL.
RIGHT. YOU'VE NEVER FLOWN WITH ME.
DON'T CALL IT CRAZY, GUY. CALL IT ENTHUSIASM.
WHERE THE HELL'S THE SEATBEL--?!
BOOOOOOOOOMMM

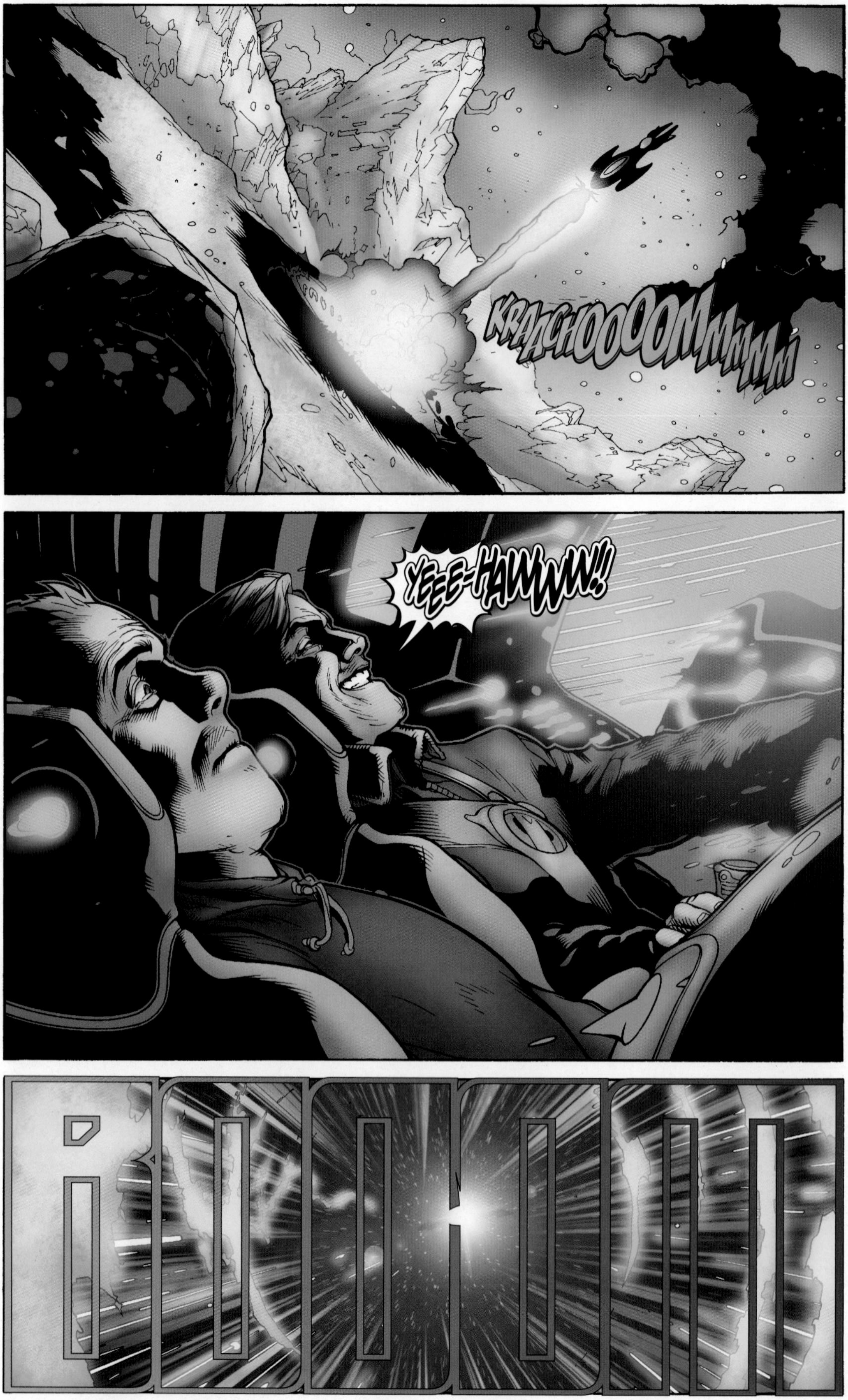
KRACHOOOOMMMMM
YEEE-HAWWW!!
BOOOM

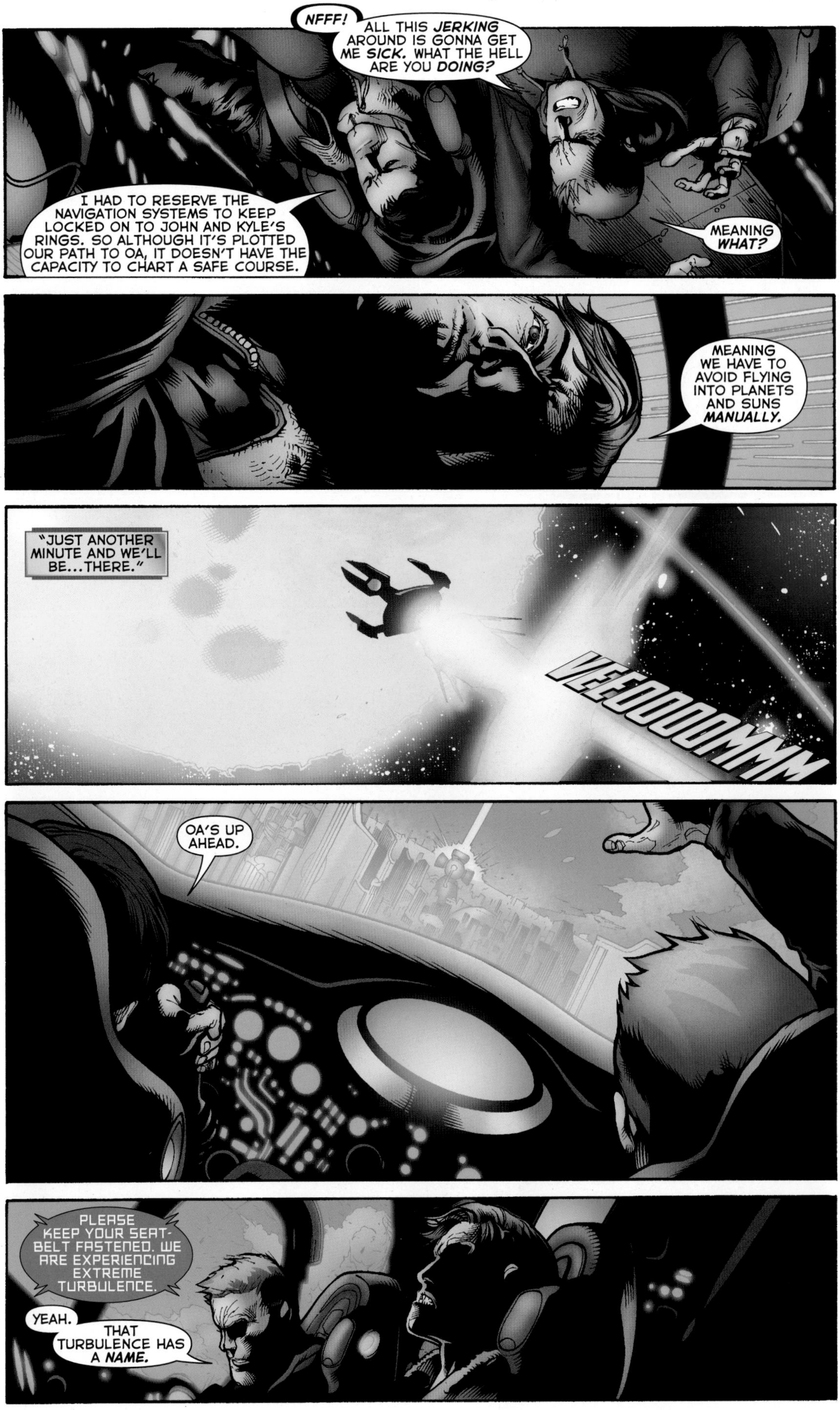

NFFF!
ALL THIS JERKING AROUND IS GONNA GET ME SICK. WHAT THE HELL ARE YOU DOING?
I HAD TO RESERVE THE NAVIGATION SYSTEMS TO KEEP LOCKED ON TO JOHN AND KYLE'S RINGS. SO ALTHOUGH IT'S PLOTTED OUR PATH TO OA, IT DOESN'T HAVE THE CAPACITY TO CHART A SAFE COURSE.
MEANING WHAT?
MEANING WE HAVE TO AVOID FLYING INTO PLANETS AND SUNS MANUALLY.
"JUST ANOTHER MINUTE AND WE'LL BE...THERE."
VEEOOOOMMM
OA'S UP AHEAD.
PLEASE KEEP YOUR SEAT-BELT FASTENED. WE ARE EXPERIENCING EXTREME TURBULENCE.
YEAH.
THAT TURBULENCE HAS A NAME.

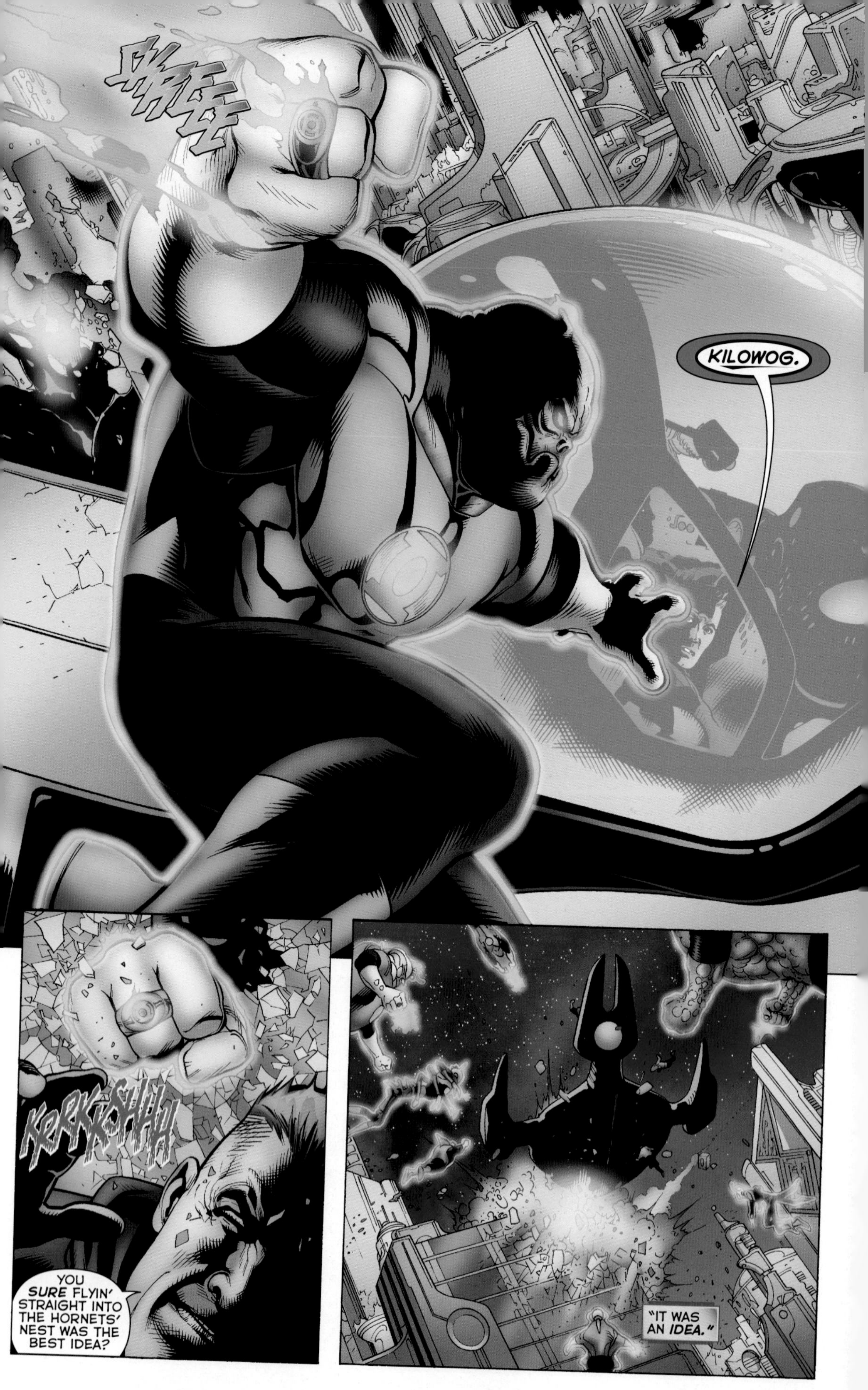
KILOWOG.
YOU SURE FLYIN' STRAIGHT INTO THE HORNETS' NEST WAS THE BEST IDEA?
"IT WAS AN IDEA."

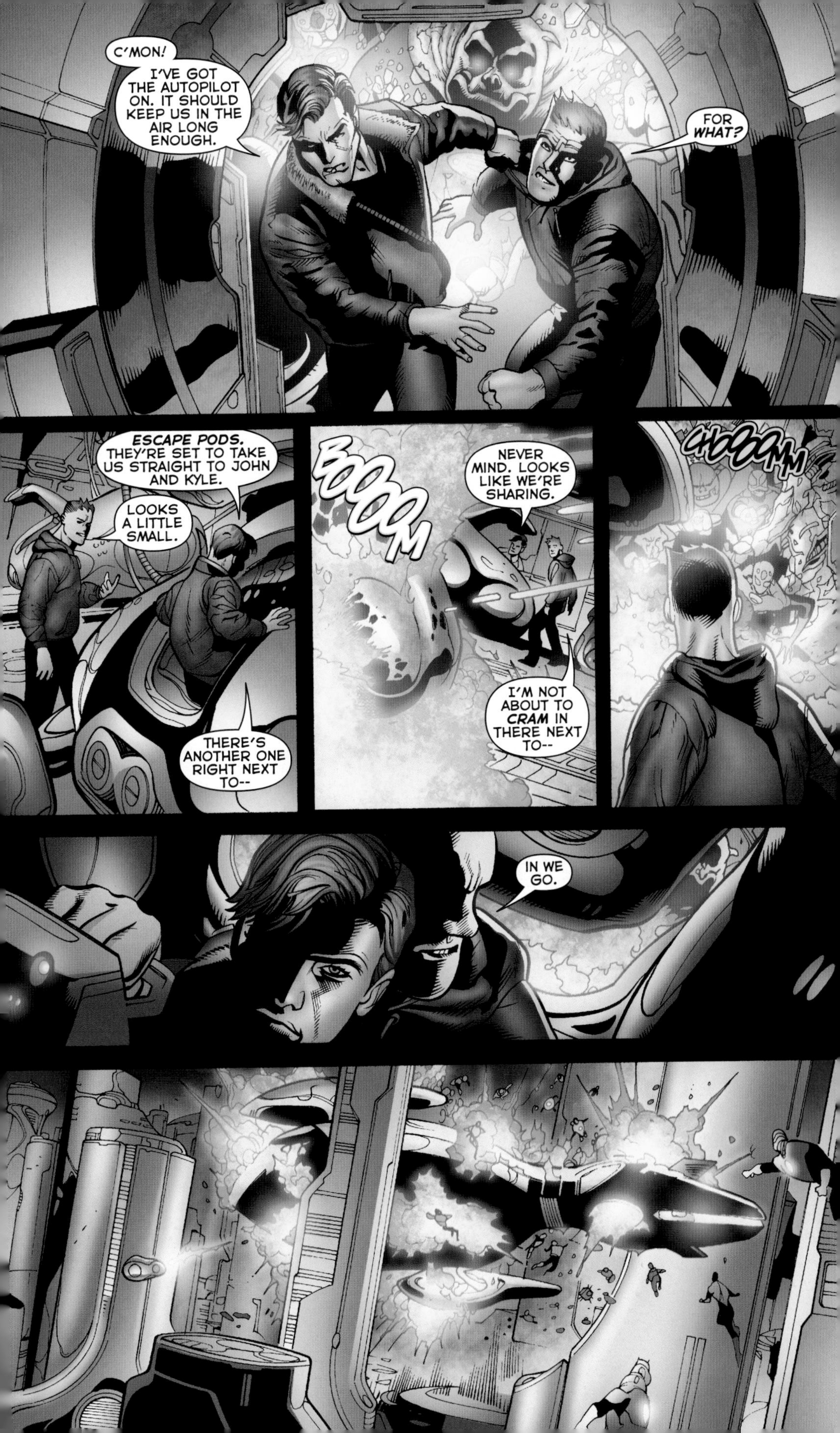
C'MON!
I'VE GOT THE AUTOPILOT ON. IT SHOULD KEEP US IN THE AIR LONG ENOUGH.
FOR WHAT?
ESCAPE PODS. THEY'RE SET TO TAKE US STRAIGHT TO JOHN AND KYLE.
LOOKS A LITTLE SMALL.
THERE'S ANOTHER ONE RIGHT NEXT TO--
BOOOOM
NEVER MIND. LOOKS LIKE WE'RE SHARING.
I'M NOT ABOUT TO CRAM IN THERE NEXT TO--
CHOOOOMM
IN WE GO.

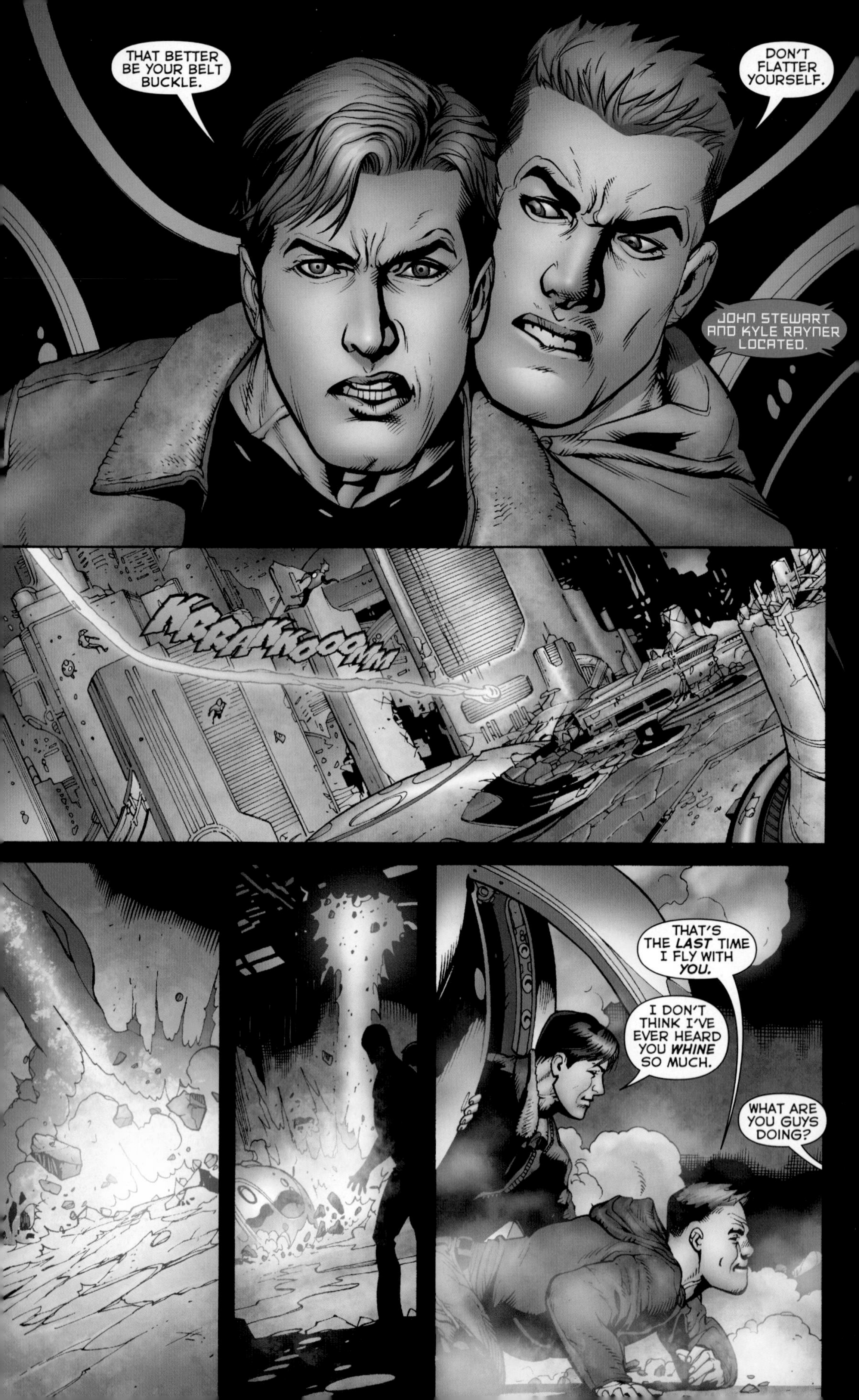

THAT BETTER BE YOUR BELT BUCKLE.
DON'T FLATTER YOURSELF.
JOHN STEWART AND KYLE RAYNER LOCATED.
KRRAKOOOMM
THAT'S THE *LAST* TIME I FLY WITH *YOU.*
I DON'T THINK I'VE EVER HEARD YOU *WHINE* SO MUCH.
WHAT ARE YOU GUYS DOING?

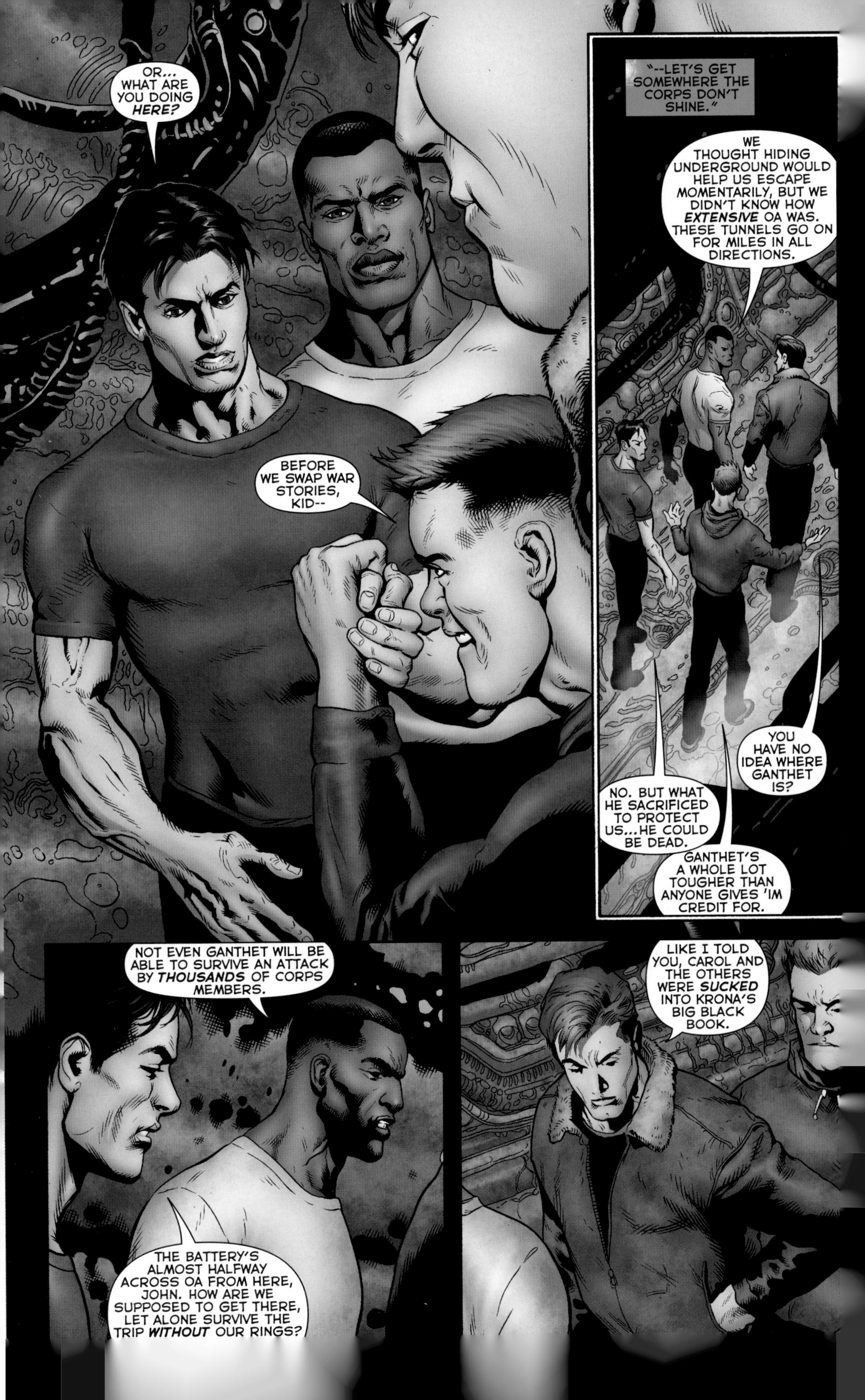
OR... WHAT ARE YOU DOING HERE?
BEFORE WE SWAP WAR STORIES, KID--
"--LET'S GET SOMEWHERE THE CORPS DON'T SHINE."
WE THOUGHT HIDING UNDERGROUND WOULD HELP US ESCAPE MOMENTARILY, BUT WE DIDN'T KNOW HOW EXTENSIVE OA WAS. THESE TUNNELS GO ON FOR MILES IN ALL DIRECTIONS.
YOU HAVE NO IDEA WHERE GANTHET IS?
NO. BUT WHAT HE SACRIFICED TO PROTECT US...HE COULD BE DEAD.
GANTHET'S A WHOLE LOT TOUGHER THAN ANYONE GIVES 'IM CREDIT FOR.
NOT EVEN GANTHET WILL BE ABLE TO SURVIVE AN ATTACK BY THOUSANDS OF CORPS MEMBERS.
THE BATTERY'S ALMOST HALFWAY ACROSS OA FROM HERE, JOHN. HOW ARE WE SUPPOSED TO GET THERE, LET ALONE SURVIVE THE TRIP WITHOUT OUR RINGS?
LIKE I TOLD YOU, CAROL AND THE OTHERS WERE SUCKED INTO KRONA'S BIG BLACK BOOK.

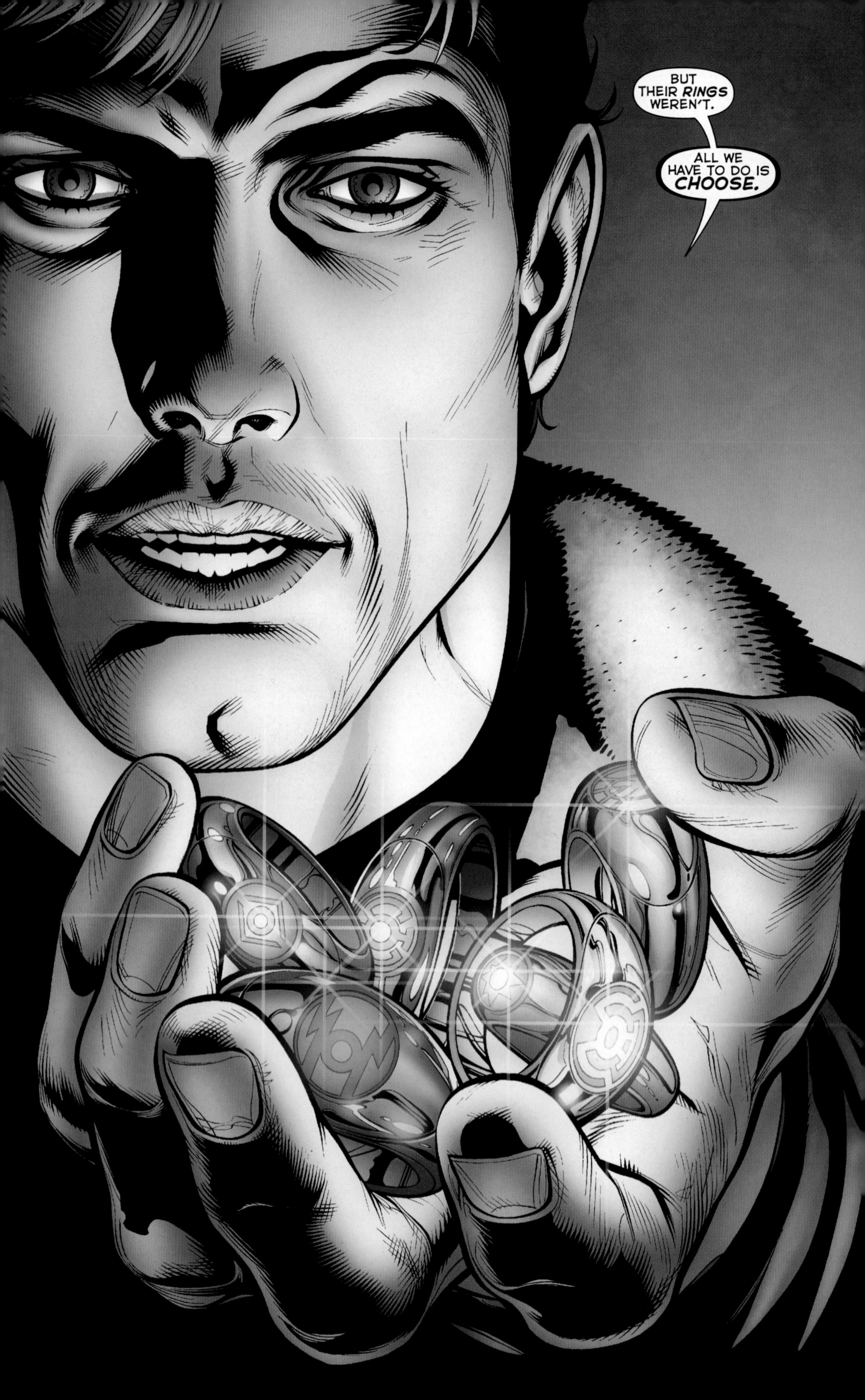
BUT THEIR RINGS WEREN'T.
ALL WE HAVE TO DO IS CHOOSE.

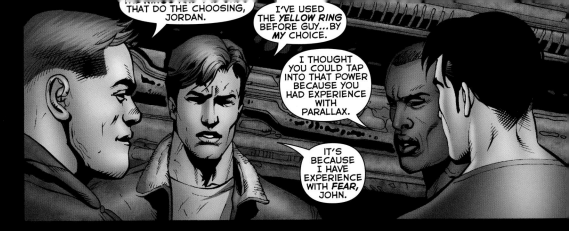

THAT DO THE CHOOSING, JORDAN.

I'VE USED THE *YELLOW RING* BEFORE GUY...BY *MY* CHOICE.

I THOUGHT YOU COULD TAP INTO THAT POWER BECAUSE YOU HAD EXPERIENCE WITH PARALLAX.

IT'S BECAUSE I HAVE EXPERIENCE WITH *FEAR*, JOHN.

I'M NOT SAYING THIS'LL BE EASY. HELL, WE MIGHT NOT EVEN GET THEM TO WORK, BUT WE HAVE TO *TRY*.

TO LIGHT THEM UP, WE JUST NEED TO ACKNOWLEDGE OUR FEELINGS...I KNOW IT'S NOT IN OUR NATURE, BUT--

TELL THAT TO *MR. THOUGHTFUL* OVER HERE.

GEE, *THANKS*, GUY.

RELAX, KYLE, IT'S A COMPLIMENT. MOSTLY.

ALL RIGHT. IF WE'RE CHOOSIN' I'M GOIN' *FIRST*. I DON'T WANNA GET STUCK WEARIN' A *CRYSTAL THONG*.

PINK AIN'T MY COLOR.

I'VE HAD A FEW ROUNDS WITH RED. I ALREADY KNOW RAGE LIKE HAL KNOWS FEAR.

GUY, YOU NEARLY *DIED* TRYING TO GET A RED RING *OFF* OF YOU LAST TIME.

WE'RE TALKING ABOUT *SAVING* THE ENTIRE DAMN CORPS, KYLE. WE'LL WORRY ABOUT ME *AFTER* IT.

BUT--

WE'RE *ALL* TAKING A CHANCE WITH THIS.

PICK YOUR POISON.

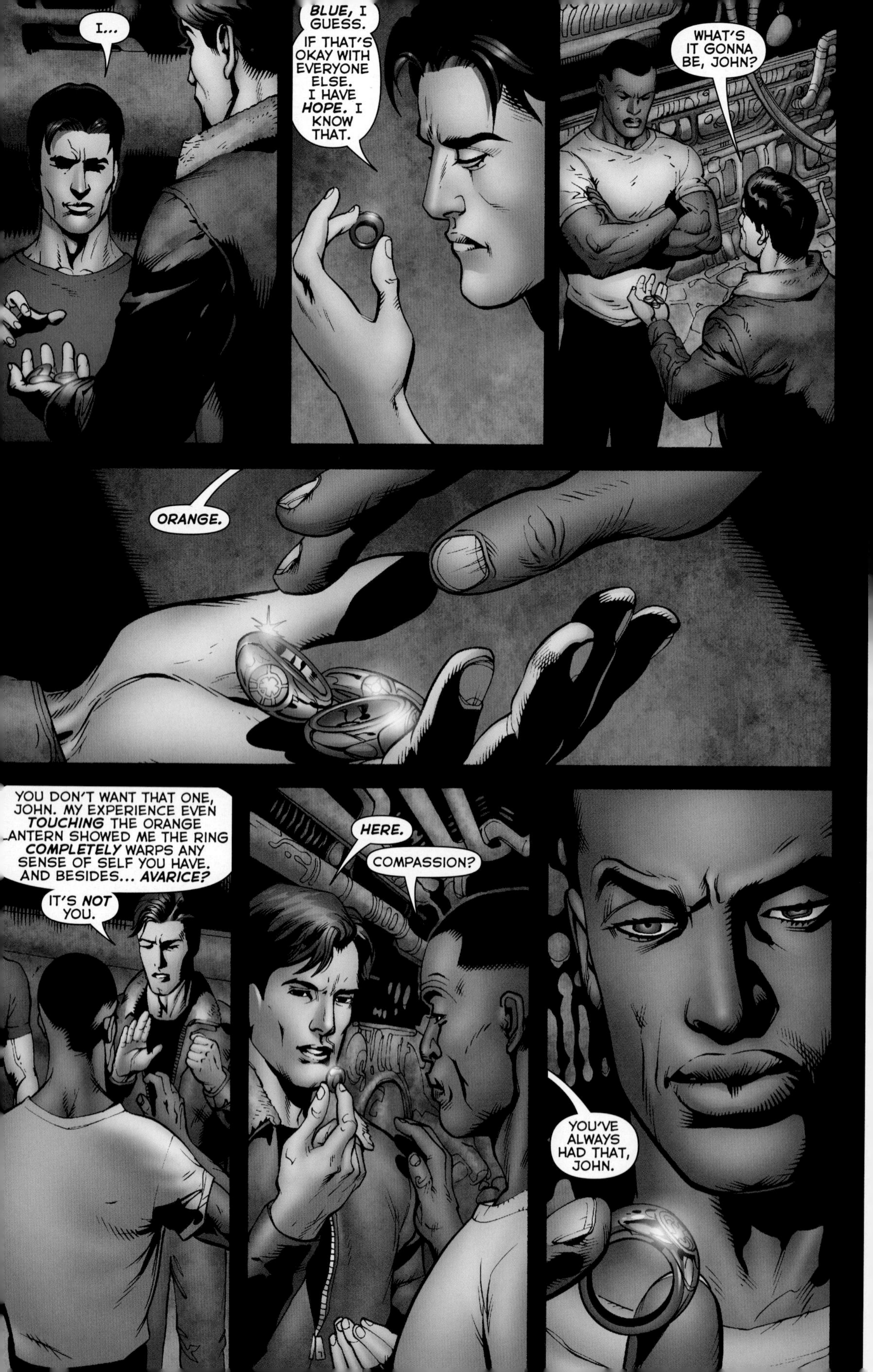
I...
BLUE, I GUESS. IF THAT'S OKAY WITH EVERYONE ELSE. I HAVE HOPE. I KNOW THAT.
WHAT'S IT GONNA BE, JOHN?
ORANGE.
YOU DON'T WANT THAT ONE, JOHN. MY EXPERIENCE EVEN TOUCHING THE ORANGE LANTERN SHOWED ME THE RING COMPLETELY WARPS ANY SENSE OF SELF YOU HAVE. AND BESIDES... AVARICE?
IT'S NOT YOU.
HERE.
COMPASSION?
YOU'VE ALWAYS HAD THAT, JOHN.

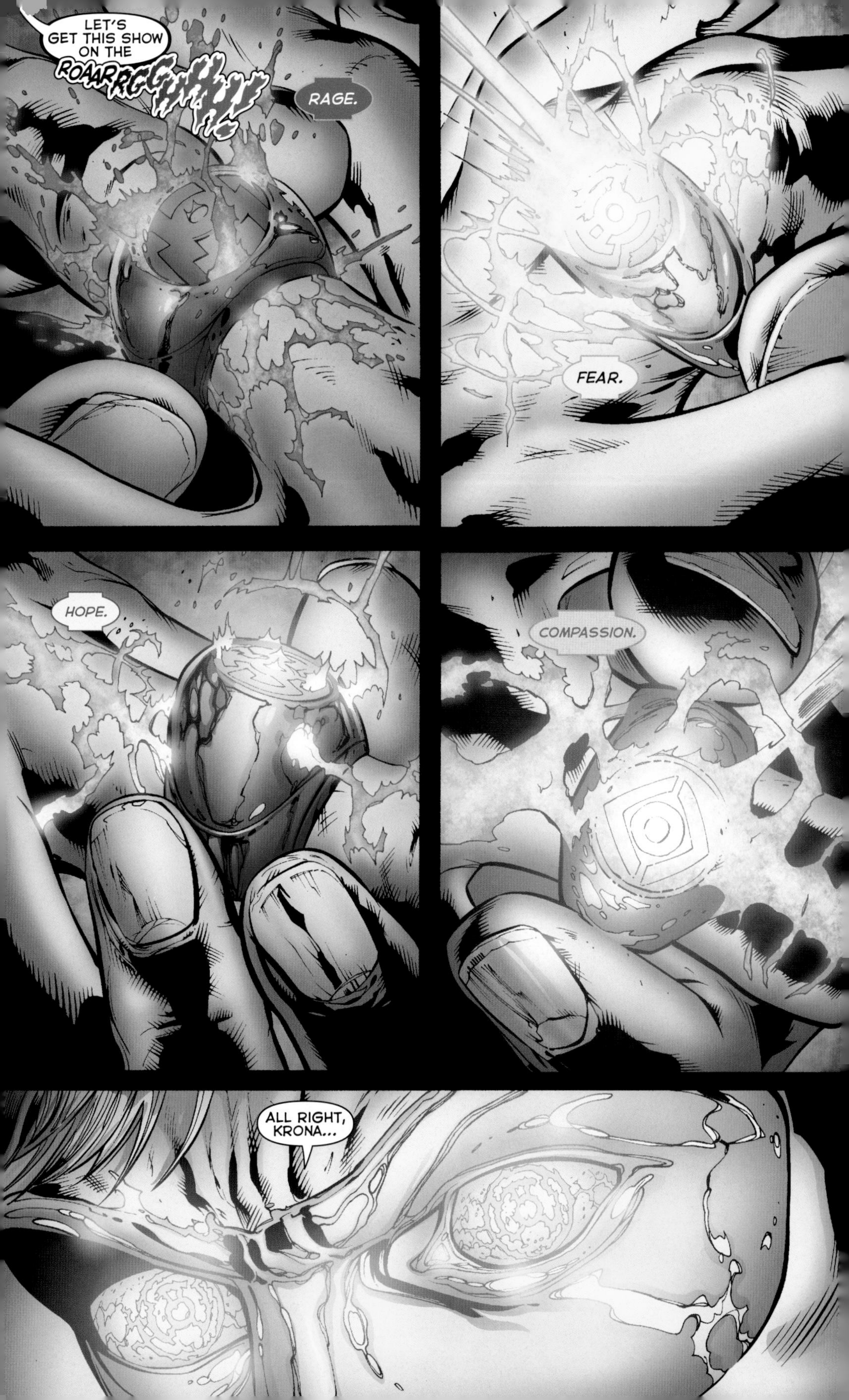
LET'S GET THIS SHOW ON THE
ROAARRGGHHH
RAGE.
FEAR.
HOPE.
COMPASSION.
ALL RIGHT, KRONA...

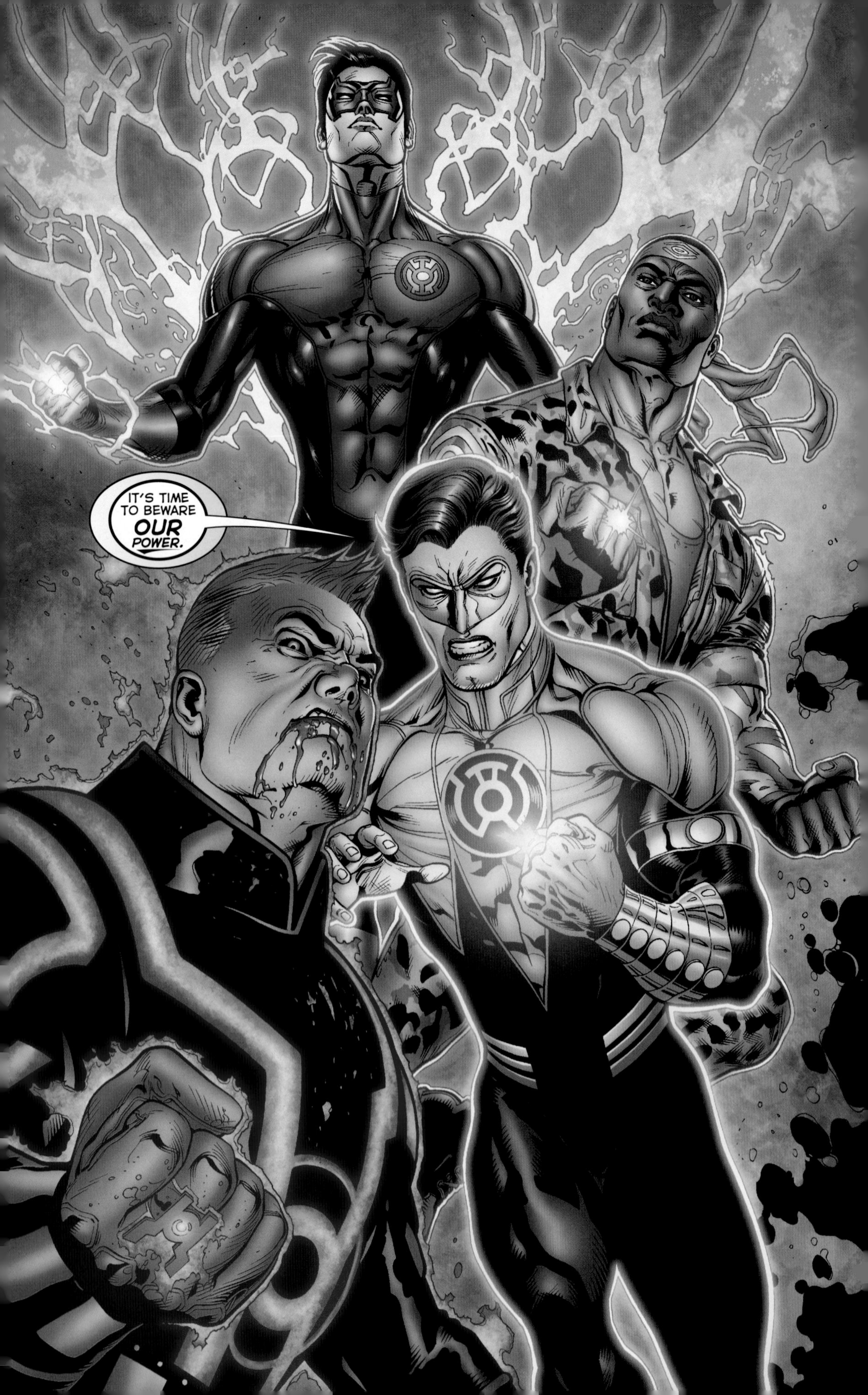
IT'S TIME TO BEWARE OUR POWER.

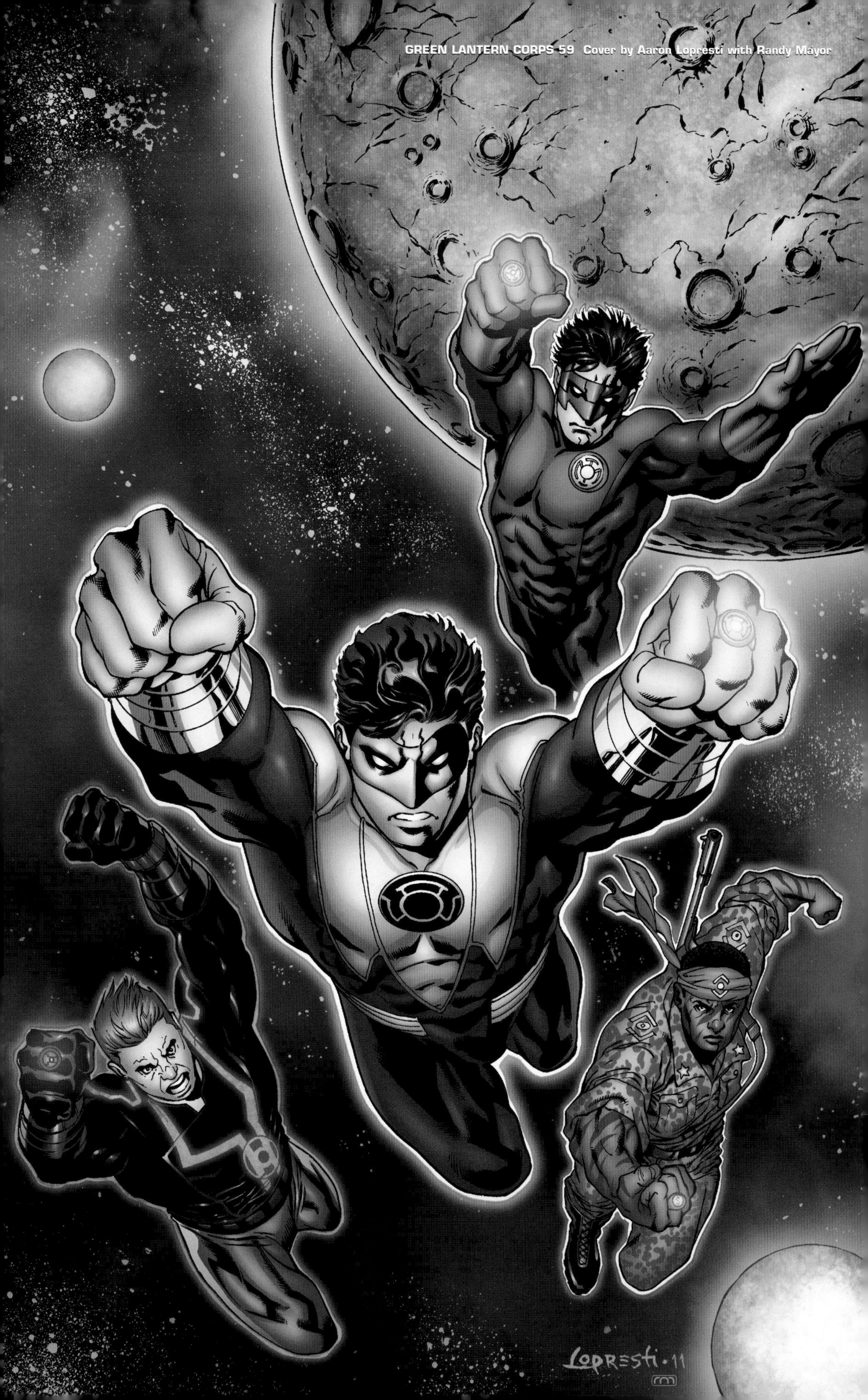
LOPRESTI·11

GREEN LANTERN CORPS 59 Cover by Aaron Lopresti with Randy Mayor

WAR OF THE GREEN LANTERNS
PART FIVE

Tony Bedard Writer
Tyler Kirkham Penciller
BATT Inker

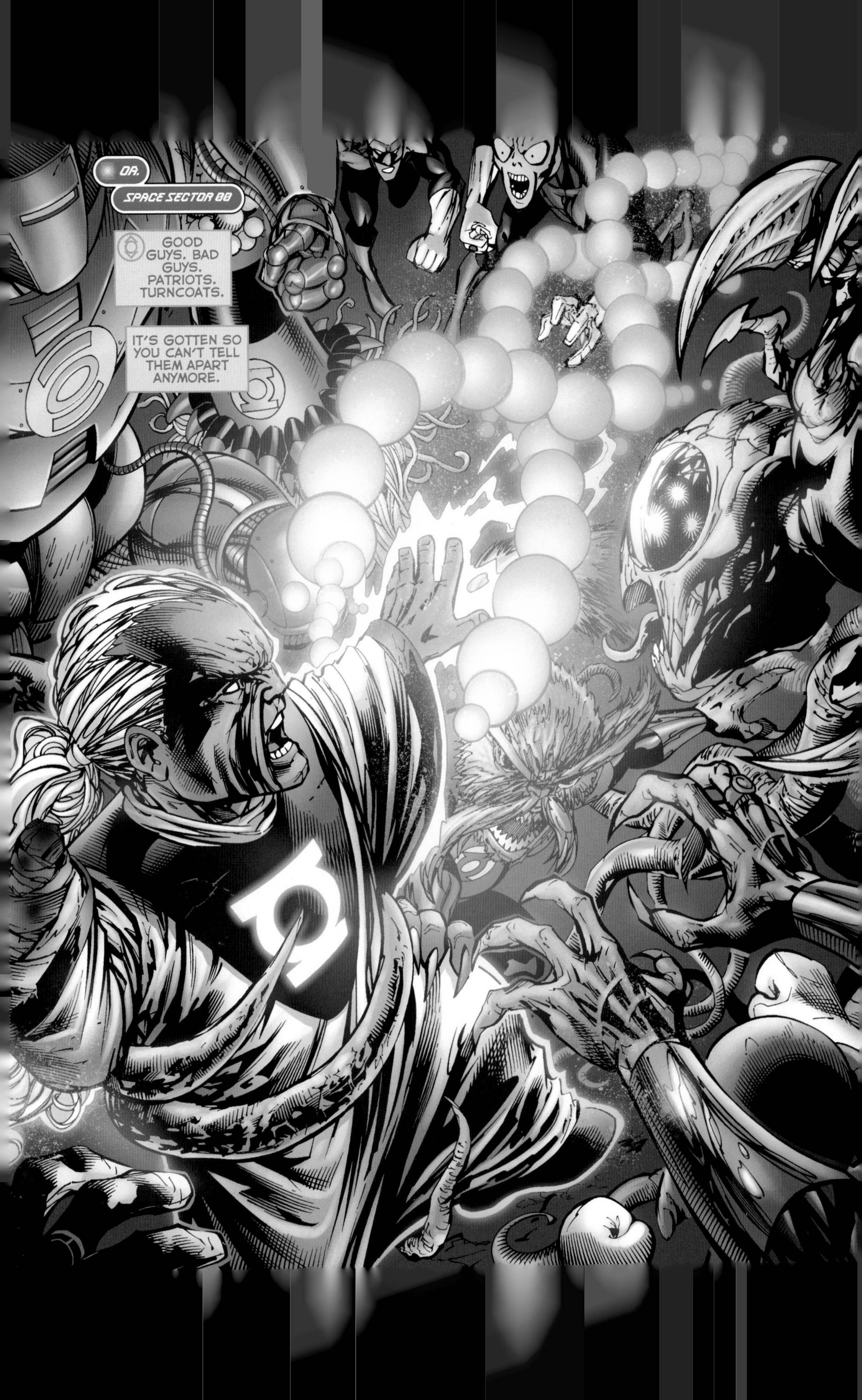
OA.
SPACE SECTOR 00
GOOD GUYS. BAD GUYS. PATRIOTS. TURNCOATS.
IT'S GOTTEN SO YOU CAN'T TELL THEM APART ANYMORE.

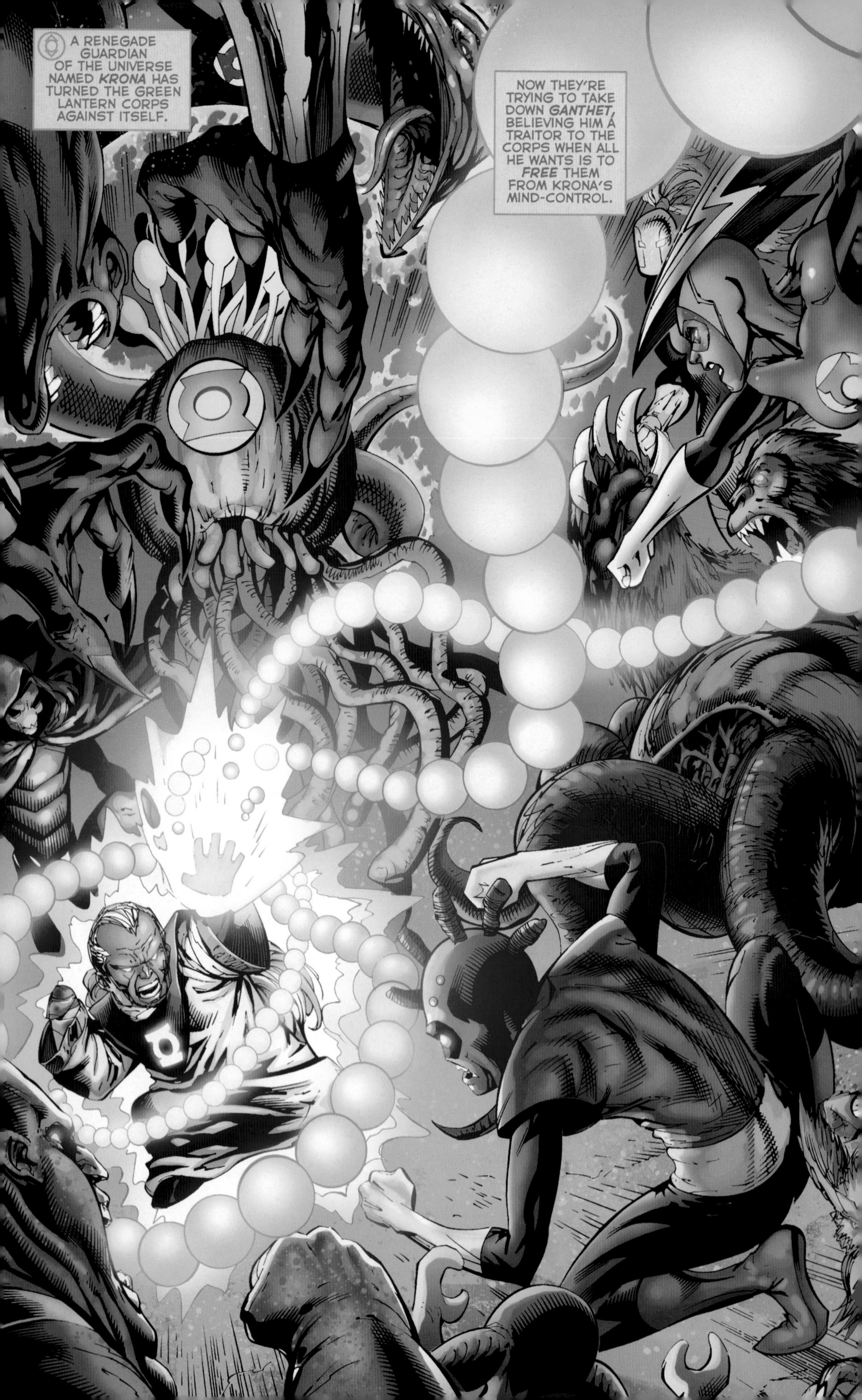
A RENEGADE GUARDIAN OF THE UNIVERSE NAMED KRONA HAS TURNED THE GREEN LANTERN CORPS AGAINST ITSELF.
NOW THEY'RE TRYING TO TAKE DOWN GANTHET, BELIEVING HIM A TRAITOR TO THE CORPS WHEN ALL HE WANTS IS TO FREE THEM FROM KRONA'S MIND-CONTROL.

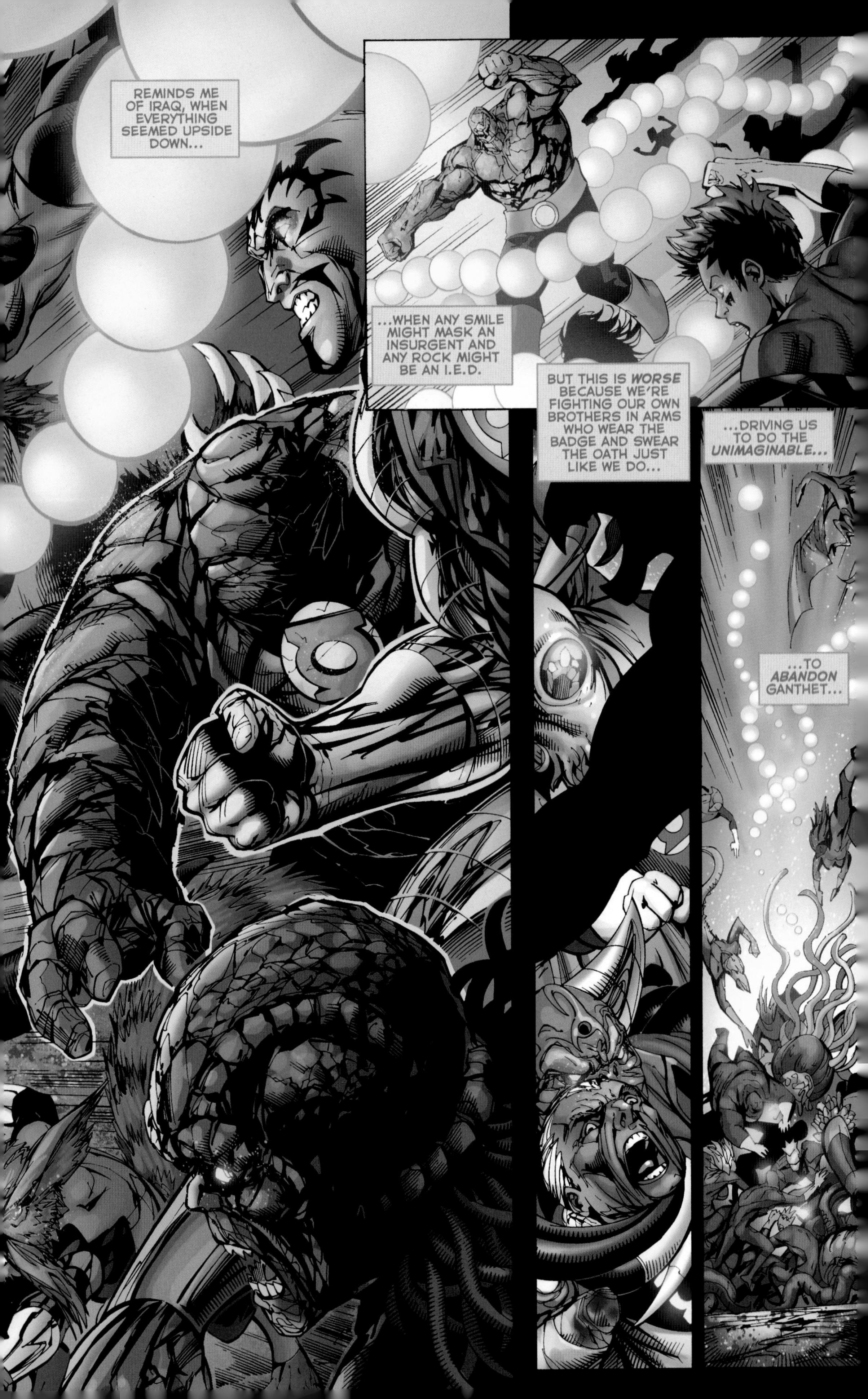
REMINDS ME OF IRAQ, WHEN EVERYTHING SEEMED UPSIDE DOWN...
...WHEN ANY SMILE MIGHT MASK AN INSURGENT AND ANY ROCK MIGHT BE AN I.E.D.
BUT THIS IS *WORSE* BECAUSE WE'RE FIGHTING OUR OWN BROTHERS IN ARMS WHO WEAR THE BADGE AND SWEAR THE OATH JUST LIKE WE DO...
...DRIVING US TO DO THE *UNIMAGINABLE*...
...TO *ABANDON* GANTHET...

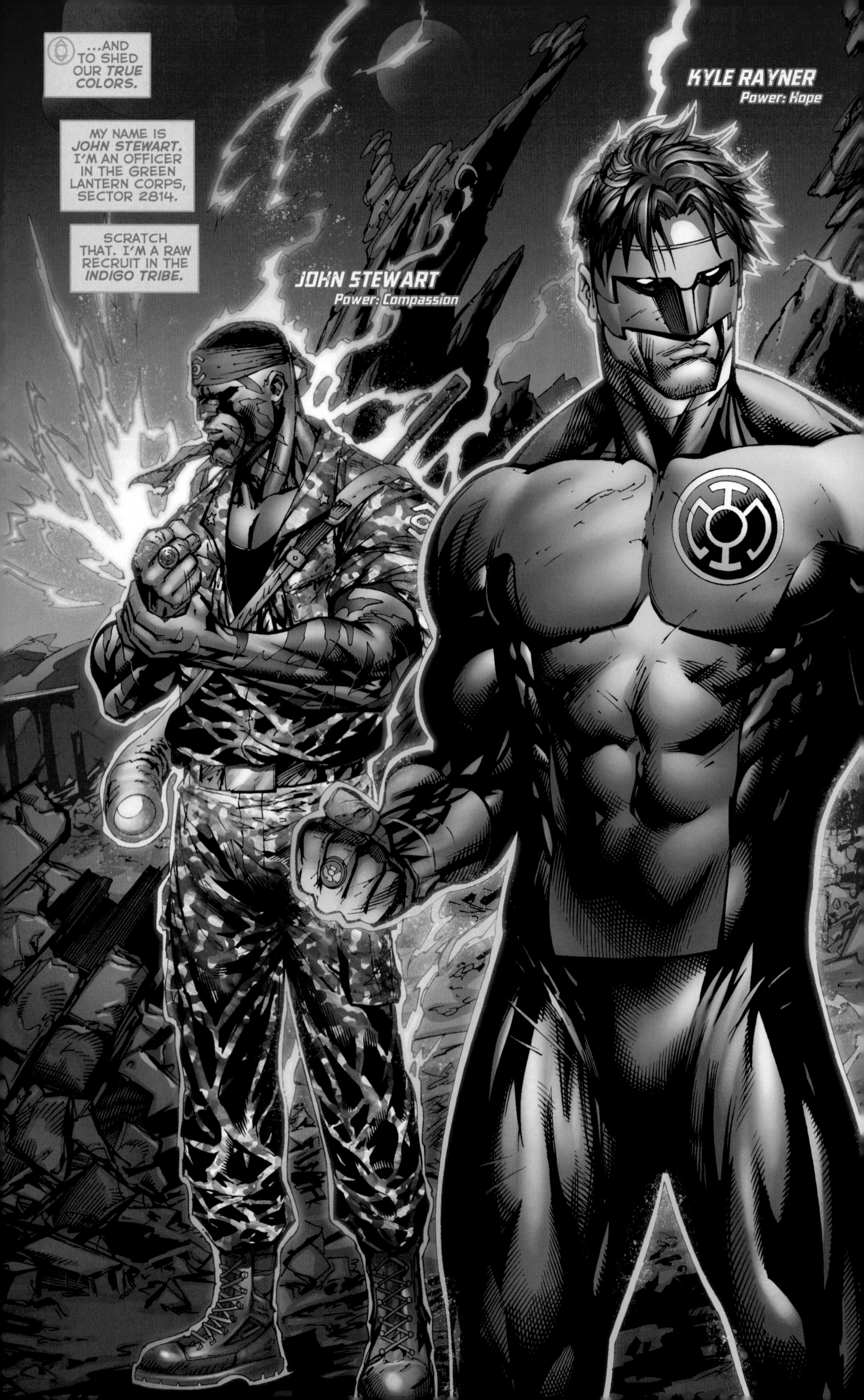
...AND TO SHED OUR TRUE COLORS.
MY NAME IS JOHN STEWART. I'M AN OFFICER IN THE GREEN LANTERN CORPS, SECTOR 2814.
SCRATCH THAT. I'M A RAW RECRUIT IN THE INDIGO TRIBE.
JOHN STEWART
Power: Compassion
KYLE RAYNER
Power: Hope

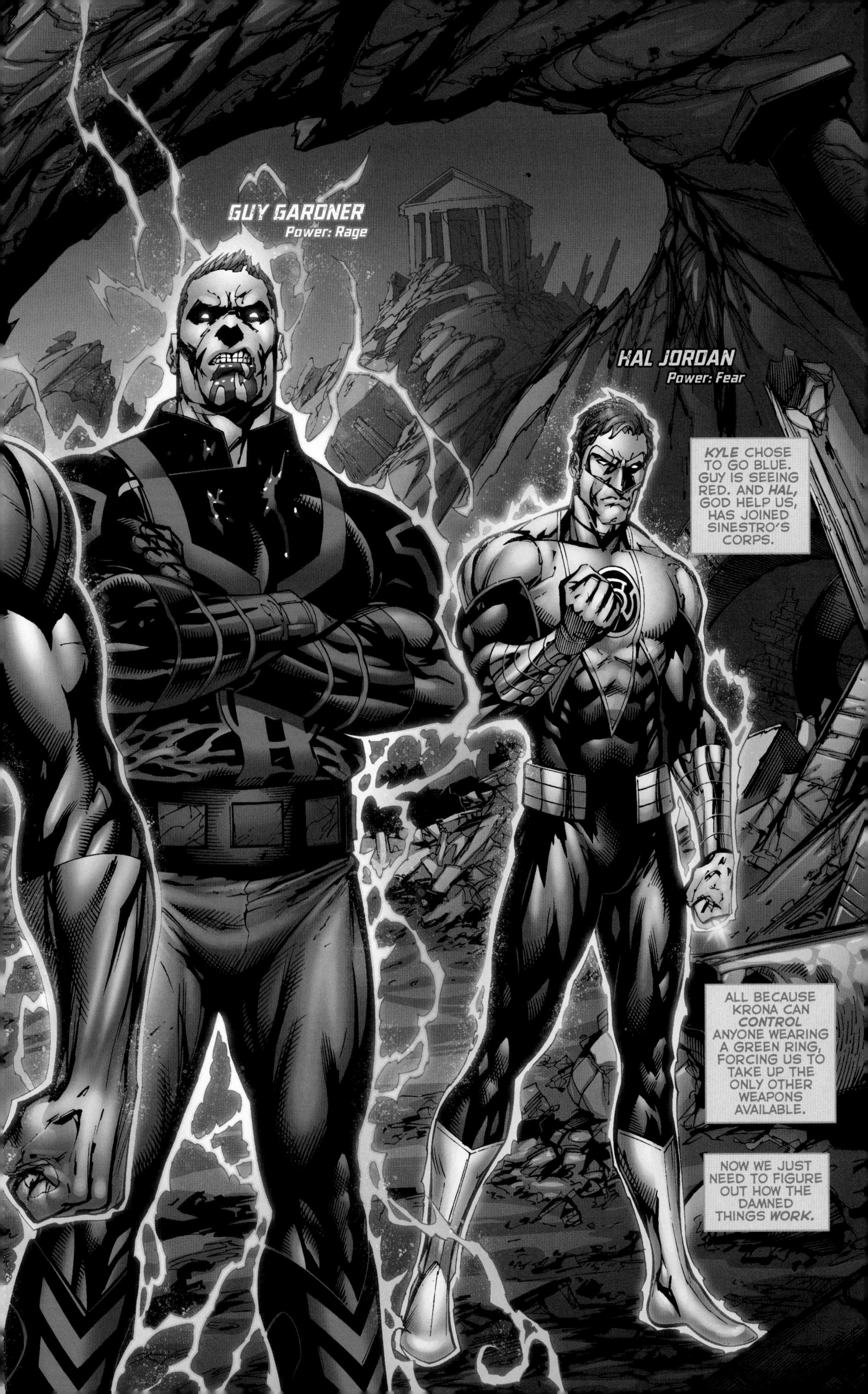
GUY GARDNER
Power: Rage
HAL JORDAN
Power: Fear
KYLE CHOSE TO GO BLUE. GUY IS SEEING RED. AND HAL, GOD HELP US, HAS JOINED SINESTRO'S CORPS.
ALL BECAUSE KRONA CAN CONTROL ANYONE WEARING A GREEN RING, FORCING US TO TAKE UP THE ONLY OTHER WEAPONS AVAILABLE.
NOW WE JUST NEED TO FIGURE OUT HOW THE DAMNED THINGS WORK.

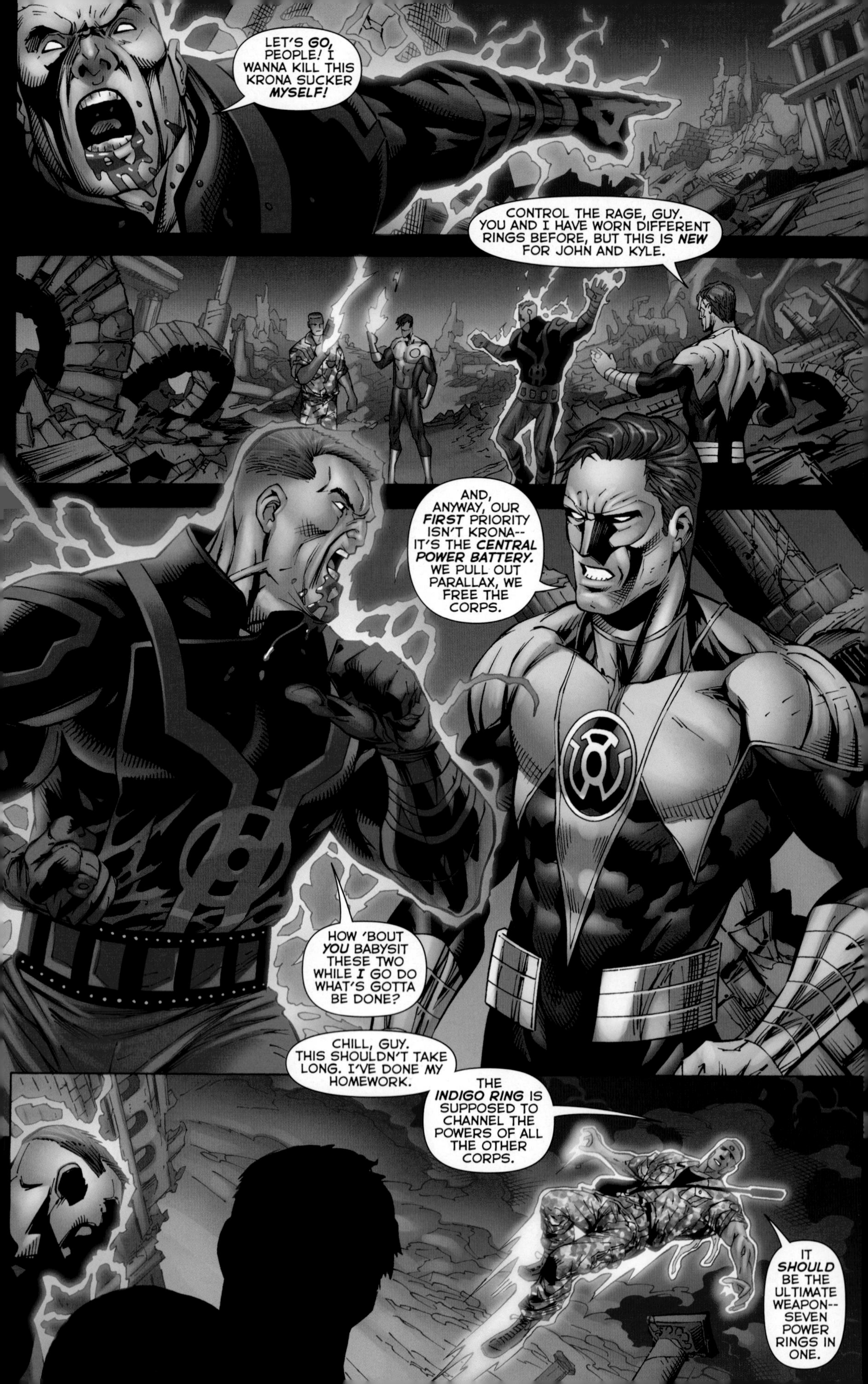
LET'S GO, PEOPLE! I WANNA KILL THIS KRONA SUCKER MYSELF!
CONTROL THE RAGE, GUY. YOU AND I HAVE WORN DIFFERENT RINGS BEFORE, BUT THIS IS NEW FOR JOHN AND KYLE.
AND, ANYWAY, OUR FIRST PRIORITY ISN'T KRONA-- IT'S THE CENTRAL POWER BATTERY. WE PULL OUT PARALLAX, WE FREE THE CORPS.
HOW 'BOUT YOU BABYSIT THESE TWO WHILE I GO DO WHAT'S GOTTA BE DONE?
CHILL, GUY. THIS SHOULDN'T TAKE LONG. I'VE DONE MY HOMEWORK.
THE INDIGO RING IS SUPPOSED TO CHANNEL THE POWERS OF ALL THE OTHER CORPS.
IT SHOULD BE THE ULTIMATE WEAPON-- SEVEN POWER RINGS IN ONE.

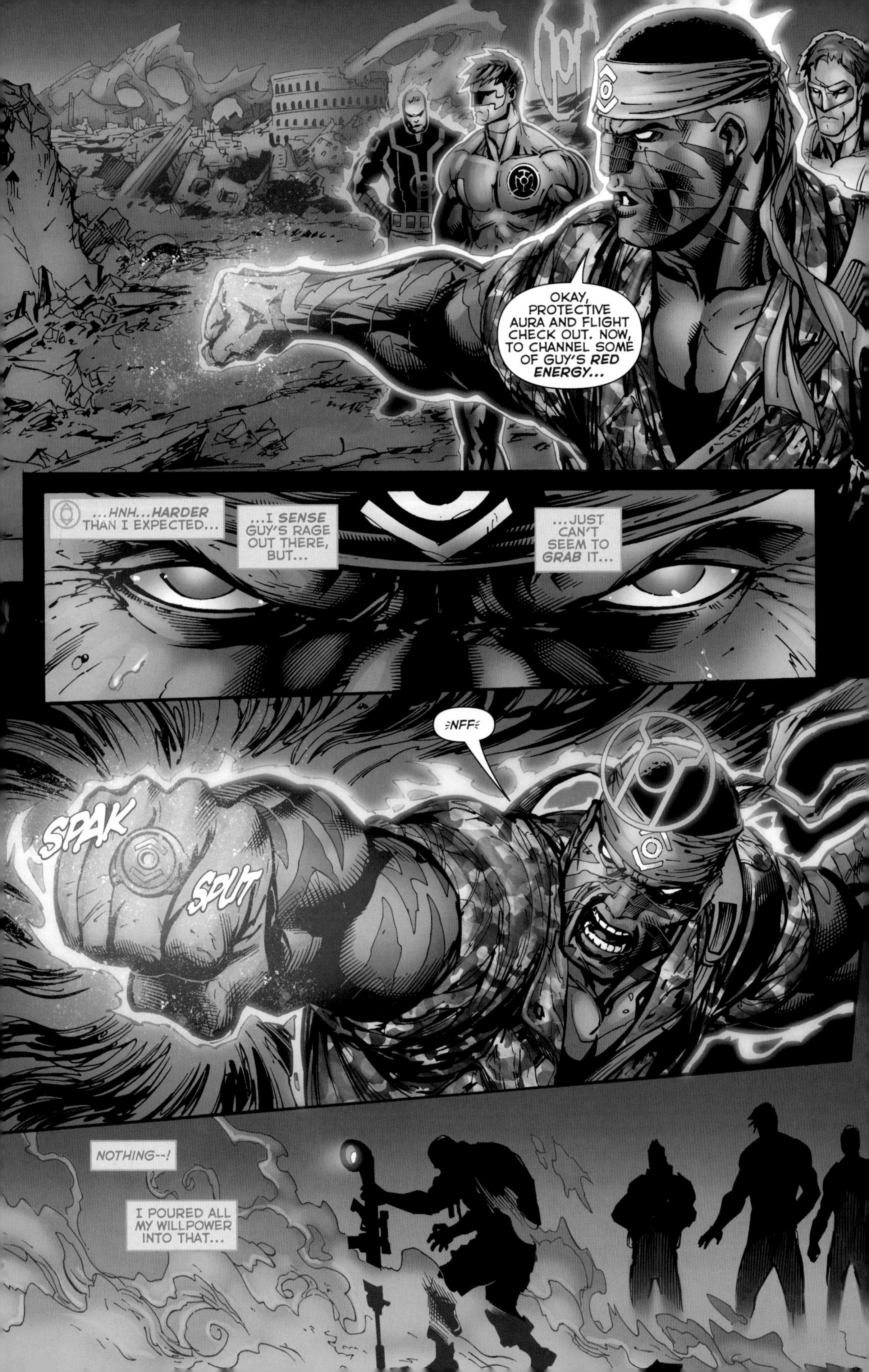
OKAY, PROTECTIVE AURA AND FLIGHT CHECK OUT. NOW, TO CHANNEL SOME OF GUY'S RED ENERGY...
...HNH...HARDER THAN I EXPECTED...
...I SENSE GUY'S RAGE OUT THERE, BUT...
...JUST CAN'T SEEM TO GRAB IT...
NFF
SPAK
SPUT
NOTHING--!
I POURED ALL MY WILLPOWER INTO THAT...

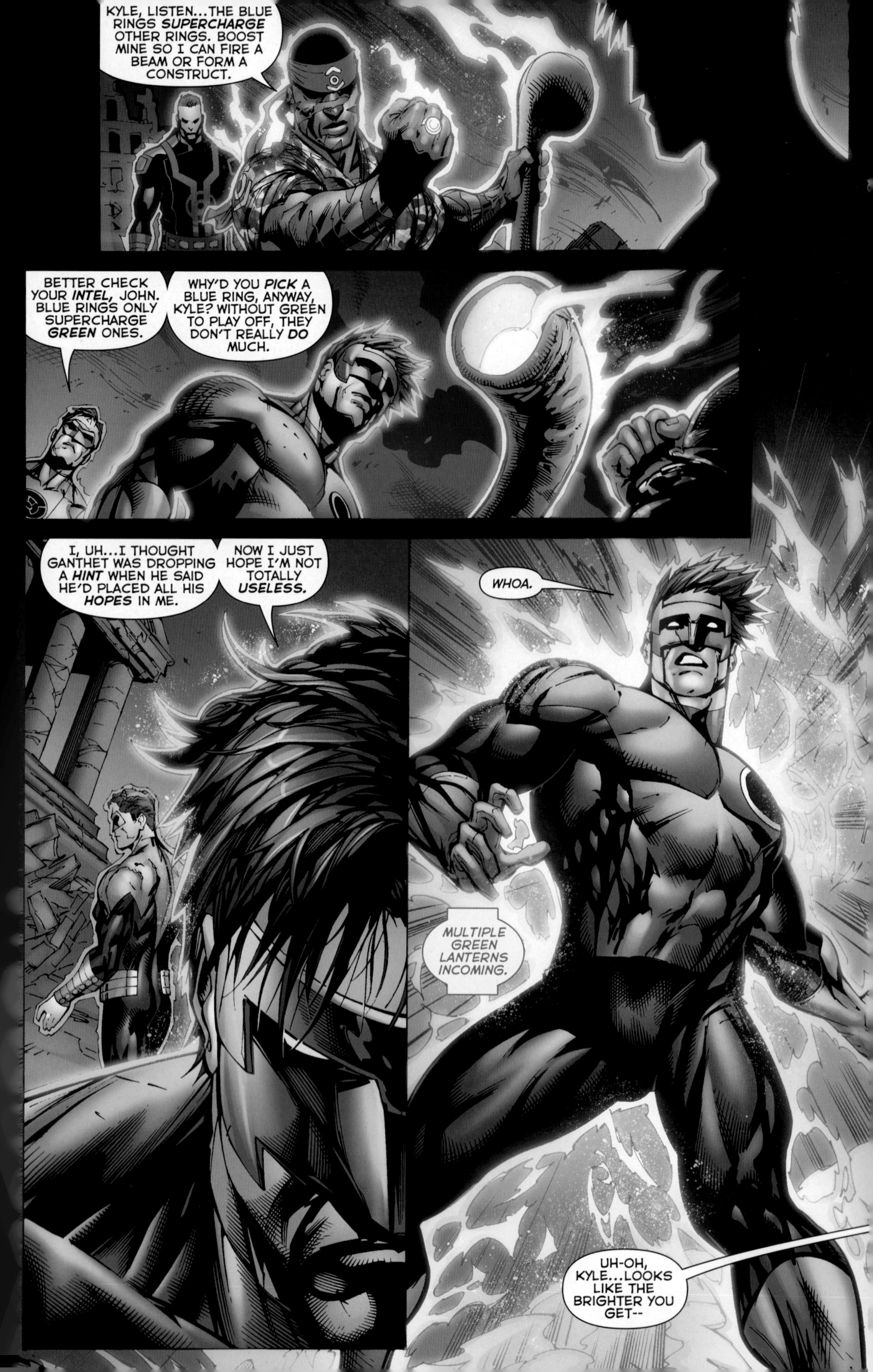
KYLE, LISTEN...THE BLUE RINGS SUPERCHARGE OTHER RINGS. BOOST MINE SO I CAN FIRE A BEAM OR FORM A CONSTRUCT.
BETTER CHECK YOUR INTEL, JOHN. BLUE RINGS ONLY SUPERCHARGE GREEN ONES.
WHY'D YOU PICK A BLUE RING, ANYWAY, KYLE? WITHOUT GREEN TO PLAY OFF, THEY DON'T REALLY DO MUCH.
I, UH...I THOUGHT GANTHET WAS DROPPING A HINT WHEN HE SAID HE'D PLACED ALL HIS HOPES IN ME.
NOW I JUST HOPE I'M NOT TOTALLY USELESS.
WHOA.
MULTIPLE GREEN LANTERNS INCOMING.
UH-OH, KYLE...LOOKS LIKE THE BRIGHTER YOU GET--

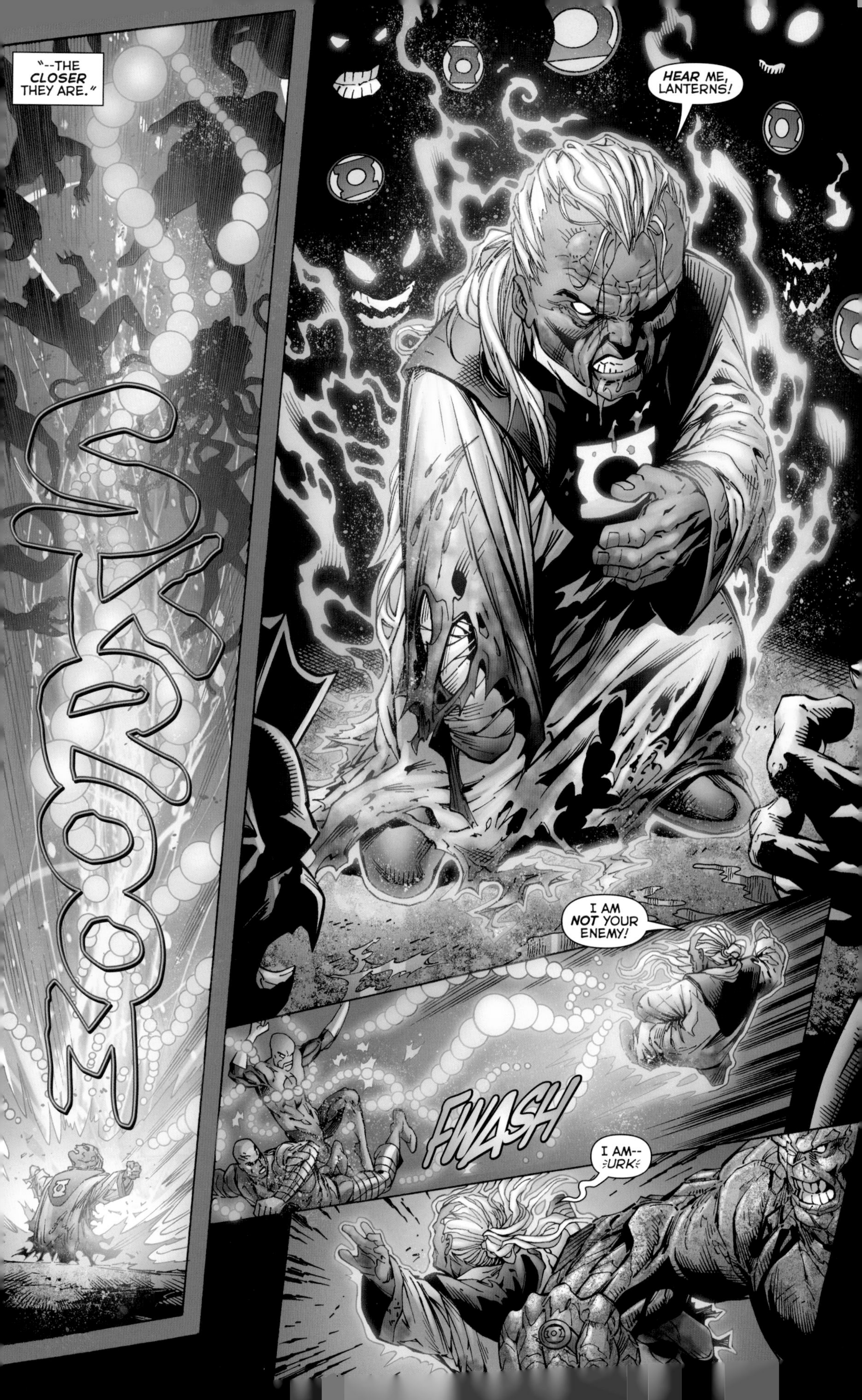
"--THE CLOSER THEY ARE."
HEAR ME, LANTERNS!
I AM NOT YOUR ENEMY!
FWASH
I AM-- URK

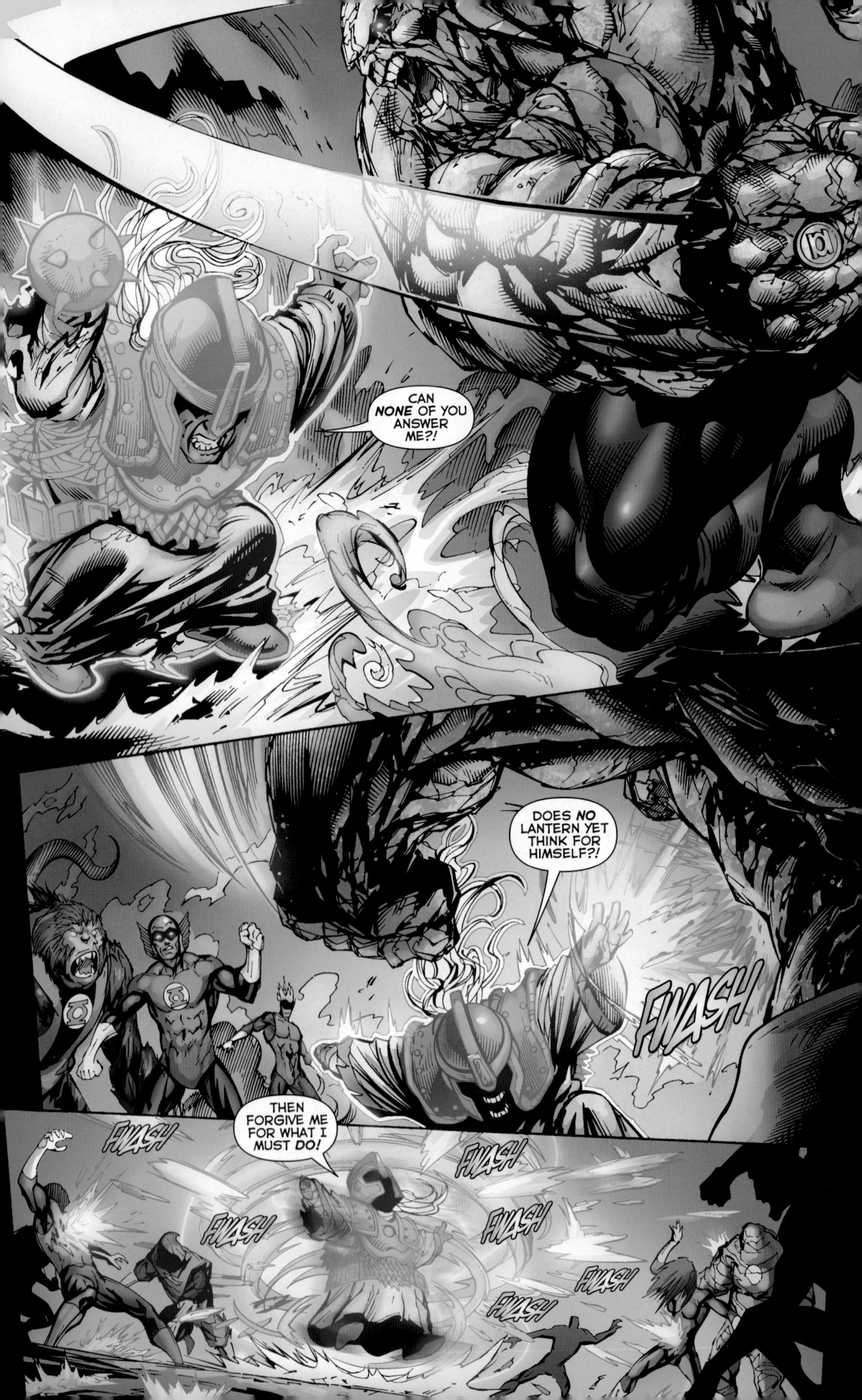
CAN NONE OF YOU ANSWER ME?!
DOES NO LANTERN YET THINK FOR HIMSELF?!
FWASH
THEN FORGIVE ME FOR WHAT I MUST DO!
FWASH
FWASH
FWASH
FWASH
FWASH
FWASH

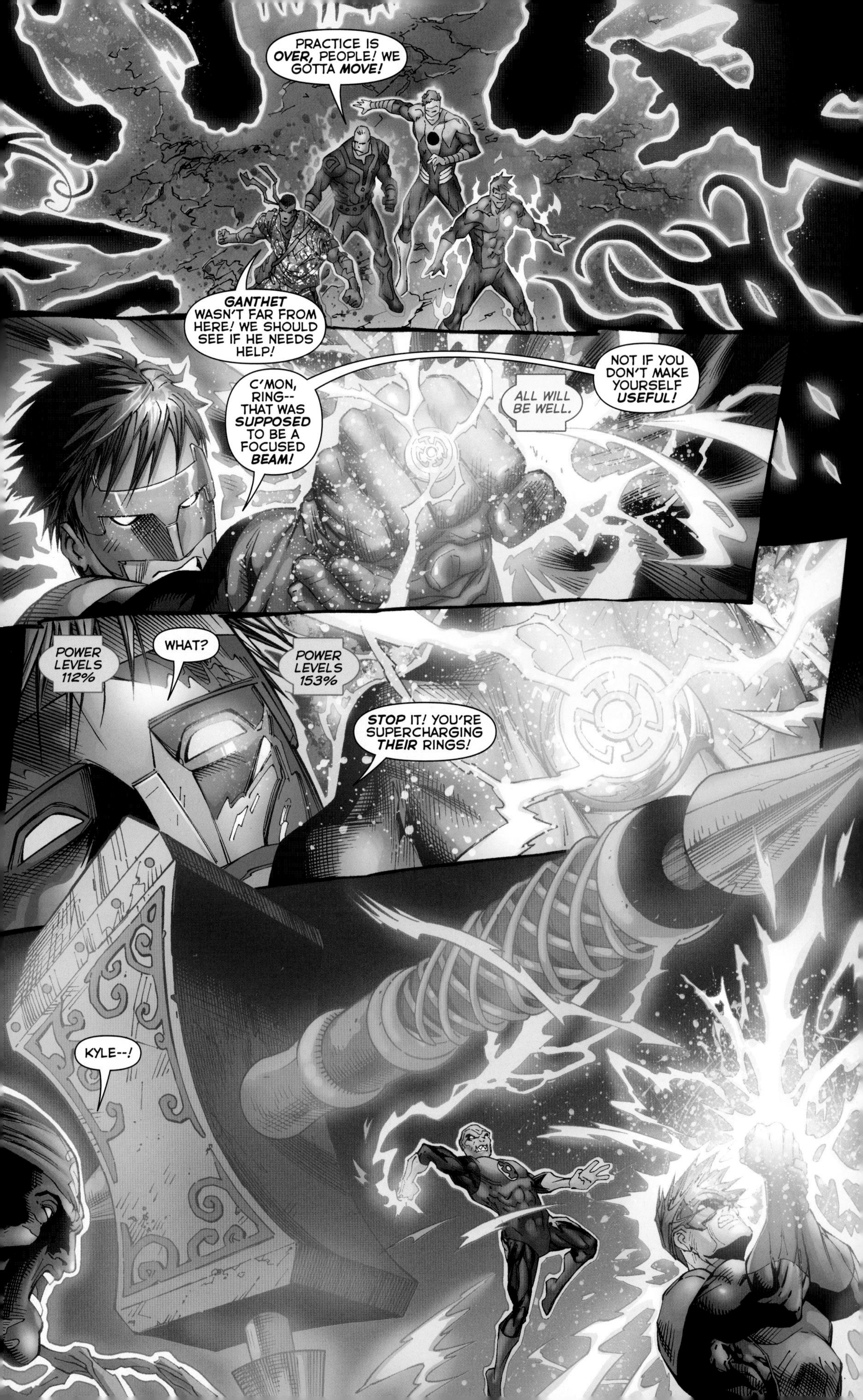
PRACTICE IS OVER, PEOPLE! WE GOTTA MOVE!
GANTHET WASN'T FAR FROM HERE! WE SHOULD SEE IF HE NEEDS HELP!
C'MON, RING-- THAT WAS SUPPOSED TO BE A FOCUSED BEAM!
ALL WILL BE WELL.
NOT IF YOU DON'T MAKE YOURSELF USEFUL!
POWER LEVELS 112%
WHAT?
POWER LEVELS 153%
STOP IT! YOU'RE SUPERCHARGING THEIR RINGS!
KYLE--!

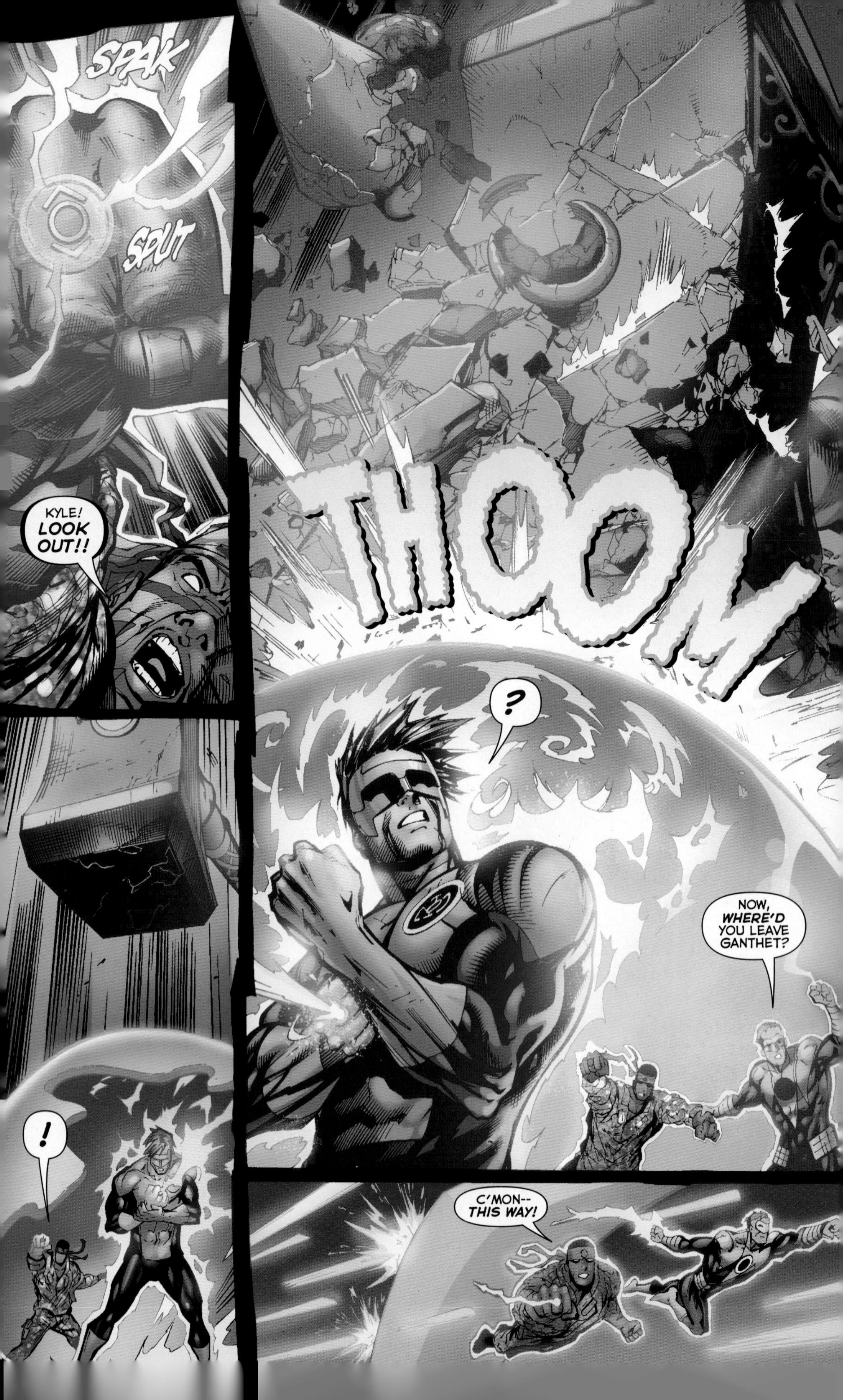
SPAK
SPUT
KYLE! LOOK OUT!!
THOOM
?
NOW, WHERE'D YOU LEAVE GANTHET?
!
C'MON-- THIS WAY!

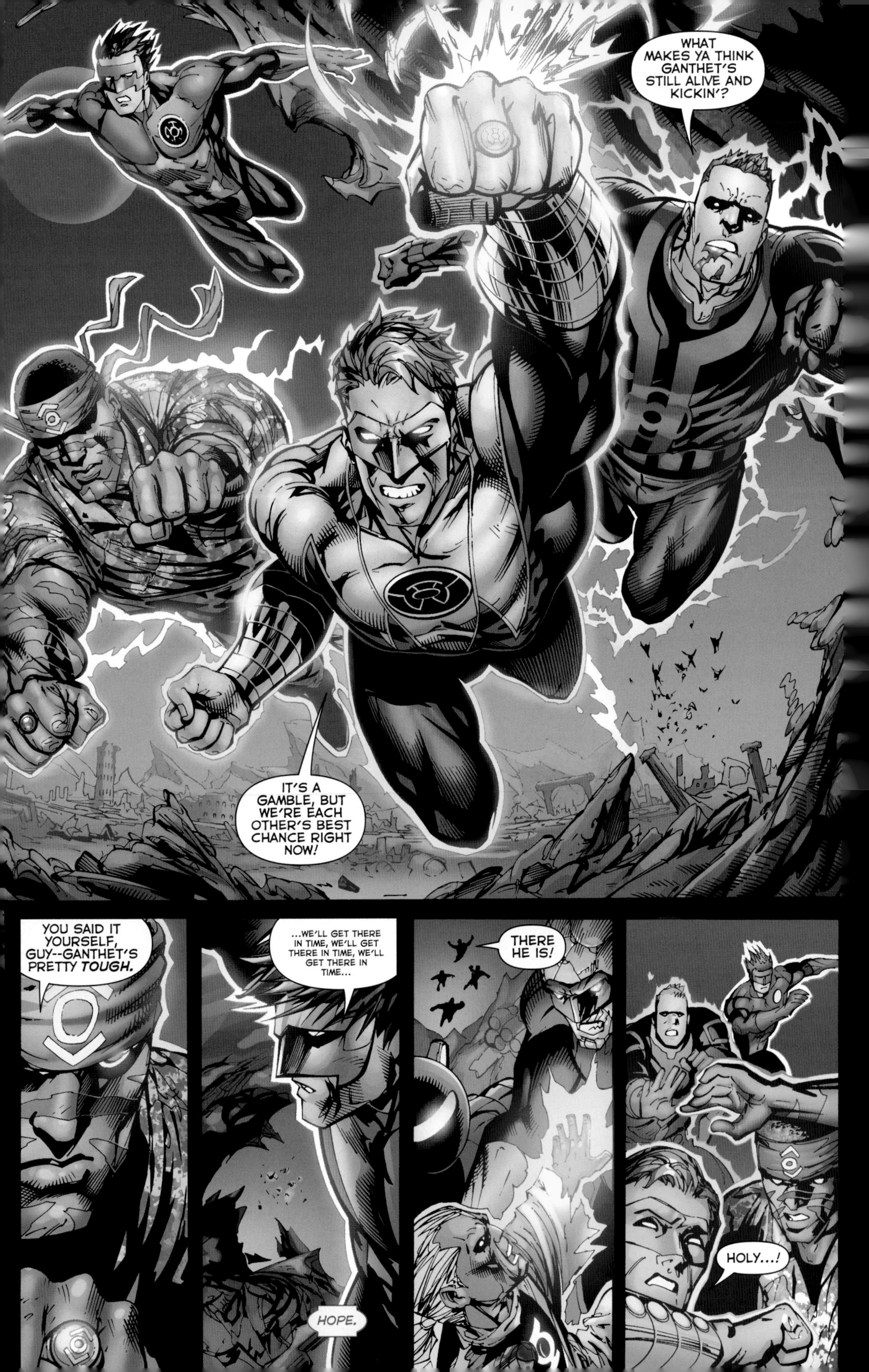

WHAT MAKES YA THINK GANTHET'S STILL ALIVE AND KICKIN'?
IT'S A GAMBLE, BUT WE'RE EACH OTHER'S BEST CHANCE RIGHT NOW!
YOU SAID IT YOURSELF, GUY--GANTHET'S PRETTY TOUGH.
...WE'LL GET THERE IN TIME, WE'LL GET THERE IN TIME, WE'LL GET THERE IN TIME...
HOPE.
THERE HE IS!
HOLY...!

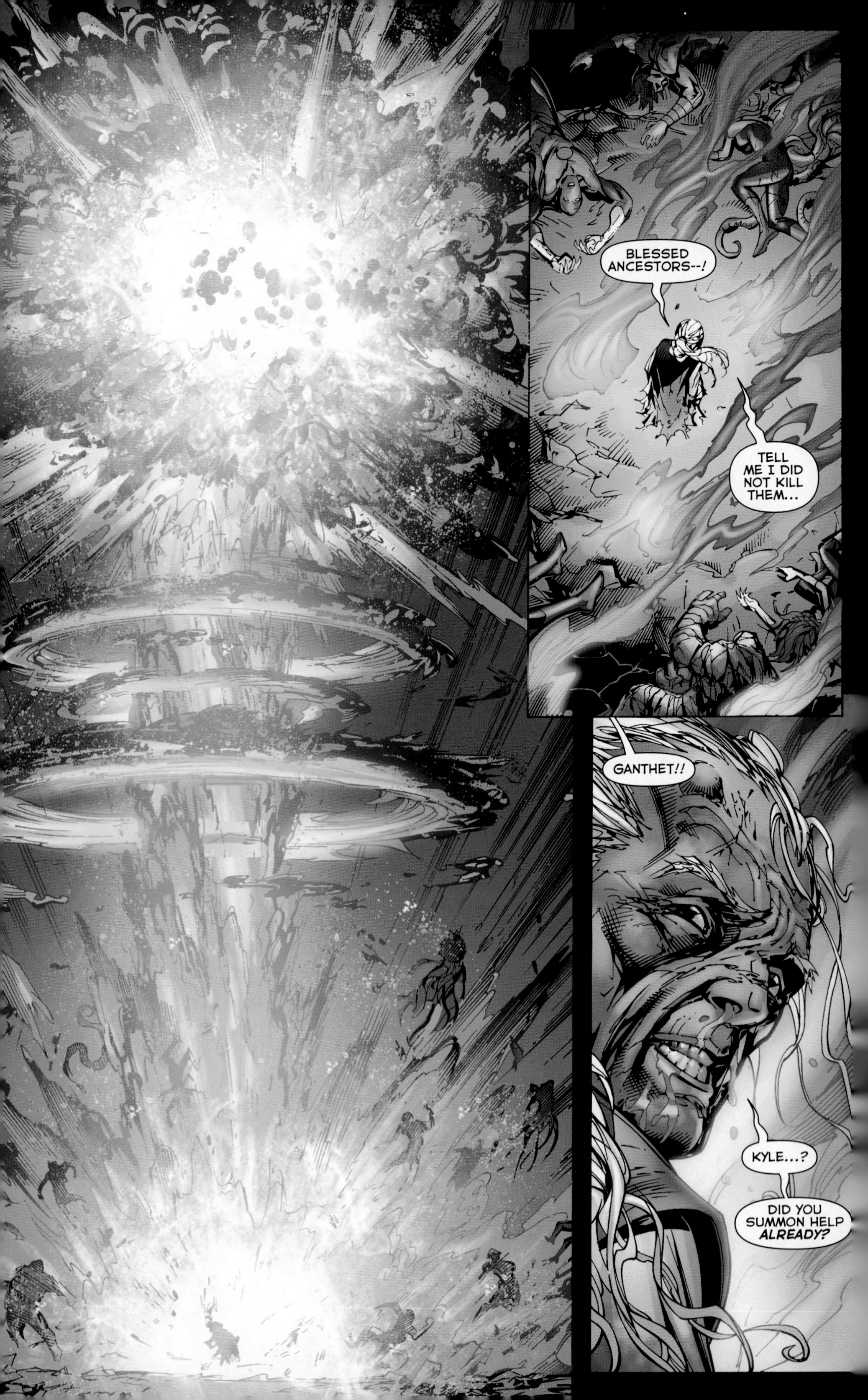

BLESSED ANCESTORS--!
TELL ME I DID NOT KILL THEM...
GANTHET!!
KYLE...?
DID YOU SUMMON HELP *ALREADY?*

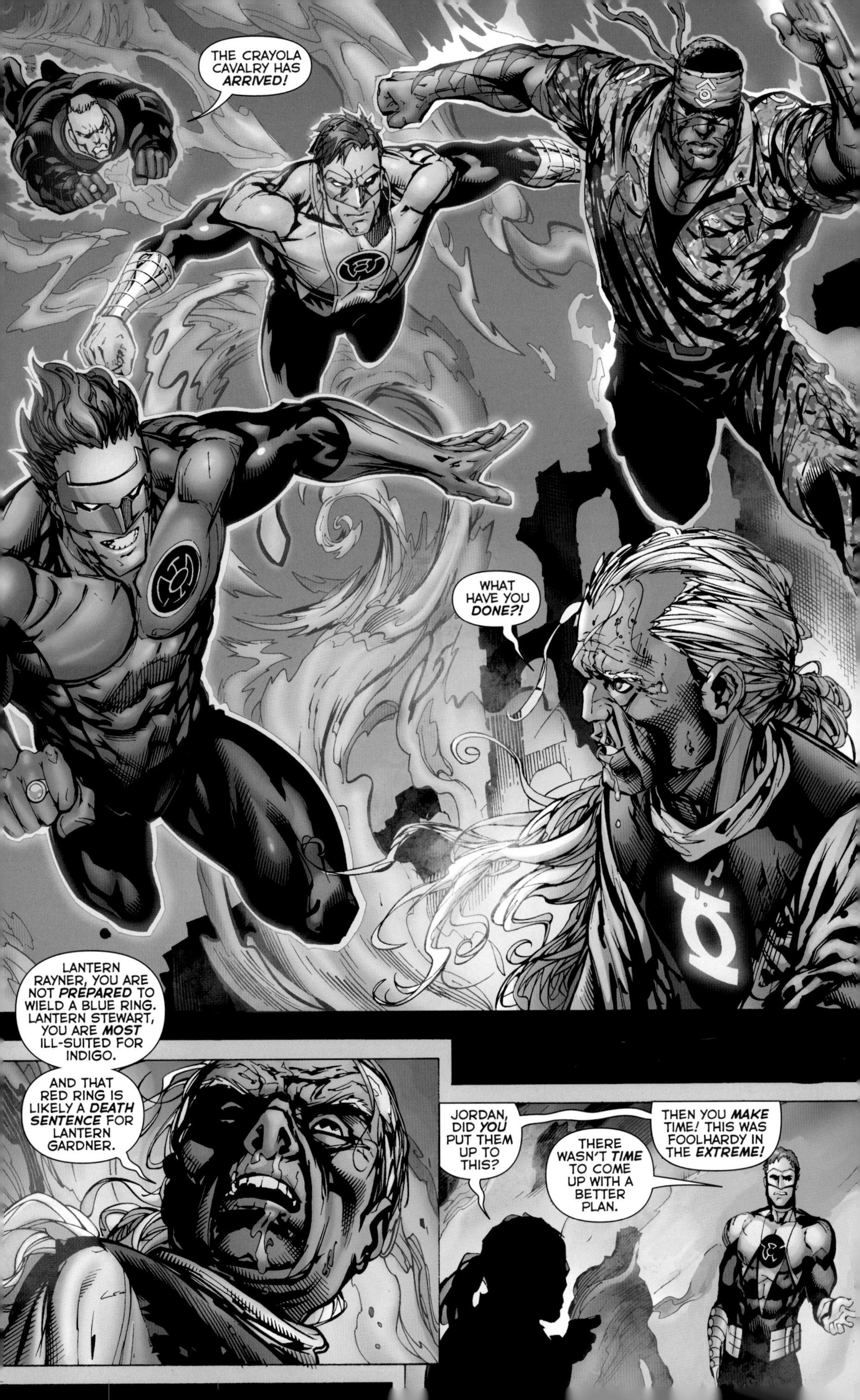

THE CRAYOLA CAVALRY HAS ARRIVED!
WHAT HAVE YOU DONE?!
LANTERN RAYNER, YOU ARE NOT PREPARED TO WIELD A BLUE RING. LANTERN STEWART, YOU ARE MOST ILL-SUITED FOR INDIGO.
AND THAT RED RING IS LIKELY A DEATH SENTENCE FOR LANTERN GARDNER.
JORDAN, DID YOU PUT THEM UP TO THIS?
THERE WASN'T TIME TO COME UP WITH A BETTER PLAN.
THEN YOU MAKE TIME! THIS WAS FOOLHARDY IN THE EXTREME!

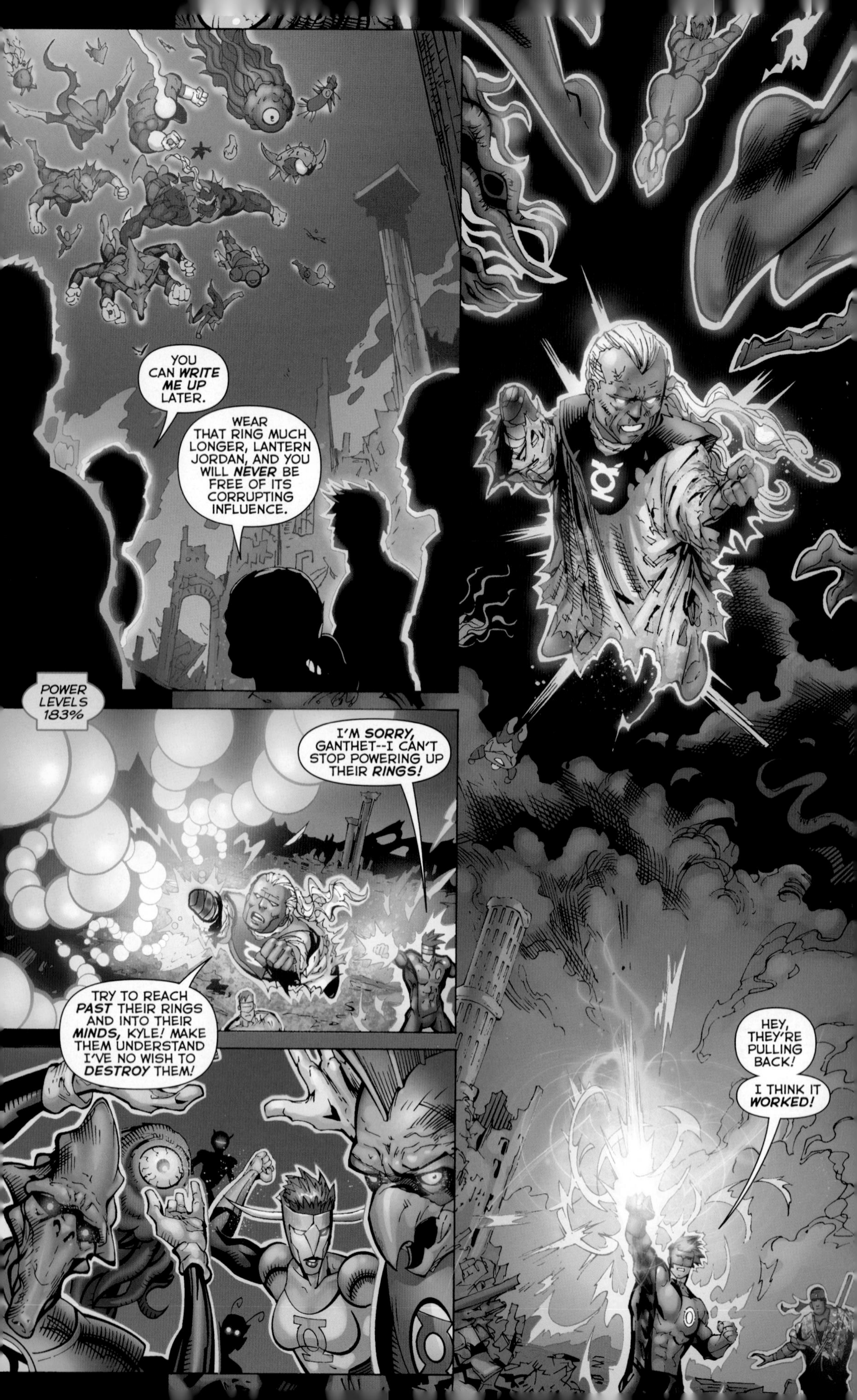
YOU CAN WRITE ME UP LATER.
WEAR THAT RING MUCH LONGER, LANTERN JORDAN, AND YOU WILL NEVER BE FREE OF ITS CORRUPTING INFLUENCE.
POWER LEVELS 183%
I'M SORRY, GANTHET--I CAN'T STOP POWERING UP THEIR RINGS!
TRY TO REACH PAST THEIR RINGS AND INTO THEIR MINDS, KYLE! MAKE THEM UNDERSTAND I'VE NO WISH TO DESTROY THEM!
HEY, THEY'RE PULLING BACK!
I THINK IT WORKED!

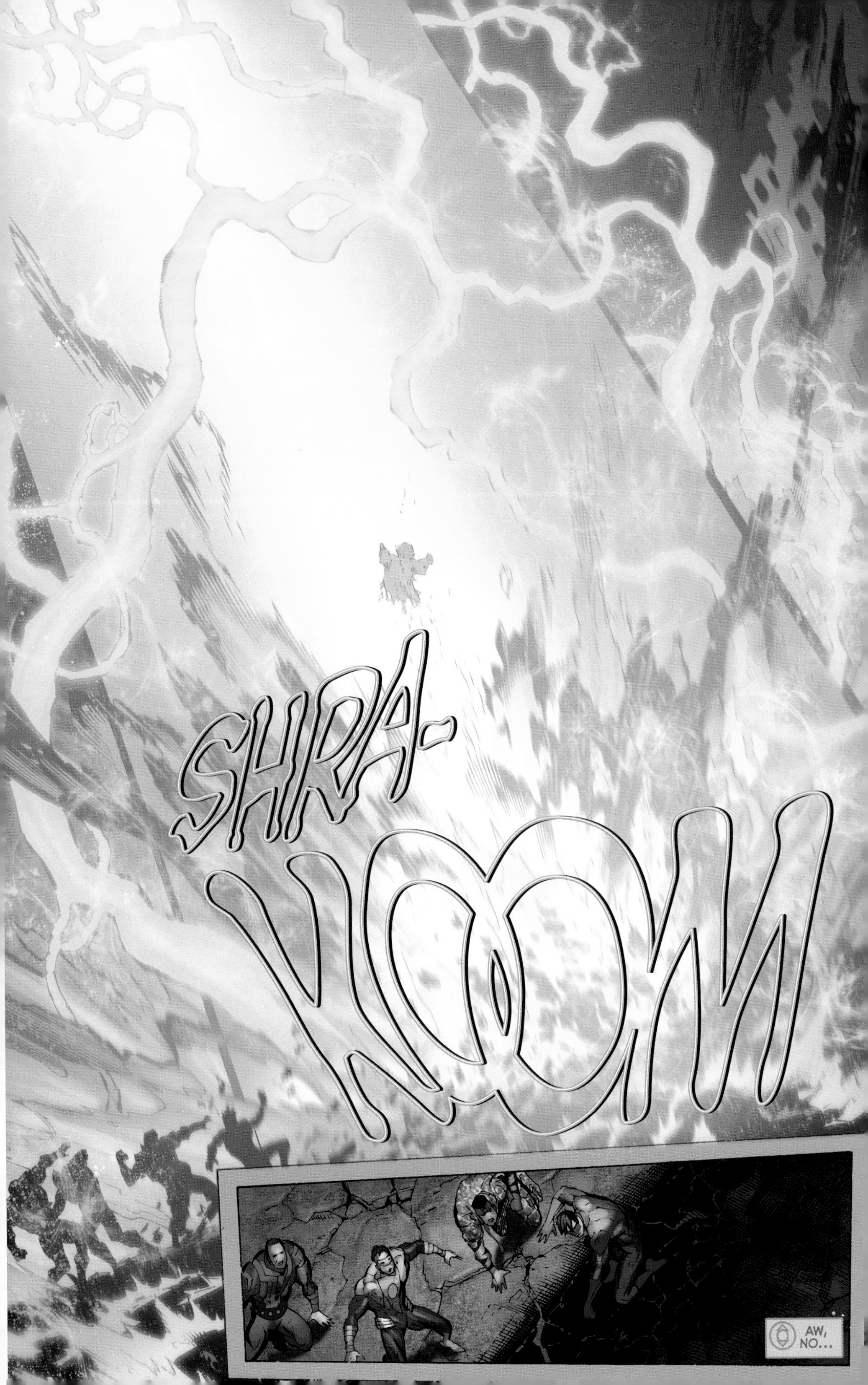
SHRA-
KOOM
AW, NO...

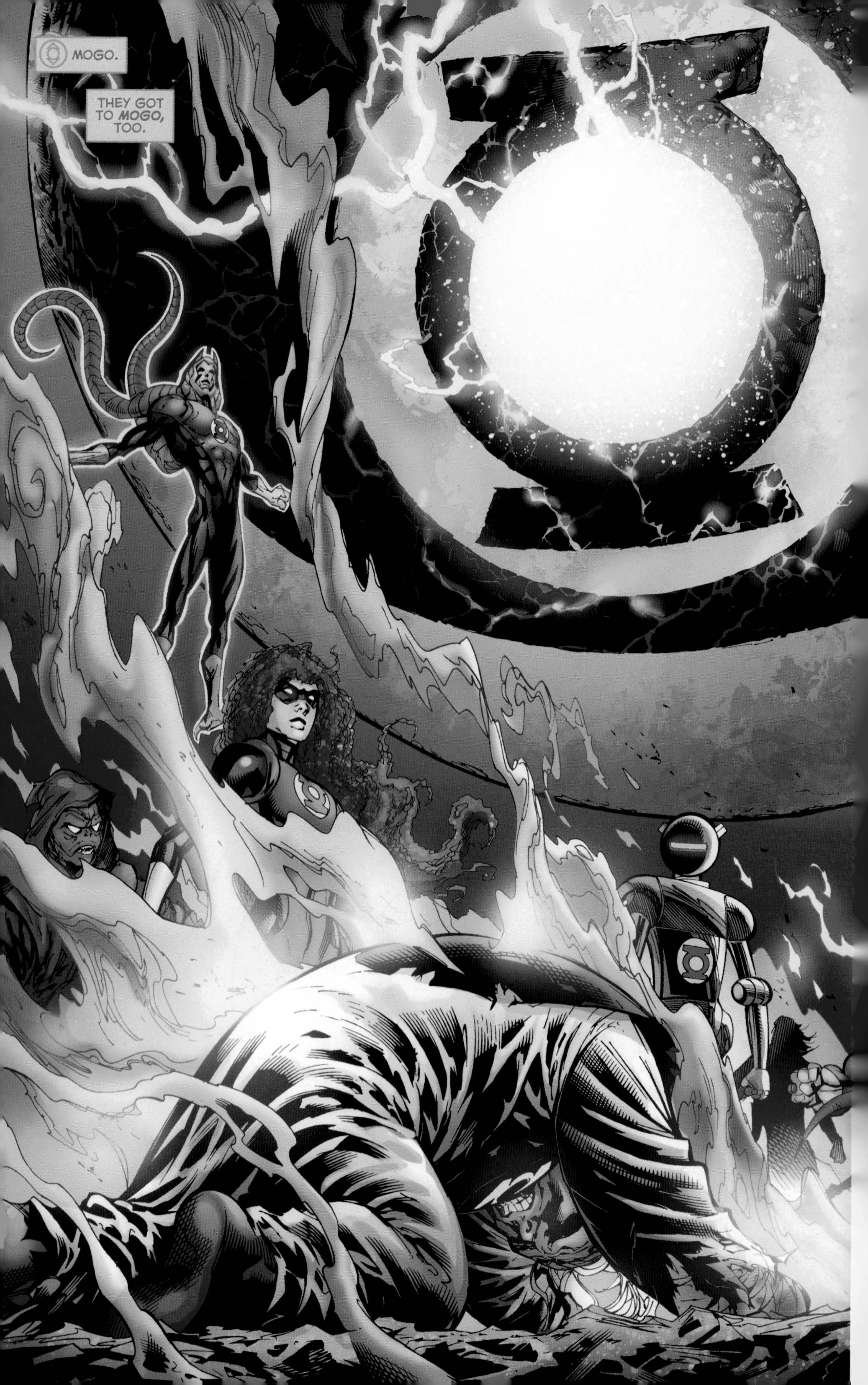

MOGO.
THEY GOT TO MOGO, TOO.

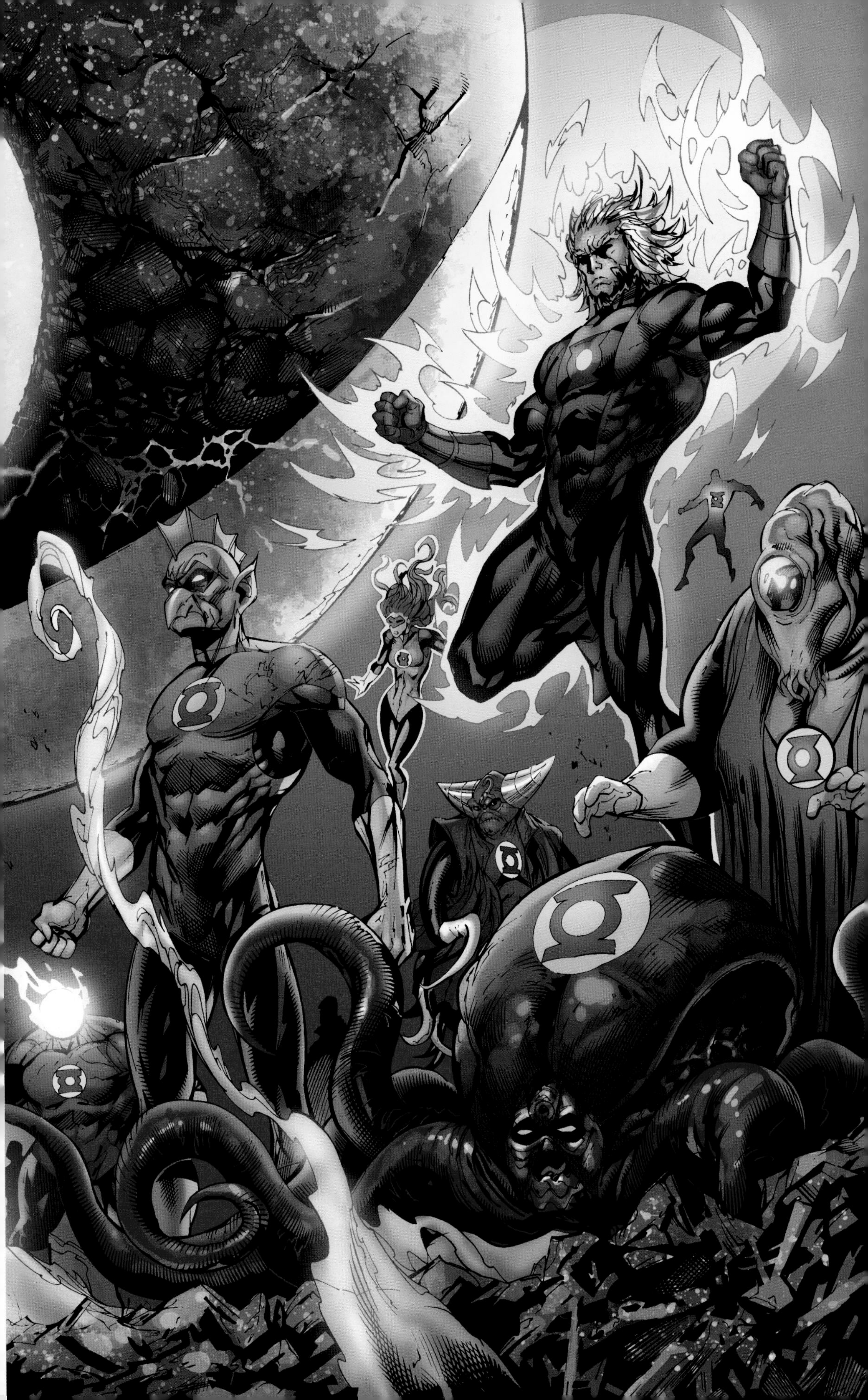

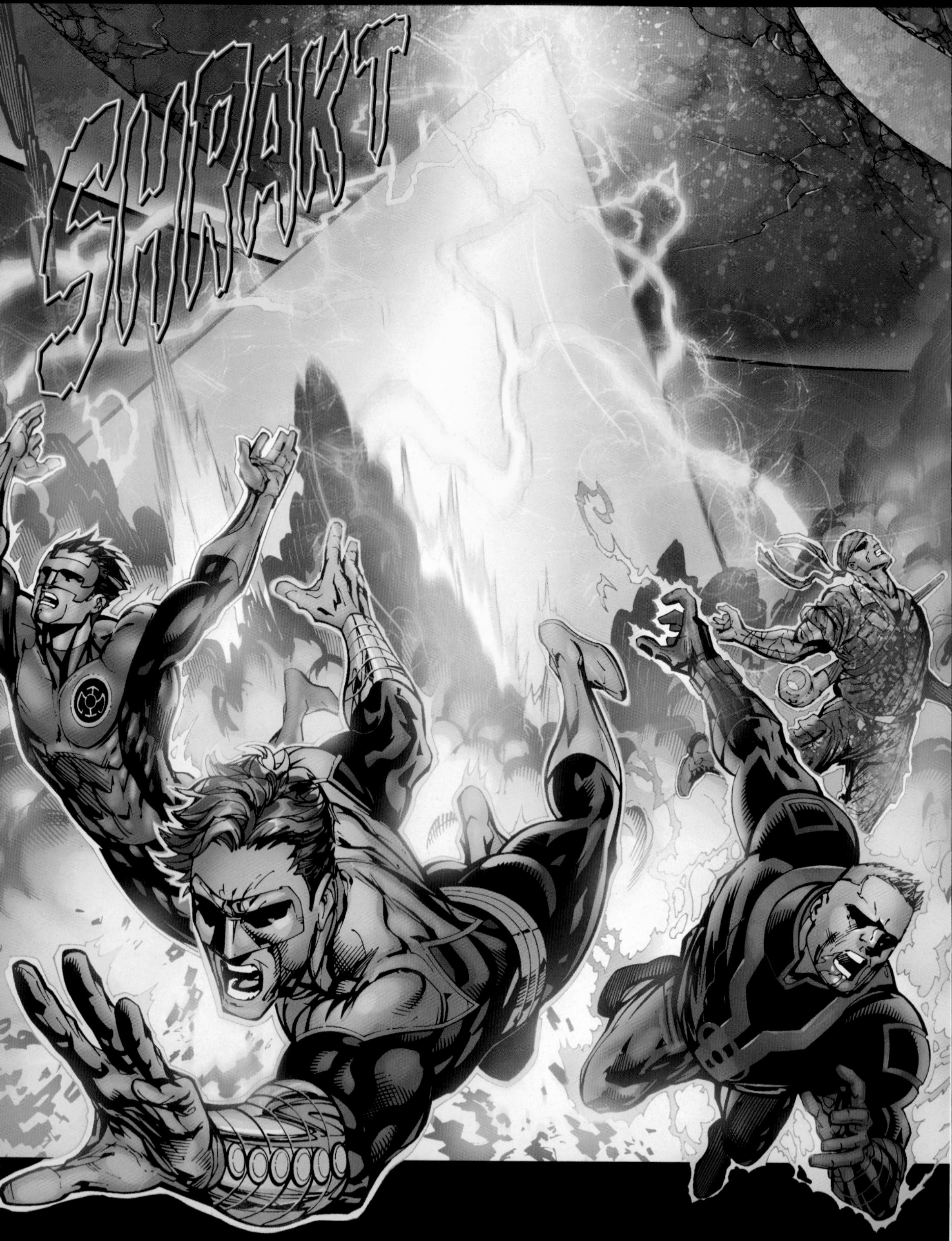
SHRAKT

GREEN LANTERN: EMERALD WARRIORS 8
Cover by Miguel Sepulveda with Gabe Eltaeb

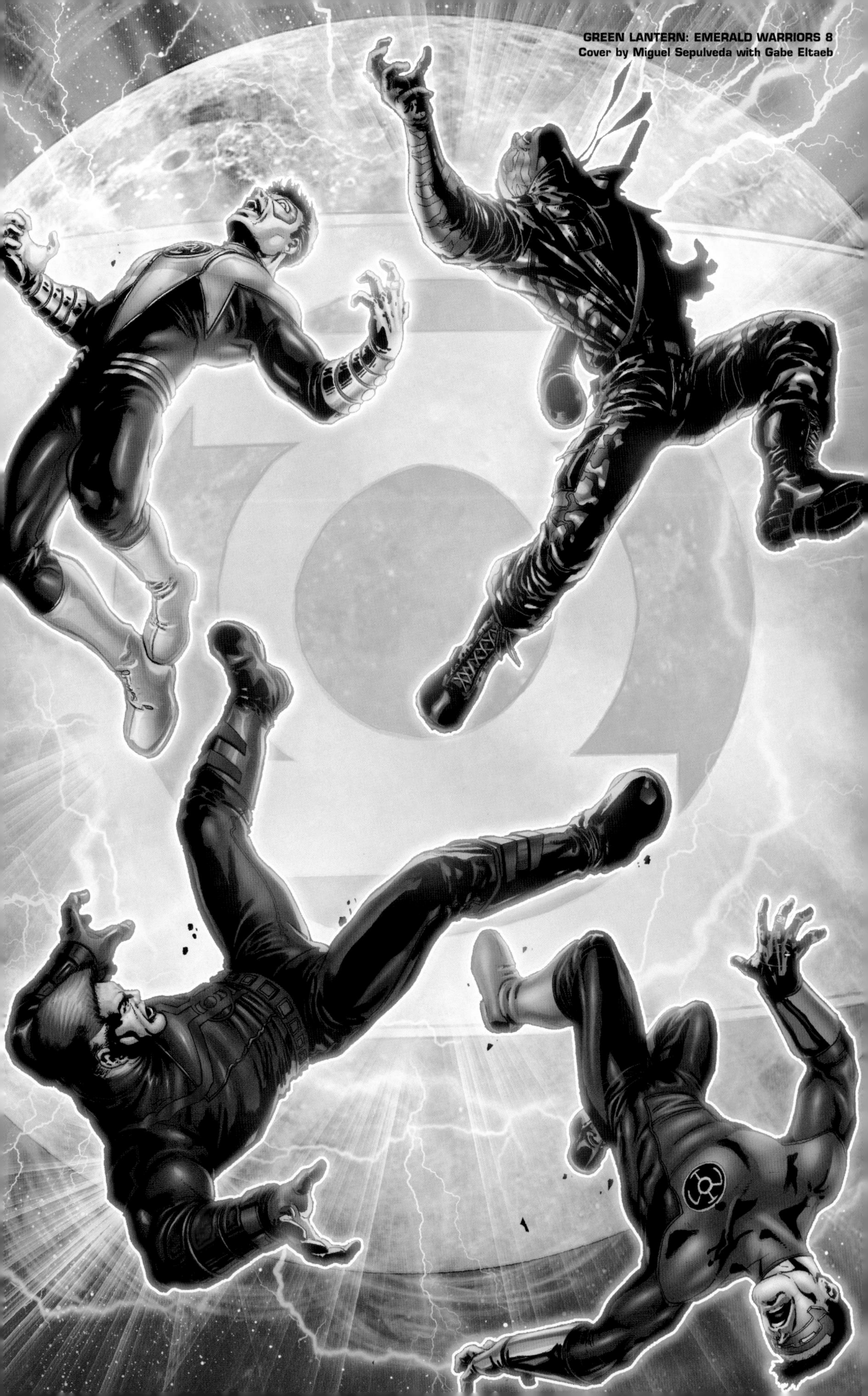

WAR OF THE GREEN LANTERNS
PART SIX

Peter J. Tomasi Writer
Fernando Pasarin Penciller
Cam Smith Inker

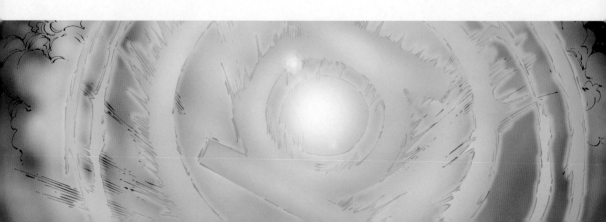

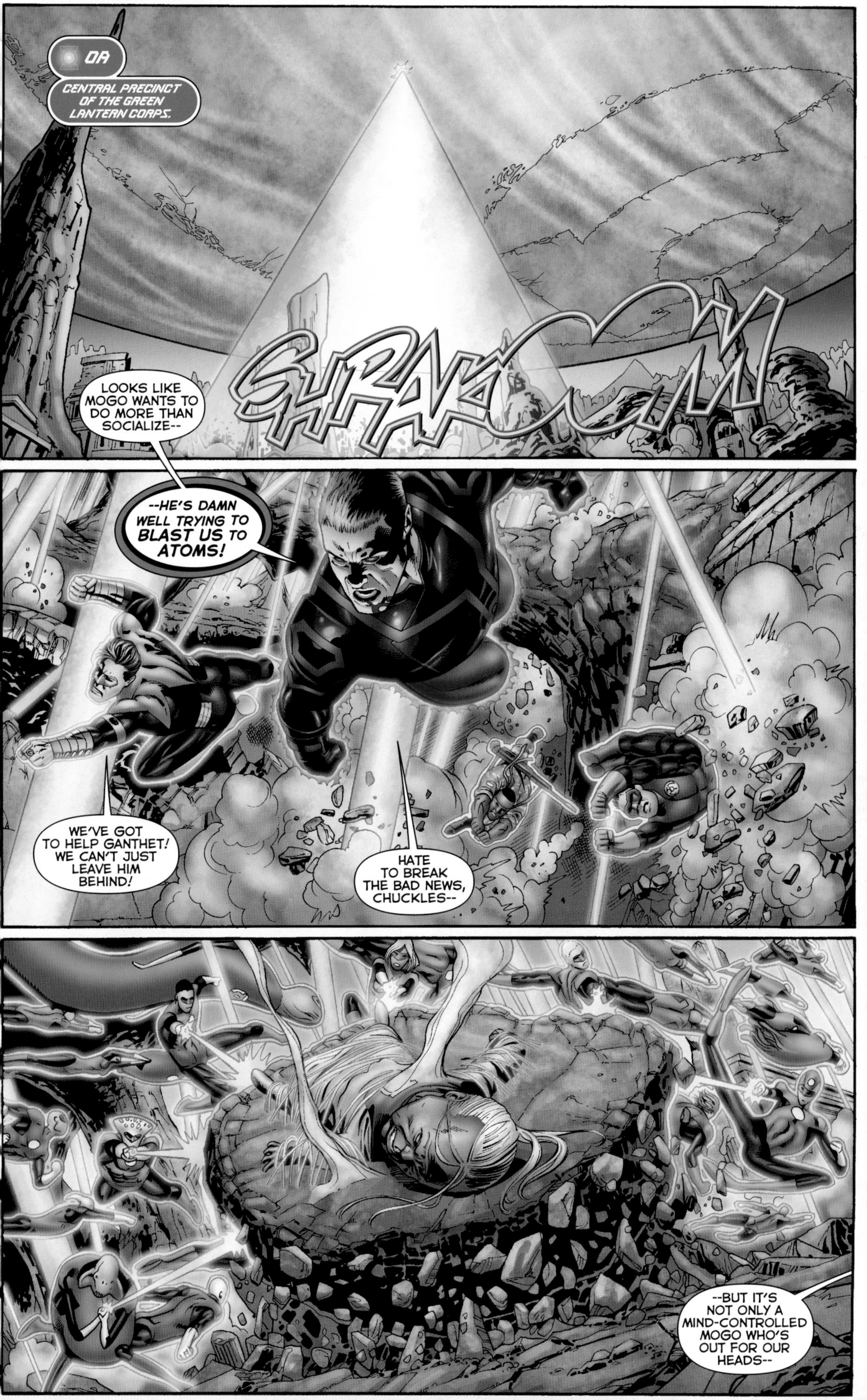
OA
CENTRAL PRECINCT OF THE GREEN LANTERN CORPS.
SHRAKOOOM
LOOKS LIKE MOGO WANTS TO DO MORE THAN SOCIALIZE--
--HE'S DAMN WELL TRYING TO BLAST US TO ATOMS!
WE'VE GOT TO HELP GANTHET! WE CAN'T JUST LEAVE HIM BEHIND!
HATE TO BREAK THE BAD NEWS, CHUCKLES--
--BUT IT'S NOT ONLY A MIND-CONTROLLED MOGO WHO'S OUT FOR OUR HEADS--

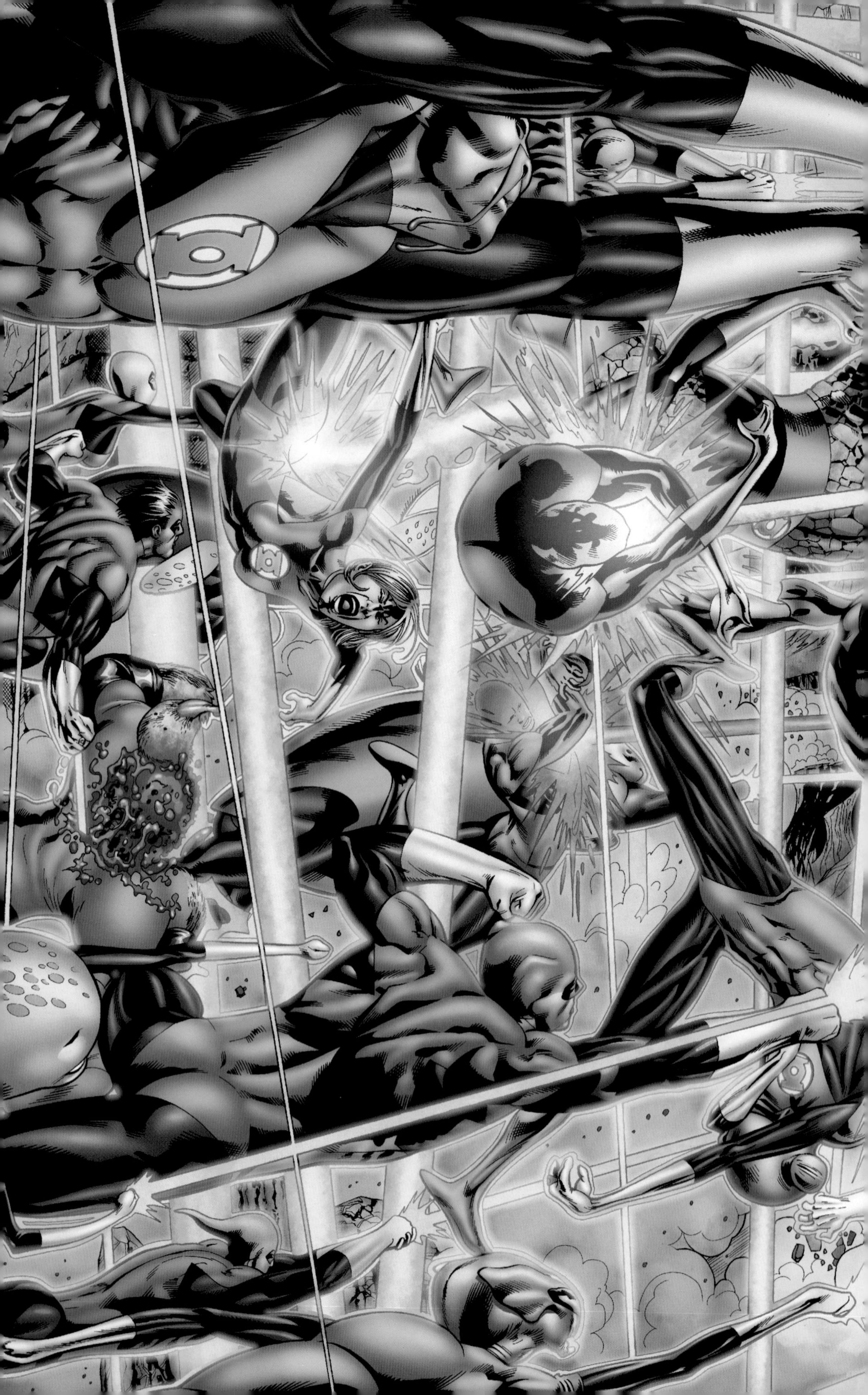

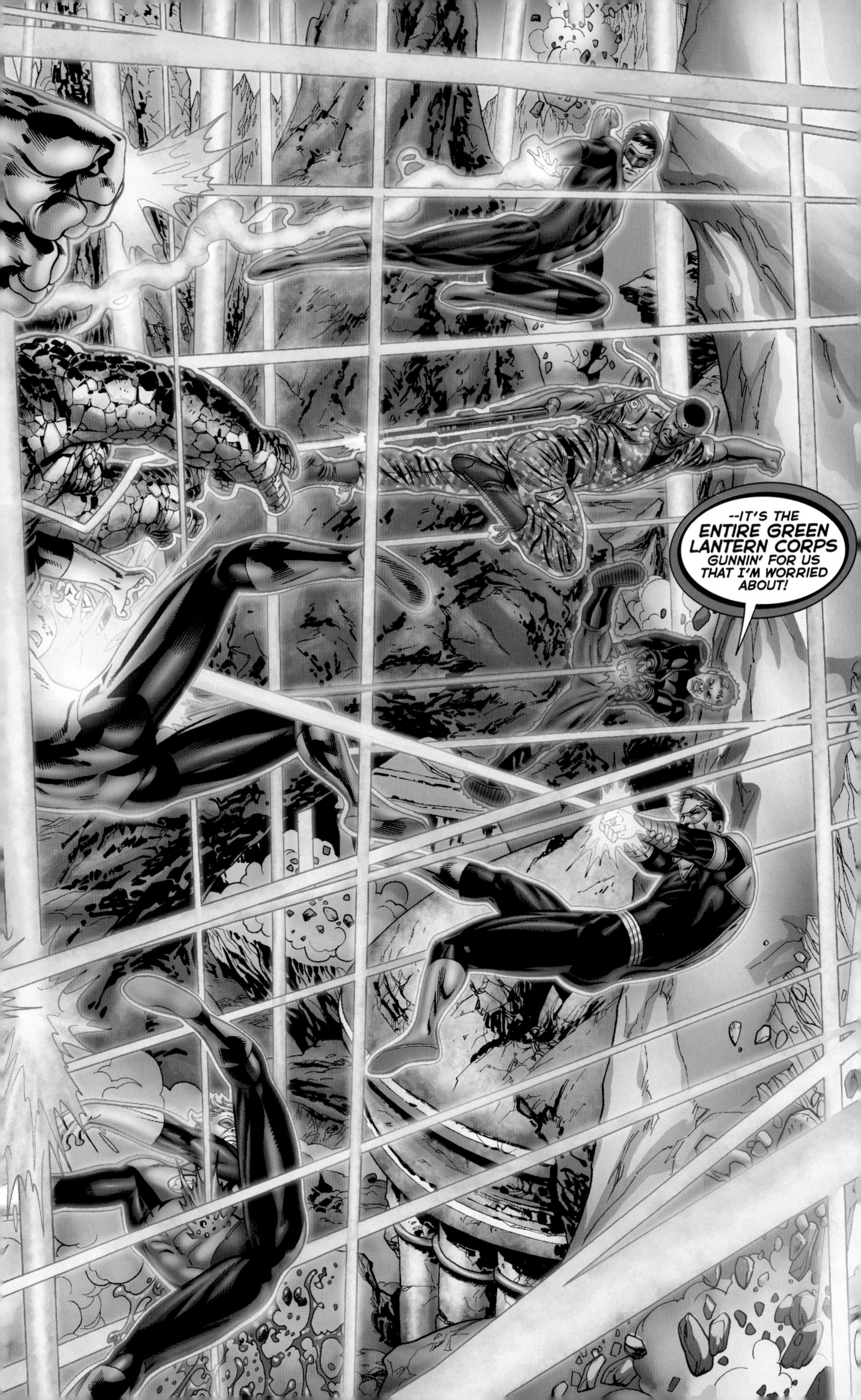
--IT'S THE ENTIRE GREEN LANTERN CORPS GUNNIN' FOR US THAT I'M WORRIED ABOUT!

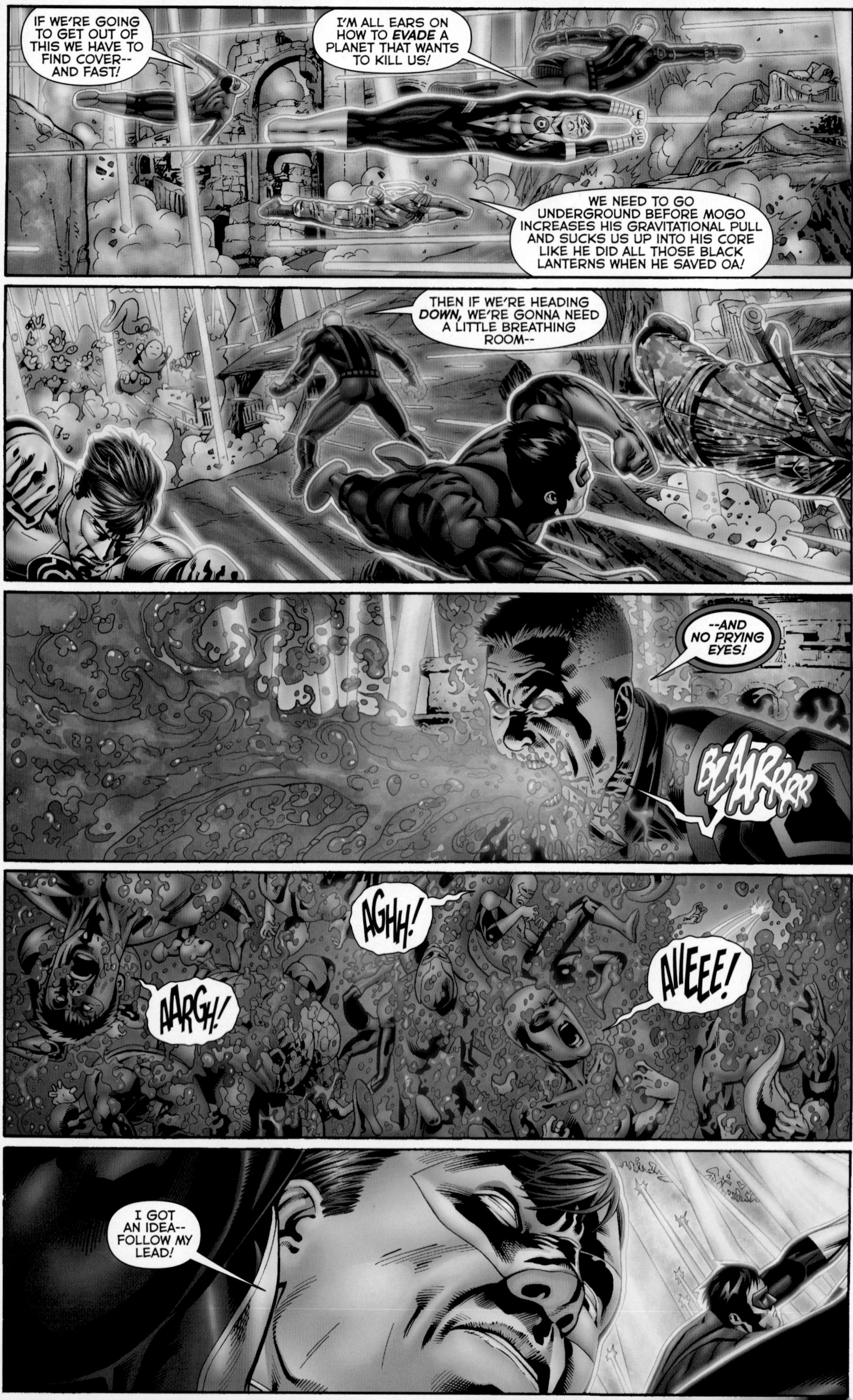
IF WE'RE GOING TO GET OUT OF THIS WE HAVE TO FIND COVER-- AND FAST!
I'M ALL EARS ON HOW TO EVADE A PLANET THAT WANTS TO KILL US!
WE NEED TO GO UNDERGROUND BEFORE MOGO INCREASES HIS GRAVITATIONAL PULL AND SUCKS US UP INTO HIS CORE LIKE HE DID ALL THOSE BLACK LANTERNS WHEN HE SAVED OA!
THEN IF WE'RE HEADING DOWN, WE'RE GONNA NEED A LITTLE BREATHING ROOM--
--AND NO PRYING EYES!
BLAARRRR
AGHH!
AARGH!
AIIEEE!
I GOT AN IDEA-- FOLLOW MY LEAD!

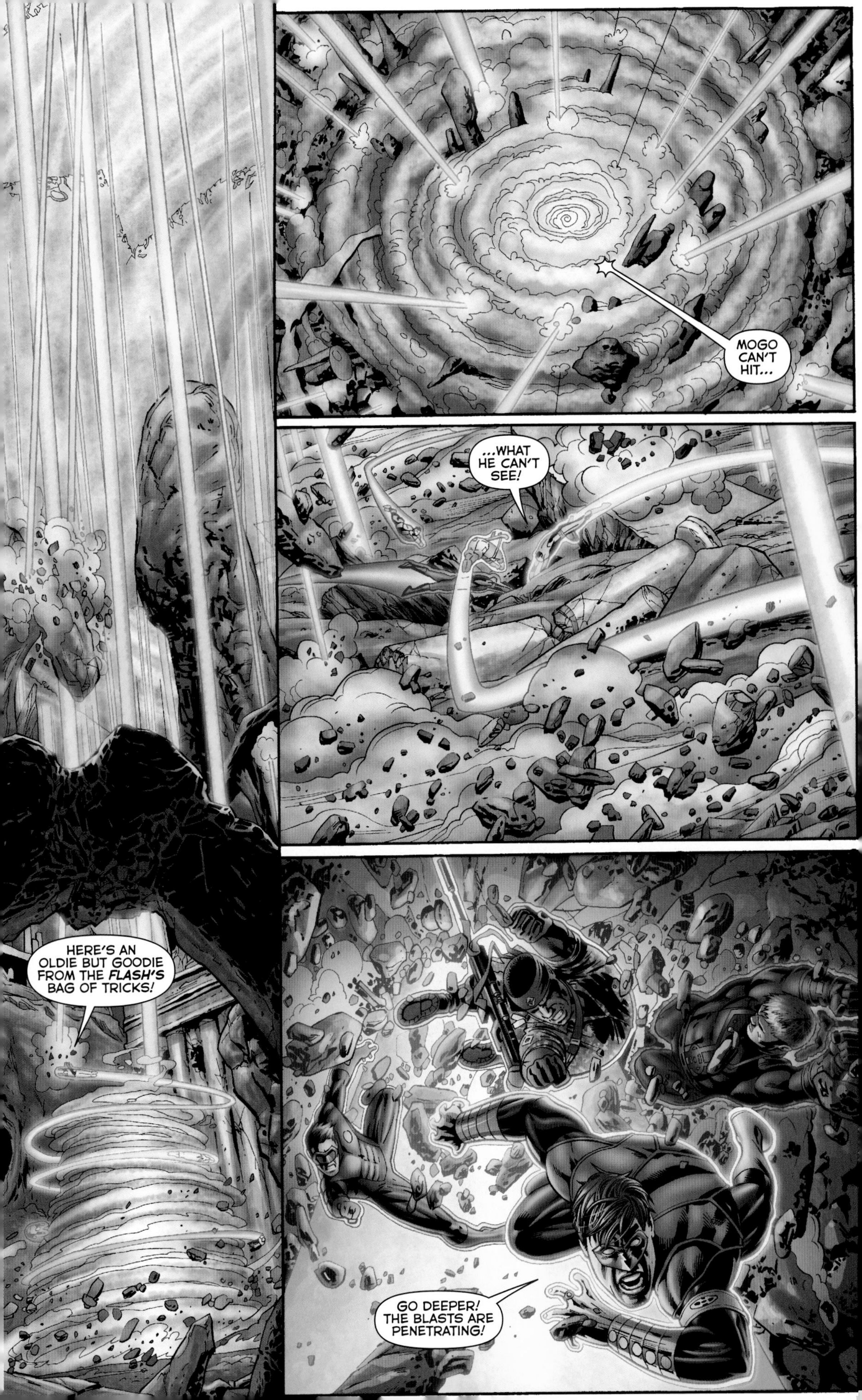
MOGO CAN'T HIT...
...WHAT HE CAN'T SEE!
HERE'S AN OLDIE BUT GOODIE FROM THE FLASH'S BAG OF TRICKS!
GO DEEPER! THE BLASTS ARE PENETRATING!

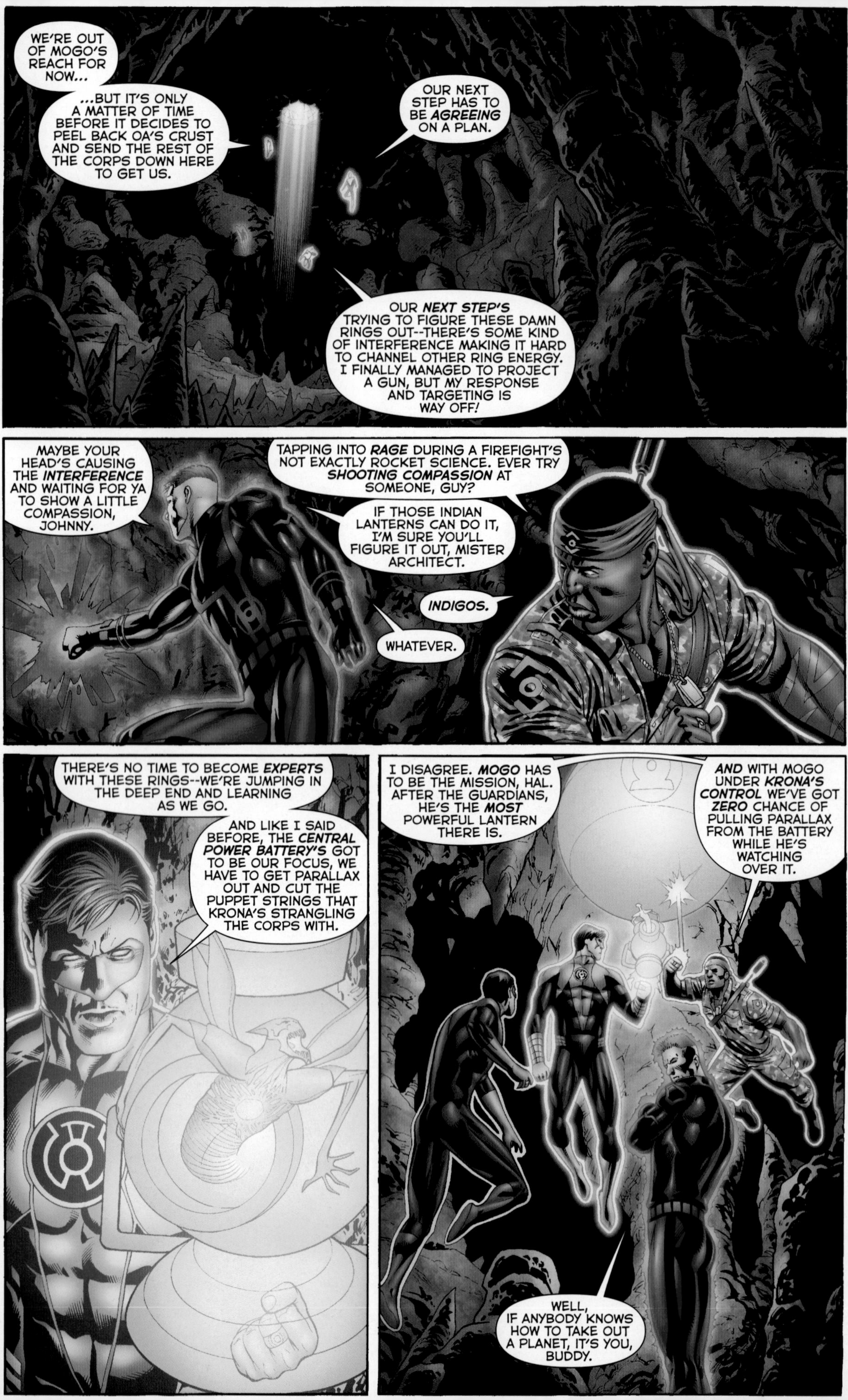
WE'RE OUT OF MOGO'S REACH FOR NOW...
...BUT IT'S ONLY A MATTER OF TIME BEFORE IT DECIDES TO PEEL BACK OA'S CRUST AND SEND THE REST OF THE CORPS DOWN HERE TO GET US.
OUR NEXT STEP HAS TO BE AGREEING ON A PLAN.
OUR NEXT STEP'S TRYING TO FIGURE THESE DAMN RINGS OUT--THERE'S SOME KIND OF INTERFERENCE MAKING IT HARD TO CHANNEL OTHER RING ENERGY. I FINALLY MANAGED TO PROJECT A GUN, BUT MY RESPONSE AND TARGETING IS WAY OFF!
MAYBE YOUR HEAD'S CAUSING THE INTERFERENCE AND WAITING FOR YA TO SHOW A LITTLE COMPASSION, JOHNNY.
TAPPING INTO RAGE DURING A FIREFIGHT'S NOT EXACTLY ROCKET SCIENCE. EVER TRY SHOOTING COMPASSION AT SOMEONE, GUY?
IF THOSE INDIAN LANTERNS CAN DO IT, I'M SURE YOU'LL FIGURE IT OUT, MISTER ARCHITECT.
INDIGOS.
WHATEVER.
THERE'S NO TIME TO BECOME EXPERTS WITH THESE RINGS--WE'RE JUMPING IN THE DEEP END AND LEARNING AS WE GO.
AND LIKE I SAID BEFORE, THE CENTRAL POWER BATTERY'S GOT TO BE OUR FOCUS, WE HAVE TO GET PARALLAX OUT AND CUT THE PUPPET STRINGS THAT KRONA'S STRANGLING THE CORPS WITH.
I DISAGREE. MOGO HAS TO BE THE MISSION, HAL. AFTER THE GUARDIANS, HE'S THE MOST POWERFUL LANTERN THERE IS.
AND WITH MOGO UNDER KRONA'S CONTROL WE'VE GOT ZERO CHANCE OF PULLING PARALLAX FROM THE BATTERY WHILE HE'S WATCHING OVER IT.
WELL, IF ANYBODY KNOWS HOW TO TAKE OUT A PLANET, IT'S YOU, BUDDY.

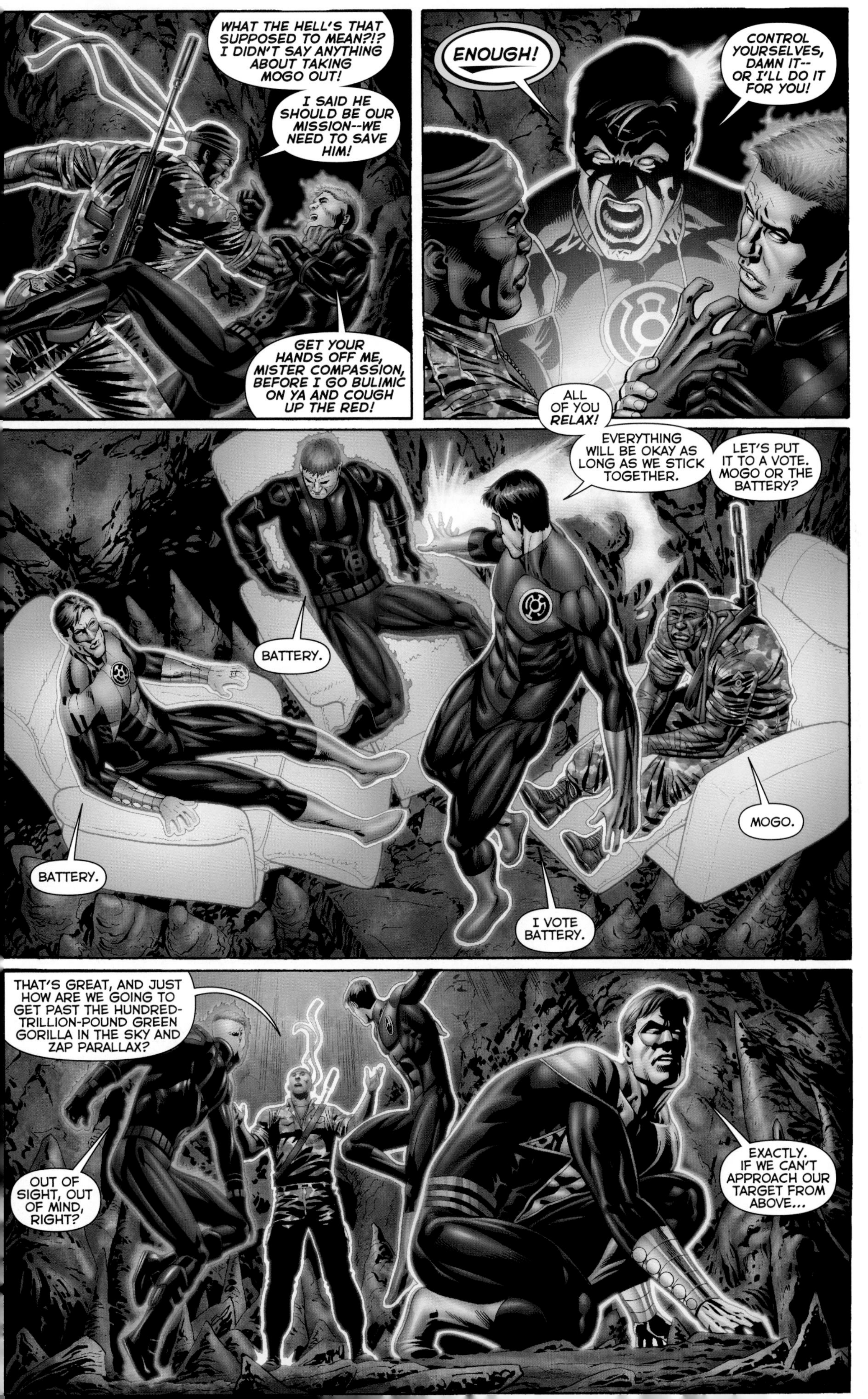
WHAT THE HELL'S THAT SUPPOSED TO MEAN?!? I DIDN'T SAY ANYTHING ABOUT TAKING MOGO OUT!
I SAID HE SHOULD BE OUR MISSION--WE NEED TO SAVE HIM!
GET YOUR HANDS OFF ME, MISTER COMPASSION, BEFORE I GO BULIMIC ON YA AND COUGH UP THE RED!
ENOUGH!
CONTROL YOURSELVES, DAMN IT-- OR I'LL DO IT FOR YOU!
ALL OF YOU RELAX!
EVERYTHING WILL BE OKAY AS LONG AS WE STICK TOGETHER.
LET'S PUT IT TO A VOTE. MOGO OR THE BATTERY?
BATTERY.
BATTERY.
MOGO.
I VOTE BATTERY.
THAT'S GREAT, AND JUST HOW ARE WE GOING TO GET PAST THE HUNDRED-TRILLION-POUND GREEN GORILLA IN THE SKY AND ZAP PARALLAX?
OUT OF SIGHT, OUT OF MIND, RIGHT?
EXACTLY. IF WE CAN'T APPROACH OUR TARGET FROM ABOVE...

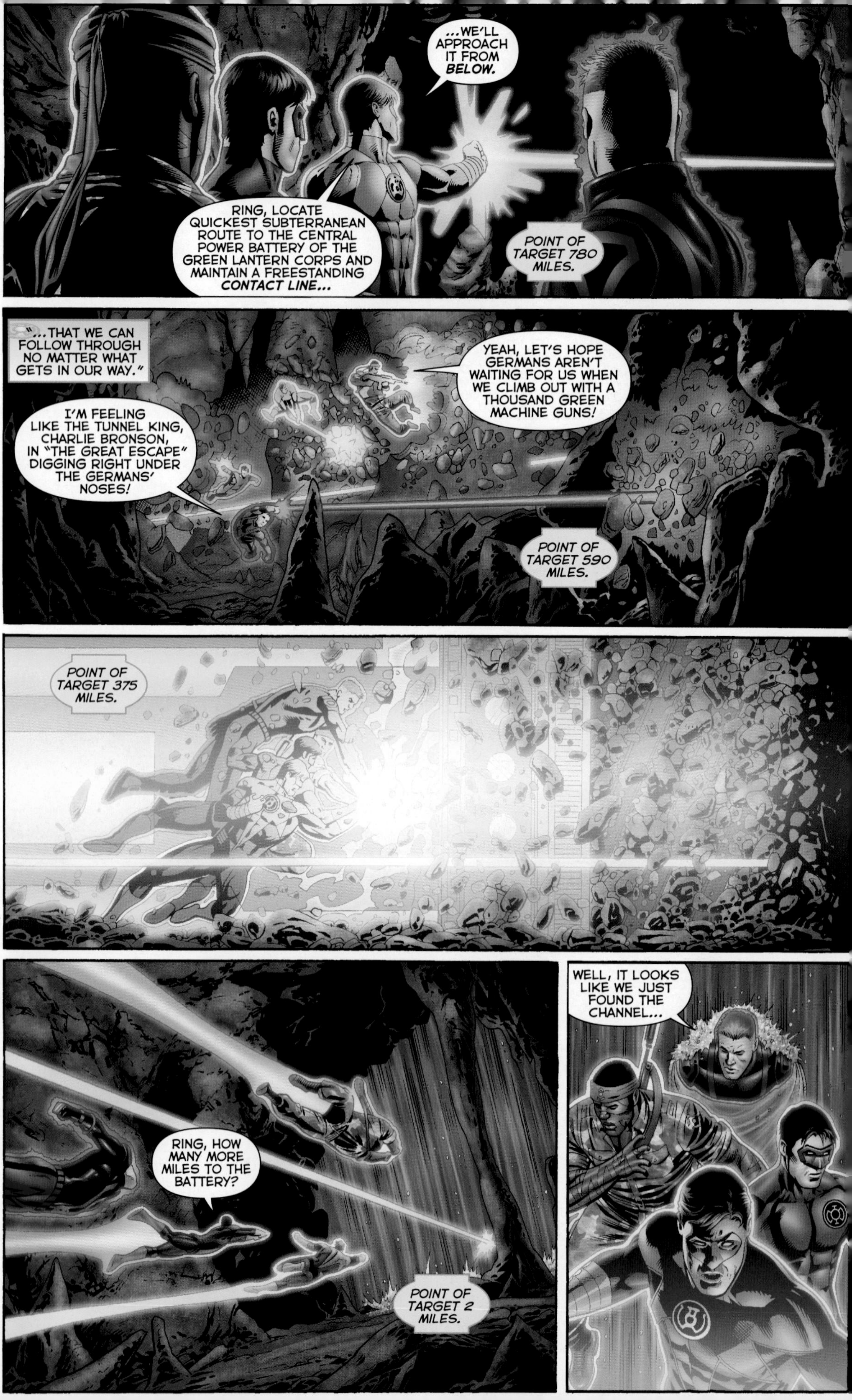

...WE'LL APPROACH IT FROM BELOW.
RING, LOCATE QUICKEST SUBTERRANEAN ROUTE TO THE CENTRAL POWER BATTERY OF THE GREEN LANTERN CORPS AND MAINTAIN A FREESTANDING CONTACT LINE...
POINT OF TARGET 780 MILES.
"...THAT WE CAN FOLLOW THROUGH NO MATTER WHAT GETS IN OUR WAY."
YEAH, LET'S HOPE GERMANS AREN'T WAITING FOR US WHEN WE CLIMB OUT WITH A THOUSAND GREEN MACHINE GUNS!
I'M FEELING LIKE THE TUNNEL KING, CHARLIE BRONSON, IN "THE GREAT ESCAPE" DIGGING RIGHT UNDER THE GERMANS' NOSES!
POINT OF TARGET 590 MILES.
POINT OF TARGET 375 MILES.
RING, HOW MANY MORE MILES TO THE BATTERY?
POINT OF TARGET 2 MILES.
WELL, IT LOOKS LIKE WE JUST FOUND THE CHANNEL...

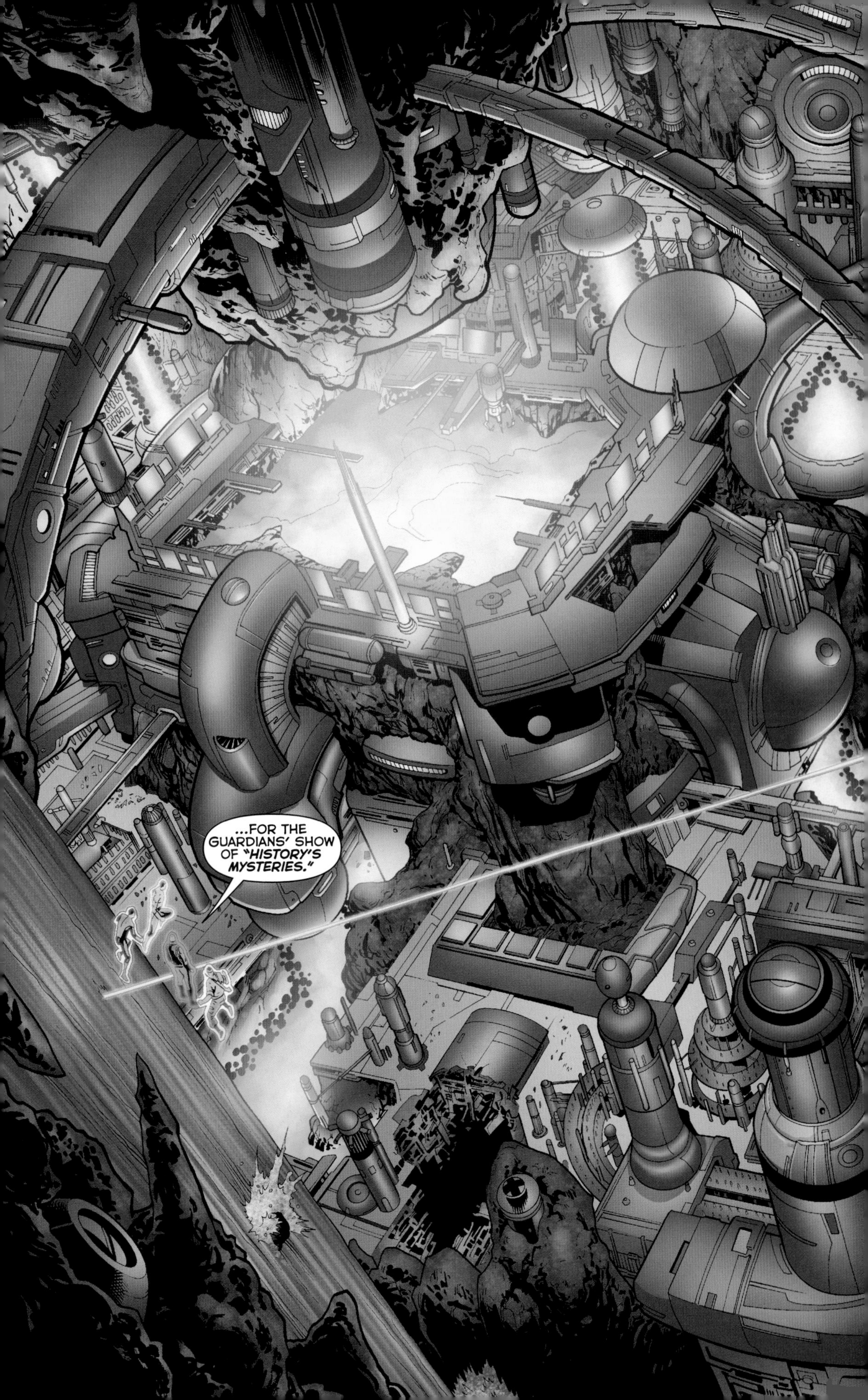
...FOR THE GUARDIANS' SHOW OF "HISTORY'S MYSTERIES."

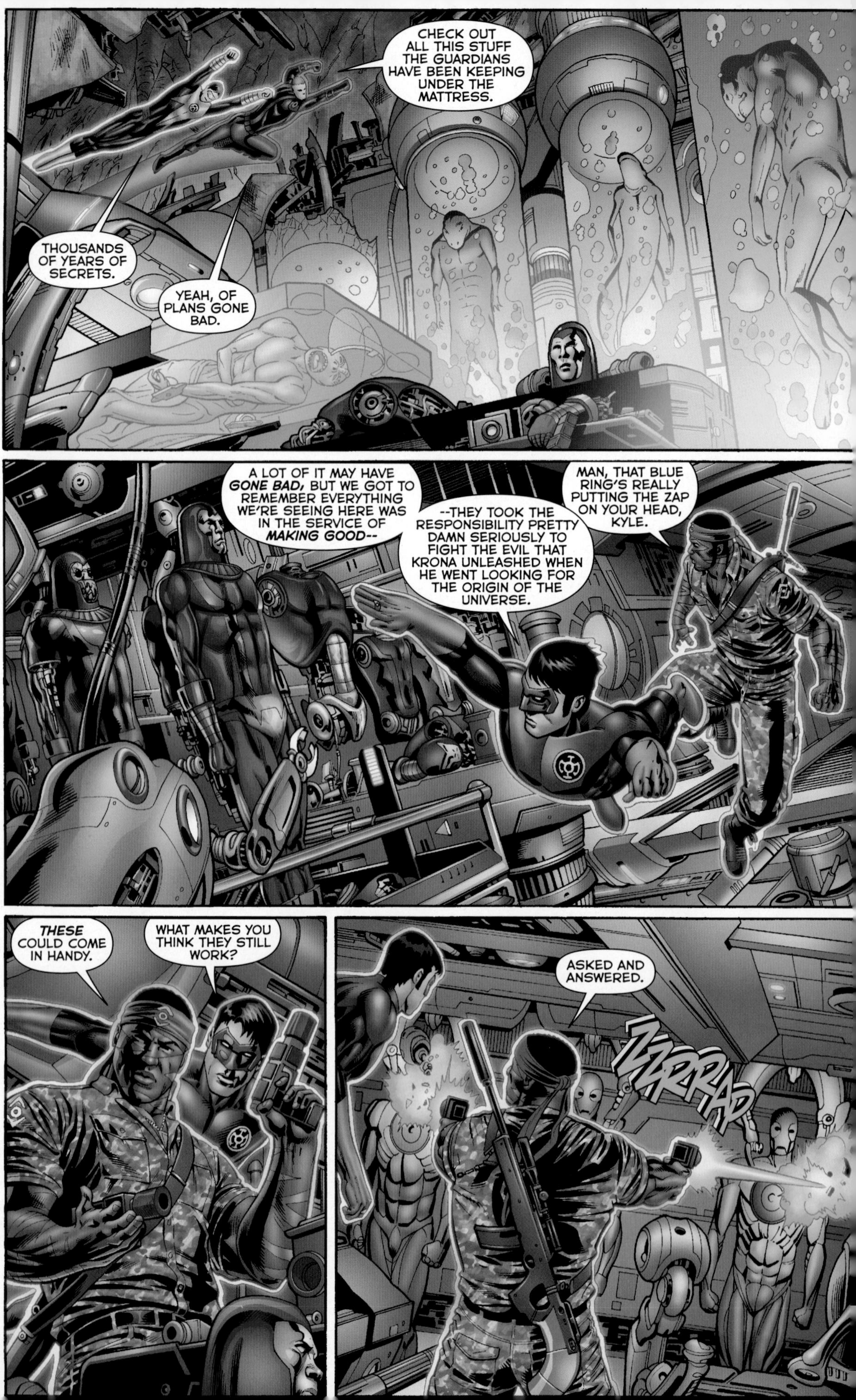
CHECK OUT ALL THIS STUFF THE GUARDIANS HAVE BEEN KEEPING UNDER THE MATTRESS.
THOUSANDS OF YEARS OF SECRETS.
YEAH, OF PLANS GONE BAD.
A LOT OF IT MAY HAVE GONE BAD, BUT WE GOT TO REMEMBER EVERYTHING WE'RE SEEING HERE WAS IN THE SERVICE OF MAKING GOOD--
--THEY TOOK THE RESPONSIBILITY PRETTY DAMN SERIOUSLY TO FIGHT THE EVIL THAT KRONA UNLEASHED WHEN HE WENT LOOKING FOR THE ORIGIN OF THE UNIVERSE.
MAN, THAT BLUE RING'S REALLY PUTTING THE ZAP ON YOUR HEAD, KYLE.
THESE COULD COME IN HANDY.
WHAT MAKES YOU THINK THEY STILL WORK?
ASKED AND ANSWERED.
ZZZRRAP

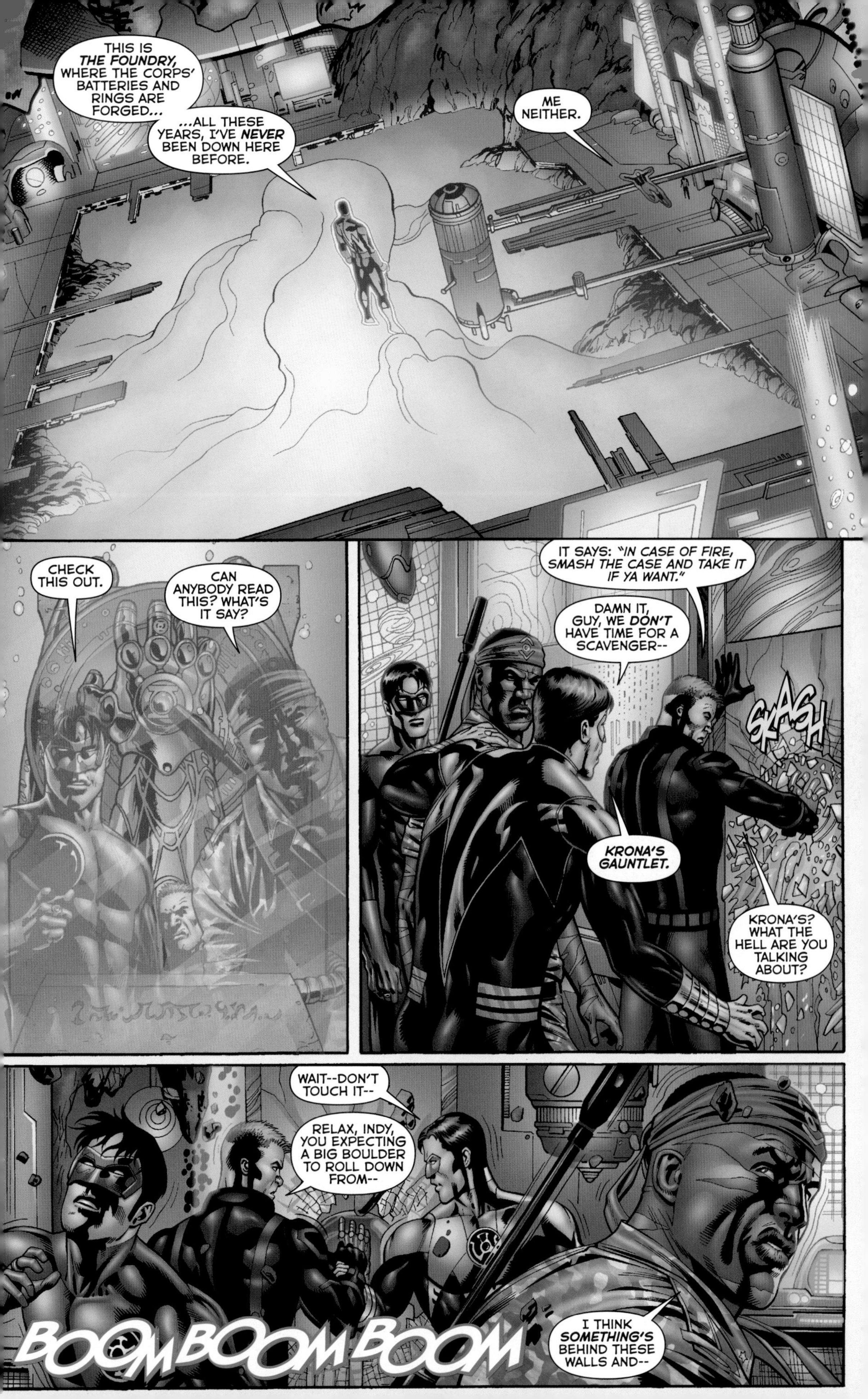
THIS IS THE FOUNDRY, WHERE THE CORPS' BATTERIES AND RINGS ARE FORGED...
...ALL THESE YEARS, I'VE NEVER BEEN DOWN HERE BEFORE.
ME NEITHER.
CHECK THIS OUT.
CAN ANYBODY READ THIS? WHAT'S IT SAY?
IT SAYS: "IN CASE OF FIRE, SMASH THE CASE AND TAKE IT IF YA WANT."
DAMN IT, GUY, WE DON'T HAVE TIME FOR A SCAVENGER--
SKASH
KRONA'S GAUNTLET.
KRONA'S? WHAT THE HELL ARE YOU TALKING ABOUT?
WAIT--DON'T TOUCH IT--
RELAX, INDY, YOU EXPECTING A BIG BOULDER TO ROLL DOWN FROM--
BOOM BOOM BOOM
I THINK SOMETHING'S BEHIND THESE WALLS AND--

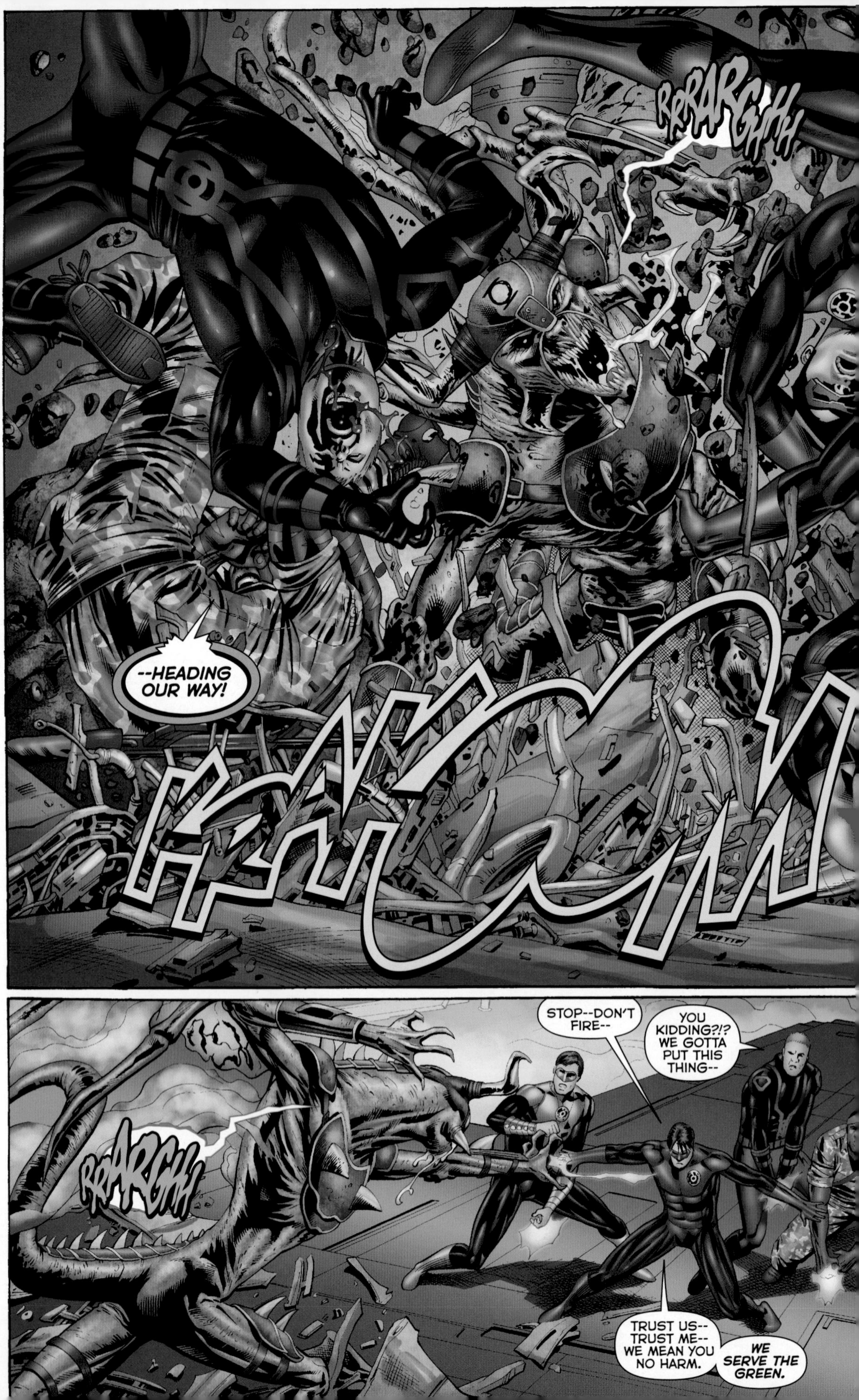
RRRARGHHH
--HEADING OUR WAY!
KRAKOOM
STOP--DON'T FIRE--
YOU KIDDING?!? WE GOTTA PUT THIS THING--
RRARGHH
TRUST US-- TRUST ME-- WE MEAN YOU NO HARM.
WE SERVE THE GREEN.

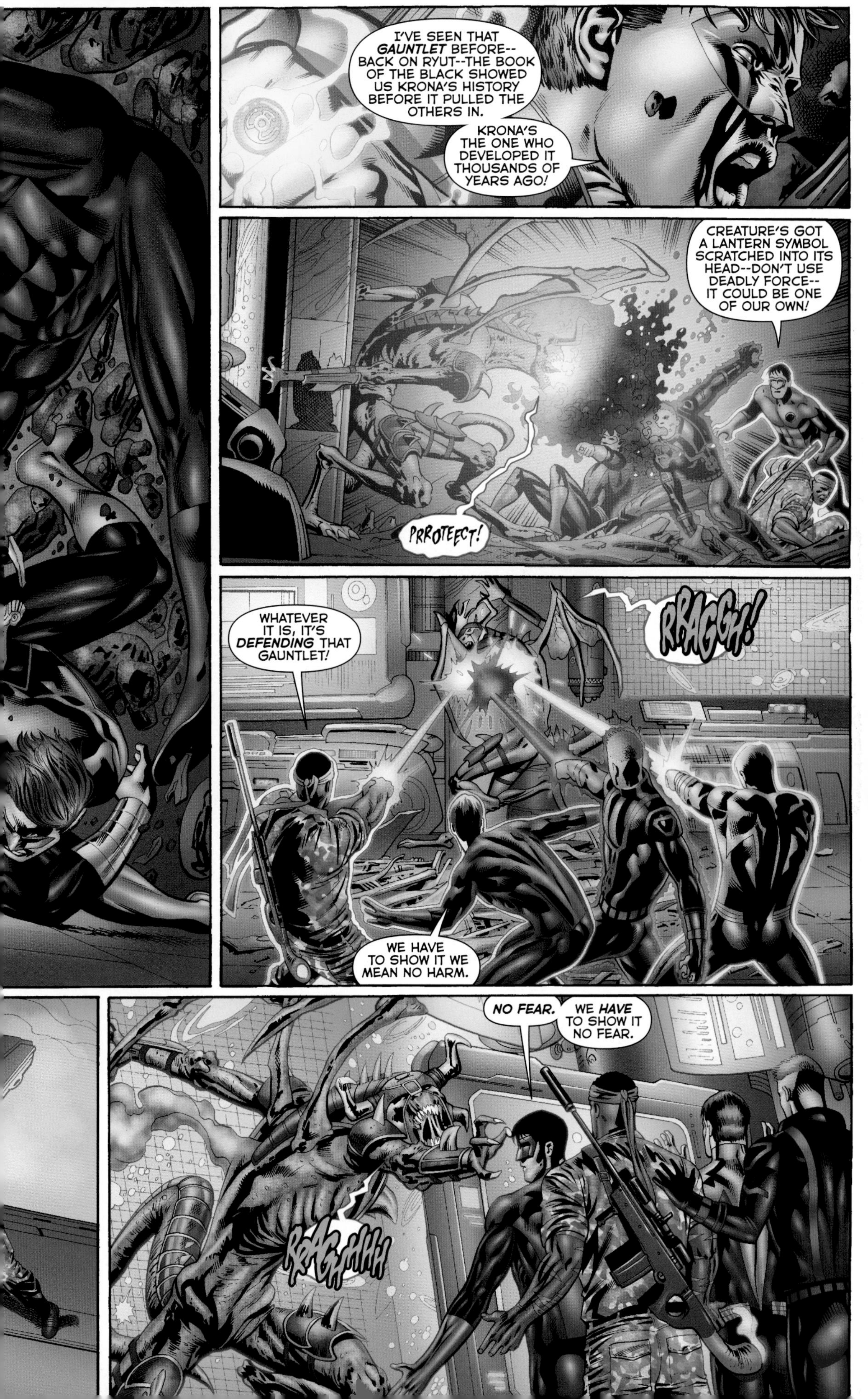
I'VE SEEN THAT GAUNTLET BEFORE--BACK ON RYUT--THE BOOK OF THE BLACK SHOWED US KRONA'S HISTORY BEFORE IT PULLED THE OTHERS IN.
KRONA'S THE ONE WHO DEVELOPED IT THOUSANDS OF YEARS AGO!
CREATURE'S GOT A LANTERN SYMBOL SCRATCHED INTO ITS HEAD--DON'T USE DEADLY FORCE--IT COULD BE ONE OF OUR OWN!
PRROTEECT!
WHATEVER IT IS, IT'S DEFENDING THAT GAUNTLET!
RRAGGH!
WE HAVE TO SHOW IT WE MEAN NO HARM.
NO FEAR.
WE HAVE TO SHOW IT NO FEAR.
RRAGHHHH

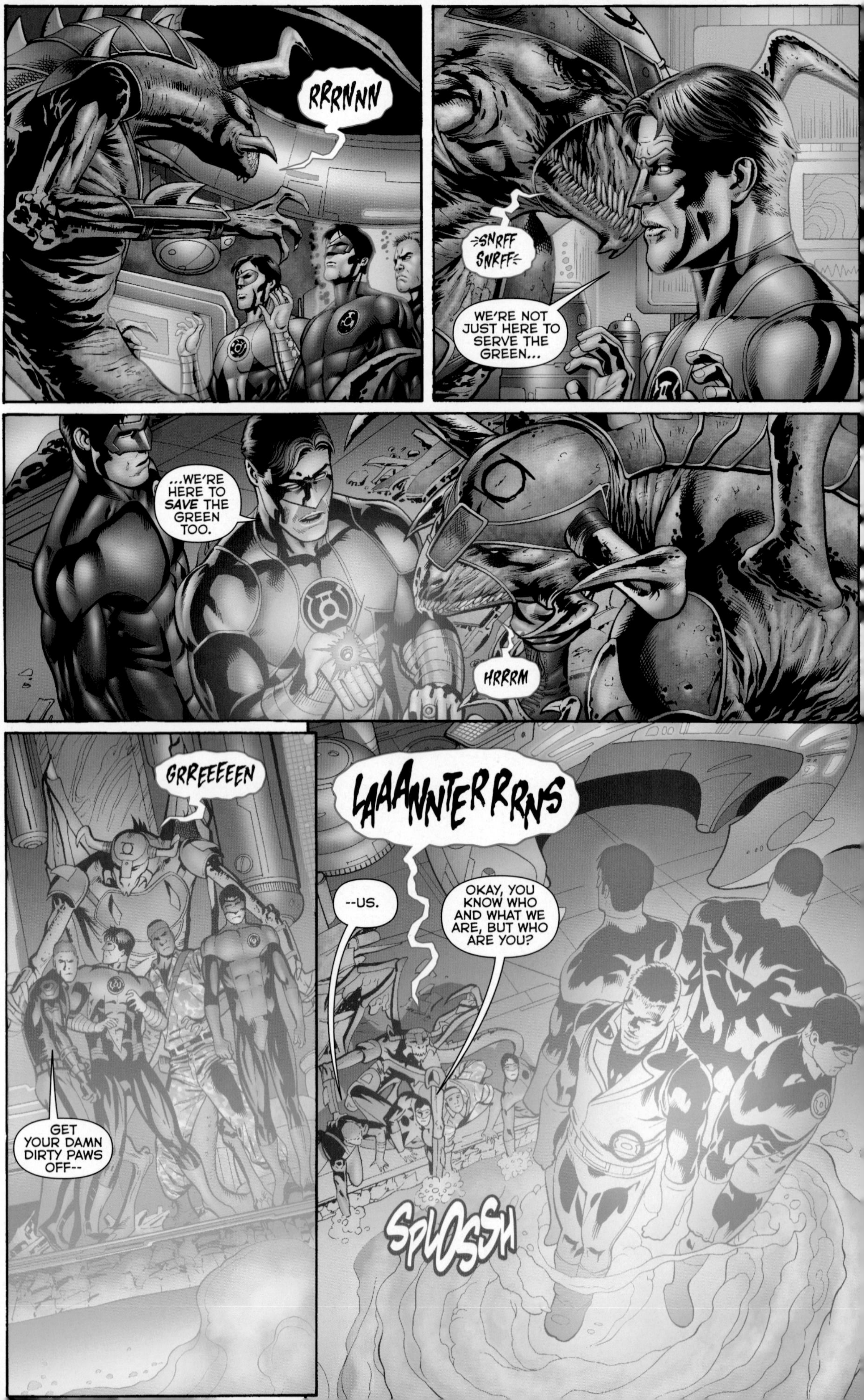
RRRNNN
SNRFF SNRFF
WE'RE NOT JUST HERE TO SERVE THE GREEN...
...WE'RE HERE TO SAVE THE GREEN TOO.
HRRRM
GRREEEEEN
GET YOUR DAMN DIRTY PAWS OFF--
LAAANNTERRRNS
--US.
OKAY, YOU KNOW WHO AND WHAT WE ARE, BUT WHO ARE YOU?
SPLOSSH

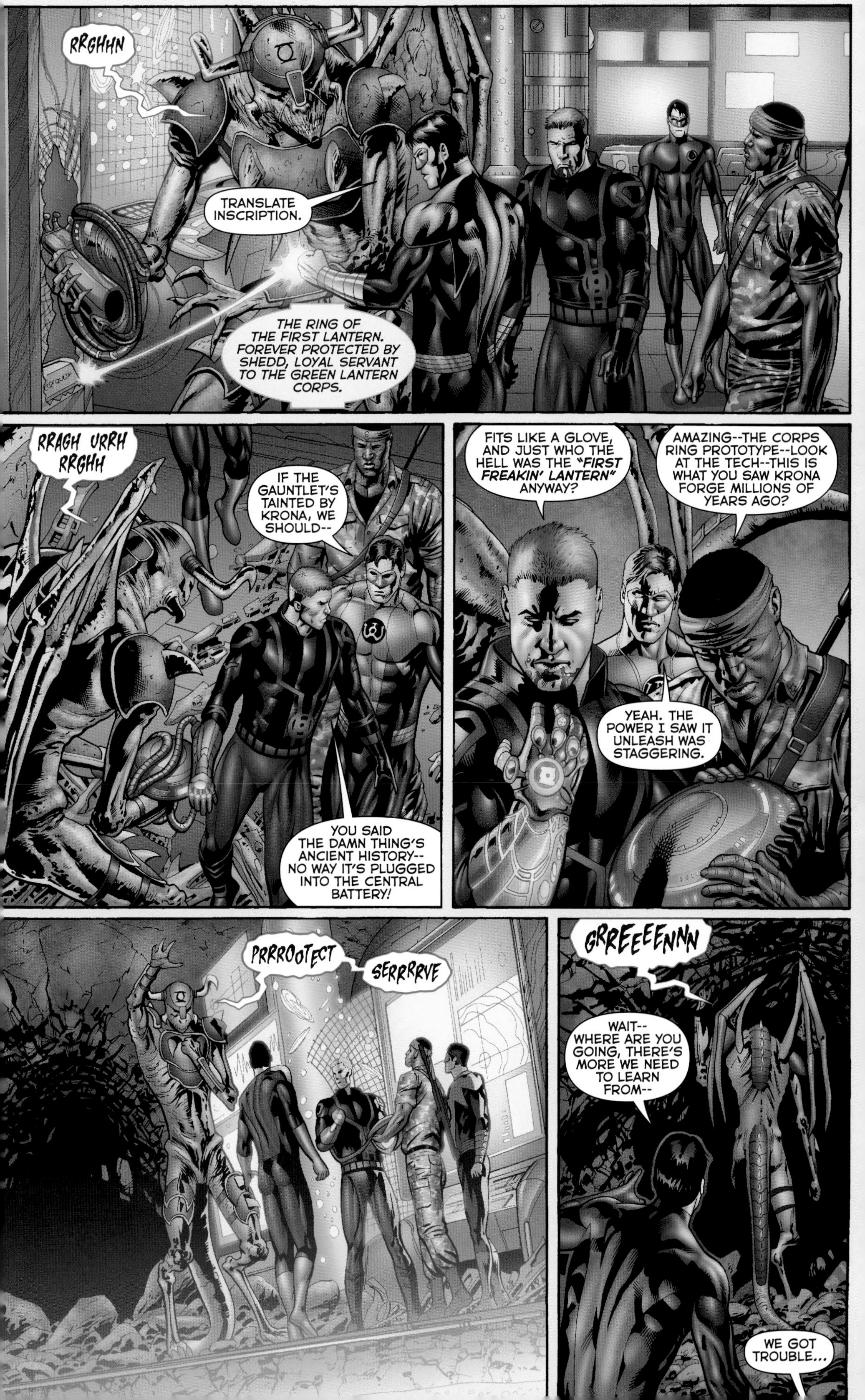
RRGHHN
TRANSLATE INSCRIPTION.
THE RING OF THE FIRST LANTERN. FOREVER PROTECTED BY SHEDD, LOYAL SERVANT TO THE GREEN LANTERN CORPS.
RRAGH URRH RRGHH
IF THE GAUNTLET'S TAINTED BY KRONA, WE SHOULD--
YOU SAID THE DAMN THING'S ANCIENT HISTORY-- NO WAY IT'S PLUGGED INTO THE CENTRAL BATTERY!
FITS LIKE A GLOVE, AND JUST WHO THE HELL WAS THE "FIRST FREAKIN' LANTERN" ANYWAY?
AMAZING--THE CORPS RING PROTOTYPE--LOOK AT THE TECH--THIS IS WHAT YOU SAW KRONA FORGE MILLIONS OF YEARS AGO?
YEAH. THE POWER I SAW IT UNLEASH WAS STAGGERING.
PRRROOTECT
SERRRRVE
GRREEEENNN
WAIT-- WHERE ARE YOU GOING, THERE'S MORE WE NEED TO LEARN FROM--
WE GOT TROUBLE...

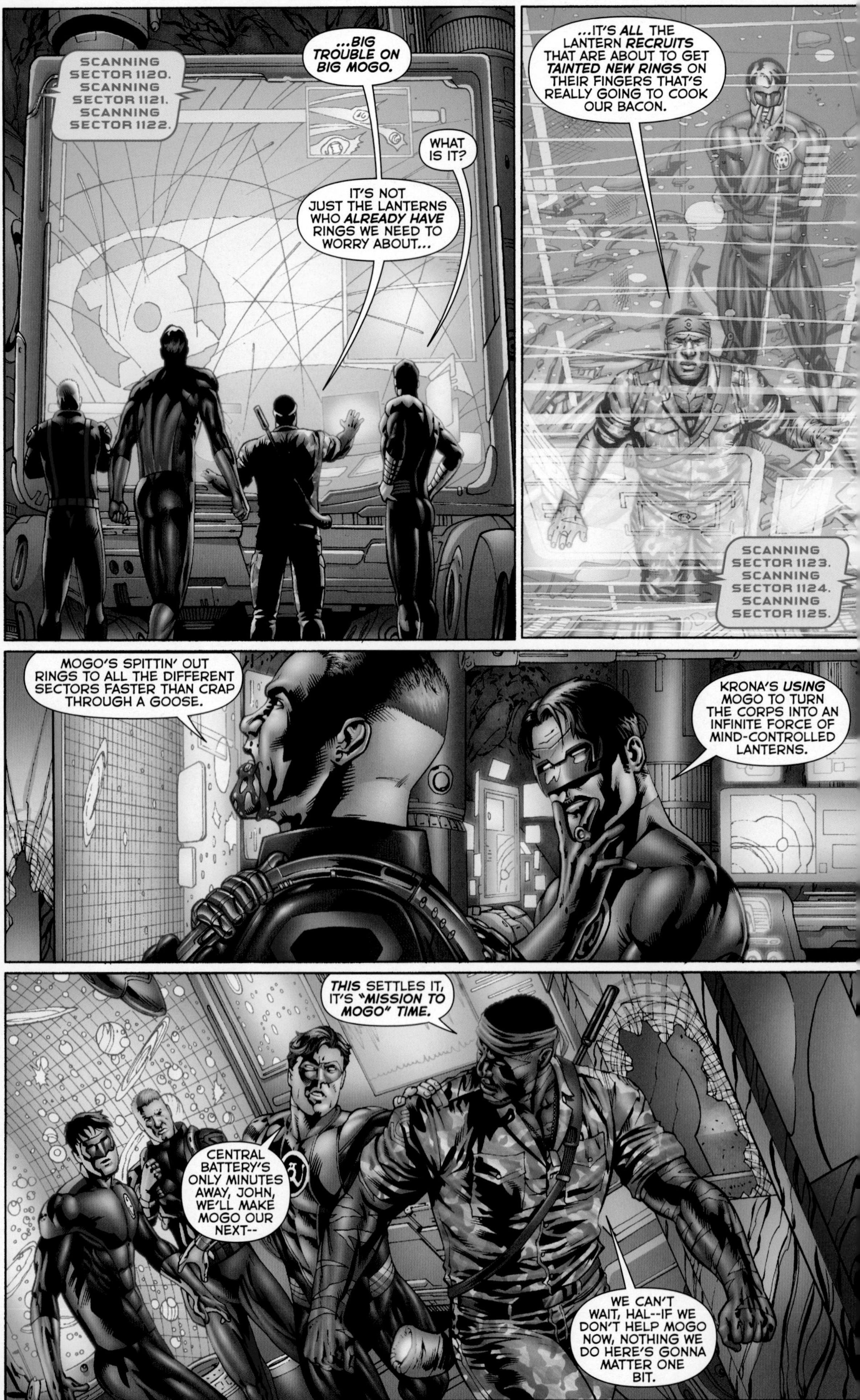
SCANNING SECTOR 1120. SCANNING SECTOR 1121. SCANNING SECTOR 1122.
...BIG TROUBLE ON BIG MOGO.
WHAT IS IT?
IT'S NOT JUST THE LANTERNS WHO ALREADY HAVE RINGS WE NEED TO WORRY ABOUT...
...IT'S ALL THE LANTERN RECRUITS THAT ARE ABOUT TO GET TAINTED NEW RINGS ON THEIR FINGERS THAT'S REALLY GOING TO COOK OUR BACON.
SCANNING SECTOR 1123. SCANNING SECTOR 1124. SCANNING SECTOR 1125.
MOGO'S SPITTIN' OUT RINGS TO ALL THE DIFFERENT SECTORS FASTER THAN CRAP THROUGH A GOOSE.
KRONA'S USING MOGO TO TURN THE CORPS INTO AN INFINITE FORCE OF MIND-CONTROLLED LANTERNS.
THIS SETTLES IT, IT'S "MISSION TO MOGO" TIME.
CENTRAL BATTERY'S ONLY MINUTES AWAY, JOHN, WE'LL MAKE MOGO OUR NEXT--
WE CAN'T WAIT, HAL--IF WE DON'T HELP MOGO NOW, NOTHING WE DO HERE'S GONNA MATTER ONE BIT.

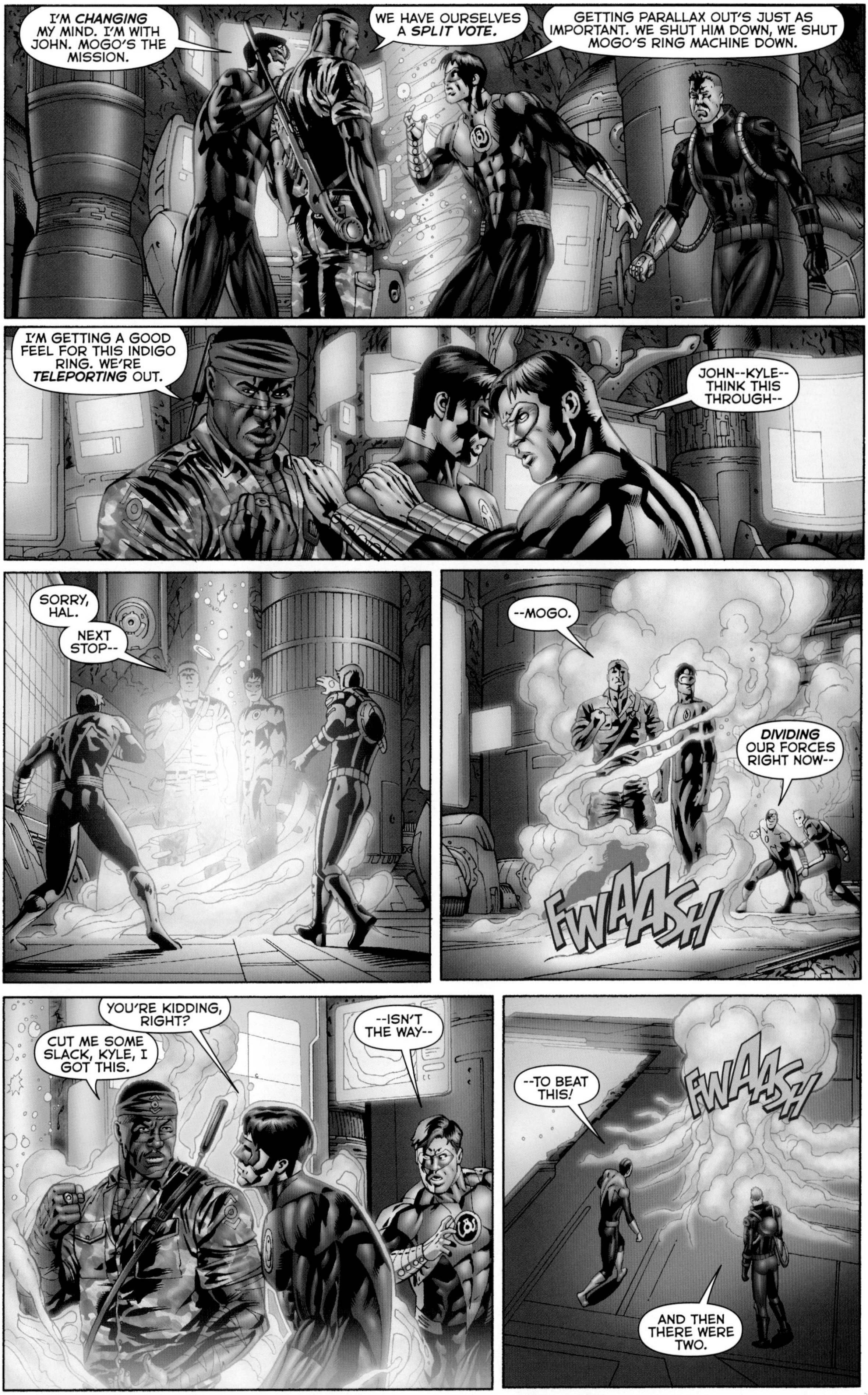
I'M CHANGING MY MIND. I'M WITH JOHN. MOGO'S THE MISSION.
WE HAVE OURSELVES A SPLIT VOTE.
GETTING PARALLAX OUT'S JUST AS IMPORTANT. WE SHUT HIM DOWN, WE SHUT MOGO'S RING MACHINE DOWN.
I'M GETTING A GOOD FEEL FOR THIS INDIGO RING. WE'RE TELEPORTING OUT.
JOHN--KYLE--THINK THIS THROUGH--
SORRY, HAL.
NEXT STOP--
--MOGO.
DIVIDING OUR FORCES RIGHT NOW--
FWAAASH
YOU'RE KIDDING, RIGHT?
CUT ME SOME SLACK, KYLE, I GOT THIS.
--ISN'T THE WAY--
--TO BEAT THIS!
FWAASH
AND THEN THERE WERE TWO.

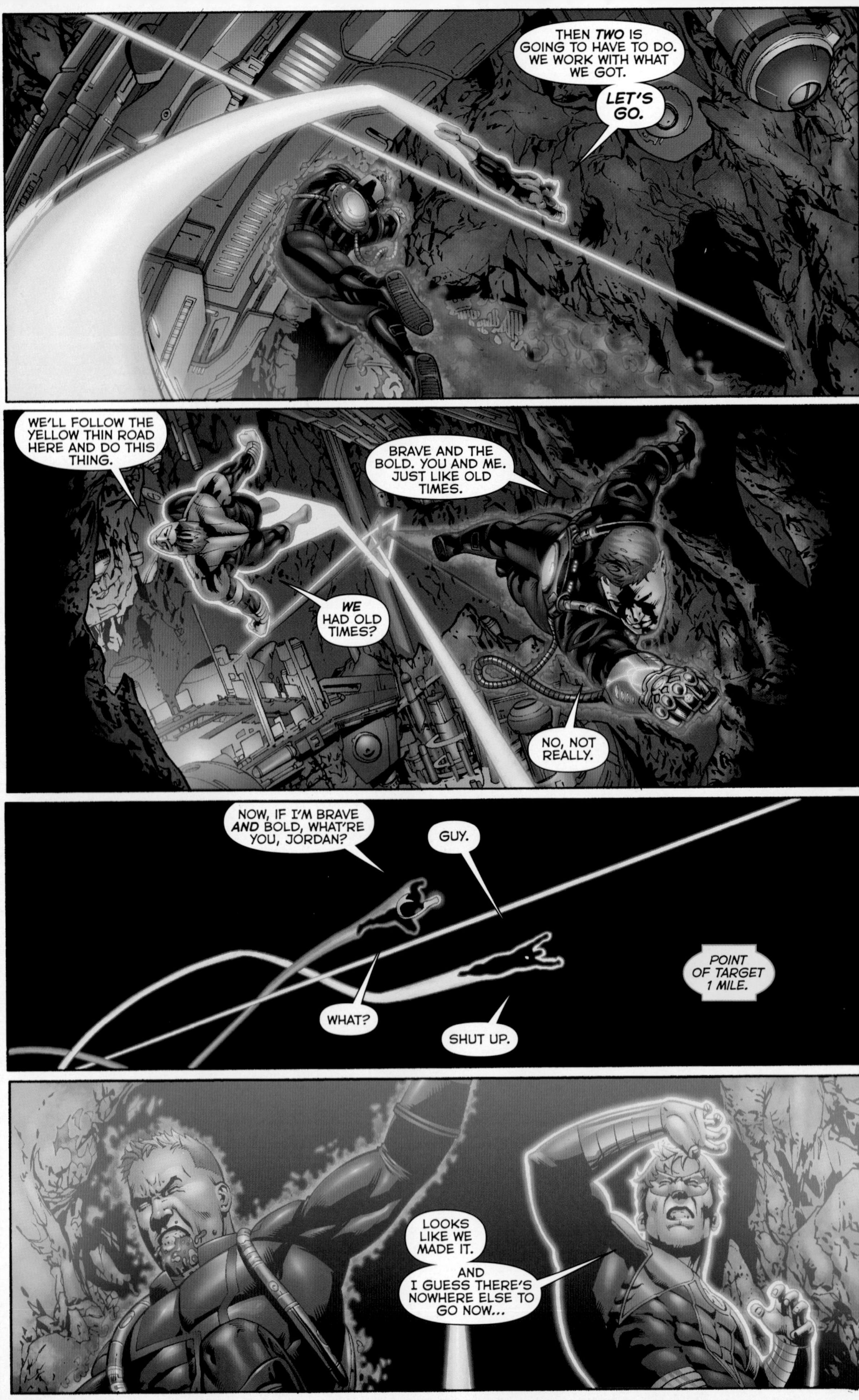
THEN *TWO* IS GOING TO HAVE TO DO. WE WORK WITH WHAT WE GOT.
LET'S GO.
WE'LL FOLLOW THE YELLOW THIN ROAD HERE AND DO THIS THING.
BRAVE AND THE BOLD. YOU AND ME. JUST LIKE OLD TIMES.
WE HAD OLD TIMES?
NO, NOT REALLY.
NOW, IF I'M BRAVE *AND* BOLD, WHAT'RE YOU, JORDAN?
GUY.
WHAT?
SHUT UP.
POINT OF TARGET 1 MILE.
LOOKS LIKE WE MADE IT.
AND I GUESS THERE'S NOWHERE ELSE TO GO NOW...

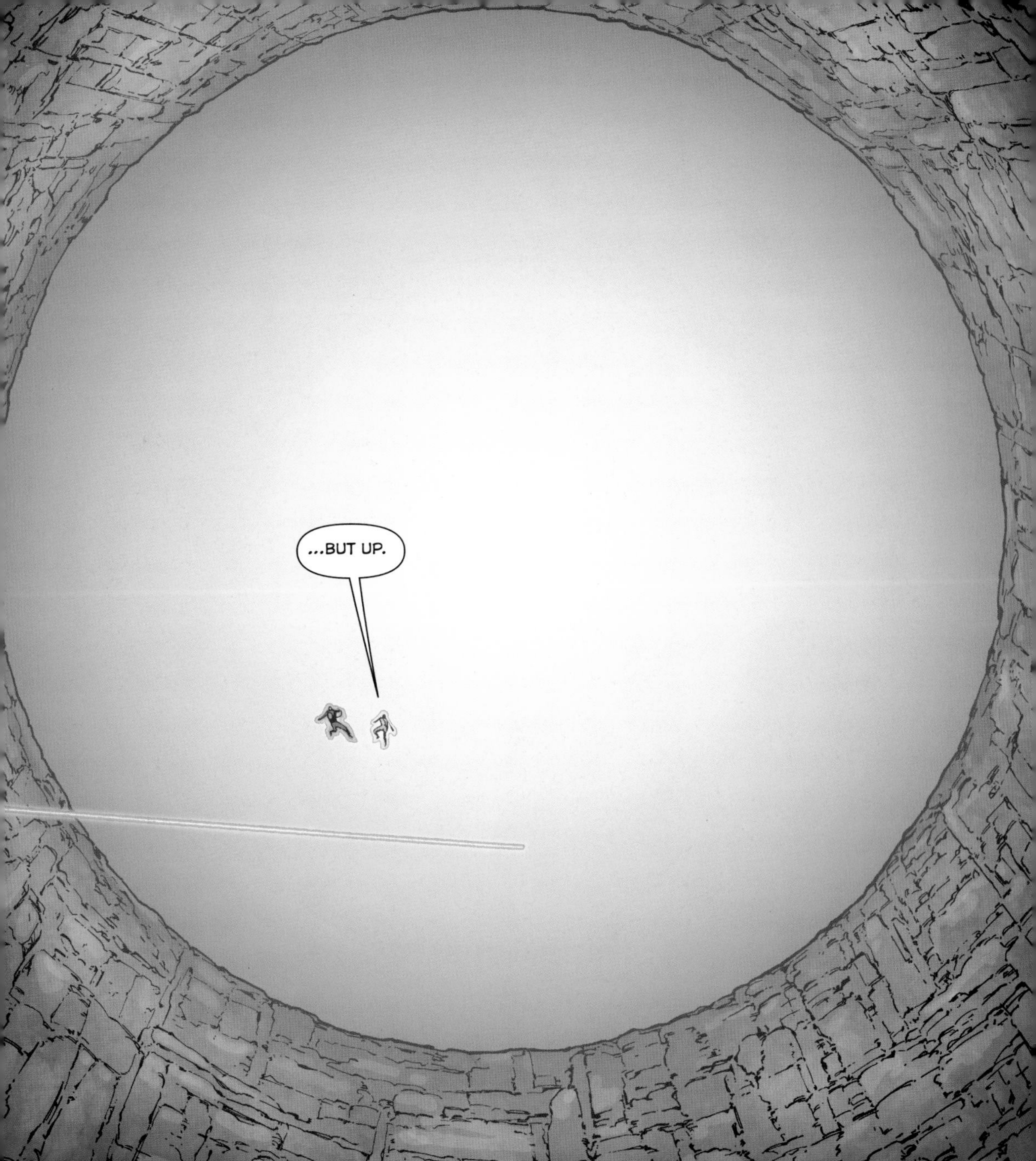
...BUT UP.

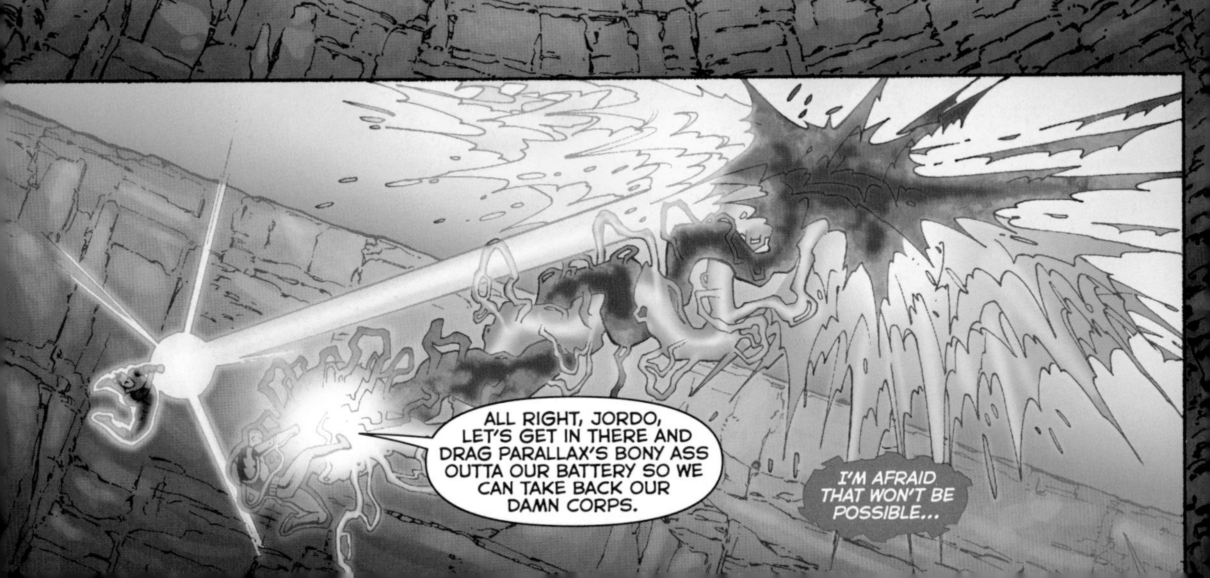
ALL RIGHT, JORDO, LET'S GET IN THERE AND DRAG PARALLAX'S BONY ASS OUTTA OUR BATTERY SO WE CAN TAKE BACK OUR DAMN CORPS.
I'M AFRAID THAT WON'T BE POSSIBLE...

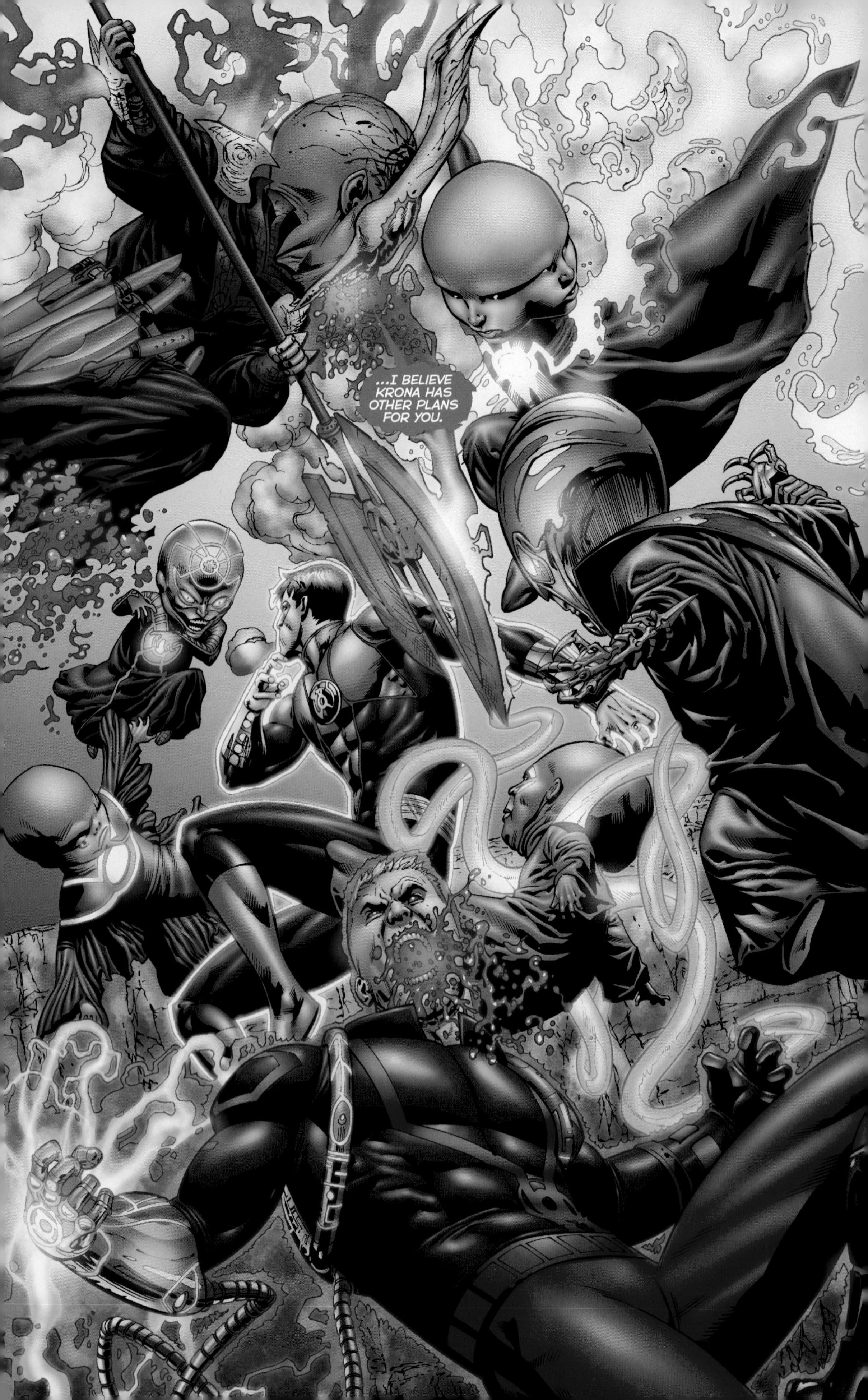
...I BELIEVE KRONA HAS OTHER PLANS FOR YOU.

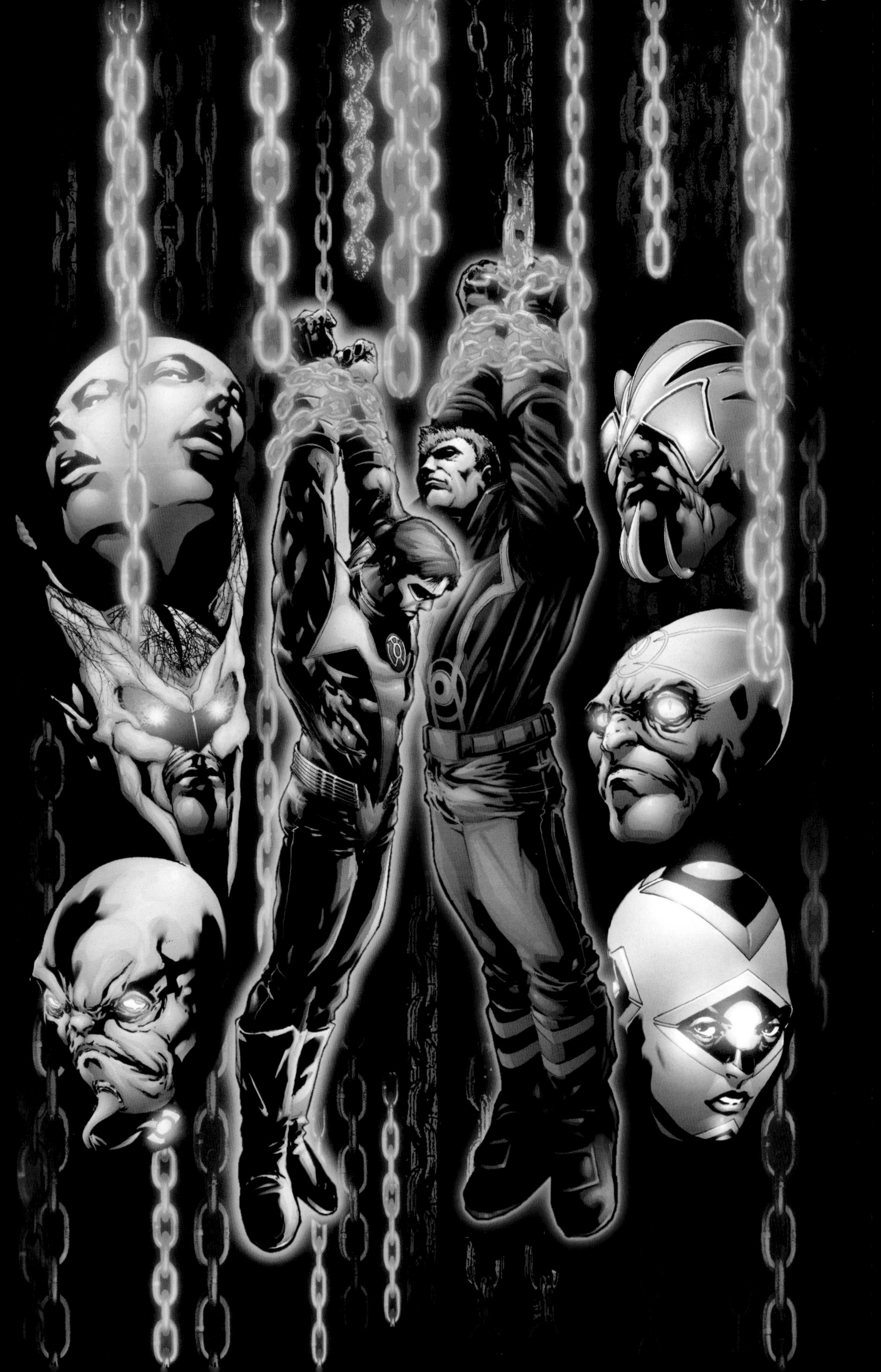

GREEN LANTERN 66 Cover by Miguel Sepulveda with Nathan Eyring

WAR OF THE GREEN LANTERNS
PART SEVEN

Geoff Johns Writer
Doug Mahnke Penciller
Keith Champagne, Christian Alamy, Mark Irwin & Tom Nguyen Inkers

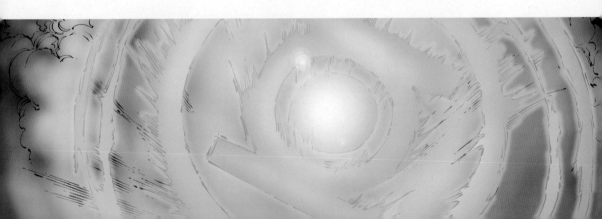

NO ONE KNOWS HOW LONG *MOGO* HAS BEEN A GREEN LANTERN.

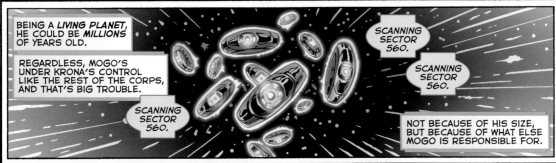

BEING A *LIVING PLANET,* HE COULD BE *MILLIONS* OF YEARS OLD.

REGARDLESS, MOGO'S UNDER KRONA'S CONTROL LIKE THE REST OF THE CORPS, AND THAT'S BIG TROUBLE.

SCANNING SECTOR 560.

SCANNING SECTOR 560.

SCANNING SECTOR 560.

NOT BECAUSE OF HIS SIZE, BUT BECAUSE OF WHAT ELSE MOGO IS RESPONSIBLE FOR.

YOU HAVE THE ABILITY TO OVERCOME GREAT FEAR.

YOU HAVE THE ABILITY TO OVERCOME GREAT FEAR.

WHEN RINGS ARE SEARCHING FOR NEW RECRUITS, MOGO'S CORE IS WHAT GUIDES THEM. HE'S THEIR *MORAL COMPASS.*

BUT WITH PARALLAX INFECTING MOGO, THAT COMPASS IS *BROKEN.*

WELCOME TO THE GREEN LANTERN CORPS.

WELCOME TO THE GREEN LANTERN CORPS.

OA.

OA.

OA.

IF JOHN AND KYLE CAN'T FREE MOGO--KRONA'S ARMY IS GOING TO KEEP *GROWING.*

AND THE UNIVERSE IS GOING TO BE OVERRUN WITH *MINDLESS* AND *VIOLENT* GREEN LANTERNS.

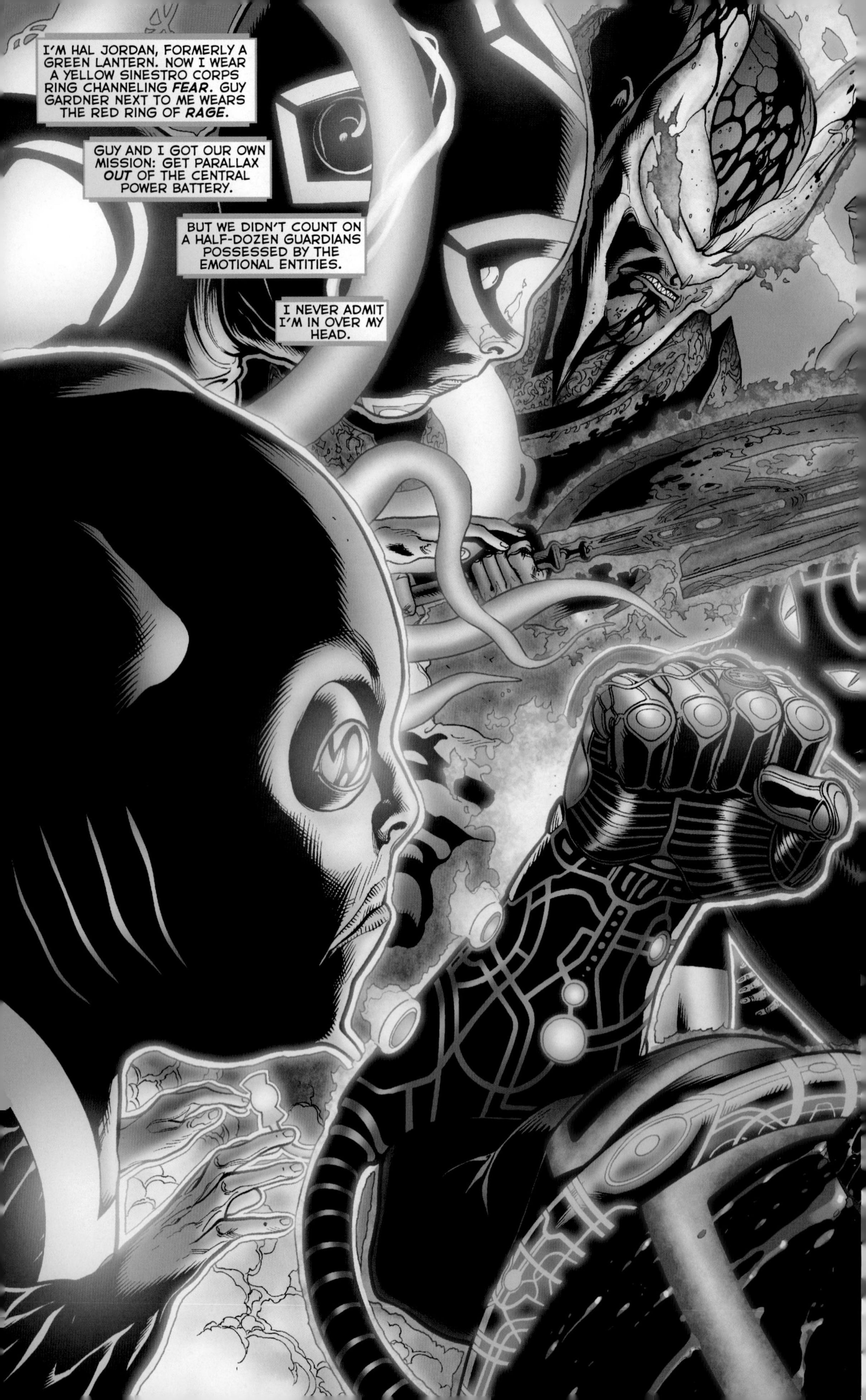
I'M HAL JORDAN, FORMERLY A GREEN LANTERN. NOW I WEAR A YELLOW SINESTRO CORPS RING CHANNELING *FEAR*. GUY GARDNER NEXT TO ME WEARS THE RED RING OF *RAGE*.
GUY AND I GOT OUR OWN MISSION: GET PARALLAX *OUT* OF THE CENTRAL POWER BATTERY.
BUT WE DIDN'T COUNT ON A HALF-DOZEN GUARDIANS POSSESSED BY THE EMOTIONAL ENTITIES.
I NEVER ADMIT I'M IN OVER MY HEAD.

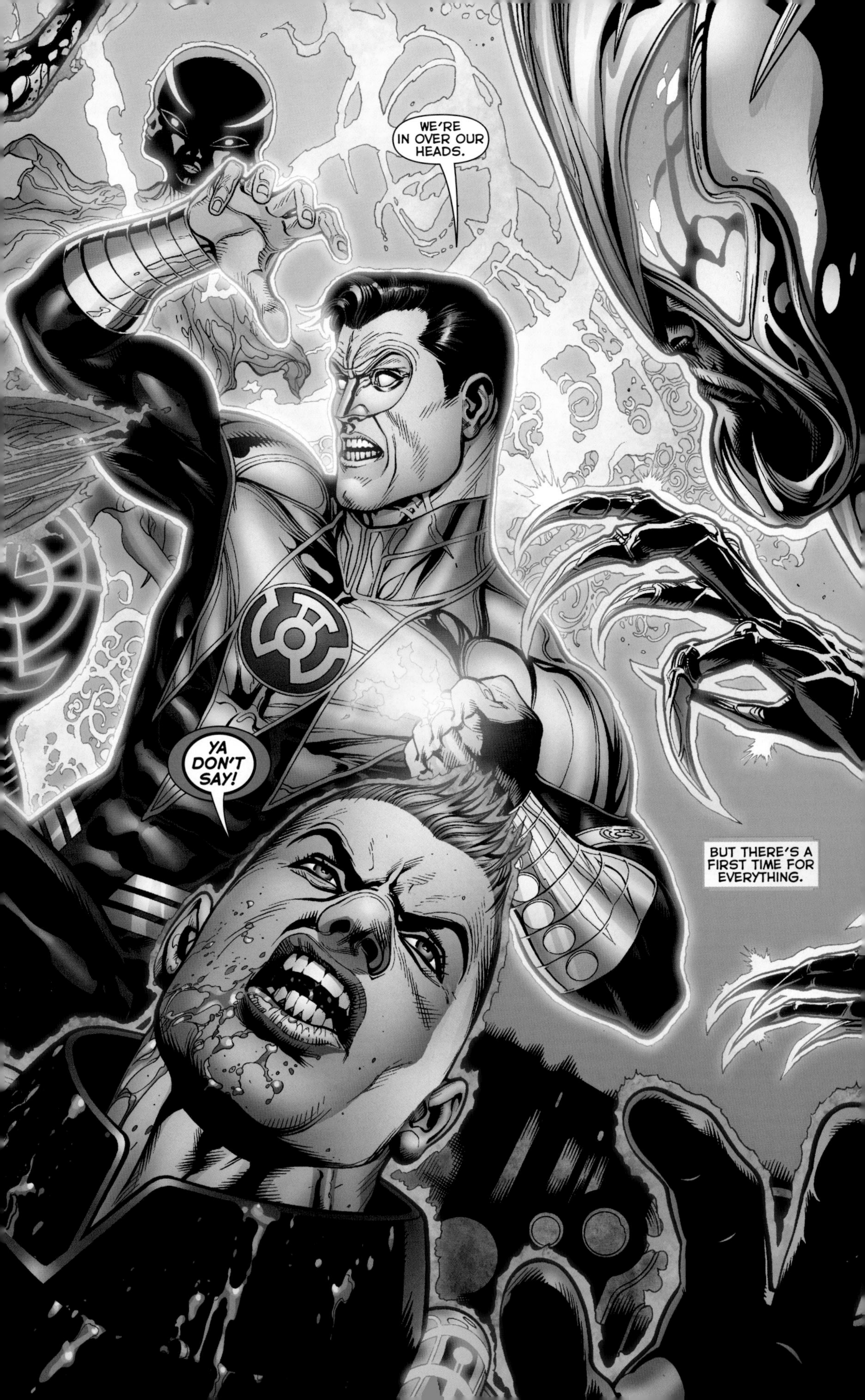
WE'RE IN OVER OUR HEADS.
YA DON'T SAY!
BUT THERE'S A FIRST TIME FOR EVERYTHING.

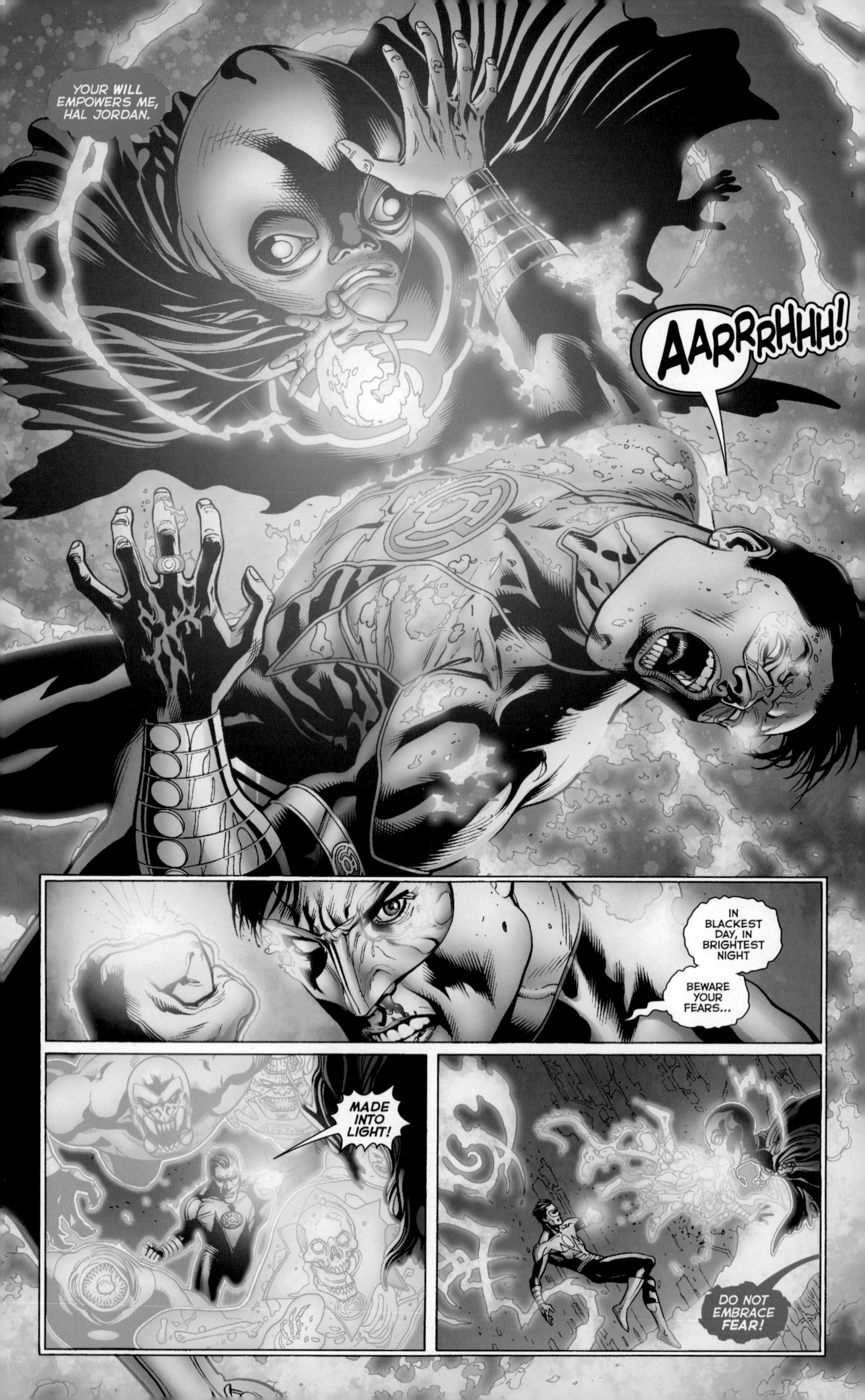
YOUR WILL EMPOWERS ME, HAL JORDAN.
AARRRHHH!
IN BLACKEST DAY, IN BRIGHTEST NIGHT
BEWARE YOUR FEARS...
MADE INTO LIGHT!
DO NOT EMBRACE FEAR!

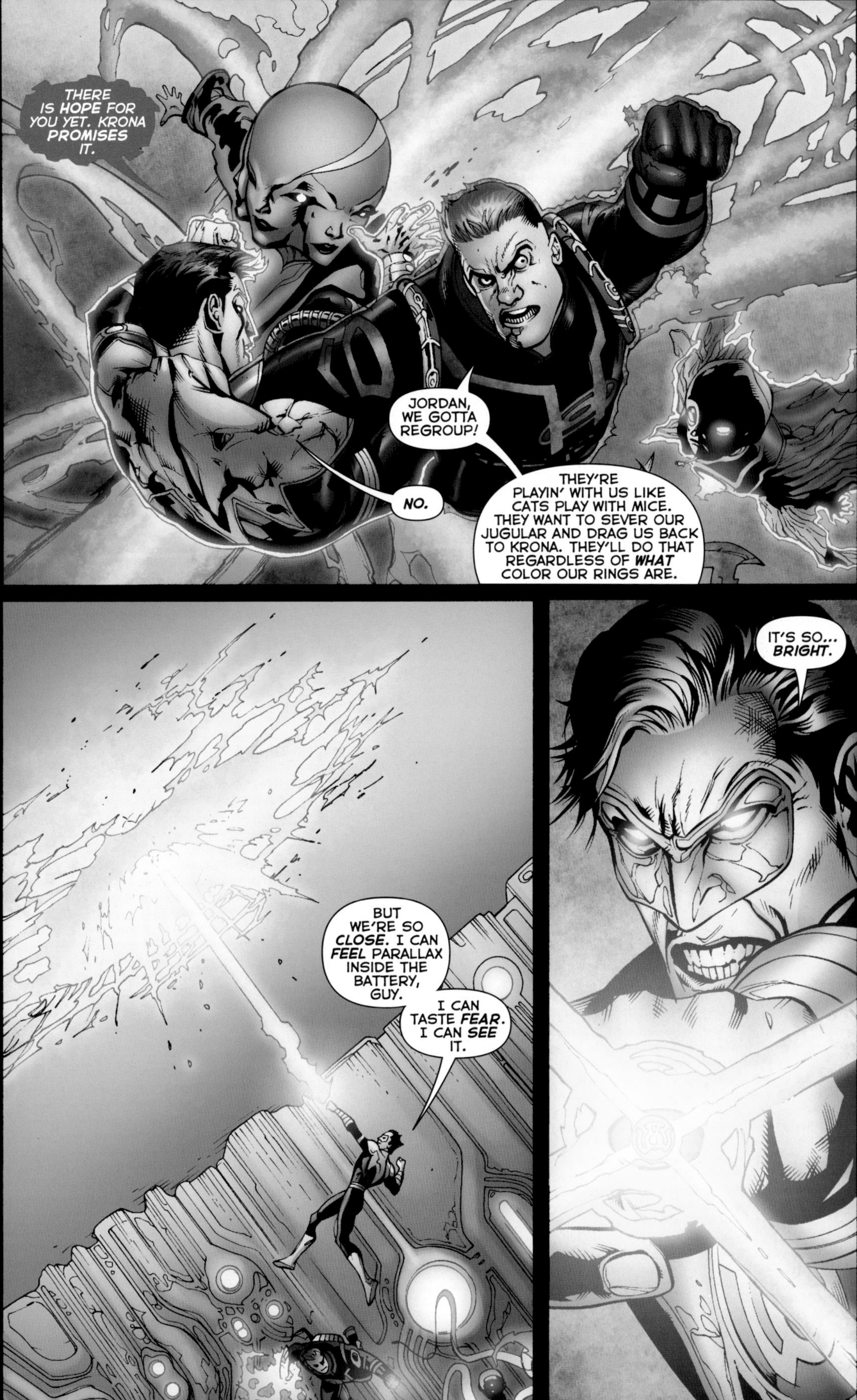
THERE IS HOPE FOR YOU YET. KRONA PROMISES IT.
JORDAN, WE GOTTA REGROUP!
NO.
THEY'RE PLAYIN' WITH US LIKE CATS PLAY WITH MICE. THEY WANT TO SEVER OUR JUGULAR AND DRAG US BACK TO KRONA. THEY'LL DO THAT REGARDLESS OF WHAT COLOR OUR RINGS ARE.
BUT WE'RE SO CLOSE. I CAN FEEL PARALLAX INSIDE THE BATTERY, GUY.
I CAN TASTE FEAR. I CAN SEE IT.
IT'S SO... BRIGHT.

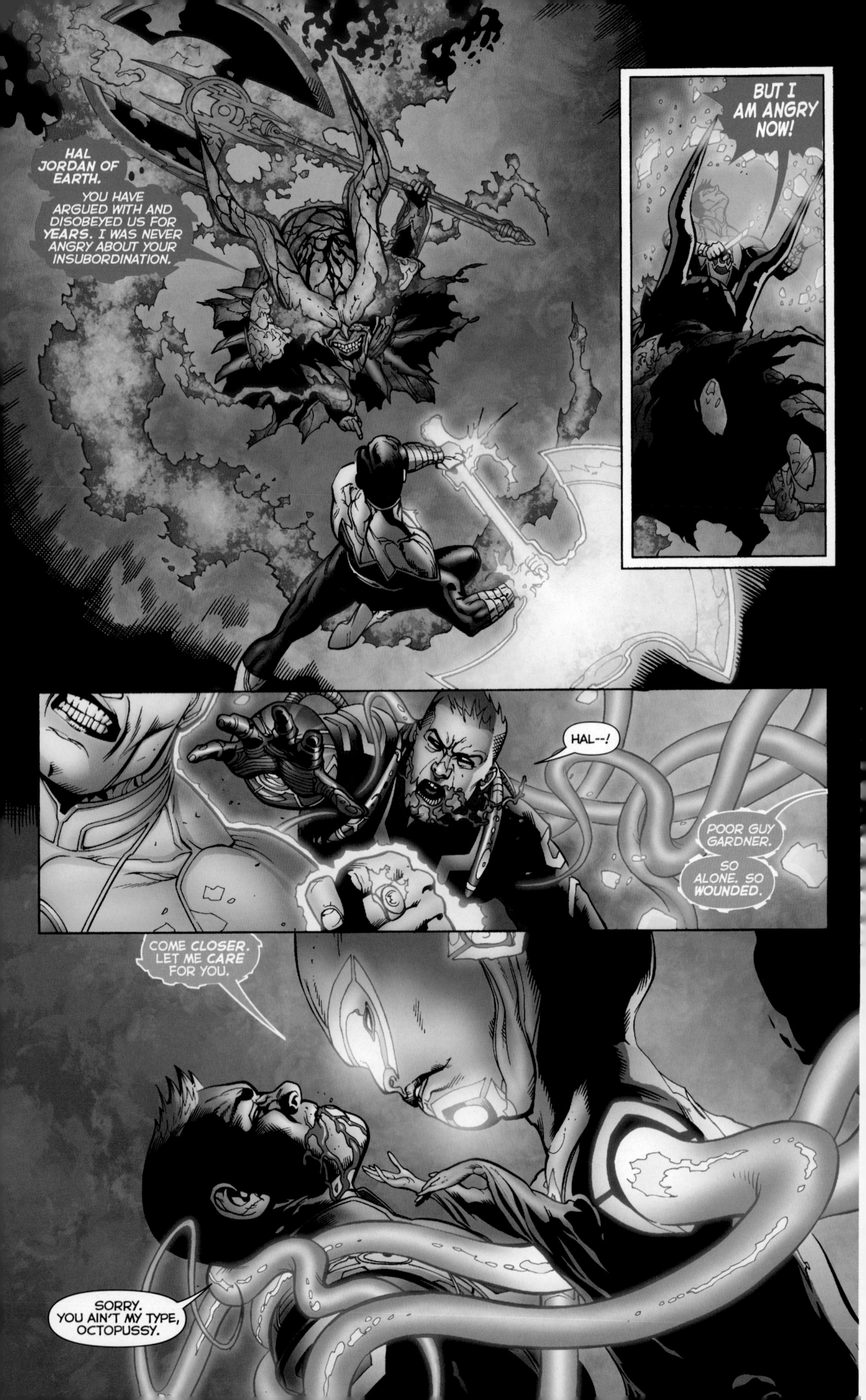
HAL JORDAN OF EARTH.
YOU HAVE ARGUED WITH AND DISOBEYED US FOR YEARS. I WAS NEVER ANGRY ABOUT YOUR INSUBORDINATION.
BUT I AM ANGRY NOW!
HAL--!
POOR GUY GARDNER.
SO ALONE. SO WOUNDED.
COME CLOSER. LET ME CARE FOR YOU.
SORRY. YOU AIN'T MY TYPE, OCTOPUSSY.

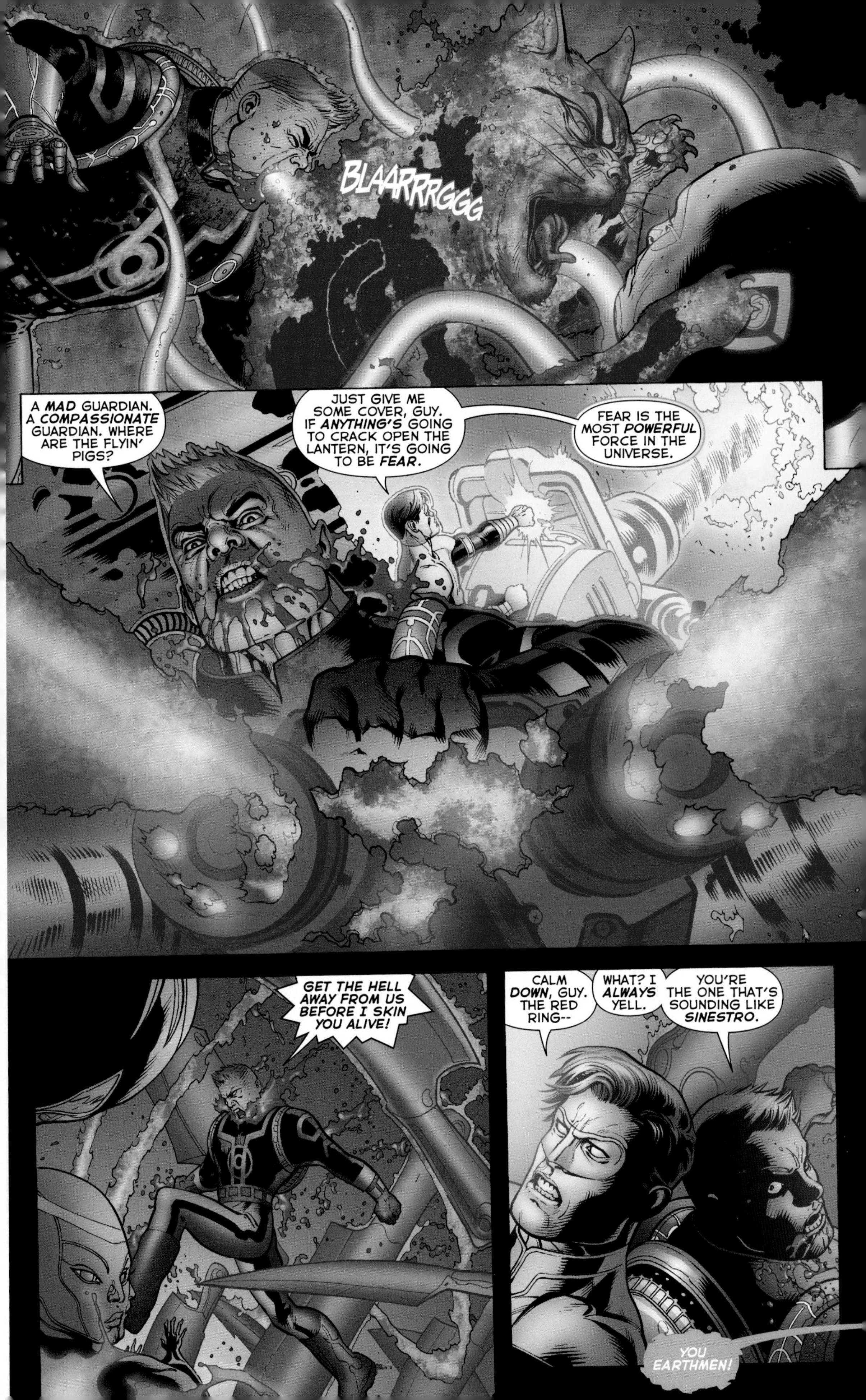
BLAARRRGGG
A MAD GUARDIAN. A COMPASSIONATE GUARDIAN. WHERE ARE THE FLYIN' PIGS?
JUST GIVE ME SOME COVER, GUY. IF ANYTHING'S GOING TO CRACK OPEN THE LANTERN, IT'S GOING TO BE FEAR.
FEAR IS THE MOST POWERFUL FORCE IN THE UNIVERSE.
GET THE HELL AWAY FROM US BEFORE I SKIN YOU ALIVE!
CALM DOWN, GUY. THE RED RING--
WHAT? I ALWAYS YELL.
YOU'RE THE ONE THAT'S SOUNDING LIKE SINESTRO.
YOU EARTHMEN!

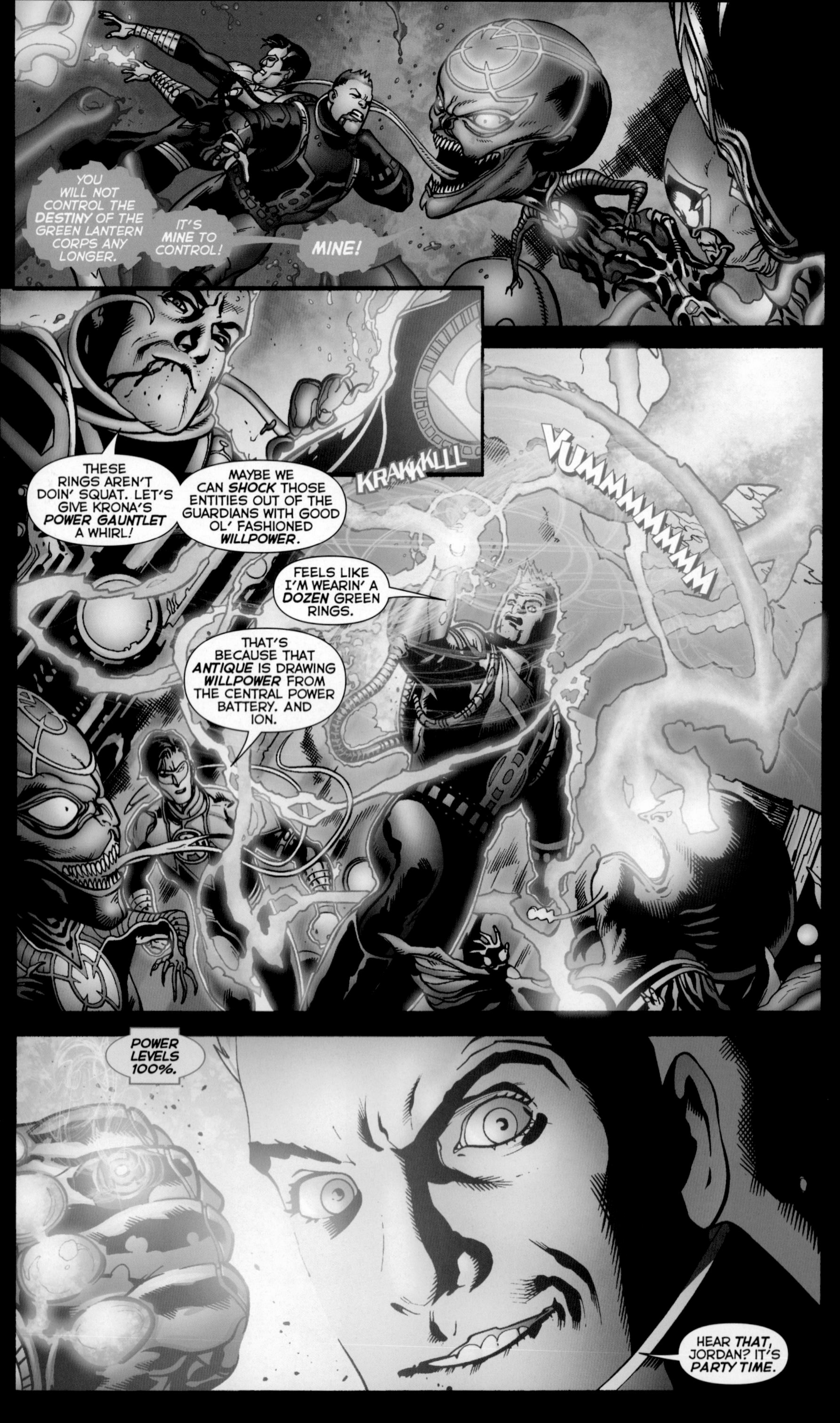
YOU WILL NOT CONTROL THE DESTINY OF THE GREEN LANTERN CORPS ANY LONGER.
IT'S MINE TO CONTROL!
MINE!
THESE RINGS AREN'T DOIN' SQUAT. LET'S GIVE KRONA'S POWER GAUNTLET A WHIRL!
MAYBE WE CAN SHOCK THOSE ENTITIES OUT OF THE GUARDIANS WITH GOOD OL' FASHIONED WILLPOWER.
KRAKKKLLL
VUMMMMMMMMM
FEELS LIKE I'M WEARIN' A DOZEN GREEN RINGS.
THAT'S BECAUSE THAT ANTIQUE IS DRAWING WILLPOWER FROM THE CENTRAL POWER BATTERY. AND ION.
POWER LEVELS 100%.
HEAR THAT, JORDAN? IT'S PARTY TIME.

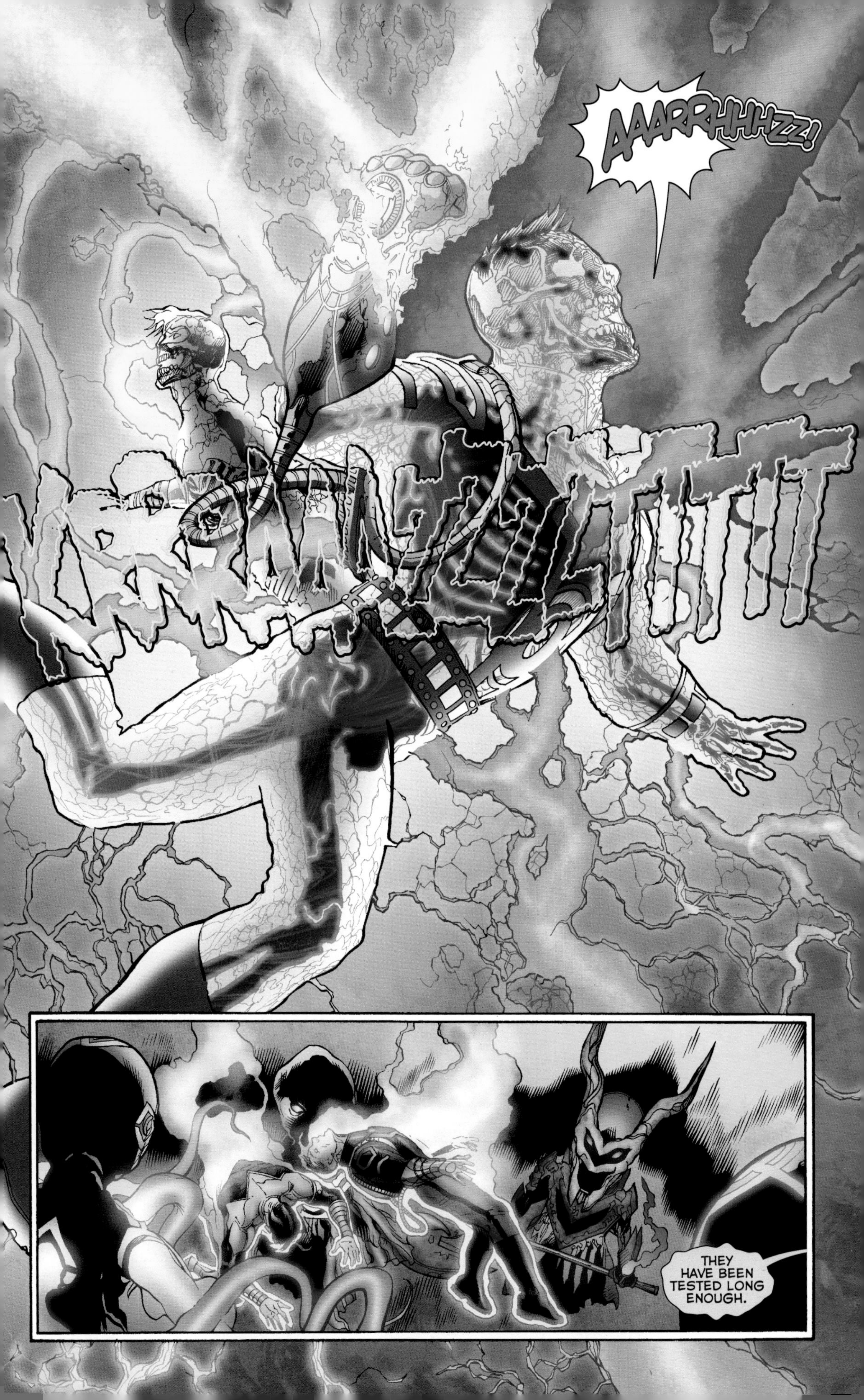
AAARRHHHZZ!
THEY HAVE BEEN TESTED LONG ENOUGH.

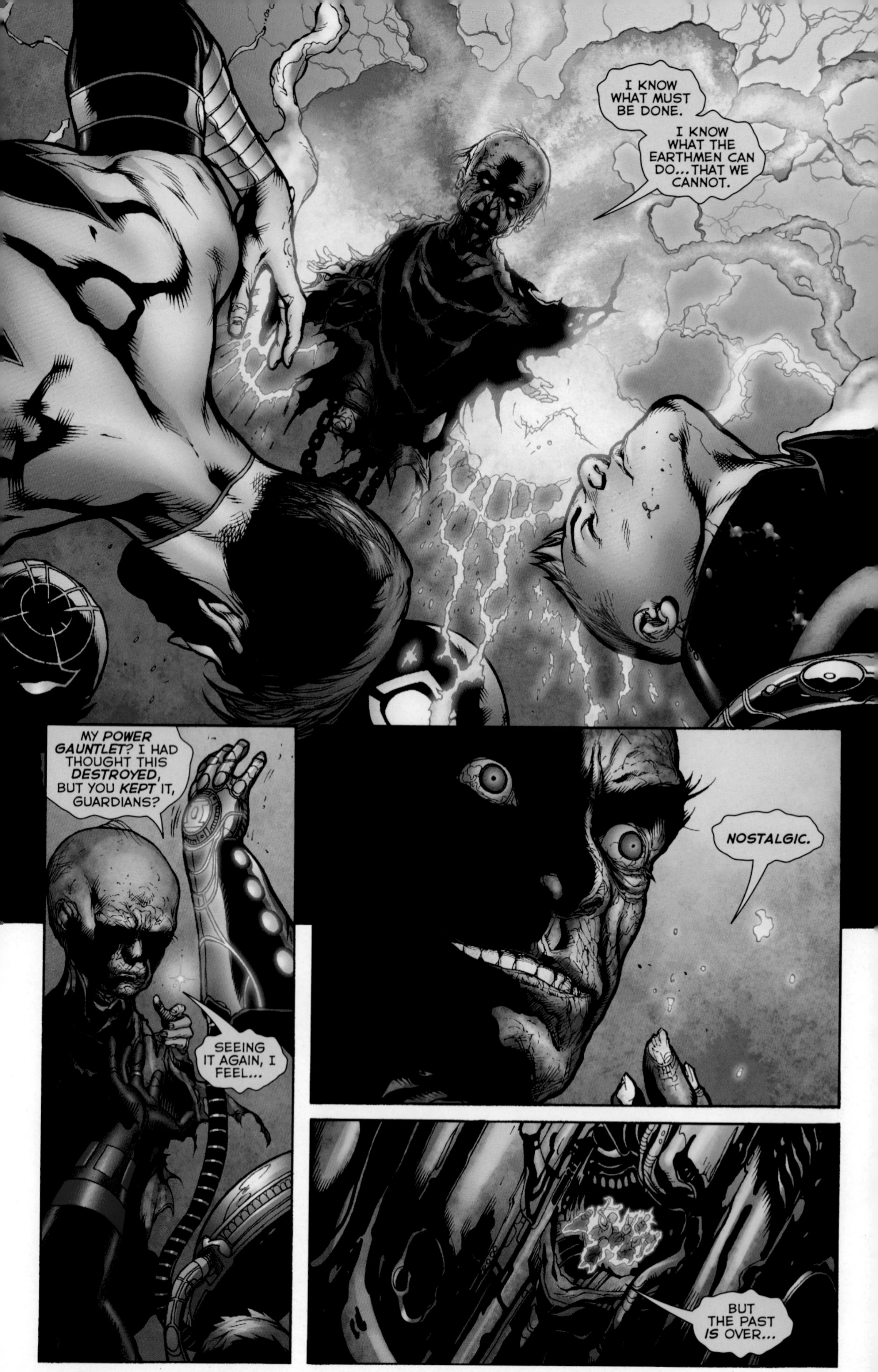
I KNOW WHAT MUST BE DONE.
I KNOW WHAT THE EARTHMEN CAN DO...THAT WE CANNOT.
MY *POWER GAUNTLET*? I HAD THOUGHT THIS *DESTROYED*, BUT YOU *KEPT* IT, GUARDIANS?
SEEING IT AGAIN, I FEEL...
NOSTALGIC.
BUT THE PAST *IS* OVER...

"...THE *FUTURE* IS ON THE HORIZON."

THE CITADEL OF THE GUARDIANS.

NGGG.

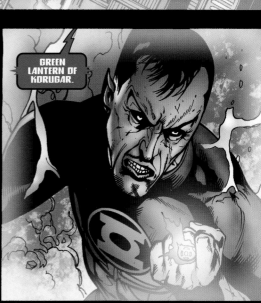

GREEN LANTERN OF KORUGAR.

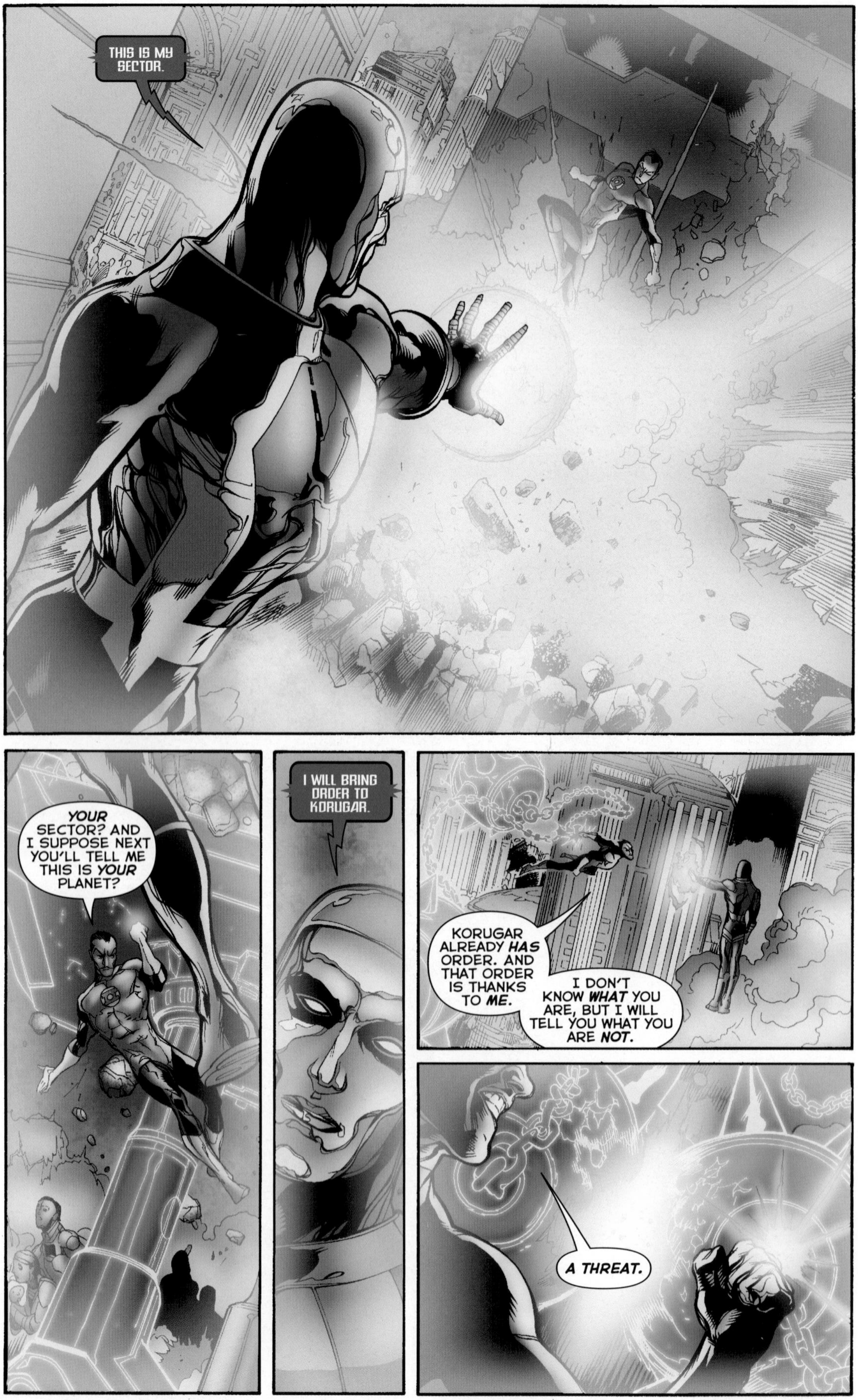
THIS IS MY SECTOR.
YOUR SECTOR? AND I SUPPOSE NEXT YOU'LL TELL ME THIS IS YOUR PLANET?
I WILL BRING ORDER TO KORUGAR.
KORUGAR ALREADY HAS ORDER. AND THAT ORDER IS THANKS TO ME.
I DON'T KNOW WHAT YOU ARE, BUT I WILL TELL YOU WHAT YOU ARE NOT.
A THREAT.

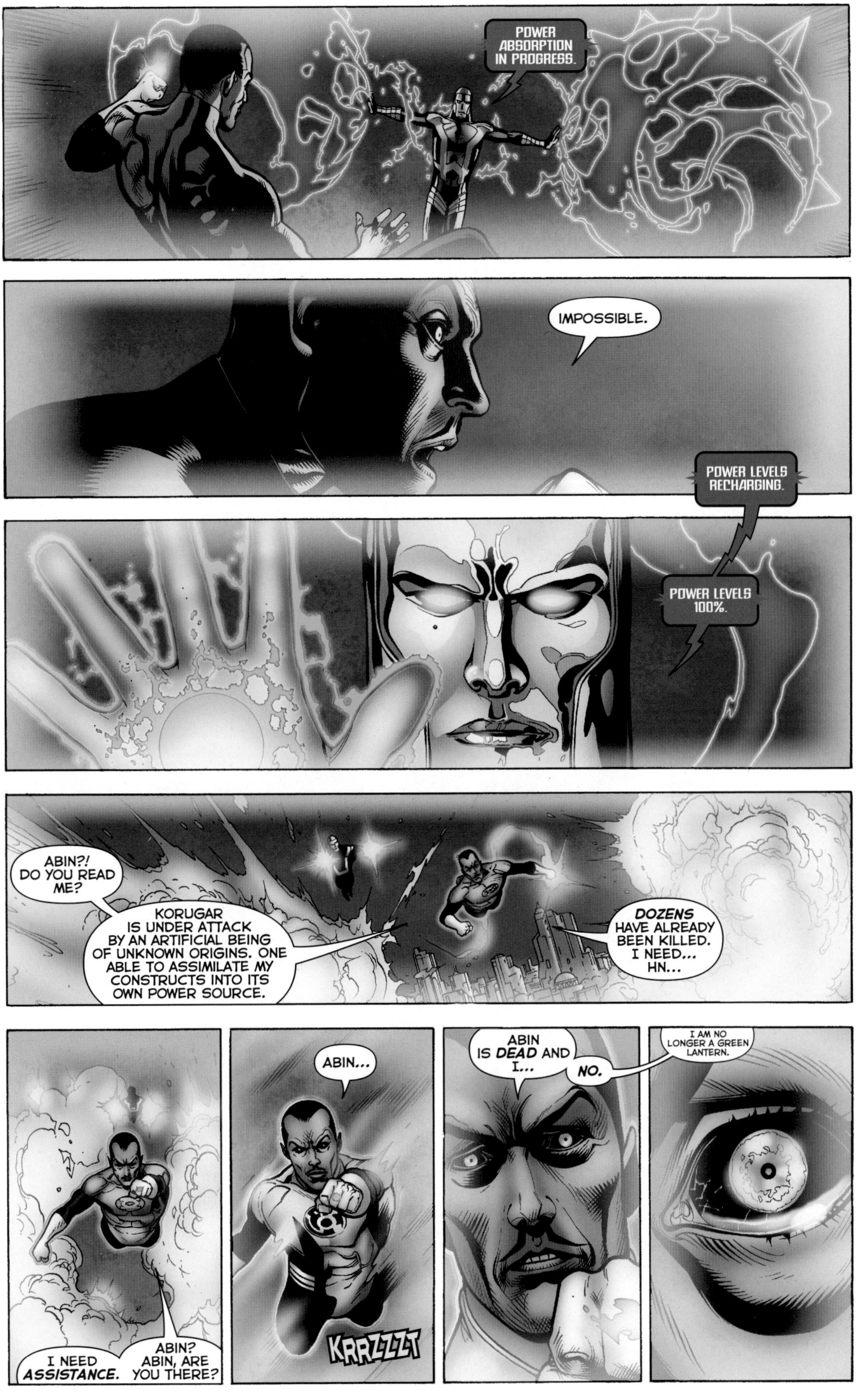
POWER ABSORPTION IN PROGRESS.
IMPOSSIBLE.
POWER LEVELS RECHARGING.
POWER LEVELS 100%.
ABIN?! DO YOU READ ME?
KORUGAR IS UNDER ATTACK BY AN ARTIFICIAL BEING OF UNKNOWN ORIGINS. ONE ABLE TO ASSIMILATE MY CONSTRUCTS INTO ITS OWN POWER SOURCE.
DOZENS HAVE ALREADY BEEN KILLED. I NEED... HN...
I NEED ASSISTANCE.
ABIN? ABIN, ARE YOU THERE?
ABIN...
KRRZZZT
ABIN IS DEAD AND I...
NO.
I AM NO LONGER A GREEN LANTERN.

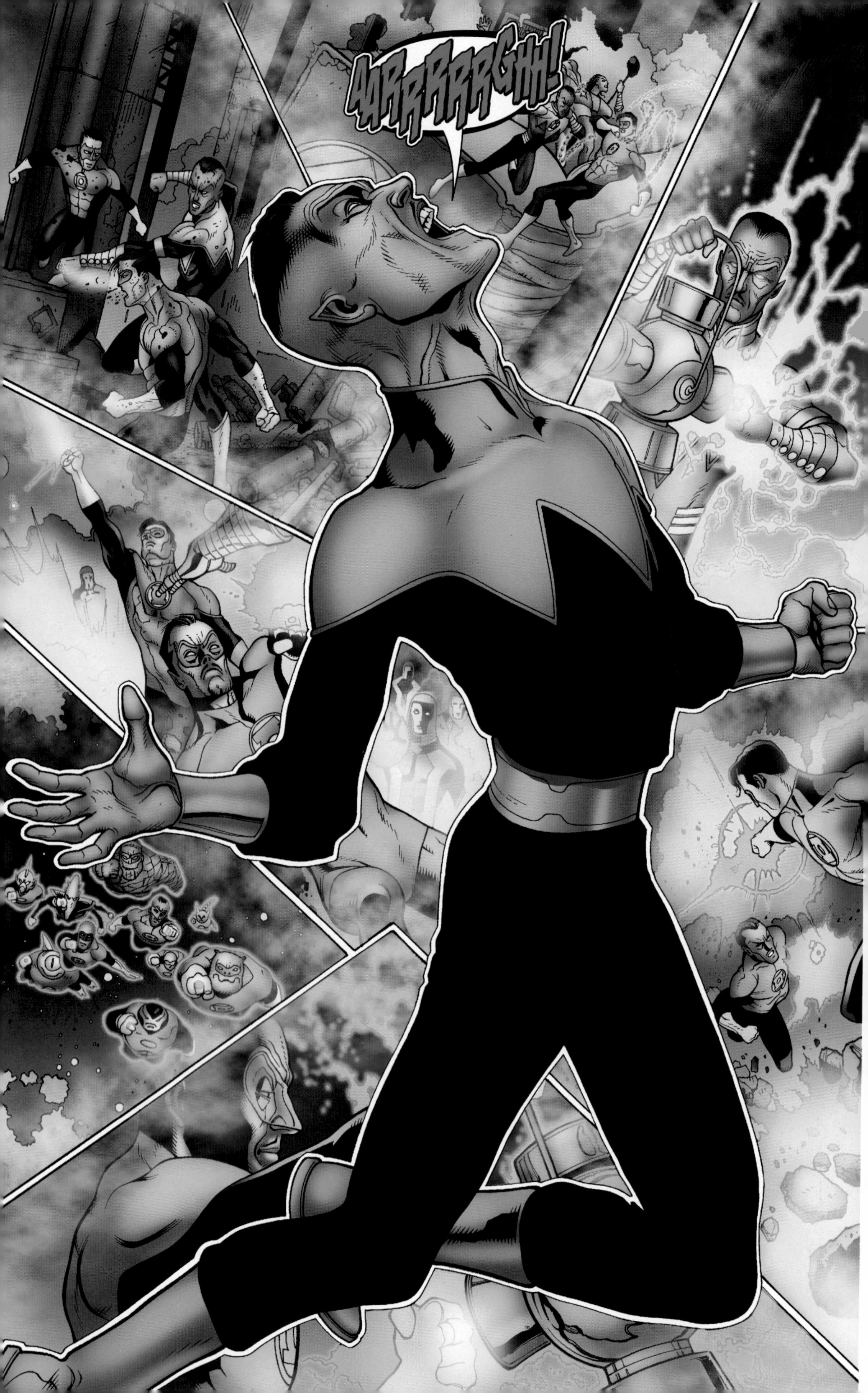
AARRRRRGHH!

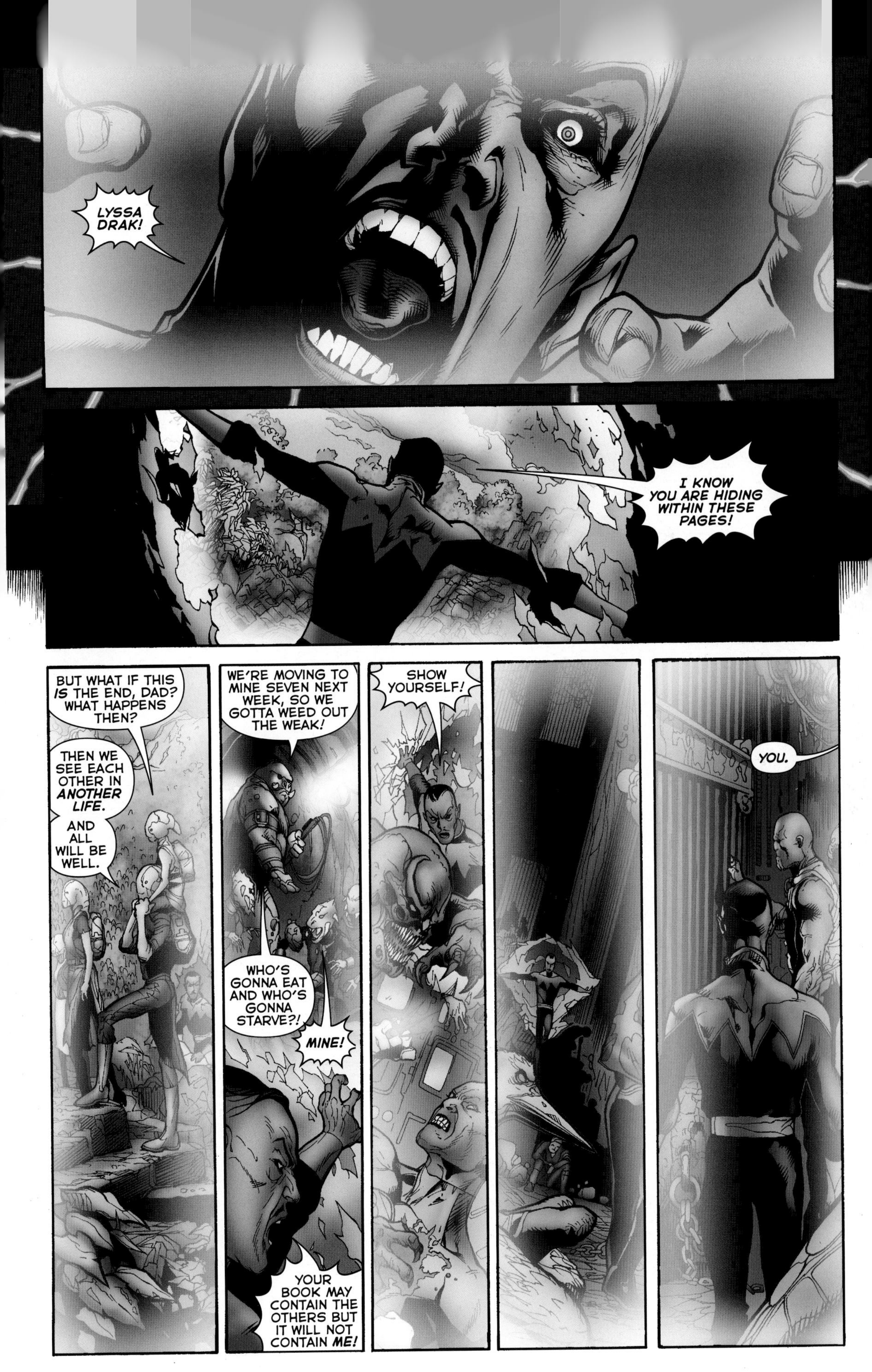
LYSSA DRAK!
I KNOW YOU ARE HIDING WITHIN THESE PAGES!
BUT WHAT IF THIS *IS* THE END, DAD? WHAT HAPPENS THEN?
THEN WE SEE EACH OTHER IN ***ANOTHER LIFE***.
AND ALL WILL BE WELL.
WE'RE MOVING TO MINE SEVEN NEXT WEEK, SO WE GOTTA WEED OUT THE WEAK!
WHO'S GONNA EAT AND WHO'S GONNA STARVE?!
MINE!
YOUR BOOK MAY CONTAIN THE OTHERS BUT IT WILL NOT CONTAIN ***ME!***
SHOW YOURSELF!
YOU.

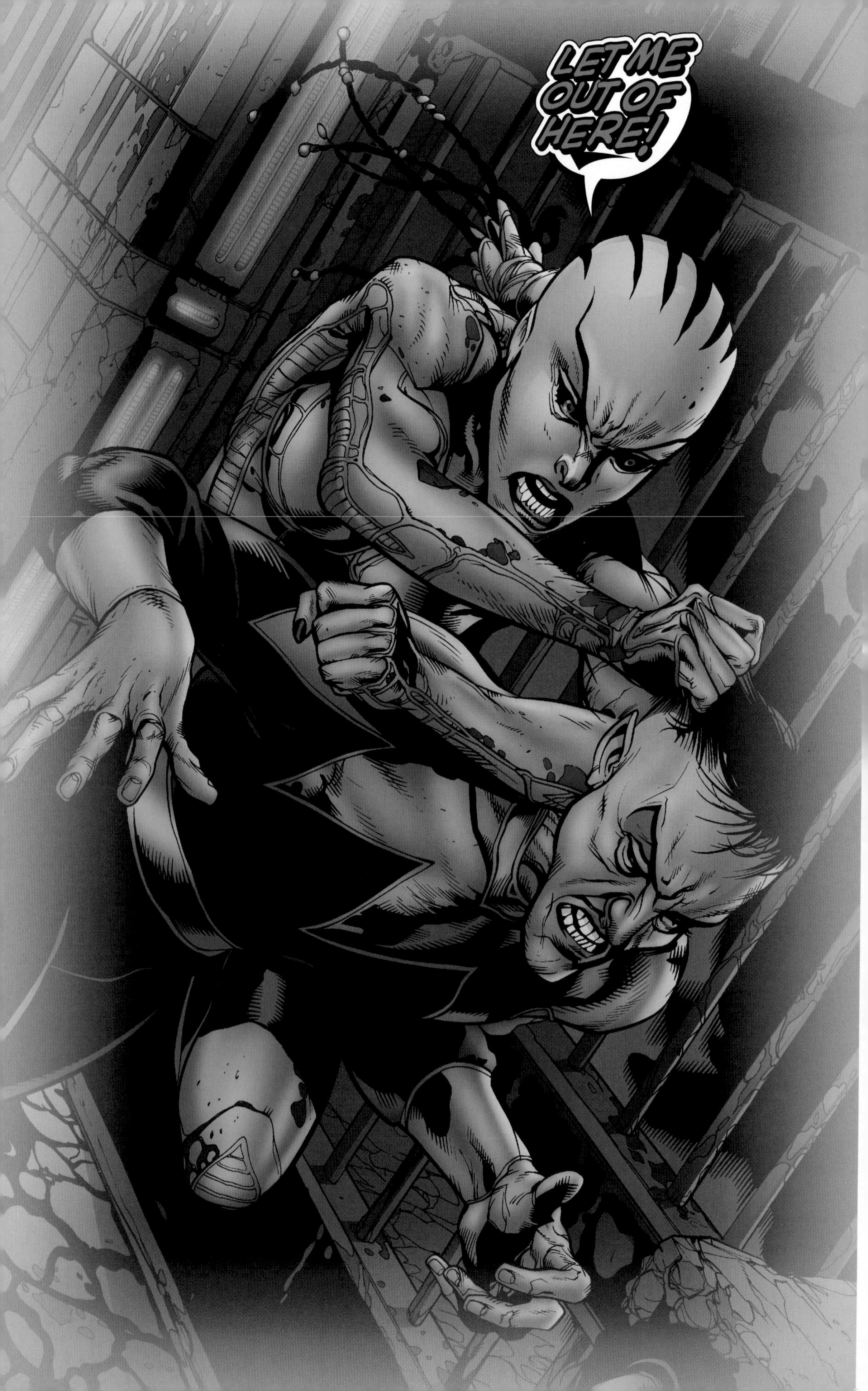
LET ME OUT OF HERE!

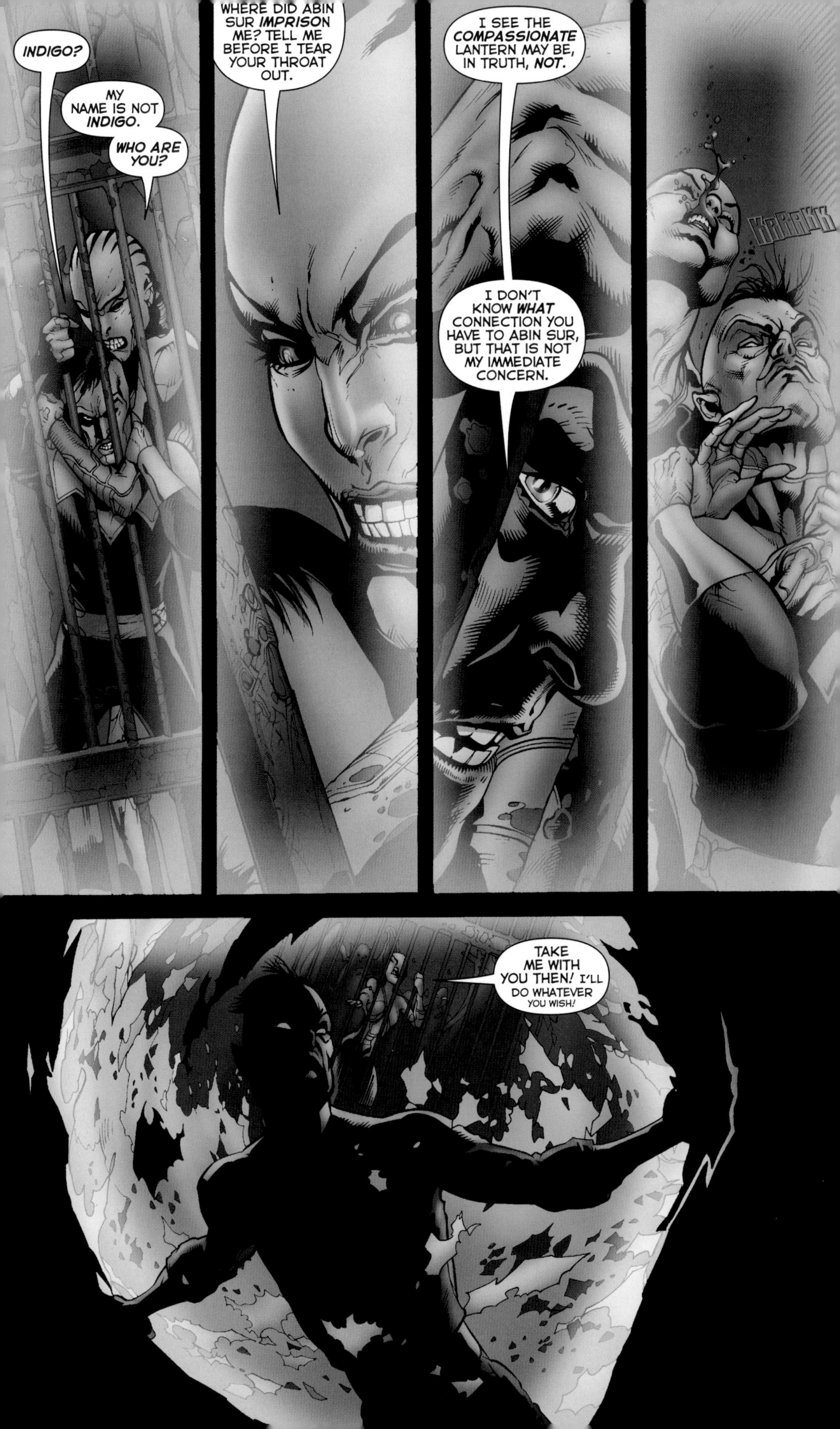
INDIGO?
MY NAME IS NOT INDIGO.
WHO ARE YOU?
WHERE DID ABIN SUR IMPRISON ME? TELL ME BEFORE I TEAR YOUR THROAT OUT.
I SEE THE COMPASSIONATE LANTERN MAY BE, IN TRUTH, NOT.
I DON'T KNOW WHAT CONNECTION YOU HAVE TO ABIN SUR, BUT THAT IS NOT MY IMMEDIATE CONCERN.
KRAKK
TAKE ME WITH YOU THEN! I'LL DO WHATEVER YOU WISH!

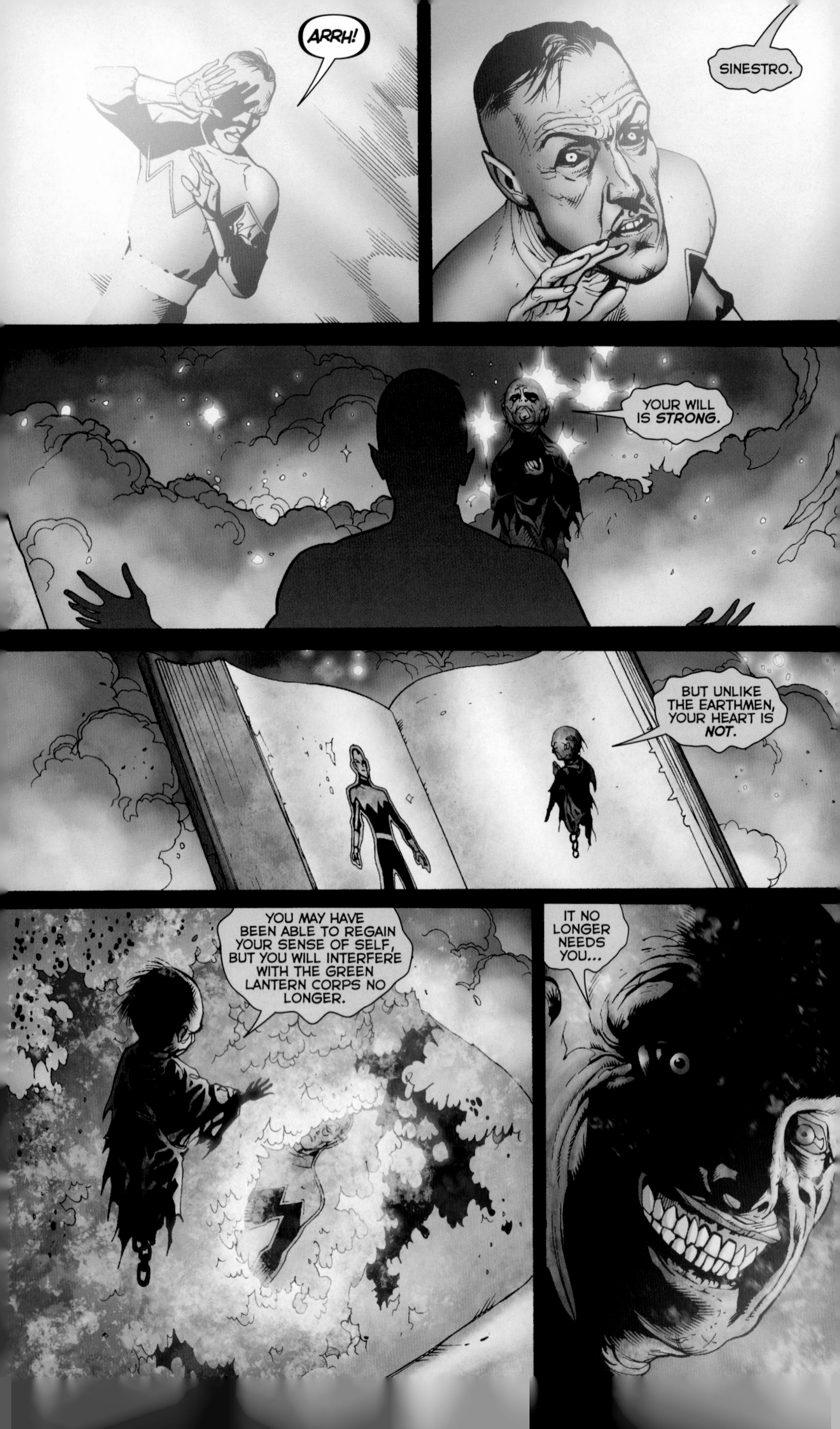
ARRH!
SINESTRO.
YOUR WILL IS STRONG.
BUT UNLIKE THE EARTHMEN, YOUR HEART IS NOT.
YOU MAY HAVE BEEN ABLE TO REGAIN YOUR SENSE OF SELF, BUT YOU WILL INTERFERE WITH THE GREEN LANTERN CORPS NO LONGER.
IT NO LONGER NEEDS YOU...

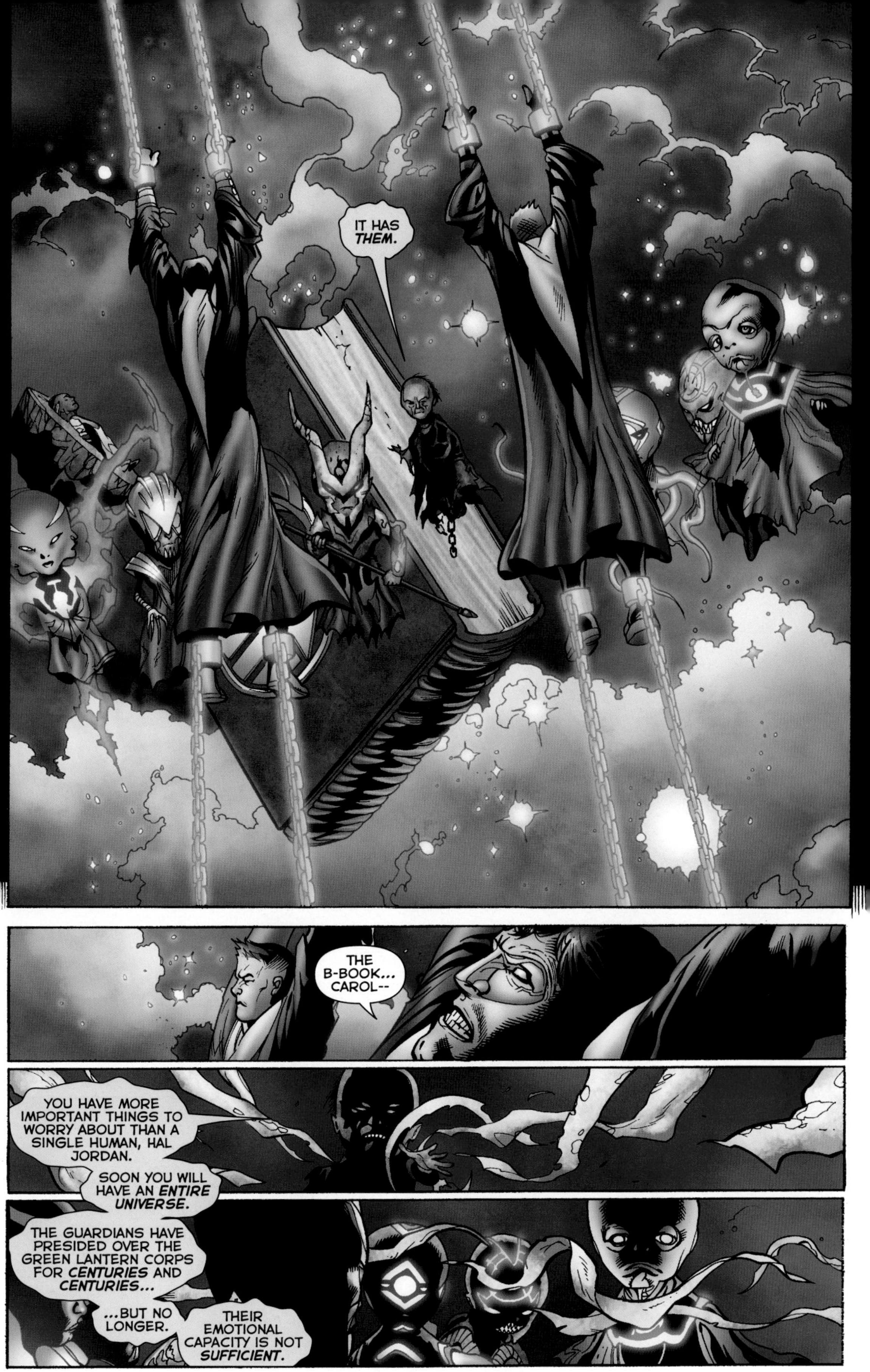
IT HAS THEM.
THE B-BOOK... CAROL--
YOU HAVE MORE IMPORTANT THINGS TO WORRY ABOUT THAN A SINGLE HUMAN, HAL JORDAN.
SOON YOU WILL HAVE AN ENTIRE UNIVERSE.
THE GUARDIANS HAVE PRESIDED OVER THE GREEN LANTERN CORPS FOR CENTURIES AND CENTURIES...
...BUT NO LONGER.
THEIR EMOTIONAL CAPACITY IS NOT SUFFICIENT.

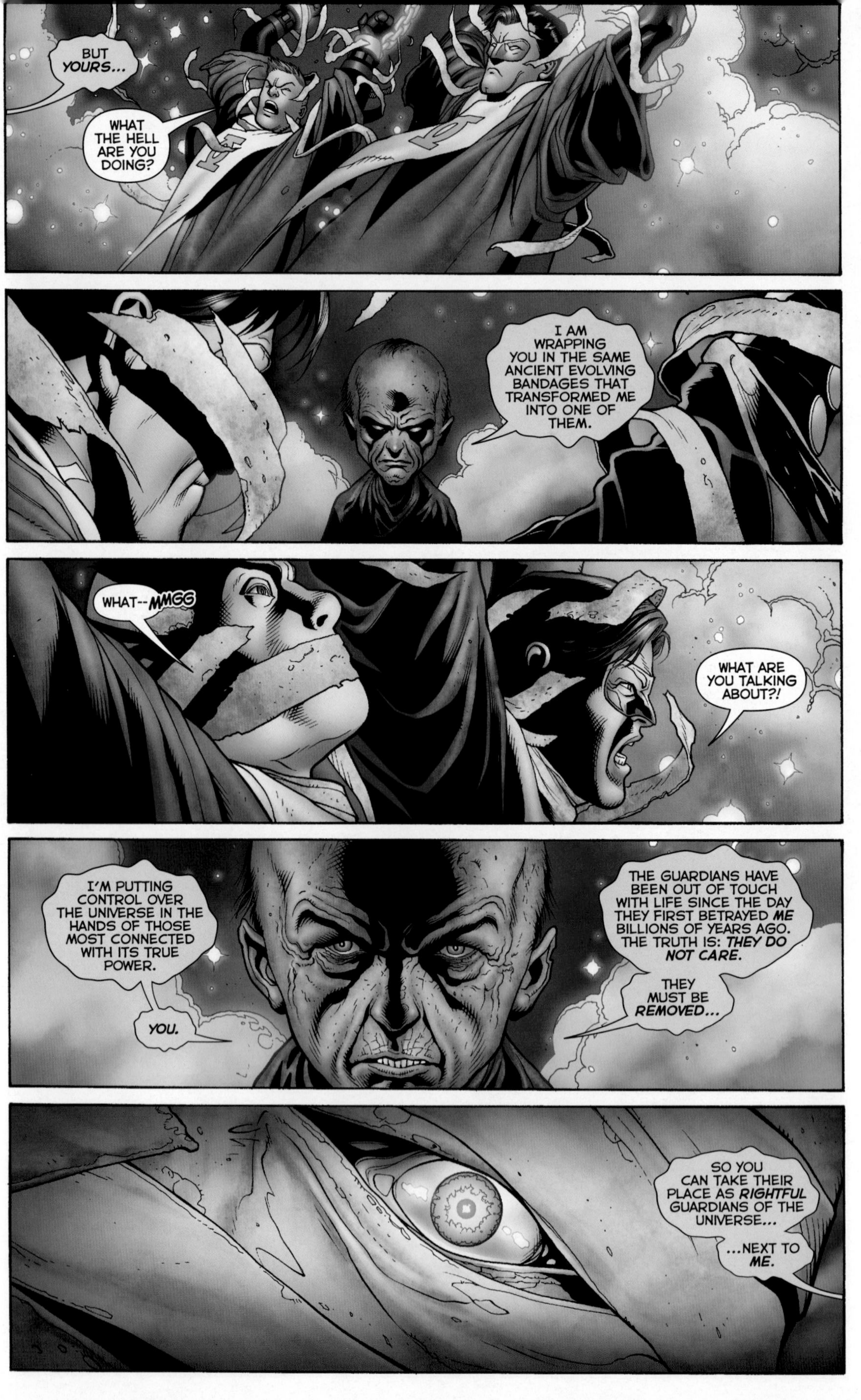

BUT YOURS...
WHAT THE HELL ARE YOU DOING?
I AM WRAPPING YOU IN THE SAME ANCIENT EVOLVING BANDAGES THAT TRANSFORMED ME INTO ONE OF THEM.
WHAT--MMGG
WHAT ARE YOU TALKING ABOUT?!
I'M PUTTING CONTROL OVER THE UNIVERSE IN THE HANDS OF THOSE MOST CONNECTED WITH ITS TRUE POWER.
YOU.
THE GUARDIANS HAVE BEEN OUT OF TOUCH WITH LIFE SINCE THE DAY THEY FIRST BETRAYED ME BILLIONS OF YEARS AGO. THE TRUTH IS: THEY DO NOT CARE.
THEY MUST BE REMOVED...
SO YOU CAN TAKE THEIR PLACE AS RIGHTFUL GUARDIANS OF THE UNIVERSE...
...NEXT TO ME.

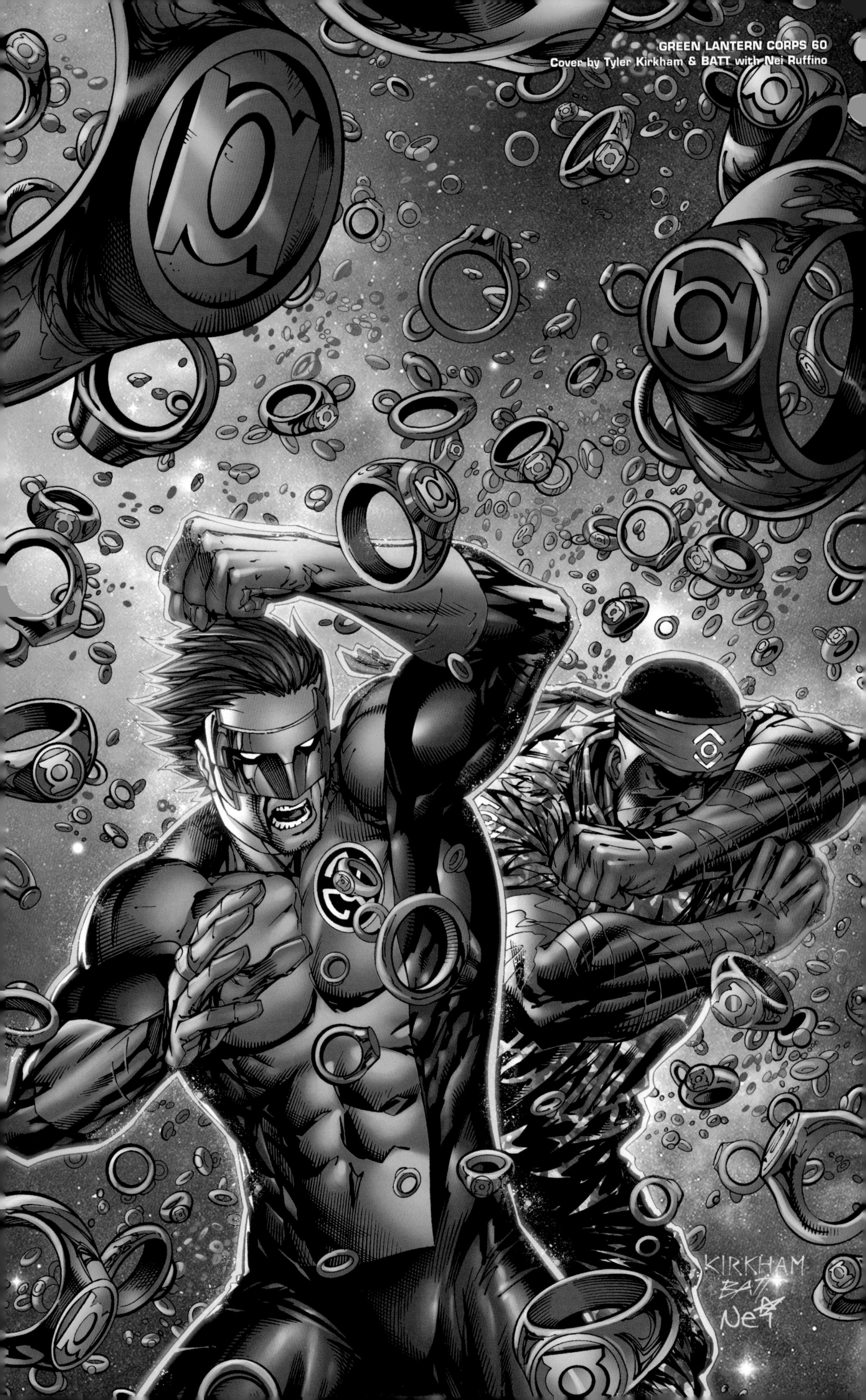
KIRKHAM
BATT
Nei

GREEN LANTERN CORPS 60
Cover by Tyler Kirkham & BATT with Nei Ruffino

WAR OF THE GREEN LANTERNS
PART EIGHT

Tony Bedard Writer
Tyler Kirkham Penciller
BATT Inker

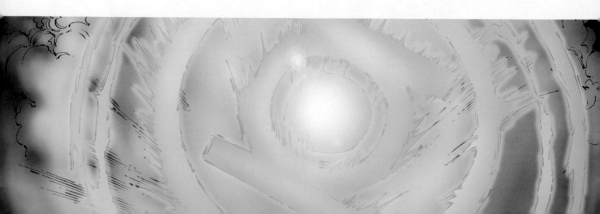

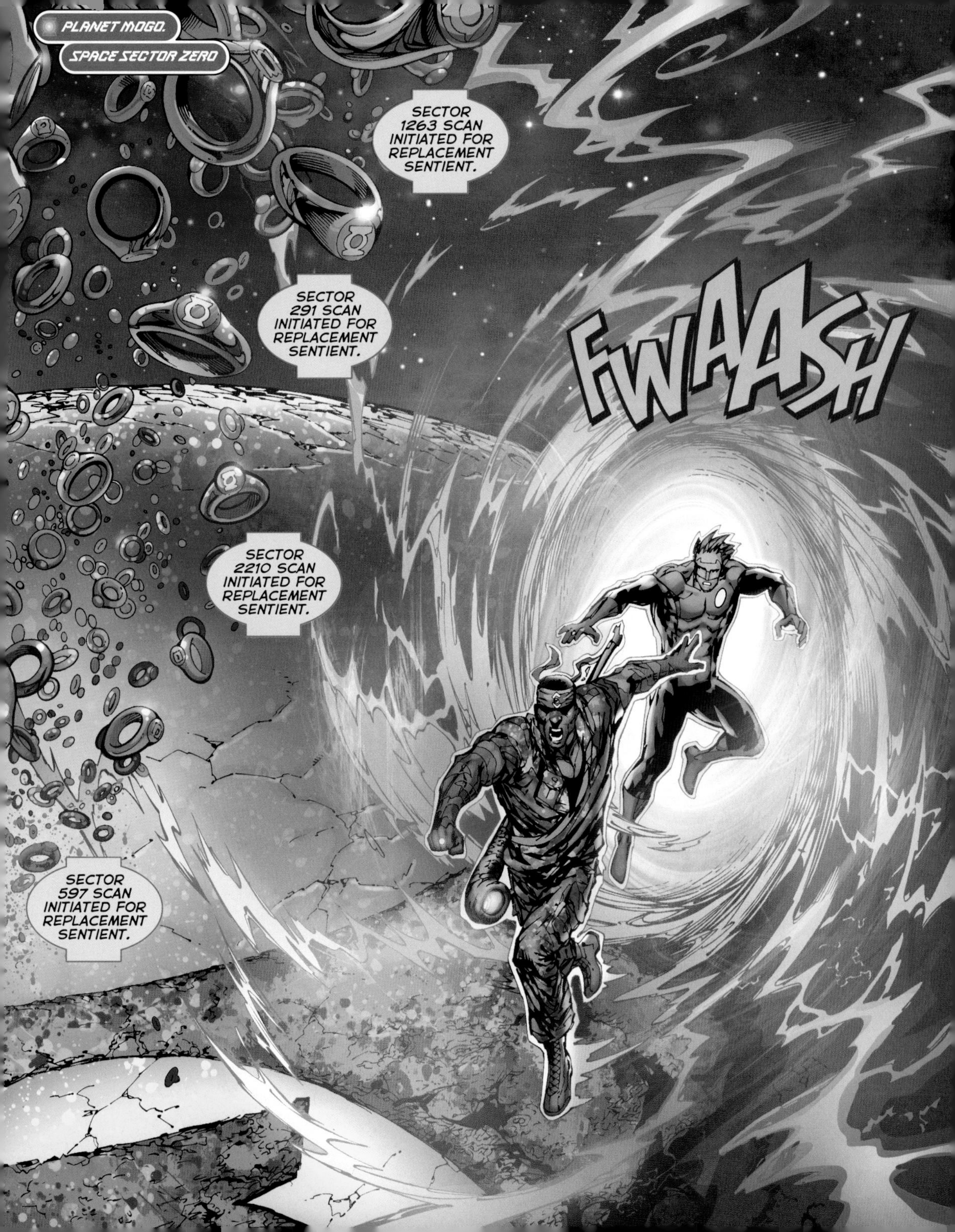
PLANET MOGO.
SPACE SECTOR ZERO
SECTOR 1263 SCAN INITIATED FOR REPLACEMENT SENTIENT.
SECTOR 291 SCAN INITIATED FOR REPLACEMENT SENTIENT.
FWAASH
SECTOR 2210 SCAN INITIATED FOR REPLACEMENT SENTIENT.
SECTOR 597 SCAN INITIATED FOR REPLACEMENT SENTIENT.

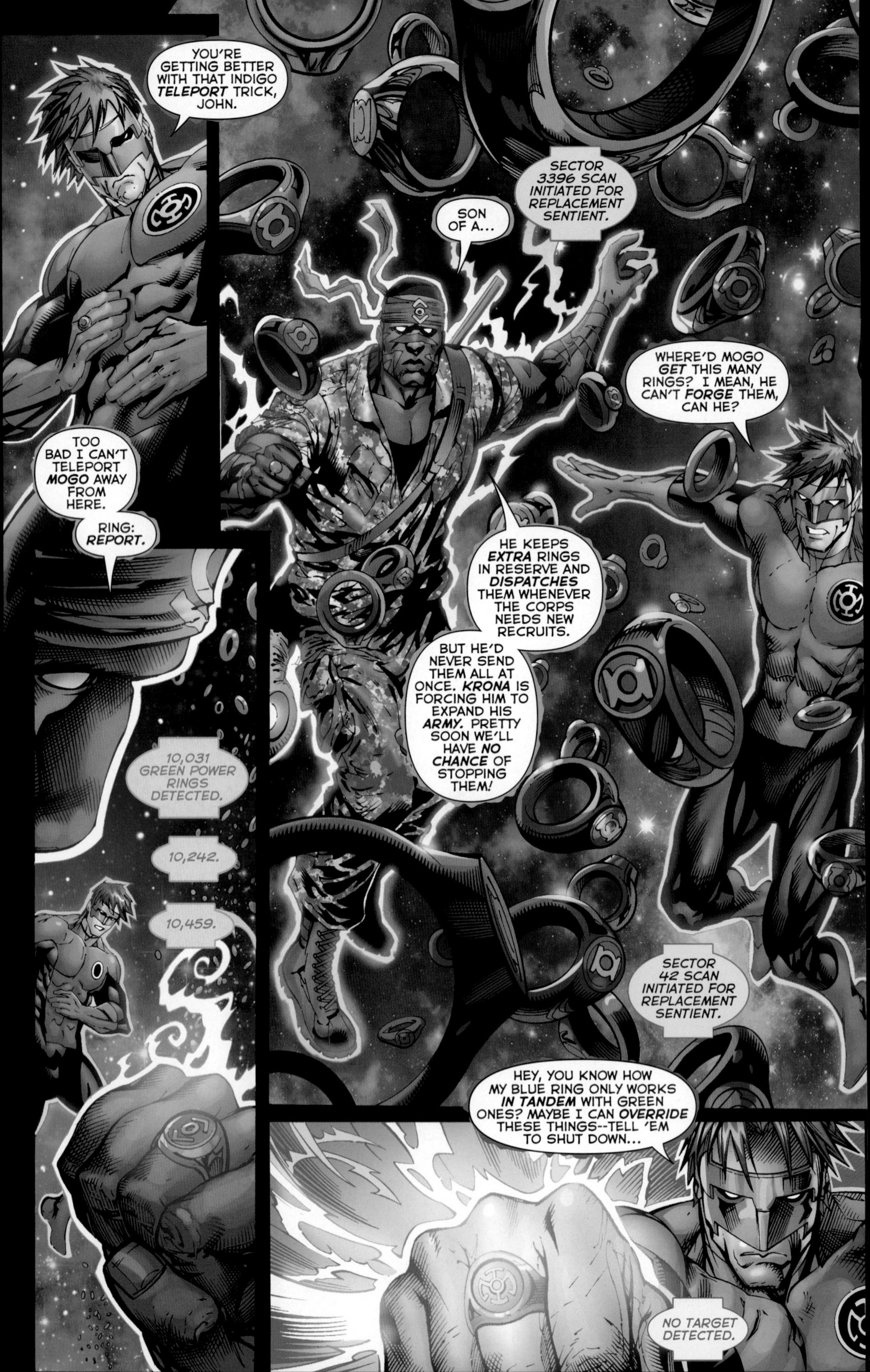

YOU'RE GETTING BETTER WITH THAT INDIGO TELEPORT TRICK, JOHN.
TOO BAD I CAN'T TELEPORT MOGO AWAY FROM HERE.
RING: REPORT.
SON OF A...
SECTOR 3396 SCAN INITIATED FOR REPLACEMENT SENTIENT.
WHERE'D MOGO GET THIS MANY RINGS? I MEAN, HE CAN'T FORGE THEM, CAN HE?
HE KEEPS EXTRA RINGS IN RESERVE AND DISPATCHES THEM WHENEVER THE CORPS NEEDS NEW RECRUITS.
BUT HE'D NEVER SEND THEM ALL AT ONCE. KRONA IS FORCING HIM TO EXPAND HIS ARMY. PRETTY SOON WE'LL HAVE NO CHANCE OF STOPPING THEM!
10,031 GREEN POWER RINGS DETECTED.
10,242.
10,459.
SECTOR 42 SCAN INITIATED FOR REPLACEMENT SENTIENT.
HEY, YOU KNOW HOW MY BLUE RING ONLY WORKS IN TANDEM WITH GREEN ONES? MAYBE I CAN OVERRIDE THESE THINGS--TELL 'EM TO SHUT DOWN...
NO TARGET DETECTED.

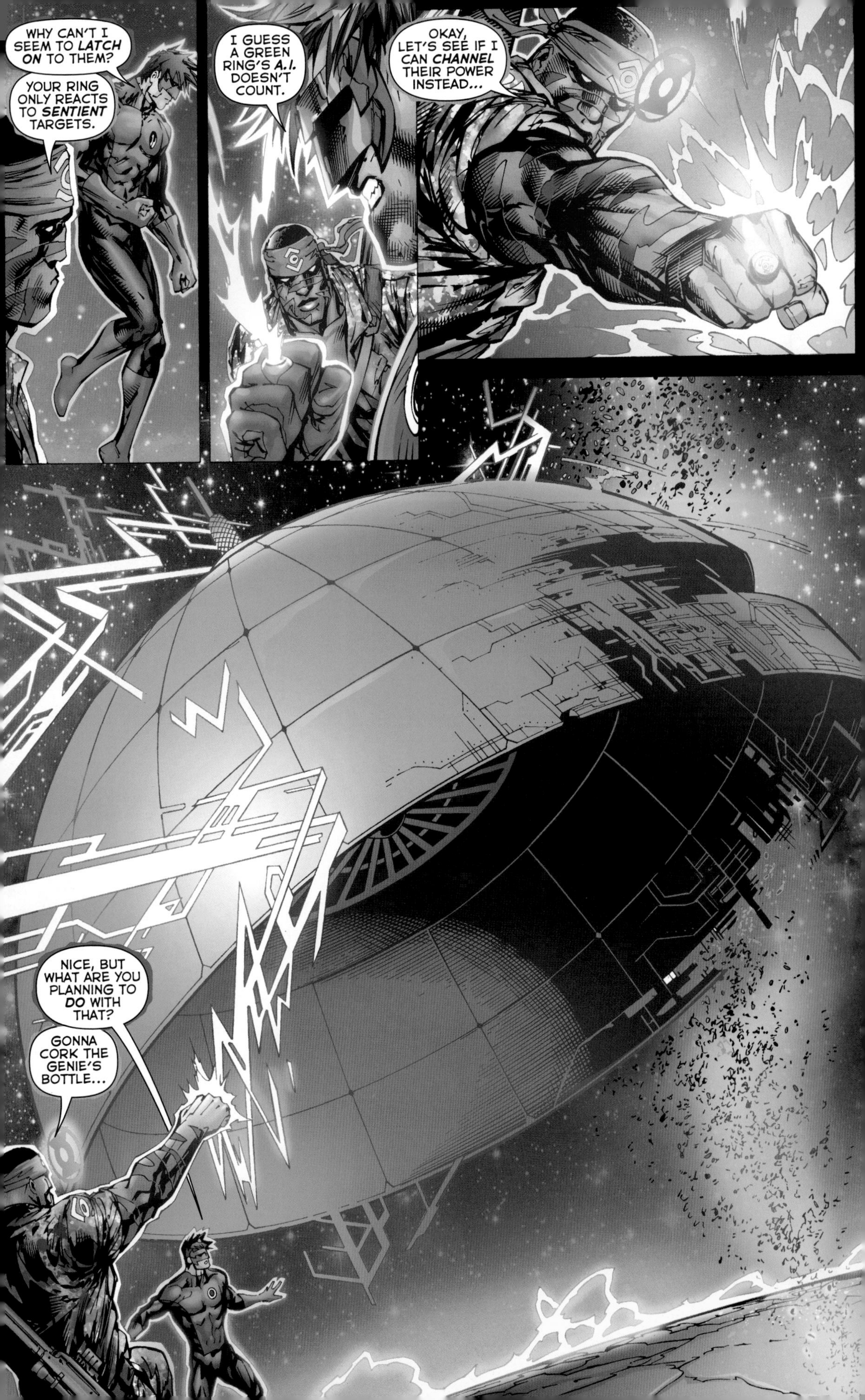
WHY CAN'T I SEEM TO LATCH ON TO THEM?
YOUR RING ONLY REACTS TO SENTIENT TARGETS.
I GUESS A GREEN RING'S A.I. DOESN'T COUNT.
OKAY, LET'S SEE IF I CAN CHANNEL THEIR POWER INSTEAD...
NICE, BUT WHAT ARE YOU PLANNING TO DO WITH THAT?
GONNA CORK THE GENIE'S BOTTLE...

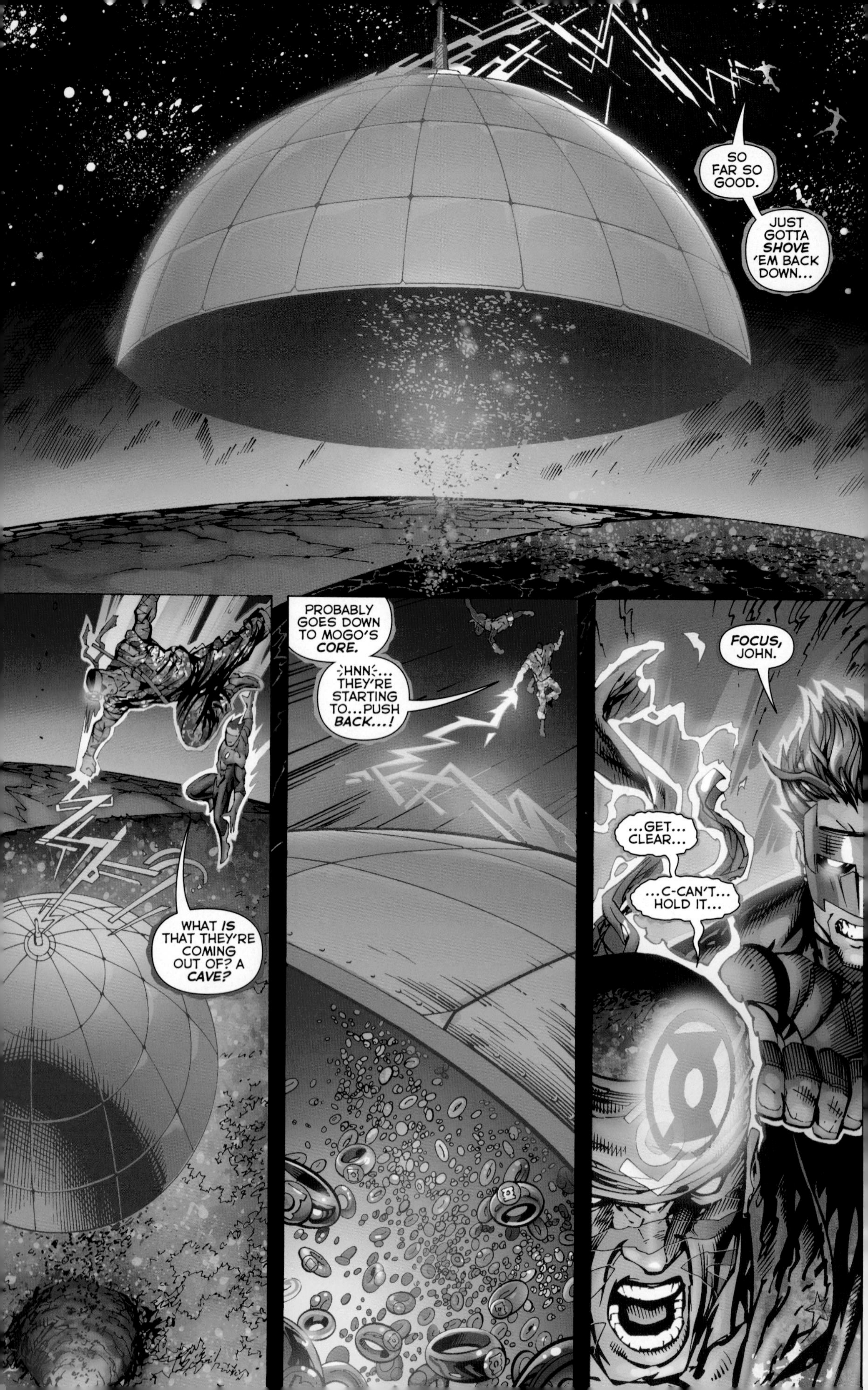
SO FAR SO GOOD.
JUST GOTTA SHOVE 'EM BACK DOWN...
WHAT IS THAT THEY'RE COMING OUT OF? A CAVE?
PROBABLY GOES DOWN TO MOGO'S CORE.
HNN... THEY'RE STARTING TO...PUSH BACK...!
FOCUS, JOHN.
...GET... CLEAR...
...C-CAN'T... HOLD IT...

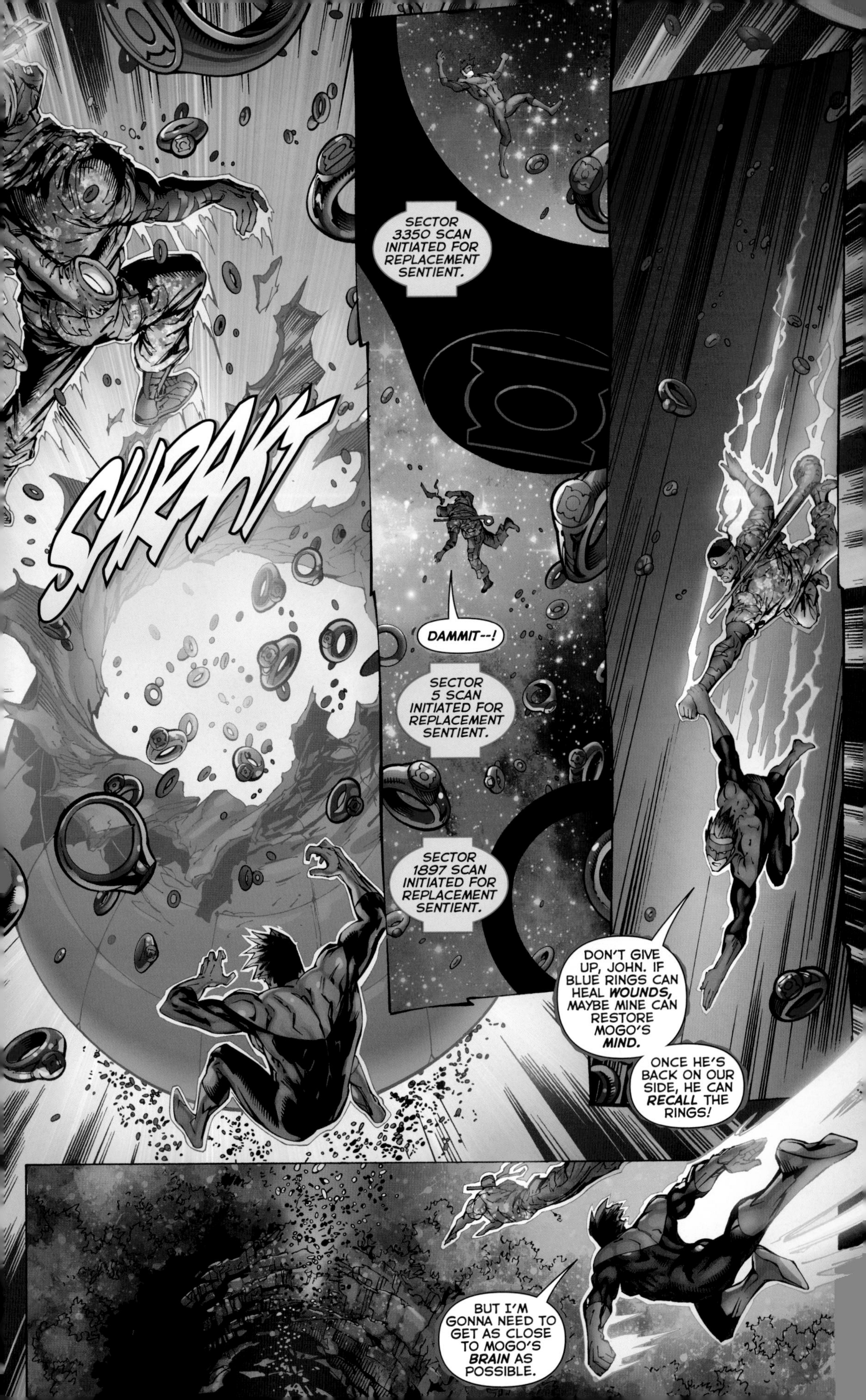
SHRAKT
SECTOR 3350 SCAN INITIATED FOR REPLACEMENT SENTIENT.
DAMMIT--!
SECTOR 5 SCAN INITIATED FOR REPLACEMENT SENTIENT.
SECTOR 1897 SCAN INITIATED FOR REPLACEMENT SENTIENT.
DON'T GIVE UP, JOHN. IF BLUE RINGS CAN HEAL WOUNDS, MAYBE MINE CAN RESTORE MOGO'S MIND.
ONCE HE'S BACK ON OUR SIDE, HE CAN RECALL THE RINGS!
BUT I'M GONNA NEED TO GET AS CLOSE TO MOGO'S BRAIN AS POSSIBLE.

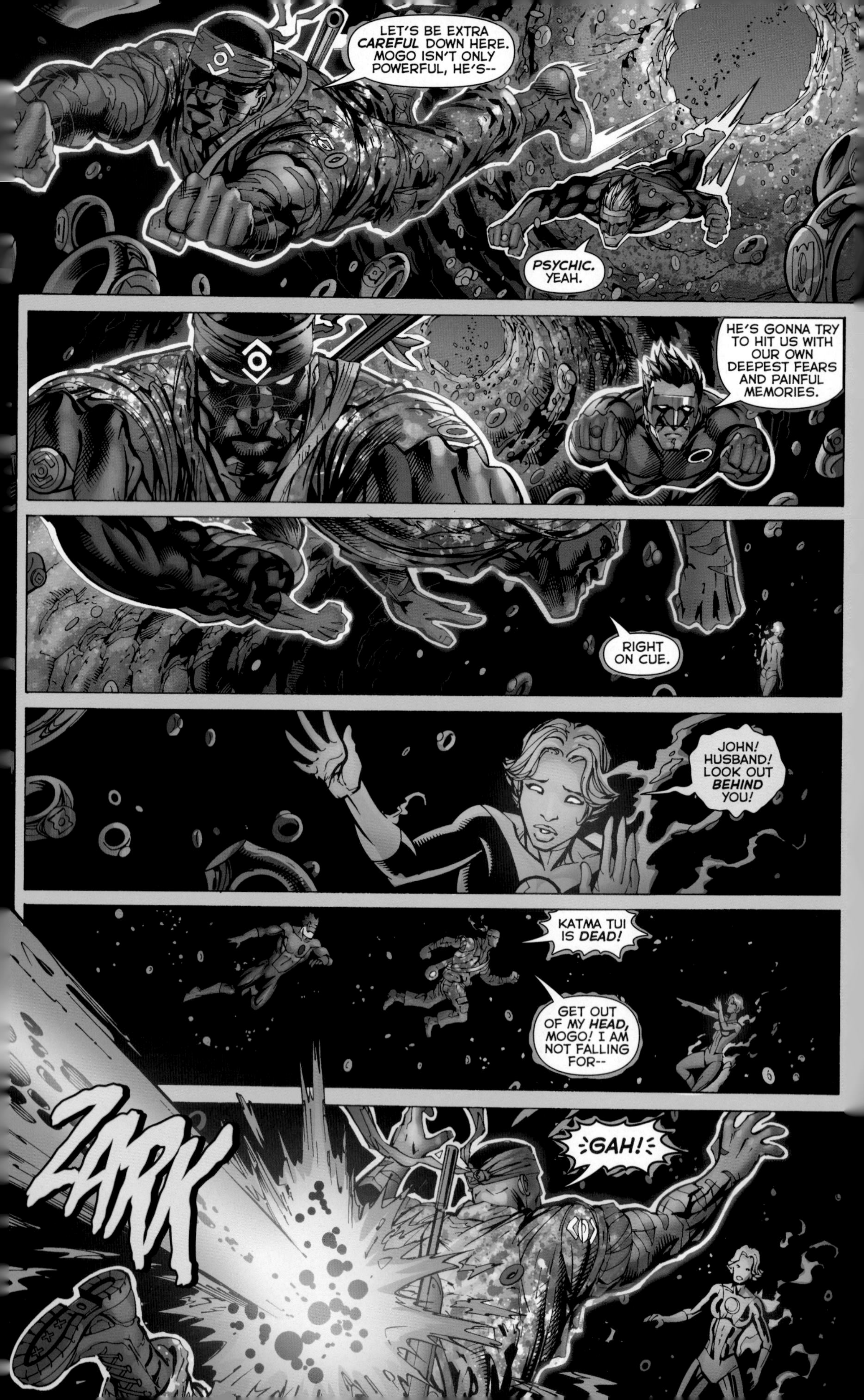
LET'S BE EXTRA *CAREFUL* DOWN HERE. MOGO ISN'T ONLY POWERFUL, HE'S--
PSYCHIC. YEAH.
HE'S GONNA TRY TO HIT US WITH OUR OWN DEEPEST FEARS AND PAINFUL MEMORIES.
RIGHT ON CUE.
JOHN! HUSBAND! LOOK OUT *BEHIND* YOU!
KATMA TUI IS *DEAD!*
GET OUT OF MY *HEAD,* MOGO! I AM NOT FALLING FOR--
ZARK
GAH!

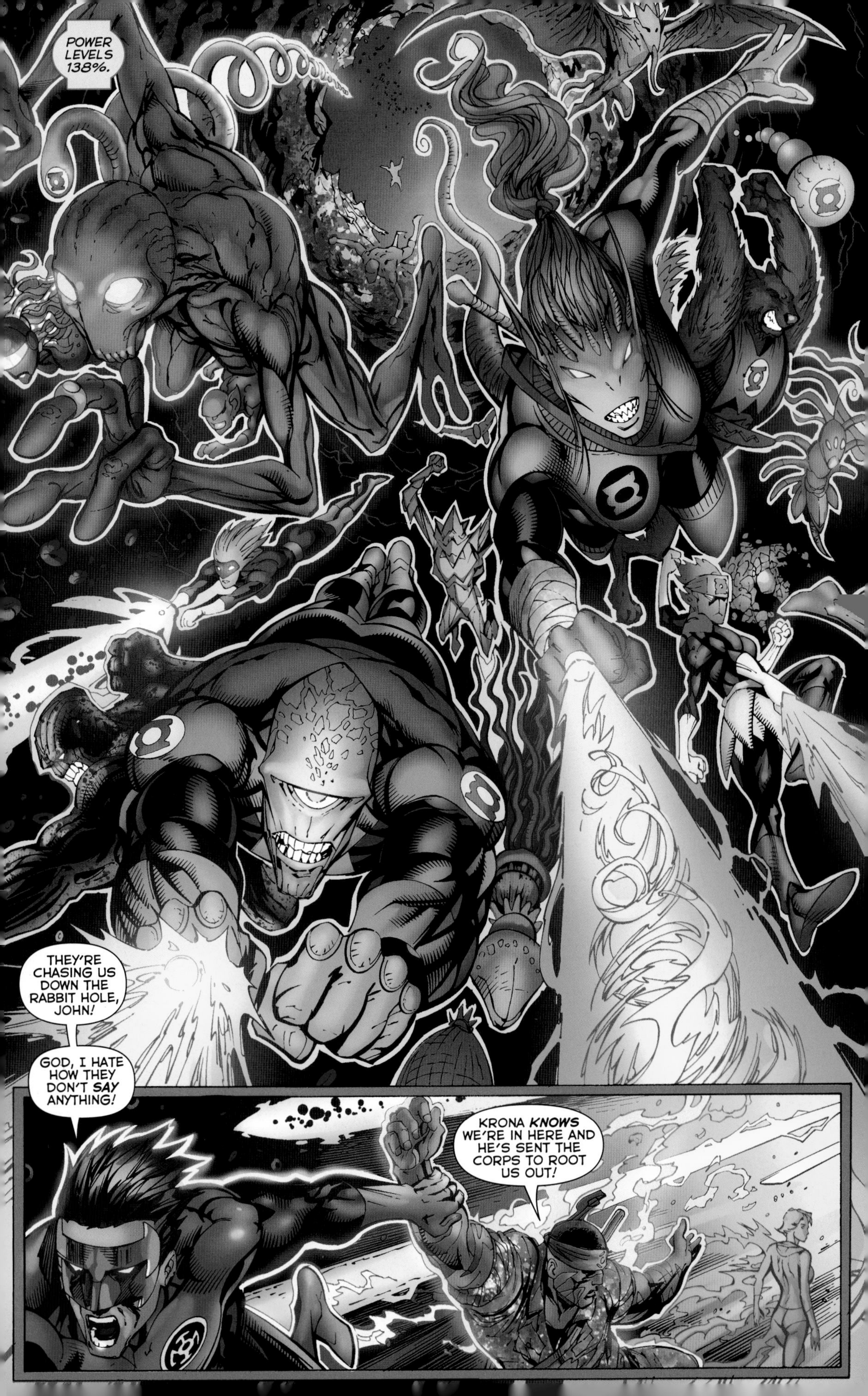
POWER LEVELS 138%.
THEY'RE CHASING US DOWN THE RABBIT HOLE, JOHN!
GOD, I HATE HOW THEY DON'T SAY ANYTHING!
KRONA KNOWS WE'RE IN HERE AND HE'S SENT THE CORPS TO ROOT US OUT!

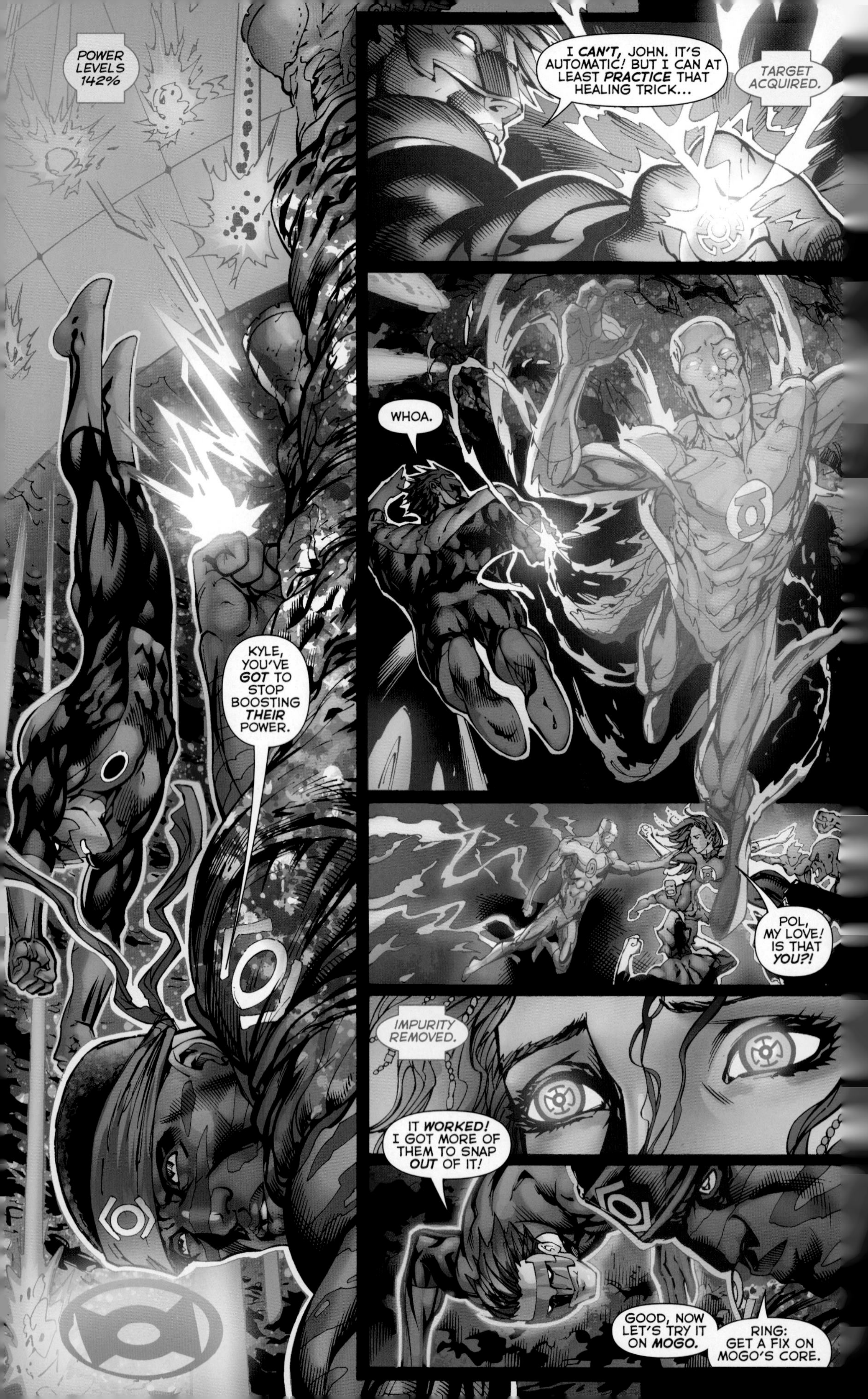
POWER LEVELS 142%
I CAN'T, JOHN. IT'S AUTOMATIC! BUT I CAN AT LEAST PRACTICE THAT HEALING TRICK...
TARGET ACQUIRED.
WHOA.
KYLE, YOU'VE GOT TO STOP BOOSTING THEIR POWER.
POL, MY LOVE! IS THAT YOU?!
IMPURITY REMOVED.
IT WORKED! I GOT MORE OF THEM TO SNAP OUT OF IT!
GOOD, NOW LET'S TRY IT ON MOGO.
RING: GET A FIX ON MOGO'S CORE.

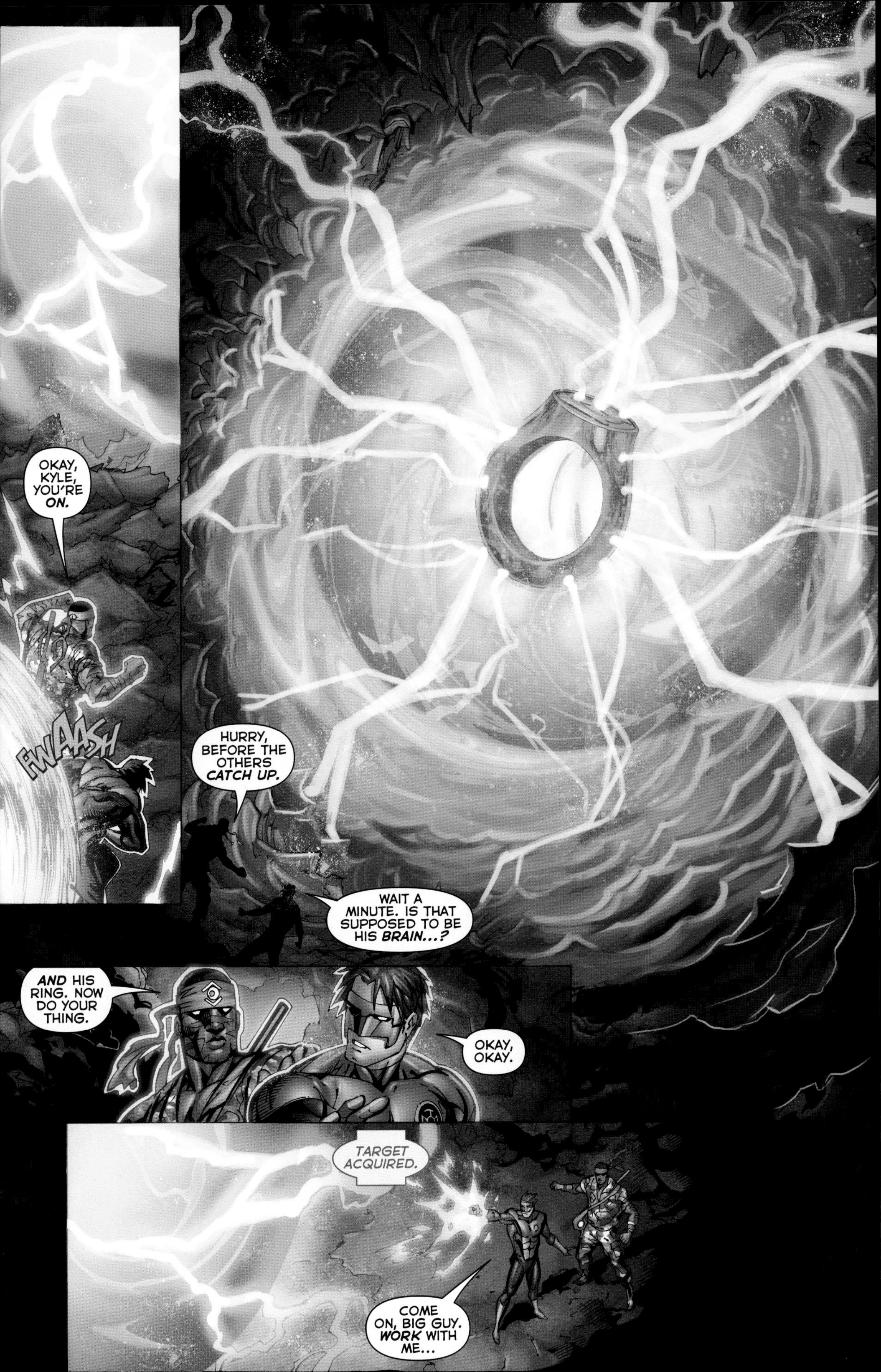
OKAY, KYLE, YOU'RE ON.
FWAASH
HURRY, BEFORE THE OTHERS CATCH UP.
WAIT A MINUTE. IS THAT SUPPOSED TO BE HIS BRAIN...?
AND HIS RING. NOW DO YOUR THING.
OKAY, OKAY.
TARGET ACQUIRED.
COME ON, BIG GUY. WORK WITH ME...

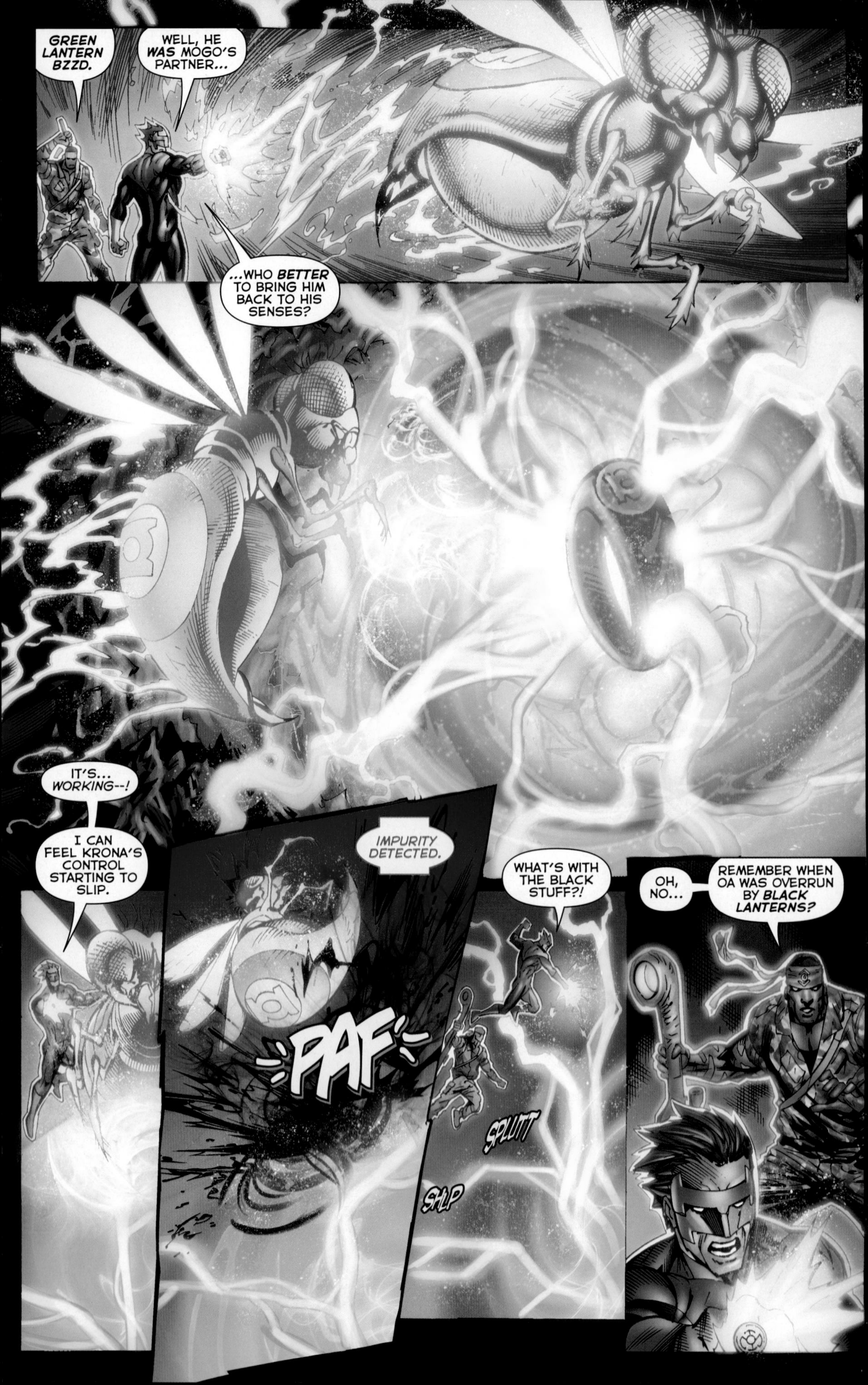
GREEN LANTERN BZZD.
WELL, HE WAS MOGO'S PARTNER...
...WHO BETTER TO BRING HIM BACK TO HIS SENSES?
IT'S... WORKING--!
I CAN FEEL KRONA'S CONTROL STARTING TO SLIP.
IMPURITY DETECTED.
PAF
WHAT'S WITH THE BLACK STUFF?!
SPLUTT
SHLP
OH, NO...
REMEMBER WHEN OA WAS OVERRUN BY BLACK LANTERNS?

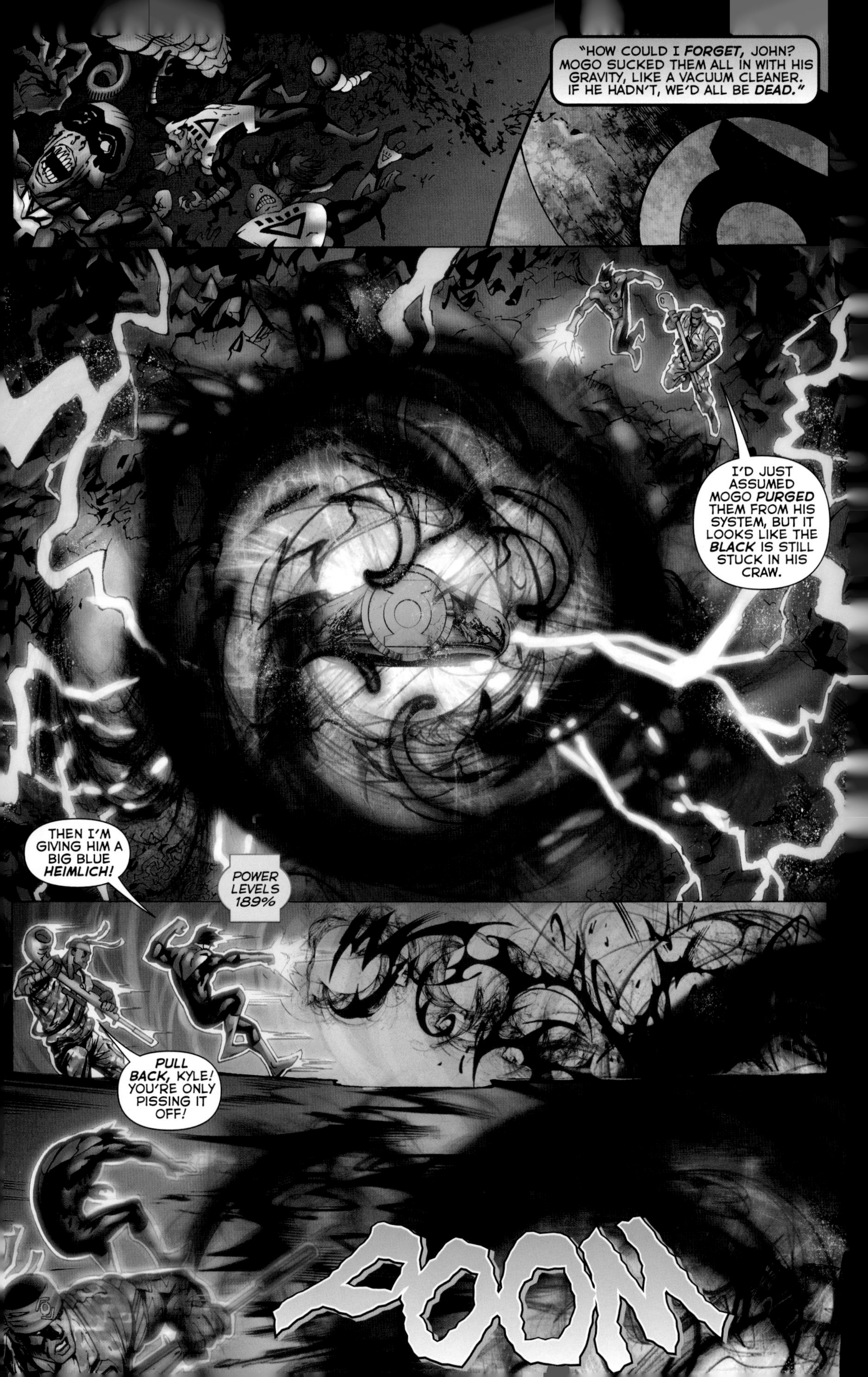

"HOW COULD I FORGET, JOHN? MOGO SUCKED THEM ALL IN WITH HIS GRAVITY, LIKE A VACUUM CLEANER. IF HE HADN'T, WE'D ALL BE DEAD."
I'D JUST ASSUMED MOGO PURGED THEM FROM HIS SYSTEM, BUT IT LOOKS LIKE THE BLACK IS STILL STUCK IN HIS CRAW.
THEN I'M GIVING HIM A BIG BLUE HEIMLICH!
POWER LEVELS 189%
PULL BACK, KYLE! YOU'RE ONLY PISSING IT OFF!
DOOM

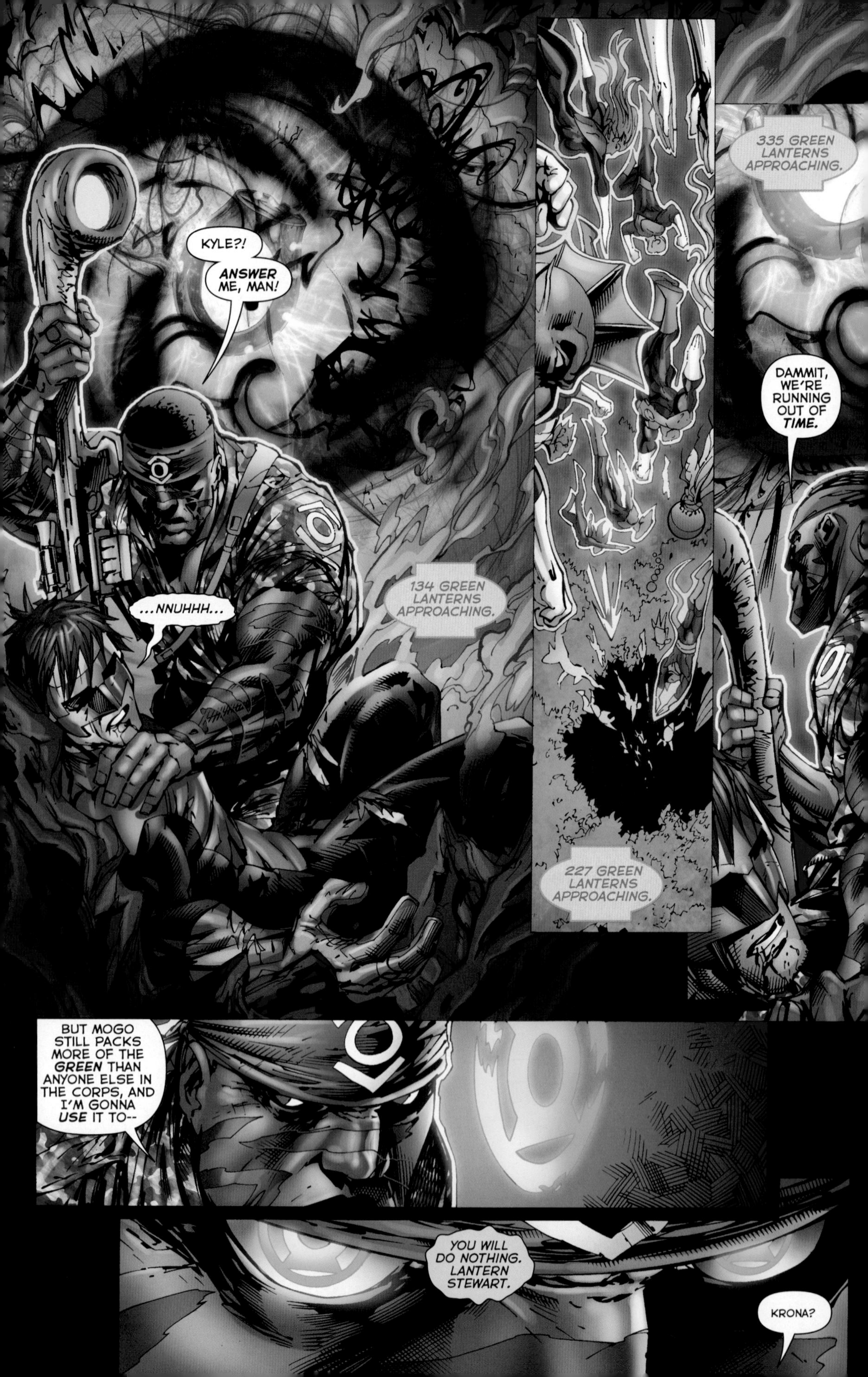
KYLE?!
ANSWER ME, MAN!
...NNUHHH...
134 GREEN LANTERNS APPROACHING.
227 GREEN LANTERNS APPROACHING.
335 GREEN LANTERNS APPROACHING.
DAMMIT, WE'RE RUNNING OUT OF TIME.
BUT MOGO STILL PACKS MORE OF THE GREEN THAN ANYONE ELSE IN THE CORPS, AND I'M GONNA USE IT TO--
YOU WILL DO NOTHING. LANTERN STEWART.
KRONA?

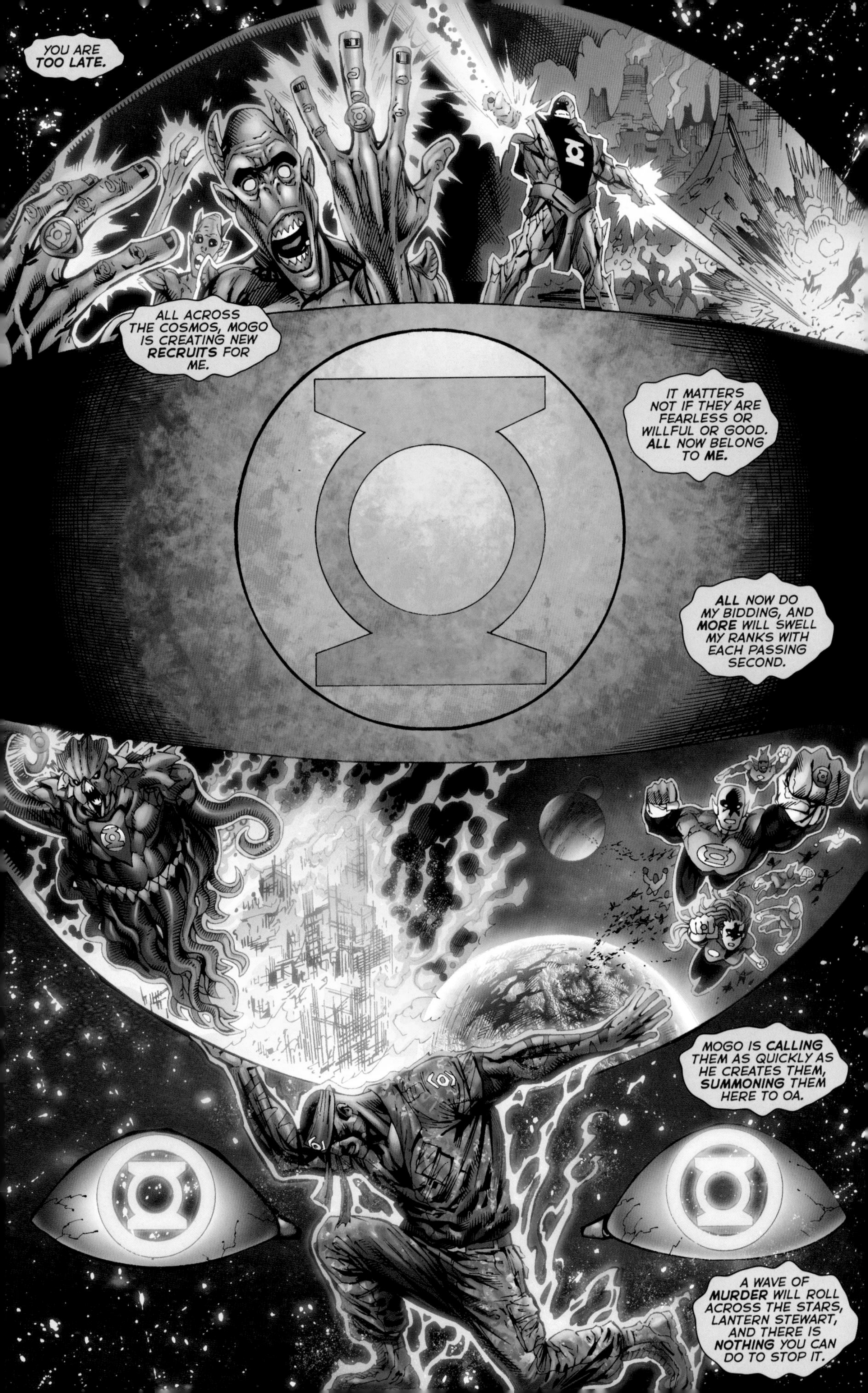
YOU ARE TOO LATE.
ALL ACROSS THE COSMOS, MOGO IS CREATING NEW RECRUITS FOR ME.
IT MATTERS NOT IF THEY ARE FEARLESS OR WILLFUL OR GOOD. ALL NOW BELONG TO ME.
ALL NOW DO MY BIDDING, AND MORE WILL SWELL MY RANKS WITH EACH PASSING SECOND.
MOGO IS CALLING THEM AS QUICKLY AS HE CREATES THEM, SUMMONING THEM HERE TO OA.
A WAVE OF MURDER WILL ROLL ACROSS THE STARS, LANTERN STEWART, AND THERE IS NOTHING YOU CAN DO TO STOP IT.

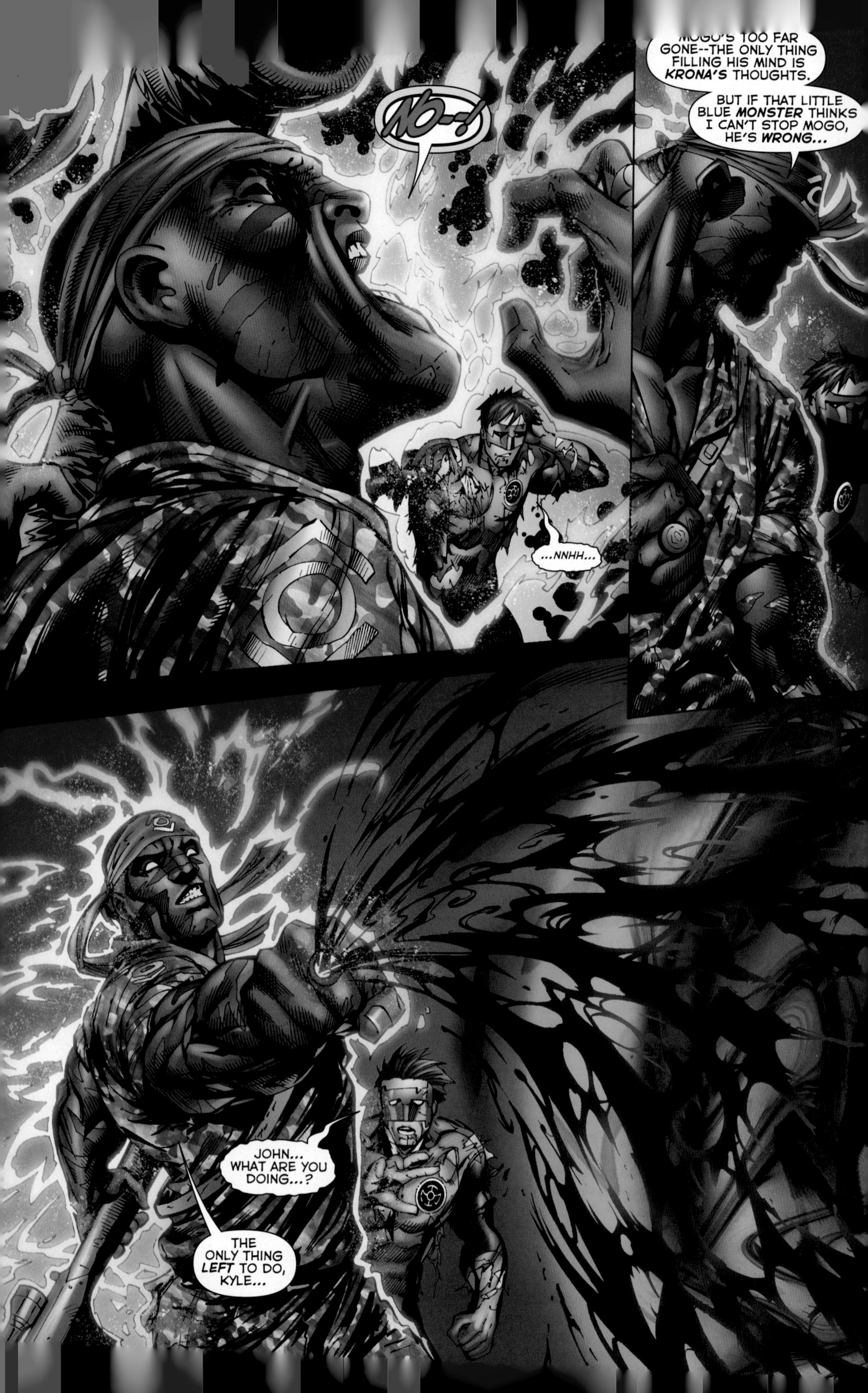
NO--!
...NNHH...
MOGO'S TOO FAR GONE--THE ONLY THING FILLING HIS MIND IS KRONA'S THOUGHTS.
BUT IF THAT LITTLE BLUE MONSTER THINKS I CAN'T STOP MOGO, HE'S WRONG...
JOHN... WHAT ARE YOU DOING...?
THE ONLY THING LEFT TO DO, KYLE...

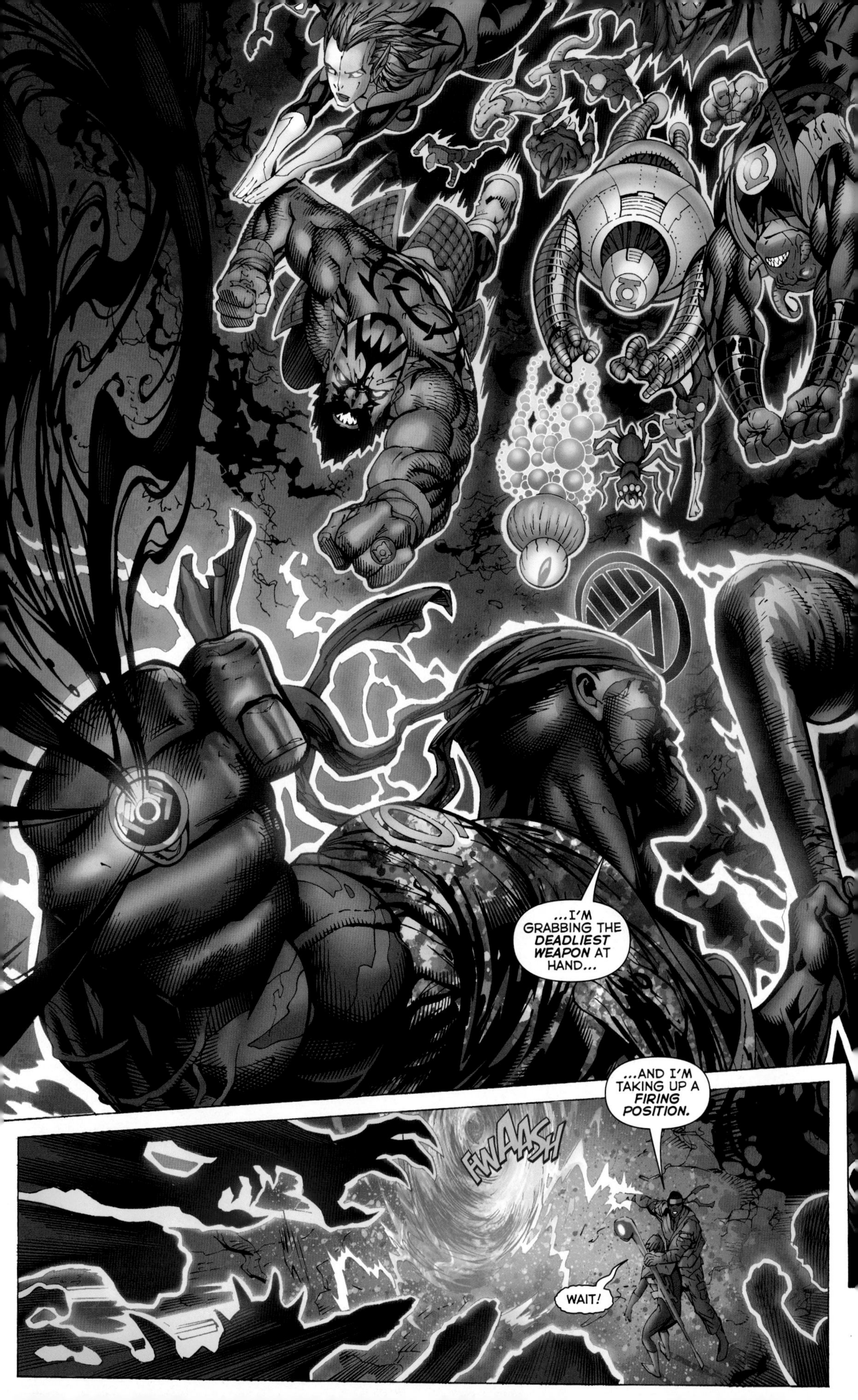
...I'M GRABBING THE DEADLIEST WEAPON AT HAND...
...AND I'M TAKING UP A FIRING POSITION.
FWAASH
WAIT!

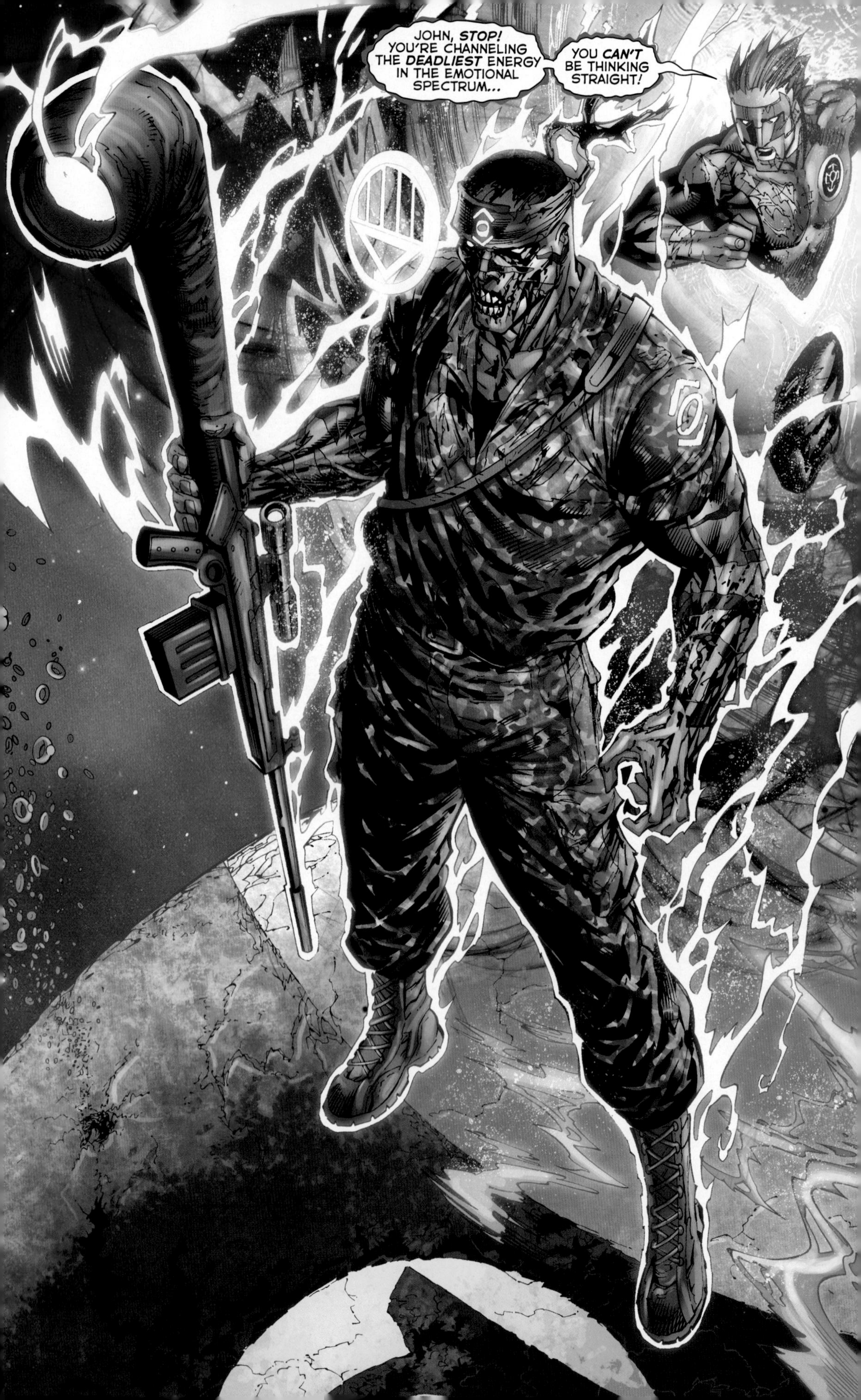
JOHN, STOP! YOU'RE CHANNELING THE DEADLIEST ENERGY IN THE EMOTIONAL SPECTRUM...
YOU CAN'T BE THINKING STRAIGHT!

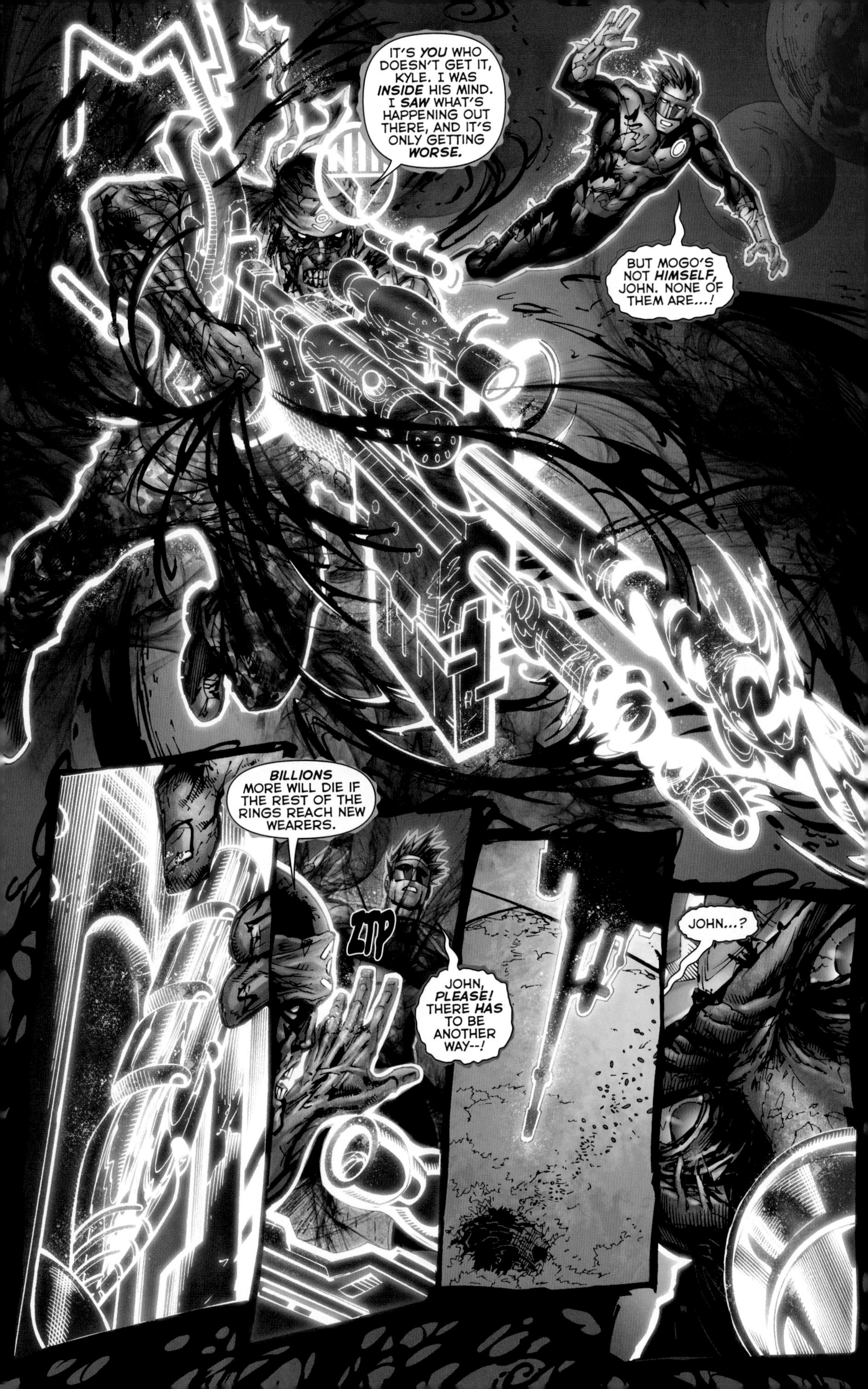
IT'S *YOU* WHO DOESN'T GET IT, KYLE. I WAS *INSIDE* HIS MIND. I *SAW* WHAT'S HAPPENING OUT THERE, AND IT'S ONLY GETTING *WORSE.*
BUT MOGO'S NOT *HIMSELF,* JOHN. NONE OF THEM ARE...!
BILLIONS MORE WILL DIE IF THE REST OF THE RINGS REACH NEW WEARERS.
ZZIP
JOHN, *PLEASE!* THERE *HAS* TO BE ANOTHER WAY--!
JOHN...?

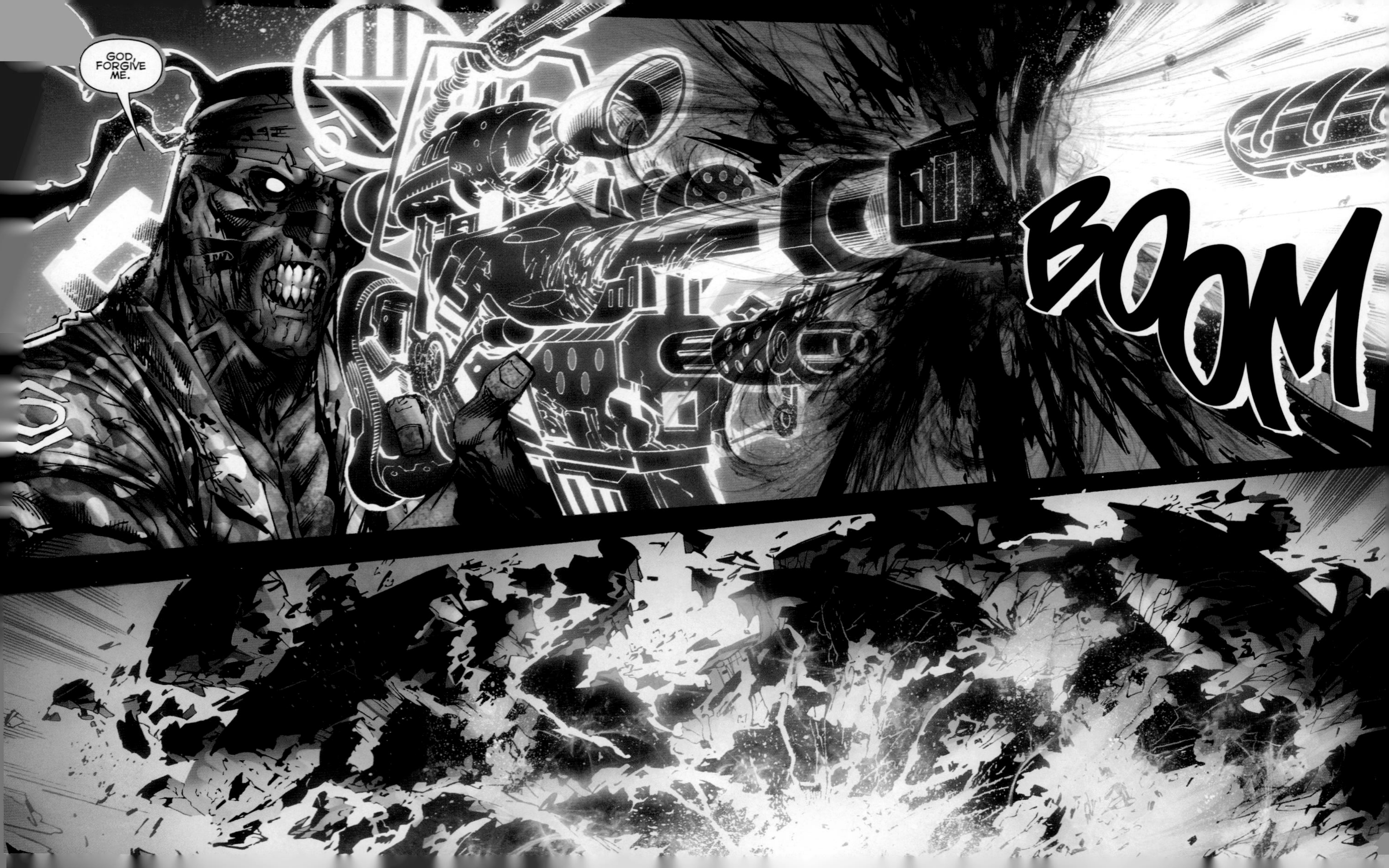
GOD, FORGIVE ME.
BOOM

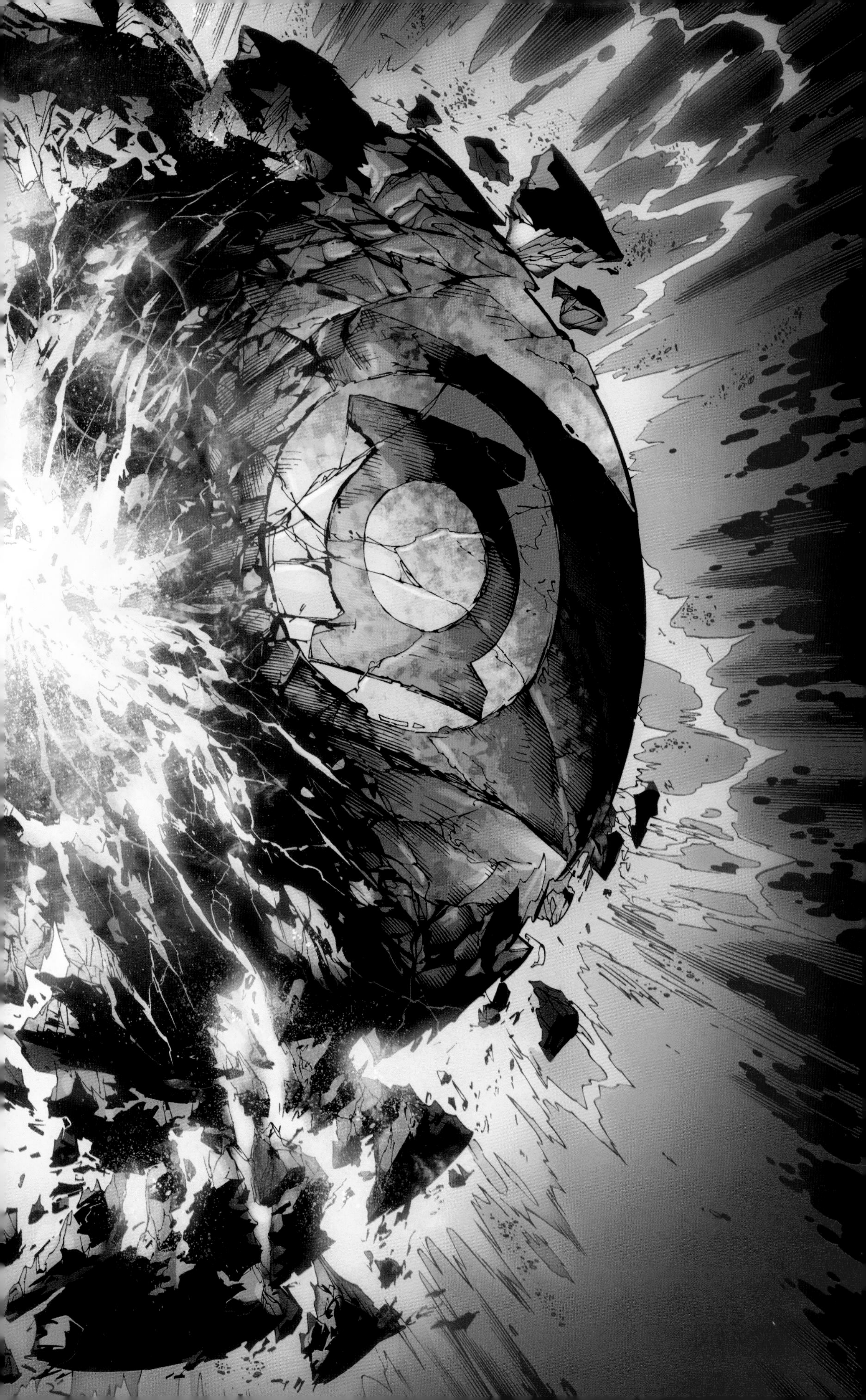

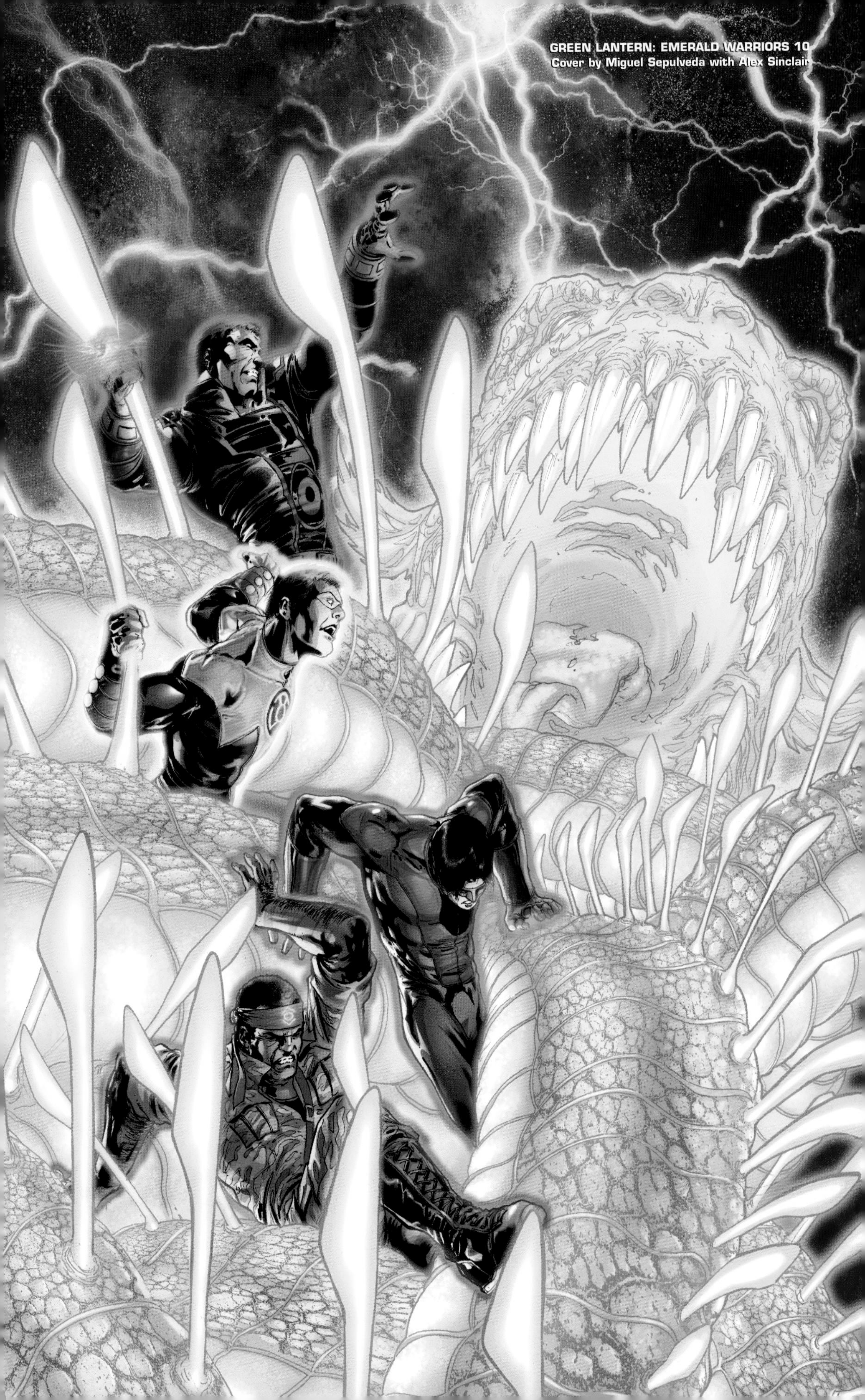
GREEN LANTERN: EMERALD WARRIORS 10
Cover by Miguel Sepulveda with Alex Sinclair

WAR OF THE GREEN LANTERNS
PART NINE

Peter J. Tomasi Writer
Fernando Pasarin Penciller
Cam Smith, Keith Champagne, Andy Owens,
Sean Parsons, Jack Purcell & Jay Leisten Inkers

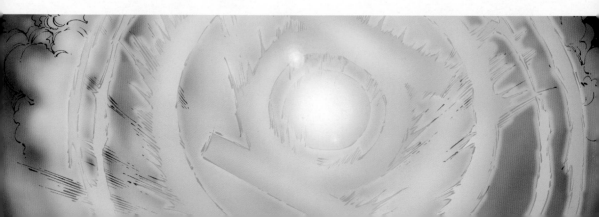

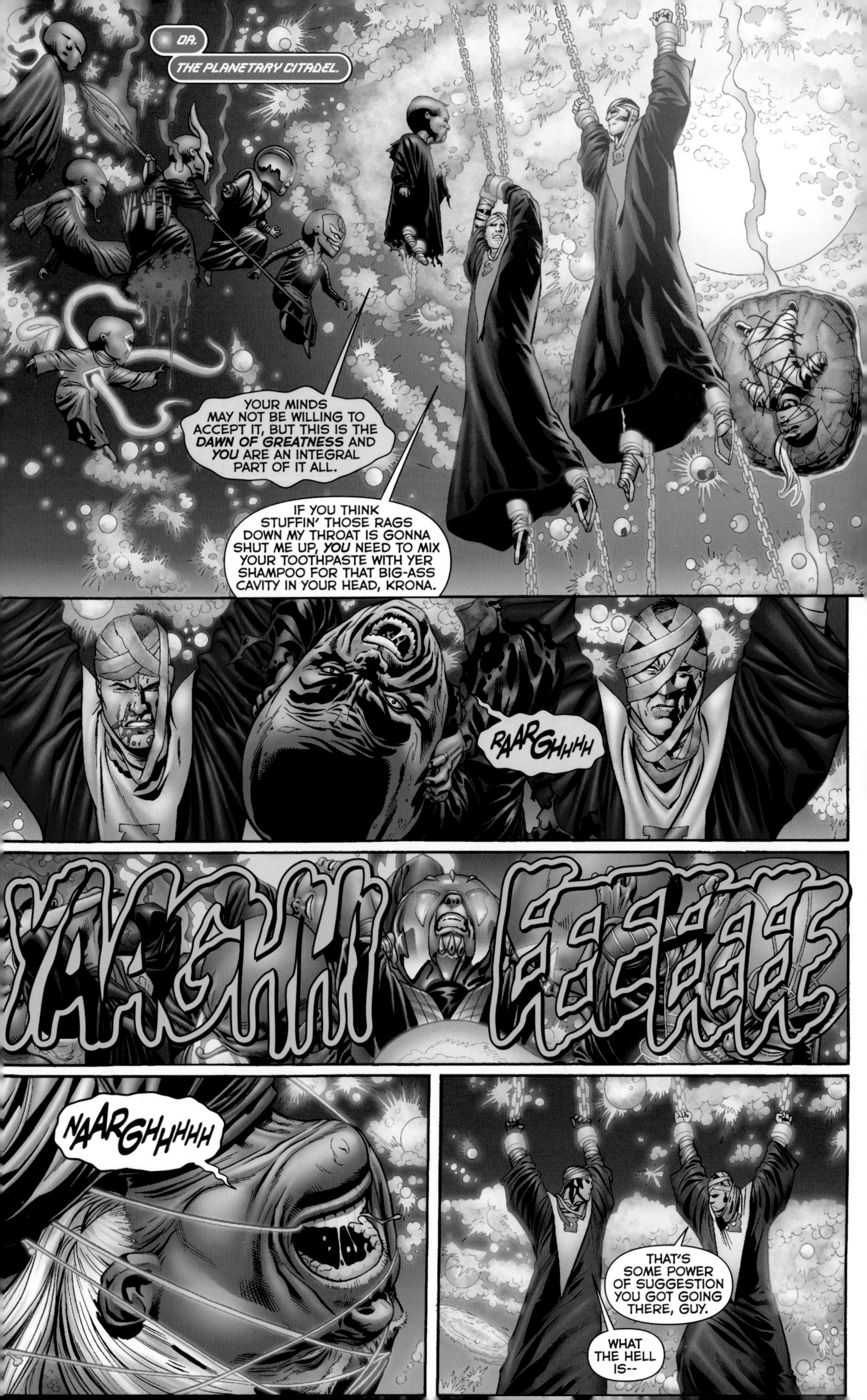

OA.
THE PLANETARY CITADEL.
YOUR MINDS MAY NOT BE WILLING TO ACCEPT IT, BUT THIS IS THE *DAWN OF GREATNESS* AND *YOU* ARE AN INTEGRAL PART OF IT ALL.
IF YOU THINK STUFFIN' THOSE RAGS DOWN MY THROAT IS GONNA SHUT ME UP, *YOU* NEED TO MIX YOUR TOOTHPASTE WITH YER SHAMPOO FOR THAT BIG-ASS CAVITY IN YOUR HEAD, KRONA.
RAARGHHHH
NAARGHHHHH
THAT'S SOME POWER OF SUGGESTION YOU GOT GOING THERE, GUY.
WHAT THE HELL IS--

WE GOT A GIFT HORSE OPENING ITS YAP WIDE, JORDAN!

NOW'S A GOOD TIME TO GET OUR ASSES OUTTA HERE!

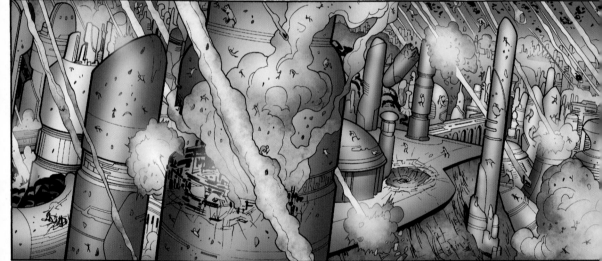

YARRGH

NOOOO

AAIEEE

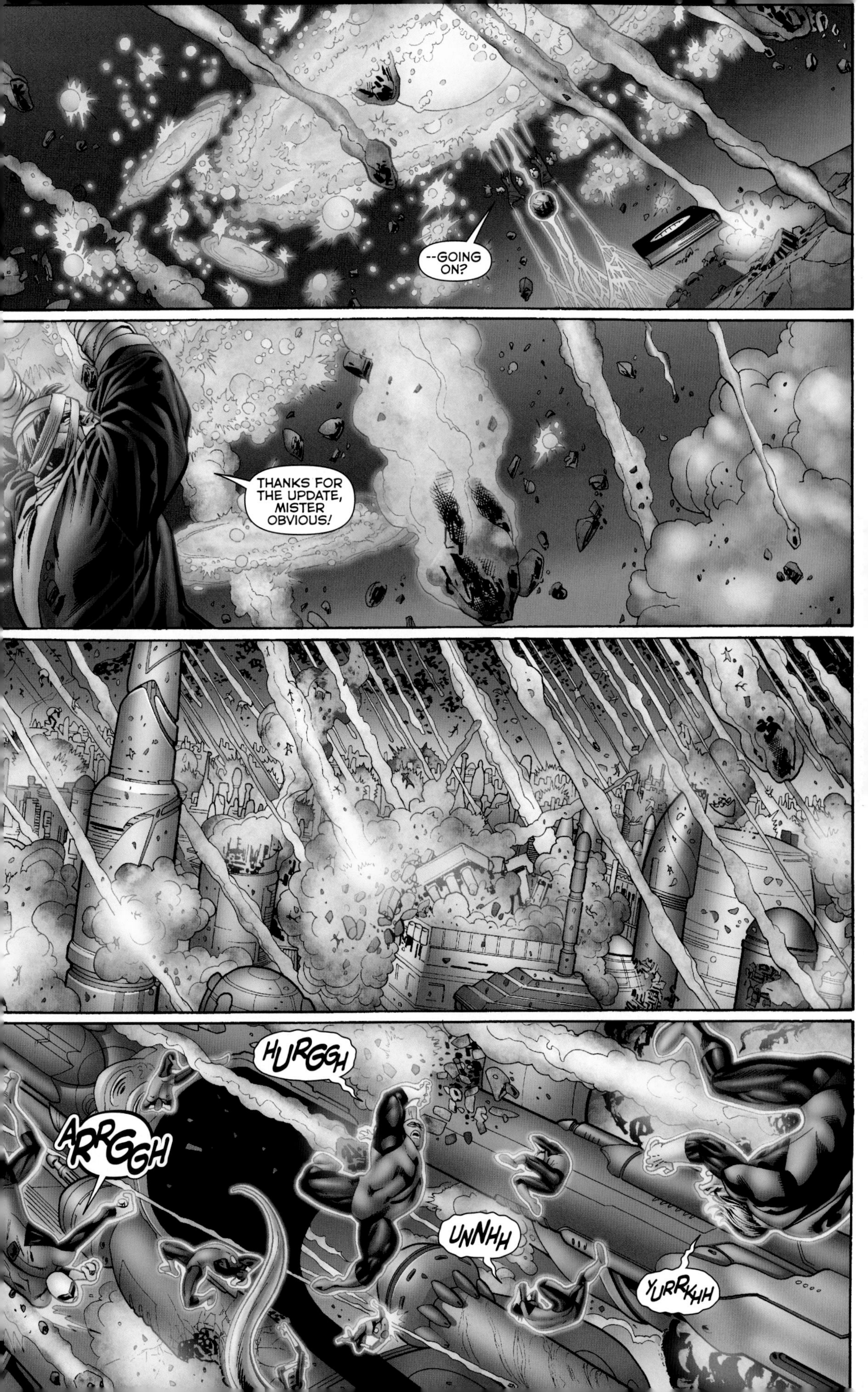
--GOING ON?
THANKS FOR THE UPDATE, MISTER OBVIOUS!
HURGGH
ARRGGH
UNNHH
YURRKHH

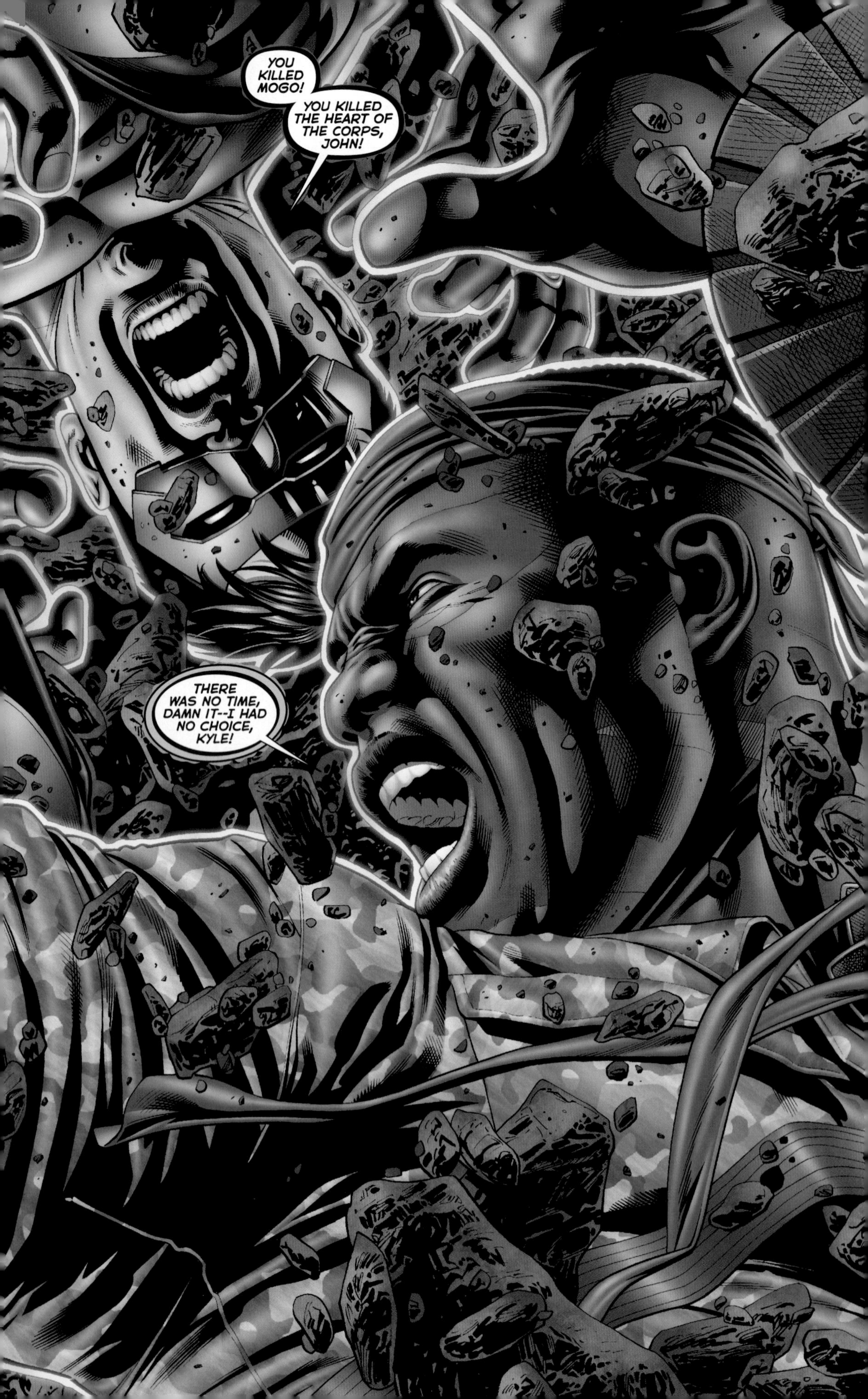
YOU KILLED MOGO!
YOU KILLED THE HEART OF THE CORPS, JOHN!
THERE WAS NO TIME, DAMN IT--I HAD NO CHOICE, KYLE!

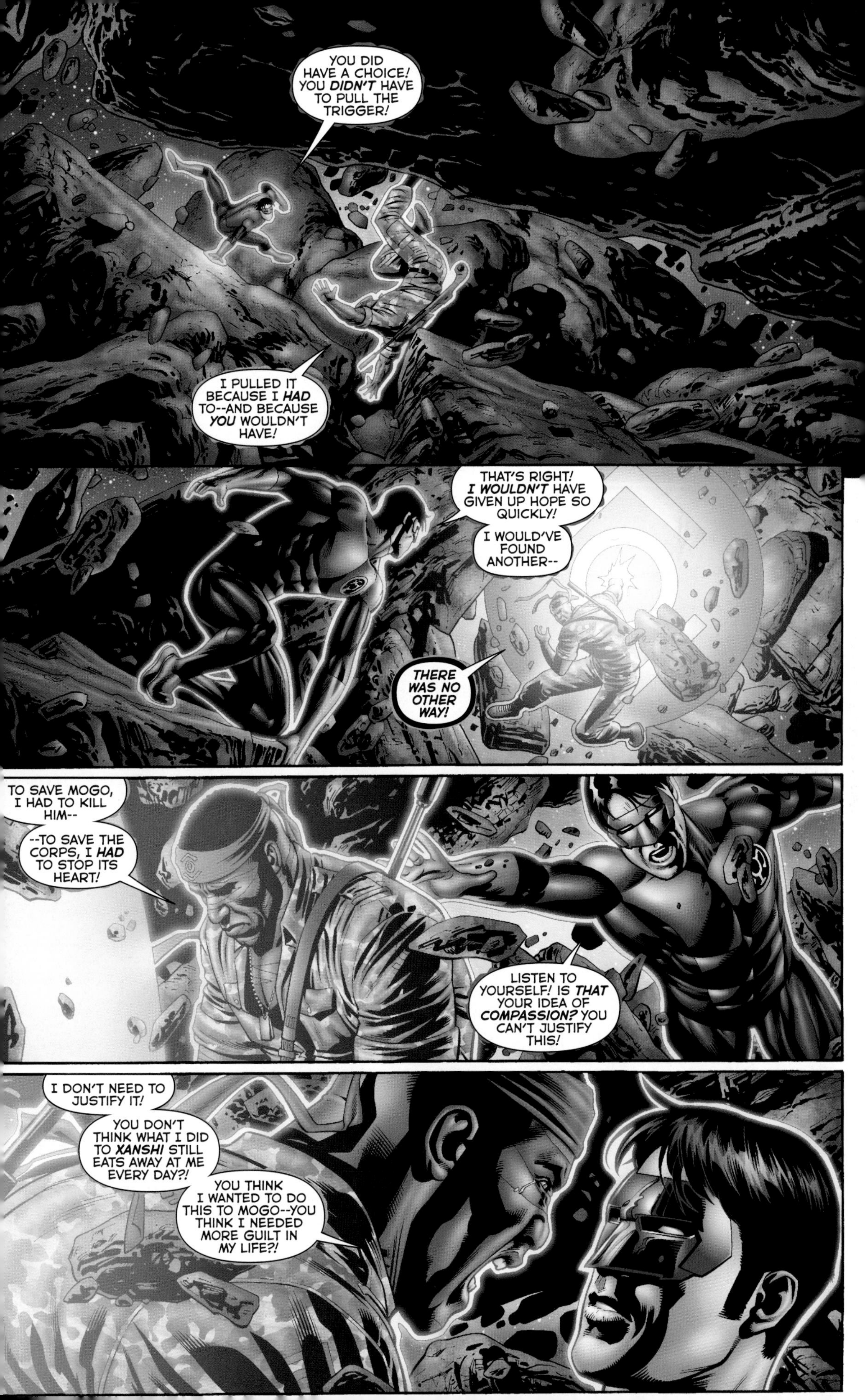
YOU DID HAVE A CHOICE! YOU DIDN'T HAVE TO PULL THE TRIGGER!
I PULLED IT BECAUSE I HAD TO--AND BECAUSE YOU WOULDN'T HAVE!
THAT'S RIGHT! I WOULDN'T HAVE GIVEN UP HOPE SO QUICKLY!
I WOULD'VE FOUND ANOTHER--
THERE WAS NO OTHER WAY!
TO SAVE MOGO, I HAD TO KILL HIM--
--TO SAVE THE CORPS, I HAD TO STOP ITS HEART!
LISTEN TO YOURSELF! IS THAT YOUR IDEA OF COMPASSION? YOU CAN'T JUSTIFY THIS!
I DON'T NEED TO JUSTIFY IT!
YOU DON'T THINK WHAT I DID TO XANSHI STILL EATS AWAY AT ME EVERY DAY?!
YOU THINK I WANTED TO DO THIS TO MOGO--YOU THINK I NEEDED MORE GUILT IN MY LIFE?!

GET AWAY FROM ME.

MAYBE IF I PULL ENOUGH PIECES OF MOGO TOGETHER--

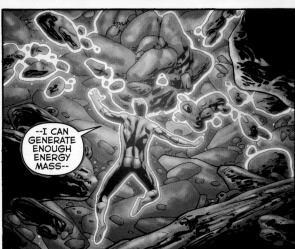

--I CAN GENERATE ENOUGH ENERGY MASS--

--AND HELP HIM RESTART HIS CORE!

NO!

I CAN DO THIS! I KNOW I CAN!

WHAT I'VE DONE'S IRREPARABLE, KYLE, MOGO'S GONE.

MOGO IS NOT GONE! WE'RE STAYING HERE UNTIL--

HAL AND GUY NEED US!

WE'RE LEAVING!

FAASH!

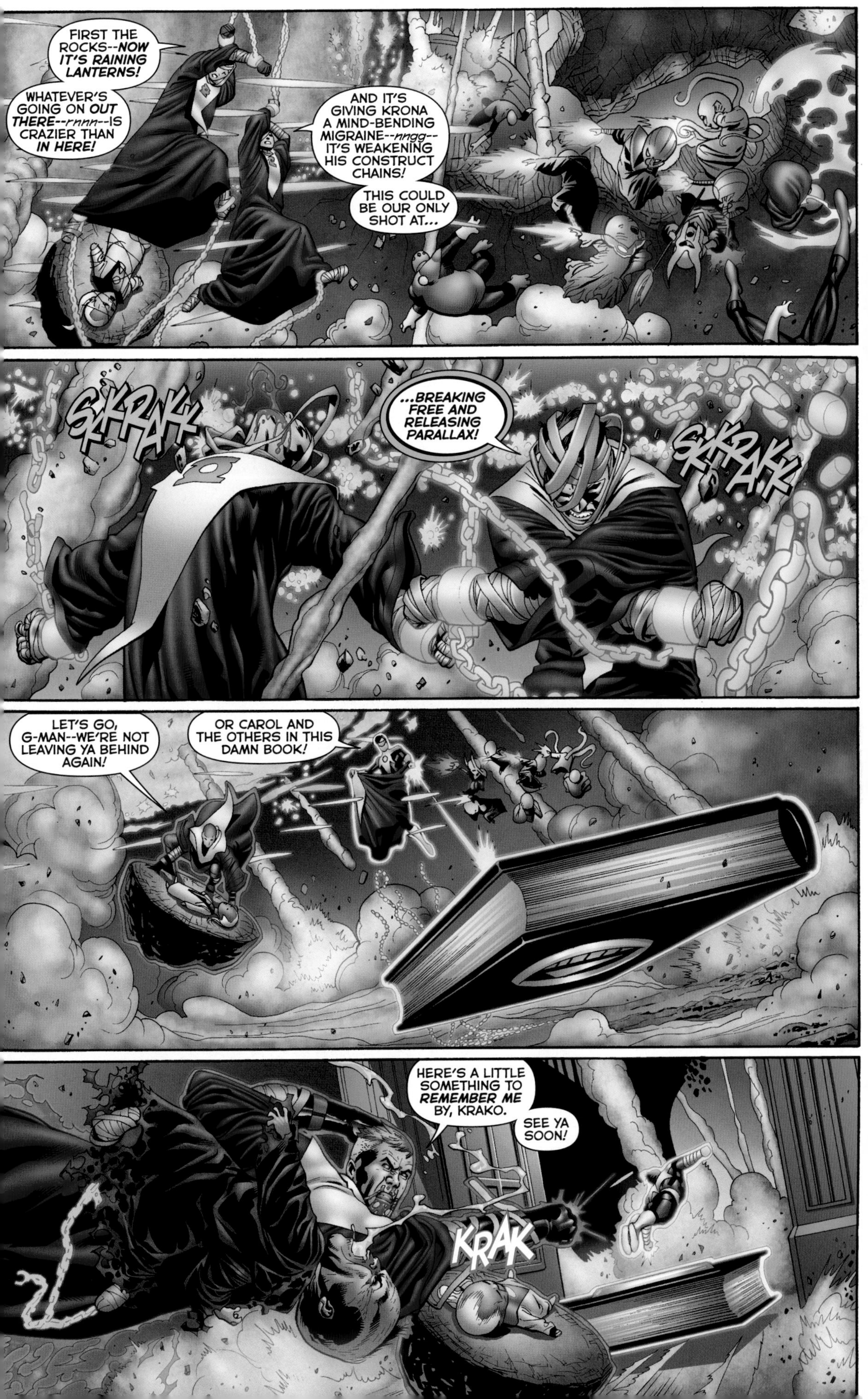

FIRST THE ROCKS--NOW IT'S RAINING LANTERNS!
WHATEVER'S GOING ON OUT THERE--rnnn--IS CRAZIER THAN IN HERE!
AND IT'S GIVING KRONA A MIND-BENDING MIGRAINE--nngg--IT'S WEAKENING HIS CONSTRUCT CHAINS!
THIS COULD BE OUR ONLY SHOT AT...
SKKRAKK
...BREAKING FREE AND RELEASING PARALLAX!
SKKRAKK
LET'S GO, G-MAN--WE'RE NOT LEAVING YA BEHIND AGAIN!
OR CAROL AND THE OTHERS IN THIS DAMN BOOK!
HERE'S A LITTLE SOMETHING TO REMEMBER ME BY, KRAKO.
SEE YA SOON!
KRAK

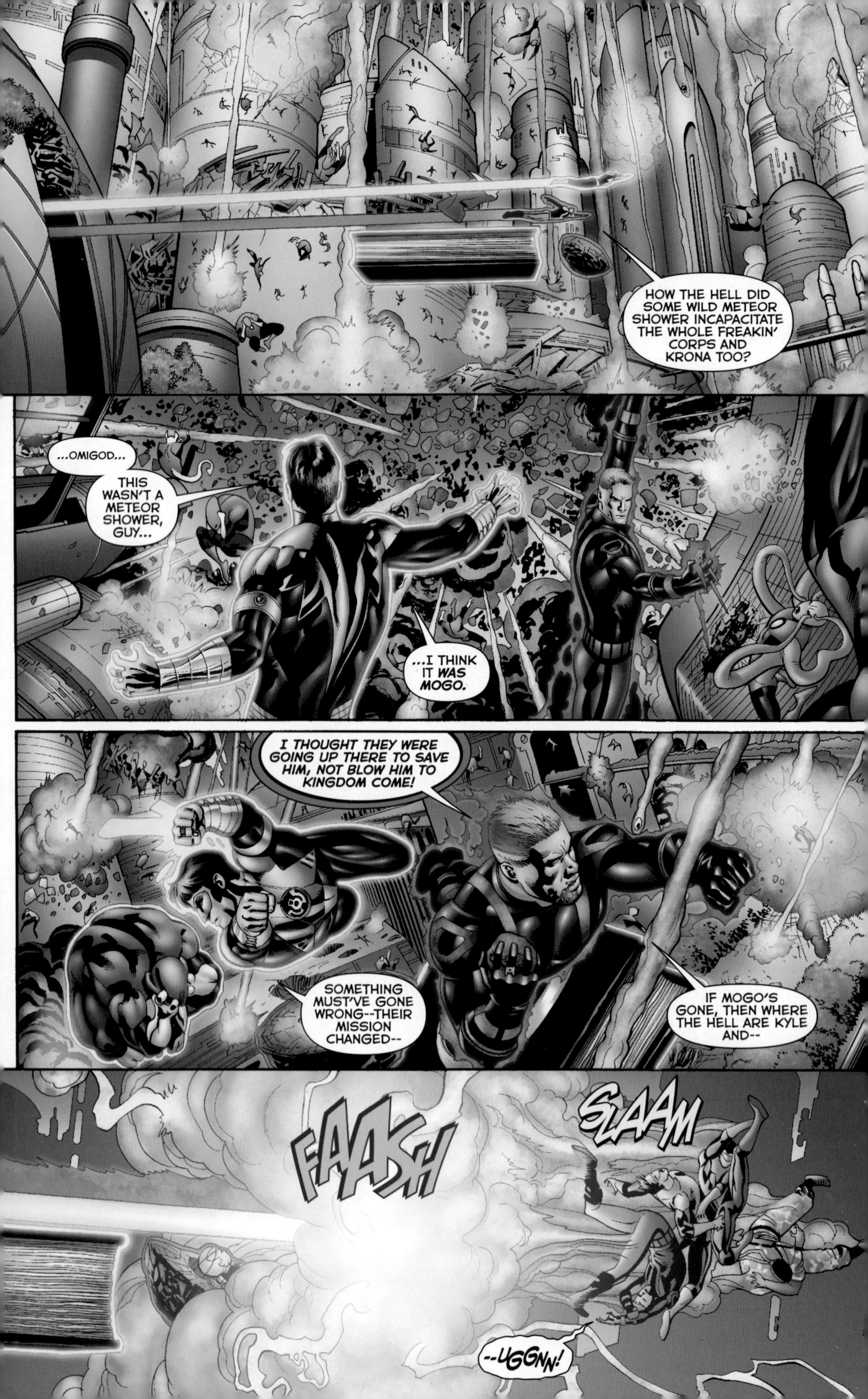
HOW THE HELL DID SOME WILD METEOR SHOWER INCAPACITATE THE WHOLE FREAKIN' CORPS AND KRONA TOO?
...OMIGOD...
THIS WASN'T A METEOR SHOWER, GUY...
...I THINK IT WAS MOGO.
I THOUGHT THEY WERE GOING UP THERE TO SAVE HIM, NOT BLOW HIM TO KINGDOM COME!
SOMETHING MUST'VE GONE WRONG--THEIR MISSION CHANGED--
IF MOGO'S GONE, THEN WHERE THE HELL ARE KYLE AND--
FAASH
SLAAM
--UGGNN!

STILL GETTING THE *HANG* OF TELEPORTING, *huh?*

MOGO'S *DEAD.*

YEAH, AND JOHN KILLED HIM.

PARALLAX'S STILL INSIDE?

WITH ALL THESE LANTERNS FLOATING AROUND, IT LOOKED LIKE--

IT WAS MOGO-- WHEN HE BLEW UP, HE MUST'VE RELEASED SOME KINDA *PSYCHIC FEEDBACK*--

--EVERYONE BUT US IS OUT OF COMMISSION-- EVEN KRONA AND THE GUARDIANS ARE FEELING THE PAIN.

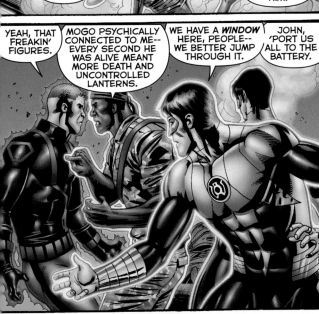

YEAH, THAT FREAKIN' FIGURES.

MOGO PSYCHICALLY CONNECTED TO ME-- EVERY SECOND HE WAS ALIVE MEANT MORE DEATH AND UNCONTROLLED LANTERNS.

WE HAVE A *WINDOW* HERE, PEOPLE-- WE BETTER JUMP THROUGH IT.

JOHN, 'PORT US ALL TO THE BATTERY.

THE GUARDIANS?

THEY PUT THE HURT ON US. THEY'RE UNDER KRONA'S CONTROL AND POSSESSED BY THE ENTITIES.

IS GANTHET--

BLUEBERRY'S A TOUGH NUT-- HE'S STILL ALIVE.

I CAN'T SAY THE SAME FOR US IF WE DON'T GET PARALLAX OUT.

JOHN, I DON'T KNOW WHAT THE HELL WENT ON UP THERE, BUT GET US TO THE BATTERY-- *NOW!*

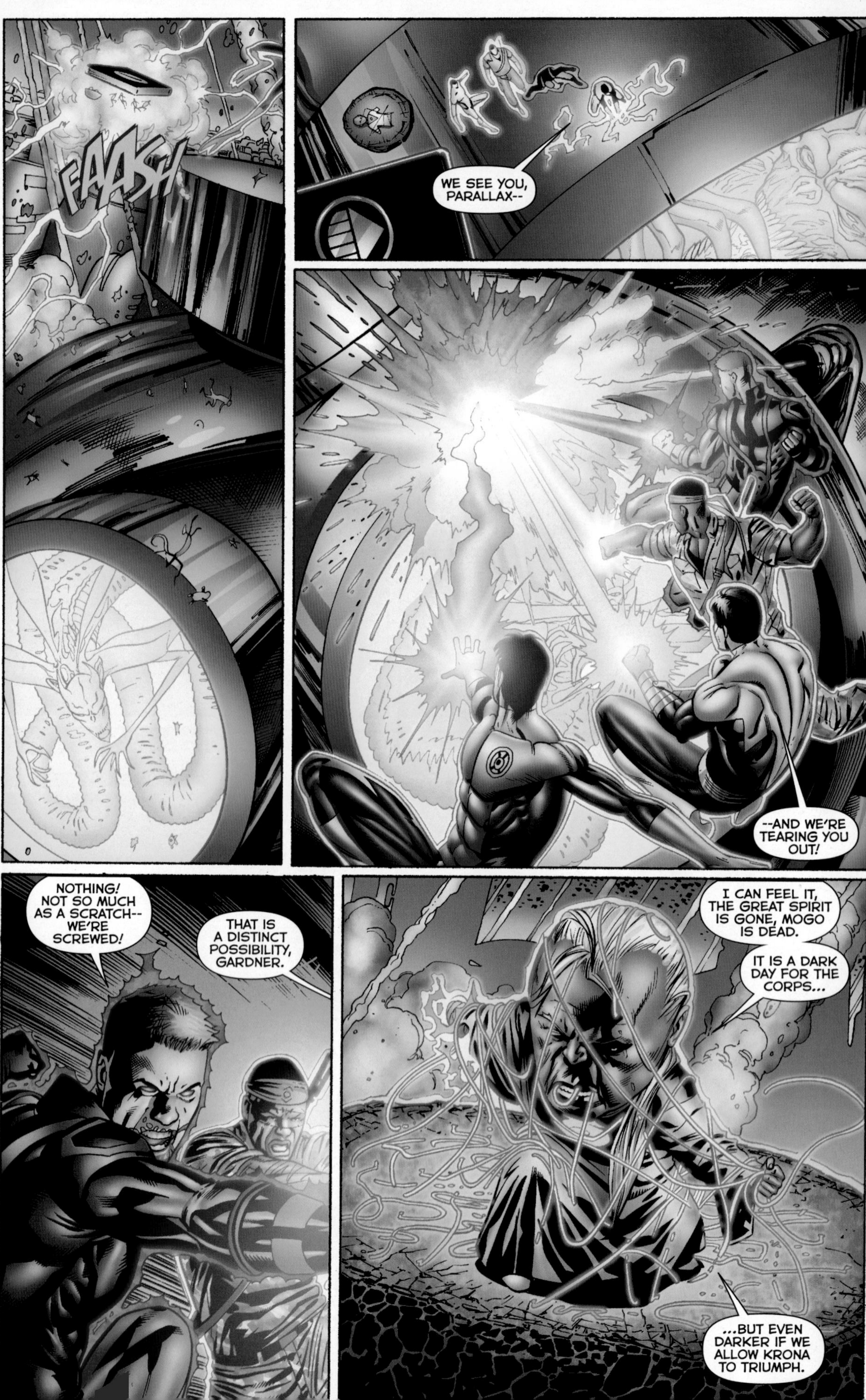
FAASH
WE SEE YOU, PARALLAX--
--AND WE'RE TEARING YOU OUT!
NOTHING! NOT SO MUCH AS A SCRATCH-- WE'RE SCREWED!
THAT IS A DISTINCT POSSIBILITY, GARDNER.
I CAN FEEL IT, THE GREAT SPIRIT IS GONE, MOGO IS DEAD.
IT IS A DARK DAY FOR THE CORPS...
...BUT EVEN DARKER IF WE ALLOW KRONA TO TRIUMPH.

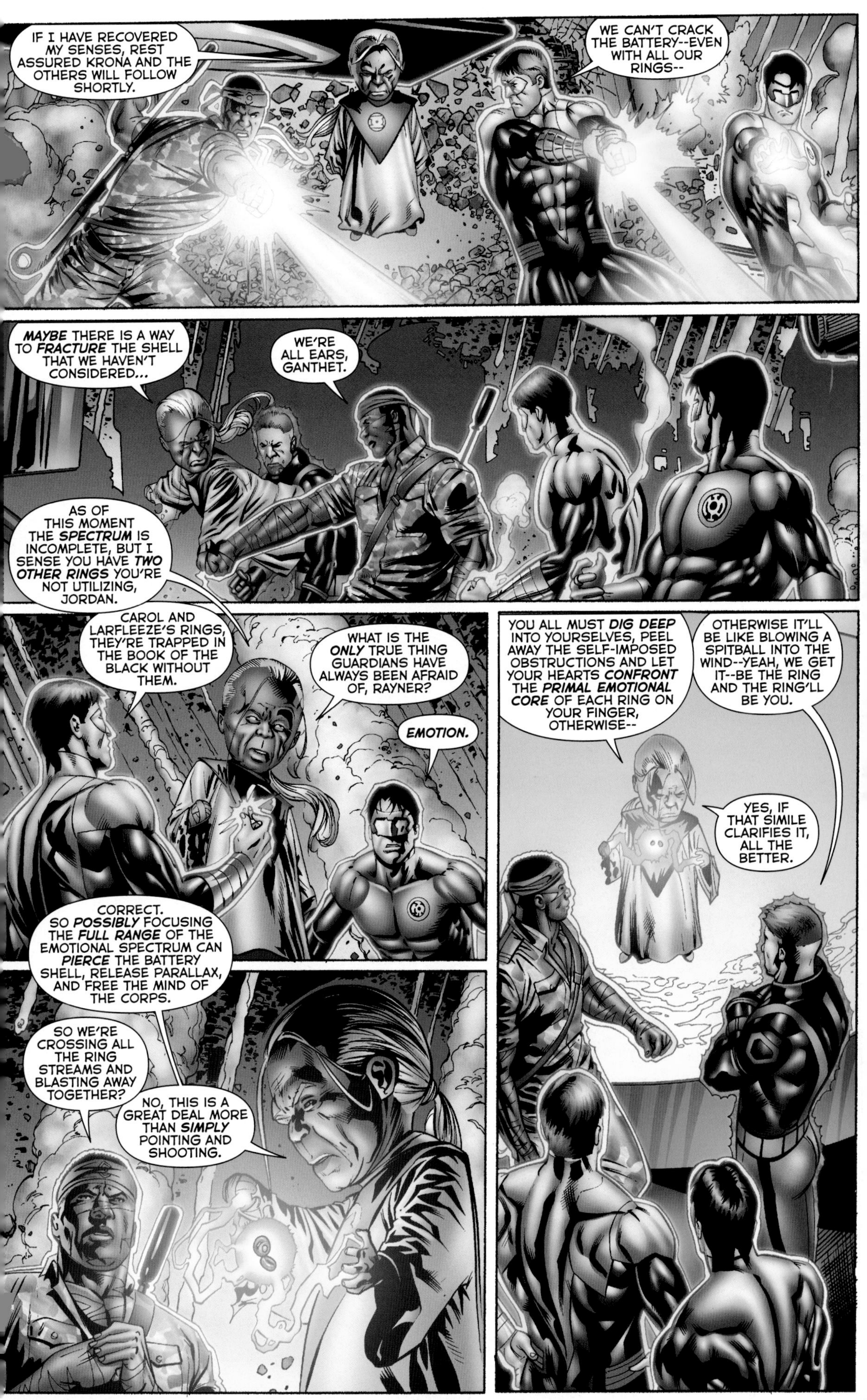
IF I HAVE RECOVERED MY SENSES, REST ASSURED KRONA AND THE OTHERS WILL FOLLOW SHORTLY.
WE CAN'T CRACK THE BATTERY--EVEN WITH ALL OUR RINGS--
MAYBE THERE IS A WAY TO *FRACTURE* THE SHELL THAT WE HAVEN'T CONSIDERED...
WE'RE ALL EARS, GANTHET.
AS OF THIS MOMENT THE *SPECTRUM* IS INCOMPLETE, BUT I SENSE YOU HAVE *TWO OTHER RINGS* YOU'RE NOT UTILIZING, JORDAN.
CAROL AND LARFLEEZE'S RINGS, THEY'RE TRAPPED IN THE BOOK OF THE BLACK WITHOUT THEM.
WHAT IS THE *ONLY* TRUE THING GUARDIANS HAVE ALWAYS BEEN AFRAID OF, RAYNER?
EMOTION.
CORRECT. SO *POSSIBLY* FOCUSING THE *FULL RANGE* OF THE EMOTIONAL SPECTRUM CAN *PIERCE* THE BATTERY SHELL, RELEASE PARALLAX, AND FREE THE MIND OF THE CORPS.
SO WE'RE CROSSING ALL THE RING STREAMS AND BLASTING AWAY TOGETHER?
NO, THIS IS A GREAT DEAL MORE THAN *SIMPLY* POINTING AND SHOOTING.
YOU ALL MUST *DIG DEEP* INTO YOURSELVES, PEEL AWAY THE SELF-IMPOSED OBSTRUCTIONS AND LET YOUR HEARTS *CONFRONT* THE *PRIMAL EMOTIONAL CORE* OF EACH RING ON YOUR FINGER, OTHERWISE--
OTHERWISE IT'LL BE LIKE BLOWING A SPITBALL INTO THE WIND--YEAH, WE GET IT--BE THE RING AND THE RING'LL BE YOU.
YES, IF THAT SIMILE CLARIFIES IT, ALL THE BETTER.

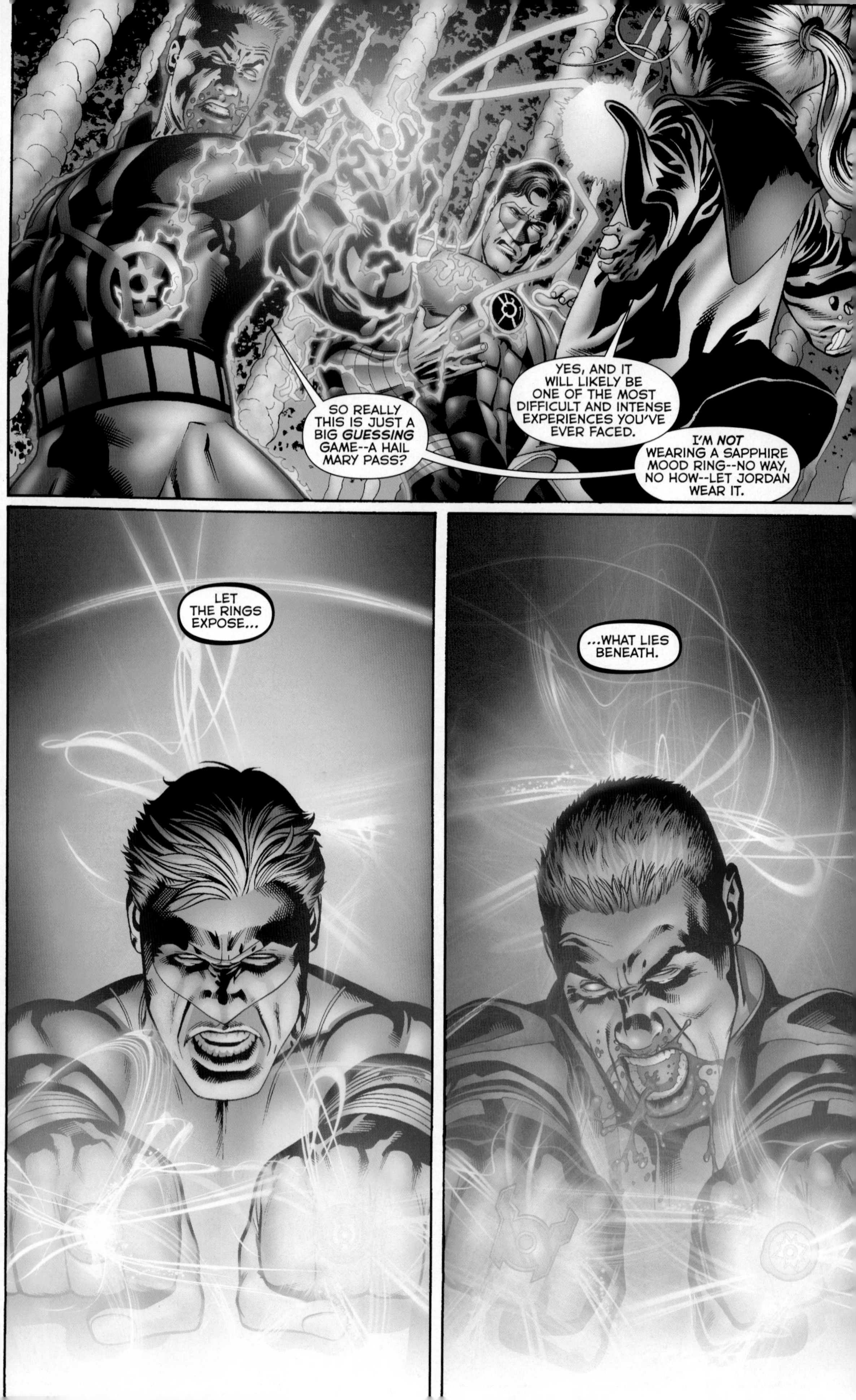
SO REALLY THIS IS JUST A BIG *GUESSING* GAME--A HAIL MARY PASS?
YES, AND IT WILL LIKELY BE ONE OF THE MOST DIFFICULT AND INTENSE EXPERIENCES YOU'VE EVER FACED.
I'M *NOT* WEARING A SAPPHIRE MOOD RING--NO WAY, NO HOW--LET JORDAN WEAR IT.
LET THE RINGS EXPOSE...
...WHAT LIES BENEATH.

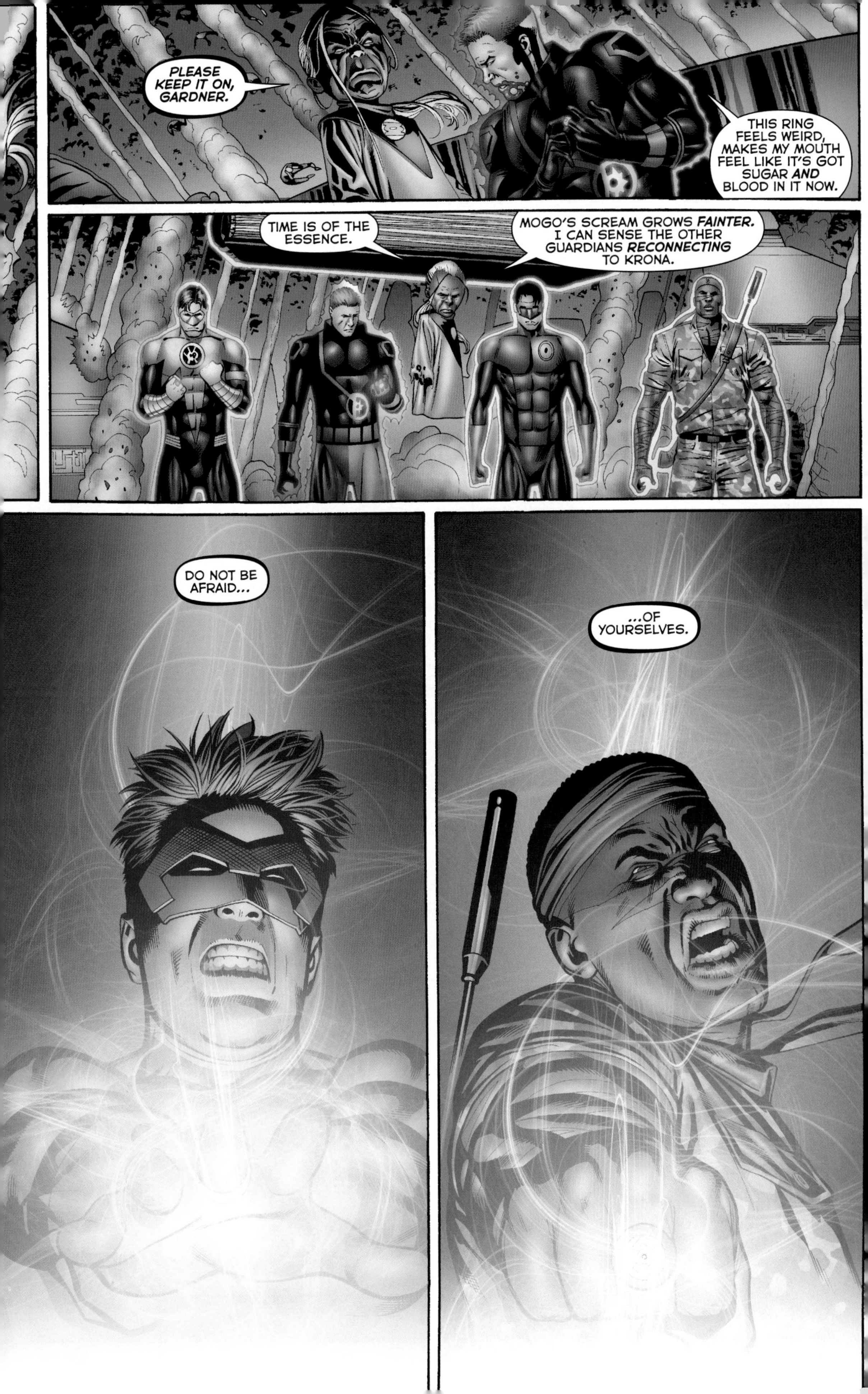
PLEASE KEEP IT ON, GARDNER.
THIS RING FEELS WEIRD, MAKES MY MOUTH FEEL LIKE IT'S GOT SUGAR AND BLOOD IN IT NOW.
TIME IS OF THE ESSENCE.
MOGO'S SCREAM GROWS FAINTER. I CAN SENSE THE OTHER GUARDIANS RECONNECTING TO KRONA.
DO NOT BE AFRAID...
...OF YOURSELVES.

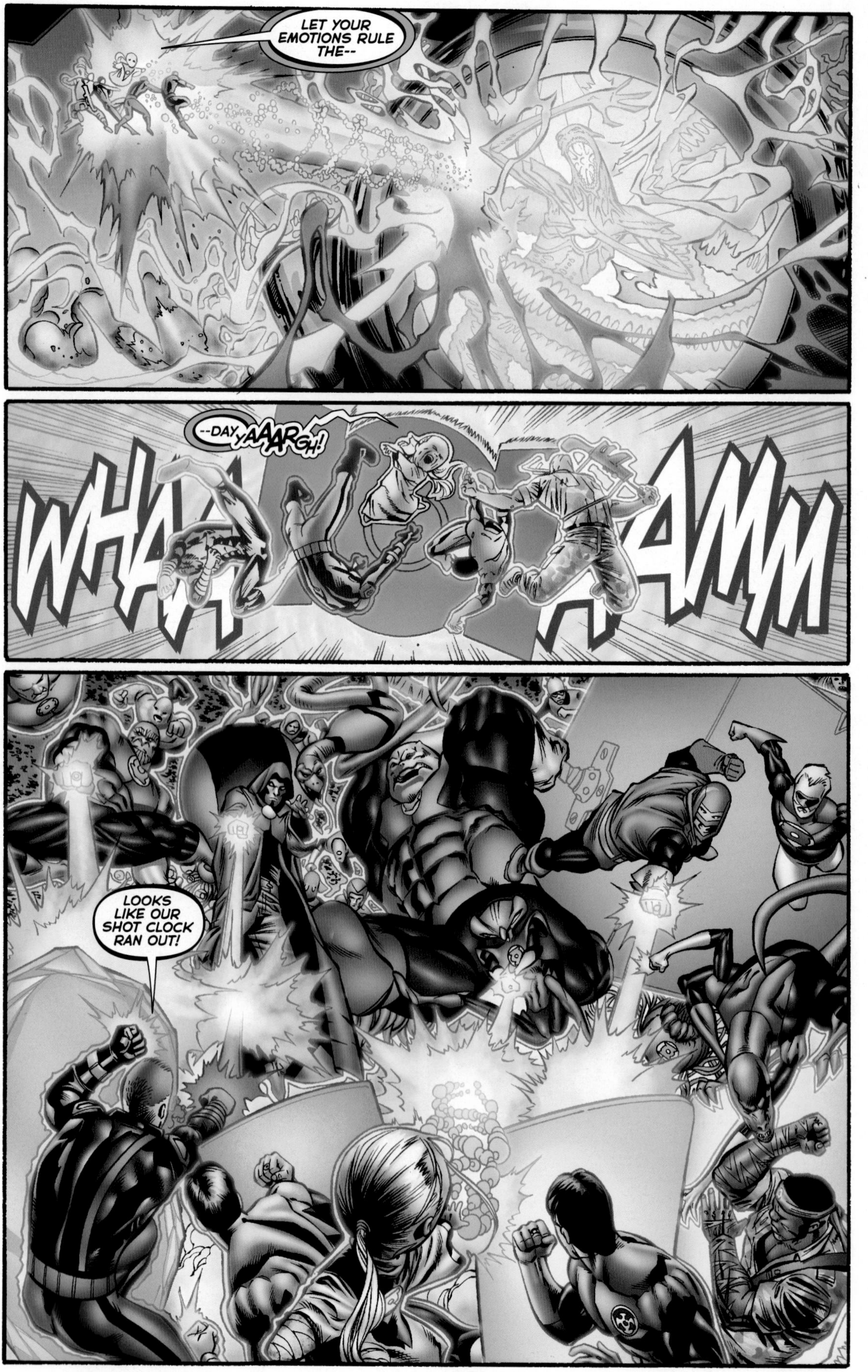
LET YOUR EMOTIONS RULE THE--
--DAY YAAARGH!
WHAAAKKAMM
LOOKS LIKE OUR SHOT CLOCK RAN OUT!

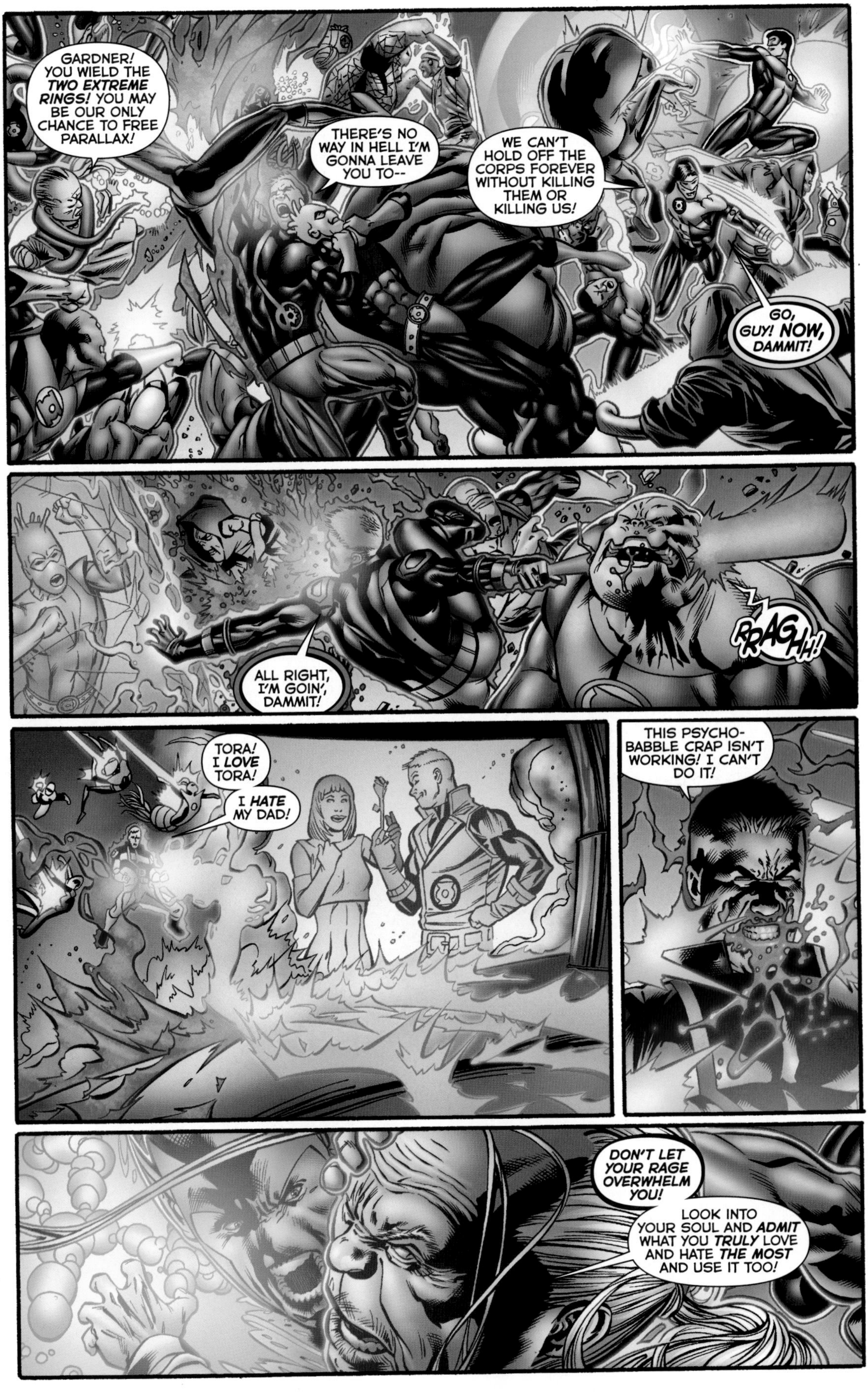
GARDNER! YOU WIELD THE TWO EXTREME RINGS! YOU MAY BE OUR ONLY CHANCE TO FREE PARALLAX!
THERE'S NO WAY IN HELL I'M GONNA LEAVE YOU TO--
WE CAN'T HOLD OFF THE CORPS FOREVER WITHOUT KILLING THEM OR KILLING US!
GO, GUY! NOW, DAMMIT!
ALL RIGHT, I'M GOIN', DAMMIT!
RRAGHH!
TORA! I LOVE TORA!
I HATE MY DAD!
THIS PSYCHO-BABBLE CRAP ISN'T WORKING! I CAN'T DO IT!
DON'T LET YOUR RAGE OVERWHELM YOU!
LOOK INTO YOUR SOUL AND ADMIT WHAT YOU TRULY LOVE AND HATE THE MOST AND USE IT TOO!

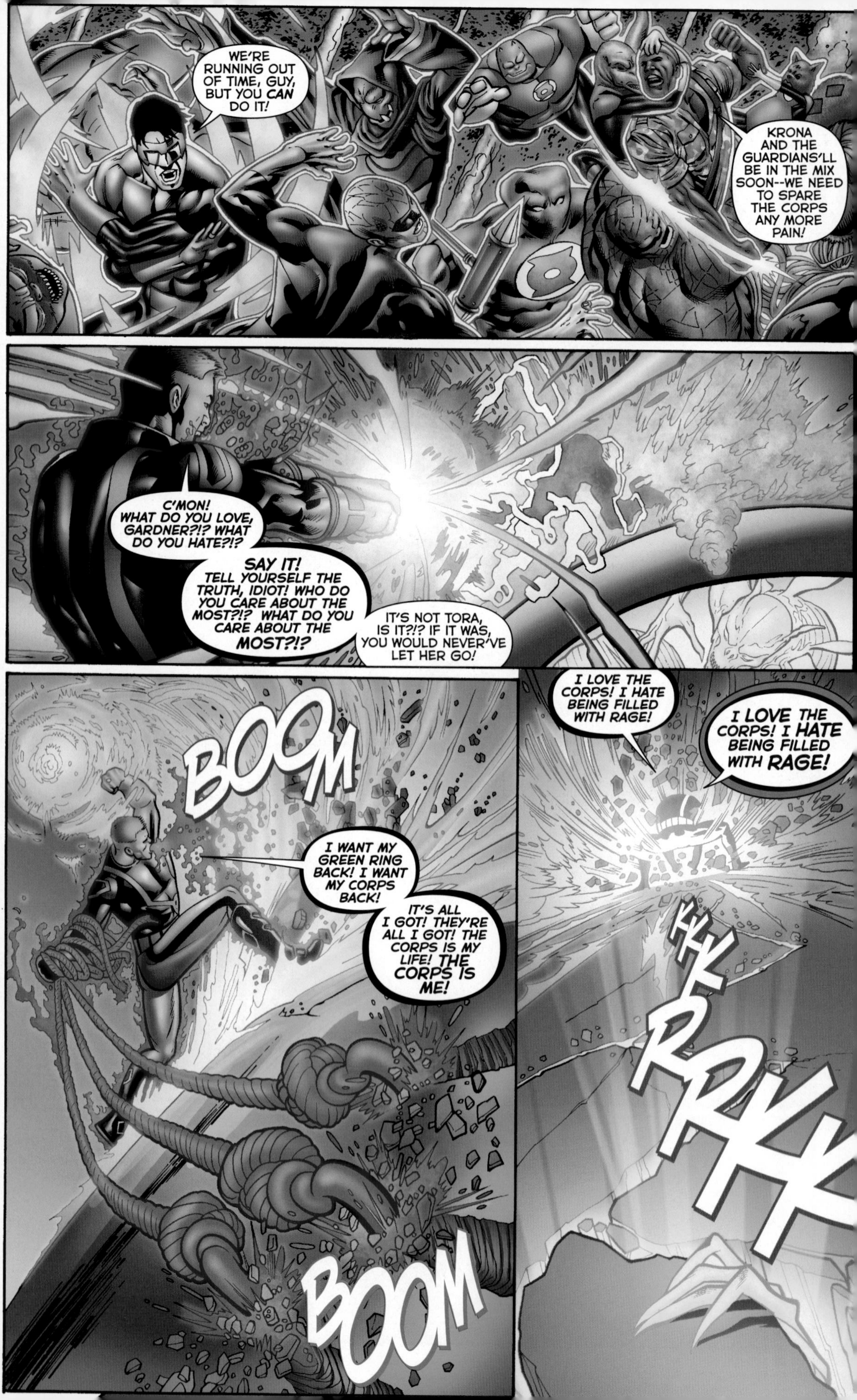
WE'RE RUNNING OUT OF TIME, GUY, BUT YOU CAN DO IT!
KRONA AND THE GUARDIANS'LL BE IN THE MIX SOON--WE NEED TO SPARE THE CORPS ANY MORE PAIN!
C'MON! WHAT DO YOU LOVE, GARDNER?!? WHAT DO YOU HATE?!?
SAY IT! TELL YOURSELF THE TRUTH, IDIOT! WHO DO YOU CARE ABOUT THE MOST?!? WHAT DO YOU CARE ABOUT THE MOST?!?
IT'S NOT TORA, IS IT?!? IF IT WAS, YOU WOULD NEVER'VE LET HER GO!
BOOM
I WANT MY GREEN RING BACK! I WANT MY CORPS BACK!
IT'S ALL I GOT! THEY'RE ALL I GOT! THE CORPS IS MY LIFE! THE CORPS IS ME!
BOOM
I LOVE THE CORPS! I HATE BEING FILLED WITH RAGE!
I LOVE THE CORPS! I HATE BEING FILLED WITH RAGE!
KKKRRKK

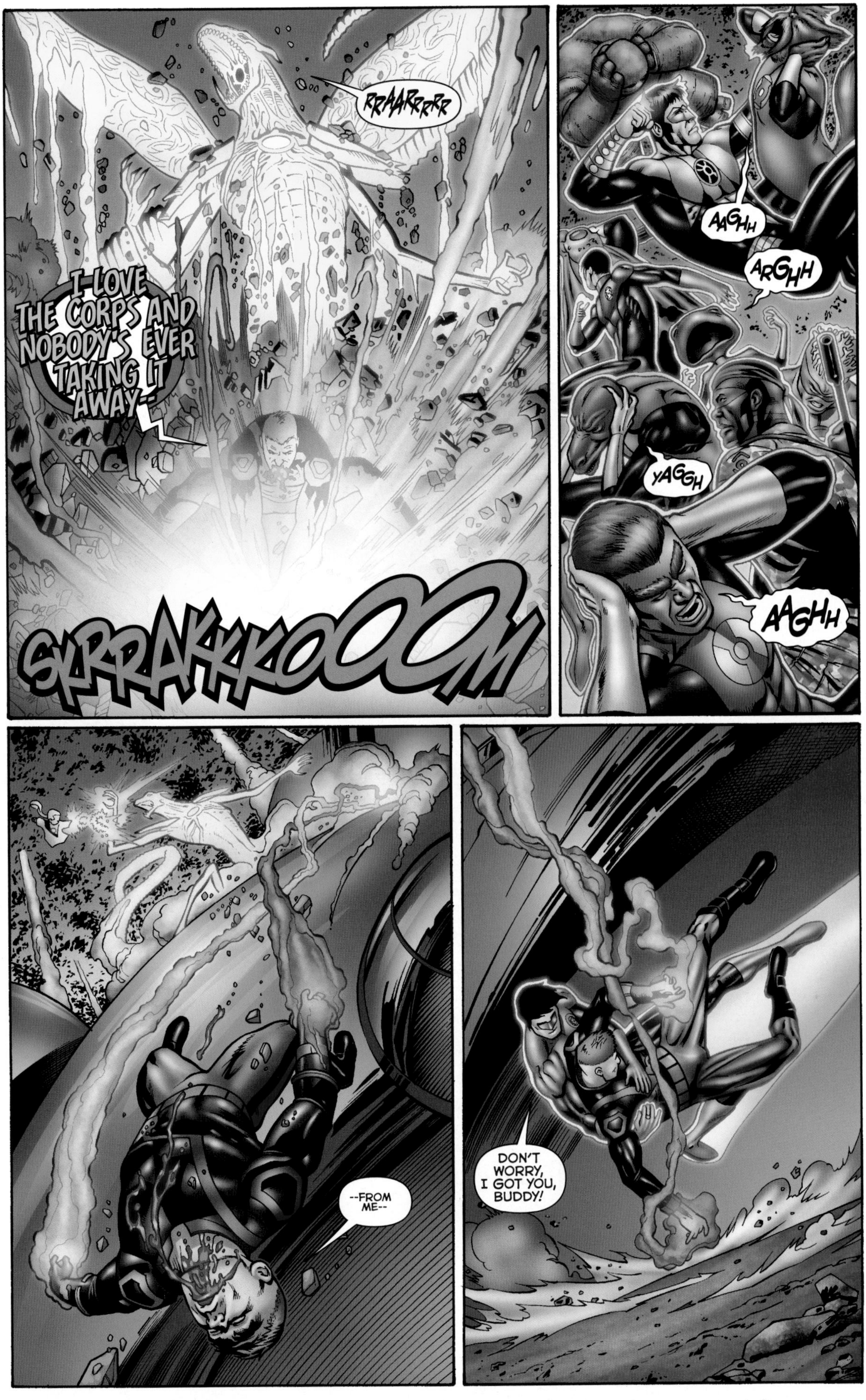
RRAARRRR
I LOVE THE CORPS AND NOBODY'S EVER TAKING IT AWAY-
SKRRAKKKOOOOM
AAGHH
ARGHH
YAGGH
AAGHH
--FROM ME--
DON'T WORRY, I GOT YOU, BUDDY!

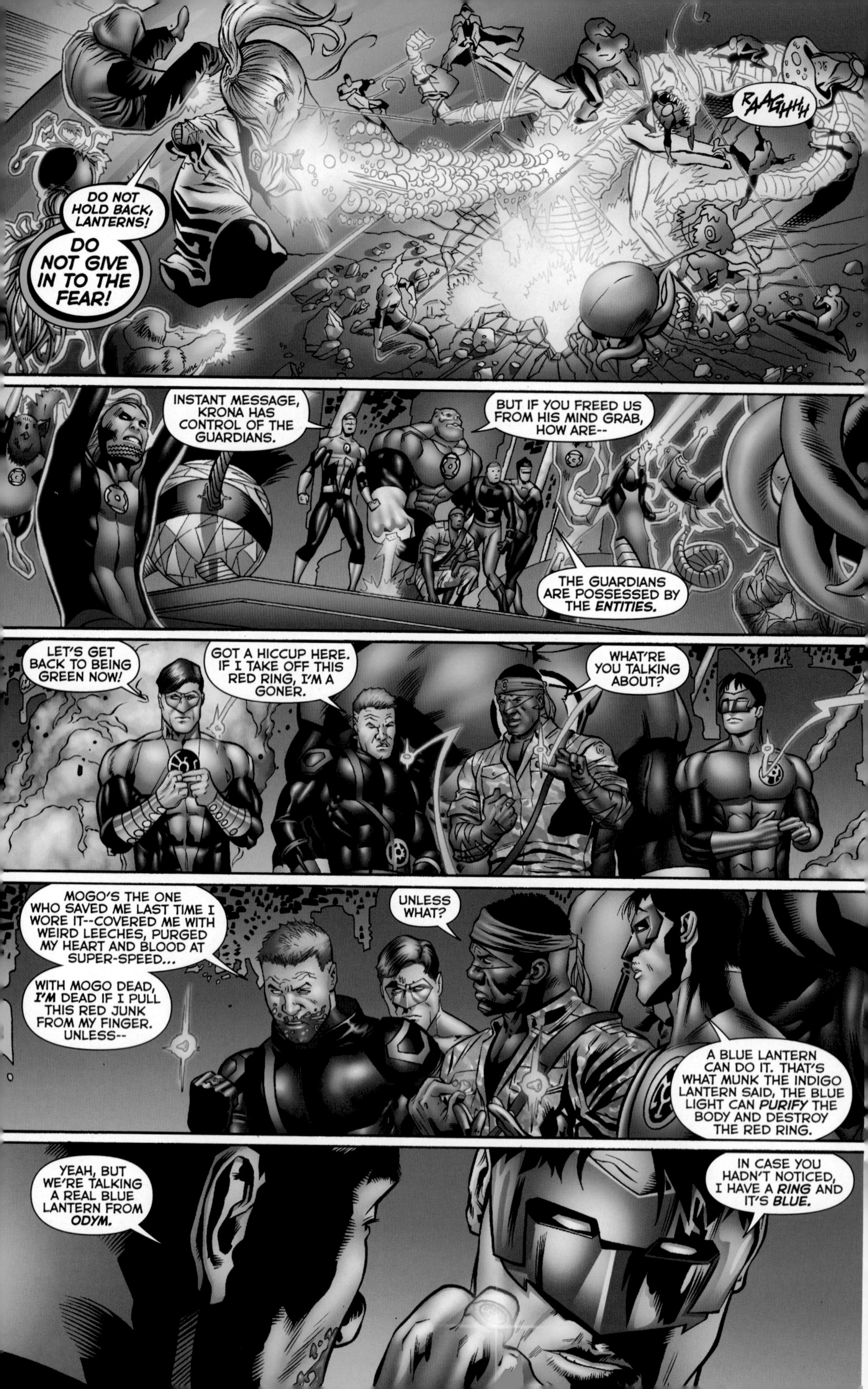
DO NOT HOLD BACK, LANTERNS!
DO NOT GIVE IN TO THE FEAR!
RAAGHHH
INSTANT MESSAGE, KRONA HAS CONTROL OF THE GUARDIANS.
BUT IF YOU FREED US FROM HIS MIND GRAB, HOW ARE--
THE GUARDIANS ARE POSSESSED BY THE ENTITIES.
LET'S GET BACK TO BEING GREEN NOW!
GOT A HICCUP HERE. IF I TAKE OFF THIS RED RING, I'M A GONER.
WHAT'RE YOU TALKING ABOUT?
MOGO'S THE ONE WHO SAVED ME LAST TIME I WORE IT--COVERED ME WITH WEIRD LEECHES, PURGED MY HEART AND BLOOD AT SUPER-SPEED...
WITH MOGO DEAD, I'M DEAD IF I PULL THIS RED JUNK FROM MY FINGER. UNLESS--
UNLESS WHAT?
A BLUE LANTERN CAN DO IT. THAT'S WHAT MUNK THE INDIGO LANTERN SAID, THE BLUE LIGHT CAN PURIFY THE BODY AND DESTROY THE RED RING.
YEAH, BUT WE'RE TALKING A REAL BLUE LANTERN FROM ODYM.
IN CASE YOU HADN'T NOTICED, I HAVE A RING AND IT'S BLUE.

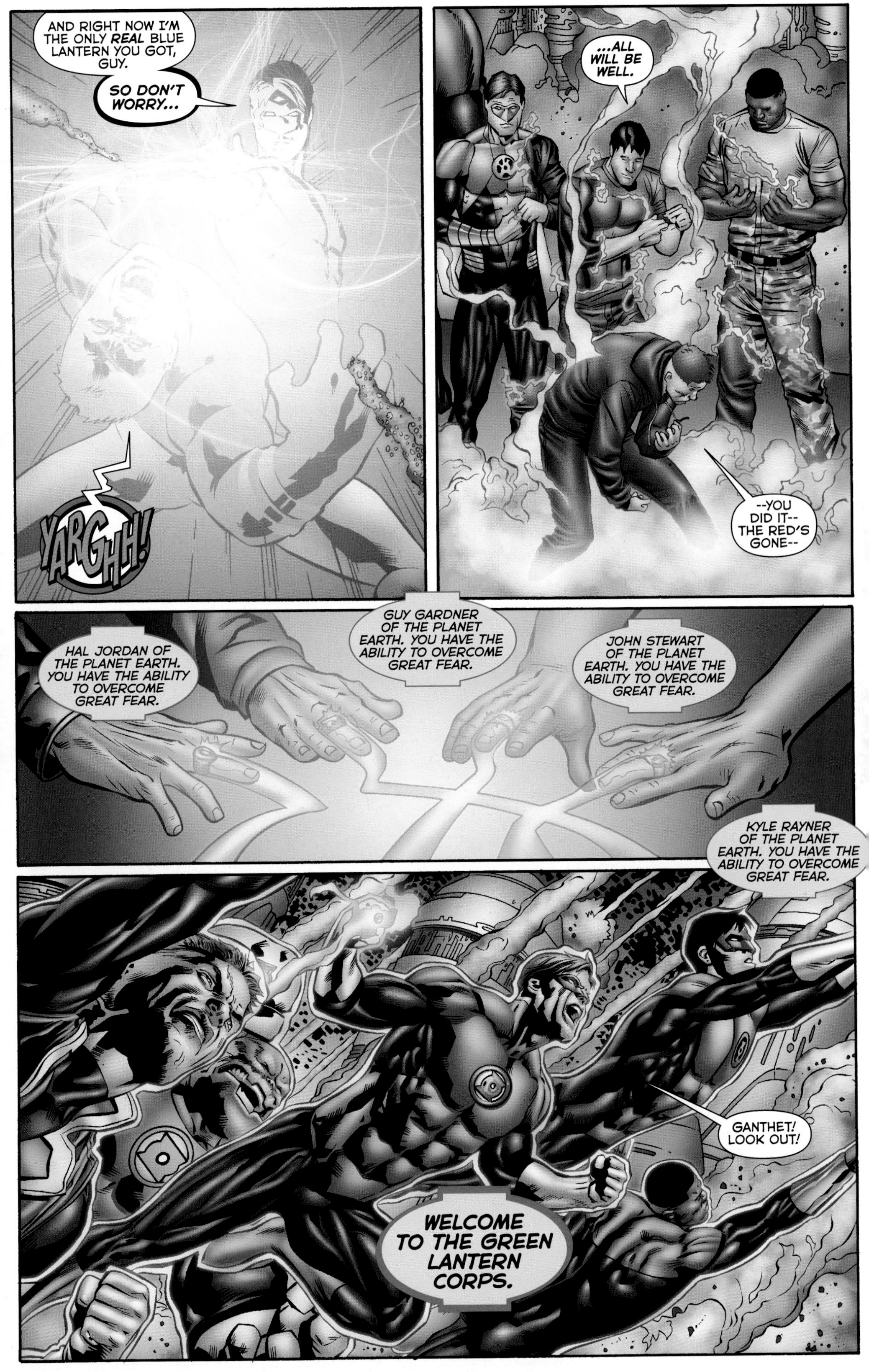

AND RIGHT NOW I'M THE ONLY REAL BLUE LANTERN YOU GOT, GUY.
SO DON'T WORRY...
YARGHH!
...ALL WILL BE WELL.
--YOU DID IT-- THE RED'S GONE--
HAL JORDAN OF THE PLANET EARTH. YOU HAVE THE ABILITY TO OVERCOME GREAT FEAR.
GUY GARDNER OF THE PLANET EARTH. YOU HAVE THE ABILITY TO OVERCOME GREAT FEAR.
JOHN STEWART OF THE PLANET EARTH. YOU HAVE THE ABILITY TO OVERCOME GREAT FEAR.
KYLE RAYNER OF THE PLANET EARTH. YOU HAVE THE ABILITY TO OVERCOME GREAT FEAR.
GANTHET! LOOK OUT!
WELCOME TO THE GREEN LANTERN CORPS.

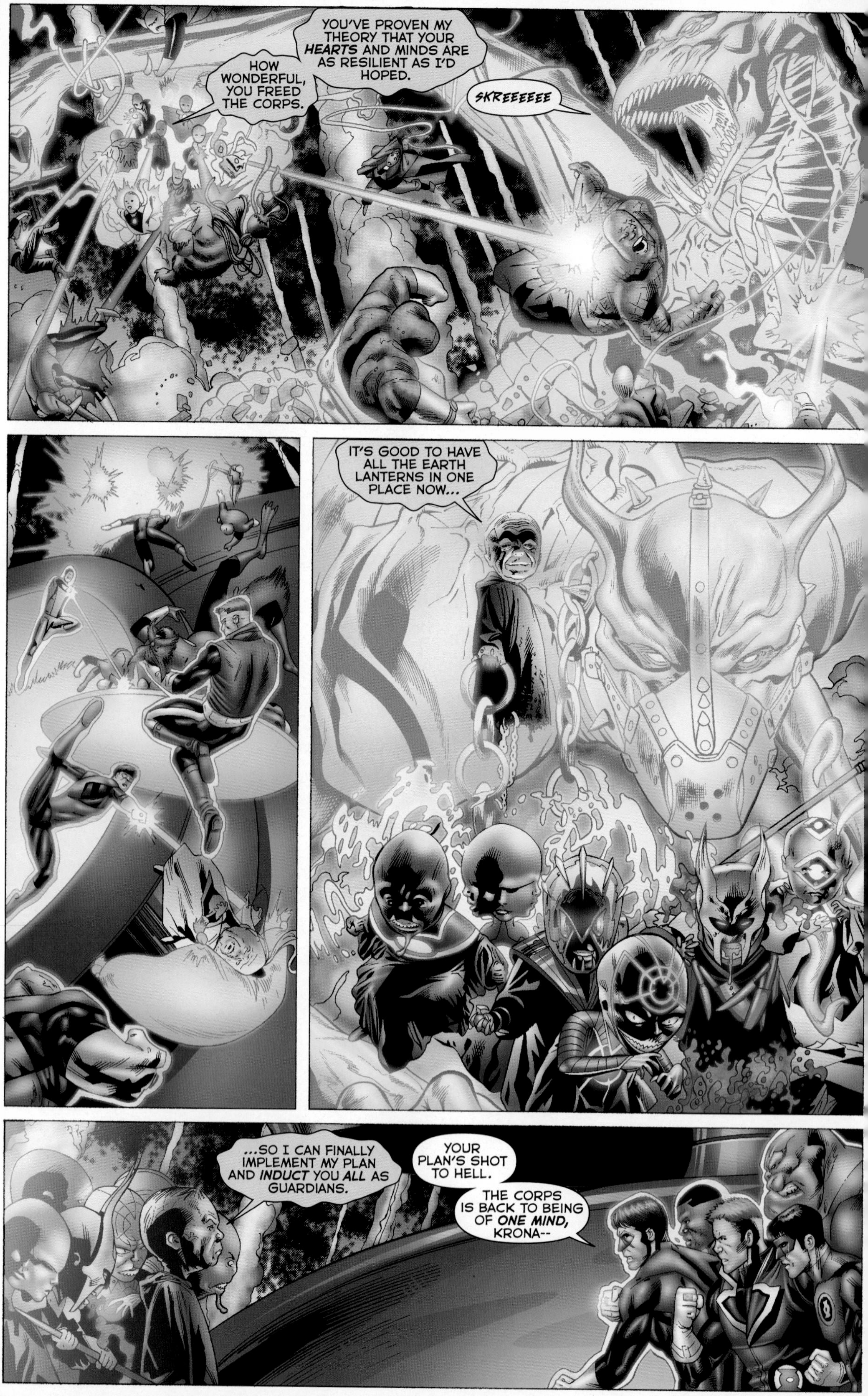
HOW WONDERFUL, YOU FREED THE CORPS.
YOU'VE PROVEN MY THEORY THAT YOUR HEARTS AND MINDS ARE AS RESILIENT AS I'D HOPED.
SKREEEEEEE
IT'S GOOD TO HAVE ALL THE EARTH LANTERNS IN ONE PLACE NOW...
...SO I CAN FINALLY IMPLEMENT MY PLAN AND INDUCT YOU ALL AS GUARDIANS.
YOUR PLAN'S SHOT TO HELL.
THE CORPS IS BACK TO BEING OF ONE MIND, KRONA--

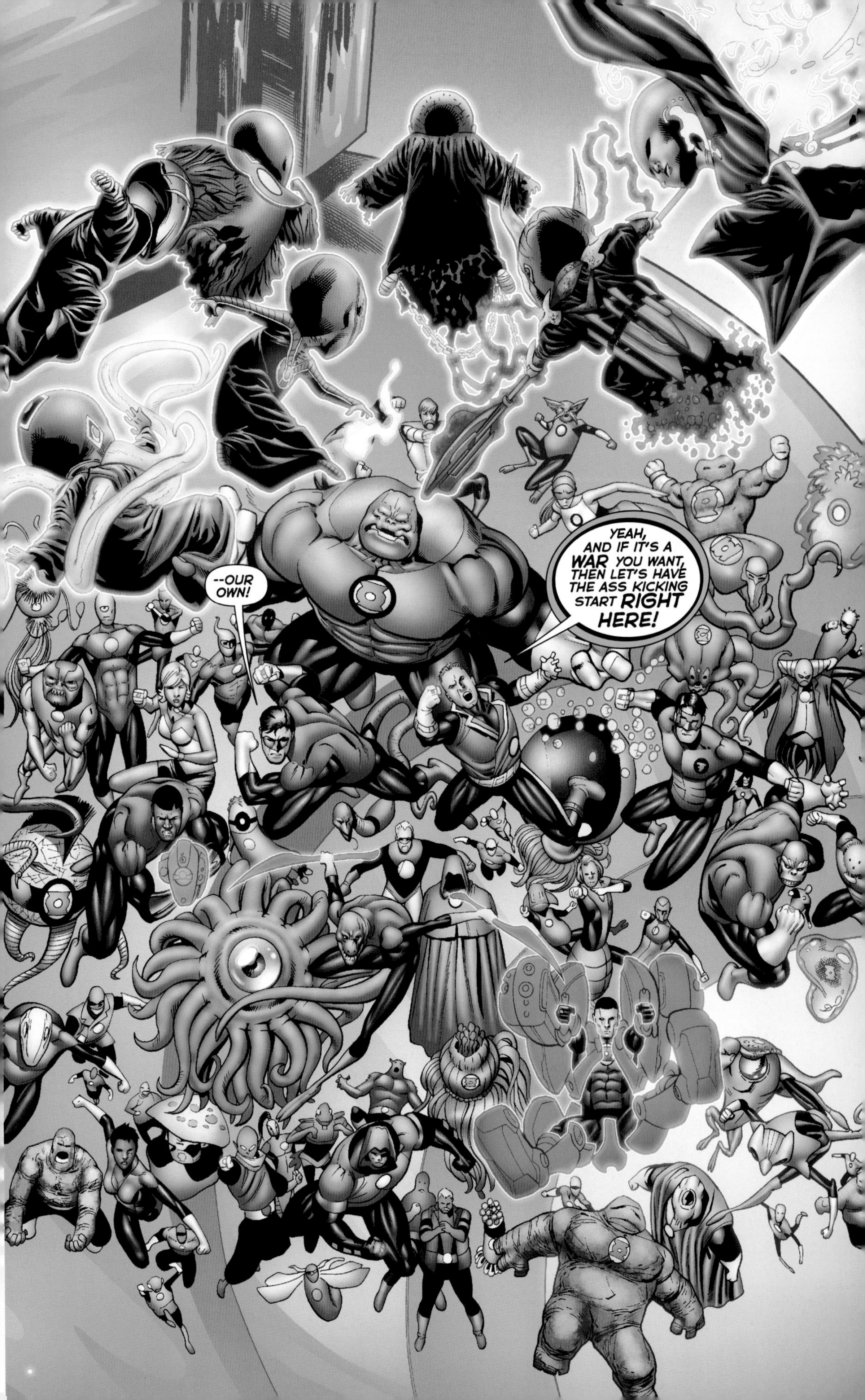
--OUR OWN!
YEAH, AND IF IT'S A WAR YOU WANT, THEN LET'S HAVE THE ASS KICKING START RIGHT HERE!

GREEN LANTERN 67 Cover by Doug Mahnke & Christian Alamy with Randy Mayor

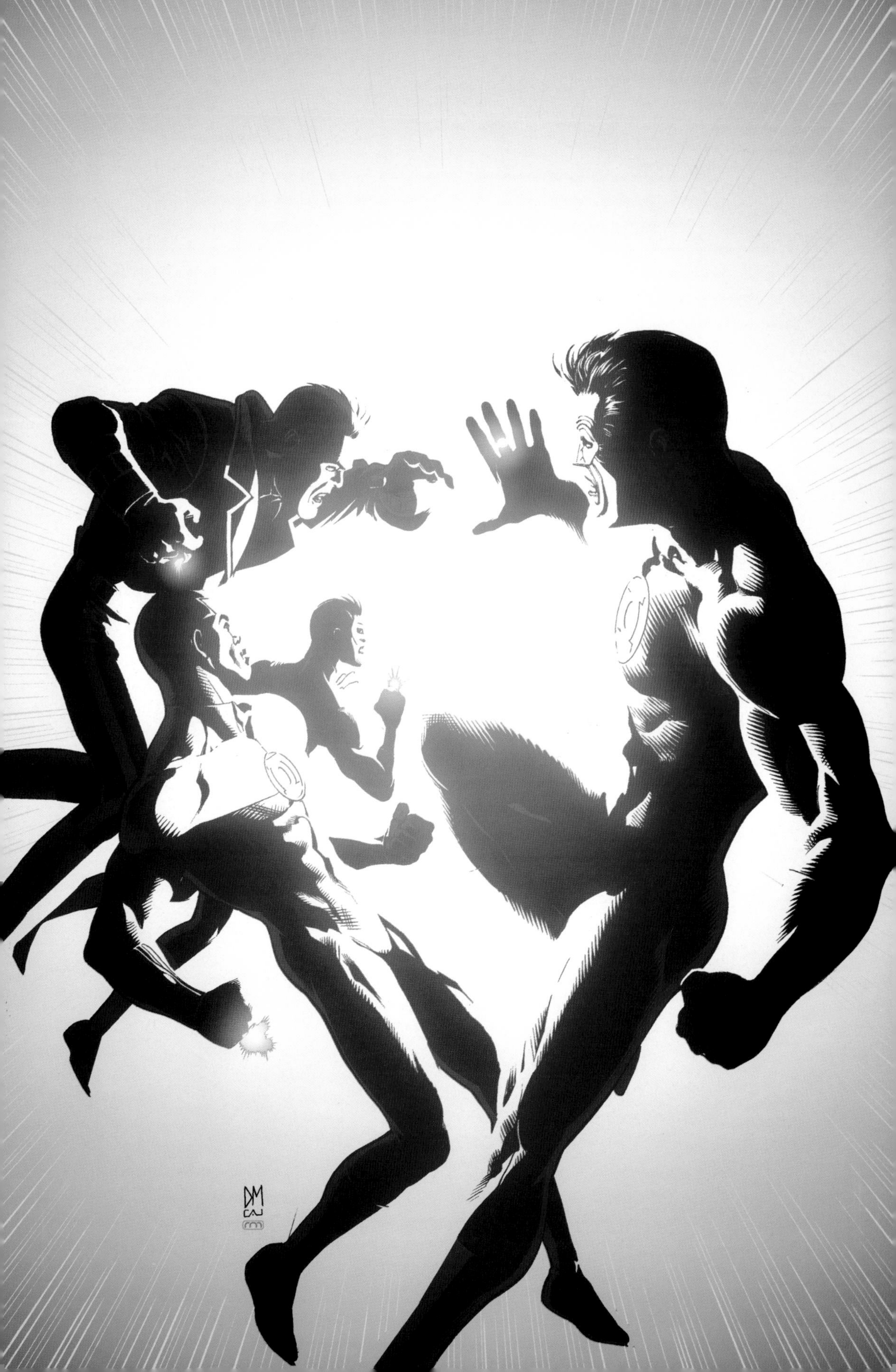

WAR OF THE GREEN LANTERNS
CONCLUSION

Geoff Johns Writer
Doug Mahnke Penciller
Christian Alamy, Keith Champagne, Tom Nguyen & Mark Irwin Inkers

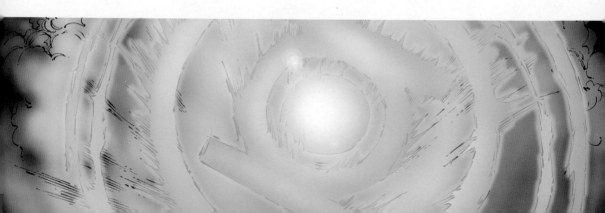

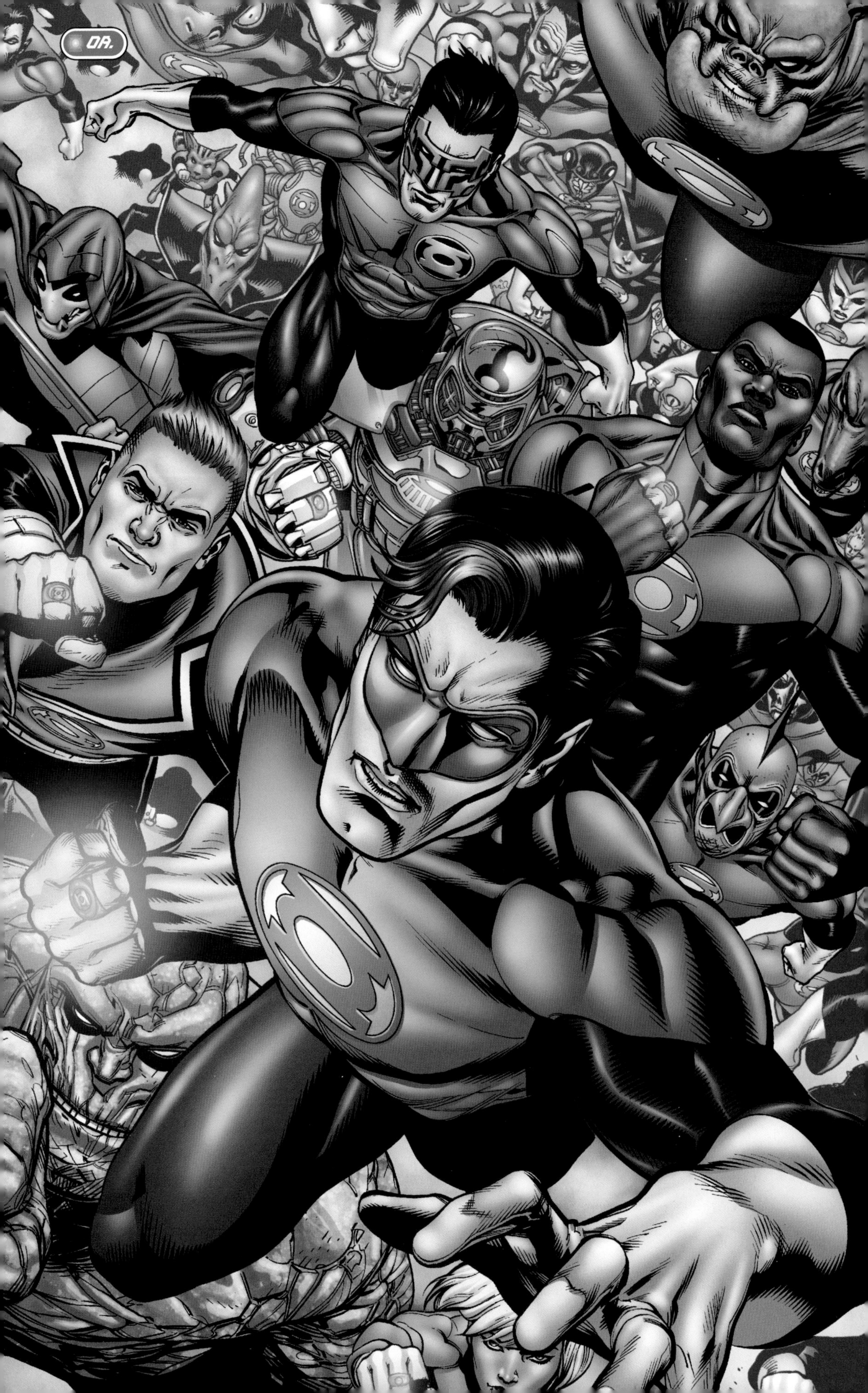
DA.

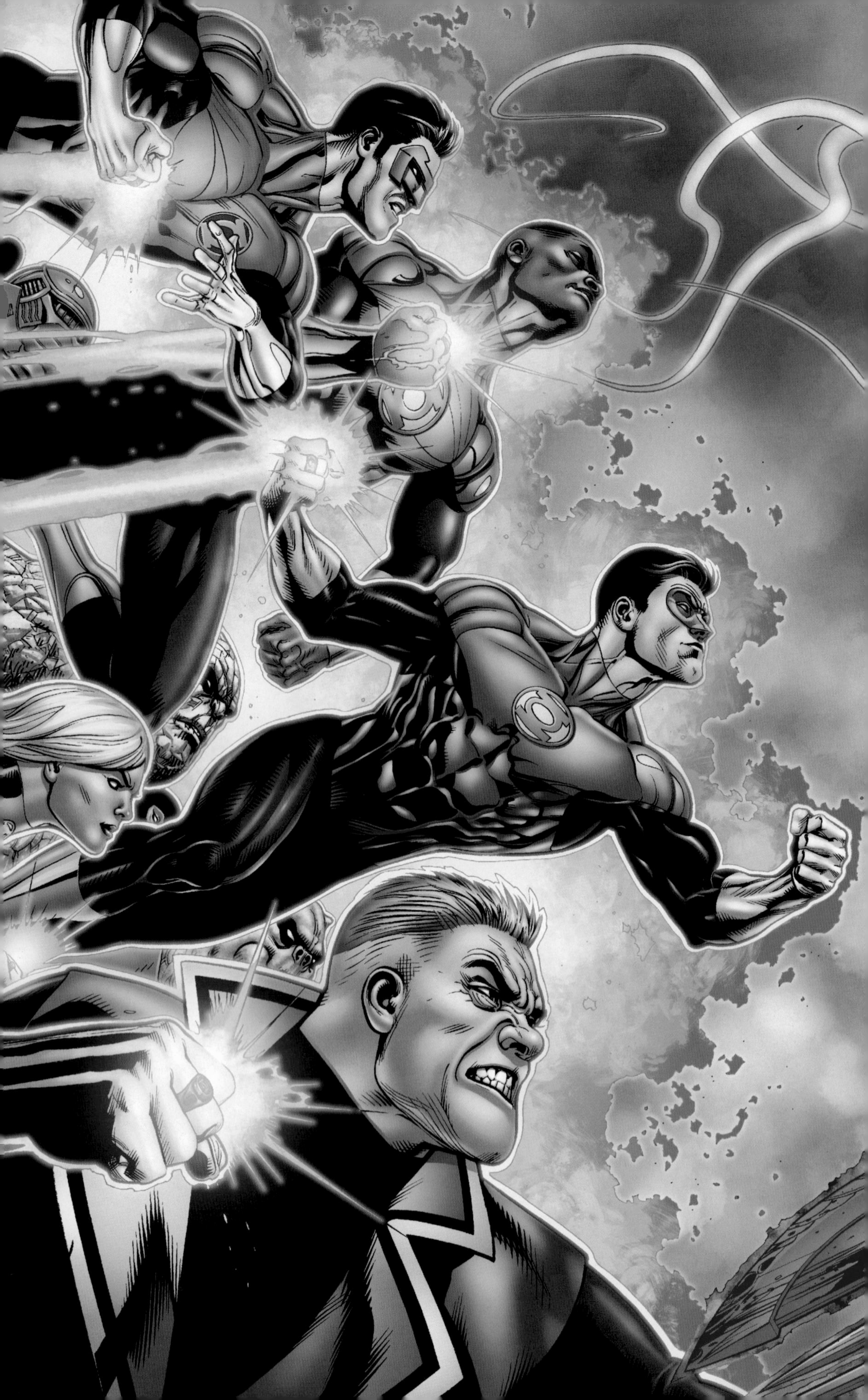

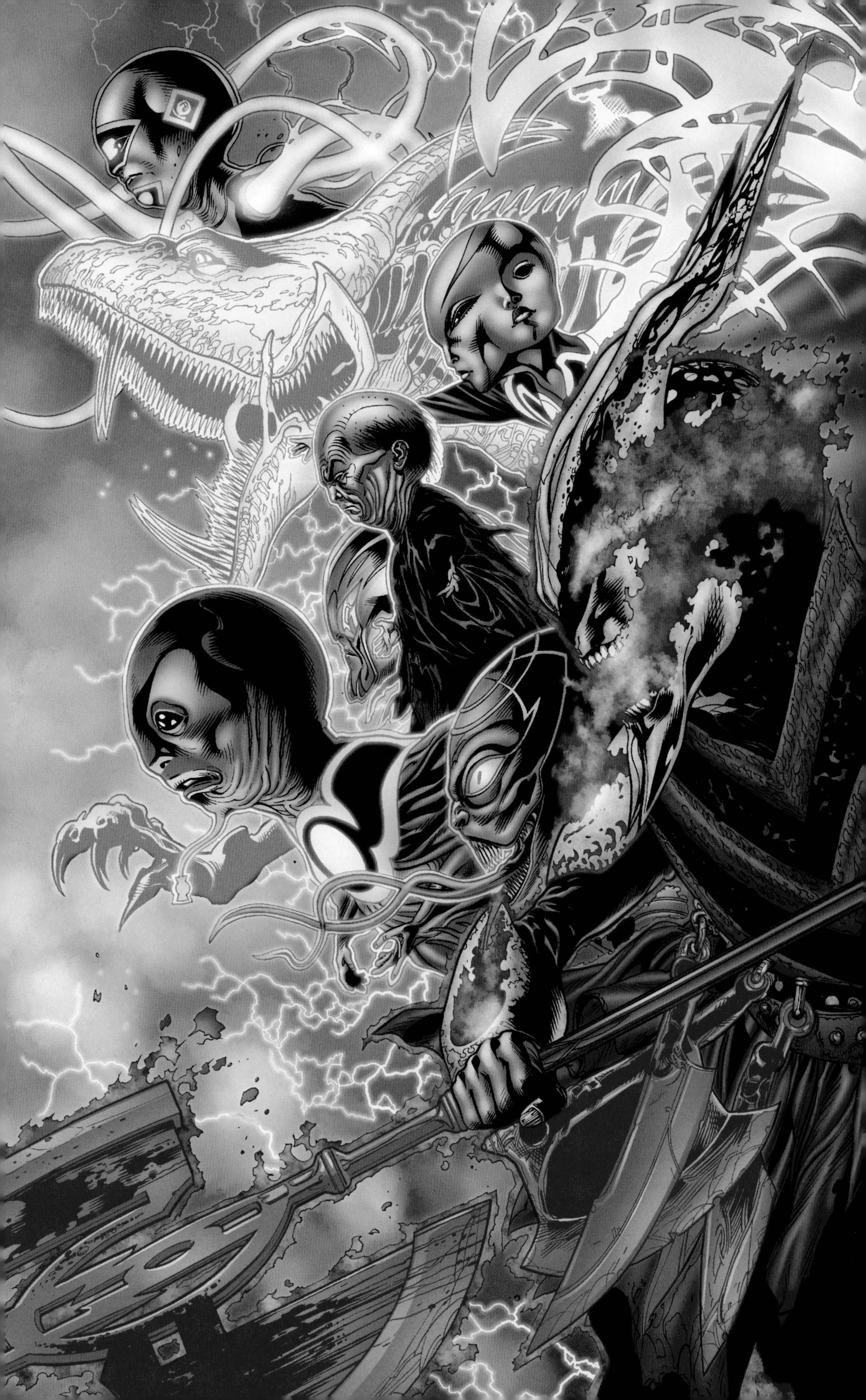

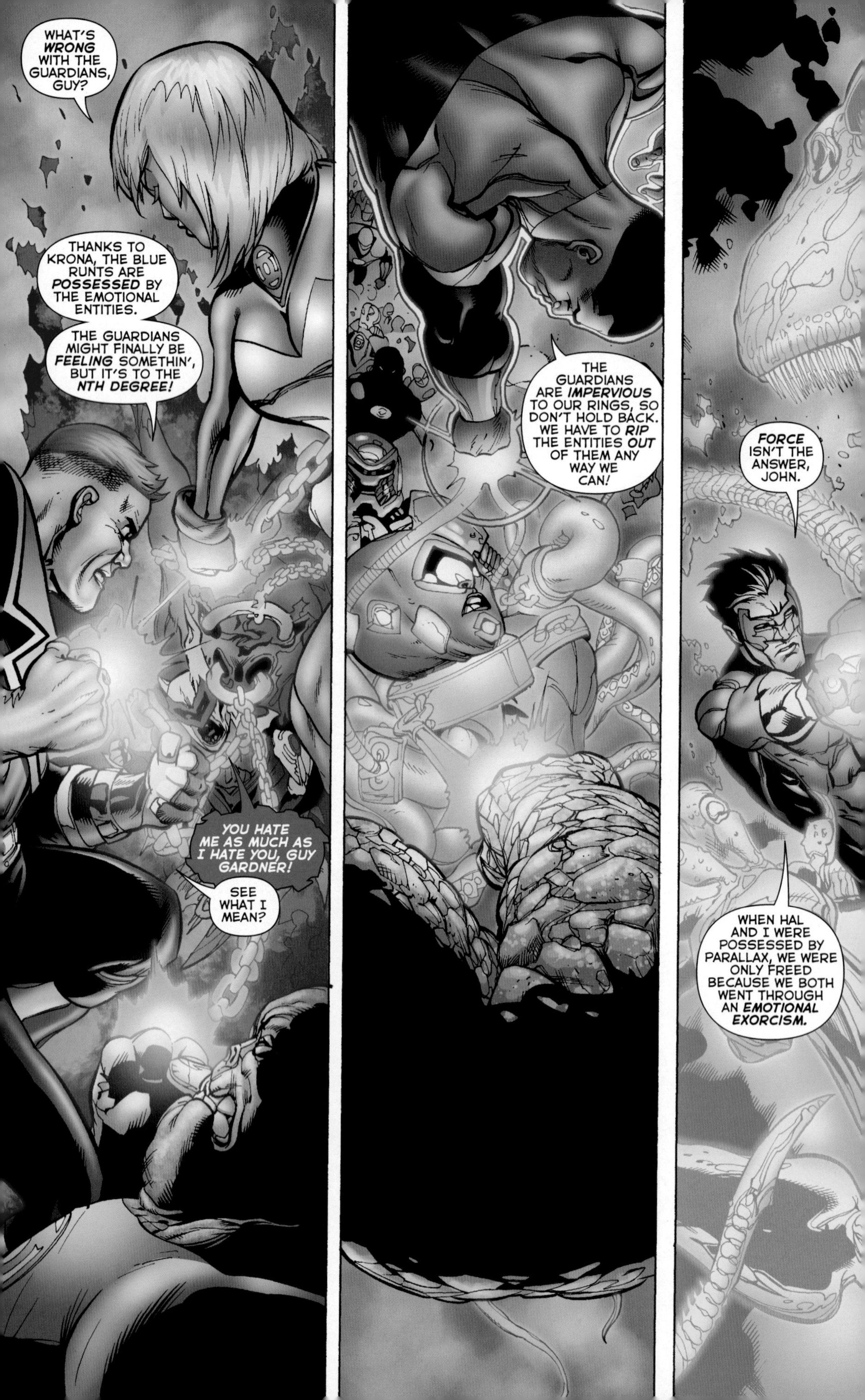
WHAT'S WRONG WITH THE GUARDIANS, GUY?
THANKS TO KRONA, THE BLUE RUNTS ARE POSSESSED BY THE EMOTIONAL ENTITIES.
THE GUARDIANS MIGHT FINALLY BE FEELING SOMETHIN', BUT IT'S TO THE NTH DEGREE!
YOU HATE ME AS MUCH AS I HATE YOU, GUY GARDNER!
SEE WHAT I MEAN?
THE GUARDIANS ARE IMPERVIOUS TO OUR RINGS, SO DON'T HOLD BACK. WE HAVE TO RIP THE ENTITIES OUT OF THEM ANY WAY WE CAN!
FORCE ISN'T THE ANSWER, JOHN.
WHEN HAL AND I WERE POSSESSED BY PARALLAX, WE WERE ONLY FREED BECAUSE WE BOTH WENT THROUGH AN EMOTIONAL EXORCISM.

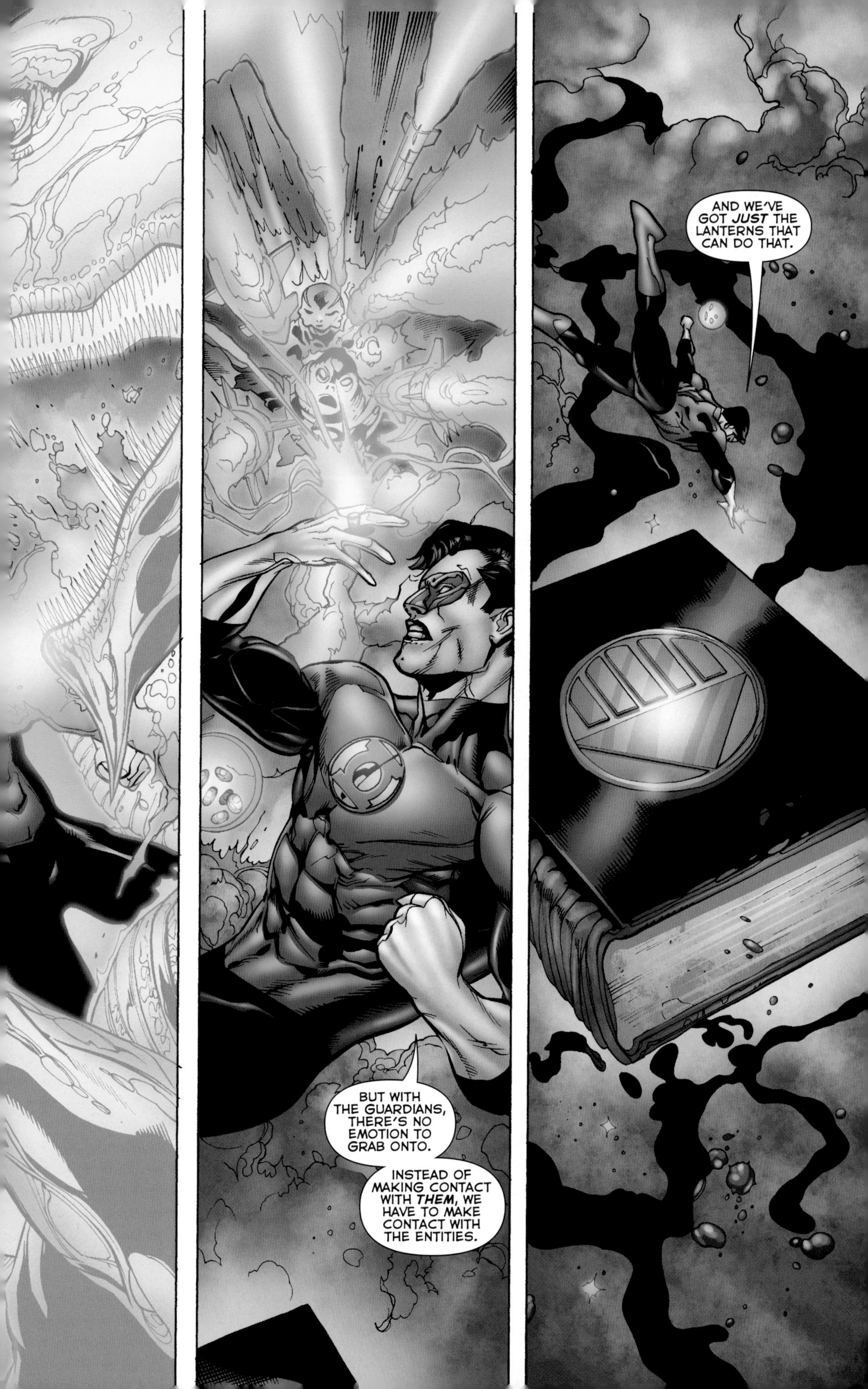
BUT WITH THE GUARDIANS, THERE'S NO EMOTION TO GRAB ONTO.
INSTEAD OF MAKING CONTACT WITH *THEM*, WE HAVE TO MAKE CONTACT WITH THE ENTITIES.
AND WE'VE GOT *JUST* THE LANTERNS THAT CAN DO THAT.

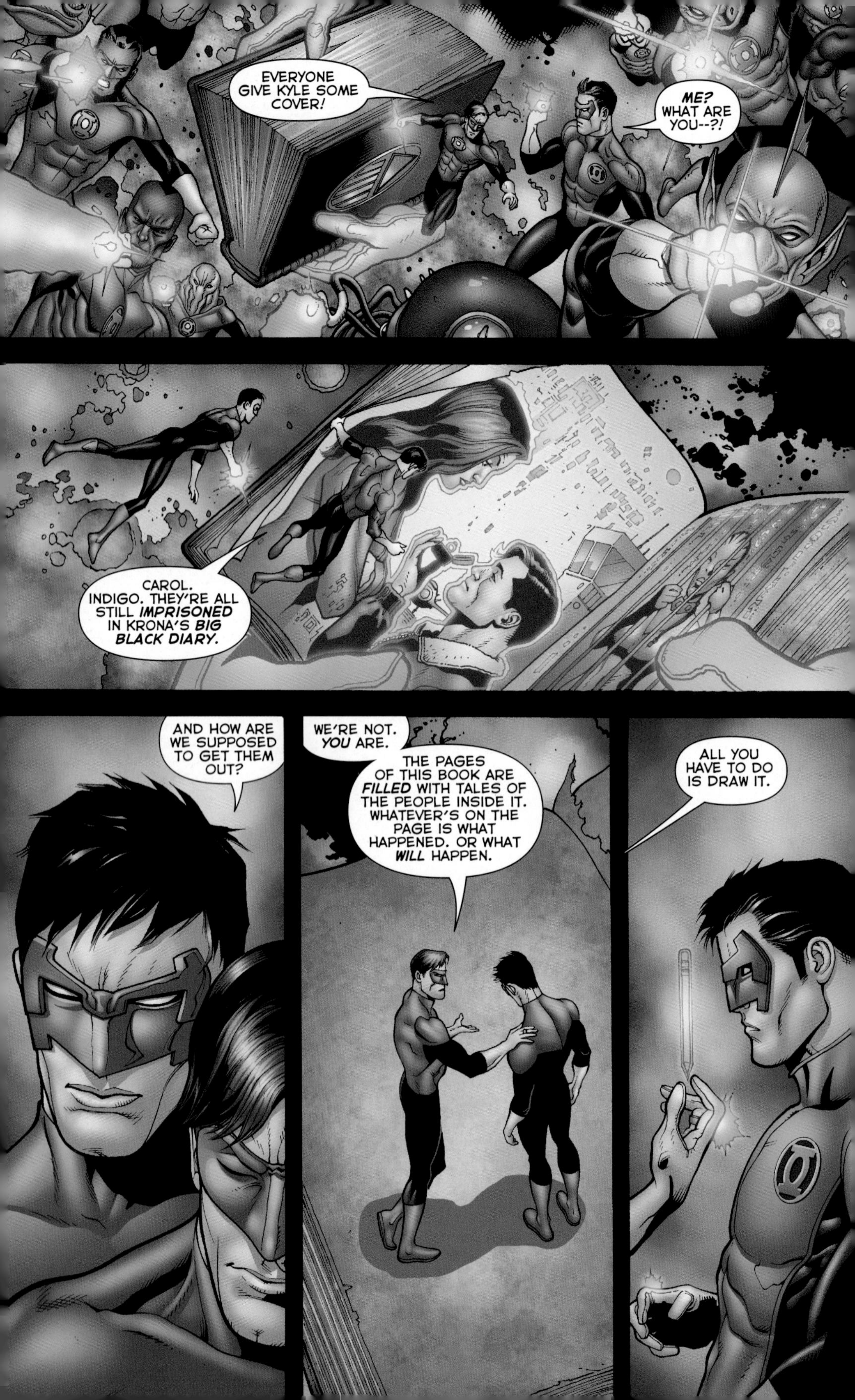

EVERYONE GIVE KYLE SOME COVER!
ME? WHAT ARE YOU--?!
CAROL. INDIGO. THEY'RE ALL STILL IMPRISONED IN KRONA'S BIG BLACK DIARY.
AND HOW ARE WE SUPPOSED TO GET THEM OUT?
WE'RE NOT. YOU ARE.
THE PAGES OF THIS BOOK ARE FILLED WITH TALES OF THE PEOPLE INSIDE IT. WHATEVER'S ON THE PAGE IS WHAT HAPPENED. OR WHAT WILL HAPPEN.
ALL YOU HAVE TO DO IS DRAW IT.

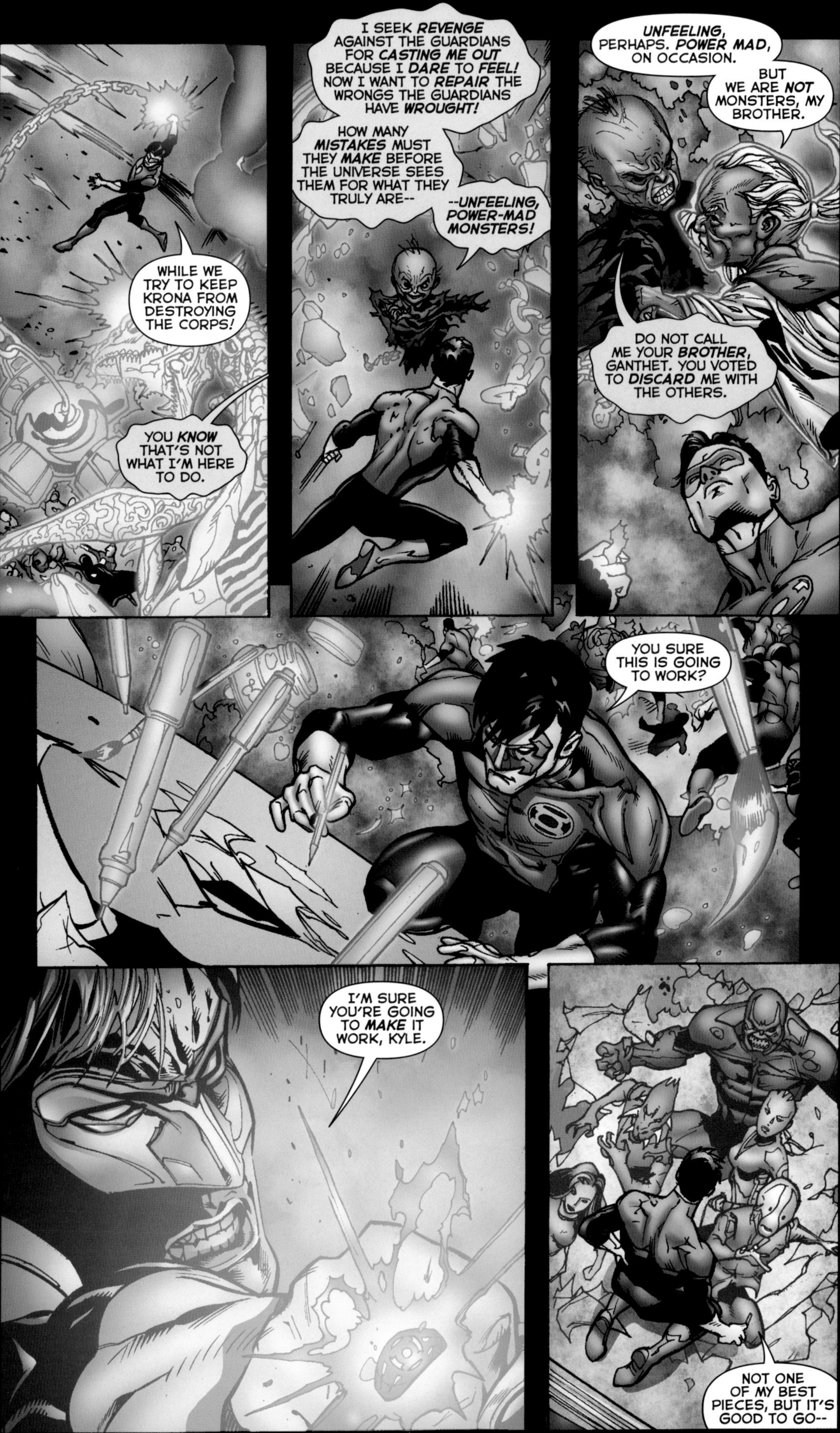
WHILE WE TRY TO KEEP KRONA FROM DESTROYING THE CORPS!
YOU KNOW THAT'S NOT WHAT I'M HERE TO DO.
I SEEK REVENGE AGAINST THE GUARDIANS FOR CASTING ME OUT BECAUSE I DARE TO FEEL! NOW I WANT TO REPAIR THE WRONGS THE GUARDIANS HAVE WROUGHT!
HOW MANY MISTAKES MUST THEY MAKE BEFORE THE UNIVERSE SEES THEM FOR WHAT THEY TRULY ARE--
--UNFEELING, POWER-MAD MONSTERS!
UNFEELING, PERHAPS. POWER MAD, ON OCCASION.
BUT WE ARE NOT MONSTERS, MY BROTHER.
DO NOT CALL ME YOUR BROTHER, GANTHET. YOU VOTED TO DISCARD ME WITH THE OTHERS.
YOU SURE THIS IS GOING TO WORK?
I'M SURE YOU'RE GOING TO MAKE IT WORK, KYLE.
NOT ONE OF MY BEST PIECES, BUT IT'S GOOD TO GO--

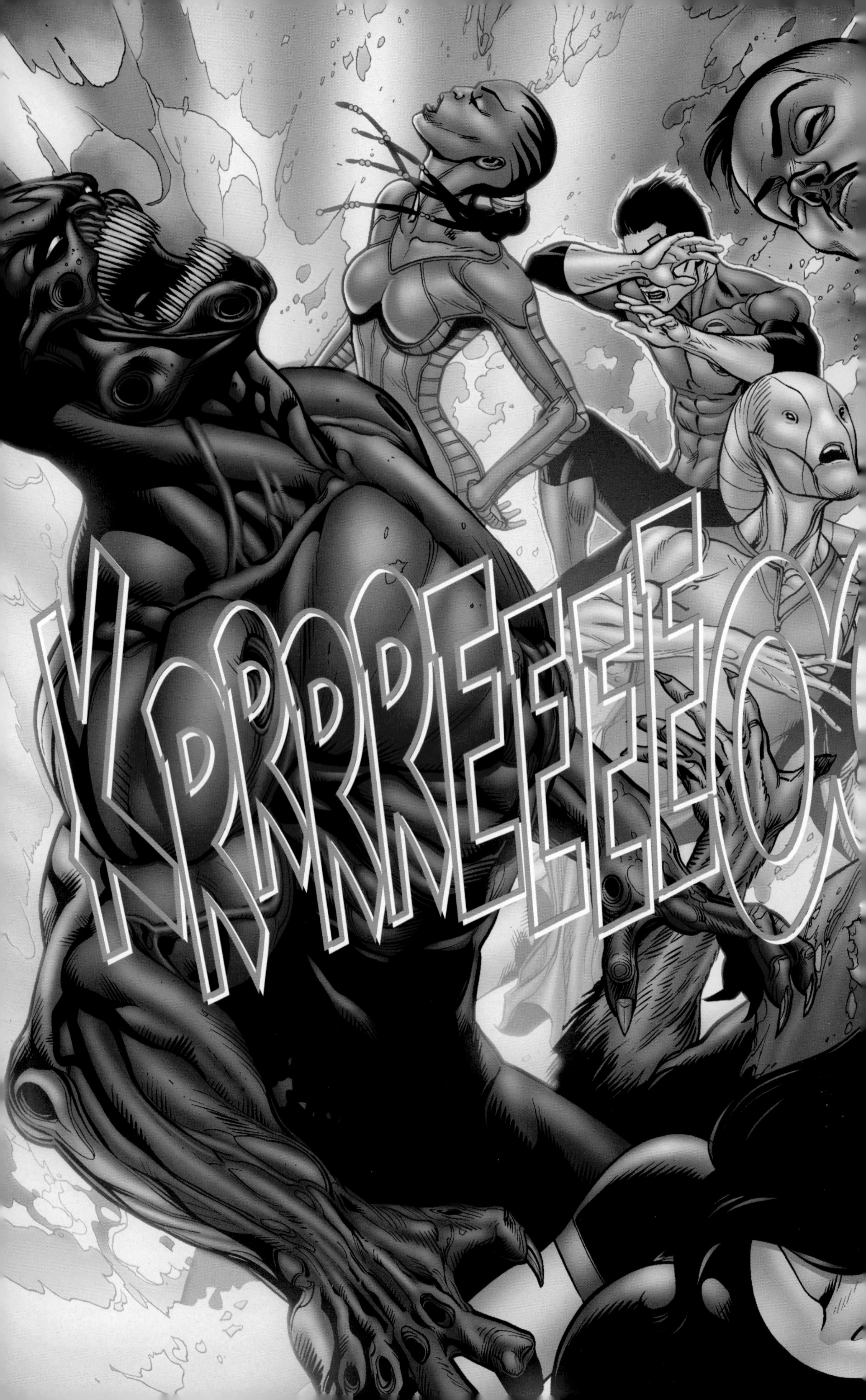

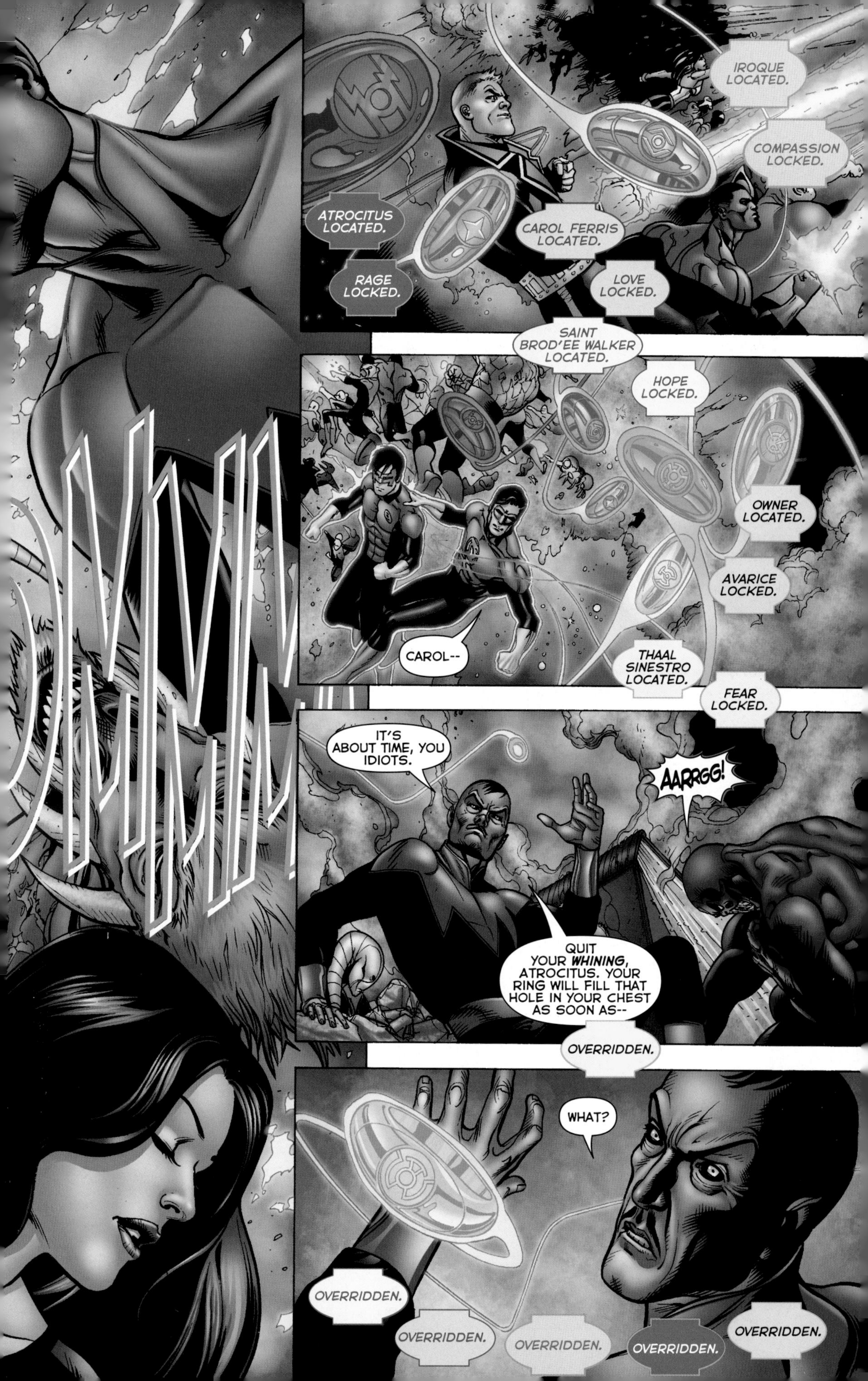
IROQUE LOCATED.
COMPASSION LOCKED.
ATROCITUS LOCATED.
RAGE LOCKED.
CAROL FERRIS LOCATED.
LOVE LOCKED.
SAINT BROD'EE WALKER LOCATED.
HOPE LOCKED.
OWNER LOCATED.
AVARICE LOCKED.
CAROL--
THAAL SINESTRO LOCATED.
FEAR LOCKED.
IT'S ABOUT TIME, YOU IDIOTS.
AARRGG!
QUIT YOUR WHINING, ATROCITUS. YOUR RING WILL FILL THAT HOLE IN YOUR CHEST AS SOON AS--
OVERRIDDEN.
WHAT?
OVERRIDDEN.
OVERRIDDEN.
OVERRIDDEN.
OVERRIDDEN.
OVERRIDDEN.

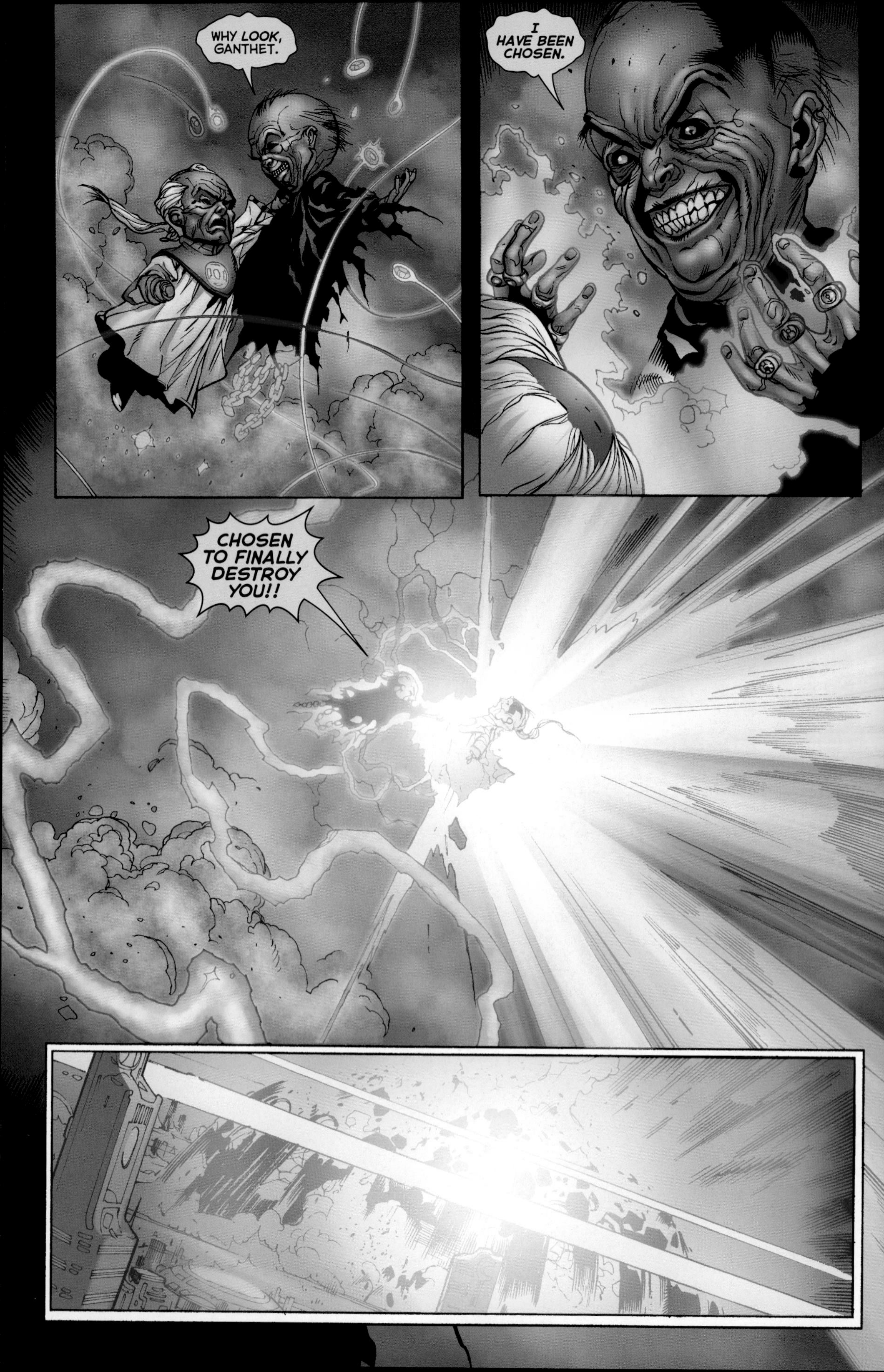
WHY LOOK, GANTHET.
I HAVE BEEN CHOSEN.
CHOSEN TO FINALLY DESTROY YOU!!

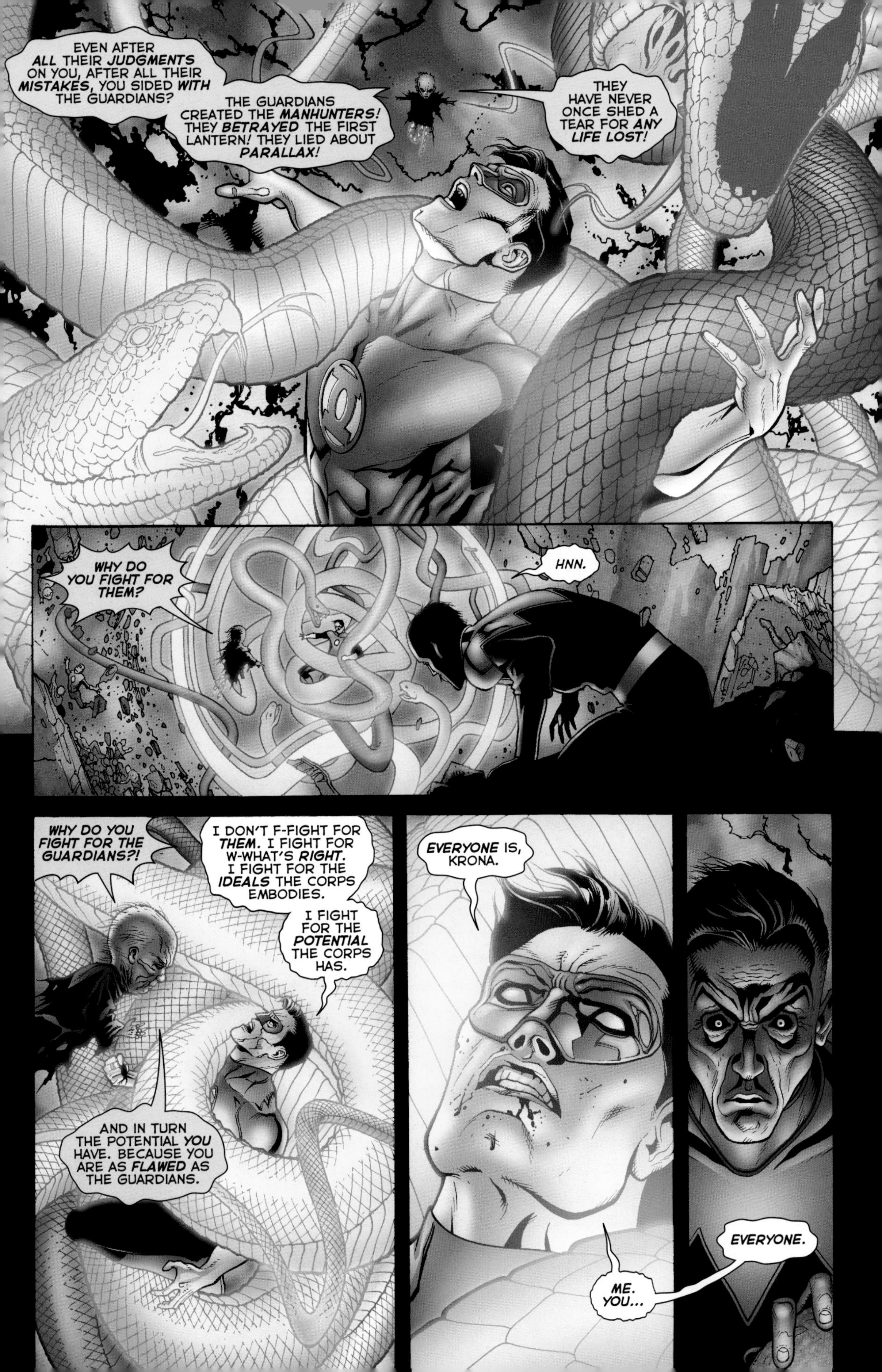
EVEN AFTER ALL THEIR JUDGMENTS ON YOU, AFTER ALL THEIR MISTAKES, YOU SIDED WITH THE GUARDIANS?
THE GUARDIANS CREATED THE MANHUNTERS! THEY BETRAYED THE FIRST LANTERN! THEY LIED ABOUT PARALLAX!
THEY HAVE NEVER ONCE SHED A TEAR FOR ANY LIFE LOST!
WHY DO YOU FIGHT FOR THEM?
HNN.
WHY DO YOU FIGHT FOR THE GUARDIANS?!
I DON'T F-FIGHT FOR THEM. I FIGHT FOR W-WHAT'S RIGHT. I FIGHT FOR THE IDEALS THE CORPS EMBODIES.
I FIGHT FOR THE POTENTIAL THE CORPS HAS.
AND IN TURN THE POTENTIAL YOU HAVE. BECAUSE YOU ARE AS FLAWED AS THE GUARDIANS.
EVERYONE IS, KRONA.
ME. YOU...
EVERYONE.

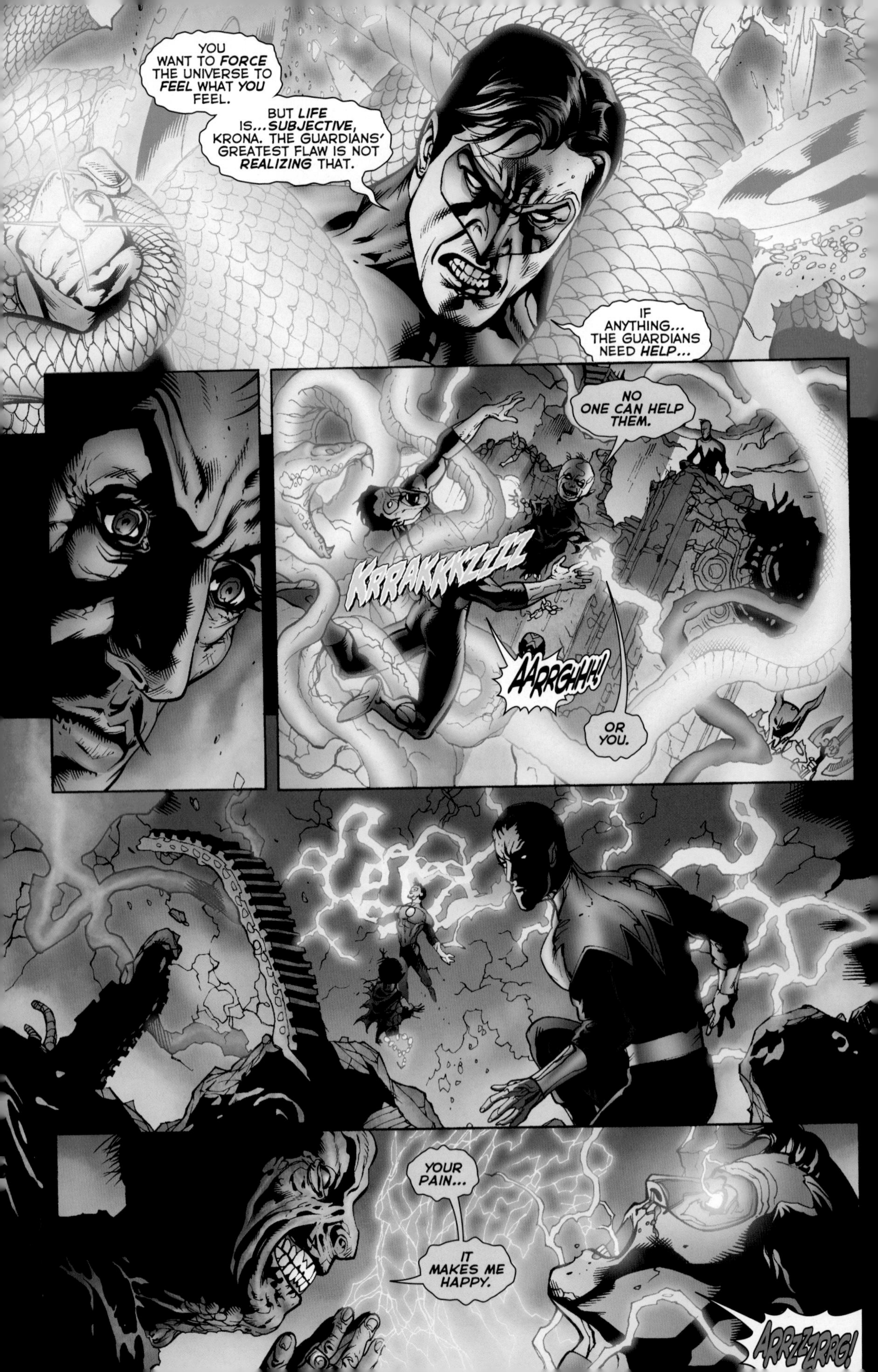
YOU WANT TO FORCE THE UNIVERSE TO FEEL WHAT YOU FEEL.
BUT LIFE IS... SUBJECTIVE, KRONA. THE GUARDIANS' GREATEST FLAW IS NOT REALIZING THAT.
IF ANYTHING... THE GUARDIANS NEED HELP...
NO ONE CAN HELP THEM.
KRRAKKKZZZZ
AARRGHHH!
OR YOU.
YOUR PAIN...
IT MAKES ME HAPPY.
ARRZZZRRG!

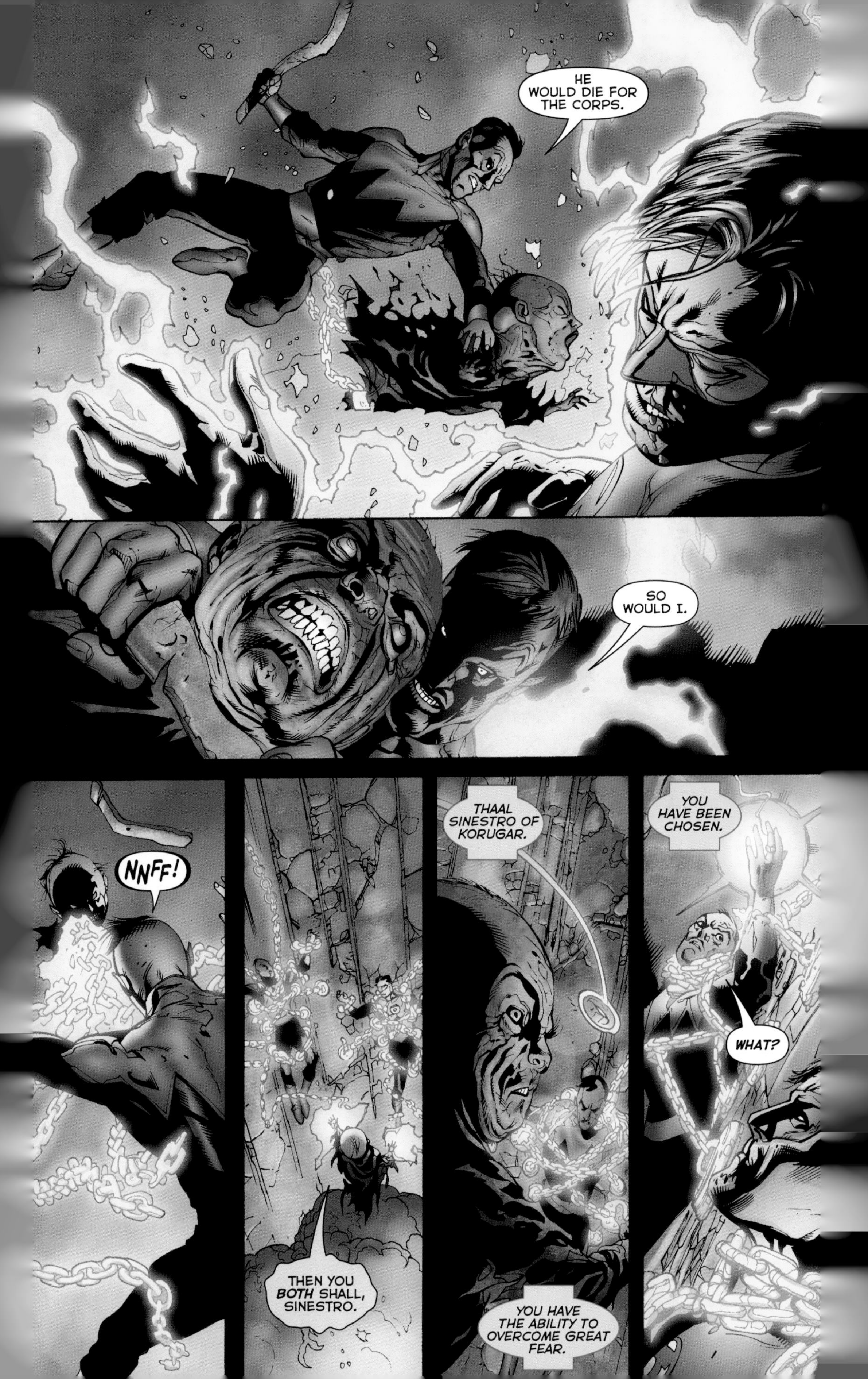
HE WOULD DIE FOR THE CORPS.
SO WOULD I.
NNFF!
THEN YOU *BOTH* SHALL, SINESTRO.
THAAL SINESTRO OF KORUGAR.
YOU HAVE THE ABILITY TO OVERCOME GREAT FEAR.
YOU HAVE BEEN CHOSEN.
WHAT?

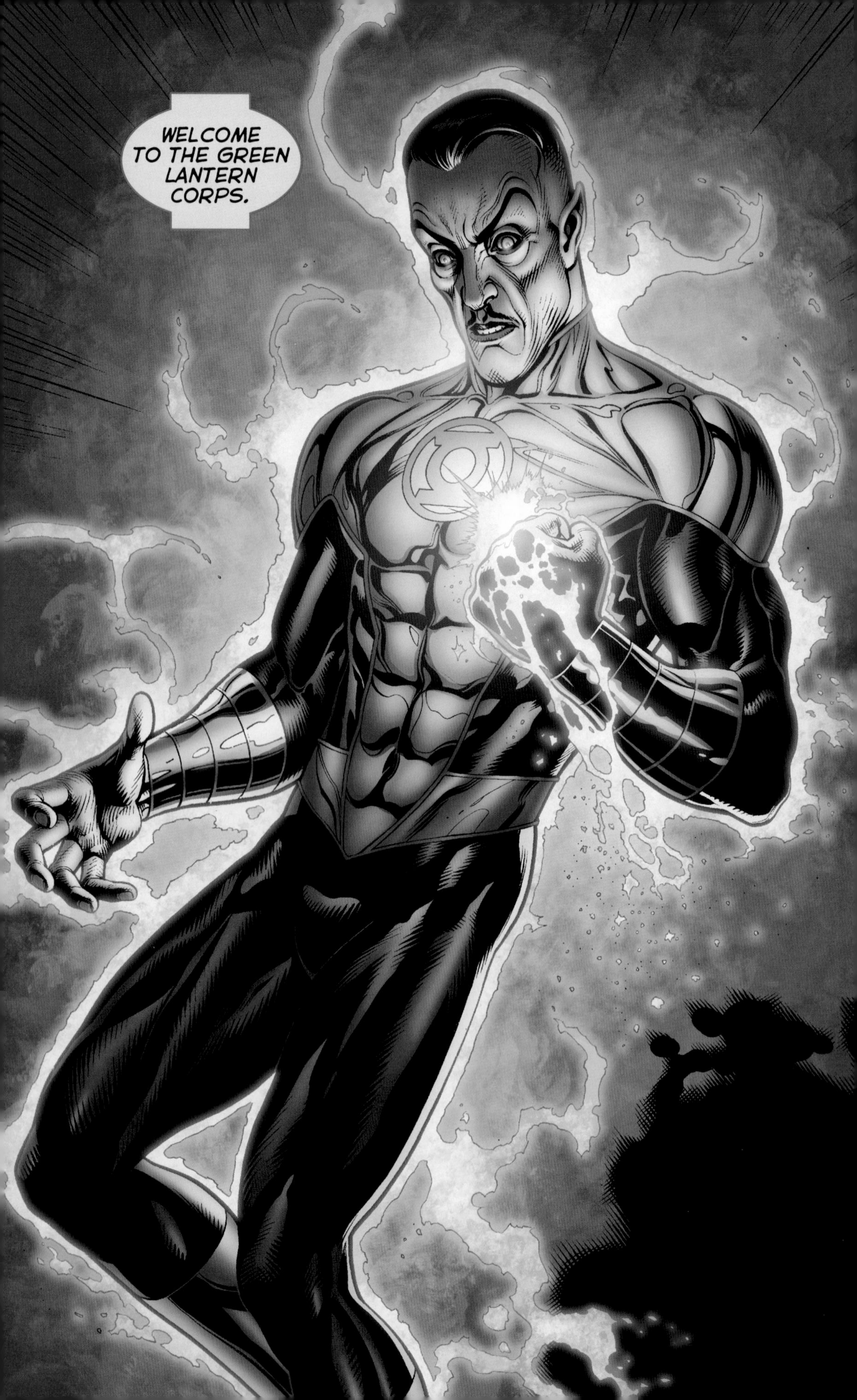
WELCOME TO THE GREEN LANTERN CORPS.

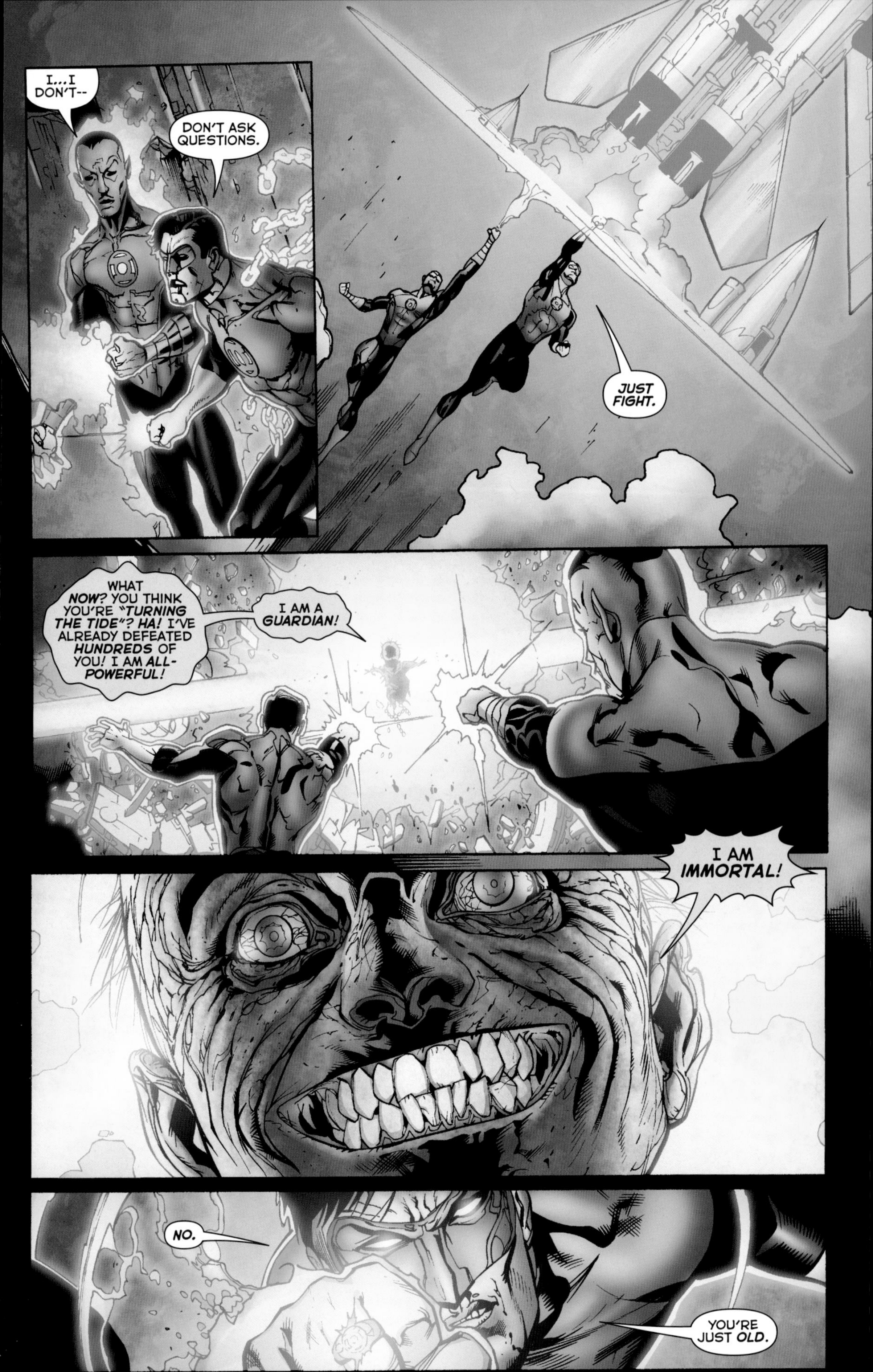
I...I DON'T--
DON'T ASK QUESTIONS.
JUST FIGHT.
WHAT NOW? YOU THINK YOU'RE "TURNING THE TIDE"? HA! I'VE ALREADY DEFEATED HUNDREDS OF YOU! I AM ALL-POWERFUL!
I AM A GUARDIAN!
I AM IMMORTAL!
NO.
YOU'RE JUST OLD.

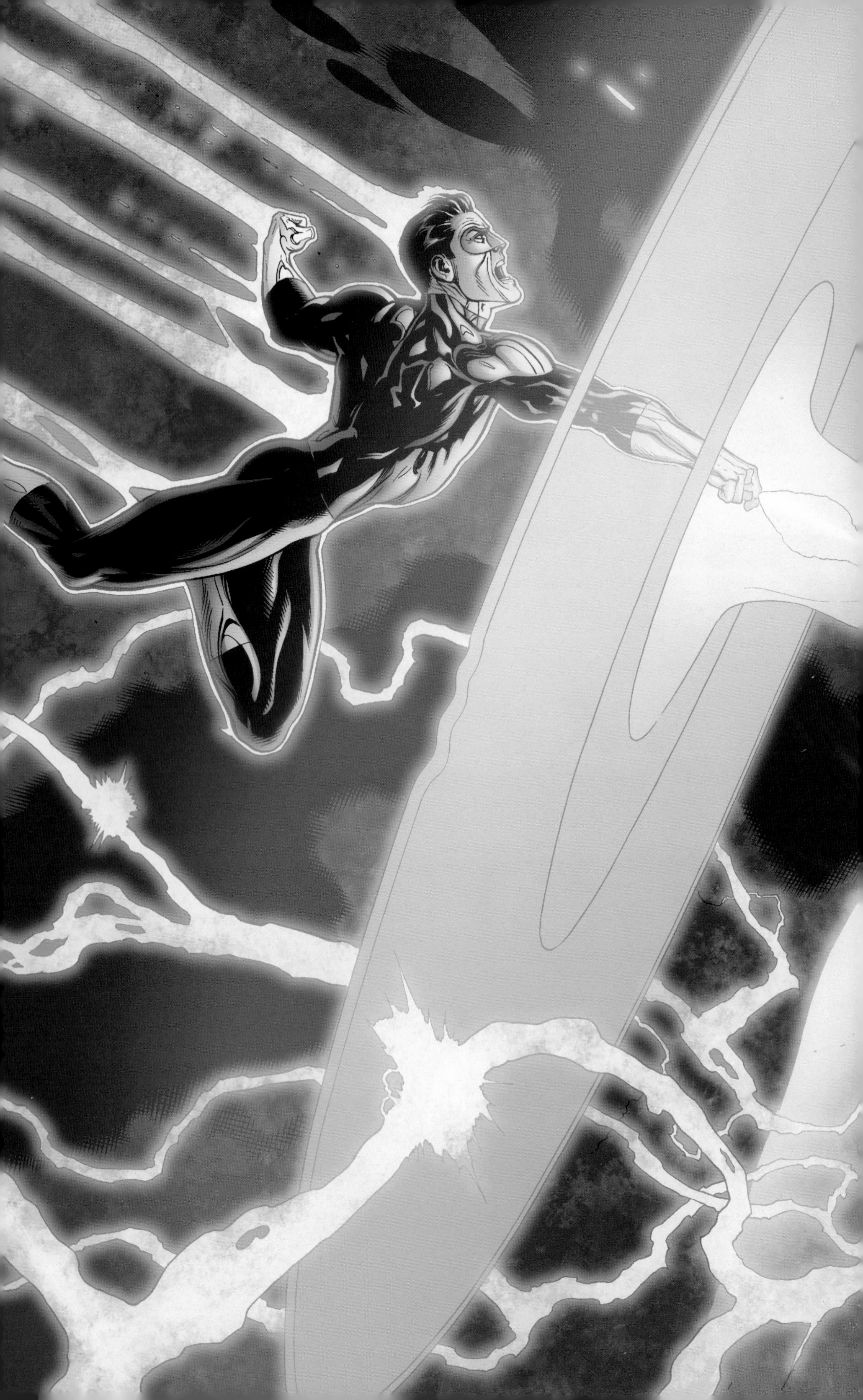

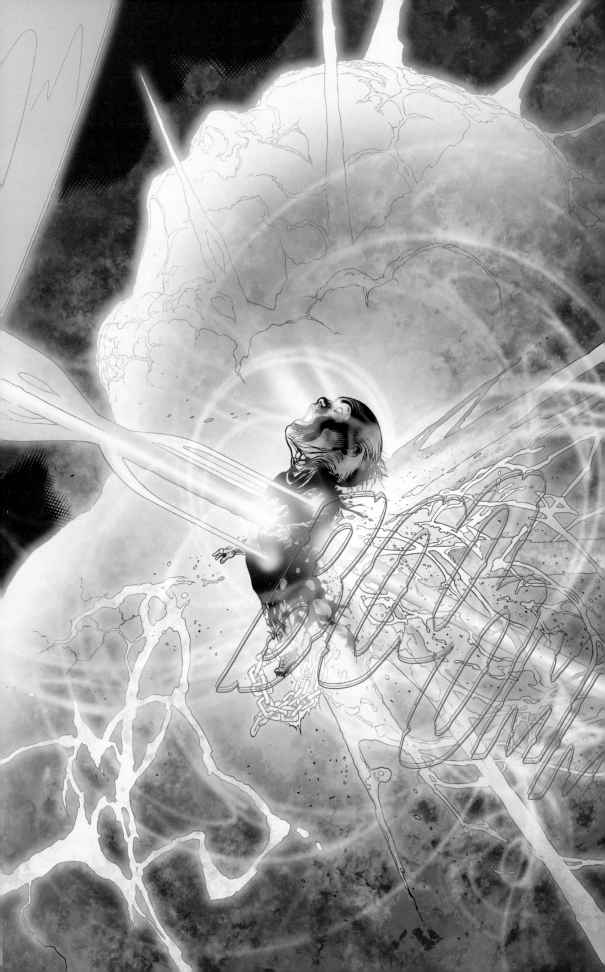

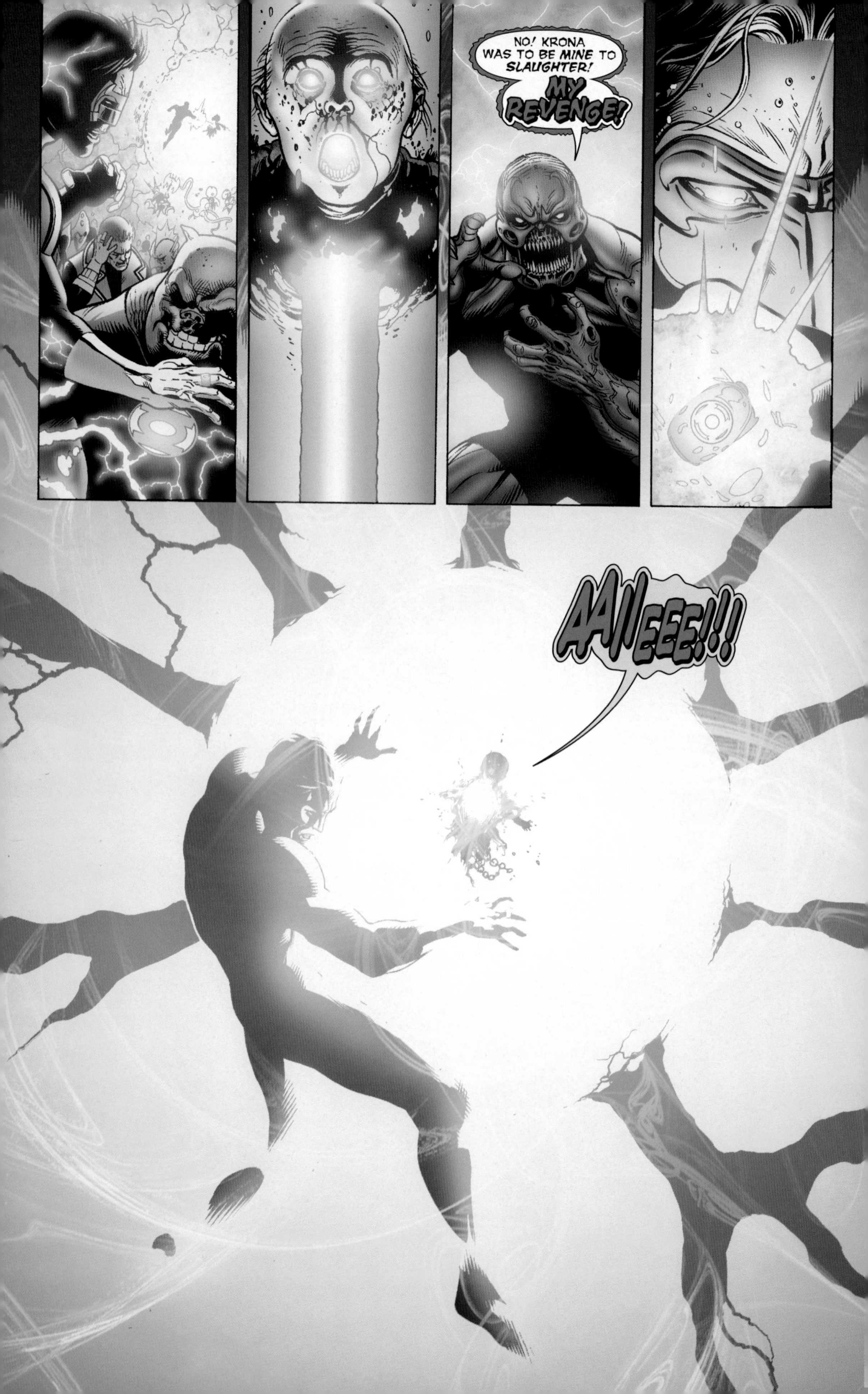
NO! KRONA WAS TO BE MINE TO SLAUGHTER!
MY REVENGE!
AAIIEEE!!!

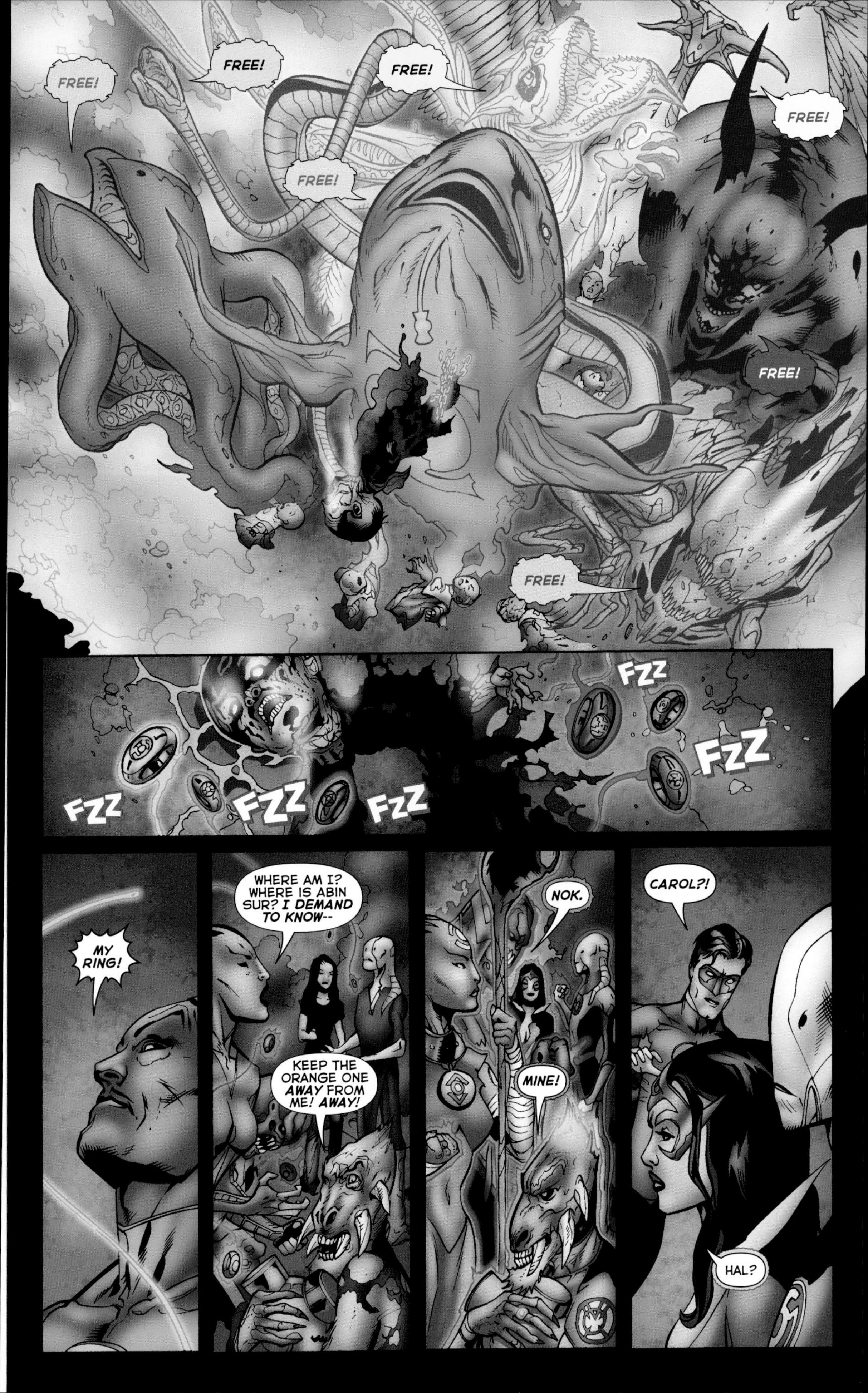
FREE!
FREE!
FREE!
FREE!
FREE!
FREE!
FREE!
FZZ
FZZ
FZZ
FZZ
FZZ
MY RING!
WHERE AM I? WHERE IS ABIN SUR? I DEMAND TO KNOW--
KEEP THE ORANGE ONE AWAY FROM ME! AWAY!
NOK.
MINE!
CAROL?!
HAL?

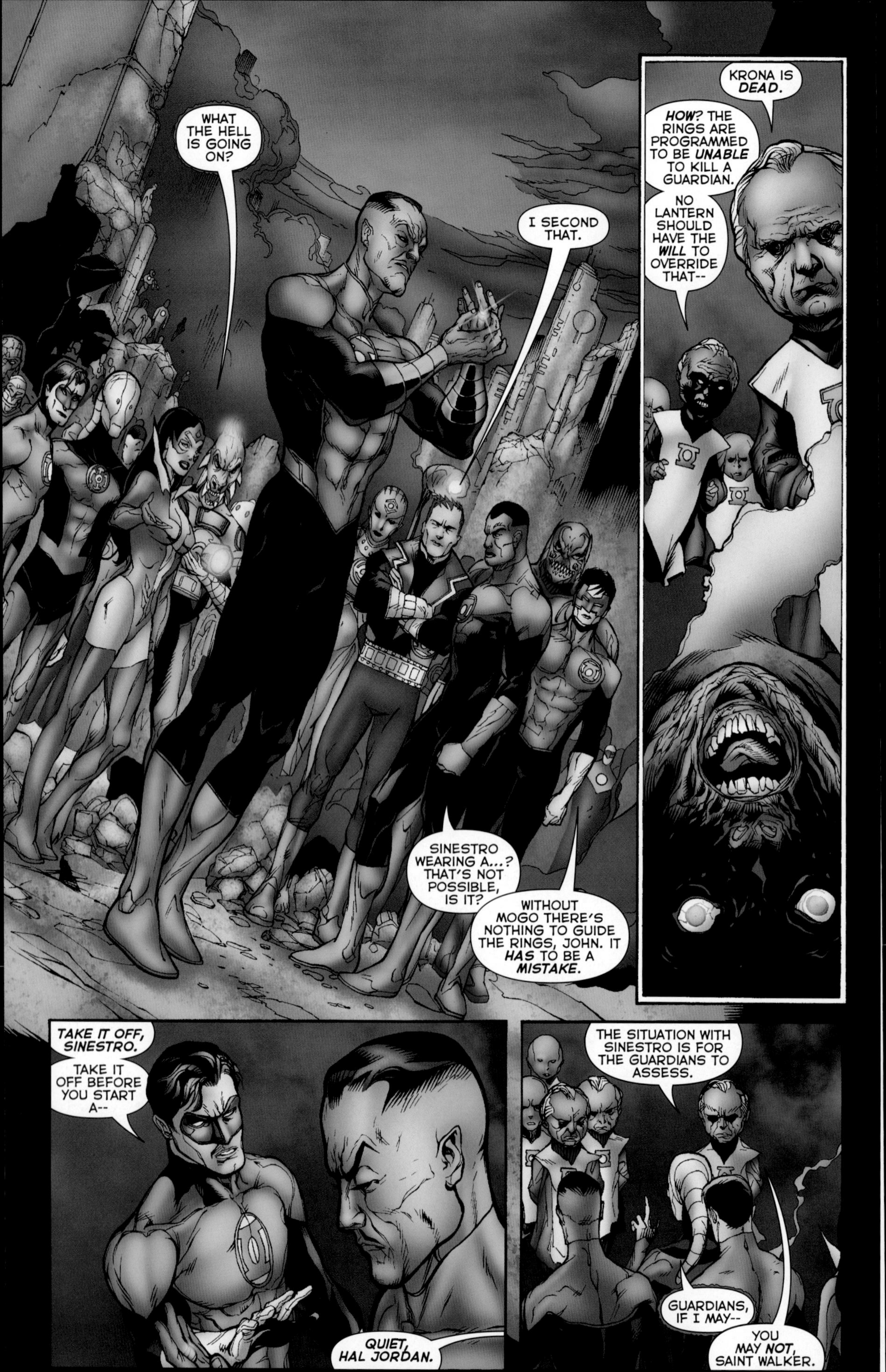

WHAT THE HELL IS GOING ON?
I SECOND THAT.
KRONA IS DEAD.
HOW? THE RINGS ARE PROGRAMMED TO BE UNABLE TO KILL A GUARDIAN.
NO LANTERN SHOULD HAVE THE WILL TO OVERRIDE THAT--
SINESTRO WEARING A...? THAT'S NOT POSSIBLE, IS IT?
WITHOUT MOGO THERE'S NOTHING TO GUIDE THE RINGS, JOHN. IT HAS TO BE A MISTAKE.
TAKE IT OFF, SINESTRO.
TAKE IT OFF BEFORE YOU START A--
QUIET, HAL JORDAN.
THE SITUATION WITH SINESTRO IS FOR THE GUARDIANS TO ASSESS.
GUARDIANS, IF I MAY--
YOU MAY NOT, SAINT WALKER.

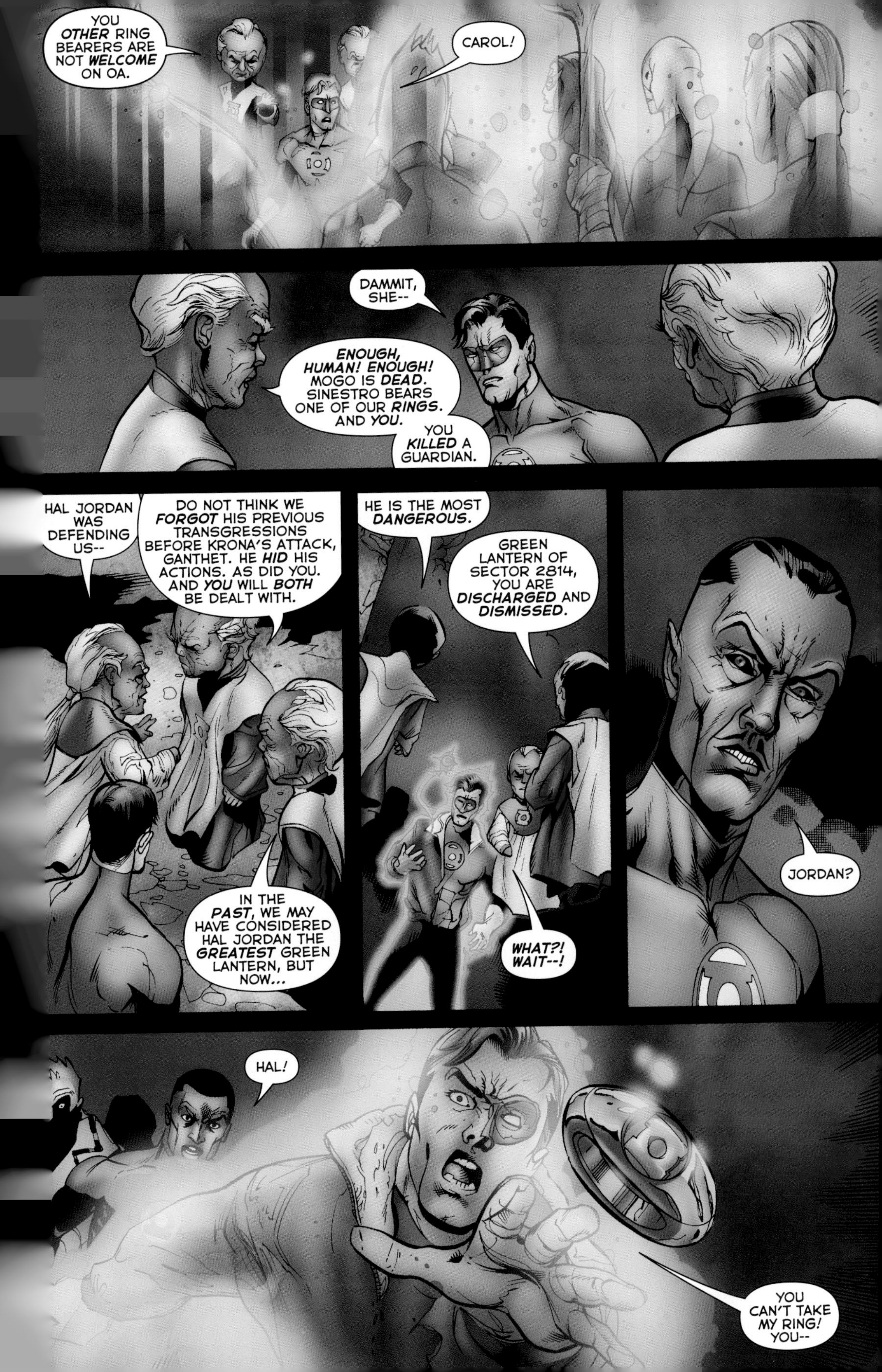
YOU OTHER RING BEARERS ARE NOT WELCOME ON OA.
CAROL!
DAMMIT, SHE--
ENOUGH, HUMAN! ENOUGH! MOGO IS DEAD. SINESTRO BEARS ONE OF OUR RINGS. AND YOU.
YOU KILLED A GUARDIAN.
HAL JORDAN WAS DEFENDING US--
DO NOT THINK WE FORGOT HIS PREVIOUS TRANSGRESSIONS BEFORE KRONA'S ATTACK, GANTHET. HE HID HIS ACTIONS. AS DID YOU. AND YOU WILL BOTH BE DEALT WITH.
IN THE PAST, WE MAY HAVE CONSIDERED HAL JORDAN THE GREATEST GREEN LANTERN, BUT NOW...
HE IS THE MOST DANGEROUS.
GREEN LANTERN OF SECTOR 2814, YOU ARE DISCHARGED AND DISMISSED.
WHAT?! WAIT--!
JORDAN?
HAL!
YOU CAN'T TAKE MY RING! YOU--

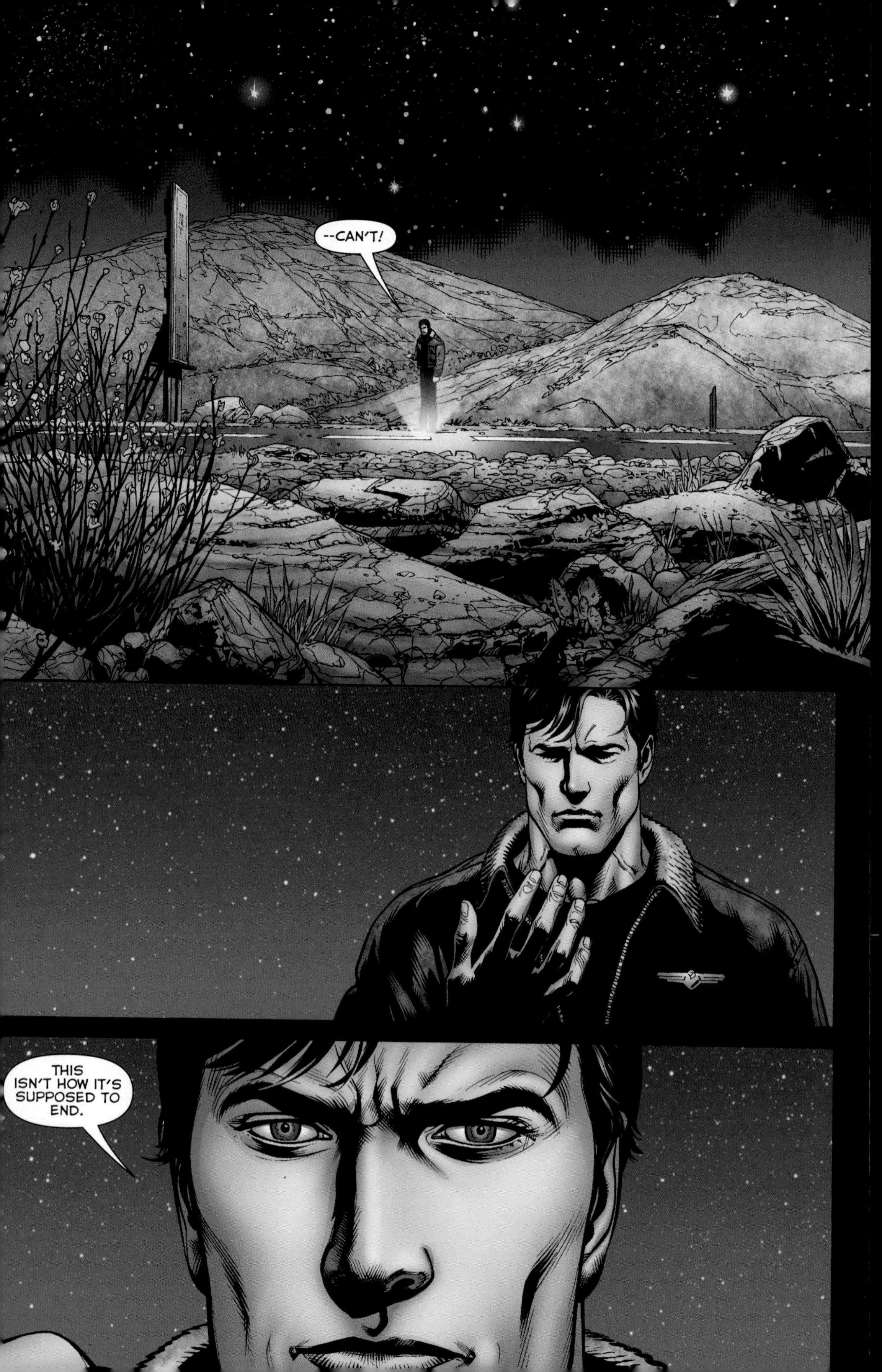
--CAN'T!
THIS ISN'T HOW IT'S SUPPOSED TO END.

WAR OF THE GREEN LANTERNS
VARIANT COVER GALLERY

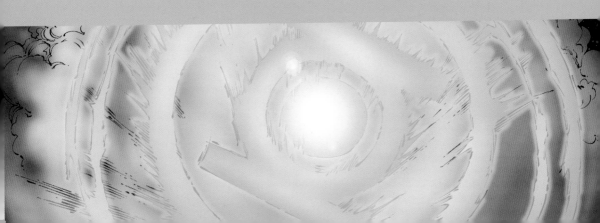

GREEN LANTERN 63 Variant cover by Brett Booth & Norm Rapmund with Andrew Dalhouse

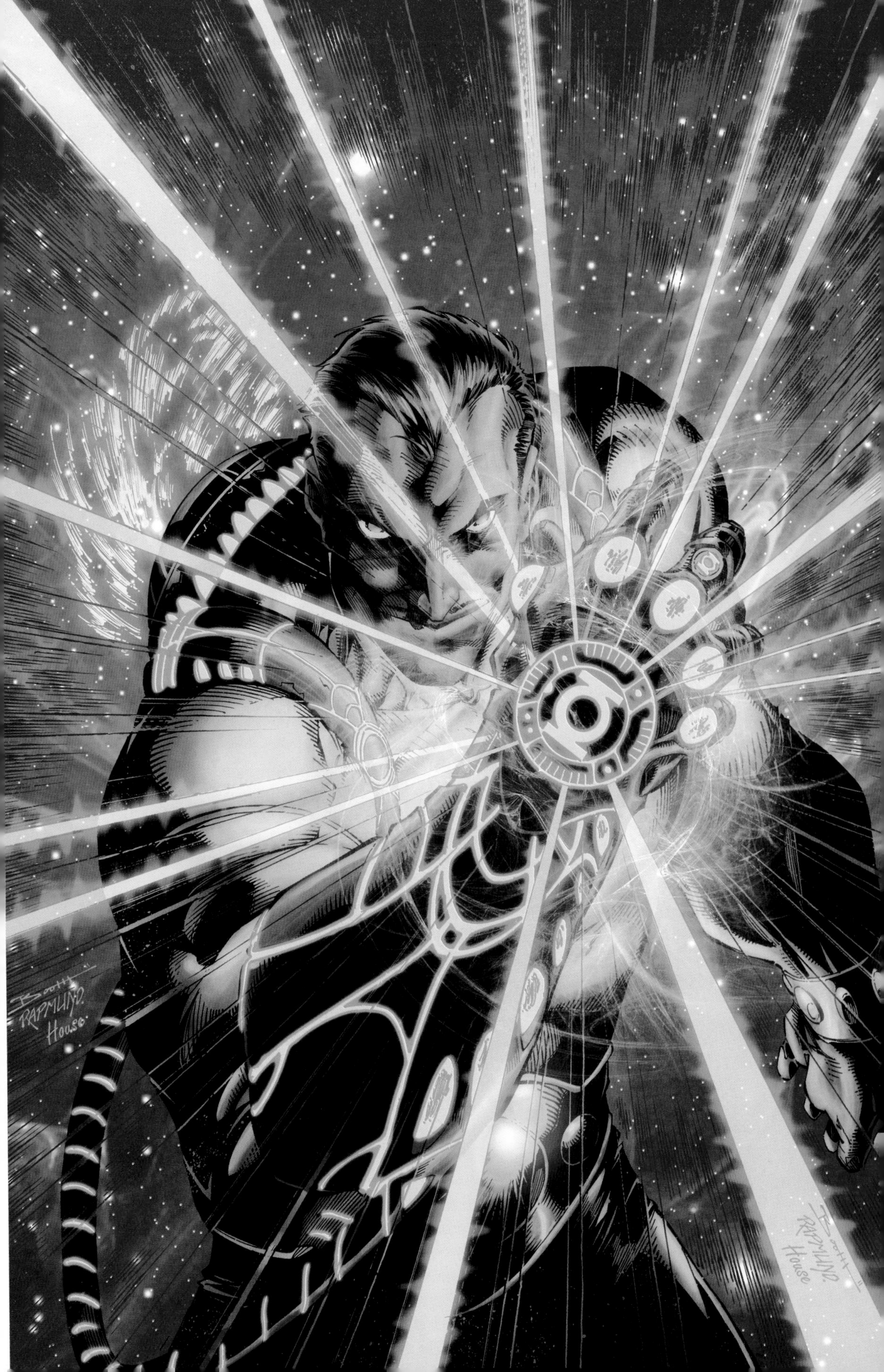
Booth
RAPMUND.
House

GREEN LANTERN 64 Variant cover by Tyler Kirkham & BATT with Brian Buccellato

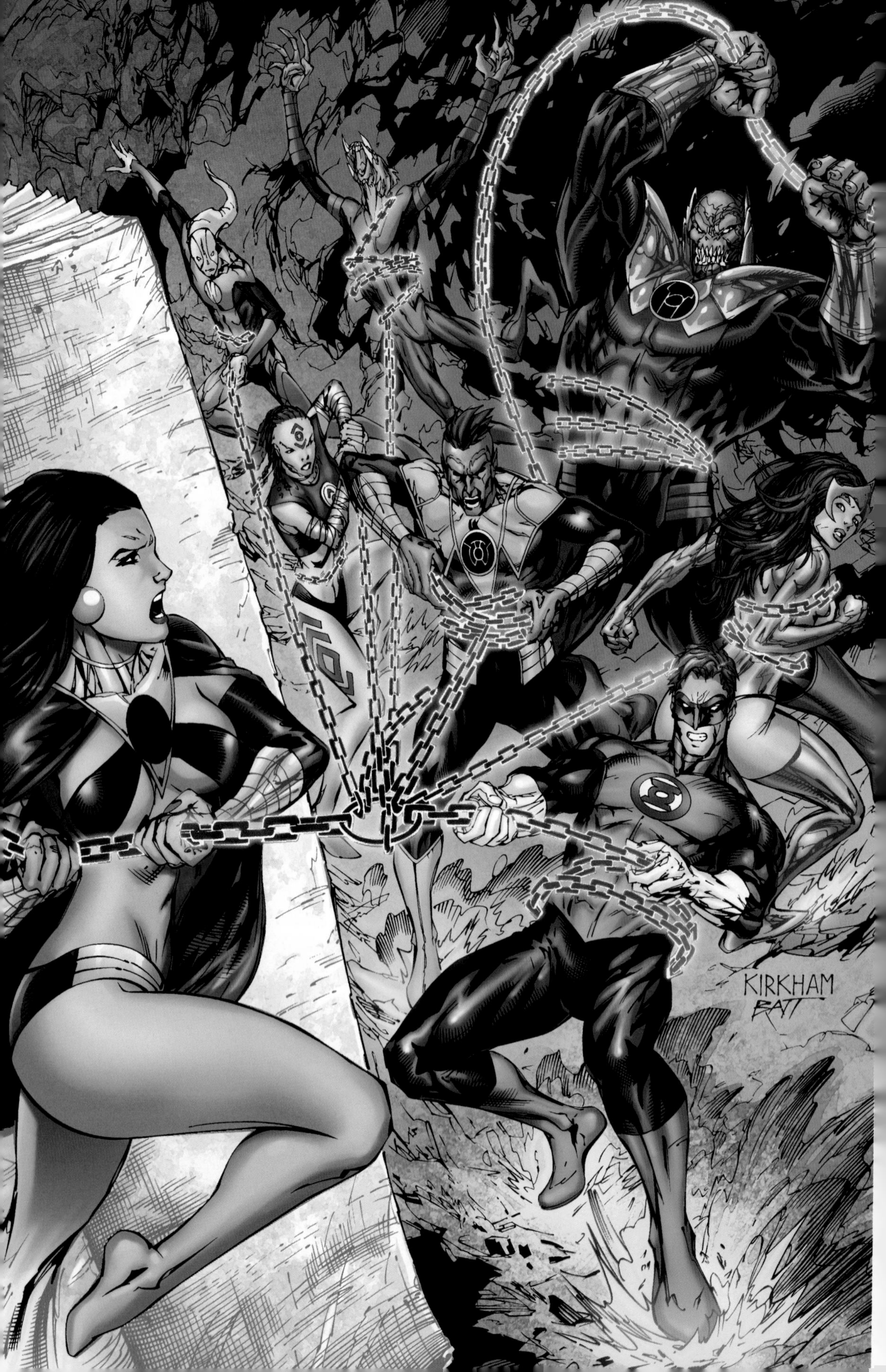
KIRKHAM
BATT

iREEN LANTERN CORPS 58 Variant cover by Tyler Kirkham & BATT with Nei Ruffino

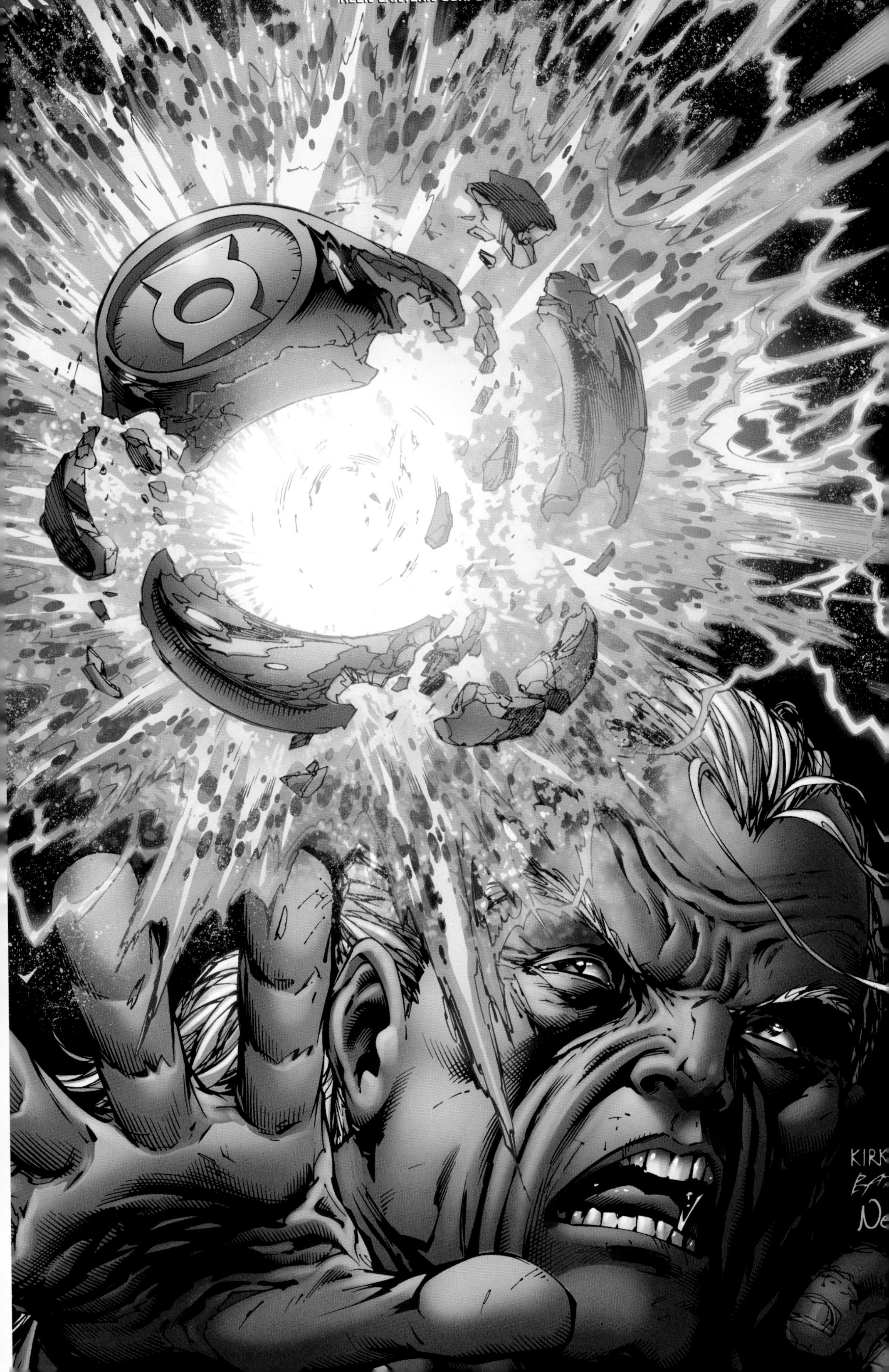
KIRK

GREEN LANTERN: EMERALD WARRIORS 8 **Variant cover by Tyler Kirkham & BATT with Nei Ruffino**

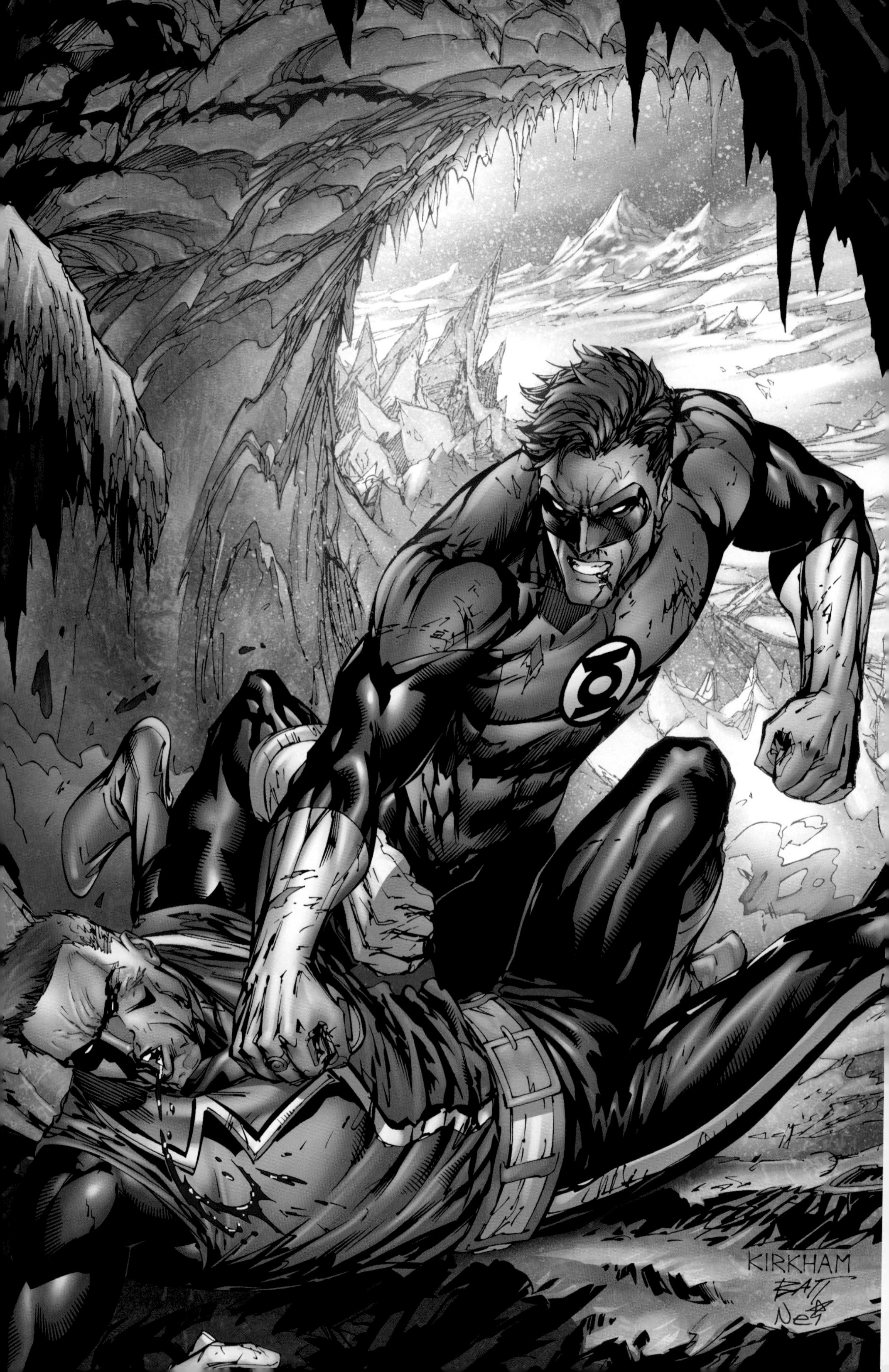
KIRKHAM

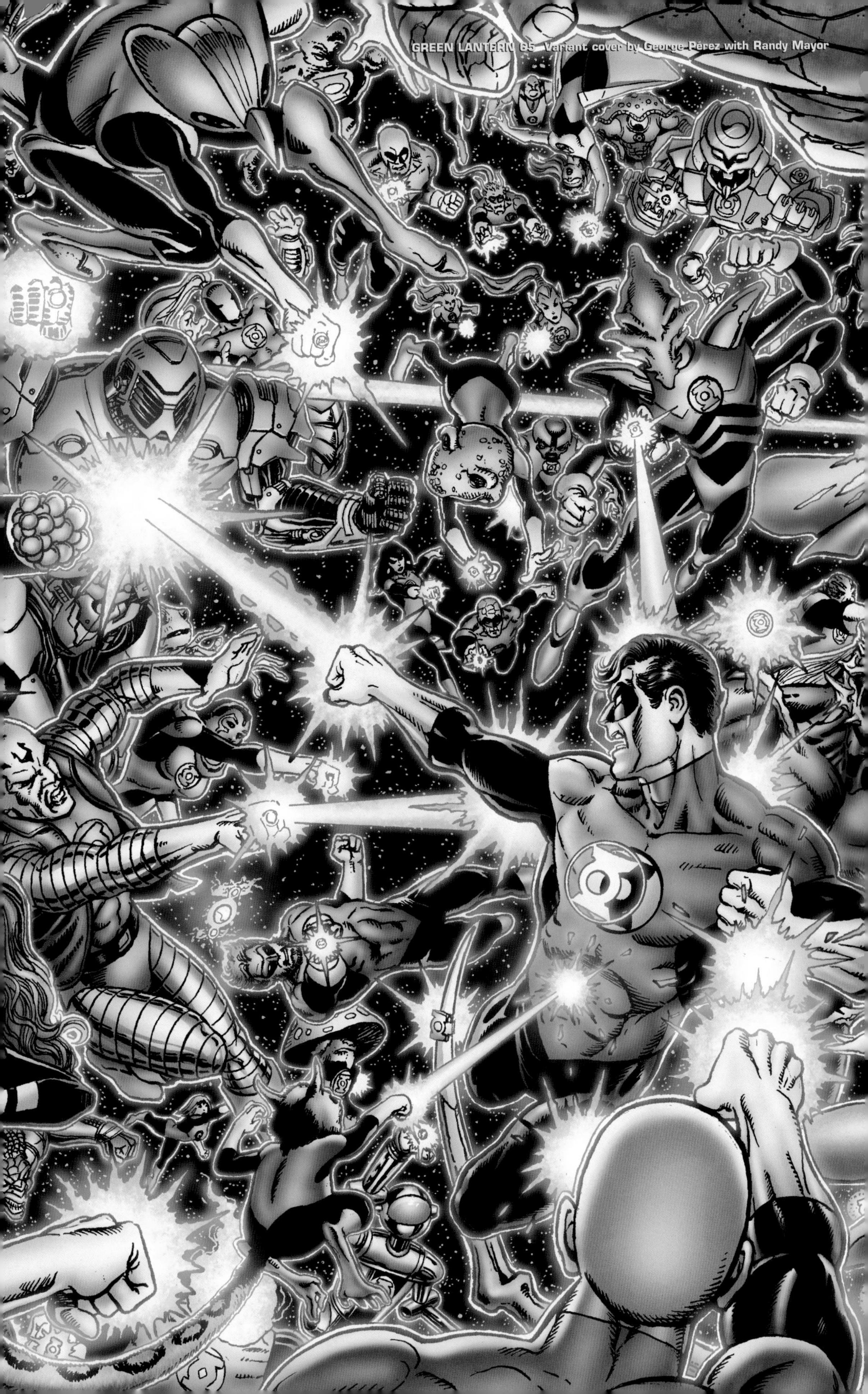
GREEN LANTERN 65 Variant cover by George Pérez with Randy Mayor

GREEN LANTERN CORPS 59 Variant cover by George Pérez with Randy Mayor

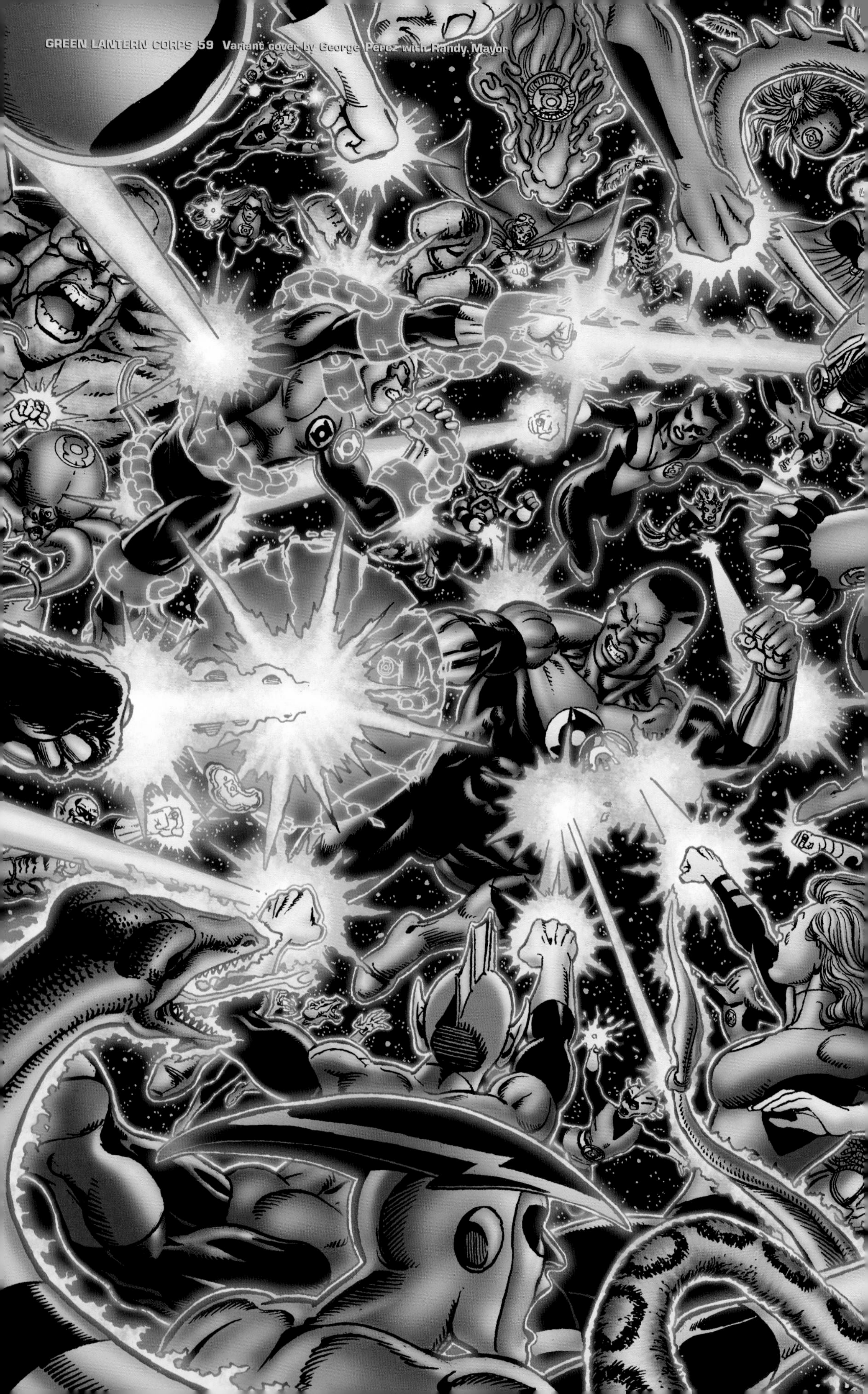

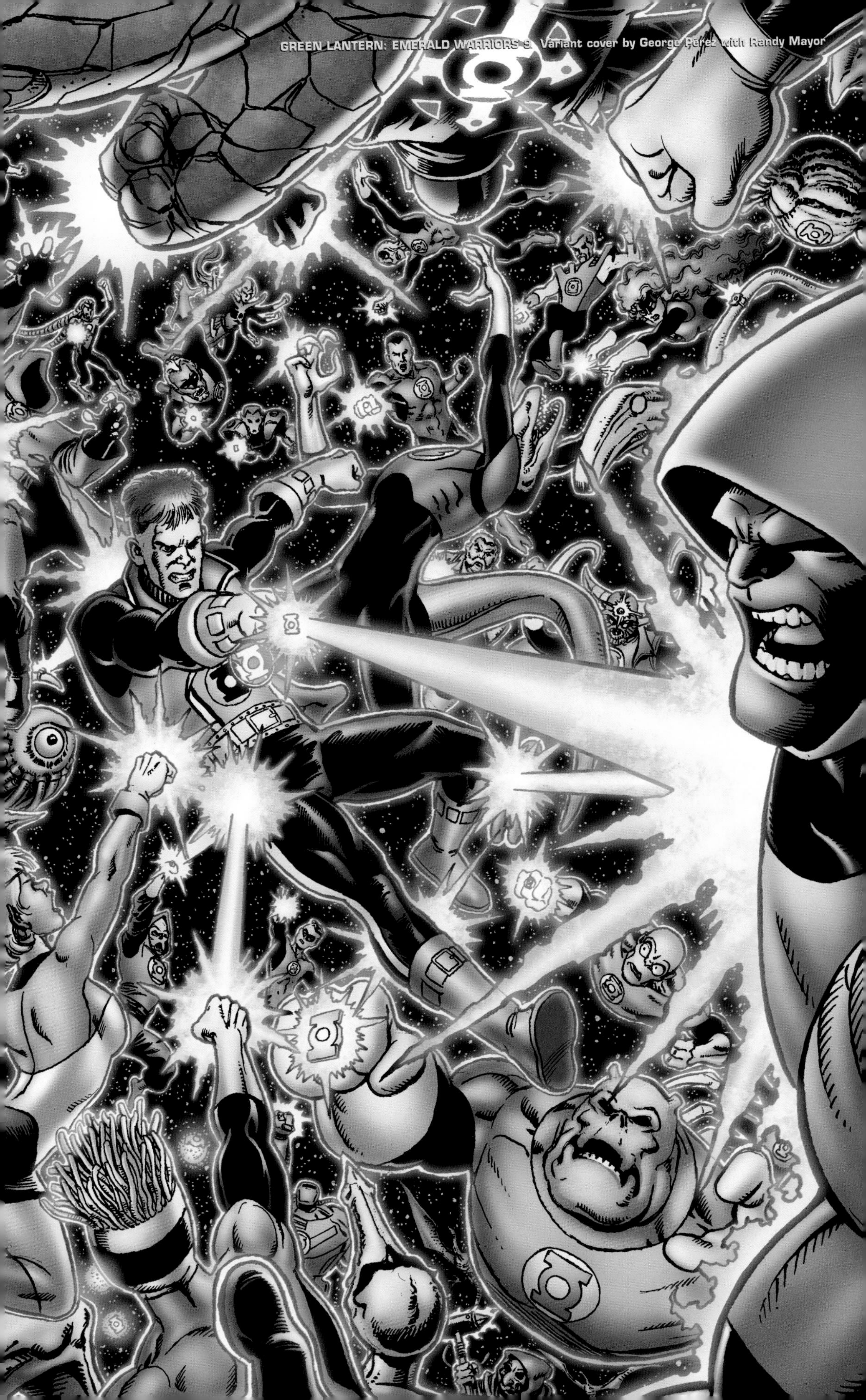

GREEN LANTERN: EMERALD WARRIORS 9 Variant cover by George Pérez with Randy Mayor

GREEN LANTERN 66 Variant cover by Clayton Crain

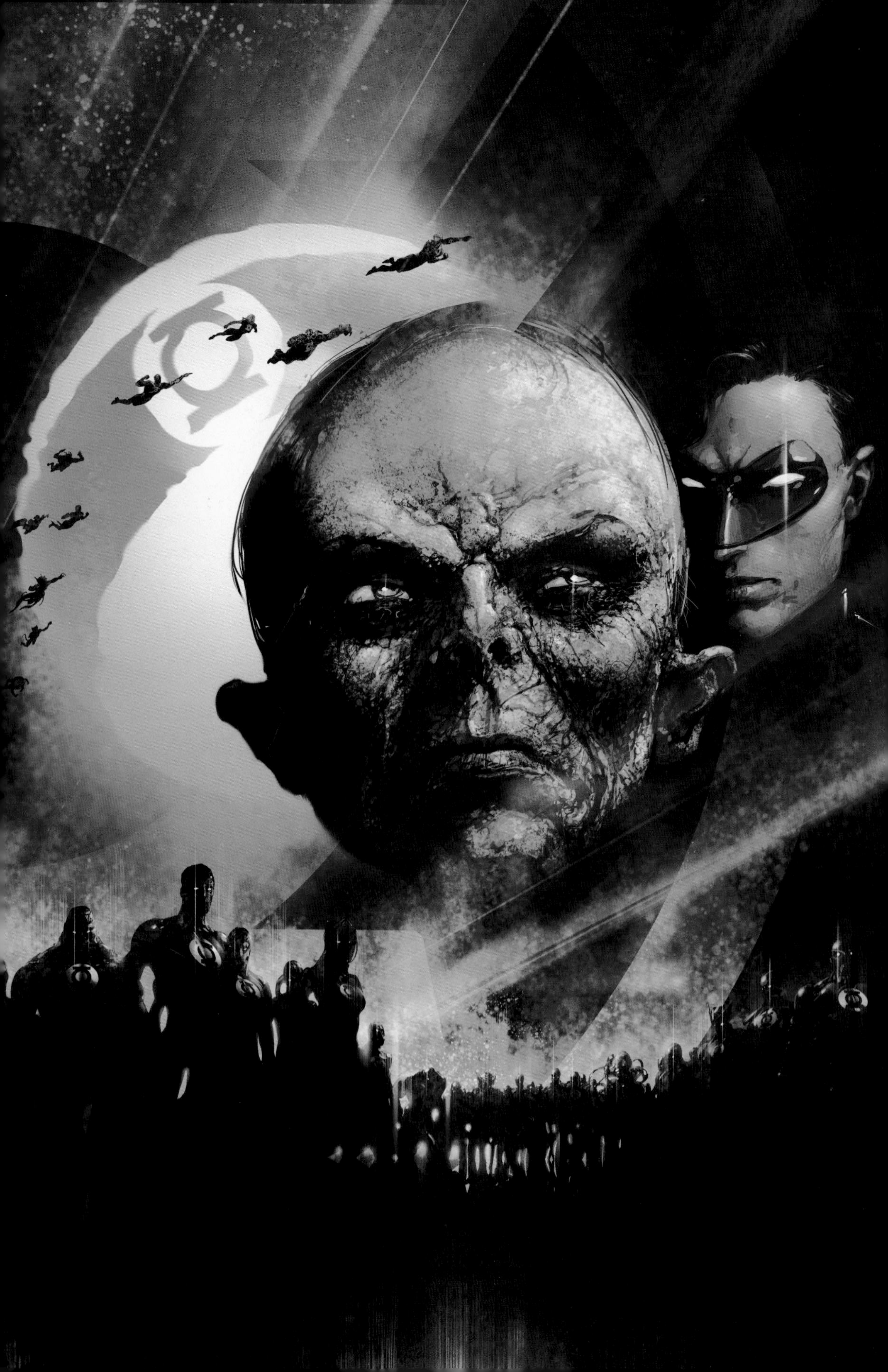

GREEN LANTERN CORPS 60 Variant cover by Clayton Crain

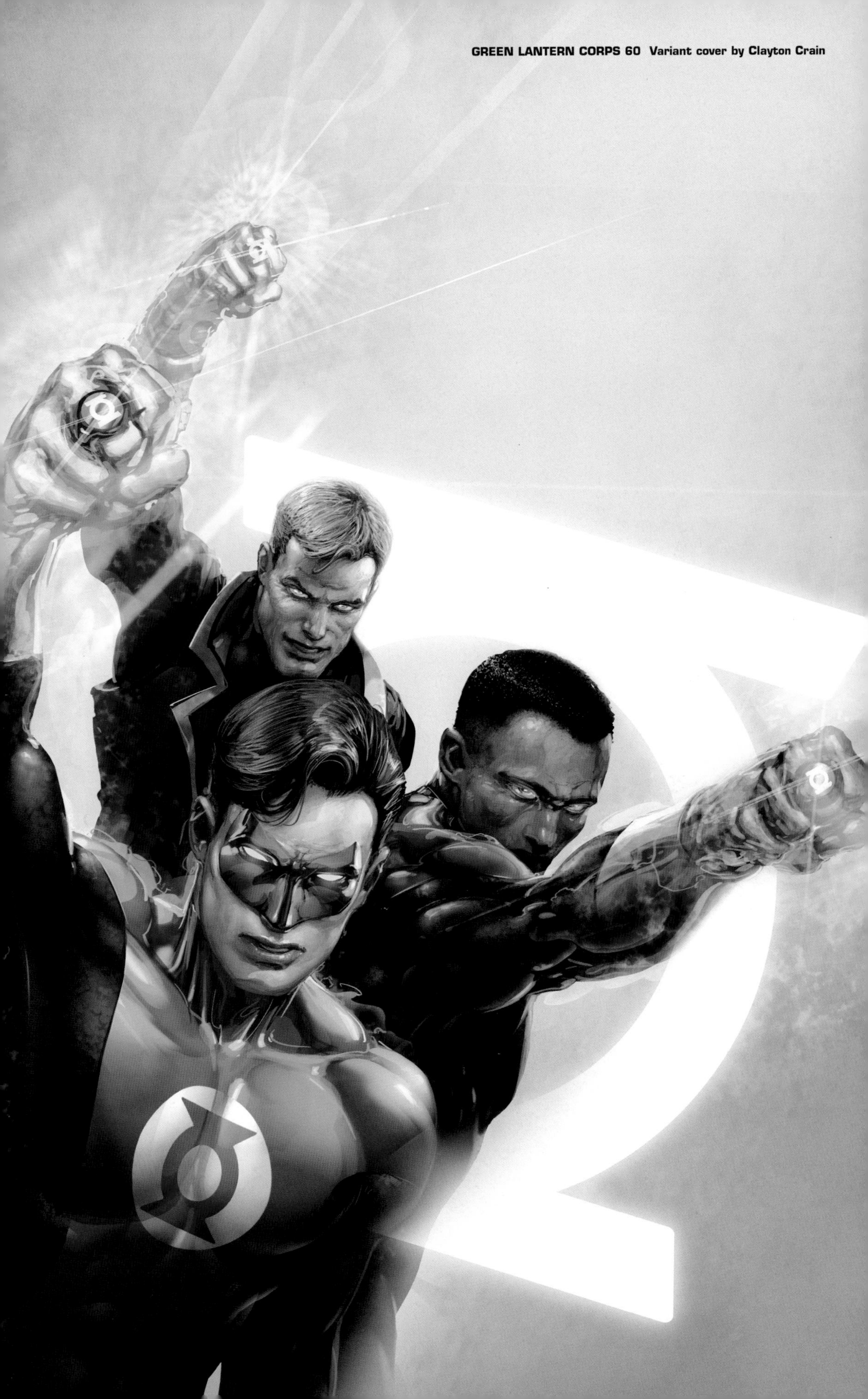

GREEN LANTERN: EMERALD WARRIORS 10 Variant cover by Clayton Crain

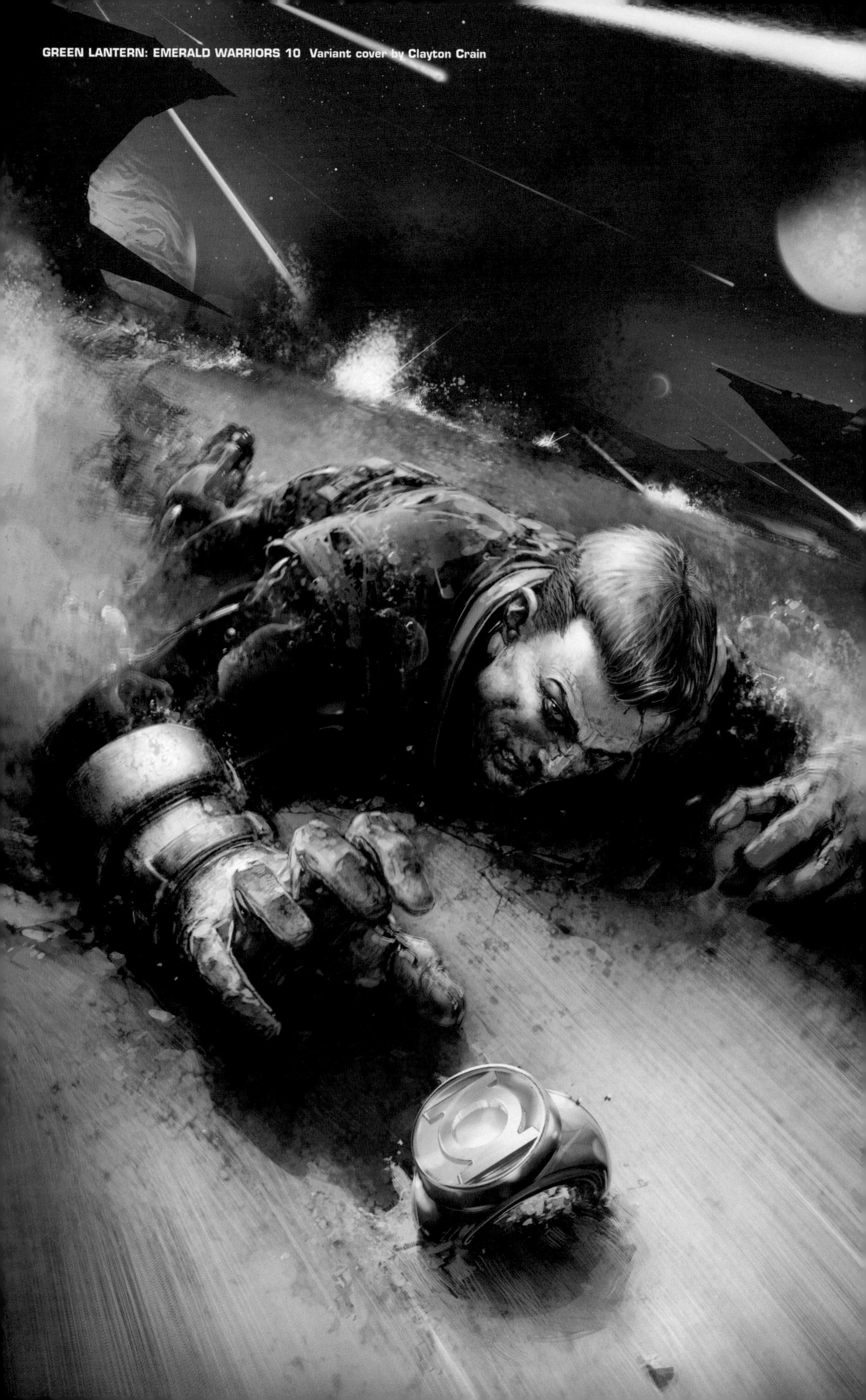

GREEN LANTERN 67 Variant cover by J.G. Jones with Alex Sinclair

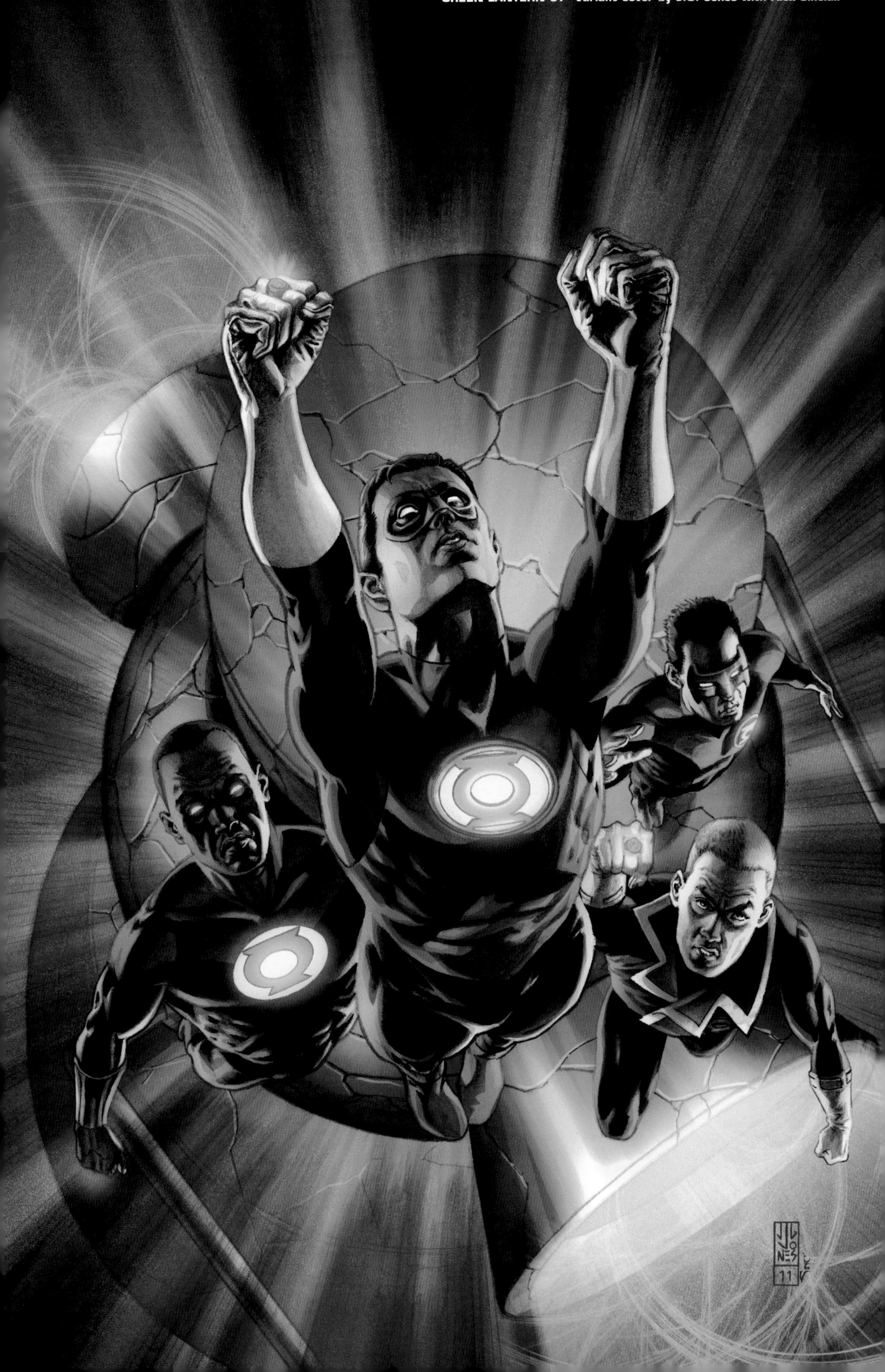

BIOGRAPHIES

WRITERS

GEOFF JOHNS

Geoff Johns is one of the most prolific and popular contemporary comic book writers. He has written highly acclaimed stories starring Superman, Green Lantern, the Flash, Teen Titans, and the Justice Society of America. He is the author of *The New York Times* best-selling graphic novels GREEN LANTERN: RAGE OF THE RED LANTERNS, GREEN LANTERN: SINESTRO CORPS WAR, JUSTICE SOCIETY OF AMERICA: THY KINGDOM COME, SUPERMAN: BRAINIAC and BLACKEST NIGHT.

Johns was born in Detroit and studied media arts, screenwriting, film production and film theory at Michigan State University. After moving to Los Angeles, he worked as an intern and later an assistant for film director Richard Donner, whose credits include *Superman: The Movie, Lethal Weapon 4* and *Conspiracy Theory*.

Johns began his comics career writing STARS AND S.T.R.I.P.E. and creating Stargirl for DC Comics. He received the Wizard Fan Award for Breakout Talent of 2002 and Writer of the Year for 2005, 2006, 2007 and 2008 as well as the CBG Writer of the Year 2003 through 2005 and 2007 and 2008, and CBG Best Comic Book Series for JSA 2001 through 2005.

After acclaimed runs on THE FLASH, TEEN TITANS and the best-selling INFINITE CRISIS miniseries, Johns co-wrote a run on ACTION COMICS with his mentor Donner. In 2006, he co-wrote 52: an ambitious weekly comic book series set in real time, with Grant Morrison, Greg Rucka and Mark Waid. Johns has also written for various other media, including the acclaimed "Legion" episode of SMALLVILLE and the fourth season of ROBOT CHICKEN. He is writing the story of the DC Universe Online massively multiplayer action game from Sony Online Entertainment LLC and has recently joined DC Entertainment as its Chief Creative Officer.

Johns currently resides in Los Angeles, California.

TONY BEDARD is a former editor at DC Comics, who has gone on to write comics for Valiant, GrossGen and Marvel Comics. For DC Comics he has written BIRDS OF PREY, COUNTDOWN, R.E.B.E.L.S. and FLASHPOINT: EMPEROR AQUAMAN. Tony is also the inaugural author of GREEN LANTERN: THE NEW GUARDIANS and BLUE BEETLE.

PETER J. TOMASI

Peter J. Tomasi was an editor with DC Comics for fourteen years. One of his proudest moments was bringing KINGDOM COME to DC's attention and also relaunching JSA for a new generation. Tomasi has also written the critically acclaimed graphic novel LIGHT BRIGADE and runs on GREEN LANTERN CORPS and BATMAN & ROBIN.

ARTISTS

DOUG MAHNKE

Born in 1963 in the Year of the Rabbit, Doug Mahnke embarked on a love affair with comics at the age of five, having received a pile of Spider-Man issues from a rugby-playing college student named Mike who lived in his basement. A consistent interest in the medium, coupled with some art skill, landed Doug a job drawing comics for Dark Horse at the age of 24 (the date is known precisely, as it occurred just two weeks before he wed his lovely bride). His first gig was illustrating a moody detective one-shot entitled *Homicide*, written by John Arcudi. The two went on to collaborate on Dark Horse's *The Mask* and their creator-owned series MAJOR BUMMER, originally published by DC.

Since then Doug has worked on a wide variety of titles, including SUPERMAN: THE MAN OF STEEL, JLA, BATMAN, SEVEN SOLDIERS: FRANKENSTEIN, BLACK ADAM: THE DARK AGE and STORMWATCH: P.H.D.. After contributing to 2009's FINAL CRISIS, he took over art chores on GREEN LANTERN. He resides in the Midwest with his wife and seven kids, one dog, and a bunny named Suzie.

TYLER KIRKHAM wanted to be a comic book artist since childhood. Before coming to DC Comics, he made a name for himself at Top Cow Studios and at Marvel, where he drew for *Tomb Raider, Amazing Spiderman, X-Men: Phoenix Warsong* and *Ultimate Fantastic 4*. Tyler lives and works in Utah.

FERNANDO PASARIN

Fernando Pasarin is a Spanish artist who has worked on *Phenix* and *Strangers* for Semic France and *Les Fils de la Louve* for Belgian publisher Le Lombard. For DC Comics, his work has appeared in GREEN LANTERN CORPS, ION, TANGENT: SUPERMAN'S REIGN and ORACLE: THE CURE.

ED BENES

Ed Benes was born in a small town in the state of Ceará, Brazil. He started to work for the U.S. comics market in the '90s, with *Samuree*. From that point on he never stopped! His credits include GUNFIRE, DEATHSTROKE, ARTEMIS: REQUIEM, *Glory*, W.I.L.D. CATS, *Sci-Tech*, GEN 13, *Thundercats*, CAPTAIN MARVEL, SUPERGIRL, BIRDS OF PREY, SUPERMAN and most recently JUSTICE LEAGUE OF AMERICA. Benes still lives in Brazil, in the city of Limoeiro do Norte with his lovely family.

ARDIAN SYAF

Ardian Syaf is an Indonesian comic book artist. He has worked on *The Dresden Files* for Random House and BLACKEST NIGHT: BATMAN, BRIGHTEST DAY, GREEN LANTERN CORPS and BIRDS OF PREY for DC Comics.

FROM THE WRITER OF
GREEN LANTERN *AND* INFINITE CRISIS

GEOFF JOHNS
IVAN REIS

**BLACKEST NIGHT:
GREEN LANTERN**

with
**GEOFF JOHNS
DOUG MAHNKE**

**BLACKEST NIGHT:
GREEN LANTERN CORPS**

with
**PETER J. TOMASI
PATRICK GLEASON**

READ THE COMPLETE EPIC IN THESE GRAPHIC NOVELS

**BLACKEST NIGHT:
BLACK LANTERN CORPS
VOL. 1**

with
**JAMES ROBINSON,
J.T. KRUL, ARDIAN SYAF,
& EDDY BARROWS**

**BLACKEST NIGHT:
BLACK LANTERN CORPS
VOL. 2**

with
**GEOFF JOHNS, JAMES ROBINSON,
GREG RUCKA, SCOTT KOLINS,
EDDY BARROWS & NICOLA SCOTT**

**BLACKEST NIGHT:
RISE OF THE
BLACK LANTERNS**

with
**GEOFF JOHNS, PETER TOMASI,
JAMES ROBINSON
& OTHERS**

**BLACKEST NIGHT:
TALES OF THE CORPS**

with
**GEOFF JOHNS,
PETER TOMASI
& OTHERS**

SEARCH THE GRAPHIC NOVELS SECTION OF
DCCOMICS.COM
FOR ART AND INFORMATION ON ALL OF OUR BOOKS!

FROM *THE WRITER OF* GREEN LANTERN *AND* SUPERMAN

GEOFF JOHNS

with DALE EAGLESHAM

"This is a flawless book."
– PHILADELPHIA DAILY NEWS

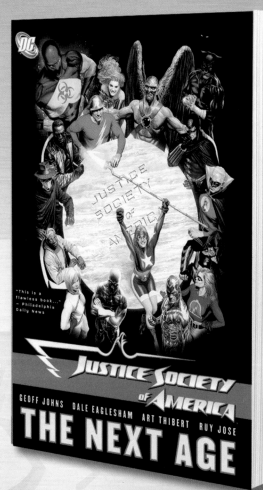

JUSTICE SOCIETY
OF AMERICA
THY KINGDOM COME PART 1

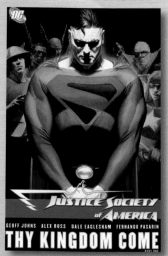

with
**DALE EAGLESHAM
& ALEX ROSS**

JUSTICE SOCIETY
OF AMERICA
THY KINGDOM COME PART 2

with
**DALE EAGLESHAM
& ALEX ROSS**

JUSTICE SOCIETY
OF AMERICA
THY KINGDOM COME PART 3

with
**DALE EAGLESHAM
& ALEX ROSS**

SEARCH THE GRAPHIC NOVELS SECTION OF
DCCOMICS.COM
FOR ART AND INFORMATION ON ALL OF OUR BOOKS!

FROM THE PAGES OF
GREEN LANTERN

GREEN LANTERN CORPS

"The Green Lantern franchise is currently the best in the superhero genre."
– THE WASHINGTON EXAMINER

GEOFF JOHNS
DAVE GIBBONS
PATRICK GLEASON

RECHARGE
TO BE A LANTERN
THE DARK SIDE OF GREEN
RING QUEST
SINS OF THE STAR SAPPHIRE
EMERALD ECLIPSE

GREEN LANTERN CORPS: TO BE A LANTERN

GREEN LANTERN CORPS: RING QUEST

GREEN LANTERN CORPS: SINS OF THE STAR SAPPHIRE

GREEN LANTERN CORPS: EMERALD ECLIPSE

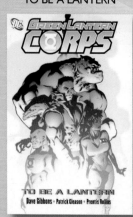

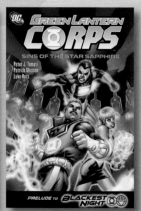

DAVE GIBBONS
with
PATRICK GLEASON

PETER J. TOMASI
with
PATRICK GLEASON

PETER J. TOMASI
with
PATRICK GLEASON

PETER J. TOMASI
with
PATRICK GLEASON

SEARCH THE GRAPHIC NOVELS SECTION OF
DCCOMICS.COM
FOR ART AND INFORMATION ON ALL OF OUR BOOKS!